Moccas:
an English deer park

The history, wildlife and management
of the first parkland National Nature Reserve

Edited by Paul T. Harding and Tom Wall

D0898717

Dedicated to the memory of Richard Chester-Master (1927-1994)
who made possible the establishment of Moccas Park as the first
parkland National Nature Reserve.

Contents

The views expressed are those of the authors and not necessarily shared by English Nature.

Foreword

When my late husband, Richard Chester-Master, inherited the Moccas Estate 36 years ago, Moccas Park had slept undisturbed for over a century. The ancient trees, so aptly described by Kilvert, were engulfed in head-high bracken, there was sparse grass for the deer, and the contours of the landscape were hidden from view. He set about the task of reclamation with great care, well aware that the Park was of very special interest to naturalists in many fields. Whilst the precipitous hillside was left undisturbed, the bracken was cleared from the lower slopes and the shapes of the ancient trees were revealed at last.

Long term planning for the future was vital, and in 1978 an Agreement was made with the Nature Conservancy Council (whose duties in England have now been assumed by English Nature) which made Moccas the first parkland National Nature Reserve. Extensive replanting was undertaken, and the interests of grazing stock and of conserving the habitat were interwoven.

The fact that the wildlife in Moccas Park is considered to be of a rarity to merit this publication is a source of both satisfaction and delight to our family. The in-depth studies undertaken over the last 21 years are now to be shared with the public in a way we had never envisaged. The partnership with English Nature, from whom the widest possible source of expertise will always be available, coupled with the continuity of family ownership, will ensure the safekeeping of this very special landscape into the new century.

I am proud and grateful that *Moccas: an English deer park* is dedicated to my husband.

Priscilla Chester-Master
Moccas, December 1999

Foreword

The opportunity to write a monograph on a single wood arises only rarely, but when it does, we realise just how much there is to know about the British countryside and, by implication, how little we know about most of the woods we manage, survey, or just visit. Compilations such as Bryan Sage's *Northaw Great Wood* (Hertfordshire County Council, 1966), Richard Steele and Colin Welch's *Monks Wood* (Nature Conservancy, 1973), Oliver Rackham's *Hayley Wood* (Cambridgeshire and Isle of Ely Naturalists' Trust, 1975), join with earlier works, such as St John Marriott's *Lessness Abbey Woods* (George Routledge, 1925) and John Crowther's *Silva Gars* [Grass Wood] (Rydal Press, 1930) to provide bench marks against which we can measure, not only our ignorance of woods elsewhere, but also the intricacies of a wood's ecology, the diversity of its wildlife, and the character of its prolonged interaction between people and nature. This new work by Paul Harding and Tom Wall extends a rare but fine tradition, which is just as important as the much more publishable broad-scale syntheses and overviews in understanding aspects of our environment.

This publication gives me particular pleasure because I was in at the start. Paul and I visited Moccas Park together for the first time in August 1972, when parkland nature conservation strategies and the Veteran Trees Initiative were inconceivable. At that time, Francis Rose was waxing enthusiastic about parkland lichens, and Alan Stubbs was trying to interest the Nature Conservancy in insect conservation, but 'saproxylics' (Chapter 5.1) had not been invented, and we were still up against ecologists who simply did not regard parkland as a form of woodland, nor recognise parks as worthy of conservation effort. We had, for example, been enjoined to omit parklands from *A Nature Conservation Review* (Cambridge University Press, 1977), compiled mainly from 1968 to 1971, though fortunately we stood our ground.

While Paul was working with me, I asked him to concentrate on what we called 'mature timber habitats', and in that connection we visited Moccas Park, then, as now, regarded as one of the most important examples. Later, in 1976, I commissioned him to undertake a detailed tree survey as part of the Nature Conservancy Council's programme of research and survey. Paul went on to complete *Pasture-woodlands in lowland Britain* (Institute of Terrestrial Ecology, 1986) with Francis Rose, and now he and Tom Wall have brought together an impressively wide range of talents and interests in *Moccas: an English deer park*.

As it happens, that first visit to Moccas Park stays in my memory as much for people as for trees and wildlife. At the end of one day, Paul and I decided to visit Bredwardine Church, where we were amazed to see a large crowd walking out of the churchyard. This turned out to be the annual gathering of the Kilvert Society, formed in memory of the nineteenth century parson who served at both Bredwardine and nearby Clyro. This led me to Kilvert's magical but sad *Diary* and the magnificently evocative description of Moccas Park as it was in 1876, now an obligatory quote for all self-respecting woodland ecologists. To read his description while standing on the steep slopes of Moccas Park, where he came "slipping, tearing and sliding" down through the oaks, birches and piles of fallen wood, is to feel the continuity of place and the passing of generations.

On a personal and more trivial note, Moccas Park holds the record so far for the most unusual request for advice during my years as a consultant. Tom Wall wrote asking if Sir Velters Cornewall could conceivably have won his bet to hit 'The Hundred Pound Oak' from 2,500 yards (see Chapter 3.2). After a youth (and middle age) mis-spent at Bisley and other ranges, I ought to have known. I decided that he could have hit the tree somewhere, but that he would have needed a sheet as large as the tree to prove it. Bill Harriman later provided far more detailed technical advice on the firearms of the time, and it is a pity that even this monograph does not have space enough to set it out in full.

I hope this book has many readers, and that they are all, like me, beguiled by the wealth of detail it contains.

Dr George Peterken, OBE
St Briavels Common, December 1999

Rationale and background

Paul T. Harding and Tom Wall

.... a young member of the Cornewall family sits under the ancient tree, emphasizing the continuity of past with present.

Thomas Hearne's painting of c.1788-9 *Moccas Deer Park with a Large Oak Tree* as described by David Morris.[1]

Et in Arcadia ego

Moccas Park in Herefordshire is a beautiful, fascinating and significant place; the essence of the classic English deer park. Thomas Hearne's portrait of the Moccas Oak captures the spirit of the Park: the veteran tree with a huge fallen limb, mature and younger trees in the middle distance, the vista to the Lawn Pool and a distant view across the valley of the River Wye (Figure 1.1.1). A small group of deer emerges from behind the mighty oak, beside which a well dressed figure rests, with hat and stick in hand and his dog nearby. This is a landscape that has been developed and maintained by man to be both useful and enjoyable; as it was in the 1780s, so it is over 200 years later. The Park is the product of centuries of active management and is of great interest for its history, landscape and wildlife. It has been seen as a notable example for 200 years and has been studied for more than a century. This book celebrates the beauty and importance of Moccas Park and explores the issues surrounding their maintenance for future generations.

Figure 1.1.1

An oak at Moccas Park Herefordshire. An etching by Benjamin Pouncy, published in 1798, after the watercolour by Thomas Hearne (c.1788-9).

The importance of Moccas Park

The Park has been known for its veteran trees for more then 200 years, but despite the long-standing involvement of the Woolhope Club (see below) and others, it was not until the early 1940s that Moccas Park was recognised as being of national importance. At that time the importance was not for the trees themselves, but for the beetles associated with them (see Chapters 5.1, 5.2 and 5.3). In 1962, the Nature Conservancy started to take an interest in the site (see Chapter 6.1), largely because of the presence of three species of saproxylic beetles, which were then known only from Moccas Park. Even today the Park is home to one species known from no other British site (see Chapter 5.2).[2] Moccas Park was notified as a Site of Special Scientific Interest in September 1963 and was listed as a Grade 1 site in the Nature Conservation Review in 1977.[3]

A Nature Reserve Agreement was eventually concluded between the owners and the Nature Conservancy Council;[4] this ran from 1978, Moccas Park being declared a National Nature Reserve in 1981, the first and for long the only parkland to have this status (see Chapter 6.1).[5] This declaration recognised the position of Moccas Park as the most important parkland and, even when forests and woodlands are taken into account, the third most important site in Britain for saproxylic beetles (see Chapter 5.1).[6] Moccas Park is rated as one of only five sites in Britain that is of international importance for its saproxylic fauna.[7] The veteran trees of the Park are important as the habitat of rare and threatened insects, but they are also recognised as being important in their own right, and younger generations of trees are important to maintain the character of the site and its long term importance for nature conservation (Figure 1.1.2).

Figure 1.1.2

Moccas Park National Nature Reserve. View south across the Lawn Pool towards the Upper Park. Photograph by Peter Wakely, May 1994.

Moccas Park is of historic significance too. It was included on English Heritage's *Register of parks and gardens* in 1986 as part of the Moccas Court Grade II★ site, signifying its great historic interest.[8] As is explained in Chapter 3.1, part of the particular landscape importance of the Park lies in it having been touched to some degree by the three main currents of landscape design in the late eighteenth century. This was the heyday of the English landscape park, which some consider to be England's most significant contribution to European aesthetics.

During the period since 1962, the Park has served as an open-air workshop and classroom, where knowledge of nature conservation in parklands has been extended and practitioners have, for the first time, experienced some of the complexities of parkland management. Model management agreements have been explored and practical trials in nature conservation have been carried out. Later chapters of the book, in Section 6, describe the management and maintenance of the nature conservation and historic heritage interests of the Park and, in particular, chart the progress and successes of the 21-year Nature Reserve Agreement that ran from 1978 to 1999 and is currently being re-negotiated.

Rationale for a book on Moccas Park

This book records the knowledge and experience that has been gained at Moccas Park, a prime example of the English deer park. In doing so the book seeks also to identify what more needs to be learned in order to enhance the conservation of this park and English parks in general. And, not least, it seeks to celebrate this beautiful, fascinating and significant place with its distinctive air of continuity of the past with the present. The reasoning behind this book may be explained by analysing the meaning of the individual words of the title, *Moccas: an English deer park*.

Park

The noun *park* is used in many contexts and with several meanings. Parks as places of beauty and utility are a truly ancient concept; Assyrian parks existed three thousand years ago, and, in the 5th century BC, the Buddha preached his first sermon in the old deer park of Varanasi (Benares) in India, sitting under a tree. Lasdun recognises many different stages of development in English parks:[9] from their medieval origins as hunting grounds (and larders), for wealthy and highly privileged landowners, to the recreational areas preserved or created in urban areas for those who otherwise would be almost totally deprived of contact with any local natural environment.[10] In the following chapters we shall see that Moccas Park fits into several of Lasdun's stages of the development of English parks.

Deer

We define the park as a *deer park* to establish that it is one of the relatively small number of parks in the United Kingdom that still contain a managed deer herd and to distinguish it from other parkland at Moccas (eg that leading to Moccas Court).[11] The Deer Park at Moccas was formerly more extensive (see Chapter 3.1), but unless indicated to the contrary the name Moccas Park, as applied in this book, refers to the present day Deer Park.

English

Deer parks have been a feature of the British landscape from the Middle Ages onwards and many fewer comparable examples existed (let alone survive) in other European countries.[12] The vast majority of deer parks always was, and still is in England, rather than in other parts of the United Kingdom. Moccas Park exemplifies the English deer park as a place of social, aesthetic, economic and sporting importance within a substantial country estate. There is something especially English too about those whose interests and enthusiasms are recorded in this book, be they ambitious and fashionable Georgian land owners, Victorian clerics or twentieth century amateur naturalists. They have all added further layers of Englishness to the identity of Moccas Park.

Moccas

Moccas Park is, in so many respects, a particularly good example of an English deer park to place on record.

It was one of Britain's first parkland Sites of Special Scientific Interest and the first parkland National Nature Reserve (Chapter 6.1). This status is a consequence of entomological studies carried out from the 1930s onwards, which identified the special importance of the Park. This status has led to many further investigations across a broad range of natural history.

The record of Moccas Park presented here is not, however, intended as a definitive statement; several chapters are interim reports of work in progress.[13] Indeed, part of the rationale for this book is to stimulate further recording, study, research and re-evaluation of existing information. To this end we highlight the many areas in which knowledge is sparse or even absent.

But Moccas Park also presents an example of the range of management history and the links of that history to the lives, successes and difficulties of landowners (Section 2). It also allows us to examine how past management has shaped what we see today (Chapter 3.1).

Moccas Park also enables us to examine what has been learned about parkland management for nature conservation, including the inter-relationship with the present-day owners who manage the Park as part of a working agricultural and sporting estate (Section 6).

Finally, Moccas Park provides a case study for the future consolidation and enhancement of the nature conservation and landscape value of parkland (Figure 1.1.3) as envisaged in the Habitat Action Plan for *Lowland wood-pasture and parkland* prepared as part of the UK Biodiversity Action Plan process.[14] In the final chapter we offer a 'Vision for the future', in which we take up the challenge of the Habitat Action Plan and look to a future in which the value of a park such as Moccas is both recognised and built on at a landscape scale.

Figure 1.1.3

Moccas Park from the south west. Aerial photograph taken in May 1978. The Park lies in the foreground, Moccas Court stands left of centre towards the top and on the left hand edge the River Wye is visible. Photograph courtesy of the University of Cambridge Committee for Aerial Photography.

Background - Moccas Park in the local context

Long before Moccas Park came to attention nationally, its beauty and interest were known to and commented upon by local naturalists, historians and writers. Much of this locally compiled information is covered in other chapters, but it has a special place in providing a background to all subsequent work on the Park.

The Kilvert connection

The description of Moccas Park quoted on the inside front cover of this book is taken from the diary of the Reverend Francis Kilvert (1840-1879). First published sixty years ago, *Kilvert's diary* is now acknowledged as a minor classic.[15] It is celebrated for many qualities, not least Kilvert's vibrant descriptions of the people and countryside of the Clyro district in mid-Victorian times.[16]

The surviving parts of *Kilvert's diary* contain six references to Moccas Park (see Chapter 2.4), of which the most significant is the entry of 22 April 1876. This is one of the more celebrated passages and has done much to raise awareness of Moccas Park. Richard Mabey refers to it as "the most graphic account we have of the feel of an ancient wood-pasture" and notes that it is a "forceful demonstration that the features responsible for their [wood-pastures'] ecological importance and aesthetic appeal are not so very far removed from each other".[17]

Kilvert's eye focused sharply on the aesthetic appeal of the picturesque elements of the Park, particularly on the ancient but still vigorous and highly individual trees. These and other features of the Park on which he commented - "fallow wood", hawthorns and the seeming immortality of the "grey old men" - are regarded today as being of critical importance to the ecological interest of the park, as we shall see in later chapters.

It is this conjunction of aesthetic appeal and ecological importance, as noted by Richard Mabey, which is one of the particular themes of this book.[18] Mabey points out that "Kilvert's presence and the record he left .... have added their own indefinable trace". For many, they are integral to the experience of a visit to the Park.

When viewed today the Park differs in a number of respects from the scene that Kilvert recorded, and this is even after due allowance is made for the distilled and romanticised nature of the description that Kilvert has left us. The amount of "fallow wood" appears much reduced, the hawthorns have almost all gone and the number of ancient trees seems fewer than is suggested by Kilvert. Whether there are actually fewer ancient trees in the Park today is questionable (see Chapter 3.3).

The Woolhope Naturalists' Field Club connection

Kilvert recorded in his diary that he disliked sharing his countryside walks with "a herd" and certainly declined the opportunity to go out with the Woolhope Naturalists' Field Club.[19] This is somewhat ironic in the context of the present book because the Club's *Transactions* are such a significant source of information concerning the Park and its trees, which were cherished by the Club as well as by Kilvert. The Club has made many visits to Moccas Park over the years, including several hosted by the Park's owner, the Reverend Sir George Cornewall (1833-1908). Cornewall was Honorary Secretary and later President of the Woolhope Club and allowed a particularly fine oak which stills stands in the Park today, to be named 'The Woolhope Club Oak' (see Chapter 3.2).

Six years before Kilvert's description, an anonymous 'commissioner' of the Woolhope Club girthed 90 trees in the Park and these measurements were published in the Club's *Transactions,* together with photographs.[20] Some drawings followed and in later years a few repeat girthings and photographs.[21] Together with Kilvert's description, the Woolhope Club's record is a rare and important insight into an English deer park as it was a century or more ago. The Club's observations are discussed in more detail in Chapters 3.2. and 3.4.

The Woolhope Club's interests have always been broad; they remain so today and Club members have contributed to chapters in this book covering a wide range of topics. Numerous past publications in the Club's *Transactions* concerning various aspects of the ecology and history of the Park are discussed in later chapters.[22]

Derivation of the name Moccas

It is an unusual name, almost certainly a corruption of the Welsh *Mochros*, meaning the promontory, moor or place of pigs, a place name which occurs at a few locations in Wales.[23] The place name has associations with the 5th century Welsh saint variously named Dyfrig (in Welsh), Dubricius (in Latin) or Devereux (in Norman French), who is believed to have founded a religious settlement at Moccas and to have lived there. One legend (among many) is that Dubricius was told by an angel to found a monastery. The place for it should be where he would find a white sow and her piglets. Leaving his monastery at Ross on the River Wye, he found such a place further up the river, described as well wooded and abounding in fish, which he called Mochros. The life of Dubricius is described in the *Liber Landavensis* and by Canon Doble.[24] However, the legends of Dubricius are complicated by the fact that *Moccoss* was a Celtic god - the Holy Boar - possibly suggesting an example of cross-referral between pre-Christian, Celtic traditions and early Christian hagiology.

Notes

1   Morris (1989).
2   Saproxylic species are those that depend on wood, usually but not always dead and decaying wood, for some part of their life cycle; for a full definition see Chapter 5.1.
3   Ratcliffe (1977).
4   This was backed by a report (Harding 1977) which drew together for the first time the available information concerning the Park; this report has been the starting point for the present book.
5   Duncombe Park, Yorkshire, the second parkland National Nature Reserve, followed in 1994. Nature reserves managed directly by Britain's statutory nature conservation bodies or with their formal approval are 'declared' to be National Nature Reserves. They are nationally important examples of wildlife habitats and/or geological formations and are managed on behalf of the nation.
6   See also Harding & Alexander (1994).
7   Speight (1989).
8   The significance of this designation is explained more fully in Chapter 6.3.
9   Lasdun (1991).
10   "The parks were the lungs of London." Attributed to William Pitt, Earl of Chatham, by William Windham in a speech in the House of Commons, 1808.
11   It is difficult to give a precise figure for the number of deer parks in England. Cantor (1983) lists more than 1800 parks in England during the medieval period (defined as from the Domesday Survey to 1485), the majority of which will have been deer parks. Shirley (1867) lists 334 parks stocked with deer. Whitaker (1892) lists nearly 400, but includes some very small 'deer paddocks', whilst noting that 50 parks described by Shirley (op. cit.) 'no longer contain deer'. By 1949 the number in England had dwindled to 135 parks with deer (Whitehead 1950). According to Hingston (1988), C.J. Lucas in 1969 recorded only 112 parks with deer in the whole of Great Britain. The turning point for the decline in numbers of deer parks probably came in the late 1970s and 1980s with an increase in commercial deer farming. Hingston (op. cit.) lists nearly 200 deer parks and farms in Great Britain (and Northern Ireland), but omits an unspecified number that the owners did not wish to be publicised.
12   The few surviving deer parks in Denmark are important sites for nature conservation (eg Martin 1989).
14   Most of the chapters were drafted in 1997, but the species lists have been updated with new information up to the end of October 1998.
14   UK Biodiversity Group (1998).
15   Plomer (1938, 1939, 1940).
16   Kilvert was curate at Clyro between 1865 and 1872 and subsequently vicar of Bredwardine from 1877 to 1879, respectively 13 km and 2 km from Moccas Park.
17   Mabey (1980).
18   Mabey (1980).
19   The Woolhope Naturalists' Field Club was founded in Hereford in 1851 "for the practical study, in all its branches, of the Natural History of Herefordshire and the districts immediately adjacent". It is referred to hereafter simply as 'the Woolhope Club' or 'the Club'. The Club, which still flourishes, is named after the Woolhope Dome, an area celebrated for its geology, which lies 10 km south east of Hereford.

20 Anon (1870).
21 Anon (1873).
22 These publications and a wide range of others were listed as an annotated bibliography of Moccas Park (Simpson 1994), which has been an important source of reference in the preparation of this book.
23 Barber (1916), Burgoyne (1977).
24 The book of Llan Dâv or Llandaff (*Liber Landavensis*) is a 12th century compilation inspired by Urban, Bishop of Llandaff, to assert the rights and privileges of the newly constituted see of Llandaff over territories claimed by the see of Hereford and by acquisitive, lay Norman landowners. Doble (1984) provides a well-documented summary of what is known of the life of St Dubricius, including numerous references to Moccas and the saint's association with an early religious settlement there. St Dubricius resigned as primate of Wales in favour of St David and he died on Bardsey Island circa 550 AD. According to Burgoyne (1977) the fate of St Dubricius' religious settlement at Moccas is uncertain and no archaeological evidence of its location is known.

References relating to Moccas Park

ANON. 1870. Incidental notes on remarkable trees in Herefordshire. *Transactions of the Woolhope Naturalists' Field Club*, 288-321.

ANON. 1873. The remarkable trees of Herefordshire. *Transactions of the Woolhope Naturalists' Field Club*, 100-155.

HARDING, P.T. 1977. *Moccas deer park, Hereford and Worcester: a report on the history, structure and natural history.* Unpublished report to the Nature Conservancy Council by the Institute of Terrestrial Ecology, Huntingdon. A slightly revised version of Appendix 2 in HARDING, P.T. 1977. *Second report to the Nature Conservancy Council on the fauna of the mature timber habitat* (CST Report No. 103). Banbury: Nature Conservancy Council. (Hereafter this is referred to only in the revised, unpublished but widely circulated version.)

HARDING P.T. & ALEXANDER, K.N.A. 1994. The use of saproxylic invertebrates in the selection and evaluation of areas of relic forest in pasture-woodlands. *In*: P.T. HARDING, ed. Invertebrates in the landscape: invertebrate recording in site evaluation and countryside monitoring. *British journal of entomology and natural history*, 7 (Supplement 1), 21-26.

HINGSTON, F. ed. 1988. *Deer parks and deer in Great Britain.* Buckingham: Sporting and Leisure Press.

MABEY, R. 1980. *The Common Ground. A place for nature in Britain's future?* London: Hutchinson.

MORRIS, D. 1989. *Thomas Hearne and his landscape.* London: Reaktion Books.

PLOMER, W. 1938, 1939, 1940. *Kilvert's diary.* 3 volumes. London: Jonathan Cape.

RATCLIFFE, D.A. 1977. *A Nature Conservation Review.* 2 volumes. Cambridge: Cambridge University Press.

SHIRLEY, E.P. 1867. *Some account of English deer parks.* London: John Murray.

SIMPSON, D.A. 1994. *Moccas Park National Nature Reserve: an annotated bibliography.* Unpublished report to English Nature.

SPEIGHT, M.C.D. 1989. *Saproxylic invertebrates and their conservation.* (Nature and Environment Series, No. 42). Strasbourg: Council of Europe.

WHITAKER, J. 1892. *A descriptive list of the deer-parks and paddocks of England.* London: Ballantyne, Hanson.

WHITEHEAD, G.K. 1950. *Deer and their management in the deer parks of Great Britain and Ireland.* London: Country Life.

Other references

BARBER, W.D. 1916. The Book of Llandaff and Herefordshire place names. *Transactions of the Woolhope Naturalists' Field Club*, 158-164.

BURGOYNE, G. 1977. *A short history of the church of St Michael and All Angels Moccas.* Privately published.

CANTOR, L. 1983. *The medieval parks of England, a gazetteer.* Loughborough: Department of Education, Loughborough University of Technology.

DOBLE, G.H., edited by D.S. EVANS. 1984. *Lives of the Welsh saints.* Cardiff: University of Wales Press.

LASDUN, S. 1991. *The English park, royal, private and public.* London: Andre Deutsch.

MARTIN, O. 1989. Click beetles (Coleoptera, Elateridae) from old deciduous forests in Denmark. *Entomologiske Meddelelser*, 57, 1-107. (In Danish with abstract in English.)

UK BIODIVERSITY GROUP. 1998. Lowland wood-pasture and parkland: a Habitat Action Plan. *In*: UK BIODIVERSITY GROUP, *Tranche 2 Action Plans Volume II - terrestrial and freshwater habitats.* Peterborough: English Nature on behalf of the UK Biodiversity Group.

Environmental context

Paul T. Harding and Tom Wall

$\dfrac{1}{2}$

*We came tumbling and plunging down the
steep hillside of Moccas Park ....*

From the diary of the Reverend Francis Kilvert, 22 April 1876.[1]

Topography and habitats

Moccas Park lies 17 km west of Hereford (Figure 1.2.1). It extends to 139 ha and occupies much of the north east facing slope of Dorstone Hill, part of a long ridge that separates a section of the valley of the River Wye from the Golden Valley (River Dore) and forms the north eastern limit of the Black Mountains range. The ground of the Park falls from 276 m above sea level to just under 78 m at the lowest point on The Lawn (Figure 1.2.2). The former south western boundary of the Park, as shown on Figure 1.2.3, ran in a straight, north west to south east, line from just north of Burnt Coppice to just west of Butler's Coppice. The boundary encompassed much of the plateau at the top of the steep north east facing slopes of the Park, but including some areas with a southerly aspect. Today, virtually all the Park has a northern or north eastern aspect.

The vegetation of the Park defines three main areas (Figure 1.2.2). These are referred to throughout the following chapters: the Upper Park is uphill from the northern edge of the bracken line that divides the Park; the Lower Park which is downhill from the northern edge of the bracken line, and the Lawn Pool. Moccas Park is first and foremost a habitat for fallow deer. This was its original *raison d'être* and, to a considerable extent, it remains so today. Fallow deer require grass, foliage, mast, cover and water, which are provided in varying amounts by these three main areas of the Park.

The Upper Park is mostly steep and mainly wooded, often with tree canopies meeting, but with substantial glades too; bracken is common almost throughout and is often dominant. The upper slopes are very steep in places (Figure 1.2.2) and there are rocky outcrops near the crest of the ridge. Two permanent streams run off the ridge, in the south of the Park, and several periodic streams drain off the central hillside.

The Lower Park includes the flatter ground and more gentle slopes from which bracken has been cleared and a continuous grass sward established; it is dotted with parkland trees growing in varying densities, sometimes singly, sometimes in groups. Within this area lies The Lawn, the lowest and flattest part of the Park, surrounding the Lawn Pool. This is the only permanent water body in the Park, but it all but disappears in dry summers and although its outline encompasses some 4.4 ha, it is only at the wettest of times that all of this area is flooded. Usually the area of open water is shallow and restricted to a ring only 5-20 m wide around an island of fen and carr woodland. Three smaller pools fill only when water levels are high.

The evidence of old aerial photographs (e.g. Figure 1.2.3) indicates that the plateau area that formerly lay within the Park had a sparse cover of trees; the ground cover was probably a mixture of bracken and grass.

Pedunculate oak

Deer parks are amongst the most artificial of our wildlife habitats.[2] Created and managed for an introduced species of deer, the structure and the detail of the habitat is in turn significantly influenced by the deer themselves, with far reaching consequences for other organisms. The effect of the deer, intensified by that of the livestock, which also have long been run in the Park, is to reduce the habitat diversity and simplify the structure. The grassland tends to be tightly grazed and flowering plants are suppressed. In the woodland, the herb layer is suppressed and the shrub layer almost totally eliminated; natural regeneration is virtually non-existent and all trees show a marked browse line. The only area where the herb layer is more luxuriant and saplings prosper, is on the island in the Lawn Pool, to which deer and livestock have access only when the Pool dries up. The vascular plant communities of the Park are discussed in Chapter 4.3.

Figure 1.2.1

Moccas Park - general location. The park lies in the valley of the River Wye, to the west of Hereford City, close to the Welsh border. The three weather stations referred to under 'Climate' are identified.

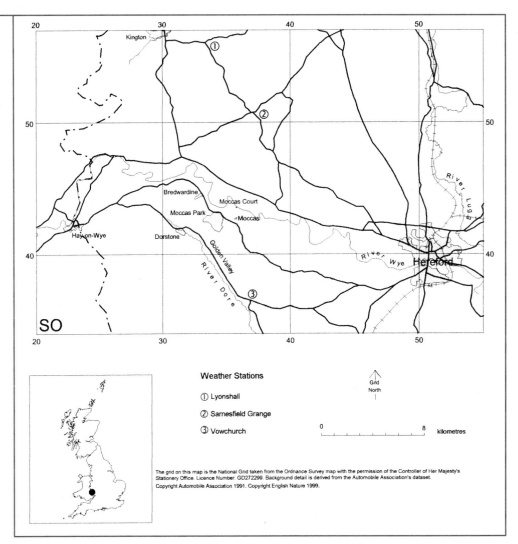

Given this picture, one might be tempted to ask whether deer parks really are important wildlife habitats. But whilst deer have reduced biodiversity in some ways, they have indirectly increased it in others. The term wood-pasture, describes the two essential elements of a deer park, but the attempt to combine these two elements restricts the woodman's options. Cutting down trees and letting them grow again (coppicing) is likely to be frustrated by the deer, as would be cutting and replanting. The alternative option is to cut trees repeatedly above grazing height (pollarding); in time, this leads to the development of a series of aging trees that are rich in micro-habitats for other organisms.

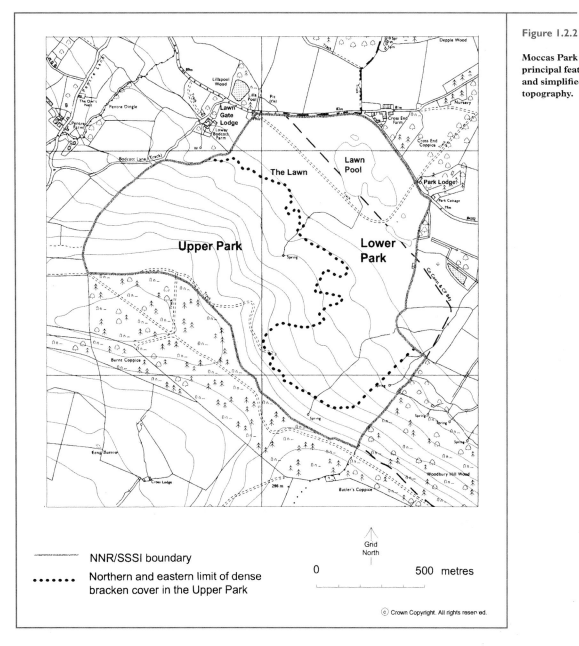

Figure 1.2.2

Moccas Park - principal features and simplified topography.

NNR/SSSI boundary

•••••• Northern and eastern limit of dense
bracken cover in the Upper Park

Grid
North

0   500   metres

© Crown Copyright. All rights reserved.

Evidence of pollarding can be identified in some trees at Moccas Park, but the practice ceased long ago. Nevertheless trees have been allowed to survive to and beyond maturity, presumably for aesthetic and cultural reasons. The consequence is that Moccas Park is well endowed, as are many other parks, with over mature and ancient trees, and with dead and rotting wood. It is these habitat elements, present continuously over centuries and probably millennia, which make for the actual or potential importance of the Park for lichens, bryophytes and fungi (Section 4), for insects, especially beetles, and for birds and bats (Section 5).

The area of The Lawn and its pool may be at the upper end of an ancient area of wetland, at the foot of the ridge. Evidence for the extent of this wetland is somewhat circumstantial.[3] Place names to the south east of Moccas, for example Blakemere and Shenmore, may denote wetland, such as possible former water bodies including 'The Black Mere' (Figure 1.2.4). 'Mere' or 'Meere' also occurs in the field names Upper Meere, Lower Meere and Mere Field shown immediately to the east of The Lawn, on John Lambe Davis's *Survey of the Manor of Moccas* of 1772 (Chapter 2.3). The Soil Survey records that the series of hollows and linear depressions (including the Lawn Pool) running from Turner's Boat (SO312458) to Mere Pool (SO361409), may represent a partly filled marginal channel along the foot of the Merbach-Woodbury Hill ridge.[4] Brown and grey, Silurian-derived, Wye alluvium occurs in some of the hollows around the Lawn Pool, which are now 15 m above the river.

Geology[5]

There are few good rock exposures within the Park; all of them are in the Upper Park and most are overgrown and rather inaccessible. The bedrock underlying the Park is Old Red Sandstone, consisting of a succession of conglomerates, sandstones, siltstones, mudstones and cornstones (calcretes or caliches). The Old Red Sandstone was deposited in semi-arid to arid continental conditions during the final stages of the Silurian Period and throughout the Devonian Period. These rocks represent deposits laid down mainly in the channels and flood plains of ephemeral rivers and on the floors of ephemeral lakes.

The rocks underlying Moccas Park consist of the Ledbury Group (also known as the Raglan Mudstone Formation). These rocks are Silurian (Prídolí or Downtonian Stage). The Ledbury Group underlies the lower part of the scarp at Moccas Park and consists predominantly of soft mudstones, subordinate sandstones, and a few cornstones. The sedimentary structures observed in the Ledbury Group, as well as the fossil fauna, indicate that these rocks may have been deposited in a marine environment on the margins of arid land surfaces.

The St Maughan's Formation rests upon the Ledbury Group and forms the upper parts of the scarp and the top of the hill in the Park. This formation belongs to the earliest part of the Devonian Period, known in Britain as the Dittonian Stage. Whilst mudstones form parts of

Figure 1.2.3

Moccas Park in July 1946 showing the former southern boundary. The present park is the tree-covered area on the right hand side of the photograph. RAF photograph.

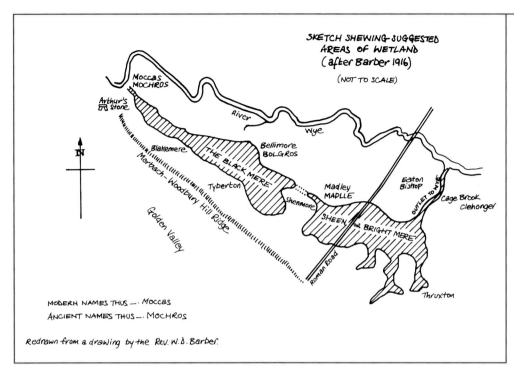

Figure I.2.4

Suggested areas of ancient wetlands to the south east of Moccas Park. Redrawn from a drawing by the Rev W.D.Barber (1916) (not to scale).

the St Maughan's Formation, sandstones are more dominant and cornstones are much commoner than in the Ledbury Group, with no marine elements. Tufa, produced by the solution and subsequent redeposition of lime from the cornstone layers has been noted in some streams in the Park.[6]

Geomorphology and soils

The glacial and immediately post-glacial history of the area is complex. Much of the Park is covered by Pleistocene till and other fluvio-glacial deposits. These are products of the Late-Devensian glaciation, when the area was glaciated by a lobe of ice pushing eastwards down what is now the valley of the Wye, from the Welsh ice sheet to the west. At its maximum, this ice reached over 150 m in depth near Moccas.[7] The retreat of the 'Wye glacier' is marked by features such as the Staunton Moraine from Bredwardine north east to near Staunton on Wye and north to Norton Canon. The decaying ice of the 'Wye glacier' deposited debris contained in and on the glacier. A terrace of soils of the Dore Series, which are brown, silty, slightly stony, outwash deposits, forms the ridge of slightly higher land between the Lawn Pool and the Moccas to Bredwardine road, near Cross End Farm.[8]

Buried within these clay, sand and gravel deposits were blocks of ice, which eventually formed kettle-holes as they melted during deglaciation, which may have taken place around 13 000 B.P.[9] The Staunton Moraine impounded a temporary lake upstream from Moccas.[10] Presumed evidence of a marine incursion some time before the maximum extension of the Devensian ice sheet, based on the presence of grey foraminiferous clays found near Bredwardine,[11] has now been discounted.[12]

Throughout the Park, the soils are typically neutral to weakly acidic, reddish loams derived from this glacial drift and downwash and from the underlying marls and sandstones. The Soil Survey classifies the soils of the Park as follows:[13]

❖ Lower Park (below the bracken line) - Wootton Series, brown earths, silty and stony drift derived from Devonian and Silurian rocks;

- Upper Park (above the bracken line) - Bromyard Series, brown earths, fine silty, over Devonian marl with occasional interbedded fine-grained sandstones and siltstones;
- Surrounding the Lawn Pool - non-calcareous gley soils of the Vernolds (surface-water gley, silty and stony drift) and Hollington (ground-water gley, silty alluvium) Series;
- Low-lying area, south east of the Lawn Pool, leading towards the Castle mound - Kingsland Series, non-calcareous ground-water gley soils, silty alluvium.

Climate

In hilly terrain, such as that surrounding Moccas Park, local weather conditions can vary considerably over small distances. There is no meteorological station at or near Moccas so that information about the climate of the site must be extrapolated using data from weather stations nearby. The location of Moccas Park will inevitably result in differences from nearby weather stations and the aspect, slope and elevation of the site causes subtle differences within the site.[14]

The Soil Survey Record summarised data for nearby weather stations for the period 1916-1960.[15] More recent, monthly meteorological averages have been provided by the National Agromet Unit of ADAS.[16] These are for the period 1961-1990 and include an element of correction for altitude.

Table 1.2.1 Monthly long term (1961-1990) meteorological averages (excluding rainfall).

	Jan	Feb	Mar	Apr	May	Jun	Jul	Aug	Sep	Oct	Nov	Dec
Maximum temperature (°C)	6.3	6.4	8.9	11.8	15.2	18.3	20.3	19.8	17.1	13.6	9.3	7.3
Minimum temperature (°C)	1.0	0.6	1.9	3.5	6.1	8.9	10.7	10.5	8.6	6.4	3.1	1.7
Sunshine (hours)	1.4	2.1	3.2	4.6	5.5	5.8	5.7	5.2	4.1	2.7	1.9	1.3
Days of air frost	11	11	7	4	1	0	0	0	0	1	5	10
30 cm soil temperature (°C)	4.4	4.3	5.4	8.0	11.2	14.3	16.1	16.1	14.4	11.6	8.1	5.7
Windspeed (knots)	9.6	9.5	9.7	8.8	8.3	7.9	7.5	7.5	7.7	8.1	8.9	9.4

Temperatures in the area were moderate, without extremes. The mean annual range in 1961-1990 was just 12°C rising from 3.5°C in February to 15.5°C in July and the pattern and range of temperatures is broadly similar in both periods for which weather records are available. Air frost was experienced during the winter months (December to February) on an average of only 35% of days, and soil temperatures were at or above 8°C from April to November.

Table 1.2.2 Monthly long term rainfall averages for 1916-1950 and 1961-1990 (in mm).

	Jan	Feb	Mar	Apr	May	Jun	Jul	Aug	Sep	Oct	Nov	Dec	Total
Sarnesfield Grange	76	54	49	50	57	45	62	68	58	77	80	66	739
Moccas Park	85	62	65	57	63	55	45	64	69	69	71	87	792

The annual sunshine average, 3.7 hours/day, is comparatively low, with the highest monthly averages in June and July, but this is probably to be expected in an inland area with varied topography.

Table 1.2.2 shows average monthly rainfall data for the nearest weather station for 1916 to 1950,[17] and as calculated monthly rainfall averages for 1961 to 1990.[18] These two sets of data show well-distributed, moderate rainfall throughout the year. The average annual rainfall for 1961-1990 was 792 mm with December and January being the wettest months and June and July the driest, but with a range of only about 50% between the wettest and driest months. Rainfall data for the period 1916-1950, show a slightly different pattern of rainfall distribution, but this may reflect differences in the topography as much as any changes in seasonality of rainfall between the two periods.

Using data from the period 1920-1960, the Soil Survey calculated the average growing season as being 257 days (14 March to 25 November) at Lyonshall and 261 days at Hereford.[19] A cumulative potential moisture deficit has been calculated at Vowchurch which shows a deficit from May to September of 279 mm, about 30% of the annual rainfall. Potential transpiration and evaporation exceed average rainfall only from May to July at Vowchurch, although this area may have a slightly higher average rainfall than Moccas. These data suggest a long growing season and conditions in which the availability of water to plants would cause generally low stress during the hotter, drier summer months.

Land use capability

The land use capability map, using the Soil Survey Land Use Classification, shows that Moccas Park, in common with much of the land on either side of the Merbach-Woodbury Hill ridge, is of limited use for cultivation. Only the area of The Lawn is shown as Capability Class 1.[20] The lower slopes and flatter land on the ridge in the Park are Class 3g and the steeper area below the bracken line, in the south of the Park, is Class 4g. About 30% of the Park, mainly on the steepest slopes is Class 5.

Long distance atmospheric pollution

The flora of the Park has been altered by past management practices, such as the fertilisation of the pasture and use of herbicides, and by high numbers of livestock (Section 4). Neither the incidence of, nor the effects of, on-site agricultural nutrient inputs or long distance atmospheric pollution have been studied in any detail at Moccas Park. The somewhat impoverished state of the lichen flora of the Park that is observed today (Chapter 4.1) is, however, thought to be partly attributable to long distance atmospheric pollution by sulphur and other compounds from industrial and urban sources. Increased levels of nitrogen compounds, particularly from vehicle exhausts, and other forms of pollution such as acid clouds and rain, are thought to be affecting the natural and economic vegetation of many parts of Britain.

Annual mean concentrations of sulphur dioxide gas in the atmosphere are declining nationally and the Moccas area was probably always in a zone of lower concentrations. It may however, be on the eastern edge of a zone with damaging sulphate ion and hydrogen ion concentrations in hill clouds and on the western edge of a zone of raised atmospheric ammonia concentrations. Moccas Park is also on the eastern edge of a zone of raised ozone levels.[21]

Firm conclusions about the effects of atmospheric pollution on the Park, its wildlife or its appearance cannot be drawn due to the inadequacy of data. We lack information about either the concentrations of atmospheric pollutants (and their interaction or combined effects) at the site, or the long term changes in most aspects of the flora of the Park. These are issues that could be the subject of further work.

Notes

1   Plomer (1940).
2   This point is brought out in *Lowland wood-pasture and parkland: A Habitat Action Plan* (UK Biodiversity Group 1998). It refers to wood-pasture and parklands as representing "A vegetation structure rather than a plant community... this structure consists of large, open-grown or high forest trees (often pollards) at various densities, in a matrix of grazed grassland, heathland and/or woodland floras".
3   Barber (1916).
4   Palmer (1972).
5   This account of the geology is based on information kindly supplied by David Evans (English Nature) and Peter Thomson (Woolhope Club).
6   Also known as travertine, tufa is common in the area and was used to build the 12th century parish church of St. Michael and All Angels near Moccas Court. According to Burgoyne (1977) in his short history of the church, Sir George Cornewall obtained some supplies of tufa, for 19th century repairs to the church, from Depple Wood on the banks of the Wye, west of Moccas Court.
7   Luckman (1970).
8   Palmer (1972).
9   Robinson & Haworth (1994).
10 Millward & Robinson (1978).
11 Earp & Hains (1971).
12 Sumbler *et al* (1985).
13 Palmer (1972).
14 It is not uncommon to experience local cloud or light rain in the Upper Park whilst The Lawn is dry or in sunshine.
15 Palmer (1972). Meteorological stations include Lyonshall (SO339576 & 335558), Vowchurch (SO349362) and Sarnesfield Grange (SO368509).
16 Averages are for the nearest point (SO350400 at 158 m altitude) in the ADAS 5 km database. Source: ADAS National Agromet Unit at Wolverhampton.
17 Sarnesfield Grange (SO368509) is about 9 km north north east of Moccas Park.
18 Averages are calculated for the specific site (SO341426 at 143 m altitude) from the ADAS database. Source: ADAS National Agromet Unit at Wolverhampton.
19 The period when the mean temperature exceeds 5.6°C.
20 Palmer (1972). Land Use Capability classifications:
    1 - Suitable for cultivation with no limitations or only very minor limitations;
    3g - Suitable for cultivation with moderate gradient and soil pattern limitations;
    4g - Suitable for cultivation with severe gradient and soil pattern limitations;
    5 - Generally unsuitable for cultivation with severe gradient and soil pattern limitations.
21 Much of the information about levels of atmospheric pollutants was derived from a report of the Critical Loads Advisory Group (1996).

References relating to Moccas Park

BARBER, W.D. 1916. The Book of Llandaff and Herefordshire place names. *Transactions of the Woolhope Naturalists' Field Club*, 158-164.

BURGOYNE, G. 1977. *A short history of the church of St Michael and All Angels Moccas.* Privately published.

PALMER, R.C. 1972. *Soils of Herefordshire III Sheet SO 34 (Staunton-on-Wye).* Soil Survey Record No. 11. Harpenden: Soil Survey.

PLOMER, W. 1940. *Kilvert's diary.* Volume 3. London: Jonathan Cape.

ROBINSON, M. & HAWORTH, E.Y. 1994. Survey and management proposals for the 'Lawn Pool', Moccas Park National Nature Reserve in Herefordshire. Part II: Outline pollen analysis. Unpublished report by the Institute of Freshwater Ecology to English Nature.

Other references

CRITICAL LOADS ADVISORY GROUP. 1996. *Critical levels of air pollutants for the United Kingdom.* Penicuik: Institute of Terrestrial Ecology.

EARP, J.R. & HAINS, B.A. 1971. *British Regional Geology: The Welsh Borderland.* London: HMSO.

LUCKMAN, B.H. 1970. The Hereford Basin. *In*: C. A. LEWIS, ed. *The glaciations of Wales and adjoining regions.* London: Longman.

MILLWARD, R. & ROBINSON, A. 1978. *The Welsh Borders.* London: Eyre Methuen.

SUMBLER, M.G., BRANDON, A. & GREGORY, D.M. 1985. Grindley's flood: a report of a marine clay in the Wye Valley near Hereford. *Quaternary Newsletter*, 46, 18-25.

UK BIODIVERSITY GROUP. 1998. Lowland wood-pasture and parkland: a Habitat Action Plan. *In*: UK BIODIVERSITY GROUP, *Tranche 2 Action Plans Volume II - terrestrial and freshwater habitats.* Peterborough: English Nature on behalf of the UK Biodiversity Group, 63-68.

The Lawn Pool:
sediment stratigraphy and pollen analysis

Lisa Dumayne-Peaty

And God said, 'Let the earth bring forth grass, the herb yielding seed, and the fruit tree yielding fruit after his kind, whose seed is in itself, upon the earth': and it was so.

Genesis 1:11

Five studies have been undertaken of sediments from the Lawn Pool and their pollen and spore content. These have investigated the history of the Pool and of the vegetation in the surrounding area, including what is now Moccas Park. The studies have focused on several questions: the origin of the Pool, the possible presence of Late-glacial sediment and vegetation sequences,[1] the establishment and composition of woodland during the Holocene,[2] the status of lime (*Tilia* spp.)[3] woodland at Moccas Park and the possible landscaping of the Pool in the eighteenth century. This chapter summarises findings to date.

The origin of the Lawn Pool

The first study of sediments from the Lawn Pool was undertaken in 1993 by Elizabeth Haworth and colleagues from the Institute of Freshwater Ecology.[4] Three sediment cores (93-1, 93-2 and 93-3) were obtained (Figure 1.3.1) which, along with a soil pit, were used to determine the depth and nature of the sediments and the origin of the basin in which the Pool lies. Four different and complex stratigraphies were identified, but the profiles were difficult to correlate. Analysis of the sediments led Haworth *et al.* to the view that the Pool consisted of two separate basins which coalesced or were merged artificially. They concluded that the adjacent basins (kettle holes) could have formed between moraines which originated as a result of melting glacier ice in the Wye Valley at the end of the Devensian. Grey - pink clays were found; they thought these were deposited in the Pool during deglaciation and

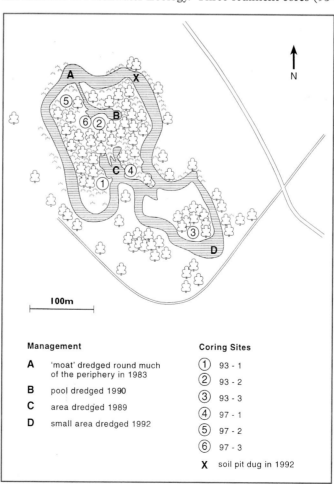

Figure 1.3.1

Coring sites. A plan of the Lawn Pool showing the location of coring sites and management works. Adapted from Haworth *et al.* (1994) and reproduced by courtesy of the Institute of Freshwater Ecology.

100m

Management

A   'moat' dredged round much of the periphery in 1983
B   pool dredged 1990
C   area dredged 1989
D   small area dredged 1992

Coring Sites

(1)   93 - 1
(2)   93 - 2
(3)   93 - 3
(4)   97 - 1
(5)   97 - 2
(6)   97 - 3

X   soil pit dug in 1992

that the organic layer, which was discovered between two clay layers in the soil pit, was deposited during the Late-glacial interstadial. The organic deposits above this were thought to represent gradual in-filling of the Pool as a result of natural hydroseral vegetation succession,[5] which had resulted in the present day carr woodland, although several clay layers in the upper sediments might have been the result of erosion events which washed minerogenic sediment into the Pool.[6] Haworth *et al.* speculated that these layers might have been a result of disturbance associated with the digging of a drainage ditch at the south eastern end of the Pool.

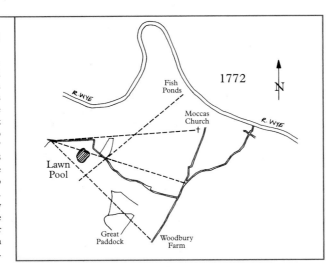

Figure 1.3.2

The Lawn Pool, 1772. The Lawn Pool and other features as shown on John Lambe Davis's map of 1772. The transect lines link points which are also shown on 'Capability' Brown's plan of 1778 (Figure 1.3.3) and the Ordnance Survey map of 1886 (Figure 1.3.4). Reproduced, by courtesy of the Institute of Freshwater Ecology, from Haworth *et al.* (1994).

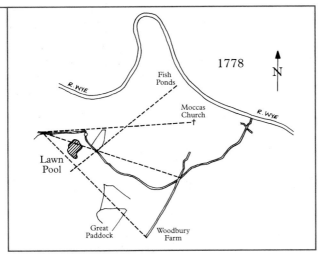

Figure 1.3.3

The intended outline of the Lawn Pool, 1778. The Lawn Pool and other features as shown on 'Capability' Brown's 'A Plan for the intended Alterations at Moccas Court in Herefordshire', 1778. The transect lines link points which are also shown on Figures 1.3.2 and 1.3.4. Reproduced, by courtesy of the Institute of Freshwater Ecology, from Haworth *et al.* (1994).

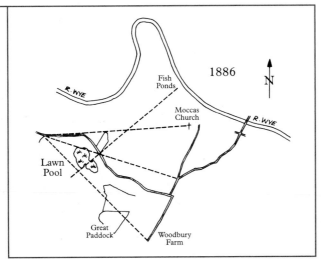

Figure 1.3.4

The Lawn Pool, 1886. The Lawn Pool and other features as shown on the Ordnance Survey map of 1886 (6 inches to 1 mile). The transect lines link points which are also shown on Figures 1.3.2 and 1.3.3. Reproduced, by courtesy of the Institute of Freshwater Ecology, from Haworth *et al.* (1994).

Haworth and her colleagues also examined the recent history of the Lawn Pool using eighteenth and nineteenth century maps. A map drawn by John Lambe Davis in 1772 (see Chapter 2.3) shows the Pool as a small, almost square feature (Figure 1.3.2). This contrasts with the considerably more extensive and sinuous outline shown on the Ordnance Survey map of 1886 (Figure 1.3.4). Such an outline was already evident on the earliest 1 inch Ordnance Survey map (not reproduced) which was based on a survey undertaken in 1828-9. The outline persists, little changed, today.

It is tempting to suggest that the apparent change in the shape and size of the Lawn Pool between 1772 and 1886 is attributable to landscaping works undertaken on the recommendation of Lancelot 'Capability' Brown, whose advice was sought in the 1770s (see Chapter 2.3). However, Brown's 'A Plan for the intended Alterations at Moccas Court' of 1778 (Figure 1.3.3) shows an outline for the Lawn Pool which differs little from that drawn by Davis and is nothing like that shown on the 1886 Ordnance Survey map. In other respects, the maps by Davis and Brown correspond well with the 1886 Ordnance Survey map (Figures 1.3.2 to 1.3.4) and it could be that the Pool was extended to the south east between 1778 and 1828 even though such an extension did not form part of Brown's Plan. Haworth *et al.* point out, however, that the hollow is shown on the 1886 map as being in-filled with swamp vegetation, suggesting that any excavation that might have taken place was fairly superficial. Further collection and examination of sediment cores from the south eastern end of the Pool is necessary before a firm conclusion can be reached as to the possible rôle of landscaping works in determining its shape and extent.

James Strutt furthered the work on the origin and sediment stratigraphy of the site by obtaining two more cores (97-1 and 97-2), both approximately 3.5 metres in depth (Figure 1.3.1).[7] His conclusions do not differ from those of Haworth *et al.*

Vegetation history

Marie Robinson and Elizabeth Haworth analysed pollen from 10 samples which were obtained from the four metres of sediment in core 93-2 (Figure 1.3.1) in order to reconstruct the vegetation history of Moccas Park. Their main conclusions, based on the outline vegetation profile they obtained, were that the basal sediments in the Pool date from the Late-glacial interstadial, that Holocene woodland development at the site was similar to that which is represented in pollen diagrams from the region, and that human impact, particularly during the Bronze Age, had an important influence on the vegetation of Moccas Park. However, in the absence of radiocarbon dates, it was difficult for them to determine the chronology of vegetation change.

The conclusions drawn by Robinson and Haworth were justified by the palynological data available to them from core 93-2,[8] but Luci Allen and Christina Gardner have taken their work further by undertaking more detailed investigations.[9] Gardner's study was aimed at elucidating further the nature of the Late-glacial vegetation described by Robinson and Haworth, by undertaking a higher resolution pollen study of the lower sediments, whilst Allen examined Holocene woodland development, particularly the status of lime (*Tilia* spp.) woodland at the site. Allen and Gardner worked on the same core (core 97-3) (Figure 1.3.1) and their pollen results have been combined into a single pollen profile that is discussed here. The pollen diagram is divided into 6 periods of vegetation development, namely MCPa to MCPf, where the initials MCP stand for Moccas Park, and 'a' to 'f' are the designated stages of vegetation development (Figure 1.3.5). The profile is not radiocarbon-dated, but the dates mentioned below and labelled on the pollen diagram are derived from correlation with other pollen diagrams for the area and regional pollen maps.[10] The work of Allen and Gardner has led to an interpretation of the vegetation history of Moccas Park which differs from that proposed by Robinson and Haworth.

9,600 to 9,000 years Before Present

The pollen evidence from core 97-3 (Figures 1.3.1 and 1.3.5) suggests that a woodland dominated by *Betula*, but in which some *Pinus* and *Corylus* occurred, was present at Moccas Park when the sediments began accumulating in the Lawn Pool (MCPa). Correlation with regional pollen maps suggests that this relates to the period around 9,600 BP.[11] The pollen types in MCPa also suggest that the Pool contained peaty water and that there was an extensive community of plants, some of which are characteristic of wet or damp places (Chenopodiaceae, *Persicaria maculosa*, Filicales, *Pedicularis*, *Pteridium*, *Typha angustifolia*, *Riccia* type). The presence of woodland taxa and the absence of pollen representative of both snow-patch vegetation and climatic warming at the end of the Late-glacial (e.g. *Artemisia*, *Rumex acetosa*, *Juniperus*), suggest that the basal sediments of 97-3 are from the early Holocene. The early part of the pollen diagram is clearly not representative of the Late-glacial interstadial,[12]

Figure1.3.5

Pollen diagram, the Lawn Pool.

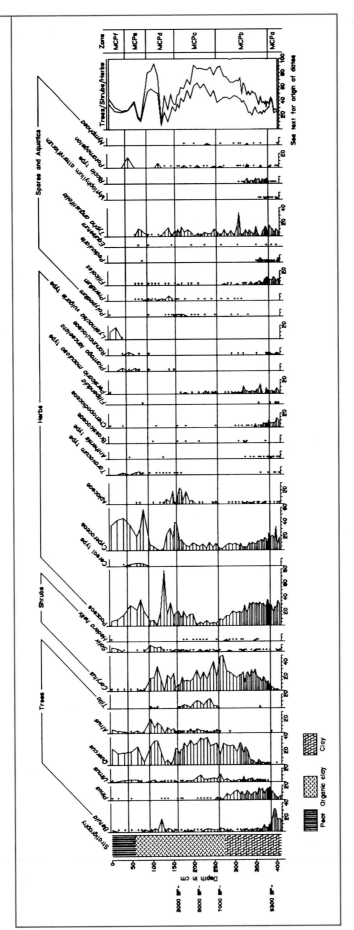

and there appears, from Gardner's work, to be no pollen evidence for Late-glacial stadial flora as proposed by Robinson and Haworth from core 93-2. Core 97-3 studied by Gardner was taken from a location approximately one metre away from 93-2 and is similar in stratigraphic detail, and therefore the pollen diagrams should have been directly comparable. Gardner also analysed the pollen content of several samples from the base of the cores studied by Strutt (97-1 and 97-2) and the results also suggest that these sediments are rich in arboreal pollen types characteristic of the Holocene.

These findings could indicate that the sediments in the Lawn Pool began accumulating in the early Holocene and that the basin may not be a feature that originated from ice wastage during the Late-glacial. An alternative explanation offered by the current author is that the basin may be a Holocene palaeochannel of the River Wye or a fluvio-glacial channel.[13] Tentative support for this interpretation is provided by the presence in the lower sediments of mollusc assemblages which are representative of flowing water (Andrew Moss, pers. comm.). Of possible relevance to this is the description by Parker and Chambers of how the rivers in Herefordshire adjusted to a meandering form *circa* 9,000 BP,[14] when valley alluviation commenced and former channels became in-filled with intercalated silts and peats.[15] However, more detailed geomorphological and palaeoecological investigations supported by radiocarbon dates are necessary in order to confirm the origins of the basin.

9,000 to 7,000 years Before Present

The lowest level of MCPb (core 97-3) probably dates to 9,000 years BP as *Ulmus* and *Quercus* appear in the pollen spectra for the first time. *Betula* and Poaceae decline, *Pinus* remains an important component of the woodland and *Corylus* increases significantly, suggesting that this was a time of woodland development. The woodland continues to develop in MCPc as *Alnus* and *Tilia* appear and this probably dates the beginning of the zone to approximately 7,000 years BP.

7,000 to 5,000 years Before Present

The mid Holocene (approximately 7,000 - 5,000 years BP) appears to have been a period of mixed woodland with a more or less closed canopy. Oak dominates in this zone, but the record for two other pollen types is particularly noteworthy. Firstly, there is a significant decline in *Ulmus* at 205 cm which probably represents the mid Holocene elm decline that is characteristic of many pollen diagrams from the British Isles around 5,000 years BP; the possible causes of the decline remain contentious.[16] Secondly, the relatively high percentage of *Tilia* (*circa* 17%) suggests that it was an important component of the woodland at Moccas Park, especially as *Tilia*, being a low pollen producer, is usually under-represented in pollen diagrams, and because its relatively large pollen grains are not dispersed over long distances.[17] *Ernoporicus caucasicus*, a scarce beetle species which feeds solely on lime, occurs in the Park today (see Chapter 5.3). Lime is now rare at Moccas Park and the presence of this beetle may be a carry over from a time when lime was more common. Many of the taxa indicative of standing water and wet ground have disappeared, although *Typha angustifolia* and *Potamogeton* are still present, and the presence of *Polypodium*, Apiaceae and *Persicaria maculosa* may indicate that the Pool was becoming in-filled.

5,000 years Before Present onwards

The pollen diagram from core 97-3 suggests that MCPd is characterized by the significant decline and disappearance of *Tilia* which probably occurred around 3, 000 years BP.[18] Such a rapid and marked decline suggests that *Tilia* must have become rare in the area. The *Tilia* decline is a feature which is common to many pollen diagrams from Great Britain and may be attributed to either climatic deterioration or human impact.[19] Several lines of evidence could be used to examine the possible cause of the *Tilia* decline at Moccas Park. The rise in *Alnus* in MCPd might suggest that the area became wetter as a consequence of climatic deterioration, but *Alnus* is characteristic of fen carr which may have been developing at this time around the Lawn Pool irrespective of climate change. The decline in *Quercus* and *Corylus* and increase in Poaceae which occur in MCPd (i.e. after the *Tilia* decline), may support an anthropogenic interpretation, although there is not a corresponding rise in taxa which are indicative of agricultural activity, and *Quercus* and *Corylus* quickly regain their former percentages. However, human impact on the vegetation clearly occurs in MCPe when there is a substantial decline in trees and a corresponding increase in Poaceae, suggesting that considerable deforestation occurred and that the amount of open ground increased. The presence of cereals may indicate that arable activity took place close to the Pool and herbs indicative of pastoralism (*Taraxacum* type, *Plantago lanceolata* and Ranunculaceae) are also present. In the absence of radiocarbon dates it is difficult to determine when this episode of human activity took place, but correlation with the archaeological record may suggest that it was Iron Age or Romano-British in date. During MCPf Poaceae declines, cereals disappear and there is some increase in *Alnus* and *Salix* which indicates a reduction in human activity. However, *Quercus* remains the most important taxa in the pollen profile.

Conclusion

The studies outlined above shed important light on issues surrounding the origin of the Lawn Pool and the vegetation history of Moccas Park. Although Haworth *et al*, Robinson & Haworth, and Strutt, all propose that the Pool originated in the Late-glacial,[20] the results presented by Gardner suggest that this was not the case and that a Holocene woodland was present at the site when the sediments began accumulating in the basin. The pollen evidence for Holocene woodland development, and in particular for the presence of an extensive lime woodland, is important in terms of elucidating the history of woodland at Moccas Park. Clearly, the environmental and vegetation record is complex and worthy of further study, and the author proposes to undertake a comprehensive programme of coring and pollen analysis combined with radiocarbon dating.

Notes

1   The Late-glacial encompassed the final stages of the last ice age, approximately 15,000 to 13,000 years Before Present.
2   The Holocene is the present interglacial period which began 10,000 years BP.
3   Nomencalture is that of Stace (1997), names cited in the text are as follows:

Alnus	Alder
Anthemis type	Chamomiles
Apiaceae	Carrot family (Umbellifers)
Artemisia	Mugworts
Betula	Birch
Brassicaceae	Cabbage family (Crucifers)
Chenopodiaceae	Goosefoot family
Corylus	Hazel
Cyperaceae	Sedge family
Equisetum	Horsetails
Filicales	Ferns
Filipendula	Meadowsweet
Hedera	Ivy
Juniperus	Juniper
Lysimachia vulgaris type	Loosestrife
Myriophyllum alterniflorum	Alternate water-milfoil
Nymphaea	White water-lily
Pedicularis	Louseworts
Persicaria maculosa	Redshank
Pinus	Pine
Plantago lanceolata	Ribwort plantain
Poaceae	Grass family
Polypodium	Polypody fern
Potamogeton	Pondweeds
Pteridium	Bracken
Quercus	Oak
Ranunculaceae	Buttercup family
Riccia type	Liverwort
Rumex acetosa	Common sorrel
Salix	Willow
Taraxacum type	Dandelions
Tilia	Lime
Typha angustifolia	Lesser bulrush
Ulmus	Elm

4   Haworth *et al* (1994).
5   A hydrosere is a succession of plant communities which commences in fresh water.
6   Minerogenic sediment is sediment composed mainly of mineral material with a low organic content.
7   Strutt (1997).
8   Palynology is the analysis of pollen remains in order to determine vegetation history.
9   Allen (1997), Gardner (1998).
10 Birks (1989).
11 Birks (1989).
12 The Late-glacial stadial was a short cold period between *circa* 11,000 and 10,000 years BP when glaciers returned to highland areas.
13 A palaeochannel is a river channel which no longer carries water as part of a present day river system. A fluvio-glacial channel is one formed by glacial melt waters.
14 Parker & Chambers (1997).
15 Alluviation is the accumulation of sediment deposited by running water.
16 Peglar (1993).
17 Andersen (1970).
18 Turner (1962).
19 Pigott & Huntley (1980).
20 Haworth *et al.* (1994), Robinson & Haworth (1994), Strutt (1997).

References relating to Moccas Park

ALLEN, L. 1997. *A reconstruction of the vegetation history of Moccas Park, Herefordshire: was this the western limit of* Tilia cordata *during the Holocene?* University of Birmingham, School of Geography BSc Dissertation.

GARDNER, C. 1998. *Is there evidence of Late-glacial deposition at Moccas Park in Herefordshire? An investigation to reconstruct a past environment using pollen and sediment analysis.* University of Birmingham, School of Geography BA Dissertation.

HAWORTH, E.Y., GUNN, I.D.M., CUBBY, P.R. & CARLOS, R. 1994. *Survey and management proposals for the 'Lawn Pool', Moccas Park National Nature Reserve in Herefordshire.* Institute of Freshwater Ecology report to English Nature.

ROBINSON, M. & HAWORTH, E. Y. 1994. *Survey and management proposals for the 'Lawn Pool', Moccas Park National Nature Reserve in Herefordshire, Part II: Outline pollen analysis.* Institute of Freshwater Ecology report to English Nature.

STRUTT, J.A. 1997. *Ice melt channels, dead ice hollows and/or a landscaped pool? A stratigraphic investigation of the depth and nature of deposits to determine the shape and origin of the aquatic basin of the Lawn Pool, Moccas Park National Nature Reserve.* Lancaster University BSc Dissertation.

Other references

ANDERSEN, S. Th. 1970. The relative pollen productivity and pollen representation of north European trees and correction factors for tree pollen spectra. *Danmarks Geologiske Undersøgelse*, 96, 1-99.

BIRKS, H.J.B. 1989. Holocene isochrone maps and patterns of tree-spreading in the British Isles. *Journal of Biogeography*, 16, 503-539.

PARKER, A.G. & CHAMBERS, F.M. 1997. Late-Quaternary palaeoecology of the Severn, Wye and Upper Thames. *In*: S. G. LEWIS & D. MADDY, eds. *The Quaternary of the Midlands and Welsh Marches: Field Guide.* London: Quaternary Research Association, 31- 48.

PEGLAR, S. 1993. The mid-Holocene *Ulmus* decline at Diss Mere, Norfolk, UK: a year-by- year pollen stratigraphy from annual laminations. *The Holocene*, 3, 1-14.

PIGOTT, C.D. & HUNTLEY, J.P. 1980. Factors controlling the distribution of *Tilia cordata* at the northern limits of its geographical range II: History in north west England. *New Phytologist*, 84, 145-164.

STACE, C. 1997. *New Flora of the British Isles.* Second edition. Cambridge: Cambridge University Press.

TURNER, J. 1962. The *Tilia* decline: an anthropogenic interpretation. *New Phytologist*, 61, 328-341.

Early history:
Arthur's Stone to Domesday

David Whitehead

Countless the larks, hysterically singing
In this wind-worried place of heather and grass
Where the ancients buried one of their number,
A chieftain, a warrior, a tamer of men.
Folklore would have us believe it was Arthur
But names become garbled when mumbled through beards.

From *Note on History*, a poem about Arthur's Stone by Edward Kaulfuss.[1]

This chapter describes the early history of the area surrounding what is now Moccas Park. It traces what is known of the story of human occupation and exploitation of the area from the earliest times through to the twelfth century. The evidence is often fragmentary but, particularly in the later years, a picture of occasional conflict and not infrequent change emerges, contrasting with the period of stability that is chronicled in later chapters. The present chapter ranges from Moccas in the Wye Valley across to Dorstone in the Golden Valley, because it is at Dorstone rather than at Moccas, that the story of Moccas Park itself, as told in the next chapter, will eventually begin.

Figure 2.1.1

Arthur's Stone, Dorstone. A wood engraving by Robert Gibbings of the neolithic long barrow, which illustrates his book *Coming down the Wye* (1942). Reproduced by courtesy of Laurence Pollinger Limited.

From the Mesolithic period to the time of the Romans

Arthur's Stone (Figure 2.1.1), one of the best known Neolithic long barrows in the British Isles, stands 1.5 km west of the Park on Dorstone Hill, and the summit of the hill (SO327422) shows evidence of fairly intensive occupation in prehistoric times.[2] Surface finds of some 4,000 fragments of flint implements were made prior to the commencement of exploratory excavations which yielded evidence of occupation over an extended period.[3] The earliest report includes mention of 11 flint artefacts dated to the Mesolithic period,[4] as well as numerous Neolithic ones.[5] Subsequent reports outline evidence of occupation through to Romano-British times.

Another Neolithic long barrow lies near Cross Lodge (otherwise known as Lodge Farm or Lodge Ground) immediately adjacent to what, in the eighteenth century, was the south western corner of the Park,[6] and in Hereford Museum there is a finely worked Neolithic flint

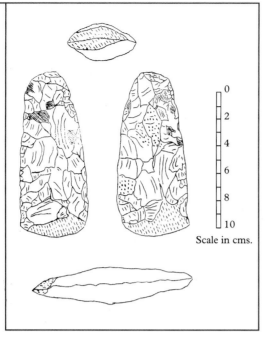

Figure 2.1.2

Neolithic flint axe.
The axe, found at the
site of Moccas Castle
in 1971, is now in
Hereford Museum.
The drawing, from
Pye (1971), is
reproduced by
courtesy of the
Woolhope Club.

axe (Figure 2.1.2) found at the site of the former Moccas Castle which lies adjacent to the north eastern corner of the Park.[7] In contrast to the ample Neolithic evidence, that from the Bronze Age is restricted to the unusual indentations – referred to as 'cupmarks' – on Arthur's Stone, and to the standing stone near Dorstone village (2 km south west of the Park).[8]

Despite the considerable evidence of earlier human activity, pollen analyses of core samples taken from the Lawn Pool suggest that significant human interference in the woodlands of Moccas may not have begun until the Iron Age (see Chapter 1.3).[9] At this period the Herefordshire landscape was dominated by hillforts as well as lowland farmsteads. Two models have been applied to the hillforts: defended villages or grain repositories for lowland farmers, guarded by a military élite. Both models suggest a high population making great demands upon the countryside, including both woodland clearance for grazing and cereals and controlled regeneration of woodland and its management for fuel and building materials.[10]

There was an Iron Age hillfort on Poston Hill, 4.5 km to the south east of the Park;[11] there are remains of what are believed to be Iron Age earthworks on Dorstone Hill,[12] and it has been suggested that the heavily forested Woodbury Hill – 'wood-fort' – lying on the eastern edge of the Park, hides evidence of another Iron Age enclosure.[13]

After the heroic expansion of the Iron Age "there was something of an agricultural retreat" in Herefordshire during the Roman period (43 AD - 400 AD),[14] and this probably led to the regeneration of woodland. Although no significant Roman site is known anywhere close to Moccas Park, the main Roman road from Chester to Caerleon (near Newport, Monmouthshire) passed some 8 km to the east of the Park. A second road leading into Wales followed the north side of the River Wye and a minor road running from Abbey Dore through the Golden Valley to the fort at Clyro, has also been suggested.[15] Evidence of occupation during the Roman period was found during the excavations at Poston Hill.[16]

St Dyfrig and St Guthlac's

During the post-Roman period the area was ruled by petty kings, one of whom, Peibio, gave Moccas to St Dyfrig (*floruit* late fifth century) as a monastic settlement.[17] The saint, also known as Dubricius, was, we are told, attracted to the site because it was well wooded and abounding in fish.[18] At about the same time, Dorstone and Bredwardine also became monasteries under the patrimony of St Dyfrig;[19] their continued presence in the seventh century suggests that this land was relatively undeveloped and not subject to any pressure from the English settlements east of the Wye.

An English raid, in about 745, during the reign of the Mercian king, Aethelbald, disturbed the peace briefly, but the *Book of Llandaff,*[20] which contains early material relating to this area of west Herefordshire, states that it was not until the mid-ninth century that the area was finally annexed by the English kings.[21] They had founded a minster church dedicated to St Guthlac at Hereford to whom they probably gave Moccas. The majority of St Guthlac's lands were in the Lugg and Frome valleys and thus a stretch of what was presumably a fairly well wooded landscape was a valuable addition to the minster's estates.[22]

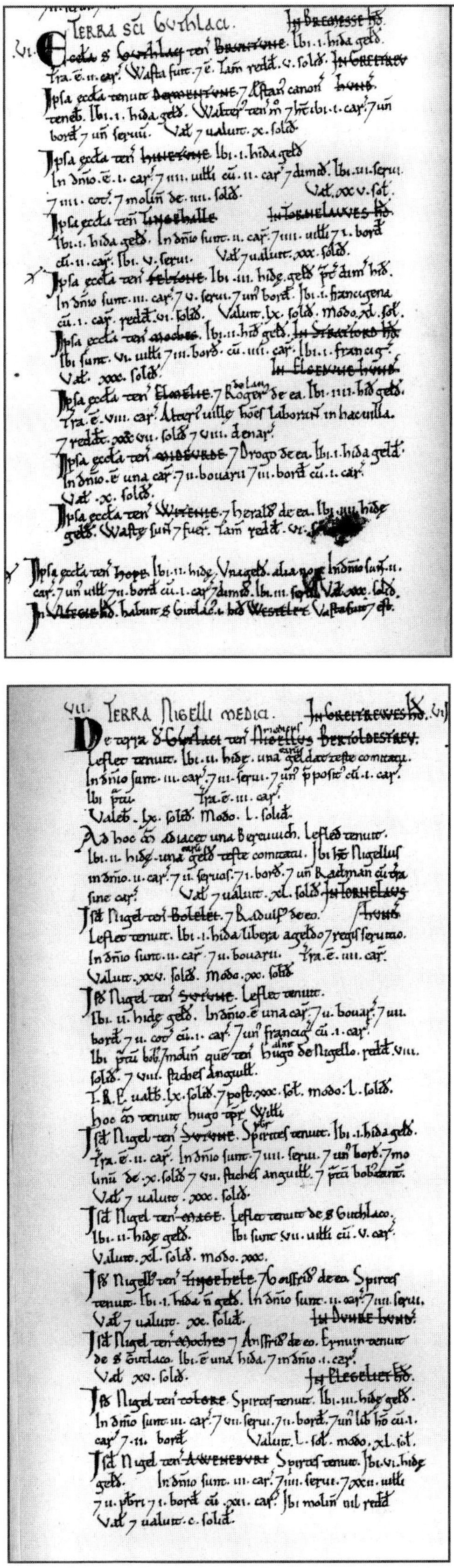

Domesday Book

Meanwhile, from the evidence of *Domesday*,[23] Dorstone and Bredwardine were secularised and integrated into the English kingdom, as is indicated by Dorstone's change of name from 'Cum Barruc', which is Old Welsh, to 'Dodintune', 'estate of Doda' (an Englishman).[24] All three estates paid tax before the Norman Conquest and thus had become essentially English communities, probably by the early tenth century.

The Golden Valley became the front line in the wars between the English and the Welsh in the 1050s and Earl Harold's presence was well established in the area on the eve of Hastings. He acquired both Bredwardine and Dorstone.[25] Harold, perhaps out of deference to St Guthlac's, left Moccas alone. Dorstone was, however, a far more valuable estate being assessed at seven hides in *Domesday* (Figure 2.1.3) compared to Moccas's three.[26] Thus it seems that even before the Conquest, Dorstone completely eclipsed the minor settlement of Moccas and its lord already dominated the top end of the Golden Valley.

Harold had won the battle for west Herefordshire, but it was left to the Normans to re-colonise. Soon after Hastings, Ralf de Tosny, the standard bearer of the Conqueror, was established by his brother-in-law, William fitz Osbern, earl of Hereford, at the advanced post of Clifford on the River Wye. One of his companions, Drogo fitz Pons, held Dorstone and it was presumably he who built the large castle mound close to the centre of the village. The minor motte and bailey castles which surround it no doubt represent the holdings of his knights.[27] *Domesday* has little information about Dorstone apart from its ownership and

Figure 2.1.3

Extracts from *Domesday*. The two entries for 'Moches' (Moccas) refer respectively to land held by the church of St Guthlac, Hereford, and by Nigel, William the Conqueror's physician. They have been translated as follows:'In Stretford Hundred. Moccas. 2 hides which pay tax. 6 villagers and 3 smallholders with 4 ploughs. 1 Frenchman. Value 30s.' and 'In Dinedor Hundred. Moccas. Ansfrid holds from him. Ernwin held from St. Guthlac's. 1 hide. In lordship 1 plough. Value 15s.' (Thorn & Thorn 1983).

the seven hides on which tax was paid. Drogo's family flourished and eventually in the early twelfth century became lords of Clifford, Llandovery and Cantref Bychan.[28] They took the name Clifford and by circa 1160 had established Richard de Solers as their tenant at Dorstone.[29] Dorstone remained an important baronial estate and the de Solers re-built the castle in stone and established an unchartered market and fair in the village.[30]

Bredwardine also stayed in secular hands and was bestowed by William fitz Osbern on an Englishman, Alfred de Marlborough, from whom it passed in the twelfth century to Ralph de Baskerville of Eardisley who probably built the castle here which is mentioned in 1199. Soon after Bredwardine became part of the great lordship of Brecknock, its importance declined, and in 1227 the castle was said to be "old".[31]

In *Domesday* (Figure 2.1.3) the major part of the manor of Moccas was still in the hands of the church of St Guthlac but this ancient minster, which was served by secular canons, was an anachronism in the new era of Norman monasticism and so it was soon absorbed by the regular Benedictine abbey of St Peter's at Gloucester.[32] St Guthlac's weakness is revealed in *Domesday* where one hide of Moccas had already been absorbed by the predatory Nigel, William the Conqueror's physician, who had acquired much of St Guthlac's land elsewhere in Herefordshire. It was held by his tenant Ansfrid.

In agricultural terms, Moccas was a fairly average manor; in relation to its hides it was well populated, with plenty of ploughs, an arable estate with no sign of any woodland or a game reserve. By the middle of the twelfth century both parts of Moccas were in the hands of Nigel's successor Walter del Fresne, and the manor had become part of the great lordship of Kington.[33]

Notes

1   Kaulfuss (1983).
2   The Neolithic period in Herefordshire ran from approximately 4200 to 2300 BC (Children & Nash 1994).
3   Kay (1967), Pye (1958, 1969), Shoesmith (1967-69), Stanford (1965).
4   The Mesolithic period in Herefordshire ran from approximately 10000 to 4200 BC (Children & Nash 1994).
5   Pye (1958).
6   Grinsell (1993).
7   Pye (1971).
8   Children & Nash (1994). The Bronze Age in Herefordshire ran from approximately 2300 to 800 BC (Children & Nash 1994).
9   The Iron Age in Herefordshire ran from approximately 800 BC to AD 48 (Children & Nash 1994).
10 Darvill (1987).
11 Anthony (1958).
12 Kay (1967).
13 Coplestone-Crow (1989).
14 Stanford (1980).
15 Margary (1967).
16 Anthony (1958).
17 Doble (1984).
18 Coplestone-Crow (1989).
19 Davies (1978).
20 The Book of Llandaff (*Liber Landavensis*) is a collection of charters relating to the diocese of Llandaff. They were collected in the twelfth century to resist the encroachments of the Bishop of Hereford upon the ancient territory of Llandaff in west Herefordshire.
21 Davies (1978).
22 Hooke (1985).
23 *Domesday Book* or the Great Survey of England, made by order of William the Conqueror, 1086.
24 Coplestone-Crow (1989).
25 Bredwardine also now has an English name. It was originally 'Lann Iunabui' after an obscure Welsh saint, but it has become 'Brocheurdie' which has been interpreted as 'plank enclosure' suggesting a fortification overlooking the important ford across the River Wye (Thorn & Thorn 1983, Coplestone-Crow 1989).
26 A 'hide' is an obscure and variable Old English measure of land thought to represent anything from 60 to 120 acres (24 to 48 ha)
27 Round (1908), Cathcart King (1983).
28 Cantref Bychan is the upper Tywi Valley below Llandovery.
29 Galbraith & Tait (1950).
30 O'Donnell (1971).
31 Cathcart King (1983).
32 Martin (1953).
33 Galbraith & Tait (1950).

References

ANTHONY, L.E. 1958. *The Iron Age Camp at Poston, Herefordshire*. Woolhope Club Occasional Publication.

CATHCART KING, D.J. 1983. *Castellarium Anglicanum*. New York: Kraus International.

CHILDREN, G. & NASH, G. 1994. *Prehistoric sites of Herefordshire*. Almeley: Logaston Press.

COPLESTONE-CROW, B. 1989. Herefordshire place-names. *British Archaeological Reports,* 214.

DARVILL, T. 1987. *Prehistoric Britain*. London: Batsford.

DAVIES, W. 1978. *An early Welsh microcosm*. Royal Historical Society Studies in History, 9. London: Royal Historical Society.

DOBLE, G.H. 1984. *Lives of the Welsh saints*. Cardiff: University of Wales Press.

GALBRAITH, V.H. & TAIT, J. 1950. Herefordshire Domesday. *The Pipe Roll Society*, ns 25, 1947-1948.

GIBBINGS, R. 1942. *Coming down the Wye*. London: Dent.

GRINSELL, L.V. 1993. Herefordshire Barrows. *Transactions of the Woolhope Naturalists' Field Club,* 47, 299-317.

HOOKE, D. 1985. *The Anglo-Saxon landscape*. Manchester: Manchester University Press.

KAULFUSS, E. 1983. *Roses at Midnight*. Madley: Castlebury Books.

KAY, R.E. 1967. Three unrecorded earthworks from south-west Herefordshire. *Transactions of the Woolhope Naturalists' Field Club*, 39, 40-43.

MARGARY, I.D. 1967. *Roman roads in Britain*. London: John Baker.

MARTIN, S.H. 1953. St. Guthlac, Hereford's forgotten saint. *Transactions of the Woolhope Naturalists' Field Club*, 34, 62-69.

O'DONNELL, J. 1971. Market centres in Herefordshire, 1200-1400. *Transactions of the Woolhope Naturalists' Field Club*, 40, 186-194.

PYE, W.R. 1958. Report on prehistoric finds in north-west Herefordshire. *Transactions of the Woolhope Naturalists' Field Club*, 36, 80-83.

PYE, W.R. 1969. Dorstone Hill, Herefordshire. *Herefordshire Archaeological News-sheet*, number 14, August 1969.

PYE, W.R.. 1971. A flint axe from Moccas. *Herefordshire Archaeological News-sheet*, number 23, October 1971.

ROUND, J.H. 1908. Introduction to the Herefordshire Domesday. *In:* W. PAGE, ed. *Victoria County History, Herefordshire I*. London: Constable, 263-307.

SHOESMITH, R. 1967-1969. Reports of sectional recorders: Archaeology, 1967, 1968, 1969. *Transactions of the Woolhope Naturalists' Field Club*, 157-159, 362-364, 475-477.

STANFORD, S.C. 1965. Reports of sectional recorders: Archaeology, 1965. *Transactions of the Woolhope Naturalists' Field Club*, 38, 156-159.

STANFORD, S.C. 1980. *The archaeology of the Welsh Marches*. London: Collins.

THORN, F. & THORN, C. 1983. *Domesday Book: Herefordshire*. Chichester: Phillimore.

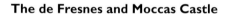
The de Fresnes, Vaughans and Cornewalls:
1160-1771

David Whitehead

2
—
2

He lay very still and quiet with his legs crossed and his feet resting against his faithful hound. There was a look of deep calm upon his face .... the Great Crusade, the Battle of Life, was over .... his hands were clasped in silent prayer. And so in the dim light of the choir of the old Norman church he [de Fresne] *had lain silently praying night and day for seven hundred years.*

Francis Kilvert's description of the effigy (Figure 2.2.1) in Moccas Church, 10 April 1875.[1]

Moccas Park appears to breathe antiquity but no firm evidence has yet emerged for its existence prior to the seventeenth century. Much of what follows is a reconstruction of the manorial history of Moccas and the adjoining parishes of Dorstone and Bredwardine. The evolution of Moccas as a gentry estate with a deer park, is very firmly tied up with the rise and decline of these adjoining baronial centres, both of which had deer parks long before the time when one can be evidenced at Moccas.

Figure 2.2.1

Effigy in Moccas Church. It is thought to be of a member of the de Fresne family. The photograph was taken in 1933 by Alfred Watkins, it is reproduced by courtesy of Hereford City Library.

The de Fresnes and Moccas Castle

The first de Fresne to live at Moccas was Walter, who appears in the margin of the *Balliol Domesday* of *circa* 1160 as "W. de Mocres".[2] He also gave his name to Freen's Court in the parish of Sutton St Michael in central Herefordshire. Walter was the successor of Nigel, William the Conqueror's physician, at both Sutton and Moccas, but since he called himself 'de Mocres' he was probably domiciled there, perhaps at the castle adjoining the park.[3] He shared a fishery on the Wye with the prior of St Guthlac's.[4]

Figure 2.2.2

The de Fresne family arms. "Or, a lion rampant gules langued azure within a bordure sable" (Strong 1848).

The motte and bailey castle at Moccas (Figure 2.2.3), lying adjacent to the eastern boundary of the present day Park, was noted in the mid nineteenth century by the Reverend Sir George Cornewall. Robinson, following local tradition, had no hesitation in associating the earthwork with the de Fresnes.[5] It is strange that the castle is remote from the twelfth century church, because elsewhere in Herefordshire castles provide a manorial focus alongside the church. This is probably explained by the division of Moccas between St Guthlac's and Nigel as noted in *Domesday* (see Chapter 2.1).

The productive three hide estate in the hands of the minster was probably close to the church of which they were the patrons.[6] The one hide estate in Nigel's hands no doubt provided the site for the castle. In the thirteenth century the adjoining settlement – Woodbury Farm – was

Figure 2.2.3

Moccas Castle.
The site of the motte and bailey castle photographed by Alfred Watkins in 1925; very little survives today. Reproduced by courtesy of Hereford City Library.

one of those manors to which Gloucester Abbey laid claim as part of the ancient patrimony of St Guthlac's.[7] The castle therefore seems to be on the original portion of Nigel's holding and was probably built by his tenant, a de Mocres, in the late eleventh or early twelfth century, that is to say before the de Fresnes gained complete control of the manor.

The de Fresnes prospered and although they owned a moated manor house at Sutton Freen together with many other properties, they continued to regard Moccas as their principal residence. In 1294 Hugh de Fresne was granted a royal crenellation licence which allowed him "to strengthen with a stone wall without a tower or turret and not exceeding ten feet in height below the battlements" his manor house at Moccas. Either Hugh failed to adhere to these limitations or started work prematurely, for later in the year the sheriff of Hereford was instructed to seize his fortified house at Moccas.[8]

Robinson and others have assumed that the work took place upon the site of the motte and bailey castle and that this enhancement, together with the right of free warren, granted in 1291, which allowed him to hunt small game animals on all of his estates, implied that the Park may well have come into existence at this time.[9] Crenellation licences frequently went hand in hand with imparking,[10] moreover, Hugh had very little room to manoeuvre at Sutton Freen which was located in an area of intense arable farming, surrounded by open fields.[11] Moccas, on the other hand, was set in a landscape where there was probably plenty of residual woodland, indicated in *Domesday* by the large number of adjoining estates with "waste", thus providing a suitable location for a park.[12]

Notwithstanding the lack of documentary evidence for the scenario sketched out above, it provides a reasonable explanation for the arrival of the deer park at Moccas.[13] And the position of the castle in proximity to what is now the Park would seem to demonstrate a classic relationship between castle and deer park commented upon at Devizes, Windsor and elsewhere,[14] and repeated in Herefordshire where at least 14 deer parks are associated with castles.[15]

There are, however, certain problems with this scenario. Archaeologists question whether the earthwork castle was ever re-edified in stone. They have found no traces of mortared or cut stone on the site,[16] and the puny mound, which had summit dimensions of 12 feet x 9 feet and rose less than 12 feet above the bailey, seems too insubstantial to have received a tower. Kay, who surveyed the site in 1953 before it was deeply ploughed, concluded: "It seems unlikely, from the surface evidence remaining, that any portion of the 'castle' was of masonry construction".[17]

Moccas Castle may have been the earliest focus of the de Mocres (Fresne) holding at Moccas, but with the demise of St Guthlac's estate, made evident by the *Balliol Domesday* in circa 1160, the opportunity for developing a new residence, close to the church and at the centre of a community, may have appealed to later generations of the de Fresnes.[18] The first member of the family recorded as patron of the church was Hugh's son John (*floruit* 1306-46).[19] Perhaps his father's crenellation licence relates to the building or re-building of a stone castle close to the church rather than beside the Park.[20]

Did Moccas Park originate in the Golden Valley?

It is entirely possible that there was no park at Moccas in the Middle Ages. The Inquisition of Sir Richard de Fresne in 1375 mentions: "One ruinous house which is worth nothing....two plough lands of (arable) land which are worth approximately 30s per annum....twelve acres of meadow which are worth approximately 12s per annum....twelve acres of wood etc".[21] This is remarkably little land, by no means accounting for the *Domesday Book* estate of four hides, and there is no mention of a park.

However, nearly all Richard's neighbours had parks and it would therefore be surprising if there had not been one at Moccas. The park of Ralph de Baskerville III (d.1210) at

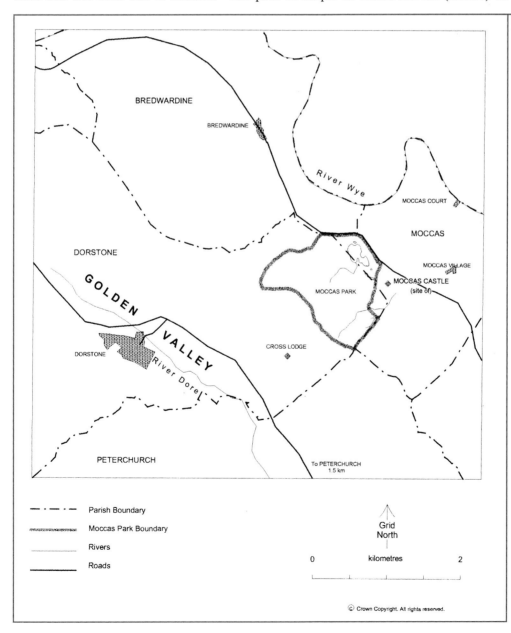

Figure 2.2.4

Local features. The location of Moccas Park in relation to the boundaries of local civil parishes, villages, roads, rivers and other features.

— ·· — ·· —   Parish Boundary

~~~~~~~~~   Moccas Park Boundary

————   Rivers

————   Roads

Grid North

0   kilometres   2

© Crown Copyright. All rights reserved.

Bredwardine is mentioned in the late twelfth century, whilst another in the parish of Dorstone is referred to in 1317 as belonging to Geoffrey de Bella Fago.[22] Geoffrey complained to the king that several persons, including John de Solers, had carried away hay from his park. It has not been possible to trace Geoffrey de Bella Fago elsewhere in Herefordshire (the family's property seems to have been confined to Oxfordshire and the adjoining counties), but John de Solers was the lord of Dorstone Castle and his carrying away of hay suggests that he had some claim upon the park.[23] Unfortunately however, although Dorstone is relatively well documented in the Middle Ages, finding evidence for the site of the park has proved impossible.

If there was a park associated with the lordship of Dorstone it had either disappeared by the mid-fourteenth century or it was very remote from the village centre. Thus, Dorstone/Moccas Park may have started its life as marginal land on the Dorstone ridge, attached to the manor of Dorstone rather than to that of Moccas.[24] Paul Harding and Trevor Rowley may well be right in suggesting that the de Bella Fago park was situated not at Dorstone itself but on and over the ridge in that enclave of Dorstone parish which now forms the largest portion of the present-day Moccas Park (Figure 2.2.4).[25] The presence of Cross Lodge (previously known as Lodge Grounds and Lodge Farm) in the Golden Valley, implies that at one point the Park may have been approached from Dorstone. Indeed, it is possible, as is pointed out later (see Chapter 3.1), that the Park may originally have run from as far down in the Golden Valley as the Dorstone to Peterchurch road.

The Park – if it existed – was unlikely to move towards Moccas during the greater part of the twelfth century when we have assumed that the Castle was occupied by the de Fresnes. The most likely date for these changes was not until the late twelfth or early thirteenth century, when, seemingly, the de Fresnes had abandoned their earthwork castle and had moved towards Moccas church or, perhaps, were domiciled at their other property, Freen's Court.

Figure 2.2.5

Parish boundaries. The location of Moccas Park in relation to the boundaries of Dorstone and other local civil parishes before 1950, and altitude in feet.

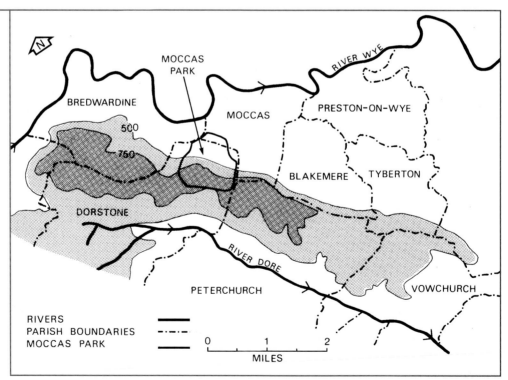

Trevor Rowley suggests that the parish boundary between Moccas and Dorstone originally followed the ridge – as it does for the adjoining parishes of Peterchurch and Vowchurch (Figure 2.2.5) – but was deliberately extended to the north east to embrace the enlarged park of Dorstone.[26] Yet it carefully avoids Moccas Castle, cutting it off from the land at its foregate. Such an action could only have occurred when the Castle was deserted, but leaving the Castle in Moccas parish perhaps had symbolic value for the lord of Moccas.

The Vaughans: parvenu gentry

Following the death of Richard de Fresne in about 1375, Moccas ceased to be the centre of a discrete lordship and a variety of men are found holding the estate. Sometime in the early sixteenth century it became part of a new powerful lordship, focused upon Bredwardine, founded by Sir Roger Vaughan (*circa* 1388-1415).[27] Sir Roger's family were to dominate the social and political life of west Herefordshire and Brecknock between the late fifteenth and early seventeenth centuries. Bredwardine Castle was re-built and celebrated in the patrimony of the second son.[28] A Walter Vaughan was settled at Moccas in about 1550.

Figure 2.2.6

The Vaughan family arms. "Tradition tells us that he [the ancestor of the house of Vaughan] was born with a snake round his neck ... from this supposed event his posterity took their arms:- Sable, three boys' heads couped at the shoulder, each having a snake wreathed round his neck, proper" (Leather 1912).

It is probably during this era that we can assume – for direct documentary evidence is still lacking – that Dorstone Park became Moccas Park and was attached to the Vaughan lordship. The Vaughans were a classic example of the parvenu gentry, thrown up by the Wars of the Roses, for whom a park would be the ultimate chivalric symbol. When Sir George Cornewall acquired the estate in 1772, it included property in Moccas, Bredwardine, Dorstone, Peterchurch, Cusop, Clifford and Cluttuck, indicating the extent of the Vaughan inheritance. The collapse of the major medieval lordships in the Golden Valley had provided plenty of opportunities for the Vaughan family to gorge itself upon property on the Dorstone side of the ridge. The park must have come with these earlier prizes and probably achieved its greatest extent at this time; but the symbolic acquisition of Dorstone Castle did not occur until Sir George Cornewall purchased it in 1780.[29]

All over England in the fifteenth century there was a retreat from arable farming; land was being enclosed, put down to pasture and imparked.[30] The royal records of this period are full of grants to the new gentry to embattle their houses and create parks. Three Herefordshire parks came into existence in this era, each associated with a family which had benefited from the "intestine broils" of the later Middle Ages. Hampton Court (1438) for Sir Roland Leinthall (1,000 acres imparked); Bronsil near Eastnor (1460) for Richard de Beauchamp (1,300 acres imparked) and Brampton Bryan, without specific licence, for the Harleys, probably after 1470.[31]

Moccas Park is not marked on Saxton's county map of 1577, but nor is Hampton Court or Bronsil, for which firm fifteenth century evidence exists. Saxton's imitators, Camden (in 1607), Speede (in 1610), Blome (in 1673) and Morden (in 1690), also ignore the Park, and it makes its first cartographic appearance on Saxton "resurveyed & enlarged" in 1665. By this date there is other evidence, the earliest dates from 1617, when Henry Vaughan of Moccas sent deer to stock the park of his cousin (Richard Boyle, Earl of Cork) in Youghal, Co. Cork.[32]

The Cornewalls: poachers turned park keepers

The story of the Cornewall succession to the Moccas estate specifically involves the deer park. Edward, the third son of John Cornewall of Berrington in Herefordshire, after fighting for the king in the Civil War, was in 1650 caught poaching deer in Moccas Park. Fortunately for Edward, Henry Vaughan's widow, his second wife Frances, "was so much struck by the prisoner's appearance" that she married him.[33] Edward Cornewall died in

Figure 2.2.7

The Cornewall family arms. "Argent, a lion rampant gules, ducally crowned or, within a bordure engrailed sable bezantée" (Strong 1848). The crest is a Cornish chough.

1708 and, according to Robinson, his son Henry (d.1716) acquired the rest of the Vaughan property including Bredwardine.[34]

The succession of the Cornewalls was a signal moment in the history of the Moccas Estate and may have had some impact upon the management of the Park. In 1677, a few years after the Park had appeared on 'Saxton resurveyed', the park pale is referred to on an ecclesiastical survey concerned with land close to Woodbury Farm. A similar survey of 1607 had failed to mention this feature and indicates that the adjoining land was in open fields. This suggests that there may have been some extension of the Park in the period between these two surveys, or at least its boundaries had been formalised.[35] It is suggested that the loose alignments of sweet chestnuts in the upper parts of the Park may date from the late seventeenth century (see Chapter 3.1) and the Cornewall succession may have ended a period of neglect and inaugurated improvements prompted by aesthetic considerations. The rows of sweet chestnuts in the Herefordshire parks of Brampton Bryan and Croft, which arrive in the seventeenth century seem to reflect such a change in the appreciation of medieval deer parks.

Moccas Park appears in detail on John Lambe Davis's survey of 1772 for Sir George Cornewall (see Chapter 2.3). Sir George (born Amyand) acquired the estate and his new surname, following his marriage in 1771 to the only daughter of Velters Cornewall M.P. who had died in 1768 without male heirs. The Park which Davis depicts, stretches from the Lawn south westwards up and over the Dorstone ridge and encloses Lodge Grounds. An approach from the Peterchurch to Dorstone road enters the Park below the lodge. Thus, the orientation of the park still seems to emphasise its apparent Dorstone origins. The western quarter of the park is depicted without trees, perhaps indicating that, like the park at Brampton Bryan in this period, it was divided into compartments to produce a succession of coppice.[36] A clear division is also indicated between the Park proper and The Lawn. A prominent feature of The Lawn is its pool, which at this date has a fairly regular shape. To the south east is the Upper and Lower Meer, another wet area where the remains of the castle stood, but the remains are at this date ignored, being left unmapped.

Notes

1   Plomer (1939). It is not definitely known whose effigy it is, but Kilvert, in common with others, attributes it to the de Fresne family (early sources use the spelling 'del Fresne', later ones 'de Fresne'). Kilvert believed it to be of Sir Reginald (dates not known) but Robinson (1869) on the authority of Silas Taylor, thought it to be of Richard (died *circa* 1375). Kilvert's grandmother's maiden name was Ashe, and he speculates spuriously on a family connection with the de Fresnes: "The thing that interested me most in the Church was the beautiful tomb of Sir Reginald de Fresne (Fraxinus = Ashe) the Crusader, perhaps an ancestor of my own". 'Frêne' and 'Fraxinus' are respectively the French and Latin names for an ash tree.
2   The *Balliol Domesday*, so called after Balliol College, Oxford, manuscript 350, provides an annotated transcription of the original Domesday Survey for Herefordshire. The interest lies in the annotations, which reflect changes in land ownership between 1086 and *circa* 1160.
3   Galbraith & Tait (1950).
4   St Guthlac's Cartulary, microfilm in Hereford Record Office.
5   Robinson (1869).
6   A 'hide' is an obscure and variable Old English measure of land thought to represent anything from 60 to 120 acres (24 to 48 ha).
7   St Guthlac's Cartulary, Coplestone-Crow (1979).
8   Calendar of Patent Rolls, Edward II, 23; Robinson (1869).
9   Robinson (1869), Cathcart King (1983).
10 Coulson (1979).
11 Sheppard (1979).
12 Darby (1954).
13 Whitehead (1995).
14 Crawford & Terrett (1953).
15 Cantor (1983).
16 Robinson (1869) states however that "the foundations have long formed a quarry for road metal".
17 Kay (1991).
18 The community may have included a market centre (O'Donnell 1971).
19 Capes (1909).
20 There is however no physical evidence on the ground to this effect.
21 Inquisitions Post Mortem XIV (1375-6), 124.
22 Banks (1883), Calendar of Patent Rolls 1313-17, 683.
23 Inquisitions Post Mortem IX, (1347-50), 124, 184.

24 The tendency for medieval parks to be sited on land of little value is common throughout England. The examples of Brampton Bryan and Rotherwas come to mind in Herefordshire.
25 Harding and Rowley, in correspondence in English Nature files.
26 Rowley, in correspondence in English Nature files.
27 Jones (1959).
28 Robinson (1869).
29 Robinson (1869).
30 Platt (1975), Cantor (1982).
31 Calendar of Patent Rolls 1429-36, 446; Calendar of Charter Rolls VI, 137; Whitehead (1996).
32 Townshend (1904).
33 Robinson (1869); this account suggests however that Edward may have had an ulterior motive and "have intended his shaft for nobler game than ranged in the park". By contrast, the account given by Vaughan (1904) is unreservedly romantic: Cornewall, heavily disguised under the rough garb of a country poacher is carried, bound and unconscious, to Frances Vaughan. He wakes to behold "the anxious face of an exceedingly beautiful woman [Frances] bending over him .... [whose eyes] .... forged bonds far more lasting than those of the park keepers, bonds which were rivetted for ever at the altar. So Moccas passed to the Cornewalls".
34 Robinson (1869).
35 Hereford Record Office, 6/64-68.
36 Whitehead (1996).

References relating to Moccas Park

ROBINSON, C.J. 1869. *A history of the castles of Herefordshire and their lords*. London: Longman.

TOWNSHEND, D. 1904. *The life and letters of the great Earl of Cork*. London: Duckworth.

VAUGHAN, H.F.J. 1904. The Vaughans of Herefordshire. *In*: C. READE, ed. *Memorials of old Herefordshire*. London: Hemrose and Sons.

WHITEHEAD, D. 1995. Some connected thoughts on the parks and gardens of Herefordshire before the age of landscape gardening. *Transactions of the Woolhope Naturalists' Field Club*, 193-223.

Other references

BANKS, R.W. 1883. Cartularium Prioratus S Johannis Evang. de Brecon. *Archaeologia Cambrensis*.

CALENDAR OF PATENT ROLLS. London: HMSO.

CALENDAR OF CHARTER ROLLS. London: HMSO.

CANTOR, L. 1983. *The medieval parks of England: a Gazetteer*. Loughborough: Loughborough University.

CANTOR, L. 1982. *The English medieval landscape*. London: Croome Helm.

CAPES, W.W., ed. 1909. *Richard Swinfield's registers of the bishops of Hereford*. London: Canterbury and York Society.

CATHCART KING, D.J. 1983. *Castellarium Anglicanum*. New York: Kraus International.

COPLESTONE-CROW, B. 1979. The Baskervilles of Herefordshire. *Transactions of the Woolhope Naturalists' Field Club*, 18-39.

COULSON, C. 1979. Structural symbolism in medieval castle architecture. *Journal of the British Archaeological Association*, 132, 73-90.

CRAWFORD, O.G.S. & TERRETT, I.B. 1953. *Archaeology in the field*. London: Phoenix House.

DARBY, H.C., ed. 1954. *The Domesday Geography of Midland England*. Cambridge: Cambridge University Press.

GALBRAITH, V.H. & TAIT, J. 1950. Herefordshire Domesday. *The Pipe Roll Society*, ns 25, 1947-1948.

INQUISITIONS POST MORTEM. London: HMSO.

JONES, E. 1959. Sir Roger Vaughan. *In*: ANON eds. *Dictionary of Welsh Biography*. London: Cymmrodorion Society, 992-993.

KAY, R.E. 1991. Moccas Castle. *Herefordshire Archaeological News*, 55, 5-6.

LEATHER, E.M. 1912. *The Folk-lore of Herefordshire*. Hereford: Jakeman & Carver.

O'DONNELL, J. 1971. Market centres in Herefordshire 1200-1400. *Transactions of the Woolhope Naturalists' Field Club*, 186-194.

PLATT, C. 1975. *Medieval England*. London: Secker and Warburg.

PLOMER, W. 1939. *Kilvert's Diary*. Volume two. London: Jonathan Cape.

SHEPPARD, J. 1979. *The origin and evolution of the field and settlement patterns of the Herefordshire manor of Marden.* Queen Mary College, London University, Department of Geography, Occasional Papers No 15.

STRONG, G. 1848. *The heraldry of Herefordshire.* London: Churton.

WHITEHEAD, D. 1996. Brampton Bryan Park: a documentary history. *In*: A. SCLATER, (Landskip & Prospect). *Brampton Bryan Park, Herefordshire: historical research, aesthetic evaluation, advice on replanting.* Report to English Nature, 1996.

2
2

Sir George Cornewall:
management, improvement and landscaping, 1771-1819

Susanne Seymour, Charles Watkins and Stephen Daniels

Still let utility improvement guide,
And just congruity in all preside.
While shaggy hills are left to rude neglect,
Let the rich plains with wavy corn be deck'd.

Richard Payne Knight (1795) *The Landscape.*[1]

I
n the eighteenth century the Moccas Estate was one of a number of modest gentry properties in the fertile country of the Middle Wye valley between Hereford and Hay-on-Wye. It was an established estate, densely inscribed with old features, including the Deer Park, aged pollards, an ancient British burial place called Arthur's Stone, the ruins of Moccas and Bredwardine castles and a scattering of old manors, including the house at Moccas itself. In this chapter we place the survival and management of Moccas Park within a broader estate management context.[2]

In 1771 Moccas came under the control of Sir George Cornewall (Figure 2.3.1) who had inherited from his father, Sir George Amyand, a considerable fortune of around £158,000, including a house at Carshalton in Surrey, a modest estate in Berkshire, La Taste plantation on Grenada in the West Indies, and a share in his London banking firm, Amyand, Staples and Mercer. The Moccas Estate in Herefordshire was added to this list when he married the heiress of a well-established county family, Catherine Cornewall (Figure 2.3.2) under the condition that he change his name to Cornewall.[3] The Cornewall family had been established in the county at Berrington since medieval times. A new branch of the family developed at Moccas when a younger son married the widow of its previous owners, another ancient family, the Vaughans, in 1650[4] (see Chapter 2.2).

Cornewall relinquished his position in the Amyand banking business in 1776 to adopt the established duties of the Cornewall family, as country squire and MP, having been elected for the Whigs in

Figure 2.3.1

Portrait of Sir George Amyand Cornewall (1748-1819) by George Romney, 1785. Private collection; photograph by courtesy of the National Portrait Gallery, London.

Figure 2.3.2

Portrait of Lady Catherine Cornewall (1752-1835) by Sir Joshua Reynolds, 1779. Private collection; photograph by courtesy of Sotheby's.

Herefordshire in 1774.[5] However, he did not divest himself of all his trading interests and colonial investments and concerned himself with estate management in Herefordshire and Grenada.[6]

Cornewall soon developed a reputation as an improving landlord and farmer. He was a founder member of the Herefordshire Agricultural Society in 1797 and has been praised as an agricultural innovator and promoter of technological changes on his estate.[7] He was interested in the aesthetics as well as the economics of landscape. Lancelot 'Capability' Brown was commissioned to provide plans for a new park and later Humphry Repton was consulted on changes in the immediate vicinity of the house. However Cornewall may well have preferred the 'Picturesque' style of estate management being developed locally by his neighbour, Uvedale Price, at Foxley, and at Downton in north Herefordshire by Richard Payne Knight (see Chapter 3.1). While Richard is said to have advised on landscaping at Moccas, his brother, Thomas Andrew Knight, President of the Horticultural Society and an authority on Herefordshire agriculture, was also influential. Thomas Knight celebrated his friendship with Cornewall by naming one of his new fruit varieties the Moccas Pear.[8]

The enlargement and rationalisation of the estate

Soon after inheriting the Moccas property, Cornewall commissioned a comprehensive survey of the estate and surrounding land from John Lambe Davis (Figure 2.3.3) which prepared the ground for his subsequent improvements.[9] These included purchases of new land, the promotion of enclosures, an extensive woodland planting programme, enlarging fields and farms, the introduction of new leases, the creation of a 'model' home farm and landscaping. These measures all helped to raise the gross rental more than five-fold over the following 40 years.[10]

In 1772, the Moccas Estate covered around 3,875 acres, with rights of common on an additional 362 acres, in the parishes of Moccas, Dorstone, Bredwardine, Peterchurch, Cusop, Clifford and Cluttuck. By 1818 over 3,560 acres of mainly freehold land had been added, entailing an investment of around £64,000 and, with some land sales, creating an estate of some 7,000 acres. The bulk of the land purchases were made before 1795, generally at cheap rates. Although some capital was available from his merchant inheritance and from the rent of La Taste, his West Indian plantation, by 1794 Cornewall had borrowed at least £29,000 (at an interest rate of 3.5%) to facilitate the expansion of his estates in Herefordshire.[11]

The major part of the land purchased by Cornewall lay in the vicinity of Moccas parish, as part of a deliberate policy to consolidate as well as to extend his property. Cornewall's largest single acquisition, the Monnington Estate in 1775, must be seen in the light of his broad view of estate improvement. Not only did the transaction add 857 acres of land to the Moccas Estate, it brought into Cornewall's possession the land on the north bank of the Wye immediately opposite his new mansion house, and part of Brobury Scar, arguably the most 'Picturesque' feature of his estate.[12]

As well as allowing the consolidation of his property around Moccas, Cornewall's land investments facilitated the rationalisation of his estate lands. These were generally let in larger units, a number under leases with detailed husbandry clauses. In 1772 the estate was let to 32 tenants and 46 cottagers and of the tenanted farms only nine exceeded 100 acres in size. Most of the farms were between 5 and 50 acres. By 1815 the pattern of landholdings had been significantly transformed: most of the 30 tenants held farms of over 100 acres and only seven rented less than 50 acres. These changes did not lead to the demise of cottagers on the estate; numbers increased through land purchases and it is probable that there were around 78 cottagers in 1815.[13]

Figure 2.3.3

John Lambe Davis's survey of 1772. Two pages from the survey of Sir George Cornewall's estate which show Moccas Park and adjacent land. Reproduced by courtesy of the Woolhope Club and Hereford City Library. Photographs by Kenneth J. Hoverd.

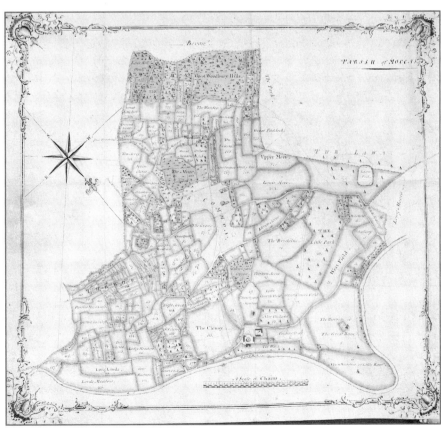

Figure 2.3.4

'A Plan for the intended Alterations at Moccas Court in Herefordshire, The Seat of Sir George Cornewall Bart by LB: 1778'. Lancelot 'Capability' Brown's plan was sold at Sotheby's in July 1986, it is now at The Getty Center for the History of Arts and the Humanities. Photograph by courtesy of Sotheby's.

Cornewall, like many landowners, promoted enclosures, although as a classic open field system probably never operated extensively in Herefordshire, which was generally enclosed early, these were mainly of limited areas of common grassland.[14] He was closely involved with that of Moccas Common in 1798 and lands in Bredwardine and Dorstone in 1819. The enclosure of Moccas Common was a small-scale affair, enacted by an informal agreement among the commoners. The enclosure of hill lands in Bredwardine and Dorstone by Act of Parliament was much more substantial and lengthy, proceedings beginning as early as 1808.

Landscaping and estate improvement

The purchase of land in the vicinity of Moccas parish allowed field and farm consolidation, the creation of new and larger farms and also facilitated Cornewall's landscaping activities.

Both the 1772 survey and Brown's parkland plan were controlling devices for these improvements. In 1772, Cornewall owned around 730 acres or 63% of the parish of Moccas and by 1815 he owned over three-quarters (76%) of the land in the parish. This territorial expansion involved Cornewall buying out completely a number of landowners listed in the 1772 survey of the parish. This survey provided the base from which these purchases and exchanges were made, fields and farms consolidated, the home farm developed, the common enclosed and new parkland laid out near the house.[15] Cornewall targeted particular areas in the parish in which to purchase land, notably the north east portion adjacent to the River Wye, the southwest fringe of wooded hillside and areas within or adjacent to the area proposed for a new park by Brown in his 1778 plans.

Lands were drained and ditches were made and kept clean, one of the principal agricultural improvements in this riverine area. On the other hand, lands were also fertilized by watering or flooding, a recognised improving practice in Herefordshire.[16] Manures generally were carefully managed on the farm and supplies of lime bought in. Ant hills were levelled, stones picked up (for subsequent use in field drainage) and both the sward and fields improved by growing trefoil, ryegrass, and white and red clover. A prominent feature of Cornewall's estate improvements was his development, from 1781, of an 'improving' home farm in the vicinity of the newly-built Moccas Court. New buildings were also erected here in 1783-84 and these were "as carefully designed as the house itself".[17] The farm included many aspects of agriculture celebrated as progressive at the time: a flock of improved breeds of sheep, the cultivation of improved grasses, hoed turnips and potatoes, experiments with swedes in 1801 and the use of new implements, including a threshing machine set up at Moccas in 1810.[18]

The heart of the farm which Cornewall was developing was located in the same area that 'Capability' Brown had suggested for a new park, when he was commissioned by Cornewall in 1778. His 'Plan for the intended Alterations at Moccas Court' (Figure 2.3.4) recommended that Cornewall remove the existing network of arable fields and meadows to create a sweeping grass prospect. Brown was not kept on to implement his plan and received only a relatively small payment of £100 for the plan itself (which can be tellingly compared to the £1,600 paid to Brown for his work at Berrington Hall north of Leominster).[19] Over the next 10 to 15 years, Cornewall and his staff adapted Brown's suggestions and gradually implemented landscaping which accommodated estate management in a way which Brown's original plan did not. A principal difference lay in the retention of substantial amounts of arable land where Brown had suggested conversion to grass. Although Cornewall laid down some of the existing arable land to grass and put in ha-has in some areas, he re-organized rather than obliterated the field pattern, transferring arable land from the main line of the prospect (from the house towards Moccas Park on the hill) to hidden or peripheral areas, and farming activity continued (Figures 2.3.5 and 2.3.6). Brown's influence on the shaping of Moccas Park itself is discussed in Chapter 3.1.

Moccas Park was also incorporated into Cornewall's strategy of estate improvements. Grazing rights were regularly let within the Deer Park, a relatively common occurrence in the county and elsewhere. Regular payments, ranging between £7,15s,6d in 1771 and £72,18s,6d in 1796, were made annually from the 1770s for the pasturing of a number of cattle and horses, and from the late 1780s of around 260 sheep, for seven months of the year in the Park. The sheep and some of the cattle and horses grazed in the Park belonged to Cornewall himself and his payments of around £17 a year for his use of the Park from 1789 reflect his rigorous accounting style for his home farm.[20] Such grazing together with the planting of woodlands was an appropriate use of this generally poor hill land, valued in 1803 for the most part at only 5s an acres (a rate of 6-7s was estimated for the 38 acres of the lower part of the Park called 'The Lawn' which lies in Moccas parish).[21] However, Cornewall did make some attempts to improve and let parts of the Park. In around 1797 nearly 53 acres were taken out of the south western part of the Park and added to Mr Williams's Llanavon Farm near

2/3

Figure 2.3.5

Land use in
1772 of the
area included
in Brown's
plan of 1778.

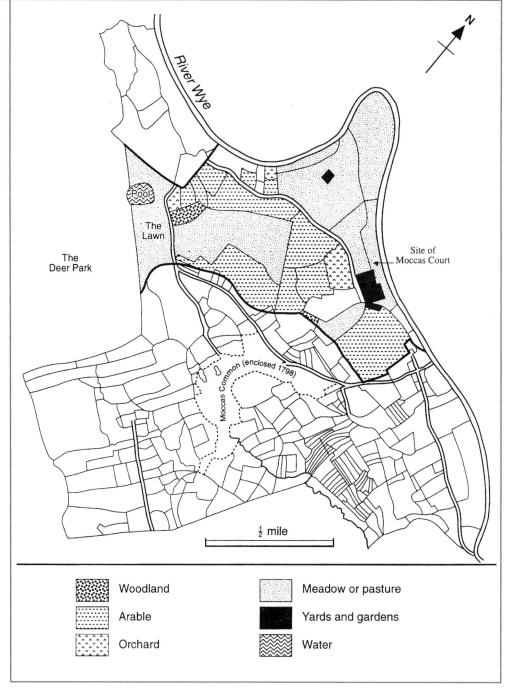

Figure 2.3.5

Land use in 1772 of the area included in Brown's plan of 1778.

Dorstone. By 1808 about 10 acres of this had been converted into arable land, mostly valued at 13s an acre (double its former value). The remainder was rough grassland, one third improved to a value of 13s an acre, the rest let at 7s an acre. A further 76 acres were let in 1797 to Mr Pritchard, consisting of nearly 18 acres converted into arable valued at 12s an acre and 58 acres of rough grassland at 7s an acre. In 1808, this land was let for £38.[22] The extent of this letting may have been even greater, as by 1807 Cornewall kept in hand only 288 acres of the Park whereas in 1803 he held 439 acres of it.[23]

Cornewall's account books, which include entries for household, personal and estate expenses (see Figure 2.3.7), provide additional evidence of improvements and landscaping within Moccas Park and to its boundaries. Payments for "raising" and "hauling" stone and for using it to build the "park wall" are likely to relate to Moccas Park as are entries for work

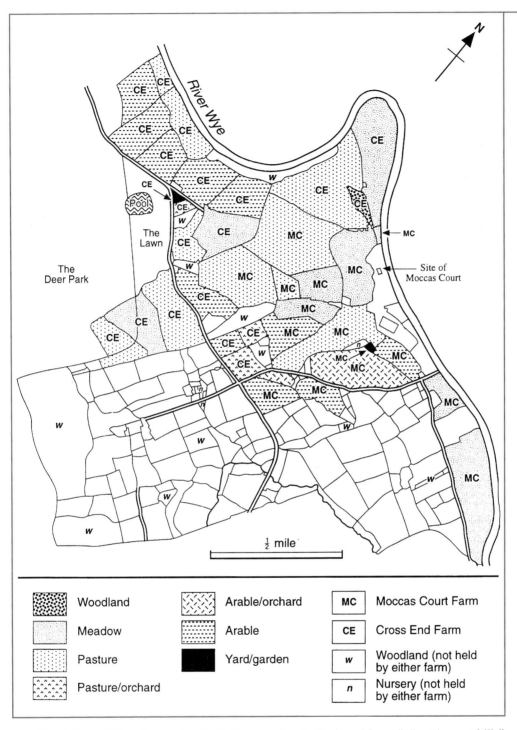

Figure 2.3.6

Land use on Moccas Court Farm and Cross End Farm in 1836.

Woodland	Arable/orchard	**MC** Moccas Court Farm
Meadow	Arable	**CE** Cross End Farm
Pasture	Yard/garden	**w** Woodland (not held by either farm)
Pasture/orchard		**n** Nursery (not held by either farm)

on a "sunk fence", "hauling park pales", "cutting fern in Park and Lawn", "cutting ant hills" (an entry in January 1784 refers to 400 of them), tree planting, road and drive making and cleaning "part of Lawn pool".[24]

Trees and woodlands

Cornewall was active in woodland management on many parts of his property. Woodland on the estate, previously accessed by tenants and many others, was systematically taken in hand, fenced, and managed in Cornewall's interest. This process may well have been partly linked to Cornewall's attempts to enhance the sporting potential of his estate.

Figure 2.3.7

Sir George Cornewall's Account Book. This double page spread is from the Account Book for 1777-1785, it covers the period July 20 to December 31 1785. A transcription is given in Appendix 10. Reproduced courtesy of the Chester-Master family and the Hereford Record Office. Photograph by Kenneth J. Hoverd.

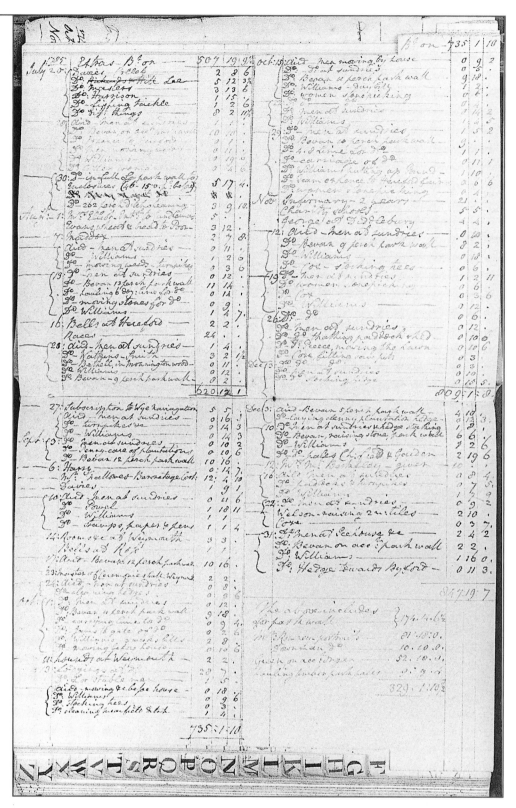

Tree planting was also carried out on a large scale. When the gardener and landscape improver John Claudius Loudon visited Moccas in 1836, he met Mr J. Webster, who had been the "gardener and forester there" since 1793.[25] Webster reported that over the past 43 years he had superintended the planting of "nearly 300,000 oaks, besides other trees, particularly on hill sides, unfit for producing either grass or corn from their steepness". Nurseries were pragmatically established on these same hillsides, so that trees were already acclimatised when transferred to plantations. According to Webster, this "made an indescribable difference in their growth when planted out" and that after thirty years' growth, larches "have attained a large size and are used for all building purposes and for fences".[26] Products included faggots, hop poles, rail poles, cord wood and timber.[27] Webster's very significant contribution to the landscaping of Moccas Park is discussed further in Chapters 3.1, 3.4 and 3.5.

Brobury Scar, a steep incision into red till, created by the River Wye, and perhaps the most conventionally 'Picturesque' of features at Moccas, was just such a site (see Figure 6.3.2). The summit of the Scar and part of its bank was planted with over 9,400 oak and sweet chestnuts, in a 'Picturesque' style, in 1812-13, with walks giving occasional views through to the Wye, house and parkland.[28] Indeed, much of the planting in the environs of Moccas was also associated with Cornewall's landscape improvements. Brick Kiln and Clenny Plantations were among a number created in the 1770s and 1780s in Moccas parish, while others, including the Warren Plantation, were extended. Large trees were also scattered through the West Field, the Warren, the Clenny and close to Moccas Court between 1786 and 1789. The ample timber resources of the parkland at Moccas in particular had been pointed out by Duncumb in 1805 when he singled it out for special mention as well-wooded, containing "very large and valuable supplies of timber for every purpose".[29] There was a "Large fall of timber at Moccas, Bredwardine, Monnington &c" in 1808-1809 when over £12,600 worth was sold in an attempt to stave off financial crisis mainly brought about by the failure of Cornewall's mercantile and colonial investments.[30] Cornewall's realisation of many of the timber assets of his estate was followed by a massive planting programme in which over 7,500 oaks and 47,500 larch and firs were set in 1817 and 1818, mainly on Weston Hill, west of Bredwardine.[31]

Cornewall commissioned the water colourist Thomas Hearne to document Moccas in a series of views which both celebrate its modern improvements and commemorate its ancient features.[32] The views include an expansive prospect over the Moccas Estate from Bredwardine Bridge, which spans the River Wye, 1 mile north of Moccas Park. The view shows a rich network of meadows, fields and woods on the hillsides at Dorstone and Bredwardine, looking towards the edge of Moccas Park in the distance and the lush riverside meadows spread along the valley floor. The Moccas Estate was typically represented in this way. Despite the heavy falls of timber in 1808-1809, an 1821 account describes the "well wooded and undulating surface" of the Moccas domain as presenting "numerous interesting scenes".[33]

One of Hearne's more sequestered views is *Moccas Deer Park with a Large Oak Tree (circa 1788-1789)* (Figure 1.1.1). Here the image is dominated by the bulk of a gnarled and storm-damaged ancient pollarded oak tree, 'the Moccas Oak', the best known of a number found in the Park and elsewhere at Moccas (see Chapter 3.2). Such isolated trees at various locations in the country were the subject of several paintings by Hearne and other 'Picturesque' artists especially from the 1780s onwards.[34] Indeed, this is just such a tree as Uvedale Price praises in his *Essay on the Picturesque* of 1794:

> "Among trees, it is not the smooth young beech, nor the fresh and tender ash, but the rugged old oak, or knotty wyche elm, that are picturesque; nor is it necessary they should be of great bulk; it is sufficient if they are rough, mossy, with a character of age, and with sudden variations in their forms. The limbs of huge trees, shattered by lightning or tempestuous winds, are in the highest degree picturesque..."[35]

By the late eighteenth century oaks had a well-established if complex symbolism. Of particular interest in relation to the Hearne watercolour are the oak's associations with ancient patrician government and naval power, both military and commercial through the provision of ship timber.[36] Both of these aspects would have been appreciated by Cornewall. From merchant and banking stock, and, as the owner of a sugar plantation in Grenada, concerned with colonial trade, any image of an oak, even such an old and damaged one as this, would have appealed to Cornewall through its associations with the merchant navy. His position as a Herefordshire estate owner strengthened Cornewall's association with merchant trade and the slave trade in particular. Most of the timber felled on well-wooded Herefordshire estates like Moccas was transported down the Wye and Severn to the port of Bristol where slave ships, specifically designed for the trade, and merchant vessels were built, and the bulk of the city's overseas trade carried out with the West Indies.[37] Similarly, the celebration of the oak's intimate connections with the Royal Navy would have raised Cornewall's commercial confidence and eased his fears of invasion, both at home and in the West Indies.

This watercolour was published as an etching in 1798, coinciding with the growing popularity of the 'Picturesque', particularly its Herefordshire connections, and the wars with Revolutionary France. It was issued as one of six *Picturesque landscapes*, etched by B. T. Pouncy (Figure 1.1.1).[38] The commentary to the engraving devotes most space to elaborating the useful associations of the oak:

> "the oak is the first in the class of deciduous trees; and it is a happiness to the lovers of the picturesque that it is as useful as it is beautiful. Because, from the utility of the oak, it is everywhere to be found; and surely, no one who is a lover of his country, but, in addition to the pleasure which he has in contemplating this noble plant, must feel his heart glow on reflecting, that from its produce springs the British Navy, which gives our Island so honourable a distinction among surrounding nations."[39]

It was the stock of the lesser compatriots of this tree, growing in Moccas Park and on other nearby estate lands, which came to Cornewall's rescue when he was struck by acute financial problems in the early nineteenth century. The trees realised over £12,600 in 1808-1809, but their very 'Picturesque' qualities, principally "the roughness of the bark" and "broken or damaged timber", had proved deceptive to the valuer, who had expected them to fetch £633 more.[40]

Conclusion

Sir George Cornewall's management of the Moccas Estate in the later Georgian period shows many of the common traits of estate management of the time. Land was accumulated by buying out lesser owners; remnants of common arable fields and grazing lands were enclosed; field boundaries were remodelled; plantations were established; new parkland was laid out and modified. Moccas Park was not unaffected by the zeal for improvement. Its boundaries were secured, its pastures were grazed by cattle, horses and sheep as well as deer, trees were planted, drives were made and small areas were incorporated in adjoining farms and even converted to arable land. However, the position of the Park on poorer land to the edge of the estate, well away from the mansion house, to some extent protected it from the excesses of Georgian parkland improvement. Moccas Park could be viewed at a distance from the house along a vista carefully managed by Cornewall, but those who wished for a closer inspection would have to make a special effort to experience it at first hand. The Park with its ancient trees was certainly valued and celebrated in the later Georgian period, but we should be careful not to give it the pre-eminent importance in the local landscape that it has subsequently achieved. Rather, it was one of an album of landscape experiences, which included other ancient trees on the estate, new enclosures and plantations, the River Wye, the new parkland around the mansion house and Brobury Scar.

Notes

1. Knight's *The Landscape, a didactic poem in three books*, was first published in 1794; it initiated 'The Picturesque Controversy'. These lines are amongst a number added for the second edition of *The Landscape* (1795) as a riposte to Humphry Repton, and others, who had, as Knight claimed in a footnote, carried their "misrepresentations .... so far as even to insinuate that my system of improvement tended 'to turn this beautiful kingdom into one huge picturesque forest'". Knight lived at Downton in the north of Herefordshire. He was a friend of Sir George Cornewall and also of Uvedale Price, who, along with Knight, was the other great advocate of 'The Picturesque' and lived at Foxley 4 miles north east of Moccas. Imperial measurements are used throughout this chapter. One mile is equivalent to 1.6 kilometres and one acre is equivalent to 0.4047 hectares.

2. We would like to thank the Leverhulme Trust for its support in funding a project on *Picturesque landscaping and estate management: the regional context of a landscape theory*, through which the research on which this chapter is based, was undertaken.

3. Thompson (1976), Namier & Brooke (1964).

4. The National Trust (1986), Robinson (1872).

5. Articles of agreement for dissolution of partnership agreement of 1770, 6 May 1774, Hereford Record Office (hereafter HCRO) J56/VI/17. Cornewall served as an MP from 1774-1796 and from 1802-1807 when he retired from parliament, see Thorne (1986), Thompson (1976) and Namier & Brooke (1964).

6. For a comparison of estate management at La Taste and Moccas see Seymour, Daniels & Watkins (1998).

7. Jones (1974).

8. Thompson (1976), Inglis-Jones (1968), Duncumb (1805), Hogg (n.d.). Thomas Andrew Knight was a protégé of Sir Joseph Banks and well-known for his agricultural and horticultural experiments. In 1805 he became a Fellow of the Royal Society and from 1811 until his death in 1838 he served as President of the Horticultural Society.

9. *A survey of the manors of Moccas, Bredwardine, Grove, Radnor, Wilmaston, and Cusop, and a farm at Crosswall; situate in the parishes of Moccas, Bredwardine, Dorston, Peter-church, Cusop, Clifford, and Cluttuck, in the county of Hereford: belonging to Sir George Cornewall Baronet.* By John Lambe Davis. 1772. Hereford City Library (hereafter HCL).

10. On average Cornewall paid around £18 an acre so that with average rents on the bulk of the estate rising from just over 11s an acre in 1772 to 20s an acre in around 1800, he paid between 18 and 33 years' purchase for his land at a time when the average was between 25 and 30 years; HCRO AF57/4/2, List of estates inherited and purchased, n.d. (c.1772-1794); HCRO BA89/9/4, Particular of lands bought by Cornewall, 1818; Beckett (1986).

11. Davis's *Survey*, 1772; HCRO AF57/4/1; HCRO AF57/5/2; Particular of estates in Herefordshire, purchased by Sir George Cornewall Bt with their present occupation and annual value, 1818, HCRO BA89/9/4; List of estates inherited and purchased, n.d. (c.1772-1794) HCRO AF57/4/2; List of lands bought, purchase money and annual value, n.d., HCRO AF57/4/2; List of payments to various persons for land, n.d., HCRO AF57/4/2; Letter from Mr Downes to George Cornewall, 7 Nov 1775, HCRO AF57/5/2; Letter from Mr Downes to George Cornewall, 14 Nov 1776, HCRO AF57/5/2; Rental of Herefordshire estates, 1794, HCRO AF57/4/2.

12. Payments for lands in Monnington are entered in the rental from Midsummer 1775; see Rentals of Moccas Estate, 1769-1786, HCRO AL33/1; List of Herefordshire estates, inherited and purchased, n.d., HCRO AF57/4/2; Particular of lands bought by George Cornewall, 1818, HCRO BA89/9/4.

13. HCL Survey of Cornewall's Herefordshire estates, 1772; HCRO BA89/9/4, Rental of Herefordshire estates, 1815; HCRO AL33/2, Rentals of the Moccas Estate, 1786-1810.

14. Jones (1974), Tate (1941).

15. A similar approach was adopted in the 1770 survey of Uvedale Price's nearby Foxley Estate for most of the parishes in which he owned land: *A book of survey containing the Manors of Yazor, Mancellacy, Bishopstone .... with the contents and yearly estimates of Uvedale Price Esq of Foxley .... in the year of our Lord 1770*, HCRO D 344; see also Daniels & Watkins (1991).

16. Duncumb (1805).

17. Thompson (1976).

18. Moccas Farm Accounts, 1781-1817, HCRO J56/III/115-117; Sir George Cornewall's account of work at Moccas from 1784, HCRO AF57/12.

19. Account Book of Sir George Cornewall containing household, personal and estate accounts, 1780, HCRO J56/IV/3. Characteristically, Brown was employed to implement the plans he suggested. Moccas, however, forms one of a small group of his commissions where payment was probably for the plan alone; other examples include Clumber (Nottinghamshire) in 1764, Grimsthorpe (Lincolnshire) in 1771 and Wardour Castle (Wiltshire) in 1780. See Seymour (1988), Hinde (1986).

20. Estate rentals and rent accounts, 1771-1799, HCRO J56/III/7-15 & 21-25; Moccas Farm Accounts, 1788-1796, HCRO J56/III/116.

21. Property tax assessment of lands in hand, 1803, HCRO AF57/7/6.

22. Wainwright's valuation and observations on the Old Park land in Llanavon, 1797, HCRO AF57/5/9-10; Letter from Benjamin Wainwright to George Cornewall, 10 Oct 1808, HCRO AF57/5/4.

23. Property tax assessments of lands in hand, 1803 and 1807-1808, HCRO AF57/7/6. A considerable portion of the southwestern part of Moccas Park in 1772 no longer forms part of the Park today and it would appear that the enclosures Cornewall made were retained; see Davis's *Survey* of 1772 and Phibbs (1993).

24. HCRO J56/IV/2, 3 and 4. The existence of other areas of parkland on the estate makes it impossible to attribute with certainty references to work "in park" to the Deer Park itself.

25. Loudon (1836).

26. Webster, cited in Loudon (1836).

27. Daniels & Watkins (1991); Monnington Coppice, amount of wood sold, 1802, HCRO AF57/4/13; Wood account at Woodbury hill, 1798, HCRO AF57/4/5; Quantity & value of timber sold at Moccas 1808-1809, HCRO LC Deeds 5214.

28. Sir George Cornewall's account of work at Moccas from 1784, HCRO AF57/12.

29. Duncumb (1805).

30. Sir George Cornewall's account of work at Moccas from 1784, HCRO AF57/12; Quantity & value of timber sold at Moccas 1808-1809, HCRO LC Deeds 5214.

31. Sir George Cornewall's account of work at Moccas from 1784, HCRO AF57/12; Weston-hill planting, 1817, HCRO AF57/12.

32 Hearne's nine watercolours of Moccas, all thought to date from the late 1780s, are as follows: (1) Moccas Deer Park with a large oak tree; (2) Monnington Oak with a view towards Moccas Court; (3) View east from the lower reaches of Moccas Deer Park (portrait); (4) Near Bodcott Farm (portrait); (5) View of Brobury Scar from Moccas Court; (6) View across Moccas Court gardens and Monnington meadows towards Hereford; (7) View from Bredwardine; (8) View of the Wye valley towards Hay-on-Wye; and (9) On the Wye at Moccas (British Museum).

33 Fielding (1821).

34 Examples by Hearne include *An oak tree* (*circa* 1786). This painting was owned by Richard Payne Knight, and Morris (1989) regards it as akin to the views of Dowton Vale painted by Hearne for Knight in 1784-1786, but in terms of subject and setting it is strongly suggestive of Moccas Park (Daniels & Watkins 1994).

35 Price (1810). In *The Landscape* (1794) Richard Payne Knight, expressed a similar enthusiam for ancient and stag-headed trees: "If years unnumber'd, or the lightning's stroke, /Have bar'd the summit of the lofty oak, /Entire and sacred let the ruin stand, /Nor fear the pruner's sacrilegious hand".

36 See Daniels (1988); James (1981); Seymour (1989).

37 Williams (1944).

38 The other etchings identified as part of this series are: *An ironwork at Downton, Herefordshire; The chestnut tree at Little Wymondley, Hertfordshire* (watercolour 1789); *An iron forge at Tintern, Monmouthshire* (drawn in 1794); *Beeham Force, Westmorland* and *In a lane at Kenilworth, Warwickshire*. All six views are bound in with the copy of Hearne & Byrne (1807) Vol.II, in the Guildhall Library, London, GR 2.2.1. Our thanks go to David Morris for this reference.

39 Letterpress accompanying the view of *An oak in Moccas Park, Herefordshire*, bound in with the copy of Hearne & Byrne (1807), as above.

40 Quantity and value of timber sold at Moccas, 1808-1809, HCRO J56/III/ LC Deeds 5214.

References relating to Moccas Park

DANIELS, S. & WATKINS, C. eds. 1994. *The Picturesque Landscape. Visions of Georgian Herefordshire.* Nottingham: University of Nottingham.

DUNCUMB, J. 1805. *General view of the Agriculture of the County of Hereford.*

HEARNE, T. & BYRNE, W. 1807. *The Antiquities of Great Britain.* Vol.II. London.

LOUDON, J.C. 1836. *The Gardener's Magazine*, 12, 368-369.

MORRIS, D. 1989. *Thomas Hearne and his landscape.* London: Reaktion Books.

PHIBBS, J.L. 1993. *Moccas Court, Herefordshire: notes on the landscaping of the deer park above the bracken line.* Report by Debois Landscape Survey Group to English Nature.

SEYMOUR, S., DANIELS, S. & WATKINS, C. 1998. Estate and empire: Sir George Cornewall's management of Moccas, Herefordshire and La Taste, Grenada, 1771-1819. *Journal of Historical Geography*, 24, 313-351.

Other references

BECKETT, J.V.1986. *The Aristocracy in England 1660-1914.* Oxford: Blackwell.

DANIELS, S. 1988. The political iconography of woodland in later Georgian England. *In*: D. COSGROVE & S. DANIELS, eds. *The iconography of landscape.* Cambridge: Cambridge University Press, 43-82.

DANIELS, S. & WATKINS, C. 1991. Picturesque landscaping and estate management: Uvedale Price at Foxley, 1770-1829. *Rural History*, 2, 141-169.

FIELDING, C. 1821. *Picturesque illustrations of the River Wye, in a series of twenty-eight views.* London: Fielding.

HINDE, T. 1986. *Capability Brown: the story of a master gardener.* London: Hutchinson.

HOGG, R. (n.d.). *Hereford Pomona.*

INGLIS-JONES, E. 1968. The Knights of Downton Castle. *The National Library of Wales Journal*, 15, 237-264, 365-388.

JAMES, N.G.D. 1981. *A history of English forestry.* Oxford: Basil Blackwell.

JONES, E.L. 1974. Agricultural conditions and changes in Herefordshire, 1660-1815. *In*: E. L. JONES ed. *Agriculture and the Industrial Revolution.* Oxford: Basil Blackwell.

KNIGHT, R.P. 1795. The landscape, a didactic poem. Addressed to Uvedale Price, Esq. Second edition. London: Bulmer & Co.

NAMIER, L. & BROOKE, J. 1964. *The history of Parliament. The Commons 1754-1790, II: Members.* London: HMSO.

PRICE, U. 1810. *Essays on the picturesque, as compared with the sublime and the beautiful, and on the use of studying pictures for the purpose of improving real landscape*, Vol.I. London: Mawman.

ROBINSON, C.J. 1872. *A history of the mansions and manors of Herefordshire.* Menston: Scolar Press

SEYMOUR, S. 1988. Eighteenth century parkland 'improvement' on the Dukeries' estates of north Nottinghamshire. PhD thesis, University of Nottingham.

SEYMOUR, S. 1989. The 'Spirit of Planting': eighteenth-century parkland 'improvement' on the Duke of Newcastle's north Nottinghamshire estates. *East Midland Geographer*, 12, 5-13.

TATE, W. E. 1941. A hand list of English enclosure Acts and awards. Part 15 - Herefordshire. *Transactions of the Woolhope Naturalists' Field Club*, 183-194.

THE NATIONAL TRUST. 1986. *Berrington Hall, Herefordshire*. London: The National Trust.

THOMPSON, N. 1976. Moccas Court, Herefordshire. *Country Life*, 160, 1474-1477, 1554- 1557.

THORNE, R. G. 1986. *The history of Parliament. The Commons 1790-1820. Vol. III: Members*. London: Secker & Warburg.

WILLIAMS, E. 1944. *Capitalism and slavery*. Chapel Hill: University of North Carolina Press.

2
—
3

From Sir George Cornewall to Lt. Col. William Chester-Master:
1819-1962

David Whitehead
and Tom Wall

2/4

*.... the landscape is singularly interesting and picturesque .... Throw into this scene
the varied effects of light and shade; a herd of deer coming to drink at the pool;
the noise of the jackdaws that haunt the hollow trees; the cries of wildfowl, and their
occasional appearance; and you have a picture to enchant an artist.*

Anon (1870). *Transactions of the Woolhope Naturalists' Field Club.*

Little in the way of documentary evidence has so far been found for the period between Sir George Amyand Cornewall's death in 1819 and 1962 when Lieutenant Colonel William Chester-Master inherited the Estate. More may come to light in due course and the history of this 150 year period can then be more adequately recorded. The present account depends on insights gained from diaries, guide books, the *Transactions* of the Woolhope Naturalists' Field Club and the reminiscences of local people.

Figure 2.4.1

Emblem of the Woolhope Naturalists' Field Club. The Club's motto is 'HOPE ON, HOPE EVER'.

The nineteenth century

'The Picturesque': from W. S. Gilpin to the Woolhope Club and Francis Kilvert

Sir George Cornewall's descendants appear to have been sensitive to the qualities of a landscape such as their own at Moccas Park. His daughters, Frances and Caroline, took delight in visiting estates famous for their scenery: in 1803 they made expeditions to Downton Vale, Herefordshire, Hawkstone Park, Shropshire and Powis Castle, Powys; at the last, we learn from the 'Greenly Diaries' that they regretted the recent felling of oaks and replanting with firs.[1] Perhaps they had been influenced by the artist William Sawrey Gilpin who had visited Moccas in August 1801.[2] Paintings of Moccas Park were amongst those that Gilpin exhibited in 1810 and 1812 at the annual exhibitions of the Society of Painters in Watercolours.[3] Such publicity made Moccas and its Deer Park well known to connoisseurs of 'Picturesque' beauty.

Several local guide books and antiquarian histories celebrated the Park. As early as 1795, John Price noticed its "finely wooded scenery" and commented on its elevated position, "the summit of which is remarkable for the variety and extent of its prospects".[4] These "prospects" are praised in every such guide book and directory for the next century implying that access to the "summit" of the Park was unrestricted and enjoyed by the general public. Presumably the "prospects" were viewed from the apparently carefully sited view points noted in Chapter 3.1.

Figure 2.4.2

The Weeping Oak by G. R. Lewis (1836). Reproduced at the same scale as in J. C. Loudon's *Arboretum et Fruticetum Britannicum* (1838): "Owing to the smallness of the scale, the weeping character is not very obvious in the figure; but it is very striking in the tree".

The fame of the estate was spread further by the celebrated gardening author and garden designer J. C. Loudon (1783-1843). There is a brief reference in his *An Encyclopaedia of Gardening* (1824) where "the large park, finely clothed with oak" is noted and a claim made that oaks here make more rapid growth than anywhere else in the country. In his *Arboretum et Fruticetum Britannicum* (1838) he describes, and reproduces in miniature, illustrations both of the 'Weeping Oak *Quercus pedunculata pendula*' (Figure 2.4.2), which stood in the Park and was the largest in England, and the 'Moccas Oak' (Figure 2.4.3), and writes of an enormous ash which may have stood in the Park too.[5]

Sir George Amyand Cornewall had died in 1819 but with England's greatest garden publicist keeping an eye on Moccas and its trees, it may be assumed that care was taken to preserve the ambiance of the Deer Park. Sir George Amyand Cornewall's son, also Sir George (1775-1835)[6] (Figure 2.4.4 shows the Cornewall family tree), continued his father's planting, perhaps with an even more well-trained 'Picturesque' eye. The second Sir George's grandson, Sir Geoffrey (1869-1951), remarked that you could detect his grandfather's work by the habit of planting in groups of three,[7] the ultimate 'Picturesque' grouping.

Figure 2.4.3

The Moccas Oak, artist unknown. Reproduced at the same scale as in J. C. Loudon's *Arboretum et Fruticetum Britannicum* (1838): "It is hollow in the trunk; but its head, though much injured by time and storms, is bushy and leafy".

The planting of a Deodar and two Wellingtonias may date from the time of Sir Velters Cornewall (1824-1868).[8] The former species was first introduced to Britain in 1831, the latter in 1853.[9] But Sir Velters was better known as a sportsman and gambler than as a silviculturalist. According to an account passed down through the family, he wagered and lost his estate when gambling in London. The winner felt so badly about his success however, that he undertook not to claim his winnings provided Sir Velters succeeded in getting back to Moccas by matins the next day. By dint of riding all night Sir Velters just made it.

Figure 2.4.4

Simplified family tree of the Cornewalls of Moccas and the Chester-Masters of The Abbey, Cirencester. Sources: Cecil & Reade (1908), funerary monuments at Moccas Church and Mrs P. M. Chester-Master.

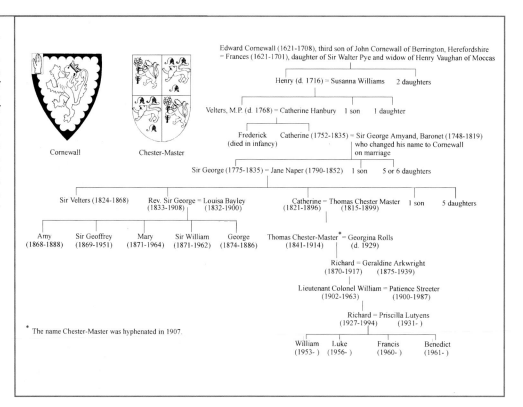

Sir Velters died a bachelor in 1868 and the estate was inherited by his younger brother, the Reverend Sir George Cornewall (Figure 2.4.5), Rector of Moccas. A member of the Woolhope Naturalists' Field Club (see Chapter 1.1), he played host on several occasions to field meetings at Moccas, when the Park was always on the itinerary. He was for some time the Club's Honorary Secretary and later its President. He allowed a very fine oak which still stands in the Park today, to be named after the Club (see Chapter 3.2).

A visit to the Park in 1870 by a 'commissioner' of the Club is especially well recorded in its *Transactions*.[10] The account (from which the epigraph is taken) exudes a typical mid-Victorian interest in observational science. Many trees are measured and recorded (further details are given in Chapters 3.2 and 3.5) but the description of the visit is almost submerged in the language of the 'Picturesque' and at each new scene a piece of pastoral poetry - Cowper, Spencer, Ovid, Virgil - is provided to elevate the aesthetic experience.

Figure 2.4.5

Portrait of the Reverend Sir George Cornewall (1833-1908). A photograph from *Herefordshire Portraits* (Anon 1908).

2/4

Approaching Moccas Park from the Court, the commissioner notes signs of benign neglect. The oaks in the Little Park (the area leading up to Moccas Park) are described as growing in "a charming bit of wilderness ... a loosely scattered undergrowth of thorn trees, sloes, eglantine, and briars"; moving on, he finds views of the "grand old trees of the Park" to be obscured by "commonplace hedgerow timber" and by the hedges themselves. Despite this initial disappointment, the commissioner is soon overcome by the charms of the place: "the landscape is singularly interesting and picturesque... you have a picture to enchant an artist".

But the Woolhope Club's commissioner makes critical comments too: "Moccas Park ... is far too much crowded with trees. Every one of the grand old Oaks is surrounded by a grove of smaller ones, until the Park itself is like a wood, and squirrels may skip from end to end without the need of touching the ground". The campaign of planting by the first Sir George and his son was having a deleterious effect upon the beauty of the Park.

The Reverend Sir George seems to have taken the commissioner's advice seriously, and during his time there are several references to timber sales from the Park.[11] Certainly the photographs of 'The Woolhope Club Oak' taken in 1870 and 1932 and reproduced in Chapter 3.4, show a transformation in this particular area of the Park over the 60 intervening years. A forest of younger trees, presumably oaks, has been thinned to a mere handful.

The Woolhope Club commissioner's lengthy text of 1870 includes much of interest but it is the description written on 22 April 1876 by the Reverend Francis Kilvert (1840-1879) (see inside front cover) which distilled for the nineteenth and twentieth centuries the quintessential character of Moccas Park; it had become ageless and sublime. The description is taken from *Kilvert's Diary* first published sixty years ago.[12] The diary includes three passing references to Moccas Park and three more substantial entries including that of 22 April 1876 which is one of the more celebrated passages in the diary and has done much to raise awareness of Moccas Park.

This was not however Kilvert's only visit to Moccas Park. An earlier one, on 30 August 1872, inspired the following vignette:

> "When we came down into the Park .... we saw the smoke of the gipsy camp-fire framing the oaks and found Lady Cornewall, Miss Newton and Mrs Berkeley Stanhope busy making teas by the shore of the rushy lake. Sir George Cornewall, who had been attending the funeral of his aunt Miss Cornewall, now joined us dressed in black with a white straw hat and black ribbon. He made himself useful by cutting bread and butter . Mrs Berkeley Stanhope had brought some splendid yellow butter and we were all so hungry that everything swiftly disappeared. Then there was a looking over and comparing of sketches and Mrs Crichton by general request sat down on the bank to make a sketch of the scene of our gipsy party."[13]

Other references are much briefer, but in 1878 we learn of the Reverend Sir George shooting at Moccas (doubtless including the Park) when "for some time the rattle of guns was almost incessant" (4 January), of another picnic (10 July) and of the keepers shooting bucks for venison (14 August).[14] Taken together these various fragments are suggestive, not surprisingly, of the Park's role in the nineteenth century as deer park and sporting and social amenity.

The twentieth century

From Cornewalls to Chester-Masters

The Reverend Sir George Cornewall died in 1908. He was succeeded by his two bachelor sons, Geoffrey (1869-1951) and William (1871-1962); the Estate then passed to their cousin Lieutenant Colonel William Chester-Master (the family tree in Figure 2.4.4 shows the relationship between the Cornewall and Chester-Master families). The story thereafter is taken up in Chapter 6.1.

Evidence for the period from 1908 to 1962 is scanty. What little there is suggests that the Park was left to its own devices for many years, although after Sir Geoffrey's death in 1951, some of the best oaks are said to have been felled to help to pay death duties,[15] and some 42 hectares of the highest ground was sold to the Forestry Commission and planted with conifers leading to a contraction of the Park on its southern boundary.

No one alive today in the small local community has recollections that extend to before the 1930s but memories, particularly of the 1940s and 1950s, remain strong. Recollections of gathering chestnuts and harvesting fern (bracken) are particularly vivid.[16] The reputation of Moccas Park for sweet chestnuts was of course well known to local people but also to many from further afield. Local lads knew of the few 'bannut' (walnut) trees and gathered 'conkers' too. Estimates of the numbers of sweet chestnut pickers range from ten or a dozen at a time to "hundreds". Whatever the figure, their presence suggests that the Cornewalls showed some tolerance towards public access.

The Park may to some extent have been open to the casual visitor but social distinctions were still maintained. Local people entering the Park to cut fern in the early autumn were denied access via the white gate (i.e. the main gate opposite the Park Lodge), and were expected to use a subsidiary entrance, an unpainted gate a little to the east which has now been dispensed with. By all accounts the fern was of prodigious height and occupied much of the Lower Park. It was harvested by several local farmers, for bedding, to protect mangel tumps from frost or as 'stools' on which to build hay ricks.[17] The most extensive area free of fern was between the Lawn Pool and the road and this was favoured by the cattle and sheep which grazed in the Park. Pigs were let in on occasion, but surreptitiously, so that they might profit from the acorn crop.

It is said that both Geoffrey and William Cornewall were keen sportsmen and employed three or four keepers (today there is just one, but the Estate is smaller than formerly). Salmon fishing on the Wye absorbed much time in season, and ducks and pheasants (wild, not released) were shot in the Park. The island in the Lawn Pool was fired, possibly annually, to control the vegetation; presumably this was regarded as beneficial to the duck shoot. When, in the 1960s, most of the Lower Park was ploughed or disced, patches of better grass resembling tees or greens were discovered suggesting that a rudimentary golf course may have been laid out at one time, as was the case at Brampton Bryan Park in the north of the county.[18]

Tracks within the Park were kept free from overgrowth and for those permitted to enter by the white gate, the track round the Lawn Pool to another white gate at the Lawn Gate Lodge (now blocked off) was well maintained. Indeed, "one Thursday", in the 1930s, when the road alongside the Park was impassable due to a fallen tree, a Midland Red Bus was diverted through the Park via the Lawn Gate, a journey which today can tax even a Land Rover!

Hillside Cottage, standing barely 20 metres beyond the eastern boundary of the Park, near Woodbury, was occupied until the late 1940s, when a workman was still living close to the top of the Park at Parkgate Cottage, overlooking Peterchurch; both buildings have now gone. This workman was responsible for repairs to the wall and perhaps to the deer paling too. A saw pit halfway up the eastern side of the Park was still being used in the early 1940s.

Moccas Park was a quiet and little changing backwater. But the wider world impinged from time to time. There are recollections of Indian soldiers in transit camping in the Park sometime during the Second World War. At the same period the corms of meadow saffron were gathered for medicinal use to meet a wartime shortage (see Chapter 4.3). And in an unseasonable snowstorm on 29 April 1945 Wellington Bomber LP 410, which was on a training flight, crashed at the top of the Park;[19] all six crew lost their lives: Flight Lieutenant H. K. Crowther, Warrant Officers E. J. Bay and E. W. Skelton, Pilot Officer E. G. M. Smith and Flight Sergeants W. Forster and G. J. Whitcombe.

Notes

1   Towards the end of her life, Elizabeth Greenly (1771-1839), of Titley Court, near Kington, Herefordshire, copied her diary and letters into the six manuscript volumes known today as the 'Greenly Diaries'; they have never been published. They include many references of local interest (Salt 1951).

2   William Sawrey Gilpin (1762-1843) was nephew of the Rev. William Gilpin, high priest of 'The Picturesque', he went on to practise as a landscape gardener, most notably at Scotney Castle, Kent, often regarded as the ultimate in 'Picturesque' design. 'The Picturesque' involved retaining the natural and preserving and enhancing intricacy, variety, irregularity and roughness but also viewing and composing the landscape in the manner of a painter (see Chapters 2.3 and 3.1).

3   Anon (1992) names 'Scene in Moccas Park' as the title of paintings exhibited in 1810 and 1812, presumably they were two different works. What is presumed to be one of these is illustrated in the catalogue of a sale held in 1980 (Witt Library, Courtauld Institute). This is the only painting of the Park by Gilpin which the authors have seen illustrated. It shows sheep under a beech tree and is dated 1810 . The painting shows only a small area of Moccas Park and gives little idea as to how the Park looked at that date. Its present whereabouts are not known.

4   Price (1795).

5   Loudon (1838), Hadfield (1969); further details of these trees are given in Chapter 3.2.

6   By reason of his marriage and change of name (see Chapter 2.3), George Amyand's baronetcy became attached to the name Cornewall. He had inherited the title from his father, also George Amyand, who was created a baronet in 1764 (Cecil & Reade 1908).

7   Anon (1933).

8   Sir Velters succeeded his father when only 11 years old (Cecil & Reade 1908); presumably his mother was influential in the management of the Estate for some years thereafter.

9   Mitchell (1978).

10 Anon (1870).

11 Hereford Record Office (hereafter HCRO) F10/156.

12 Plomer (1938, 1939, 1940). Kilvert (1840-1879) was curate at Clyro between 1865 and 1872 and vicar of Bredwardine from 1877 until his death in 1879; he is buried in Bredwardine churchyard. Clyro, near Hay-on-Wye, and Bredwardine are respectively 13 km and 2 km from Moccas Park. The extant parts of his diary include entries made over the period January 1870 to March 1879. For the entry of 22 April 1876 see Plomer (1940).

13 Plomer (1939). This is the Reverend Sir G. H. Cornewall; his aunt was Miss Anna Maria Cornewall (1779-1872). Miss Newton lived at The Cottage, now Bredwardine Hall; she was instrumental in Kilvert's appointment to the living of Bredwardine. The Reverend and Mrs Berkeley Stanhope lived at Byford Rectory 5 km east of Moccas Park and Mrs Crichton at Wye Cliff between Hay-on-Wye and Clyro (Grice 1983, Lockwood 1990).

14 Plomer (1940).

15 I.R.P. (1975); see also Chapter 3.4.

16 Recollections on this and allied topics were kindly provided by Messrs Tom Bowen, Sam Davies, Les Whittal and Lawrie Whittall.

17 The annual mowing of fern in Moccas Park may well have been of very long standing; there is an entry of 9 October 1790 in Sir George Cornewall's Account Book which refers to "mowing fern in Park" (HCRO J/56/IV/4). Fern was apparently sometimes referred to in the district as 'Radnorshire hay', presumably as a pointed reference to the poverty of the neighbouring county.

18 In the 1970s the open area of The Lawn west of the Lawn Pool, was on a short list of three possible locations for a cricket pitch for Moccas Village. It was eventually sited between the Village Hall and Moccas Court.

19 Information supplied by Mr R. Cooke, Mr W. J. L. Roberts and the Ministry of Defence.

References relating to Moccas Park

ANON. 1870. Incidental notes on remarkable trees in Herefordshire. *Transactions of the Woolhope Naturalists' Field Club*, 288-321.

ANON. 1933. First field meeting, May 25th, 1933. *Transactions of the Woolhope Naturalists' Field Club*, xi-xviii.

ANON. 1992. *The Royal Watercolour Society. The first fifty years 1805-1855.* Woodbridge: Antique Collectors' Club.

CECIL, G.S. & READE, C. 1908. *The House of Cornewall.* Hereford: Jakeman & Carver.

HADFIELD, M. 1969. Moccas Park. *Quarterly Journal of Forestry*, 63, 254-256.

I.R.P. 1975. Moccas Estate. *Quarterly Journal of Forestry*, 69, 113-115.

LOUDON, J.C. 1824. *An Encyclopaedia of Gardening.* London: A. & R. Spottiswood.

LOUDON, J.C. 1838. *Arboretum et Fruticetum Britannicum.* Vol. III. London: Longman, Brown, Green & Longman.

PLOMER, W. 1938, 1939, 1940. *Kilvert's Diary.* Three volumes. London: Jonathan Cape.

PRICE, J. 1795. *An historical account of the city of Hereford.* Hereford: Walker.

Other references

ANON. 1908. *Herefordshire Portraits (Past and Present).* Hereford: Jakeman & Carver.

GRICE, F. 1983. *Francis Kilvert and his World.* Horsham: Caliban Books.

LOCKWOOD, D. 1990. *Francis Kilvert.* Bridgend: Seren Books.

MITCHELL, A. 1978. *A field guide to the trees of Britain and northern Europe.* Second edition. London: Collins.

SALT, A.E.W. 1951. The Greenly Diaries. *Transactions of the Woolhope Naturalists' Field Club*, 238-249.

Reading the landscape

John Phibbs

The first and most material is to consult the Genius of the place.
What is, is the great guide as to what ought to be.

Joseph Spence, 1751.[1]

Moccas Park presents something of a challenge to those who would regard it as a designed ornamental landscape. For while 'Capability' Brown, Humphry Repton and Richard Payne Knight are all known to have advised at Moccas, there are no specific references to landscaping the Park in the extensive collections of estate papers. Furthermore, at first sight, nothing could look less designed - the bulk of Moccas Park consists of more or less evenly spaced trees, most of them oak, scattered in apparently random fashion over the steep north-facing hill and across The Lawn. Francis Kilvert's judgement is altogether understandable: "No human hand set those oaks. They are 'the trees which the Lord hath planted'."[2]

Figure 3.1.1

Looking west across the Lawn Pool towards the Upper Park. Photograph by Peter Wakely, May 1994.

However, this first impression is illusory, for Moccas Park does have an ornamental design: its earthworks are readily discernible in the bracken, and some of its plantings survive, embedded within the matrix of the oak trees. Furthermore, this design proves to be as intricate and varied an example of the informal English landscape style as can be found anywhere.

In this chapter I shall describe five phases in the planting of Moccas Park, pointing out the evidence noted on the ground and in the archives, that supports the argument.[3]

Moccas Park before about 1660

Moccas may well have been a medieval park, but our first reference to it is seventeenth century,[4] (see Chapter 2.2) and no matter when it was set up, about 50 veteran oaks and the scraps of ridge and furrow which survive in the Park, are most likely to pre-date it (Figures 3.1.2 and 3.1.3).[5]

This ridge and furrow is concentrated on the lower ground around the Lawn Pool and must have been arched up by ploughing before the end of the Middle Ages.[6] Most of the veteran oaks stand on the ridge and furrow, and around it. 'The *Hypebaeus* tree', or 'Stag's Horn Oak' itself (see Chapter 3.2) appears to be in origin a hedgerow tree.[7]

Before 1773, Moccas Park ran south over the hill to include Lodge Farm and Pritchard's Park in the Golden Valley, and may have run to Bodcott Lane (the road from Dorstone to Moccas), in the west.[8] The almost entire absence of ridge and furrow from the higher ground

Figure 3.1.2

Field archaeology of The Lawn. The plan, based on a partial survey carried out in *circa* 1979, shows the main areas of ridge and furrow. Reproduced by courtesy of Trevor Rowley, Oxford University.

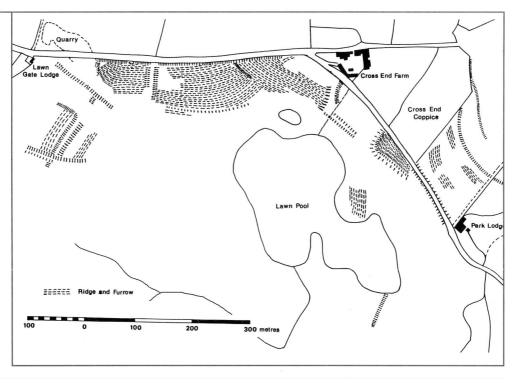

Figure 3.1.3

The Park boundaries and the relationship between ridge and furrow and the oldest oaks. This plan shows some areas of ridge and furrow not surveyed for Figure 3.1.2.

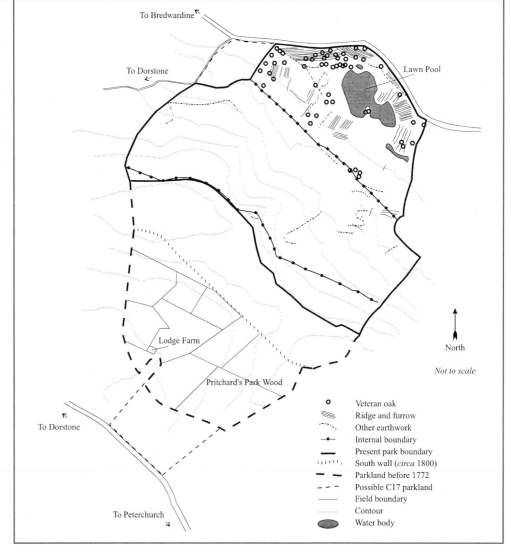

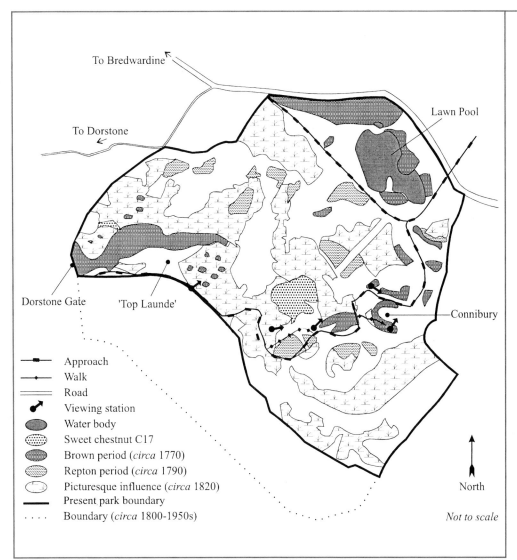

Figure 3.1.4

Walks, viewing stations and plantings, *circa* **1660-1840.**
The principal approaches, walks and associated viewing stations and the general distribution of the main phases of planting.

suggests either that it was a very early deer park or a waste, with thickets and perhaps the occasional oak pollard. Such a waste would have provided a suitable habitat for deer and one might reasonably expect such thickets, had they existed, to have been retained in the seventeenth century.

The size of some of the banks crossing the Park suggests some inner compartmentation when it was first created - one of these banks has veteran oaks on it and may therefore pre-date the Park, however we know that it remained significant into the eighteenth century, because Brown adopted it as the southern edge of his plan of 1778.[9]

Moccas Park in about 1660

Whatever the origin of Moccas Park itself, one would expect the great sweet chestnut pollards which stand in the Upper Park (Figure 3.1.4) to have been planted around the time of the Restoration (1660). At many other parks in England (Shrubland and Euston in Suffolk, and Bramshill in Hampshire, to name but three) this species was planted in the wave of nationalistic forestry that John Evelyn both encouraged and encapsulated in his *Sylva* of 1664.

The sweet chestnuts of the Upper Park have never been mapped or recorded in detail, but some at least are planted in the straight lines of a formal design and while there are occasional specimens and groups elsewhere, most grow west of the Connibury (see Figure 3.1.4). Only a thorough survey however will tell us what the design was and how it was intended to function.

There are a few surviving veteran oak maidens in the Park, and these look as if they may date from the same phase of planting as the sweet chestnuts: typically these oaks are smoother in the bole than pollards, they may have been pollarded once but the short boles could just be a consequence of growing trees in parkland.[10] The distribution of these trees does not suggest any discernible design today, but a parallel for trees being planted into wood-pasture in the seventeenth century can be found at Woodhall Park in Hertfordshire.[11]

Figure 3.1.5

Lancelot 'Capability' Brown. A portrait of 1770 by Nathaniel Dance; reproduced by courtesy of the National Portrait Gallery, London.

The Brown period (1770s and 1780s)

John Lambe Davis's survey of 1772 shows that the Park may have been reduced in size by this date and while it still stretched into the Golden Valley to the south, its other boundaries were more or less those that we find today.[12] The 1772 survey seems to have been undertaken as a preliminary to an extensive and long-term improvement of the estate and Sir George Cornewall turned to 'Capability' Brown (Figure 3.1.5) for advice.

The details of the commission at Moccas are uncertain but the round £100 sum paid to Brown,[13] though substantial, suggests an agreed fee for a plan or plans, rather than a long term contract. Whatever was decided on, will have been executed by Sir George Cornewall himself. He kept an account of the wide range of works carried out on the estate each year,[14] including tree planting, but the location of works is often not specified and their nature frequently remains unclear.

Brown's only surviving plan, 'A Plan for the intended Alterations at Moccas Court in Herefordshire, 1778' (see Chapter 2.3),[15] pre-dates this payment by 3 years and covers very little of Moccas Park, for it stops at the lower internal boundary. However, many Brownian elements in the Park are to be found well above this line, at the top of the Park, and it is on these that I shall concentrate.

In the Brown period, if not before, two new principal approaches may have been developed from the west and south: one from Dorstone and one from the Golden Valley, over Pritchard's Park.[16] Also at this time, to judge by the size of the trees, extensive plantations of beeches were made in association with oak and yew. These trees are to be found in considerable numbers around the Dorstone gate and north of the 'Top Launde' (my nomenclature, see Figure 3.1.4), but they can also be found in groups related to the Dorstone approach as it makes its way down the hill, in particular around the Connibury. Finally, although there is little obviously Brownian earth-working in the Park, the Lawn Pool may have been extended.

The design that underpinned these developments was related above all to the approach from Dorstone. A combination of earthworks and planting was employed to compose good landscapes from such principal approaches and their environs, and the visitor was presumably expected to stop the carriage, and even to walk to a particular viewing station, as to the Connibury, where the track of the path survives and is indicated on Figure 3.1.4.

Traces of such walks are seldom found today, though other examples can be followed at Alnwick in Northumberland, Chatsworth in Derbyshire and Cowdray, Trentham and Wotton in Buckinghamshire. They underline the importance attached in Brown's time to the composition of specific views.

The fine beeches at Moccas Park are nowhere more clearly associated with designed landscape than at the climactic view towards Moccas Court from the Dorstone approach, close to the point where the approach leaves the deer fence today. There is good evidence that they were planted: the group north of the 'Top Launde' includes six in a row, perhaps part of a formal planting, but probably trees put in on the edge of a plantation.

Many of these beeches branch out from the bole at about 2 metres, but they do not look like pollards. It seems more likely that they were maidens, grown in a nursery and headed on transplanting.[17] From similar examples on other sites this appears to have been common practice in the eighteenth century. Among landscapes attributed to Brown, it can be found in the beech belts at Longleat in Wiltshire, throughout the parkland at Sledmere in Yorkshire, at Trentham and elsewhere. At Moccas Park, and at these other places, occasional oak maidens are to be found with the beeches, and not all of the beeches have been headed. It may be that two planting methods were adopted to insure against failure.

A close parallel for the Moccas Park beeches can be found at King's Wood, Trentham. Here beeches are also associated with drives on high ground, there is a similar mixture of headed and timber trees, some of the beeches at the edges of the plantings also stand in straight rows and there is the same association with yew and with oak.[18] There is also a similar climactic sense of the carefully composed view, framed by the beech, from the highest and most dramatic point of the drive.

The Lawn Pool as shown on Brown's plan would never have been a dominant feature in such magnificent countryside and the River Wye, on the north side of Moccas Court, would have brought the main water interest to the design. However, similar small pools, acting as a kind of focal point to a prospect, can be found in Brownian landscapes; the Black Pool at Trentham is one good example.

Haworth has pointed out that the eastern half of the Lawn Pool as it exists today is not shown on Davis's survey (1772), nor on Brown's plan (1778), and was therefore perhaps dug during a later phase of landscaping.[19] (Haworth's observations are discussed in more detail and extracts from relevant plans are reproduced in Chapter 1.3). Indeed the present irregular outline of the Pool does seem to nod towards the kind of picturesque landscaping that Richard Payne Knight popularised at the very end of the eighteenth century. Following this reasoning, a date in the late 1790s for any presumed extension of the Lawn Pool appears quite reasonable. However, I would point out that from the climactic view point on the Dorstone approach, an eastern extension of the Pool would have brought it into the line of sight towards Moccas Court. I suggest therefore that any such extension might date from a decade or two earlier, when Brown's influence was at its peak.[20]

It seems likely that the line of oaks along the extreme north eastern shore of the Lawn Pool is contemporary with the Pool's presumed extension in the eighteenth century. These oaks look large enough to have been planted in Brown's time and similar fringes of oak can be found beside the lakes of other landscapes attributed to Brown. Ragley in Warwickshire, is a very good example, but similar effects are to be seen at Petworth in Sussex, Blenheim in Oxfordshire and Doddington in Cheshire. In these four cases, and at Moccas Park, the trees are planted on a slight lip, largely concealed by careful earth modelling. In all four cases the trees are in surprisingly straight rows, and, again in all four, a drive or approach runs behind the trees and I assume that such plantings were intended to screen the lip and the edge of the water which might be muddy or reedy.

Figure 3.1.6

Humphry Repton. A stipple engraving by H.B. Hall after S. Shelley, published in 1802; reproduced by courtesy of the National Portrait Gallery, London.

The Repton period (1790s)

'Capability' Brown died in 1783 and by the end of the decade his position as the leading place-maker or landscape gardener in England had been taken by Humphry Repton (Figure 3.1.6), who was consulted by Sir George Cornewall between 1792 and 1795.[21] Once again we have no direct evidence for Repton's influence on the development of Moccas Park; he is only recorded as having worked on the banks of the River Wye.[22] However, just as a Brownian style can be found at Moccas Park in the approaches and beech plantations, so Repton's style at least, can be recognised in the planting of the 1790s.

These plantings coincided with the arrival at Moccas of the forester Mr Webster. His work was described by J. C. Loudon in 1836. Over the preceding 43 years, Webster had planted nearly 300,000 oaks, besides other trees. Loudon states that these plantings were

" .... particularly on hill sides, unfit for producing either grass or corn from their steepness. Nurseries were made on these hills, and the trees raised there which were to be planted in the adjoining ground. Mr Webster says, that he found that these nurseries 'fitted the trees to the climate, which made an indescribable difference in their growth when planted out' .... Larch trees, 30 years planted, have attained a large size and are used for all building purposes, and for fences."[23]

While plantings are known to have taken place elsewhere on the estate (Brobury Scar for example, see Chapter 2.3), the field evidence suggests that groups of trees were established in Moccas Park too. Locations for these are surmised in Figure 3.1.4 on the basis of the girths of surviving trees (predominantly sweet chestnut, oak and beech), their distribution over steeply sloping ground, and the slight earthworks, suggesting fences or hedges, that can still be traced round some of them.[24] It also seems significant that there is no overlap between these plantings and the earlier beech plantations. Such a planting programme would read well with what appears to have been Sir George Cornewall's approach to improvement: work was carried out regularly every year but his overall scheme may constantly have been modified to take account of new ideas in landscape design and new economic and agricultural pressures.

There are two further elements that I would ascribe to the Repton period, only because they are so characteristic of his style. The first of these is the extensive though undatable network of drives that survives in the Upper Park (usually closely associated with the nurseries, if such they be),[25] and the second is the series of viewing stations invariably associated with the drives.[26] Drives and viewing stations are both shown on Figure 3.1.7.

By Repton's day, the walk from the drive had become a rarity, instead one finds a proliferation of levelled platforms at viewpoints beside his drives. I suspect that one of the main agents for change was the technical advance in carriage design.[27] By the 1790s, with the help of sprung steel suspension, the sporting car was in fashion, these fast light vehicles

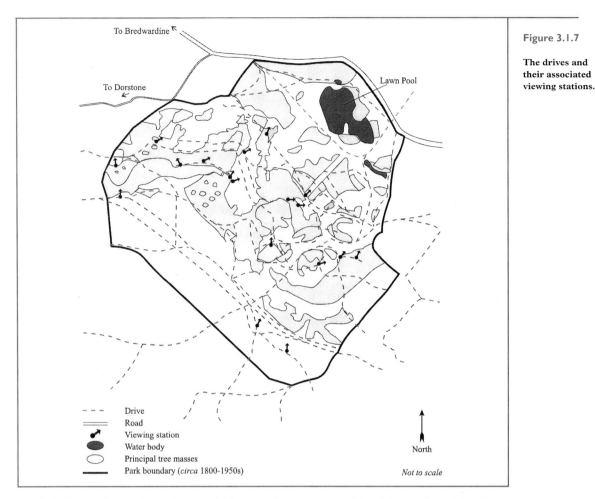

Figure 3.1.7

The drives and their associated viewing stations.

3
—
1

needed plenty of smooth tracks on which to perform, presumably with a variety of bends on them. To judge from the different gradients to be found in Brownian and Reptonian landscapes, although lighter, the cars of the 1790s could not so easily manage steep slopes, perhaps because they were pulled by lighter, quicker horses.

The platforms may have operated as parking bays where one could pull up and admire the view. They may have doubled as suitable places to fix an easel, spread a picnic or pitch a tent. Occasionally (for example at Newton Park in Somerset) one of the sketches from Repton's 'Red Book' is taken from such a viewpoint. I have found these platforms only in Reptonian landscapes (such as Endsleigh in Devon, Stoneaston in Somerset and Newton Park), but they can also be traced in Picturesque landscapes, such as Hafod in Ceredigion, and Downton Vale in Herefordshire, and at those two places the stations can only be reached on foot.

Such platforms are not the only viewing stations in the Reptonian design at Moccas Park, there are also more conventional views from bends in the drives, usually framed by Reptonian planting, and the majority of the views are towards Moccas Court, although the scale of the setting is such that the building itself can scarcely be picked out.

The Picturesque influence (1800s)

Sir George Cornewall did not consult only Repton, he also turned to Richard Payne Knight (Figure 3.1.8), of Downton Vale (now Downton Gorge National Nature Reserve) in the north of Herefordshire, and Uvedale Price, of neighbouring Foxley, the leading theoreticians and practitioners of the Picturesque.[28] Knight and Price may still have been friendly with Repton in 1793 when Sir George was following Repton's advice in respect of work near Moccas Court;[29] their friendship was to be destroyed by 'the Picturesque controversy' but this did not break into print until the following year.[30]

Figure 3.1.8

Richard Payne Knight. A portrait by Sir Thomas Lawrence exhibited in 1794; reproduced by courtesy of The Whitworth Art Gallery, The University of Manchester.

Definitions of the Picturesque are famously easy to overturn, but Thomas Hearne's pictures of Downton Vale must be a good presentation of the idea in its Herefordshire sense,[31] with their lack of focus on buildings and their emphasis on apparently casual views of the River Teme; they were, after all, commissioned by Richard Payne Knight himself. Likewise, in his pictures of Moccas Park, Hearne abandoned the classical tradition to be found in the oil paintings of Claude Lorrain,[32] fixing his easel amongst the trees, and dwelling instead on individuals and on detail.[33]

The ideas expressed by these pictures must already have been formulated by Knight and Price when Repton advised at Moccas. One would have expected them to argue for a number of things. For walks and against drives, especially sporting drives; for randomness and chance (which broadly speaking they understood to be natural) and against composed landscapes; for native tree species and against exotics; for, in fact, the very effect towards which Webster was perhaps working as described in the Woolhope Club's *Transactions* and as seen today on the ground:

> ".... some half century ago, or rather more, when the sad memory of a heavy timber fallage was green, there was a far-sighted steward at Moccas, of highly prudential 'proclivities' - probably a Scotchman - who got permission to plant all these young Oaks to take the place of the old ones as they decayed. When first planted they would look very thinly scattered over the ground, but he - good calculating soul - had measured their distance from each other to a nicety, and knew they could not be put more thickly".[34]

To judge from the surviving trees, this transmutation of the landscape was achieved by Webster in two ways: first, when the nursery clumps were ready, some of the trees within them were transplanted into the parkland adjacent and, second, a major new scheme of planting was put in hand, using oak and sweet chestnut with occasional horse chestnut. The planting seems to have been conceived with little or no attempt at design in the conventional eighteenth century sense, instead it was driven perhaps not only by Picturesque aesthetics, but also by the need, as it was perceived during the Napoleonic Wars, for future supplies of ship-building oak; for, despite its name, the Picturesque school was pre-eminently a practical one.

Later developments (1800 and after)

Some exotics, including Deodar and Wellingtonia, were planted in the nineteenth century, but these have had less impact on the landscape than the felling and forestry of the twentieth century. A comparison between tree cover as shown on the early editions of the Ordnance Survey and as it is on the ground today, suggests that there has been a good deal of felling in the south eastern part of the Lower Park. This felling seems to have brought the nineteenth century horse chestnuts towards the edge of the principal tree masses, but has otherwise made for somewhat arbitrary clearings. The major conifer plantation on the top of the hill, occupies some 41 hectares sold out of the Park in the 1950s. Four much smaller conifer plantations have been established within the Park since the 1960s, all lie on the northern edge of the Upper Park and were clearly planted in pursuit of shooting and forestry objectives.

Conclusion

Moccas is one of very few estates that I know, which were actively developed by one owner throughout the whole turbulent period between 1770 and 1820,[35] when the aesthetics of landscape was a serious issue, and when ideas about it were ceaselessly changing. This gives Moccas particular interest.

Sir George Cornewall will have had the dominant and continuing influence on the estate throughout this time, and it would be a mistake to insist too strongly on ascribing every development in Moccas Park to one or other of his advisers, particularly as the ideas of Brown, Repton and the Picturesque movement progressively changed. Nonetheless, there are distinct patterns of design within Moccas Park and it is to these that this chapter has drawn attention.

Notes

1 Joseph Spence (1699-1768) was Professor of Poetry and, later, of modern History at Oxford. This quotation is from a letter on gardening written by Spence to the Rev. Wheeler, the full text of which appears in Hunt & Willis (1988).
2 Plomer (1940). Kilvert's judgement, expressed in his diary entry of 22 April 1876, relates to the ancient trees of the Park; it is one that, subconsciously at least, many of those involved in the nature conservation management of the Park may in the past have shared.
3 Phibbs (1993a, 1993b).
4 Townshend (1904).
5 The exact number and date of the veteran oaks remains a matter of conjecture, but the distribution of the most obviously old examples is shown in Figure 3.1.3. Their dating is discussed in Chapter 3.5.
6 The width between ridges at Moccas Park appears generally to be narrow; widths of 3.8 to 6 m have been measured (Tom Wall pers. comm.). Such narrow widths are sometimes attributed to the late eighteenth and early nineteenth centuries (Rackham 1986, and Taylor *in* Hoskins 1988) but Astill (1988) points out that seven of the ten dated medieval examples of ridge and furrow known to him, all of which were dated to before 1200, range in width between 2.4 and 4.5 m.
7 The significance of the location of the ridge and furrow and its relationship to the veteran trees remains hard to judge, but does not look casual.
8 A complaint from Geoffrey de Bella Fago to the king concerning the theft of hay from his park at Dorsinton (= Dorstone) in 1317 (Calendar of Patent Rolls 1313-17, 683), confirms the presence of a park in the Golden Valley at that time, but its precise location, and hence its relationship to the formerly more extensive area of Moccas Park, is not known (see chapter 2.2).
9 'A Plan for the intended Alterations at Moccas Court in Herefordshire. The Seat of Sir George Cornewall Bart by LB: 1778'. Such compartmentation has been noticed by Rackham (1986). The exact function of these internal boundaries is often unclear, but at Moccas Park the boundary along the southern edge of The Lawn may have been used to control grazing, allowing The Lawn to be mown for hay, while after mowing the deer may have been encouraged down within sight of the road by the re-growth of this better grass. The Lawn was given a higher value than the rest of the Park in 1807 (see Chapter 2.3).
10 As noted by Harding (1977).
11 The trees shown by the watercolourist Thomas Hearne in 1789/9 (see Note 31) as background to his depiction of the Moccas Oak (see Chapter 3.2) appear to be of a size consistent with them having been planted in the seventeenth century.
12 'A Survey of the Manors of Moccas, Bredwardine, Grove, Radnor, Wilmaston, and Cusop, and a Farm at Crosswall; situate in the Parishes of Moccas, Bredwardine, Dorston, Peter-church, Cusop, Clifford, and Cluttock, in the county of Hereford belonging to Sir George Cornewall Baronet. By John Lambe Davis, 1772'. The survey is discussed in more detail in Chapter 2.3. It is held in Hereford City Library.
13 Lancelot Brown's 'Account Book', Lindley Library, London.
14 His account books are held in Hereford Record Office.
15 Now held at the Getty Center for the History of Arts and the Humanities. It is reproduced as Figure 2.3.4.
16 The term 'principal approach' is used by Brown's contemporary and admirer Thomas Whately (Whately 1770). Such approaches are often found in Brownian landscapes. They are typified by their length and by their habit of debouching into the park from the middle of nowhere (both of these characteristics are to be found at Moccas Park, and also at Caversham in Berkshire, Heveningham in Suffolk, Sandleford Priory in Berkshire and Trentham in Staffordshire, to name only four). They may well have no lodges at their ends (as for example at Heveningham, Moccas and Trentham) and it is not surprising to find that they cross public roads in their course (as at Cowdray in Sussex and Sandleford Priory). I do not know what they were for, but suspect that their function was less to provide access to the house than to provide fine driving between the house, the drives themselves (within), and the ridings (generally outside) the parkland proper. It has also occurred to me, in respect of the principal approach at Caversham, that their line may have been determined by the desire to show visitors as much of the estate as possible before entering the parkland.
17 Harding (1977) counted approximately 116 of these headed or pollarded beech trees in the Upper Park.
18 At Trentham this probably indicates a fenced clump or plantation with a yew under-storey.
19 Haworth *et al* (1994).

20 The substantial cut which survives at the south eastern corner of the Lawn Pool suggests a failed attempt to link the Pool with smaller bodies of water to the east, and may be read as evidence that there were several phases in the development of the water.

21 Hazel Fryer (pers. comm.).

22 Loudon (1840); Hazel Fryer (pers. comm.).

23 Loudon (1836).

24 It is not known for certain how such new plantings would have been protected against deer, but Repton had proffered advice at other sites. In his Red Book for Stoke Park, Buckinghamshire (1792), he suggested grazing with sheep rather than deer because "a much slighter fence" would suffice. At Stanage Park, Radnorshire (1803) he advised as follows: "… there is a mode of planting which if judiciously executed might add to the cloathing without destroying the Character viz. in the small open spaces surrounded by old thorns and birch, a few oaks from two or three to ten or twelve might be planted in groupes inclosed by a pale, which the outside bushes would hide and which the deer would not injure, because they never break into very small inclosures of this kind". The last point is one which has been rediscovered by woodland managers in recent years.

25 Figure 3.1.7 shows the routes of drives as shown on Ordnance Survey maps and as recorded in 1993 (Phibbs 1993a, 1993b). In general, drives and paths made since the second half of the nineteenth century tend to run straight and pay little respect to any contours (see for example the Portman drives at Hestercombe in Somerset). My conjecture is that the drives at Moccas Park, which do respect the contours, are Reptonian in date. It is interesting that there are relatively few on the south west side of the Park where the topography is richest, but my supposition is that this part of the Park had already been planted when the drives came to be laid out, probably after the arrival of Mr Webster in about 1793, the year that Sir George Cornewall did work near Moccas Court "by Repton's advice" (Fryer 1994). The dating of both drives and platforms is vexed however, because platforms were also established at the stations I regard as Brownian, for example the climactic view from the Dorstone approach.

26 I may be applying the term 'viewing station' anachronistically to the Brownian design, for the term is Repton's and, so far as I know, he did not use it before 1800 (see the 'Red Books' for Betchworth in Surrey, Magdalen College, Oxford and Sheringham in Norfolk).

27 Felton (1794).

28 Daniels & Watkins (1994).

29 Fryer (1994).

30 Goode (1982).

31 Thomas Hearne (1744-1817) was commissioned by Richard Payne Knight in about 1784 to paint at least 12 water colours of Downton Vale; later he provided two drawings for Knight's didactic poem *The Landscape* (1794). Morris (1989) dates Hearne's work at Moccas, where he painted nine watercolours for Sir George Cornewall, to the late 1780s (see Chapter 2.3).

32 The paintings and drawings of Claude Gellée le Lorrain (1600-82) were much sought after by English collectors of the eighteenth century.

33 But Hearne's approach may owe something to Claude Lorrain's sketches. It must be significant that Richard Payne Knight was the first collector to concentrate on Claude's drawings. In both style and subject matter they provide models for Hearne, and the cascades, brooks and ivy-clad trees that Claude drew, look more English than Italian (Whiteley 1998). Kilvert's experience of 1876 "[Those oaks] look as if they had been at the beginning and making of the world", was also fundamentally Picturesque.

34 Anon (1870).

35 Eridge, on the Kent/Sussex border is another such.

References relating to Moccas Park

ANON. 1870. Incidental notes on remarkable trees in Herefordshire, Moccas Park. *Transactions of the Woolhope Naturalists' Field Club*, 288-321.

FRYER, H. 1994. Humphry Repton in Herefordshire. *In*: S. DANIELS & C. WATKINS, eds, *The picturesque landscape*. Nottingham: University of Nottingham, 80-85.

HARDING, P.T. 1977. *Moccas Deer Park, Hereford and Worcester: a report on the history, structure and natural history*. Unpublished report to the Nature Conservancy Council by the Institute of Terrestrial Ecology, Huntingdon.

HAWORTH, E.Y., GUNN, I.D.M., CUBBY, P.R. & CARLOS, R. 1994. *Survey and management proposals for the Lawn Pool, Moccas Park National Nature Reserve in Herefordshire*. Report by the Institute of Freshwater Ecology to English Nature.

LOUDON, J.C. 1836. Planting at Moccas Court. *The gardener's magazine*, 12, 368-369.

LOUDON, J.C. 1840. *The landscape gardening and landscape architecture of the late Humphry Repton, Esq*. London.

MORRIS, D. 1989. *Thomas Hearne and his landscape*. London: Reaktion Books.

PHIBBS, J.L. 1993a. *Moccas Court, Herefordshire: notes on the landscaping of the deer park*. Report by Debois Landscape Survey Group to English Nature.

PHIBBS, J.L. 1993b. *Moccas Court, Herefordshire: notes on the landscaping of the deer park above the bracken line*. Report by Debois Landscape Survey Group to English Nature.

PLOMER, W. 1940. *Kilvert's diary*. Volume three. London: Jonathan Cape.

TOWNSHEND, D. 1904. *The life and letters of the great Earl of Cork*. London: Duckworth

Other references

ASTILL, G. 1988. Fields. *In*: G. ASTILL & A. GRANT, eds. *The countryside of medieval England*. Oxford: Blackwell, 62-85.

DANIELS, S. & WATKINS, C., eds. 1994. *The picturesque landscape*. Nottingham: University of Nottingham.

FELTON, W. 1794. *A treatise on carriages*. London.

GOODE, P. 1982. The Picturesque controversy. *In*: G. CARTER, P. GOODE & K. LAURIE, eds. *Humphry Repton, Landscape Gardener*. Norwich: Sainsbury Centre for Visual Arts, 34-41.

HOSKINS, W.G. 1988. *The making of the English countryside*. With an introduction and commentary by Christopher Taylor. London: Hodder & Stoughton.

HUNT, J.D. & WILLIS, P. 1988. *The Genius of the Place. The English Landscape Garden 1620- 1820*. Massachusetts: Massachusetts Institute of Technology.

KNIGHT, R.P. 1794. *The Landscape, a didactic poem. In three books. Addressed to Uvedale Price, Esq*. London: Nicol.

RACKHAM, O. 1986. *The history of the countryside*. London: Dent.

WHATELY, T. 1770. *Observations on modern gardening*. London.

WHITELEY, J.J.L. 1998. *Claude Lorrain. Drawings from the collections of the British Museum and the Ashmolean Museum*. London: British Museum.

$\dfrac{3}{1}$

A landscape of remarkable trees

Tom Wall

The man of science and of taste .... will .... discover beauties in a tree which the others would condemn for its decay ....

Humphry Repton (1803). *Observations on the Theory and Practice of Landscape Gardening.*

The remarkable trees of Moccas Park have been celebrated for over 200 years; they are intrinsic to its landscape and to 'the genius of the place'. There are descriptions and illustrations of various remarkable trees dating from Georgian times, the Victorian period and the twentieth century. The present account draws on material from all these periods, and in particular on an article devoted to Moccas Park in a series entitled "Incidental notes on remarkable trees in Herefordshire" written by a 'commissioner' of the Woolhope Naturalists' Field Club and published anonymously in its *Transactions* for 1870.[1] Particular 'celebrities' emerge from these various sources, and their names, natures and histories are described here.

I would, however, concur with the 'commissioner's' observation that

".... to do justice to the series of magnificent trees that luxuriate in Moccas Park is simply impossible .... there seems nothing for it but to give the facts as they were met with, and to offer a humble apology to 'the Spirit of every tree' - and there will be many of them - that does not get the full description it merits."

The Moccas Oak

'The Moccas Oak' no longer survives but it is perhaps the Park's most celebrated tree. It was depicted by Thomas Hearne, one of the most important topographical artists of the later eighteenth century, in one of nine watercolours of the Moccas Estate commissioned by Sir George Cornewall and painted in 1788-9 (see Figure 1.1.1).[2] This series includes one other of Moccas Park illustrating a fine beech tree (see cover illustration).[3] 'The Moccas Oak' was subsequently drawn and etched by J. G. Strutt for his *Sylva Britannica* (1822)[4] and was described and illustrated by J. C. Loudon in his *Arboretum et fruticetum Britannicum* (1838);[5] these two illustrations are reproduced respectively as Figures 3.4.1 and 2.4.3. In 1870 the 'commissioner' added his own description and recorded the tree's girth (36 feet at 5 feet from the ground).[6]

Figure 3.2.1

'The Moccas Oak', 1870. A sketch by Worthington G. Smith from *Transactions of the Woolhope Naturalists' Field Club,* 1873.

3/2

Figure 3.2.2

'The Stag's Horn Oak', 1873. A sketch by Worthington G. Smith from *Transactions of the Woolhope Naturalists' Field Club*, 1873. The tree is now generally referred to as 'The *Hypebaeus* Tree' and is numbered 151.

Figure 3.2.3

'The *Hypebaeus* Tree' (= 'The Stag's Horn Oak'), 1997. A sketch by Éilis Kirby.

Figure 3.2.4

'The Promontory Oak', 1873.

A sketch by Worthington G. Smith from *Transactions of the Woolhope Naturalists' Field Club*, 1873. The tree is numbered 62.

Figure 3.2.5

'The Promontory Oak', 1997. A sketch by Éilis Kirby.

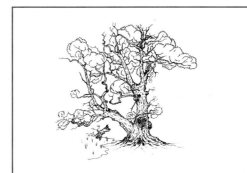

A further drawing and description appear in the Woolhope Club *Transactions* for 1873 (Figure 3.2.1) where the tree is identified as being a pedunculate oak.[7] In 1874 Worthington G. Smith wrote that it was entirely hollow, "on walking inside, and looking round, it is like being in a good-sized room."[8] Could it be that this "good sized room" had once been a family home? Dr David Boddington reports the recollection of a Mrs Watkins, born at Moccas, probably in the 1880s, concerning a hollow tree in the Lower Park in which "a whole family was reared".[9]

On 22 April 1876 the Reverend Francis Kilvert added his own poetic description:

> ".... we came upon .... what seemed at first in the dusk to be a great ruined grey tower, but which proved to be the vast ruin of the king oak of Moccas Park, hollow and broken but still alive and vigorous in parts and actually pushing out new shoots and branches. That tree may be 2000 years old. It measured roughly 33 feet round by arm stretching".[10]

The Woolhope Club girthed the tree again in 1891, noting that it was "charred internally owing to its having been accidentally set on fire".[11] That the Club failed to record a girth on the occasion of its Field Meeting of 25 May 1933, when other well-known trees were measured,[12] suggests that by then 'The Moccas Oak' was no more.

The girth of 'The Moccas Oak' in 1891 was 36 feet 6 inches, this compares with a measurement of 39 feet 7 inches for the stoutest pedunculate oak recorded in the British Isles.[13] Clearly therefore, 'The Moccas Oak' was a very substantial tree. It is estimated that it dated from about 1064.[14]

'The Stag's Horn Oak' or 'The *Hypebaeus* Tree'

In terms of character and associations this tree is a worthy successor to 'The Moccas Oak'. It is thought to be the one described by the 'commissioner' in 1870 as "a burlesque of a tree that wrapped its dark extraneous growth round itself like a frieze mantle".[15] It is illustrated for the first time in a sketch by Worthington G. Smith reproduced in both the Woolhope Club *Transactions* of 1873 and the *Gardener's Chronicle*,[16] where it is referred to as 'The Stag's Horn Oak' (Figure 3.2.2). A comparison of the sketch with Figure 3.2.3, leaves no doubt that this is the tree which nowadays is often called 'The *Hypebaeus* Tree'. This is because of its rôle in the rediscovery of the beetle *Hypebaeus flavipes*, for which Moccas Park is the only British location (see Chapter 5.2).

Whilst the form of the trunk has changed little over the last 120 years, the crown has lost much of its stag's-head. Today 'The *Hypebaeus* Tree' has a girth of 30 feet 5 inches and is the stoutest and probably the oldest tree in the Lower Park; estimates suggest that it may date from about 1400.[17]

Various oaks of note

Other sketches published in both the *Transactions* and the *Gardener's Chronicle* show 'The Promontory Oak' (Figure 3.2.4), which still stands on a promontory on the south side of the Lawn Pool and 'The Riven Oak' (Figure 3.2.6), only half of which now survives. Recent sketches of both trees are reproduced as Figures 3.2.5 and 3.2.7. Trees named in other publications,[18] but now gone or untraceable, are 'The Hundred Pound Oak' and 'The Weeping Oak' (both of which are described below), 'The Spring Oak' (from beneath which a spring issued), 'The Tall Oak' (a photograph of which is reproduced as Figure 3.4.5; it was 118 feet in height in 1870 but had fallen by 1891), 'The Broad Oak' (with a canopy diameter of 120-130 feet) and 'The Golden Bough Oak' (which produced yellow foliage each spring).

The 'commissioner' gives some details of the naming of 'The Hundred Pound Oak': it stood "on the very top of the Hill ....a very respectable oak some nine or ten feet in circumference ..... It is visible in full size... [from Moccas Court] ... and was a great

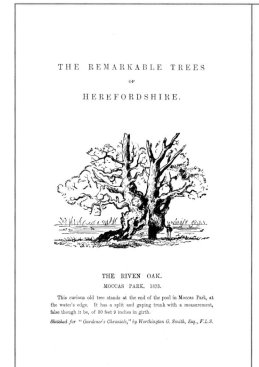

THE REMARKABLE TREES
OF
HEREFORDSHIRE.

THE RIVEN OAK.
MOCCAS PARK. 1873.

This curious old tree stands at the end of the pool in Moccas Park, at the water's edge. It has a split and gaping trunk with a measurement, false though it be, of 30 feet 9 inches in girth.

Sketched for "Gardener's Chronicle," by Worthington G. Smith, Esq., F.L.S.

Figure 3.2.6

'The Riven Oak', **1873.** A sketch by Worthington G. Smith from *Transactions of the Woolhope Naturalists' Field Club*, 1873.

Figure 3.2.7

'The Riven Oak', **1985.** A sketch by Heather Percy who drew the tree from a slightly different angle to the one chosen by Worthington G. Smith (Figure 3.2.6). The remains of the right hand side of the tree now lie in the Lawn Pool, but there is no doubt that the subject of the two drawings (tree number 22) is the same.

favourite with Lady Cornewall.[19] 'I would not lose that oak,' she said one day, 'for a hundred pounds,' and it has ever after borne the name of the 'Hundred Pound Oak'."[20]

There is another story associated with the naming of a 'Hundred Pound Oak', either the same tree or another which also stood at the top of the Park. According to local tradition it was so named because Sir Velters Cornewall (1824-1868), a renowned gambler, won a wager of a hundred pounds that he could hit it with a rifle bullet from Moccas Court, a distance of perhaps 2,500 yards.[21]

'The Weeping Oak' was, according to Elwes & Henry in their *Trees of Great Britain and Ireland*,[22] the most famous tree of its kind. Loudon who published a small figure of the tree which is reproduced as Figure 2.4.2, quotes from a description sent to him by Mr J. Webster, gardener and forester at Moccas: ".... total height of the trunk, 75 ft., with branches reaching from about the middle of its height to within 7 ft. of the ground, and hanging down like cords. Many of these branches are 30 ft long, and no thicker in any part of that length than a common wagon rope".[23]

'The Woolhope Club Oak' and 'The Knoll Oak'

'The Woolhope Club Oak' (subsequently referred to simply as 'The Club Oak') and 'The Knoll Oak' are two trees of particular silvicultural interest;[24] they were first picked out in 1870 and are still identifiable today. The former was named in 1870 in honour of the Woolhope Naturalists' Field Club of which the Reverend Sir George Cornewall, owner of Moccas Park, had been the Honorary Secretary for many years.[25] It is a particularly well proportioned tree with a tall bole and bark that twists up the trunk in the manner of a sweet chestnut. Photographs of 'The Club Oak' were printed in the Club's *Transactions* for 1870 and 1932; they are reproduced in Chapter 3.4, along with a photograph taken in 1997. The 1997 photograph reveals signs of 'die-back', the retrenchment that leads to stag-headedness; this may explain why, as shown in Table 3.2.1, the tree is apparently shorter today than it was in 1932.

'The Knoll Oak' is another fine tree; photographs of it are reproduced in Chapter 3.5. It was not particularly old when it was selected for girthing in 1870. This has allowed girth increments during the tree's mature growth phase to be measured, and because the tree's trunk is free of distortions, these measurements can be treated with some confidence. They may therefore be useful in indicating the growth rates achieved during their mature phases by other trees in the Park and calculations derived from successive measurements of this tree have, by extrapolation, been used to estimate the age of other trees, as explained in Chapter 3.5. 'The Knoll Oak' and 'The Woolhope Club Oak' are estimated to date from about 1706 and 1598 respectively.

Successive girth measurements are also available for 'The Promontory Oak' and its neighbour, and also for 'The Stag's Horn Oak ('The *Hypebaeus* Tree') and 'The Riven Oak' but in all cases growth forms, or low branches at the measuring height, make comparisons highly questionable. This is not the case however for what may be christened 'The Bredwardine Lodge Oak'. Measured in 1870 it is identifiable today from the 'commissioner's' description: "the tree next to the Bredwardine Lodge entrance, which measures 20 ft. 10 in., sends its roots above ground on every side very curiously";[26] a recent measurement is given in Table 3.2.1. This tree is estimated to date from 1502.

Newly named oaks

A more recent addition to the lexicon of Moccas trees is the 'Old Man of Moccas'. This tree is amongst a group of particularly characterful oaks standing part way up the east side of the

Lower Park; it is one of a number of trees in Moccas Park represented in paintings by the contemporary artist Diane Barker.

Another addition is a tree which, because of its size and form, has been christened 'The Bonsai Oak'(Figure 3.2.8); it grows close to the deer fence at the top of the Park. The tree germinated, probably at least 20 years ago, in a hollow in the upper side of a large fallen limb which is propped up above ground level by a projecting fork. The base of the tree's trunk stands in the hollow, but this hollow is 30 inches above the ground and the tree's roots are presumed to extend rather further, running down through one half of the projecting fork before they strike the ground.[27]

Figure 3.2.8

'The Bonsai Oak',
1994. Photograph
by Peter Wakely.

Chestnuts, beech, ash and lime trees

Sweet and horse chestnuts and beech are common both in the Lower and Upper Park. There are many very fine specimens, particularly of both species of chestnut in the Upper Park, but none that yet stands out by virtue of position, sheer size or character. By contrast Loudon describes a remarkable ash tree "... growing on the edge of a dingle, with immensely large roots, running on the surface of the ground for 50 feet and upwards, down the steep side of the dingle, [it] has a clear trunk of 30 feet, which at 15 feet from the ground, is 7 feet in diameter [22 feet in girth]; the contents of this trunk, and of three large limbs, make 1,003 [cubic] feet [of timber]".[28] Elwes & Henry knew of no larger ash anywhere, but by the time they were writing (1909) it was just a memory.[29] Today there are very few well established ash trees growing in the Park, one is however a particularly large and characterful tree (see cover illustration). In 1997 it had a girth of 26 feet 6 inches; this compares with a girth of 29 feet recorded for the stoutest ash tree currently growing in the British Isles.[30]

A photograph taken in 1932, apparently in the Upper Park, shows a large pollarded lime tree;[31] the photograph is reproduced as Figure 3.5.14. Ten limes survive here, most of which have been identified as large-leaved lime *Tilia platyphyllos*.[32] Some are now very large, with girths of up to 25 feet 6 inches; the largest may be 400 or more years old.[33] If these trees were more accessible they would certainly be amongst the more celebrated trees of Moccas Park.

Yew and Wellingtonia

Another species exclusive to the Upper Park is yew; at least 6 good specimens are to be found here with girths of up to 14 ft. 10 in. They, like the large-leaved limes, may well be relics of the former natural woodland cover of the Park. By contrast, Wellingtonias were introduced to this country in 1853,[34] and to Herefordshire in 1855,[35] at about which time the two currently growing in the Park were probably planted. If so, they will have been present in 1870 but at that time were doubtless too small to attract the attention of the Woolhope Club's 'commissioner'. By 1931 the better of the two had shot up, as shown in Figure 3.2.9. A recent photograph (Figure 3.2.10) shows that its top has blown out, nevertheless it is the tallest tree

Figure 3.2.9

Wellingtonia, *circa* 1931. A photograph by Walter Pritchard from *Transactions of the Woolhope Naturalists' Field Club*, 1931. The tree is numbered 320.

Figure 3.2.10

Wellingtonia, 1997. A photograph by Éilis Kirby of the same tree (number 320) as is shown in Figure 3.2.9.

in the Park and only two trees in the Lower Park, both of them oaks, are stouter. A series of measurements of this tree are given in Table 3.2.1.

Conclusion

The landscape of Moccas Park owes much to many remarkable trees. They have long been celebrated, but perhaps never more so than today, when interest, especially in ancient trees, is particularly strong, as is manifested, for example, in the Veteran Trees Initiative, through which this book is published. It is an interest which reflects both a growing awareness of the importance of the United Kingdom for ancient trees, and a concern for their vulnerability to pollution, changes in land use and over-zealous concerns for tidiness and safety.[36] But the interest flows from something more fundamental, a certain reverence and admiration for these ancient living things which have stood quietly through generations of human endeavour, strife and upheaval. It is to be hoped that the conservation of these veteran and other remarkable trees will enable them, in the words of Francis Kilvert, to go on "tiring down and seeing out generation after generation".[37]

Table 3.2.1: Successive measurements of 'The Woolhope Club Oak', 'The Knoll Oak', 'The Bredwardine Lodge Oak' and a Wellingtonia

For reasons of authenticity and ease of comparison, all measurements in this table are given in feet and inches. A clinometer was used to take height measurements for the 1997 survey; it is not known how previous measurements were made. The girthing of ancient trees is not straightforward and apparent anomalies in measurements are therefore not surprising. For example, in the case of 'The Woolhope Club Oak' a large boss has developed at the measuring height of five feet. The 1998 measurement was taken at the height of the boss but the boss was subtracted from the measurement and an allowance was added equivalent to the girth of the trunk that the boss occupied. It is not known how long this boss has existed, nor, if it were present, how previous recorders may have measured in relation to it. The estimation of tree heights is problematical too, but note that 'The Woolhope Club Oak' is dying back and the top has blown out of the Wellingtonia, presumably accounting for their loss of height.

Tree name	Tree number	Year	Girth (feet and inches) at 5 feet	Height (feet)	Source
The Woolhope Club Oak	259	1870	19' 5"	94'	Anon 1870
		1891	20' 10"		Anon 1891
		1932	23' 0"	circa 105'	James 1932
		1985	26' 3"	circa 78'	Percy 1985
		1997	26' 11"	89'	Hatfield & Taylor 1997
		1998	24' 7"		P. Harding and T. Wall[38]
The Knoll Oak	267	1870	14' 7"		Anon 1870
		1932	17' 7"		James 1932
		1985	20' 6"	circa 90'	Percy 1985
		1997	20' 8"		Hatfield & Taylor 1997
		1998	20' 10"		P. Harding and T. Wall[39]
The Bredwardine Lodge Oak	187	1870	20' 10"		Anon 1870
		1997	27' 9"		Hatfield & Taylor 1997
Wellingtonia	320	1931	20' 2"	108'	James 1931
		1974		123'	I.R.P. 1975
		1997	27'11"	122'	Hatfield & Taylor 1997

Notes

1   Anon (1870). The anonymous commissioner prefaces his remarks as follows: " The discovery of a new Mistletoe-Oak by the Rev. Sir George H. Cornewall, Bart., on the Moccas Estate, [it was not in the Park] had an irresistible claim on the immediate attention of your Commissioner." This, amongst other evidence, suggests that the commissioner may well have been Dr H. G. Bull, a luminary of the Woolhope Club and author of the classic paper "The mistletoe in Herefordshire", published in the Club's *Transactions* in 1864 (see Chapter 4.3).

2   Thomas Hearne (1744-1817); his commission at Moccas was preceded by one for Richard Payne Knight, a friend of Sir George Cornewall, at Downton Vale (now Downton Gorge National Nature Reserve) in north Herefordshire (Morris 1989, Wall 1994); see also Chapter 2.3. Hearne's watercolour was published as an etching in 1798 under the title *An oak in Moccas Park, Herefordshire*; the etching is reproduced as Figure 1.1.1. Loudon (1838) refers to the tree as "The Moccas Park Oak on the banks of the River Wye", but it is clear from the itinerary followed by the Woolhope Club's 'commissioner' (Anon 1870), and from later accounts (Anon 1873b, Anon 1891), that the tree stood in Moccas Park, probably south east of the Lawn Pool.

3   The full series is listed in Chapter 2.3 where the watercolour of the beech tree is described as "view east from the lower reaches of Moccas Deer Park".

4   Strutt (1822).

5   Loudon (1838).

6   Anon (1870). For reasons of historical authenticity and ease of comparison, most of the measurements in this chapter are given in feet and inches.

7   Anon (1873a).

8   Smith (1874).

9   David Boddington (pers. comm.).

10 Plomer (1940).

11 Anon (1891).

12 Anon (1933).

13 This is the largest measurement given in Mitchell, Schilling & White (1994), it is of a pedunculate oak at Bowthorpe, Lincolnshire measured in 1980.

14 This figure is derived from its girth and the application of growth rates estimated for 'The Knoll Oak', following the methodology explained in White (1994). Age estimates made for other trees named in this chapter were derived in a similar way. The ages of trees are discussed at greater length in Chapter 3.5.

15 Anon (1870).

16 Anon (1873a), Smith (1874).

17 See Chapter 3.5.

18 Anon (1870), Anon (1891).

19 It is unclear as to which Lady Cornewall the account refers, but as the past tense is used, it could well be Lady Jane Cornewall, 1790-1852.

20 Anon (1870).

21 Sam Davies and Ivor Saunders (pers. comms.); the tree in question is variously referred to as 'The Hundred Pound Oak' and 'The Hundred Guinea Oak'. Expert opinion is that even with the best rifle available at that time, a correct calculation of the aim adjustment for the distance, and a calm day, it would have taken an exceptional marksman to have hit the tree taken as a whole, let alone its trunk (Dr George Peterken, woodland ecologist and formerly a member of the Queen's Hundred, the premier rifle shooting competition at Bisley, and Bill Harriman, Head of Firearms at the British Association for Shooting and Conservation and an authority on the history of firearms (pers. comms)).

22 Elwes & Henry (1907).

23 Loudon (1836).

24 Both trees appear to be hybrids; James (1932) reports on determinations to this effect made by the Director of Kew Gardens.

25 Anon (1870).

26 Anon (1870); this former lodge was also referred to as the Lawn Gate Lodge.

27 Its girth at 1.5 m is 50 cm (but at 75 cm it is 77 cm), its height is approximately 4.8 m and its branches spread across a diameter of some 7.8 m.

28 Loudon (1838); the location of this tree is not definitely known, but as Hadfield (1969) remarks, Loudon's statement that it grew "on the edge of a dingle" is suggestive of the Park.

29 Elwes & Henry (1909).

30 Mitchell, Schilling & White (1994). The measurement, taken in 1988, was of an ash at Clapton Court, Somerset. The Moccas Park ash is numbered 97.

31 James (1932).

32 Harding (1977), C.D. Pigott (pers. comm.).

33 C.D. Pigott (pers. comm.); see Chapter 3.5.

34 Mitchell (1978).

35 The first recorded planting in Herefordshire was at Holme Lacey Park (Anon 1870). In 1931 the better of the two trees in Moccas Park was comparable in size to the largest trees at Holme Lacey (James 1931), suggesting that it may have been planted at about the same time as the original planting there.

36 Rackham (1989) states that "from Boulogne to Athens one rarely sees a tree more than 200 years old. England (and Greece) are exceptions". However, interest in ancient trees is by no means confined to the British Isles. For example, Boquete (1998) describes a catalogue of large and characterful trees established in Spain in 1917 and Fontaine (1914) describes the ancient oak of Allouville Bellefosse, Normandy, one of several celebrated trees which are shown today on road atlases of France.

37 Plomer (1940).

38 Unpublished personal records.

39 Unpublished personal records.

References relating to Moccas Park

ANON. 1870. Incidental notes on remarkable trees in Herefordshire. *Transactions of the Woolhope Naturalists' Field Club*, 288-321.

ANON. 1873a. The remarkable trees of Herefordshire. *Transactions of the Woolhope Naturalists' Field Club*, 100-154.

ANON. 1873b. The fungus foray and feast of the Woolhope Club, October 1873. *Transactions of the Woolhope Naturalists' Field Club*, 100-116.

ANON. 1891. Field meeting report. *Transactions of the Woolhope Naturalists' Field Club*, 221-223.

ANON. 1933. Field meeting report. *Transactions of the Woolhope Naturalists' Field Club*, xi-xviii.

ELWES, H.J. & HENRY, A. 1907, 1909. *The trees of Great Britain and Ireland*. Volumes II and IV. Edinburgh: privately published.

HADFIELD, M. 1969. Moccas Park. *Quarterly journal of forestry*, 63, 254-256.

HARDING, P. T. 1977. *Moccas deer park, Hereford and Worcester: a report on the history, structure and natural history*. Unpublished report to the Nature Conservancy Council by the Institute of Terrestrial Ecology, Huntingdon.

HATFIELD, D. & TAYLOR, M. 1997. Girths of all trees in the Lower Park (except those planted since 1960) together with selected height measurements. Internal English Nature report.

I.R.P. 1975. Moccas Estate. *Quarterly journal of forestry*, 69, 113-115.

JAMES, F.R. 1931. Wellingtonia trees in Herefordshire. *Transactions of the Woolhope Naturalists' Field Club*, 108-109.

JAMES, F.R. 1932. Trees in Moccas Park and elsewhere. *Transactions of the Woolhope Naturalists' Field Club*, 182-183.

LOUDON, J.C. 1836. Planting at Moccas Court. *The gardener's magazine*, 12, 368-369.

LOUDON, J.C. 1838. *Arboretum et fruticetum Britannicum*. Volumes II and III.

MORRIS, D. 1989. *Thomas Hearne and his landscape*. London: Reaktion Books.

PERCY, H. 1985. Moccas Park National Nature Reserve, Tree Inventory. Internal Nature Conservancy Council report.

PLOMER, W. 1940. *Kilvert's diary*. Volume three. London: Jonathan Cape.

SMITH, W.G. 1874. Oaks at Moccas Court. *The Gardeners' Chronicle*. February 14.

STRUTT, J.G. 1822. *Sylva Britannica; or Portraits of forest trees, distinguished for their antiquity, magnitude or beauty. Drawn from nature and etched by Jacob George Strutt.* London: Colnaghi & Co.

Other references

BOQUET, E.R. 1998. The expansion of the forest and the defence of nature: the work of forest engineers in Spain 1900-1936. *In*: C. WATKINS, ed. *European woods and forests. Studies in cultural* history. Wallingford: CAB International, 181-190.

FONTAINE, A. 1914. *Allouville Bellefosse. Le gros chêne, la paroisse, Pierre Blain d'Esnambuc.* Yvetot: Delamare.

MITCHELL, A.F. 1978. *A field guide to the trees of Britain and northern Europe.* Second edition. London: Collins.

MITCHELL, A.F., SCHILLING, V.E. & WHITE, J.E.J. 1994. *Champion trees in the British Isles.* Technical paper 7. Edinburgh: Forestry Commission.

RACKHAM, O. 1989. *The last forest. The story of Hatfield Forest.* London: Dent.

REPTON, H. 1803. *Observations on the Theory and Practice of Landscape Gardening.* London.

WALL, T. 1994. The verdant landscape: the practice and theory of Richard Payne Knight at Downton Vale. *In*: S. DANIELS & C. WATKINS, eds. *The picturesque landscape.* Nottingham: University of Nottingham, 49-65.

WHITE, J. 1994. *Estimating the age of large trees in Britain.* Research Information Note 250. Farnham: Forestry Authority.

3
2

The trees: surveys
and other sources of information

Paul T. Harding
and Tom Wall

Survey is an exercise in which a set of qualitative or quantitative observations are made without preconceptions of what the findings ought to be.

Coordinating Commission for Biological Recording (1995).
Biological recording in the United Kingdom.

C ontinuity of habitat, in particular veteran trees, is essential for almost all of the organisms that are particularly associated with wood-pastures and parks. The survival of trees to old age, progressive die-back and eventual death and decay, is a natural process not normally seen in other types of managed woodland. This is what makes wood-pastures and parklands so distinctive and important for wildlife. Although many of the wood-pastures that remain in Britain have good numbers of veteran trees, it is essential to maintain and renew this habitat over timescales that are many times the lifespan of a human.

To manage the resource of trees in Moccas Park, in order to fulfil nature conservation objectives and maintain the distinctive and historic landscape, we must know what trees are present, where they are and their age, growth form and general condition. In this and the next two chapters, we summarise the considerable body of information about the trees of the Park, which enables us to assess the trees and their history, spanning a period of more than 200 years.

Building up the picture

In seeking to build up an historical picture of the numbers, distribution, species and age structure of trees in the Park, we can draw on both representational sources (maps, paintings, book illustrations and photographs) and on written sources (surveys, historical accounts and documentary evidence). The following account lists these sources and indicates the sort of information and insights they offer.

Maps, paintings, book illustrations and ground photographs

The first detailed Estate Map of which we are aware dates from 1772. 'Capability' Brown's plan of 1778 includes The Lawn,[1] but it is a proposal rather than a record and is not therefore regarded as relevant to the present exercise. The earliest known painting of Moccas Park dates from the 1780s, since when the Park has figured on Ordnance Survey maps, and in a number of water colours, book illustrations and photographs. There has been Francis Kilvert's word picture too.[2] Many photographs have been taken since the 1970s by ourselves and others, but these overlap with the detailed tree surveys cited below which provide a more objective record.

Beech

The following table is not intended to be an exhaustive list, but identifies those representations most helpful in building up the picture of the Park and its development over the last two centuries.

Table 3.3.1. Selected maps, paintings, book illustrations and ground photographs

Date	Cartographer/ Artist/ Photographer	Detail	Source
1772	John Lambe Davis	Series of estate maps at 8" to 1 mile prepared for Sir George Cornewall which give indications of relative tree densities throughout the Park.[3]	Hereford City Library; Figure 2.3.3
1780s	Thomas Hearne	Two watercolour portraits of trees, a beech and 'The Moccas Oak'; taken at face value the background of both provide evidence of the age structure of the trees in the Lower Park.	See Chapters 1.1, 2.3 and 3.2 and cover illustration
1822	J.G. Strutt	Etching of the 'Moccas Oak' from a similar angle to that of Hearne's painting.	Strutt (1822); Figure 3.4.1
1871	Ladmore & Son	Photographs of 'The Club Oak' and 'The Tall Oak'; the backgrounds of both provide evidence of the age structure of the trees in the Lower Park.	Anon (1870); Figures 3.4.2 and 3.4.5
1873	Worthington G. Smith	Drawings of 4 individual trees in Lower Park, but without any background.	Anon (1873); Figures 3.2.1, 3.2.2, 3.2.4 and 3.2.6
1886	Ordnance Survey	First edition 6" to 1 mile map gives indications of relative tree densities throughout the Park and absolute numbers in parts of the Lower Park.	Ordnance Survey; Figure 3.3.1
1931	Walter Pritchard	Photograph of a Wellingtonia in its setting on the interface between Upper and Lower Parks.	James (1931); Figure 3.2.9
1932	Anon	Photographs of 'The Club Oak' and 'The Knoll Oak' (see below) showing parts of the Lower Park.	James (1932); Figures 3.4.3 and 3.5.12
1998	Éilis Kirby	Photographs of 'The Club Oak', 'The Knoll Oak' and a Wellingtonia; when set alongside those cited above, these photos provide important insights into changes to the tree cover of the Lower Park over the last 130 years.	Figures 3.4.4, 3.5.13 and 3.2.10 respectively

Aerial photographs

The vertical black and white aerial photographs listed below have been used to pin-point some recent changes to the Park. There are other and later photographs (vertical and oblique), some of them in colour.

1946

Those taken on 11 July 1946, provide the earliest clear evidence of the appearance of the whole of the Park (see Figures 1.2.3 and 3.3.2).[4]

At this time, part of the Park still extended over the brow of the Merbach-Woodbury ridge to the south west, as far as an area marked on present-day maps as Burnt Coppice. This part of the Park has the appearance of being covered with bracken, scattered shrubs or scrub but

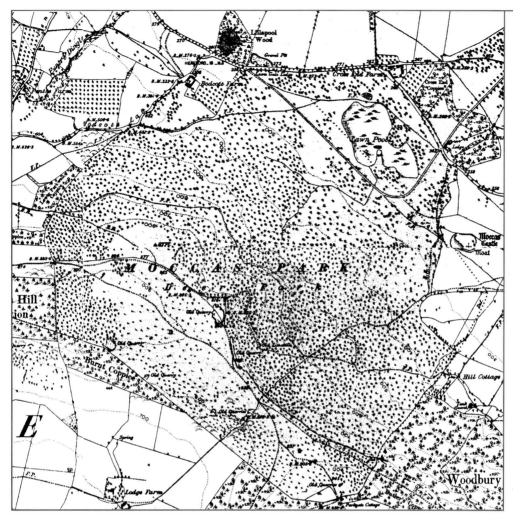

Figure 3.3.1

**Ordnance Survey
map, 1886.** Scale of
original maps 6 inches
to 1 mile.

with few trees other than at the western end where there is a sizeable group of trees with large crowns; they are understood to have been beech.[5]

1963

Photographs dating from June 1963 show that fellings have occurred around the Lawn and elsewhere in the Lower Park.[6] The whole Park still appears to be rough grazing with widespread bracken. The conifer plantation created on the former part of the Park described above is now well established.

1970s

Photographs taken on 3 May 1971 (for example Figure 3.3.3) show the Park before most trees had come into full leaf.[7] A small, shield-shaped plantation has been established within the bracken beds, to the south of Bodcott Farm. A further set of aerial photographs taken on 5 June 1973 does not show any other significant changes.[8]

Tree surveys

Eleven surveys of trees were conducted between 1870 and 1999 and one of dead wood. In 1976/77 an attempt was made for the first time to survey all trees throughout the Park. Subsequent surveys have concentrated on the Lower Park only. The surveys are listed and described in outline in Table 3.3.2.

Figure 3.3.2

**Aerial photograph
taken 11 July 1946.**
RAF photograph.

Figure 3.3.3

**Aerial photograph
taken 3 May 1971.**
This photograph is
reproduced from
Ordnance Survey
material with the
permission of the
Ordnance Survey on
behalf of Her
Majesty's Stationery
Office. © Crown
Copyright.
GD272299.1999.

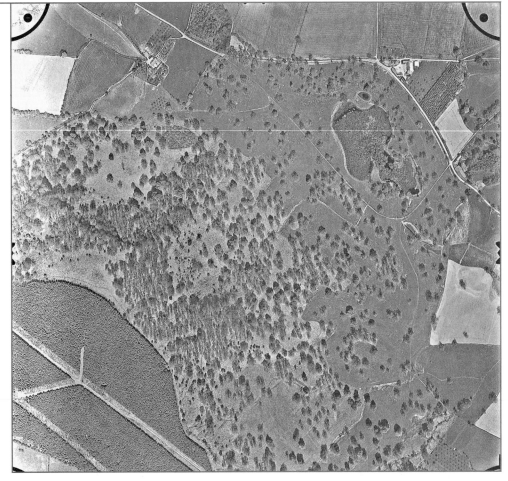

Table 3.3.2. Outline of tree surveys, 1870-1999

Surveyor	Year	Extent of survey	Information gathered
Anon, Woolhope Club[9]	1870	90 trees in Lower Park	Girths of 70 oak, 11 ash, 4 beech, 2 wych elm, 2 birch, 1 lime. Photographs of 2 trees (see above). Not a systematic survey, concentrated on the larger trees.
Dr George Peterken & Paul Harding[10]	1972	Parts of Lower Park	Brief survey (not quantitative) and report, but inadequate time was available to gain a true picture. Growth rings of tree stumps counted.
Paul Harding[11]	1976/77	Entire park	Lower Park: All trees and shrubs individually mapped and described (species, age class, growth form and condition). Upper Park: Numbers of principal tree species quantified and attributed to age classes and growth forms.
NCC staff	1978 on	Lower Park	All trees in the Lower Park were numbered, tagged and mapped (Figure 3.3.4).
Heather Percy[12]	1985/6	281 trees in Lower Park	Species, girth, estimated height, growth form, estimated crown breadth, description and note of special features; sketches of 82 trees, photos of 39 trees.
Éilis Kirby & Tom Wall[13]	1993	The 307 trees in Lower Park not covered by Percy	Species, age class and growth form.
Paul Harding[14]	1989, 1990 (twice)	Lower Park	Loss or damage following summer drought of 1989, winter storms of early 1990 and summer drought of 1990.
Heather Percy and others[15]	1985, ongoing	Lower Park	Mapping of recently planted trees; updated by Éilis Kirby in 1993, Nick Campbell in 1995 and David Hatfield and Mike Taylor in 1997.
Dave Simpson[16]	1995	Upper Park	Quantification and general distribution of recently planted trees.
Paul Harding & Tom Wall[17]	1997	Lower Park	Assessment of overall changes since Harding's survey of 1976/77.
David Hatfield & Mike Taylor[18]	1997	Lower Park	Girth measurement of all trees, including recent plantings, enabling size-class distribution to be determined for first time.
Tom Wall & Gisèle Wall[19]	1999	Lower Park	The volume and condition of dead fallen wood was assessed in three small plots.

Records of tree plantings

Prior to recent decades, documentary evidence of tree plantings is fragmentary. But there is clear evidence to be found on the ground, notably of the extensive plantings to which John

Claudius Loudon alludes in 1836.[20] Despite subsequent fellings, the contribution that these plantings make to the present-day tree stock of the Park is evident in the histograms presented in Chapter 3.5. The principal sources of information on tree plantings are detailed in Table 3.3.3.

Records of tree fellings

Again, the evidence is fragmentary, sometimes merely anecdotal and in all probability incomplete. The record for the first half of the twentieth century is particularly scanty and no

Figure 3.3.4

Map of the locations of trees in the Lower Park, *circa* **1980.** Each tree is represented by its canopy as sketched from aerial photographs.

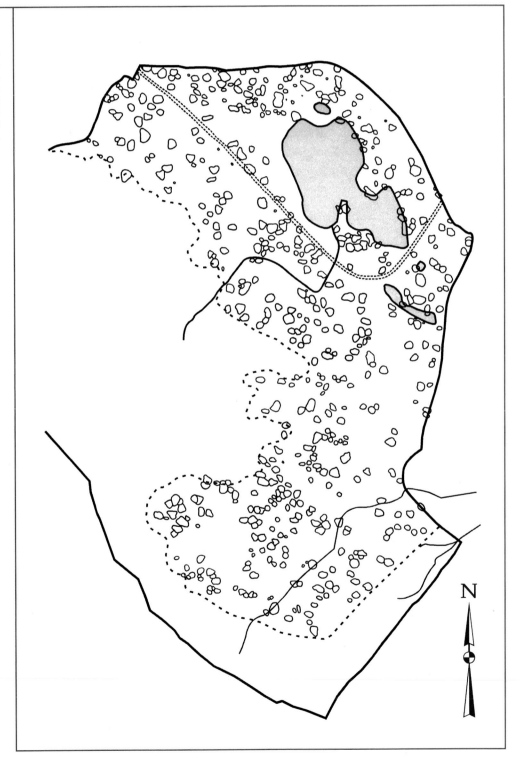

proper search has yet been made for estate records of this period. Known records are summarised in Table 3.3.4.

Tree ring counts and girthings

Counts of the annual growth rings visible on tree stumps have been used to determine the ages of some trees as detailed in Chapter 3.5. Additionally, a comparison of the girth measurements of 'The Club Oak' and 'The Knoll Oak' taken in 1870 and 1998 has enabled John White to assess potential growth rates for the Park from which tentative estimates can be made of the age of individual trees.[21]

Reviewing the evidence

In the next chapter we use these somewhat disparate sources of evidence to review the changes that have occurred in the stock of trees in the Park over the last 200 or more years. We then conclude this section with a chapter which, using the information gathered through the various tree surveys, examines the tree stock present in the Park today.

3 / 3

Table 3.3.3. Outline of records of tree plantings

Year	Location	Detail	Source
Between 1793 and 1836	Moccas Estate, presumably including the Park	"Mr Webster has planted nearly 300,000 oaks, besides other trees [including larch], particularly on hill sides".	Loudon (1836); corroborated by evidence from current size-class distribution, see Chapter 3.5.
		"Moccas Park .... is far too much crowded with trees .... some half century ago, or rather more, when the sad memory of a heavy timber fallage was green .... a far-sighted steward .... got permission to plant all these young oaks ...."	Anon (1870).
Post 1853	Lower Park	Two Wellingtonias; the earliest introduction to Britain was in 1853 (Mitchell 1978); they may be contemporary with an evergreen oak and a deodar.	Tree surveys.
1960s/1970s	Upper Park	Three small mixed plantations established by the Estate and a belt of conifers, mostly Scots pine, planted on the eastern boundary.	Tree surveys.
1968	Lower Park	74 trees planted by the Moccas Estate, of which 60 survive today.	Tree surveys.
1979-	Lower Park	694 trees planted by NCC/EN; ongoing at the rate of 10 trees per year.	Tree surveys.
1979	Upper Park	349 trees planted by NCC/EN; ongoing on an occasional basis. Additionally, 10 small exclosures planted and a one hectare natural regeneration exclosure established.	Tree surveys.

Table 3.3.4. Records of tree fellings

Year	Location	Detail	Source
?	Moccas Park	".... some half century ago, or rather more, when the sad memory of a heavy timber fallage was green." ".... many years since, on the south side of the Park, £20,000 worth of timber was felled at one time". Unclear as to whether both references are to the same felling, but presumably the former, at least, relates to 1808/9.	Anon (1870).
1808/9	Moccas Estate, probably including the Park	Over £12,600 worth of timber sold by Sir George Cornewall.	Account book and deeds, Hereford Record Office (HRO)AF 57/12 and LC Deeds 5214; see Chapter 2.4.
Between 1793 and 1836	Moccas Estate, possibly including the Park	"Mr Webster [estate gardener and forester from *circa* 1793] has removed oak trees that took ten horses to draw them".	Loudon (1836).
Post 1870	Lower Park	"The great arboreal feature of the eastern side of the Park .... consists in the number and size of the Ash trees"; by 1977 only 10 survived, suggesting felling in the interim; note 1884 and 1897 below.	Anon (1870), Harding (1977).
1870-1932	Lower Park	Photographs of 'The Woolhope Club Oak' taken in 1871 and 1932 (Table 3.3.1) show a significant reduction in the numbers of trees in the background, indicating felling within this period.	Anon (1870) and James (1932); see Chapter 3.4.
1883	Moccas Park	11 sweet chestnut, value £123.14.6d.	HRO, F10/156.
1884	Moccas Park	31 oak, 2 ash, value £265.9.6d.	HRO, F10/156.
Post late C19th	Moccas Park	Comparison of the OS 6" map of 1886 and NCC survey of 1978 onwards, suggests a 50% reduction in tree cover on The Lawn.	See Tables 3.3.1 and 3.3.2.
1897	Moccas Park and in meadows adjoining	402 oak and 13 ash with a value of £1,300.	HRO, F10/156.
Mid C20th	Lower Park	150 hardwood stumps observed 1972 and mapped in 1977. Evidence of aerial photos suggests that these were trees felled in the period 1946-63, with a few earlier; ring counts suggested these trees might have been planted during the Webster period, see above.	Peterken (1972), Harding (1977).
Early 1950s	Moccas Park	"Some of the best oaks were felled .... for death duties". Local people also refer to the felling of a "lot" of sycamores, including 40 "at one bunch", mainly on the east side; also "lots" of "great big beech" and a few oak prior to the coniferisation of an area at the top of the Park now lying outside the Park boundary.	I.R.P. (1975). Transcriptions of oral accounts, held on EN files.
1964-72	Lower Park	Local people refer to the removal of "lots" of old hawthorns, particularly on the west side but also on The Lawn.	Transcriptions of oral accounts, held on EN files.
1987	Upper Park, west side	Estate felled at least 59 mature oaks, west side.	Correspondence re felling licence application in EN files.

Notes

1   Lancelot Brown "A Plan for the intended Alterations at Moccas Court in Herefordshire, 1778". See Chapters 2.3 and 3.1.
2   Diary entry for 22 April 1876, see inside cover and Plomer (1940). An important feature of this entry is Kilvert's reference to "fallow wood"; this is discussed in Chapter 3.5.
3   "A survey of the manors of Moccas, Bredwardine, Grove, Radnor, Wilmaston, and Cusop, and a farm at Crosswall; situate in the parishes of Moccas, Bredwardine, Dorston, Peter-church, Cusop, Clifford, and Cluttuck, in the county of Hereford: belonging to Sir George Cornewall Baronet". By John Lambe Davis. 1772. Hereford City Library.
4   RAF. Library No 427. Sortie No 106G/UK/1652. Date 11 July 1946. Vertical. Print Nos 2290-2292, 4399.
5   Sam Davies (pers. comm.).
6   RAF. Library No 2170. Sortie No 543/2339. Date 31 July 1963. Vertical. Print Nos 2F21 0449-0450 and 2F22 0449-0450.
7   Ordnance Survey. Film No 71-132. Date 3 May 1971. Vertical. Print Nos 154-156, 184-187, 212-213. Much of The Lawn appears to be dissected by paths and to have many small areas of bare ground, which may be evidence of the removal of ant hills. The Lawn and other non-bracken areas are clearly improved grassland with a smooth appearance and many animal trackways. The line of the edge of the main bracken beds is similar to that mapped in 1977.
8   Cambridge University Collection. Sortie: RC8-AK. Date 5 June 1973. Vertical. Print Nos 89-97. These photographs were used as the basis for Harding's 1976/77 tree surveys.
9   Anon (1870).
10 Peterken (1972).
11 Harding (1977).
12 Percy (1986).
13 Wall (1993).
14 Harding (1990).
15 Map on English Nature files.
16 Records on English Nature files.
17 Harding (1998), Harding & Wall (1997).
18 Hatfield & Taylor (1997).
19 Wall & Wall (1999).
20 Loudon (1836).
21 White (1998).

References relating to Moccas Park

ANON. 1870. Incidental notes of remarkable trees in Herefordshire. *Transactions of the Woolhope Naturalists' Field Club*, 288-321.

ANON. 1873. The remarkable trees of Herefordshire. *Transactions of the Woolhope Naturalists' Field Club*, 100-154.

HARDING, P.T. 1977. *Moccas Deer Park, Hereford and Worcester: a report on the history, structure and natural history*. Unpublished report to the Nature Conservancy Council by the Institute of Terrestrial Ecology, Huntingdon.

HARDING, P.T. 1990. *Damage to ecologically important trees in selected pasture- woodlands resulting from winter storms and summer drought in 1990*. Unpublished report to the Nature Conservancy Council by the Institute of Terrestrial Ecology, Huntingdon.

HARDING, P.T. 1998. *Moccas Deer Park Herefordshire, survey of individual trees in the Lower Park by Paul Harding, September 1976*. Unpublished, annotated data sheets donated to English Nature.

HARDING, P.T. & WALL, T. 1997. Moccas Park NNR. tree survey 19-20 August 1997. English Nature, unpublished data sheets.

HATFIELD, D. & TAYLOR, M. 1997. Diameters of all trees and shrubs in the Lower Park, Moccas Park NNR. English Nature internal report.

I.R.P. 1975. Moccas Estate. *Quarterly Journal of Forestry*, 69, 113-115.

JAMES, F.R. 1931. Wellingtonia trees (*Sequoia gigantea*) in Herefordshire. *Transactions of the Woolhope Naturalists' Field Club*, 108-109.

JAMES, F.R. 1932. Trees in Moccas Park and elsewhere. *Transactions of the Woolhope Naturalists' Field Club*, 182-183.

LOUDON, J.C. 1836. *The gardener's magazine*, 12, 368-369.

PERCY, H. 1986. *Moccas Park National Nature Reserve - Tree inventory*. Unpublished report to the Nature Conservancy Council.

PETERKEN, G.F. 1972. *Moccas Park* (GFP/Sites/31). Nature Conservancy, internal report.

PLOMER, W. 1940. *Kilvert's diary*. Volume 3. London: Jonathan Cape.

STRUTT, J.G. 1822. *Sylva Britannica; or portraits of forest trees, distinguished for their antiquity, magnitude or beauty. Drawn from nature and etched by Jacob George Strutt*. London: Colnaghi & Co.

WALL, T. 1993. *Inventory of established trees, Lower Park 1985/86 and 1993*. English Nature, internal report.

WALL, T. & WALL, G. 1999. *Estimates of the volume of fallen wood in three sample areas of the Lower Park at Moccas.* Unpublished report to English Nature.

WHITE, J. 1998. *Estimating the age of large and veteran trees in Britain.* Forestry Commission Research Information Note.

Other reference

COORDINATING COMMISSION FOR BIOLOGICAL RECORDING. 1995. *Biological recording in the United Kingdom.* Ruislip: Department of the Environment.

The trees: recruitment, losses and changes
since the eighteenth century

Paul T. Harding
and Tom Wall

*To anyone concerned with management, forest or otherwise, one of the
greatest* lacunae *in the wider conservation field is information
on how the community has changed ....*

H. Collier Dawkins (1971).
In: *The scientific management of animal and plant communities for conservation.*

3

4

The main tree species of the Park today, as they have been for more than a century,
are oak, beech, sweet chestnut and horse chestnut. Management has been the
over-riding factor determining the numbers, age structure and species of trees.
From the 1780s onwards, as outlined in Chapter 3.3, there are scattered records and other
evidence of the plantings and fellings which have determined what is present today. Drought,
wind-throw and disease have played some part in the loss of trees but natural regeneration
appears to have had very little influence on recruitment.

In this chapter we describe recruitment, losses and changes: the main phases of planting from
the 1780s onwards; the evidence of fellings over the same period; the losses from other
causes; the losses from all causes in the Lower Park between 1976/77 and 1997; and the
overall impact these various events have had on the species composition and age structure of
the tree cover of the Park over the last 200 or more years.

RECRUITMENT

Phases of tree planting

The limited evidence of
tree planting is summarised
in Table 3.3.3; the earliest
clear evidence dates from
the end of the eighteenth
century. The origins of the
very oldest trees are not
documented, but Thomas
Hearne's two watercolours
of the 1780s (Figure 1.1.1),
if taken at face value,
provide some pointers as to
the periods when some of

Figure 3.4.1

'The Moccas-Park Oak', J. G. Strutt, 1822.
From Strutt's *Sylva Britannica.*

the older trees present today may have been planted. Hearne shows a parkland structure of
scattered groups and single trees, many of them young, but a good number of which appear to be
at least 100 years old. This would seem to support the suggestion made in Chapter 3.1 that there

was a mid seventeenth century phase of planting; it suggests planting in the mid eighteenth century too.

Webster's plantings, circa 1793 to circa 1836

The first clear evidence for a concerted phase of planting comes in the late eighteenth century. This was undertaken by Mr J. Webster, who was Sir George Cornewall's forester from about 1793 to at least 1836. John Claudius Loudon refers, in particular, to Webster's planting of oaks,[1] and ring counts on oaks felled or wind-thrown in the Park over recent years suggest that those planted in Webster's time now probably form the main cohort of maturing oak trees. The majority probably now have diameters at breast height which fall into the 80-100 and 100-120 cm diameter classes as shown for the Lower Park in Figure 3.5.5. Although there are no ring counts currently available for the other principal species (sweet chestnut, beech and horse chestnut), histograms of diameters at breast height for each of these species in the Lower Park (Figures 3.5.6, 3.5.7 and 3.5.8) show similar patterns to that for oak, and it seems likely that Webster's plantings account for the peaks evident in the size-class distribution for each species. The handful of over-mature larch trees still present in the Upper Park today (some of which have recently blown down) probably date from this period too, as, one assumes, will many of the oak, beech, sweet and horse chestnuts.

Clearly Webster, working for Sir George Cornewall, was responsible for the planting of very large numbers of trees. He must be the anonymous steward to whom the anonymous 'commissioner' of the Woolhope Club refers in his account of 1870:[2]

> ".... some half century ago, or rather more, when the sad memory of a heavy timber fallage was green, there was a far-sighted steward at Moccas, of highly prudential 'proclivities' - probably a Scotchman - who got permission to plant all these young oaks to take the place of the old ones as they decayed."

Despite significant fellings in the 1880s, 1890s and 1950s (see below) many trees planted during Webster's stewardship survive today. His contribution to the parkland resource at Moccas is unrivalled.

Plantings from 1960s onwards

A handful of exotic species was planted in the mid nineteenth century, but otherwise it was not until the 1960s, after a lapse of 130 years, that a further concerted phase of planting was initiated by the Estate. It has been carried forward, since 1978, by the Nature Conservancy Council/English Nature, under the terms of the Nature Reserve Agreement. It is detailed in Chapter 6.5 and is represented by the tall initial columns of the histograms showing the distribution by diameter size-class in the Lower Park of oak, beech, sweet chestnut, ash, field maple and hawthorn (Figures 3.5.5 to 3.5.11). A range of exotic species has been planted too, but there has been virtually no planting of horse chestnut (see Chapter 6.5). Again, this planting effort has extended to the Upper Park where, in addition to the planting of individual trees, 14 small plantations have been established, ranging in size from 0.01 to 2 ha; conifers are prominent in four of these (Chapter 6.5).

Natural regeneration

The production of seeds by the main species of trees in the Park varies each year, but there is certainly no lack, especially not of acorns, in most years. Acorns collected from the Park have shown high levels of viability,[3] but there is no current evidence of the successful natural regeneration of trees of any species in the Park, other than on the island in the Lawn Pool and in exclosures, and this has probably been the case for two centuries or more. Although the occasional hawthorn gets away on the boundaries of the Park, deer and livestock soon nibble off any other trees and shrubs that germinate.

LOSSES

Tree fellings

The documentary evidence of fellings from the 1800s onwards is summarised in Table 3.3.4. The principal episodes for which such evidence has been found were in 1808/9, 1883/84, 1897 and the 1950s. The Woolhope Club account of 1870 refers to "the sad memory of a heavy timber fallage" being green "some half century ago, or rather more", suggesting the felling of 1808/9. It is unclear however as to whether the same, or an earlier felling is referred to when two paragraphs later the account states that "many years since, on the south side of the Park, £20,000 worth of timber was felled at one time".[4]

There is no record of what are likely to have been small scale, on-going fellings, to provide posts, stakes, pales and rails for use in the Park, and probably elsewhere on the Estate too; as late as the 1970s palings were still being prepared from oak felled in the Park.[5]

Early nineteenth century

Some of the consequences of the fellings of 1808/9 appear to be shown in J. G. Strutt's etching of 'The Moccas Oak' of 1822 (Figure 3.4.1). In the 1780s, Thomas Hearne had shown, in the background of his watercolour of this tree, several groups of trees in threes, whereas Strutt depicts single trees in a more open canopy structure. John Claudius Loudon's statement (albeit referring to the Estate as a whole) that "Mr Webster has removed oaks that took ten horses to draw them",[6] suggests that other much larger trees may have been felled in the Park too.

1880s and 1890s

Details of timber sales from the Park in 1883, 1884 and 1897, indicate that again at this period both the harvesting of mature trees and the thinning of younger ones was taking place.[7] The photographic record suggests that, at least in terms of the density of younger trees, these fellings had a major impact. Photographs of the 'The Club Oak' (Figure 3.4.2) and 'The Tall Oak' (Figure 3.4.5) taken in 1871,[8] show the Lower Park burgeoning with young maiden trees. These were doubtless planted by Webster, they are quite regularly sized and spaced, mostly singly. The repeat photograph of the 'The Club Oak' published in 1932 (Figure 3.4.3) shows that by then many of the trees had been felled.[9] It is

Figure 3.4.2

'The Woolhope Club Oak', March 1871. A photograph by Ladmore and Son, photographers to the Woolhope Naturalists' Field Club from *Transactions of the Woolhope Naturalists' Field Club* (Anon 1870 (sic)).

3
___
4

Figure 3.4.3

'The Woolhope Club Oak', April 1932. A photograph, probably by Walter Pritchard, from *Transactions of the Woolhope Naturalists' Field Club* (James 1932).

Figure 3.4.4

'The Woolhope Club Oak', December 1997. A photograph by Éilis Kirby; the tree is numbered 259.

Figure 3.4.5

**'The Tall Oak',
March 1871.** A
photograph by
Ladmore and Son,
photographers to the
Woolhope Naturalists'
Field Club from
*Transactions of the
Woolhope Naturalists'
Field Club* (Anon
1870 (sic)).

not known how representative of the Lower Park as a whole were the two photographs of 1871, but today comparable tree densities in the Lower Park are exceptional.

Close comparison of the Ordnance Survey 6 inch to 1 mile map of 1886 with the tree survey map compiled by Nature Conservancy Council (NCC) some time after 1978 is revealing (Figures 3.3.1 and 3.3.4). The former shows trees mapped individually, at least in the area of The Lawn. On The Lawn and up-slope from The Lawn, there are 558 tree symbols. The NCC map also shows individual trees, and by the time it was surveyed, the number of trees in this area had been almost exactly halved, only 281 surviving. Half of this discrepancy can be accounted for by the 140 or so stumps mapped in this area by Harding in 1977 (Figure 3.4.6); these appear to be attributable to fellings which took place between 1946 and 1963. The other 140 may well have been felled in the 1880s and 1890s, their last vestiges having rotted away by the time that Harding undertook his mapping of stumps.

Most of the recorded fellings have been of oak, but a significant proportion of the stock of ash trees present in 1870 appears to have been felled too, whether at this period or later. The commissioner of the Woolhope Club refers in 1870 to the number and size of the ash trees as "the great arboreal feature of the eastern end of the Park".[10] Nothing remains of this arboreal feature today, indeed there are now fewer than 10 ash trees in the whole of the Park. Two substantial wych elms and two large birches were measured in the Lower Park by the commissioner;[11] they too have been lost, but when is not known.

1950s

A range of evidence exists for significant fellings in the 1950s and for their location and extent. Firstly, there is a report that "some of the best oaks were felled during the early 1950s for death duties"[12] (Sir Geoffrey Cornewall died in 1951). Secondly, a comparison of the air photos taken in July 1946 and May 1971 (Figures 3.3.2 and 3.3.3.), shows that in the intervening period trees had been felled around the Lawn and elsewhere in the Lower Park; furthermore, the boundaries on the eastern side of the Park seem to have hedges and some trees, but few if any of these survived to the 1970s. Thirdly, from the evidence of the aerial photographs and observations on the ground, most of the 150 hardwood stumps observed and ring counted in 1972 and mapped in 1977 (Figure 3.4.6),[13] were from trees felled after 1946, although a few, very decayed stumps, may have dated from earlier. Decay meant that it was impossible to calculate accurate ages at felling but estimates fell within the range 104 and 149 years with most less than 120 years. They seem therefore to have dated from late in the period of Webster's planting régime.

A few local people still recall something of these fellings which included "a lovely lot of sycamore" mainly on the west side of the Park, including 40 which went "at one bunch".

Figure 3.4.6

Tree stumps, 1977.
The distribution of the cut stumps of deciduous trees in the Lower Park, adapted from Harding (1977).

3
—
4

N

This may also have been the time when two or three 'bannut' (walnut) trees were lost from the south eastern sector of the Lower Park.[14] And it was in the early 1950s that some 42 ha at the top of the Park were fenced out, felled and planted with conifers. The main casualties here were "lots of great big lovely beech" as well as a few oaks.

1960s-1980s

Further fellings came in the 1960s, 1970s and 1980s. Chief amongst the casualties in the 1960s were "lots" of hawthorn bushes, "old as the hills" and many of them prostrate.[15] The late 1970s saw the disappearance from the Lower Park of seven more hawthorns and two elder,[16] and in 1987, under licence, the Moccas Estate felled 59 oaks, most of which were about 150 years old,[17] in the Upper Park.

'Natural' death and damage

Few trees in managed landscapes die naturally of old age; most succumb as a result of events such as gales or droughts, or are felled. Some notable trees have been lost from the Park since the 1870s, but we have little knowledge as to what happened to them. It was not until the survey of 1976/77 that a baseline was established and changes could be recorded. Even with this baseline, much of the information about losses due to natural factors is anecdotal or, at best, has been collected sporadically.

Hot dry summers of 1975 and 1976

The presumed effect on beech and ash of the hot, dry summers of 1975 and 1976 was noticed in the 1976/77 tree survey.[18] The drought seemed to have had a significant effect on some of the beech in the Lower Park, but markedly less effect in the Upper Park. From the total of 49 beech in the Lower Park, five were classified as dead or dying. An additional eight were classified as bole only, having lost all or almost all major limbs; most of the losses were recent. Ash also apparently suffered from the drought; from the total of 11 in the Lower Park, three were classified as dying or dead and one as bole only. Most of the surviving trees were near the stream in the south eastern part of the Park.

Droughts and gales of 1989 and 1990

Moccas Park was not affected by the notorious 1987 'hurricane' that devastated woodlands and parks in south eastern England, but other unusual weather events have had an impact on the Park in the last decade. Surveys were made at Moccas Park and two other sites as part of a rapid assessment of apparent damage to important parks during the drought summers of 1989 and 1990, and the high winds of January and February 1990.[19] The numbers of dead or wind-thrown trees recorded in Moccas Park are shown in Table 3.4.1.[20] Damage to a further 28 trees was recorded, but only one, a beech which had lost 15% of its crown following the 1990 gales, has died subsequently.

Table 3.4.1 Trees recorded as dead or wind-thrown following droughts and gales in 1989 and 1990.

Year	Cause	Species	Age class and growth form	Lower Park	Upper Park
1989	Drought	Oak	Ancient pollard	1	
1990	Gale	Oak	Mature maiden	4	
1990	Gale	Beech	Mature maiden	1	
1990	Gale	Beech	Mature maiden		2
1990	Drought	Oak	Over-mature maiden		1
1990	Drought	Beech	Over-mature maiden		1
Totals				6	4

Dutch elm disease

Knowledge of the status of elm in the Park prior to the arrival, probably in the early 1970s, of Dutch elm disease, is poor. Elms are host to the lichen *Gyalecta ulmi*, but its distribution has been severely restricted by the effects of Dutch elm disease and today it finds refuge at only two sites in England, both of them rock outcrops, one of which is at Moccas Park (see Chapter 4.1). One cannot infer from this however that elm was once common in the Park, and the Woolhope Club account of 1870 provides no clarification of its status. It mentions the presence of only two wych elms, one of them in the Lower Park, the other probably on the edge of the Upper Park, but it is not a systematic account and was largely concerned with large trees occurring in the Lower Park (both of these elms were of a good size).[21] By the time of the survey of 1976/77 only one (dead) elm remained in the Lower Park and the five trees noted in the Upper Park at that time were all dead.[22] Today a few small trees, probably half a dozen at most, might be found by diligent searching of the Upper Park, but none in the Lower Park.

Squirrel damage

The survey of 1976/77 established a baseline against which to record changes in the numbers of long-established trees. A similar baseline now exists for recently planted trees but no systematic monitoring has taken place. When it does, it is expected that it will show that in the Upper Park, but not the Lower Park, significant losses of oak and beech are occurring as a result of bark stripping by grey squirrels. The few self-seeded and planted field maple are suffering too, as are self-seeded willow species.

Recent rates of loss

The complete surveys of trees in the Lower Park in 1976/77 and 1997 have been compared directly to examine losses of established trees.[23] Each survey has also been compared with the map prepared for the Lower Park showing the location of each of the established trees after numbered tags had been attached to them; the precise date of this map is not known but it is understood to date from the early 1980s. Information from the 1990 survey of gale and drought damage and from the surveys in 1985/86 and 1993 also help to chart the steady loss of small numbers of older trees.[24] Trees that died or were wind-thrown between the 1976/77 and 1997 surveys are listed in Table 3.4.2. In this table these losses are shown in two time periods, from 1976/77 to the early 1980s, and from the early 1980s to 1997.

In 1976/77 there were 764 established trees and shrubs in the Lower Park, 38 of which were classified as dying or dead. By the time that the trees were numbered in the early 1980s, 36 trees had disappeared, but only 17 of these were considered to be viable when surveyed in 1976/77, the remainder being classified as dying, dead or reduced to a bole or stump. These losses do not include seven hawthorns and two elders that were recorded in 1976/77 but were probably removed in 1977 or 1978. Losses in the period from the early 1980s to 1997, were less significant. Losses over the last 20 years are documented in Table 3.4.2.

Evaluating recent losses

In terms of live trees there has been a loss of about 5% of the tree stock from the Lower Park over the last 20 years. This is regrettable but not alarming. The picture in the Upper Park is less clear, but rates of loss are higher. As in the Lower Park, there have been deaths and wind-throw, but additionally, 59 oaks, the majority of which were approximately 150 years old,[27] were felled under licence in 1987. If fellings on this scale were to continue to add to the small, but steady, uncontrollable and unpredictable loss of living trees from causes such as wind-throw and drought, there would be a danger of significantly weakening the long-term viability of the Park for nature conservation. The cohort of trees that was represented in this felling will, over the period of the next century or two, provide the habitat for saproxylic insects, epiphytes, fungi and other wildlife for which the Park is justly famous. Significant representation from this cohort is vital for the future. It is also vital that grey squirrel damage is not allowed to compromise the establishment of a new cohort of trees in the Upper Park and, currently at least, control measures appear to be a more pressing need here than in the Lower Park.

Evaluating the changes of the last two centuries

For at least 200 years the numbers of trees have fluctuated, and the species composition has to some extent varied, with successive phases of felling and planting. These phases have been determined by changes in fashion and by commercial considerations. Figure 3.4.7 seeks to

Table 3.4.2 Lower Park: apparent tree losses 1976/77 to 1997.

Species	Nos	Age class, growth form and condition in 1976/77	Period and nature of loss	
			1977 to early 1980s[25]	*Early 1980s to 1997*[26]
Oak	1	Recently felled	Unknown	
	1	Bole	Unknown	
	5	Dying/dead mature maidens	Unknown	
	10	Mature/over-mature maidens	Unknown	
	1	Ancient pollard	Unknown	
	1	Over-mature maiden		Wind-thrown
	3	Mature/over-mature maidens		Died
Turkey oak	1	Live bole		Removed
Beech	5	Stumps	Unknown	
	2	Dead/dying mature/over-mature maidens	Unknown	
	1	Over-mature pollard	Unknown	
	3	Live boles		Died
	1	Mature maiden		Died
	1	Mature maiden		Wind-snapped
Sweet chestnut	1	Dying over-mature maiden	Unknown	
	3	Mature/over-mature maidens	Unknown	
	2	Mature/over-mature maidens		Died
Horse chestnut	1	Dying mature maiden	Unknown	
	1	Mature maiden	Unknown	
	1	Mature maiden		Wind-thrown
Ash	1	Dead	Unknown	
	1	Bole	Unknown	
Elm	1	Dead ancient pollard	Unknown	
Sycamore	1	Over-mature pollard	Unknown	
Totals	49		36	13

convey a visual impression of the tree stock of the Park and how it appears to have changed with phases of planting and felling since the 1780s. The information available is insufficiently precise however for us to be able to offer more than this impression and the following equally tentative commentary which attempts to provide snap-shots of the Park at moments of change or when the record is good. The current situation is developed more fully in the next chapter.

The position in the 1770s and 1780s

John Lambe Davis's estate maps of 1772 (Figure 2.3.3) give an indication of relative densities of tree cover in the Park at that time. Light across The Lawn, denser throughout the remainder of the area forming today the balance of the Park, but treeless across the south

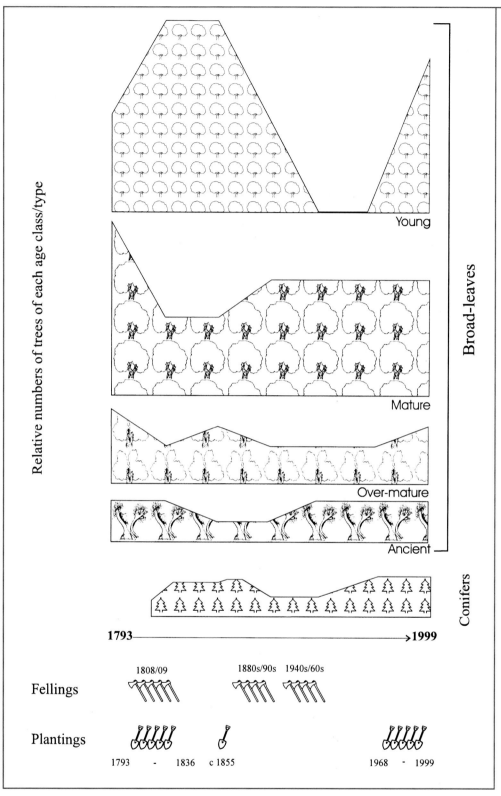

Figure 3.4.7

The number of trees in the Lower Park, 1793-1999. A pictorial representation of the relative numbers of trees by type and age class in relation to tree growth, fellings and plantings. The vertical scale shows relative rather than actual numbers.

western portion encompassing the ground lost to the Park in the 1950s and the area of Lodge Grounds excluded from the Park in the late eighteenth century.

It would be wrong to seek to deduce a great deal from Thomas Hearne's watercolours of the 1780s; they only show a limited area of the Park and are works of art not literal representations. Taken at face value they suggest however that the tree stock was then strong in terms of the younger generations, but perhaps less so in respect of large mature trees.

At this time, in the Upper Park at least, there may still have been a worthwhile representation of trees derived from the natural tree cover of the area. They would probably have included large-leaved lime and yew (both of which still survive in small numbers) oak, ash and wych elm.

The impact of the Cornewall and Webster years

Whatever the picture in the 1780s, the next 60 or so years brought marked changes - major fellings and very major plantings brought about by the financial situation and business perspective of Sir George Cornewall, and realized through the work of his forester, Mr J. Webster. As explained in Chapter 2.3, the failure of Cornewall's mercantile and colonial investments forced him to realise some of his timber assets. He believed strongly however in improvement and was also alive to the 'Picturesque' appeal of his Park so he invested considerable resources in re-planting whilst also, it seems, treasuring the Park's veteran trees.

The consequence of this period of intense activity seems likely to have been a Park richly endowed with young trees (including, perhaps for the first time, significant numbers of horse chestnut and some European larch) but with a relatively weak representation of mature ones. It seems likely too that the trees were spread relatively evenly and densely over much of the Lower Park as well as the north facing slope of the Upper Park, indeed it may well have been only the plateau area at the top of the slope (now excluded from the Park) which had really significant areas of open ground.

The position in the 1870s and 1880s

By 1870 Webster's plantings had given the Park a wooded appearance:

> "Every one of the grand old oaks is surrounded by a grove of smaller ones, until the Park itself is like a wood, and squirrels may skip from end to end without the need of touching the ground."[28]

This judgement is supported by the Ordnance Survey 6 inch to 1 mile map of 1886 (Figure 3.3.1), at least in respect of what is today the Upper Park and the south eastern area of the Lower Park. Tree symbols in this sector are fairly regularly and closely spaced. They are less so in the north eastern quarter of the Park, encompassing The Lawn. Nevertheless, in this north eastern quarter, the density of established trees appears, in 1886, to have been twice what it is today. Seemingly accurately mapped symbols for 558 trees are shown in an area which by the 1980s only supported 281 trees.

Some 42 ha at the top of the Park were fenced out, felled and planted with conifers in the 1950s. The 1886 Ordnance Survey map shows only some 25 tree symbols throughout the eastern two thirds of this area, along with a scatter of bushes, presumably like the "scrubby hawthorns" remembered locally as being present in the 1940s.[29] By contrast, tree symbols are dense in the western third where there was a stand of fine beeches.[30]

But it is the "grand old oaks" of the Lower Park which were the main theme of the descriptions written by the Woolhope Club's anonymous 'commissioner' in 1870 and Francis Kilvert in 1876.[31] The impression readily gained from Kilvert's highly evocative word picture is that the Lower Park, at least, boasted large numbers of big old oaks, and an assumption may be made that there are fewer large trees present today. The 'commissioner's' description, including as it does the girths of 70 oaks growing in the Lower Park, provides a point of comparison with the present-day situation, and enables us to explore the validity of any assumptions as to the loss of old trees over the last hundred and thirty years.

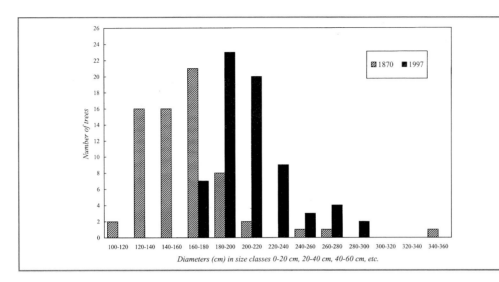

Figure 3.4.8

Diameters of large oak trees in the Lower Park. A comparison of the diameters of two different, but overlapping, samples of large oak trees in the Lower Park measured in 1870 and 1997.

The 'commissioner' makes clear by his prefatory statement, that size was his principal criterion when deciding which trees to measure: "Once in the Park .... he who would note the size of remarkable trees must set to work in earnest". His girthings are shown, converted to diameter size classes, in Figure 3.4.8; the figure uses only 68 of his girths, girths of a split tree and a double-trunked tree have been omitted. A reading of the 'commissioner's' account shows however that his selection was not systematic and consequently we cannot assume that he girthed all of the largest oaks, but it was trees remarkable by their size that interested him, and his sample is large enough for us to offer some tentative conclusions about the size and frequency of large oak trees in the Park in 1870.

Many of the oaks measured by the 'commissioner' may survive today, but he did not describe most of them in adequate detail for subsequent recognition to be possible, and only seven can be relocated today.[32] Comparison of the 'commissioner's' sample of 68 with the 68 largest oak trees growing in the Lower Park today (also shown in Figure 3.4.8), suggests however that the overall resource of oaks with large girths has probably increased over the last 130 years, not, as one might have suspected from reading Kilvert's account, decreased. There have of course been losses, notably that of 'The Moccas Oak', the largest of the trees girthed by the 'commissioner', but a substantial proportion of the trees already regarded as large in 1870 have probably survived and moved into higher diameter classes. It can be said with some confidence that there are more really big oak trees growing in the Lower Park today than in 1870.

The consequences of the fellings of the 1880s, 1890s and 1950s

Cornwall and Webster provided opportunities for subsequent harvests of timber, but their successors were not so diligent in investing for the future. Very significant quantities of timber were extracted, largely it seems from the Lower Park, in the 1880s, 1890s and 1950s. Webster's plantings had been sufficiently prolific to permit this level of fellings, but neglect of planting between the 1830s and the 1960s left a 130 year gap in the age structure which the major planting effort of recent decades cannot now bridge.

The fellings and natural losses over this period seem to have led to a general impoverishment in the range of species represented in the mature and over-mature generations. It seems that sycamore was well represented at one time and there were small numbers, at least, of wych elm and birch. Neither wych elm nor sycamore is represented in these generations today, there is only one birch and the representation of these generations in some other species has been markedly weakened too. This is particularly true of ash and hawthorn, but to some extent too of beech and, amongst minority species, of walnut and, inappropriate though the species may be, European larch too. By contrast, exotic species have gained a foothold. There are now two mature Wellingtonias, an evergreen oak and a deodar, whilst a mixed assortment, both coniferous and deciduous, was planted in the 1960s. The species and age structure of trees growing in the Park today are described in more detail in the next chapter and a full species list can be found in Appendix 4.

The situation today

Despite these reservations, our assessment is that today, in terms of balance in the age structure, whilst the overall situation is far from ideal, it may well be as favourable as at any time since the fellings of 1808/9. The stock of really large ancient trees appears to be greater than when the 'commissioner' and Kilvert described the Park in the 1870s (and quite possibly greater than for many years prior to that), Webster's plantings of 1793-1836 have now resulted in a substantial generation of mature trees, and a significant new phase of planting (albeit the first for 130 years) has been undertaken.

Notes

1 Loudon (1836).
2 Anon (1870).
3 Eric Pithers pers. comm.
4 Anon (1870).
5 Len and Shirley Slaney (pers. comm.) remember two old men working in the Park cleaving palings; they kept their technique a secret by ceasing work when anyone approached.
6 Loudon (1836).
7 Comparison of the average value per tree from these sales (1883 = £11.25/tree, 1884 = £8.04/tree, 1897 = £3.13/tree) suggests either a catastrophic (360%) decline in the price of timber in the space of 14 years or, more probably, because of the quantity (415) of trees felled in 1897, that this third felling was of thinnings from Mr Webster's plantings in the Park.
8 Anon (1870).
9 James (1931). The 'Tall Oak' had fallen by 1891 (Anon 1891) it is not known where it stood but it appears to have been somewhere in the Lower Park.
10 The girths recorded (the largest being 5.3 m) do not however appear outstanding by current standards.
11 In 1870, one of the birches had a girth of 3.075 m, only 23 cm less than the modern 'champion tree' in the British Isles (see Mitchell et al 1994).
12 I.R.P. (1975).
13 Peterken (1972), Harding (1977).
14 Tom Bowen, Sam Davies and Les Whittal (pers. comms); the walnut trees may have died rather than been felled.
15 Tom Bowen (pers. comm.).
16 These were all recorded in 1976/77 but had gone by 1997; it is thought probable that they were removed in 1977 or 1978, ie following the survey but prior to any formal agreement for the management of the Park.
17 Harding (1990).
18 At Lyonshall (SO339576 & 335558), the nearest meteorological station to Moccas Park for which 30 year records are available, the summer months (May to September) were noticeably drier than average in both years: 1975 64% of average, 1976 79% of average. Mean daily temperatures in these months were above the 30 year average: 1975 +0.6°C, 1976 +1.4°C.
19 The surveys were summarised in a report (Harding 1990). Meteorological data from Lyonshall (see Chapter 1.2) show that the summer months (May to September) were noticeably dryer than average in both years: 1989 64% of average, 1990 55% of average. Mean daily temperatures in these months were above the 30 year average: 1989 +1.3°C, 1990 +0.9°C. The summers of 1989 and 1990 were drier and hotter, compared to the 30 year averages, than the 1975 and 1976 'drought' years.
20 Much of the fallen timber resulting from storm damage in January and February 1990 (except some 'lop and top') was retained within the Park. A note for the file by John Bacon of NCC (16 March 1990) recorded that the trunks of two wind-thrown oaks (Nos 427 and 566) were to be removed by the Estate as they were of veneer quality.
21 Girths at 5 feet were given as 12 feet 6 inches and 15 feet 4 inches, corresponding to diameters of 121 and 149 cm.
22 Harding (1977).
23 Harding (1977, 1998), Harding & Wall (1997). The 1997 survey also identified individual trees that had lost branches or had otherwise suffered damage, trees which looked stressed (e.g. thin canopy foliage) and many horse chestnuts that had a 'scorched' appearance.
24 Harding (1990), Percy (1986), Wall (1993).
25 The trees were recorded in 1976/77, but are presumed not to have been present by the early 1980s because they were not tagged, numbered or mapped, and were absent in 1997.
26 These are trees which were present in the early 1980s when the trees were tagged and mapped, but which had died, been removed or had been wind-thrown/wind-snapped by 1997.
27 Harding (1990).
28 Anon (1870).
29 Sam Davies (pers. comm.).
30 Tom Bowen, Sam Davies and Les Whittal (pers. comms).
31 Plomer (1940).

32 There are three trees for which direct comparison of diameters, measured at 5 feet (1.5 m), in 1870 and 1998 is possible:'The Club Oak'(tree number 259; which increased in diameter from 188 to 239 cm), 'The Knoll Oak'(267; 142 to 202 cm) and 'The Bredwardine Lodge Oak'(187; 202 to 269 cm). Four other trees girthed in 1870 can be individually identified today, these are 'The *Hypebaeus* Tree'(151), 'The Riven Oak'(22),'The Promontory Oak'(62) and its near neighbour (61; which carries no name). However, in all cases, accurate girth comparisons are impossible: only half of 'The Riven Oak' survives and the other trees have growth forms which make measurement at the standard height impossible and there is no knowledge of the height at which these trees were measured in 1870.

References relating to Moccas Park

ANON. 1870. Incidental notes of remarkable trees in Herefordshire. *Transactions of the Woolhope Naturalists' Field Club*, 288-321.

ANON. 1891. Field meeting report. *Transactions of the Woolhope Naturalists' Field Club*, 221- 223.

HARDING, P.T. 1977. *Moccas Deer Park, Hereford and Worcester: a report on the history, structure and natural history.* Unpublished report to the Nature Conservancy Council by the Institute of Terrestrial Ecology, Huntingdon.

HARDING, P.T. 1990. *Damage to ecologically important trees in selected pasture-woodlands resulting from winter storms and summer drought in 1990.* Unpublished report to the Nature Conservancy Council by the Institute of Terrestrial Ecology, Huntingdon.

HARDING, P.T. 1998. *Moccas Deer Park Herefordshire, survey of individual trees in the Lower Park by Paul Harding, September 1976.* Unpublished, annotated data sheets donated to English Nature.

HARDING, P.T. & WALL, T. 1997. Moccas Park NNR tree survey 19-20 August 1997. English Nature, unpublished data sheets.

I.R.P. 1975. Moccas Estate. *Quarterly Journal of Forestry*, 69, 113-115.

JAMES, F.R. 1931. Wellingtonia trees in Herefordshire. *Transactions of the Woolhope Naturalists' Field Club*, 108-109.

JAMES, F.R. 1932. Trees in Moccas Park and elsewhere. *Transactions of the Woolhope Naturalists' Field Club*, 182-183.

LOUDON, J.C. 1836. *The gardener's magazine*, 12, 368-369.

PERCY, H. 1986. *Moccas Park National Nature Reserve - Tree inventory.* Unpublished report to the Nature Conservancy Council.

PETERKEN, G.F. 1972. Moccas Park (GFP/Sites/31). Nature Conservancy, internal report.

PLOMER, W. 1940. Kilvert's diary. Volume three. London: Jonathan Cape.

STRUTT, J.G. 1822. *Sylva Britannica; or portraits of forest trees, distinguished for their antiquity, magnitude or beauty. Drawn from nature and etched by Jacob George Strutt.* London: Colnaghi & Co.

WALL, T. 1993. *Inventory of established trees, Lower Park 1985/86 and 1993.* English Nature, internal report.

Other references

DAWKINS, H.C. 1971. Techniques for long-term diagnosis and prediction of forest communities. In: E. DUFFEY & A.S. WATT, eds. The scientific management of animal and plant communities for conservation. Oxford: Blackwell Scientific Publications.

MITCHELL, A.F., SCHILLING, V.E. & WHITE, J.E.J. 1994. *Champion trees in the British Isles.* Technical paper 7. Edinburgh: Forestry Commission.

3 / 4

The trees:
species, numbers, growth forms, ages and dead wood

Tom Wall and
Paul T. Harding

Lack of younger generations of trees is producing a skewed age structure, leading to breaks in continuity .... of habitat ....

UK Biodiversity Group (1998). *Lowland wood-pasture and parkland: a Habitat Action Plan.*

In this chapter we examine the overall resource of trees and dead wood at Moccas Park today. The present-day resource of trees encompasses those derived from past planting schemes and those spared during phases of tree felling (see Chapter 3.4) and it includes the particularly notable trees that have captured the imagination of visitors to the Park during the last 200 years (see Chapter 3.2). Studies of tree ages and volumes of dead wood have only recently been initiated and the first results are presented here. This chapter discusses in particular the long-established trees, further information concerning recent plantings can be found in Chapter 6.5.

Tree and shrub species

Lower Park

The present-day species composition of long established trees in the Lower Park is shown in Figure 3.5.1. Oak and, to a lesser extent, sweet chestnut, horse chestnut and beech, are the most plentiful trees; very small percentages of other species are present in the Lower Park, with only hawthorn reaching 2% of the total. Oak is dominant virtually throughout; all the other principal species are most abundant in the south eastern part of the Lower Park as shown in Figure 3.5.2. The dominance of oak has been reflected in recent plantings, begun by the Moccas Estate in 1968, and continued by the Nature Conservancy Council and English Nature since 1979 (see Chapter 6.5). The carr woodland in the Lawn Pool has never been surveyed; it includes dense stands of alders and willows. Moccas Park has fewer species in relation to its size than all but one of six ecologically (and historically) important parks surveyed by Harding in the 1970s and 1980s.[1]

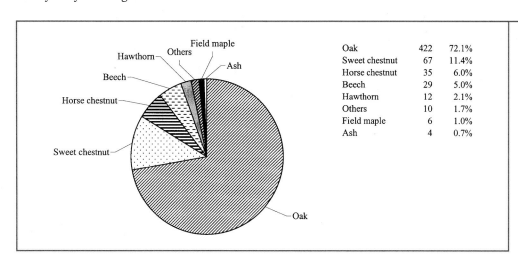

Oak	422	72.1%
Sweet chestnut	67	11.4%
Horse chestnut	35	6.0%
Beech	29	5.0%
Hawthorn	12	2.1%
Others	10	1.7%
Field maple	6	1.0%
Ash	4	0.7%

Figure 3.5.1

Tree species in the Lower Park, 1997. The numbers and percentages of tree species in the Lower Park, excluding trees planted in the period 1968-1997.

Figure 3.5.2

The distribution of beech, sweet chestnut and horse chestnut trees in the Lower Park, 1977.
The distribution of established trees of these species, adapted from Harding (1977).

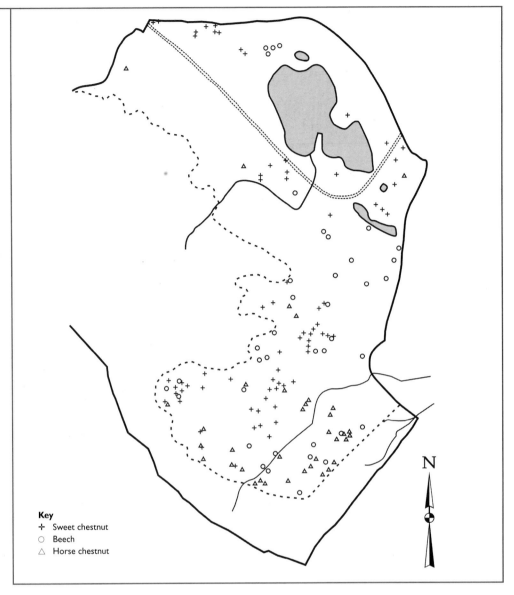

Key
+ Sweet chestnut
○ Beech
△ Horse chestnut

N

Upper Park

Much of the Upper Park is closed-canopy woodland, although there are extensive glades dominated by bracken and some areas of light tree cover. The woodland is not homogeneous; there are some pure stands of beech on the western side and, in other places, pure stands of oak. Sweet and horse chestnuts are scattered widely on the lower slopes. There are more than 60 hawthorns and also small numbers of limes,[2] ash, yew, holly, elder, field maple and birch. Figure 3.5.3 illustrates the proportions of the principal long-established species in the Upper Park in 1977; it has not been surveyed in detail since then. The species representation here is broadly similar to that in the Lower Park, but oak is not so dominant as in the Lower Park due largely to the greater numbers of beech. The dominance of oak has again been reflected in recent plantings; these are discussed in detail in Chapter 6.5.

Growth forms

In his 1976/77 survey, Harding distinguished between maiden and pollard trees.[3] He recognised however that the distinction is frequently not clear, especially with trees that have developed in open conditions. Furthermore, a tree may lose its leader and grow to appear like

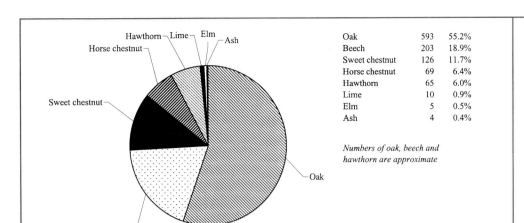

Oak	593	55.2%
Beech	203	18.9%
Sweet chestnut	126	11.7%
Horse chestnut	69	6.4%
Hawthorn	65	6.0%
Lime	10	0.9%
Elm	5	0.5%
Ash	4	0.4%

Numbers of oak, beech and hawthorn are approximate

Figure 3.5.3

Tree species in the Upper Park, 1977. The numbers and percentages of the principal tree species, excluding trees planted in the 1960s and 1970s.

a pollard through causes other than pollarding. However, it became clear from this survey that it is a very long time since pollarding was a significant activity in the Park; perhaps as much as 200 years. Latterly, where trees have been planted they have been grown on as maidens.

Harding found 90 trees that looked like pollards in the Lower Park, representing 12% of all the trees in this part of the Park. In the Upper Park he found 184 trees that looked like pollards, representing 18% of all the trees growing there. Taking the mature trees, the dominant age class, he judged that only 5% of this age class in the Park as a whole, were pollards. Table 3.5.1 summarises the proportions of maiden and pollard trees in the mature and older age classes in 1976/77. Table 3.5.2 provides a breakdown of the distribution of the apparent pollards as between the principal species in the Lower and Upper Parks. The main feature of note here is the high number of pollard beech in the Upper Park, representing in excess of 40% of pollarded trees of all species in the entire Park.

Table 3.5.1 Numbers of living maiden and pollard trees (all species) in the mature, over-mature and ancient age classes in the Park as a whole in 1976/77, expressed also as a percentage of the overall total of trees present.

	Maiden		Pollard		Totals
	No.	**%**	**No.**	**%**	
Mature	934	58	48	3	982
Over-mature	388	24	165	10	553
Ancient	7	<1	61	4	68
Totals	1329	83	274	17	1603

Table 3.5.2 Numbers of living pollards of the principal species in the Lower and Upper Parks in 1976/77, expressed also as a percentage for the Lower and Upper Parks and for the Park as a whole.

	Oak		Beech		Sweet chestnut		Horse chestnut		Total
	No.	**%**	**No.**	**%**	**No.**	**%**	**No.**	**%**	
Lower Park	77	90	4	5	5	6	0	0	86
Upper Park	51	29	116	67	4	2	2	1	173
Totals	128	49	120	46	9	3	2	<1	259

Figure 3.5.4

Diameters of trees in the Lower Park, 1997. The distribution of all trees by diameter class in cm, measured at 1.5 m above ground level.

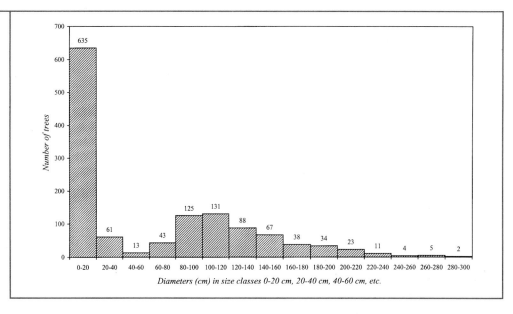

Ages and age structure

The girth of a tree has to increase each year that it lives, and unlike height and crown spread, girth is non-reversible, it therefore provides the best potential for measuring a tree's age.[4] The girths of all the trees in the Lower Park were measured in 1997, permitting the size/age distribution of all the tree species, plus hawthorns, growing in the Lower Park to be determined, as shown in Figure 3.5.4, where size is expressed as a series of diameters derived from the girth measurements.[5] Figures 3.5.5 to 3.5.11, show the size/age structure of each of the principal species of trees and hawthorn growing in the Lower Park.

The general picture which emerges is of a bimodal size/age distribution. All species except horse chestnut show high numbers of small/young trees, and all except hawthorn and ash show a subsidiary peak of medium-sized/middle-aged ones. There is in all cases a largely empty trough between these peaks, demonstrating a lengthy hiatus in recruitment, and there is also poor representation of trees in the larger size/age classes. These weaknesses in the size/age structure have significant implications for the future. Yet the generation structure of oak was rather better at Moccas Park, and that of beech was no worse than at three other ecologically (and historically) important parks surveyed by Harding in the 1970s, before tree planting programmes were completed.[6]

Figure 3.5.5

Diameters and ages of oak trees in the Lower Park, 1997. The distribution of all oak trees in the Lower Park by diameter class in cm, measured at 1.5 m above ground level, showing estimated planting/germination dates.

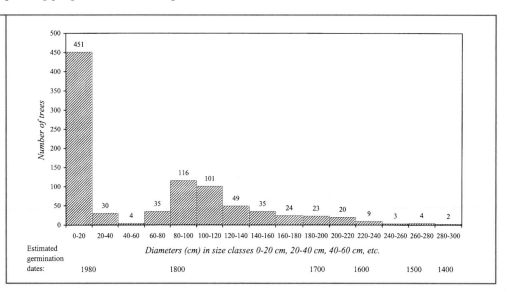

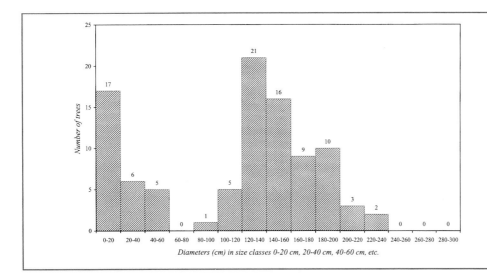

Figure 3.5.6

Diameters of sweet chestnut trees in the Lower Park, 1997. The distribution of all sweet chestnut trees in the Lower Park by diameter class in cm, measured at 1.5 m above ground level.

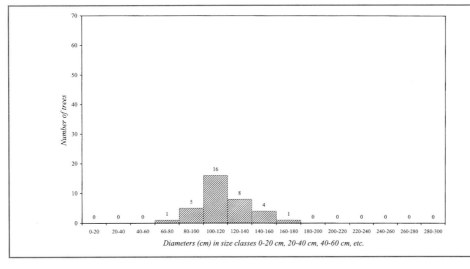

Figure 3.5.7

Diameters of beech trees in the Lower Park, 1997. The distribution of all beech trees in the Lower Park by diameter class in cm, measured at 1.5 m above ground level.

Figure 3.5.8

Diameters of horse chestnut trees in the Lower Park, 1997. The distribution of all horse chestnut trees in the Lower Park by diameter class in cm, measured at 1.5 m above ground level.

What information is there as to when the peaks were established and as to the age of individual trees? The first peak can be dated with confidence, being attributable to plantings since the late 1960s. But it is only in respect of oak that it is currently possible to date the subsidiary peak. Three trees felled or windblown in 1998 had a mean diameter at 1.5 m of 100 cm, which lies at the mid-point of the subsidiary peak of diameters, and they had a mean age (calculated by counting annual growth rings) of 176 years (ie dating from 1822).[7] This corresponds to the very extensive plantings of oak reported as having been carried out by Sir

George Cornewall's forester, Mr J. Webster, between about 1793 and 1836 (see Chapter 3.4). Whilst there are no similar data for other species, it seems likely that the comparable peaks noted for sweet chestnut, beech and horse chestnut relate to the same phase of planting.

No ring counts are available from which to age the larger trees of any species at Moccas Park, but John White has proposed a method of estimating the age of large trees in Britain from

Figure 3.5.9

Diameters of ash trees in the Lower Park, 1997. The distribution of all ash trees in the Lower Park by diameter class in cm, measured at 1.5 m above ground level.

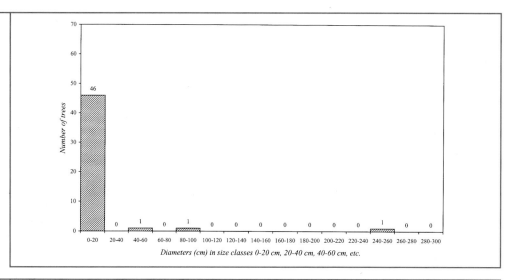

Figure 3.5.10

Diameters of field maple trees in the Lower Park, 1997. The distribution of all field maple trees in the Lower Park by diameter class in cm, measured at 1.5 m above ground level.

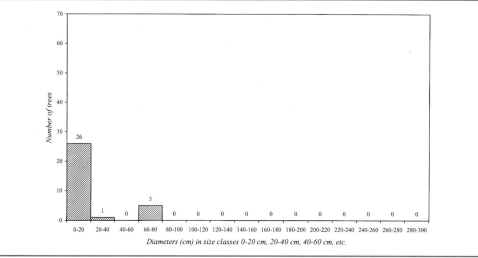

Figure 3.5.11

Diameters of hawthorn bushes in the Lower Park, 1997. The distribution of all hawthorns bushes in the Lower Park by diameter class in cm, measured at 1.5 m above ground level.

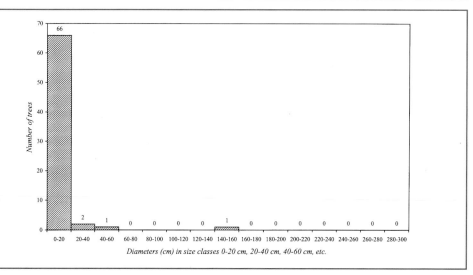

girth/diameter measurements.[8] The method is based on a wealth of recorded data and historical information held in the Forestry Commission's National Tree Register and elsewhere. It has been applied in respect of some oak trees from the Lower Park. The method depends on determining the probable rate of early growth in relation to local conditions and the duration of the development period of the tree up to optimum crown size. This allows the 'core development' of an individual tree to be defined by estimates of the likely age when it reached a mature state and the width of its first annual growth ring once it had reached maturity. These estimates are then used, along with stem diameter in order to calculate a tree's age.

Successive measurements of two trees at Moccas Park, 'The Woolhope Club Oak' and 'The Knoll Oak' (see Chapter 3.2), over the years 1870 to 1998, have assisted White in determining their likely 'core development'.[9] 'The Knoll Oak' is shown in Figures 3.5.12 and 3.5.13 and 'The Club Oak' in Figures 3.4.2, 3.4.3 and 3.4.4. Both trees have grown well, but the trunk of 'The Club Oak' is difficult to girth consistently due to a boss at the girthing height, and it is the 'core development' assessment for 'The Knoll Oak' which appears most reliable and most likely to be applicable to other open-grown mature, over-mature and ancient oaks in the Park.[10] It has been used to provide indications of the likely age of the larger diameter classes of oaks in the Lower Park (those with diameters of 200 cm or more); these indications are shown on Figure 3.5.5. The same assessment has also been used in making all the age estimates for selected individual trees shown in Table 3.5.3 which includes 'The *Hypebaeus* Tree', the largest diameter tree in the Park.

Figure 3.5.12

'The Knoll Oak', April 1932. A photograph, probably by Walter Pritchard, from *Transactions of the Woolhope Naturalists' Field Club* (James 1932).

Figure 3.5.13

'The Knoll Oak', January 1998. A photograph by Éilis Kirby; the tree is numbered 267.

White provides a series of core development categories applicable to a wide range of species growing in a variety of conditions but these have not to date been applied at Moccas Park. In a similar vein, Pigott proposes a formula for estimating the age of lime trees in parklands from their diameters, which he has developed from measurements of limes for which planting dates are known.[11] This formula has been applied to two limes growing in the Lower Park which have been identified from foliage samples as *Tilia x vulgaris* 'Pallida', a clone that was widely planted in the early eighteenth century.[12] The diameters of these two trees (144 and 147 cm) leave open the

Table 3.5.3. Diameters and age estimates in 1997 for selected oak trees in the Lower Park.

Tree name	Tree no.	Diameter in cm at 1.5 m	Estimated age at girthing	Estimated date of germination
The *Hypebaeus* Tree	151	296	590	1406
The Bredwardine Lodge Oak	187	269	495	1502
The Woolhope Club Oak	259	239	468	1598
The Knoll Oak	267	200	291	1706

Figure 3.5.14

A lime tree, 1932. A photograph taken in the Upper Park, probably by Walter Pritchard, from *Transactions of the Woolhope Naturalists' Field Club* (James 1932).

possibility that they were indeed planted at that time. However, these trees are small compared with some of the limes in the Upper Park, where diameters of a series of large-leaved limes reach as much as 247 cm, suggesting they could well be 400 or more years old.[13] A photograph of a lime taken in 1932 is reproduced as Figure 3.5.14.

Indications of maximum age are available for two conifer species on the basis of their dates of first introduction to this country. Despite their good size they prove to be relatively young compared with other species growing in the Park. Thus the single deodar, a species first introduced in 1831, must be less than 170 years old,[14] and the two Wellingtonias, first introduced to this country in 1853, and to Herefordshire in 1855, are no more than 145 years old, although comparison with trees at Holme Lacey Park, site of the original Herefordshire introduction, suggests that the larger of the two is probably not far short of this age.[15] Remarkably, it has grown so fast that there are now only two stouter trees in the Lower Park, both of them oaks and both perhaps four times its age. Photographs of this tree are reproduced as Figures 3.2.9 and 3.2.10.

Oliver Rackham has observed that "From Boulogne to Athens one rarely sees a tree more than 200 years old. England (and Greece) are the exceptions".[16] Even when age estimates are restricted just to oaks and the search area is confined to the Lower Park, a tally of in excess of 100 trees more than 200 years old is soon arrived at. Clearly Moccas Park makes a very worthwhile contribution to an internationally important resource.

Dead wood

It is dead wood, or "fallow wood" as it was called by Francis Kilvert,[17] whether as heart rot, or as attached or fallen branches, that is the prime resource for the invertebrate fauna for which Moccas Park is celebrated. Without live trees there can never be dead wood, so for the future well-being of the invertebrate fauna, the numbers, species, age structure and condition of the trees are critical, but in themselves they give only a very broad indication of the current dead wood resource.

In order to begin to establish baseline data on the dead wood resource, estimates of the quantity of fallen dead wood in excess of 5 cm in diameter have been made for three sample plots in the Lower Park.[18] Clearly, the higher the density of standing trees the greater the opportunities for fallen wood, and the three areas were selected as being representative of the range of densities of standing trees in the Lower Park. The values recorded are shown in Table 3.5.4.

We are unaware of comparable estimates of the volume of fallen dead wood made in other parklands.[19] Kirby *et al.* have, however, made preliminary estimates for British broadleaved woodlands,[20] on the basis of which they proposed provisional benchmarks as follows: low <20 cubic metres per hectare; medium, 20-40 cubic metres per hectare; high, >40 cubic metres per hectare. Whilst parkland and forest are two different habitats, it appears surprising that

Table 3.5.4. Estimates of the volume of fallen dead wood in excess of 5 cm in diameter, and counts of dead standing trees in three sample plots of the Lower Park in 1999.

The numbers of standing trees exclude those planted since 1968; the volume of fallen dead wood includes the above ground element of rooted stumps and the entire volume of up-rooted stumps.

Plot	Size (ha)	Numbers of live standing trees per ha	Volume (m³) of fallen dead wood per ha	Numbers of standing dead trees
1	3.69	5.96	5.86	1
2	1.33	11.28	3.00	1
3	3.14	20.38	14.92	1
Totals	8.16			3
Means		12.38	8.88	0.37 per ha

the highest volume of dead wood per hectare so far recorded for the classic parkland habitat at Moccas Park, one of the country's premier sites for dead wood invertebrates, would, on current information, be assessed as low for a forest site.[21] This issue requires further study. A larger area of the Lower Park should be surveyed and comparative measures gathered from other sites; estimates need to be made too of the volume of dead wood present in the Upper Park, which is in essence a woodland habitat. Volumes here are likely to be higher, but are unlikely now to attain those observed by Francis Kilvert in 1876: "We came tumbling and plunging down the steep hillside of Moccas Park, slipping, tearing and sliding through oak and birch and fallow wood of which there seemed to be underfoot an accumulation of several feet, the gathering ruin and decay probably of centuries".[22]

Kirby *et al.* also proposed benchmarks for the number of standing dead trees in British woodlands, as follows: low, 0-10 per ha (all below 10 cm diameter); medium, 11-50 per ha (of which some are more than 10 cm diameter); high, more than 50 per ha (of which some are

Figure 3.5.15

Standing and fallen dead wood. Dead and decaying timber from an oak tree in the Lower Park, May 1994, photograph by Peter Wakely.

more than 40 cm diameter). Each of the sample areas in the Lower Park held only one standing dead tree, although in each case it was 40 cm or more in diameter.

A study of the ancient oaks of Sherwood Forest provides another point of comparison.[23] Here Watkins and Lavers found that almost a third of all the ancient oaks were standing dead trees greater than one metre in height and that in Sherwood Country Park, the area of Sherwood Forest which has the largest number of ancient oaks, 55% of the trees were dead. In contrast, there are currently no standing dead ancient oaks in the Lower Park at Moccas; some may have been removed during the agricultural improvement of the Park that took place in the 1960s and one disappeared in the late '70s (Table 3.4.2).

Dead wood attached to the standing tree, particularly the decaying heartwood, is almost certainly of equal or greater importance for the specialist fauna than fallen timber. The Sherwood Forest study made estimates of the numbers of dead, but attached, limbs per tree and the proportion of trees with heart rot. No comparable figures are available for Moccas Park and it is an aspect which needs to be explored. Those who made the estimates at Sherwood highlight however "the difficulty of taking accurate measurements that can be compared over time and can be made consistently by different surveyors".[24]

Looking to the future: the need for continuity

Ancient trees are part of 'the genius' of Moccas Park and their continued presence is vital in respect both of landscape and nature conservation. To this end there are a series of management objectives, which are already in hand (see Chapter 6.5) and which need to be pursued assiduously, some over the very long term, and some indefinitely; they all relate to the need to maintain continuity in the stock of over-mature and ancient trees and their associated dead wood habitats, standing and fallen. They are as follows:

❖ Sustain the existing stock of ancient and over-mature trees long enough for 'the Webster generation' (the many survivors of the major cohort planted between about 1790 and 1840) to 'catch up' and achieve senility. Strategies to achieve this may include tree surgery, both to safeguard ancient and over-mature trees and to speed the creation of dead wood niches in younger trees.

❖ Sustain, in its turn, 'the Webster generation' long enough for the trees planted over the last 30 years to 'catch up' and 'bridge' the 130 year generation gap, that period between about 1840 and 1970 when there was virtually no planting or natural regeneration. This may in due course involve strategies similar to those mentioned above, but in the short term it should include the creation and management, from an early age, of new young pollards, so as to promote trees in which dead wood niches may develop in quantity and diversity at a younger age than might otherwise be the case.

❖ Maintain an ample and continuous supply of dead wood both in the trees and on the ground. This involves continuing arrangements for the safeguard of fallen dead wood through the Nature Reserve Agreement. It could also include deliberate injury, without severance, of healthy limbs.

❖ Maintain a continuous cycle of planting throughout the Park so that there are no more generation gaps in the future.

Continuity is the watchword. If we look again at Thomas Hearne's atmospheric paintings of the Park in the 1780s, we find many features that are familiar to us today, including old trees, and younger generations too, dead wood (standing and fallen), deer and bracken; there has been a significant element of continuity in the landscape over the last 200 years. It needs to be sustained and enhanced into the future.

Notes

1   Harding & Alexander(1993).

2   The lime trees of the Park are of interest. Those in the Upper Park include a group of large-leaved lime and one other in the extreme south east corner of the Park which is a hybrid and, judging by its location, probably a natural one. In the Lower Park there are two old, planted, hybrid limes by the 'Lawn Gate' and nearby a young small-leaved lime has sprouted from the roots of a mature tree which blew down in 1976. We are grateful to C.D.Pigott who made all the identifications of lime species from foliage and, in some cases, seed samples.

3   Harding (1977).

4   White (1994).

5   "Diameter is actually derived from the measurement of girth, as this is the single parameter which sums the infinite number of diameters in an irregular stem cross-section." (Mitchell, Schilling & White (1994))

6   Harding & Alexander (1993).

7   John White (pers. comm.).

8   White (1994,1998).

9   White (1998 and pers. comm.) attributes core development categories of 80/5 and 90/6 respectively to 'The Knoll Oak' and 'The Woolhope Club Oak' but he observes that because of possible discrepancies in measurements the latter may be less reliable than the former.

10 White (1998 and pers. comm.) has assigned it to a category of 80/5 indicating that it reached optimum crown size at 80 years and that its first annual growth ring after reaching maturity was 5 mm in width.

11 Pigott (1989).

12 Identification by C.D. Pigott.

13 Pigott (1989 and pers. comm.).

14 Mitchell (1978) gives 1831 as the year of first introduction.

15 The first recorded planting in Herefordshire was at Holme Lacey Park (Anon 1870). In 1931 the better of the two trees in Moccas Park was comparable in size to the largest trees at Holme Lacey (James 1931), suggesting that it may have been planted at about the same time as the original planting there.

16 Rackham (1989).

17 Plomer (1940).

18 Wall & Wall (1999).

19 Watkins & Lavers (1998) provide counts of fallen "limbs" per ancient oak in Sherwood Forest, but no indications of volume.

20 Kirby et al. (1998).

21 It should be noted however that in a number of cases fallen limbs from the Lower Park have been dragged into the bracken at the edge of the Upper Park, thus reducing the volume of dead wood present in the Lower Park but not in the Park as a whole.

22 Plomer (1940).

23 Watkins & Lavers (1998).

24 Watkins & Lavers (1998).

References relating to Moccas Park

ANON. 1870. Incidental notes of remarkable trees in Herefordshire. *Transactions of the Woolhope Naturalists' Field Club*, 288-321.

HARDING, P.T. 1977. *Moccas Deer Park, Hereford and Worcester: a report on the history, structure and natural history.* Unpublished report to the Nature Conservancy Council by the Institute of Terrestrial Ecology, Huntingdon.

HARDING, P.T. & ALEXANDER, K.N.A. 1993. The saproxylic invertebrates of historic parklands: progress and problems. *In*: K.J. KIRBY & C.M. DRAKE. eds. *Dead wood matters: the ecology and conservation of saproxylic invertebrates in Britain*, 58-73. (English Nature Science No.1) Peterborough: English Nature.

JAMES, F.R. 1931. Wellingtonia trees in Herefordshire. *Transactions of the Woolhope Naturalists' Field Club*, 108-109.

JAMES, F.R. 1932. Trees in Moccas Park and elsewhere. *Transactions of the Woolhope Naturalists' Field Club*, 182-183.

PLOMER, W. 1940. *Kilvert's diary*, volume 3. London: Jonathan Cape.

WALL, T. & WALL, G. 1999. *Estimates of the volume of fallen wood in three sample areas of the Lower Park at Moccas.* Unpublished report to English Nature.

WHITE, J. 1998. *Estimating the age of large and veteran trees in Britain.* Research Information Note 250. Edinburgh: Forestry Commission.

Other references

KIRBY, K.J., REID, C.M., THOMAS, R.C. & GOLDSMITH, F.B. 1998. Preliminary estimates of fallen dead wood and standing dead trees in managed and unmanaged forests in Britain. *Journal of Applied Ecology*, 35, 148-155.

MITCHELL, A.F. 1978. *A field guide to the trees of Britain and northern Europe.* Second edition. London: Collins.

MITCHELL, A.F., SCHILLING, V.E. & WHITE, J.E.J. 1994. *Champion trees in the British Isles.* Technical paper 7. Edinburgh: Forestry Commission

PIGOTT, C.D. 1989. Estimating the age of lime-trees (*Tilia* spp.) in parklands from stem diameter and ring counts. *Arboricultural Journal*, 13, 289-302.

RACKHAM, O. 1989. *The Last Forest. The Story of Hatfield Forest.* London: Dent.

UK BIODIVERSITY GROUP 1998. *Tranche 2 Action Plans - Volume II - terrestrial and freshwater habitats.* Peterborough: English Nature on behalf of the UK Biodiversity Group.

WHITE, J. 1994. *Estimating the age of large trees in Britain.* Research Information Note 250. Farnham: Forestry Authority.

WATKINS, C. & LAVERS, C. 1998. Losing one's head in Sherwood Forest: the dead wood resource of the ancient oaks. *In*: M.A. ATHERDEN & R.A. BUTLIN, eds. *Woodland in the landscape: past and future perspectives.* Leeds: Leeds University Press, 140-151.

Lichens, mosses and liverworts

Ray Woods

Most epiphytes, whether bryophytes or lichens, are very sensitive, often extremely so, to air pollution. Over wide areas of Britain there are now almost no epiphytic lichens or bryophytes of any interest left, and even outside these areas, many epiphytes in the (at present) only slightly polluted areas are confined to relic communities on older trees.

Francis Rose (1974). *The epiphytes of oak.*

LICHENS

Britain has many more veteran trees than central Europe, and parklands, such as that at Moccas, provide notable refuges for them.[1] These veteran trees provide many niches for epiphytic lichens (those growing on trees), such as sheltered crevices, and old, bark-free wood, which are not found on young or even silviculturally mature trees. These niches have been exploited by a great range of lichen species, many of which are now nationally rare.

Parks may also provide other useful substrates for lichens such as old walls or park pales; at Moccas Park rock outcrops provide a further habitat.

Lichen recording

Robert Paulson reported on lichens noted on the Hereford Foray of the British Mycological Society of 1926.[2] Moccas Park was one of the sites visited and 37 species, most of them common, were noted from trees, rocks and the park pale. The Society revisited the site in 1951 when a brief list was produced of 18 common and widespread taxa.[3] But it was not until the 1960s that lichenologists such as Francis Rose, Peter James and Brian Coppins began to produce comprehensive lists from ancient parklands such as Moccas and to recognise just how important they are for lichens.   In April 1968 Rose and Coppins undertook the first modern lichen survey of Moccas Park.[4] Working through the Lower Park only, they noted 96 species of epiphytes, a total at that time exceeded in England only by Eridge and Ashburnham Parks in Sussex. A further visit in 1981 brought the total to 112 species of epiphytes,[5] but by that time it had become clear from more widespread survey, that Moccas Park was considerably less important in relation to other parklands, than had at first been thought.

All the epiphytic species recorded in 1968 and 1981, together with those recorded since, are listed in Appendix 1, as are lichen species recorded in other habitats. Amongst species found

Figure 4.1.1

Diploicia canescens.
A lichen of nutrient-enriched tree trunks. From a drawing by James Sowerby in *English Botany* (1790-1814) by J. E. Smith and J. Sowerby.

by Rose and Coppins, those associated mostly with old parklands included *Arthonia vinosa*, *Enterographa crassa*, *Lecanactis premnea*, *Peltigera horizontalis*, *Pyrenula chlorospila* and *Thelopsis rubella*. When Rose returned to the park in 1986, the last three species, amongst others, could not be re-found (possibly due to the loss in the intervening years of elm trees through Dutch elm disease), but a further four epiphytic taxa of more widespread distribution, were located.[6]

Surveys by Mike Gosling and Ken Sandell in 1988, 1993 and 1994 added more epiphytic taxa to provide a total of 121 species[7] (the reasons why this list is not longer are discussed later in this chapter). Additionally, Gosling reported on a survey of the two most potentially lichen-rich forms of park boundary - the stone walls and park pale; he also surveyed rock outcrops.[8]

Lichens on trees: the epiphytes

James, Hawksworth & Rose provide summary descriptions of the major types of lichen-dominated vegetation in Britain.[9] Whilst no detailed phytosociological survey of Moccas Park has been carried out, it is possible, using their descriptions, and information from the various surveys of the Park, to provide an indication of the likely range of the more notable associations present.

Dry bark crevices in veteran trees

Well-lit bark crevices, sheltered from direct rainfall by overhanging branches or on the east-facing sides of trunks, support the *Arthonietum impolitae* association. The greyish crusts of *Arthonia impolita*, *Schismatomma decolorans* and *Cliostomum griffithii* are its most frequent components. Other crevices support the *Calicietum hyperelli* association, many of its members having dark-coloured, stalked fruits, for example, *Calicium viride*, *C. salicinum*, *Chaenotheca brunneola* and *C. trichialis*. The very rare *Caloplaca lucifuga* may also form part of this association.

Sheltered bases of veteran trees

The *Lecanactidetum premneae* association favours the sheltered hollows at the base of the tree just above the root plate. The black, frequently green-tinged fruits of *Lecanactis premnea* often occurs with *Schismatomma decolorans* and rarely *Enterographa crassa* which may be its only associates. Higher up the trunk it tends to be replaced by the *Arthonietum impolitae* association.

Trunks of well-lit mature and veteran trees

The greatest diversity of lichens occurs on well-lit mature trunks of ash and oak. Whilst trunks on which *Pertusaria* species dominate might be referred to the *Pertusarietum amarae* association, a complete gradation is found through to the *Parmelietum revolutae* association. The more notable crustose species include *Pertusaria hemisphaerica*, *P. flavida*, *Rinodina roboris* and *Lecanora sublivescens*, whilst foliose lichens include a range of *Parmelia* species, such as *P. caperata* and *P. subrudecta*.

Fragments of the *Lobarion* association may be found. *Normandina pulchella* occurs on a few trees with the moss *Zygodon baumgartneri*. *Biatorina atropurpurea* may also be considered as part of this association. The best examples may have occurred on elm, a tree with a base-rich bark. *Peltigera horizontalis*, *Thelopsis rubella*, *Anisomeridium biforme* and *Gyalecta flotowii* were probably all confined to elm.

The *Physciopsidetum elaeinae* association occurs on a few of the more sheltered trees. This is a southern association, rare in Wales and infrequent in the West Midlands. *Physciopsis adglutinata*, *Physconia enteroxantha*, *P. grisea*, *P. perisidiosa*, *Physcia tribacia*, *Bacidia rubella*, *B. phacodes* and *Diploicia canescens* (Figure 4.1.1) all occur in this association. If nutrient levels rise, the last species, with *Buellia punctata* and algae, become ever more dominant to form the relatively species poor *Buellietum punctiformis* association.

Well-lit lignum

Hard, dry old wood, both on fallen trunks and standing in part-dead tree canopies is colonised by a few distinctive lichens. *Imshaugia aleurites* occurs with *Parmeliopsis ambigua*, *Trapeliopsis flexuosa*, *Cladonia* species and others to form a somewhat species-poor variant of the *Parmeliopsidetum ambiguae* association.

The willow carr

Grey willow and alder form a wet woodland on the island in the Lawn Pool. Their trunks support, in the main, the *Parmelietum revolutae* association with conspicuous foliose and fruticose lichens such as *Parmelia perlata*, *P. subrudecta*, *Ramalina farinacea*, *Usnea subfloridana* and *Evernia prunastri*. The *Lecanoretum subfuscae* association occurs on twigs, and is made up mostly of crustose species such as *Lecanora pulicaris* and *L. expallens*.

Epiphytic lichens: the regional context

The total of 121 lichen species found at Moccas Park can be compared with other notable epiphytic lichen sites in Wales and the Marches, for example Dynevor Deer Park, Carmarthenshire, 154 species; Gregynog Great Wood, Powys, 130; and in Herefordshire, Croft Castle, 202; Brampton Bryan Park, 177; Downton Gorge, 90.

The British Lichen Society has devised a system for evaluating the importance of epiphytic lichen sites in Britain.[10] Sites are placed within one of seven grades. Moccas Park, with its relatively short species list which does not include some of the rarer species, is considered by the British Lichen Society to be a Grade 4 epiphytic lichen site and only of regional importance. In comparison Croft Castle and Downton Gorge are also Grade 4, but Brampton Bryan Park, Dynevor Deer Park and Gregynog Great Wood are Grade 3 (nationally important but supplementary to other more important sites).

Rose has established a 'Revised index of ecological continuity' which is based on the occurrence of 30 indicator species of epiphytic lichen which are rarely found at sites of recent origin or at sites subject in the past to clear felling or other ecological discontinuity.[11] The number of these species recorded at a site determines the index score; the higher this score the greater the level of ecological continuity appears to have been. Moccas Park scores 35; in comparison the parks at Croft Castle and Brampton Bryan (both in north Herefordshire) score 50 and 65 respectively. If post 1982 records alone are considered, Moccas Park scores 25, a low score. Given the size of Moccas Park, and the number of ancient trees it holds, some explanation is required as to why it is not a better site for epiphytic lichens.

Epiphytic lichens and atmospheric pollution from industry and agriculture

Sulphur - an historical perspective

Until comparatively recently, large areas of industrialised Britain were so badly polluted by sulphur compounds that few lichens survived.[12] Moccas Park lay at the south western edge of the highly polluted Birmingham and West Midlands conurbation, and sulphur levels may have been high enough to kill the more sensitive species, such as the tree lungworts (*Lobaria* spp.), assuming they were present. In Herefordshire they have survived in two locations, the very sheltered gorge

of the River Teme at Downton Gorge National Nature Reserve and at Brampton Bryan Park Site of Special Scientific Interest on the extreme western edge of the county. Since the 1960s sulphur levels have fallen in those areas once most badly affected. Taller chimney stacks have now been built which emit the sulphur higher into the atmosphere where it is spread more thinly over a wider area. Lichen species have now been able to recolonise parts of the Black Country from where they have possibly been absent for over 100 years.

Acid rain

The tall chimneys ought to have brought benefits to Moccas Park. Unfortunately however, the sulphur compounds, now remaining longer in the air, turn mostly to droplets of sulphuric acid. These fine droplets can impact on trees or be deposited in mist or rain to acidify the bark. Old oak and ash trees naturally have a base-rich bark and in consequence many old parkland lichens, adapted to base-rich conditions, will not grow on highly acidified bark. The taller chimneys spread their acidic droplets widely and Moccas is well within the reach of plumes from chimneys in the Trent Valley to the north east and South Wales to the south west.

Nitrogen compounds

As levels of sulphur polluting compounds have declined in recent years, so levels of nitrogen compounds have gone up. Vehicle exhausts and agriculture are major contributors to this rise.[13] Whilst not being so directly toxic to lichens as some sulphur compounds, nitrogen compounds, particularly as the oxides, nitric acid and ammonia, can affect lichen growth and influence the species which can survive at a particular site.

The effects of agriculture

Modern agriculture uses copious quantities of fertilisers, has increased the numbers of livestock and cultivates large quantities of nitrogen-fixing clover plants. One of the consequences of these measures is increased releases of ammonia and other nitrogen compounds to the air. Moccas Park has not been immune to these effects and as a consequence there appears to have been a considerable impact on the lichen flora. Species of lichen which are more tolerant of high levels of nitrogen compounds, such as *Buellia punctata* and *Diploicia canescens,* are more frequent than might be expected and the growth of algae which is favoured by high nitrogen levels has been encouraged. On some tree trunks algae are overgrowing the lichens, and on some they are now dominant.

Since 1992, the Nature Reserve Agreement between English Nature and the Moccas Estate and its farm tenant has encompassed measures designed to reduce nitrogen inputs to the Park. In particular, fertilisers are no longer used and livestock levels have been reduced. To determine the effectiveness of these measures, 'permanent' lichen recording quadrats were established on 31 trees in the Lower Park in 1988.[14] The quadrats were resurveyed in 1992 and 1996.[15] Lichen cover expanded between 1988 and 1992 with a corresponding reduction in the area occupied by algae and bare bark, but in 1996 a considerable increase in algae was noted. The picture is confusing, but differences between observers may be a factor. In particular, the judgement as to whether, at a given intersection in the quadrat grid the bark is recorded as supporting lichen or alga, is not always straight forward.

It seems certain, however, that recovery is not going to be rapid and may require further changes in management, particularly since the background ammonia emission levels and dry deposited ammonia levels reported from this part of the West Midlands are some of the highest noted in Britain.[16] In addition to minimising or reducing sources of pollutants from within the Park, tree cover along the eastern boundary should be preserved and enhanced in order to shelter the remainder of the site and intercept pollutants from outside.

Other lichen habitats

All deer parks require a deer-proof boundary. Provided it stands long enough, it is likely, whatever the material used, to be colonised by bryophytes and lichens. Gosling reported on a survey at Moccas Park of the two most potentially lichen-rich forms of park boundary, stone walls and wooden paling; he also surveyed rock outcrops.[17]

The wall

At one time, as much as half of the boundary of the Park would have been walled, the balance being a fence of cleft hardwood pales. Today most of the boundary is a fence of stakes and wire netting but worthwhile lengths of stone wall survive along the western and south eastern boundaries. The western boundary wall supports the greater diversity of lichens, with 50 species recorded. This wall is built of thinly-bedded, doubtless locally sourced, sandstone and siltstone blocks which are, in part, naturally calcareous. Sections of the wall have been mortared using lime mortar, so providing an additional calcareous element. Three attractive and readily identifiable lichens are frequent. These are the crab's eye lichen *Ochrolechia parella* which has a white thallus and large, pinkish, muffin-like fruits with a thick margin; *Caloplaca flavescens* the thallus of which is minutely lobed and is a brilliant orange-yellow; and *Tephromela atra*, present in white colonies, bearing jet-black fruits.

Colonisation rates for most lichen species are not certainly known, but relatively newly rebuilt sections of wall stand out due to their paucity of lichen cover (Figure 4.1.2). The rock outcrops in the park are a potential nearby source of propagules and almost half of the lichen species recorded from these rocks (see below) also occur on the walls.[18] The sources of some of the rarer species found on the walls must lie further afield. *Arthonia arthonioides* is particularly noteworthy. It occurs on shaded stonework at the north end of the western wall. The nearest known colonies lie to the west in Pembrokeshire, to the south in Devon and to the northeast in the Pennines.[19]

Figure 4.1.2

The park wall. A stretch at the south east end of the Park, March 1998; the newly rebuilt section in the foreground is largely devoid of lichen cover. Photograph by Tom Wall.

Lecanora conferta, readily identified by the way its thallus turns instantly orange when a drop of bleach is applied, was until recently thought to be a very rare species. It is now known to occur frequently on the sheltered sandstone walls of old churches in lowland Britain but elsewhere it is still only rarely encountered. In mid Wales its only known sites on natural rock are on sheltered outcrops beside rivers. The colony on the Moccas Park wall is the first in the Welsh Marches to be found outside a churchyard.

The park pale

Natural, hard, bark-free lignum of considerable age is a habitat now largely confined to veteran trees in parkland settings. Yet, until recently, an alternative habitat was provided by such frequent features of the lowland agricultural landscape as the wooden weather-boards of barns, and fence posts and rails made from cleft hardwood. At Moccas Park cleft hardwood pales probably at one time made up the boundary of at least half of the Park; today it is only the roadside boundary along the north eastern edge of the Park which is fenced in this way (see Figure 5.6.2). The pales of such fences, if not treated with preservatives, can form an important substrate for lichens, and such is the case at Moccas Park. Softwood, generally treated with a copper arsenate or tanalising fluid is now the preferred timber for fencing. Although one notably robust species of lichen - *Bacidia chloroticula* - appears to favour this material, even to the extent of apparently growing better where it receives zinc salts leached from galvanised wire, it is very much in the minority of lichens. Most fail to colonise treated softwood for many years. Increasing scarcity has therefore made old, untreated hardwood a significant habitat.

Gosling found 29 species growing on the park pale.[20] Whilst the very pollution tolerant lichen *Lecanora conizaeoides* was frequent, he found a good range of other species. There were two notable species: *Imshaugia aleurites* a lichen which is characteristic of Scottish pine forests, but is of scattered occurrence in parks and ancient woodlands in England and Wales, and *Physconia perisidiosa*, largely eastern in distribution and rare in the Welsh Marches. It occurred on the pales closest to the farm, reflecting its preference for the higher nutrient status of that area, probably due to stock and vehicle movements spreading dust on the pale.

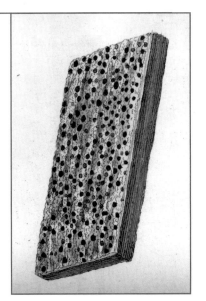

Figure 4.1.3

Cyphelium inquinans. A lichen first recorded in 1926 from the Park pale; it has a grey thallus and dark fruits. From a drawing by James Sowerby in *English Botany* (1790- 1814) by J. E. Smith and J. Sowerby.

It is interesting to compare Gosling's list of 1994 with one prepared by members of the British Mycological Society in 1926.[21] On "an old fence along one side of Moccas Old Park" they noted *Hypocenomyce caradocensis*, a species originally described by the Rev. Leighton from the Welsh Marches, *Cyphelium inquinans* (Figure 4.1.3), *Physcia hirta* (which might now be called either *P. adscendens* or *P. tenella*) and *Usnea subfloridana*. This was probably not an exhaustive list. Of the four taxa, *Physcia adscendens* and *Usnea subfloridana* still occur today; *Cyphelium inquinans* is known from the Park but not the pale, and *H. caradocensis* has never been reported again.

The rock outcrops

High up on the slopes of the Park, at an altitude of about 225 m and mostly buried in bracken, lie several outcrops of Old Red Sandstone, some of which are composed of a calcareous cornstone (see Chapter 1.2). In the summer of 1994 Gosling noted 27 lichen taxa from the outcrops he could locate amongst the dense bracken cover.[22] Competition from higher plants and bryophytes was severe. Yet the shade, shelter and humidity favoured a few notable species. These included probably the largest lichen in the park, *Peltigera horizontalis*. Considered to be an old forest indicator,[23] it was thought to have been lost from Moccas Park, having last been recorded on trees, probably elms, in the 1968 survey.[24]

A grey thallus on deeply shaded rocks proved to be *Enterographa hutchinsiae*, a lichen unknown elsewhere in the English Midlands, but of scattered occurrence to the west in Wales. But the most important find was of what is also perhaps the most visually attractive lichen in the park, *Gyalecta ulmi*, a nationally endangered species. It has a pale grey thallus with pink, often white-frosted, fruits. Only a single thallus was found in 1995, but in 1999 a substantial and thriving population was located. As its name suggests, it was once a plant of old elm trees. Dutch elm disease has killed possibly all its known hosts in Britain and apart from Moccas Park it occurs at only one other site in England, a single thallus having been found in a sheltered limestone gorge in Northumberland.[25]

The presence of a lime kiln, though now much-decayed, suggests that the lime content of these rocks has been exploited in the past. Here Gosling recorded the lichen *Peltigera rufescens*. This species was once frequently, and often erroneously, recorded; it is now known to be confined to only the most base-rich of sites.

The rock outcrops are clearly of some lichenological interest and their complete overgrowth by bracken and shrubs should be prevented by judicious pruning and cutting.

MOSSES AND LIVERWORTS - THE BRYOPHYTES

There are fewer epiphytic bryophytes than there are lichens, but trees are nevertheless important habitats for a number of species. However, it is only when the full range of habitats occurring at Moccas Park is taken into account that a worthwhile list of bryophyte species can be assembled.

Bryophyte recording

The bryophytes have not been subject to the same degree of survey as the lichens. Nevertheless, 123 taxa have been recorded; they are listed in Appendix 2.

In 1978 John and Cicely Port laid out three parallel transects starting from the road and running south west to the boundary of the Upper Park.[26] One commenced at the Park Lodge, the second bisected the Lawn Pool, whilst the third ran from a point approximately 150 m east of the Lawn Gate Lodge. Bryophytes were recorded in a quadrat of unspecified size at either 50 m or 100 m intervals along the transects.

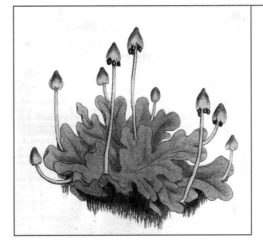

Figure 4.1.4

Conocephalum conicum. A liverwort of damp soil by streams. From a drawing by James Sowerby in *English Botany* (1790-1814) by J. E. Smith and J. Sowerby.

Epiphytic bryophytes were noted by Rose on visits in 1968 and 1986;[27] Jonathan Sleath provided species lists based on visits in 1997 and 1998, when he concentrated in particular on rock and wall habitats;[28] and the author has added additional records from his casual observations at various times over the years.

A range of common and widespread taxa occurs in the grassland, at flush sites and in bracken areas and the following comments concentrate on habitats where more noteworthy species occur: the trees, the willow carr, the Lawn Pool and the walls and rock outcrops.

The bryophyte flora of the parkland trees and willow carr

The bases of the ancient oak trees are frequently clothed in *Isothecium myosuroides*, the trunks most frequently supporting *Hypnum cupressiforme*, *Dicranoweisia cirrata* and occasionally *H. resupinatum*. But acidifying atmospheric pollutants appear to have had as considerable an effect on bryophytes in the Park as they have had on lichens, and epiphytic species are not as common as might be expected.

Species such as the mosses *Homalothecium sericeum* and *Zygodon baumgartneri* and the liverwort *Metzgeria furcata* might be expected to occur frequently on the trunks of the ancient oaks but they are uncommon, and a single oak in the Upper Park is host to the now regionally scarce *Pterogonium gracile*. Where soil splashes onto the root buttresses, *Bryum capillare* and *Orthotrichum diaphanum* occur.

Those few trees in the Park with a naturally more base-rich bark, or which grow in sheltered locations, such as the willow carr on the island in the Lawn Pool, are richer in species. Field maple in the Lower Park supports the calcicoles *Neckera complanata*, *Tortula laevipila* and *Homalothecium sericeum*, whilst the grey willows of the carr provide a substrate for *Orthotrichum affine*, *O. diaphanum*, *O. stramineum* and *O. lyellii*. The naturally higher humidity of the willow carr encourages the liverwort *Lejeunea ulicina*, a species not common in Herefordshire, as well as the more frequent *Frullania dilatata* and the moss *Ulota crispa*. The latter was known from only one station in Herefordshire a hundred years ago,[29] but it now occurs frequently in the western part of the county.

Stumps and larger pieces of dead wood have a moss flora which differs from the living trees. As the wood decays it becomes colonised by mosses more typical of peaty soils, such as *Campylopus paradoxus*, *C. introflexus*, *Orthodontium lineare* and *Dicranum scoparium*. The few species more strictly confined to trees and dead wood include *Dicranoweisia cirrata* and *Aulacomnium androgynum*.

Bryophytes of the Lawn Pool

Sedge tussocks and tree bases subject to fluctuating water levels are covered in the mosses *Amblystegium riparium*, *Brachythecium rivulare* and *Calliergon cuspidatum*. *Drepanocladus aduncus* and *Calliergon giganteum* occur in shallow water.

In summer the exposed mud of the Lawn Pool becomes colonised by a number of ephemeral species, including the moss *Physcomitrium pyriforme* and the nationally scarce thalloid liverwort *Riccia huebeneriana*, the latter unknown elsewhere in Herefordshire, but frequent on reservoir margins in central Wales. Small amounts of the locally scarce aquatic liverwort *Riccia fluitans* float in the water.

Bryophytes of walls and rock outcrops

Jonathan Sleath recorded eighteen mostly common species of lime-loving bryophytes from the walls around the Park.[30] The drier, sunny tops have been colonised by such common cushion mosses as *Tortula muralis*, *Schistidium apocarpum* and *Grimmia pulvinata*. In more shady places the apple green tufts of the much less common moss *Zygodon viridissimus* var. *stirtonii* were recorded as were the distinctive fan-shaped fronds of the liverworts *Porella platyphylla* and *Metzgeria furcata*.

Of considerably greater interest are the low sandstone outcrops, often shaded by bracken, on the upper slopes of the Park. Here Sleath recorded *Scapania scandica*, a liverwort previously unrecorded in Herefordshire, and the somewhat montane species *Blepharostoma trichophyllum*, which is rare in the Marches. He noted considerable variation in the base status of the rocks, as evidenced by the presence in some places of calcifuges such as the mosses *Isothecium myosuroides*, *Dicranum scoparium* and *Rhytidiadelphus loreus*, in contrast, elsewhere, to calcicoles such as the mosses *Anomodon viticulosus*, *Ctenidium molluscum* and the liverwort *Porella arboris-vitae*. These small rock outcrops support, in all, 76 species of bryophyte.

Conclusion

Despite its many veteran trees, Moccas Park is not a particularly good site for epiphytic lichens and bryophytes. The reasons are unclear, but pollution, whether of local or more distant origin, is thought to have played a significant part. Nevertheless, when the Lawn Pool, the park pale, the walls and rock outcrops are taken into account, the lists of lichens and bryophytes for the Park are considerably extended, encompassing a number of county and regional rarities, and, in *Gyalecta ulmi*, a nationally endangered lichen species.

Notes

1 Rose (1993); Rose quotes the late Professor J. J. Barkman, a celebrated Dutch authority on epiphytes, as saying that he had seen more ancient oaks in a drive across the Weald in the late 1960s than there were in the whole of the Netherlands.
2 Paulson (1926).
3 Smith (1952).
4 Rose & Coppins (1968).
5 Rose (1986).
6 Rose (1986).
7 Sandell & Gosling (1988), Gosling & Sandell (1993), Gosling (1994).
8 Gosling (1994).
9 James, Hawksworth & Rose (1977); the lichen communities are described as a series of 'associations' many of which have a distinctive faithful species and a group of species with a high incidence or a constant level of occurrence, reflecting subtle local variations notably in substrate, humidity and light.
10 Fletcher (1982,1993).
11 Rose (1976).
12 Hawksworth & Rose (1970).
13 Hyder Environmental & ARIC (1996).
14 Sandell & Gosling (1988). The method is as described in Looney & James (1990): aluminium nails are driven into the bark of each tree; these provide a permanent reference point onto which a quadrat frame measuring 18 x 27 cm can be positioned; ten horizontal and ten vertical wires are set into the frame; the lichens present at each of the 100 intersections are recorded. Perfect duplication of the recording location is not possible because of the tree's growth over the years, but variation will be slight.
15 Harvey & Looney (1992), Gosling (1996).
16 AEA Technology (1997).
17 Gosling (1994).
18 Gosling (1994).
19 British Lichen Society database.
20 Gosling (1994).
21 Paulson (1926).
22 Gosling (1994).
23 Rose (1976).
24 Rose & Coppins (1968).
25 Oliver Gilbert (pers. comm.).
26 Port & Port (1978).
27 Rose (1986).
28 Sleath (1998).
29 Purchas & Ley (1889).
30 Sleath (1998).

References relating to Moccas Park

GOSLING, M.M. 1994. *A survey of lichens on rocks, fences and trees at Moccas Park NNR.* Report to English Nature.

GOSLING, M.M. 1996. *Moccas Park NNR lichen survey.* Report to English Nature.

GOSLING, M.M. & SANDELL, K.A. 1993. *Lichen survey and monitoring, Moccas Park NNR Herefordshire.* Report to English Nature.

HARVEY, T. & LOONEY, J.H.H. 1992. *Lichen monitoring, Moccas Park NNR, Herefordshire.* Report to English Nature by Ecosurveys Ltd.

PAULSON, R. 1926. Lichens of the Hereford foray. *Transactions of the British Mycological Society*, 12, 87-90.

PORT, P.J. & PORT, C. 1978. *Bryophyte Survey of Moccas Deer Park Herefordshire.* Report to Nature Conservancy Council.

ROSE, F. 1974. The epiphytes of oak. *In*: M. G. MORRIS & F. H. PERRING, eds. *The British Oak.* Faringdon: Classey, 250-273,

ROSE, F. 1986. Manuscript lists of lichen and bryophyte species recorded in 1968, 1981 and 1986. In English Nature files.

ROSE, F. & COPPINS, B.J. 1968. Manuscript list of lichen species. In English Nature files.

SANDELL, K.A. & GOSLING, M.M. 1988. *Moccas Park NNR Lichen Survey.* Report to Nature Conservancy Council.

SLEATH, J. D. 1998. Manuscript list of bryophyte species. In English Nature files.

SMITH, G. 1952. The Hereford Foray. *Transactions of the British Mycological Society,* 35, 168-175.

Other references

AEA TECHNOLOGY. 1997. *Acid deposition in the UK 1992-94.* Fourth report of the review group on acid rain to the DETR.

FLETCHER, A., ed. 1982. *Survey and assessment of epiphytic lichen habitats.* CSD Report No. 384 to the Nature Conservancy Council, Peterborough.

FLETCHER, A., ed. 1993. *Revised assessment of epiphytic lichen habitats.* Report to JNCC No.99F2AO59.

HAWKSWORTH, D.L. & ROSE, F. 1970. Qualitative scale for estimating sulphur dioxide air pollution in England & Wales using epiphytic lichens. *Nature* (London) 227, 145-148.

HYDER ENVIRONMENTAL & ARIC. 1996. *The nitrogen dioxide and ammonia survey of Wales.* Final report to Welsh Office.

JAMES, P.W., HAWKSWORTH, D.L. & ROSE, F. 1977. Lichen communities in the British Isles: a preliminary conspectus. *In*: M.R.D.SEAWARD, ed. *Lichen Ecology,* Academic Press, London, 295-413.

LOONEY, J. H. & JAMES, P. M. 1990. *The effects of acidification on lichens. Final Report 1989.* Report to the Nature Conservancy Council.

PURCHAS, W.R. & LEY, A. 1889. *A flora of Herefordshire.* Hereford: Jakeman & Carver.

ROSE, F. 1976. Lichenological indicators of age and environmental continuity in woodlands. *In*: D.H.BROWN, D.L.HAWKSWORTH & R.H.BAILEY, eds. *Lichenology: progress and problems.* London: Academic Press, 279-307.

ROSE, F. 1993. Ancient British woodlands and their epiphytes. *British Wildlife,* 5, 83-93.

4

1

Fungi

Edward Blackwell

.... the life of the woodland is intimately interwoven with the lives of its fungal inhabitants .... [their] *dynamic interplay maintains the cycle of growth, death and decay.*

Alan D. M. Rayner (1993).

Forays and field clubs: a short history

Herefordshire can uniquely claim to be the birthplace of the mycological field meeting. The existence of early fungus records at Moccas Park owes something to enthusiasts based in Hereford, who, more than a century ago, initiated field excursions aimed specifically at recording fungi.

In 1868, at the instigation of a former president, Dr. Henry Bull, members of the Hereford-based Woolhope Naturalists' Field Club (generally referred to simply as the Woolhope Club), were invited to a 'Foray amongst the Funguses' (Figure 4.2.1).[1] Dr Bull thereby introduced a term which has since been adopted to designate a mycological field meeting, the 'foray'. The initial foray was sufficiently successful to be repeated annually, usually followed by a lavish dinner at the Green Dragon Hotel in Hereford, with various fungus dishes featuring prominently on the menu. While science may have been the initial spur, the delights of mycophagy were not disregarded.

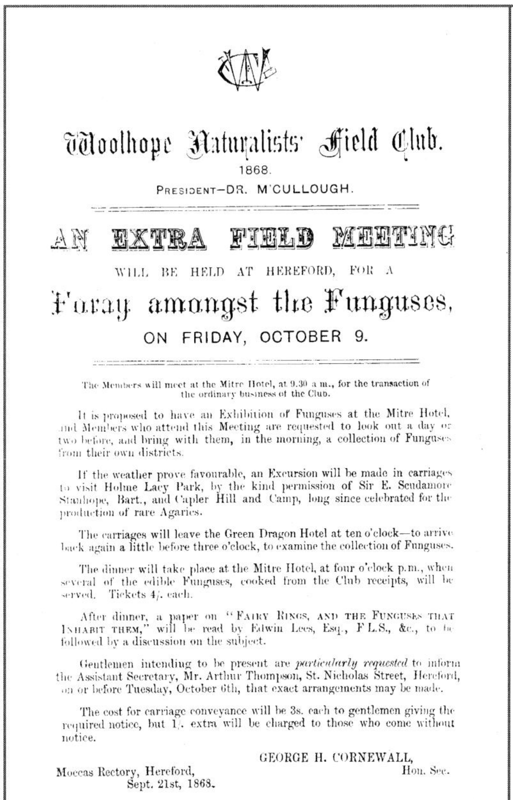

Woolhope Naturalists' Field Club.
1868.
President—Dr. M'Cullough.

AN EXTRA FIELD MEETING
WILL BE HELD AT HEREFORD, FOR A
Foray amongst the Funguses,
ON FRIDAY, OCTOBER 9.

The Members will meet at the Mitre Hotel, at 9.30 a.m., for the transaction of the ordinary business of the Club.

It is proposed to have an Exhibition of Funguses at the Mitre Hotel, and Members who attend this Meeting are requested to look out a day or two before, and bring with them, in the morning, a collection of Funguses from their own districts.

If the weather prove favourable, an Excursion will be made in carriages to visit Holme Lacy Park, by the kind permission of Sir E. Scudamore Stanhope, Bart., and Capler Hill and Camp, long since celebrated for the production of rare Agarics.

The carriages will leave the Green Dragon Hotel at ten o'clock—to arrive back again a little before three o'clock, to examine the collection of Funguses.

The dinner will take place at the Mitre Hotel, at four o'clock p.m., when several of the edible Funguses, cooked from the Club receipts, will be served. Tickets 4/. each.

After dinner, a paper on "Fairy Rings, and the Funguses that Inhabit them," will be read by Edwin Lees, Esq., F.L.S., &c., to be followed by a discussion on the subject.

Gentlemen intending to be present are *particularly requested* to inform the Assistant Secretary, Mr. Arthur Thompson, St. Nicholas Street, Hereford, on or before Tuesday, October 6th, that exact arrangements may be made.

The cost for carriage conveyance will be 3s. each to gentlemen giving the required notice, but 1/. extra will be charged to those who come without notice.

GEORGE H. CORNEWALL,
Hon. Sec.

Moccas Rectory, Hereford,
Sept. 21st, 1868.

Figure 4.2.1

'Foray amongst the Funguses'. Announcement of the first ever 'Fungus Foray', 1868. Reproduced by courtesy of the Woolhope Naturalists' Field Club.

The first foray at Moccas Park took place on 24 October 1873, when a rather modest score of about 16 species was recorded.[2] There are reports of more forays to the Park in 1880 and 1881,[3] but after the death of Dr. Bull in 1885, the event gradually lost impetus and was discontinued by the Woolhope Club after 1892.

Meanwhile interest had arisen elsewhere. The Yorkshire Naturalists' Union had begun to hold forays in various parts of Yorkshire, and in 1892 set up a Mycological Committee with the hope that their annual forays would take the place of the Hereford forays and "by avoiding the weak points of its predecessor, which were mainly confined to an excess of hospitality - prove at least equally attractive and instructive to mycologists".

With interest growing nationally, a proposal was made in 1895 to form a 'National Mycological Union' for the study of fungi, and in the following year the British Mycological Society (BMS)

Figure 4.2.2

British Mycological Society, Hereford Foray, 1926. The group includes many of the most celebrated mycologists of the time, notably G.H. Pethybridge (President), John Ramsbottom (General Secretary), Miss Gulielma Lister, Miss A. Lorrain Smith, Carlton Rea, and Miss Elsie Wakefield. Photograph by Col. C.T. Green, courtesy of the British Mycological Society.

Back row standing: S. F. Ashby, N. C. Preston, E. J. H. Corner, W. Buddin, F. M. Cory, F. G. Nutman, C. R. Metcalfe, R. W. Marsh, W. C. Moore, St J. Marriott, I. M. Roper, C. H. Grinling, S. Hastings, E. M. Day, V. Rea, F. G. Gould, W. J. Dowson, W. T. Elliott, K. St G. Cartwright, J. S. Bayliss-Elliott, E. H. Ellis, E. A. Elliot.
Front row standing: M.W. Rea, A. D. Cotton, G. Lister, A. L. Smith, G. H. Pethybridge, C. Rea, J. Ramsbottom, E. M. Wakefield, F.T. Brooks, A. A. Pearson, A. Wallis, R. Paulson, D. M. Cayley, H.R. Wakefield.
Front row: A. G. Lowndes, H. H. Knight, E. N. Carrothers, H. A. Hyde, E. M. Noel, C.A. Cooper.

was established. Links between the Woolhope Club and the new BMS remained strong due to the presence in the BMS of many who had been active in mycology in the Club.

In 1902 the Woolhope Club invited the youthful BMS to hold its sixth annual week's Fungus Foray based on Hereford,[4] placing at the disposal of the BMS their Club Room at the Public Library in Hereford, together with their numerous mycological reference works.

The historical link between the two Societies was renewed in 1926 when, on the 75th anniversary of the Woolhope Club, a series of joint forays was held in Herefordshire (Figure 4.2.2), during which Moccas Park was among the sites visited. The number of fungus species recorded at Moccas Park on this occasion was about 195.[5] Twenty-five years later, in 1951, on the occasion of the Centenary of the Woolhope Club, the BMS again met in Hereford for a week's foraying, which included Moccas Park.[6]

The tie was marked again in 1996 when it was the turn of the BMS to celebrate its Centenary, which included a week of spring forays in Herefordshire jointly with the Woolhope Club. By a now well-established tradition, Moccas Park was again included in the programme.[7] A highlight of the festivities was a Grand Dinner at the Green Dragon attended by leading members of both societies.

Sources

This review and the list of species (see Appendix 3) includes Myxomycota, but excludes lichen-forming species. It is based on 16 surveys plus a few undated records gleaned from *A flora of Herefordshire* (1889).[8] Although, as noted above, the Woolhope Club held forays in and around Herefordshire during a 25 year period ending in 1892, there were only three forays to Moccas Park and there are few systematic records of fungi at Moccas Park reported in the Club's *Transactions* prior to the joint foray with the BMS in 1926. Six of the surveys reported on here were carried out over the last eight years.

Recording: problems and biases

The process of recording fungi cannot be equated with that of recording vascular plants. What is often popularly called a 'fungus' is merely the fruiting body. Surveys of vascular plants will discover most species and certainly those that occur in quantity. Comparable completeness is almost unattainable in surveying fungi, where recording fruiting bodies is a matter of chance due to their seasonal and sporadic occurrence. In consequence, fungus surveys can do no more than record what the observer sees on a particular day in a particular year, this will generally be a mere sample of the total number of species actually present. Furthermore, many groups of microscopic fungi can be determined only by laboratory techniques and are usually the domain of the specialist. Most records in these groups are attributable to visits by the BMS.

Figure 4.2.3

Brown warty agaric, Agaricus (Amanita) rubescens. A woodland species, it is also known as the blusher. From Dr H. G. Bull's 'Illustrations of the edible funguses of Herefordshire', *Transactions of the Woolhope Naturalists' Field Club*, 1868, 196-203.

The total number of species recorded at Moccas Park in the period 1873-1998 is approximately 654. The total is necessarily approximate due to the inclusion of about a dozen records where the true identity of the taxon is uncertain and cannot now be unambiguously equated with nomenclature in current use. Points of comparison are the Dudmaston Estate in Shropshire, where regular recording of fungi over the past 30 years has produced a total of approximately 700 species and the list for Herefordshire, which currently stands at approximately 2,500 species,[9] representing about one sixth of the British fungal flora.[10]

The records exhibit bias in three ways:

❖ Towards autumn fruiting fungi; all but three of the surveys took place in the autumn.

❖ Towards groups which reflect the interests and preferences of the recorders, the larger fungi predominating, in particular the Basidiomycete Agarics (including Boletales and Russulales) such as *Amanita rubescens* (Figure 4.2.3). At 47% of the total, these are well represented, as are Aphyllophorales (brackets, polypores and allies) at 13%. Ascomycota account for about 16%, while Uredinales, Myxomycota, and mitosporic fungi each amount to just less than 4%. The remaining groups represented in the record each fall below 1%.

❖ Towards species typical of the dominant parkland and woodland habitats, but reflecting also the poor representation of certain tree species notably birch, sycamore and conifers.

Noteworthy species and communities

The wood-decomposing bracket fungi of standing and fallen trees are well represented in the records of recent years. These include both the persistent woody conks such as *Ganoderma* and *Inonotus* species, and the fleshier brackets such as beef-steak *Fistulina hepatica*, *Grifola frondosa*, sulphur polypore or chicken-of-the-woods *Laetiporus sulphureus* and dryad's saddle *Polyporus squamosus* (Figure 4.2.4), and giant polypore *Meripilus giganteus*. Species

Figure 4.2.4

Dryad's saddle, Polyporus squamosus. The Upper Park, May 1994, photograph by Frank E. Lancaster.

of particular note are *Buglossoporus quercinus*, which is only known from five sites in Britain and the uncommon *Ganoderma resinaceum*.[11] Among other agents of decomposition are many smaller brackets and fungi of fallen branches such as *Bjerkandera adusta*, *Coriolus versicolor*, *Daedaleopsis confragosa*, *Datronia mollis*, *Hymenochaete rubiginosa*, *Stereum* spp., *Schizopora paradoxa*, *Serpula himantioides* and *Vuillemina comedans*.

The following species recorded at Moccas Park appear in the BMS Red Data List,[12] and are categorised as vulnerable (V) or endangered (E):

Agaricales: *Collybia acervata* (V); *Hygrocybe calyptraeformis* (V) (Figure 4.2.5).

Aphyllophorales: *Buglossoporus quercinus* (E); *Strobilomyces floccopus* (V); *Clavaria zollingeri* (V); *Cantharellus cinereus* (V).

Russulales: *Russula solaris* (V).

Myxomycota: *Lycogala conicum* (V).

Oliveonia fibrillosa was recorded on the BMS Foray of 1996; it had only recently been added to the British list. *Podoscypha multizonata*, a rare species on soil in broadleaved woods, was recorded in 1873. The record in 1951 of rust *Puccinia buxi* on box *Buxus sempervirens* is of interest; it usually indicates the presence of old and long established box bushes, but none is known to survive in the Park today.

Ted Green and Alan Lucas have drawn attention to the following:[13]

❖ Uncommon mycorrhizal species: *Amanita aspera*, *Tricholoma sejunctum*, *Phylloporus rhodoxanthus*, *Lactarius cimicarius*, *Boletus aereus*, *Boletus albidus*, *Boletus pulverulentus*, *Gyroporus castaneus*.

❖ Uncommon species associated with old pasture: *Agaricus augustus*, *Macrolepiota konradii*, *Hygrocybe colemanniana*, *H. persistens* var. *langei*, *H. unguinosa*, *H. vitellina* and *Clavaria zollingeri*. The report of the BMS foray of 1926 refers to grassland fungi stating that "the ground proved very rich in Clavarias in spite of the dense growth of bracken" and "*Hygrophori* [grassland waxcaps, *Hygrocybe*] were also abundant".[14] Twenty-seven *Hygrocybe* species appear on the species list. In Denmark, grasslands are assessed as being of national importance where 17-32 *Hygrocybe* species are recorded.[15] In the absence of any comparative British studies, the BMS has adopted the same assessment.[16] It should be noted however that 14 of these records date from forays in 1873, 1926 or 1951.

❖ Rare or uncommon wood decomposers as noted above.

Some notable absentees and some species not recorded for a number of years

There are marked gaps in the record both of certain taxonomic groups, and of specialised habitat/substrate associations, as well as

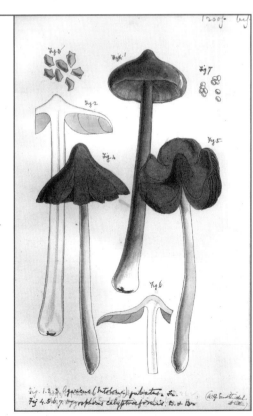

Figure 4.2.5

***Hygrocybe calyptraeformis* and *Entoloma jubatum*.** From an illustration by Worthington G. Smith in his 'New and rare Herefordshire and British Hymenomycetous fungi', *Transactions of the Woolhope Naturalists' Field Club*, 1868, 245-246. *H.calyptraeformis* (front three and spores, highly magnified, top right), a species of grassland and heath, was first recorded at Moccas Park in 1873. *E.jubatum* (other drawings) is a grassland species that has not been recorded at Moccas Park since 1926.

interesting absences of what elsewhere might be regarded as common fungi. Taxonomic groups with only token representation include, in particular, those obligate parasites infecting the living parts of vascular plants (leaves, petioles, stems, inflorescences etc.) namely the rusts, smuts, downy and powdery mildews and leaf-curl fungi. Habitat/substrate communities which are under-represented include dung-colonising fungi, fire-site fungi, aquatic Hyphomycetes (occurring on submerged vegetable debris) and fungi occurring on insects and spiders. Such gaps in both taxonomic and habitat/substrate groups are more likely to be due to the lack of visiting specialists rather than to any real deficiency of such fungi on the site.

Notable absences, at least in recent years, of species which are easily recognised and common elsewhere, include the maze gill *Daedalea quercina*, found on oak and sweet chestnut, *Phellinus igniarius,* most commonly found on willow, and tar spot *Rhytisma acerinum,* reflecting the absence of sycamore. Birch trees are rare today but may have been more common at one time.[17] Species associated with birch, such as fly agaric *Amanita muscaria*, *Russula betularum*, and *Lactarius glyciosmus* are absent from the record, and birch bracket *Piptoporus betulinus* was last recorded in 1926. *Rhodotus palmatus*, a species usually found on elm, has been recorded once only (in 1873), suggesting perhaps that elm was infrequent even before trees were lost to Dutch Elm disease in the 1970s. The death cap *Amanita phalloides* was last recorded in 1926, and the fircone fungus *Strobilomyces floccopus* in 1971. Species of *Cortinarius* are rather few (seven) and records are mainly from the past. Earthstars *Geastrum*, morels *Morchella*, truffles *Tuber* and other fungi which fruit underground, are absent from the record. Common species like *Marasmiellus ramealis*, *Mycena acicula*, *M. galopus*, *Panellus stipticus*, the scarlet caterpillar fungus *Cordyceps militaris*, grass choke *Epichloe typhina* and meadow puffball *Vascellum pratense,* were last found in 1951, while *Postia stiptica* and the common earth ball *Scleroderma citrinum* have not appeared in the record since 1926. Several species recorded in the past have not been seen in recent times, for example *Podoscypha multizonata* (1873), tawny grissette *Amanita fulva* (1951), and magpie *Coprinus picaceus* (1951), but this may just be due to chance.

Site management

Maintaining continuity of the parkland, woodland and grassland habitats in an undisturbed condition, is central to the conservation of the fungi of Moccas Park.[18] The retention of dead wood is of particular importance. The quantity of dead wood seems to have been a particular feature of Moccas Park in the past. In 1876 Francis Kilvert described "fallow wood of which there seemed to be underfoot an accumulation of several feet, the gathering ruin and decay probably of centuries".[19] Half a century later, the report of the 1926 BMS foray stated that "the park is remarkable for its fine old trees, and the many fallen, undisturbed trunks provide ample occupation for mycologists", and that "under some of the great oaks and beeches on the grassy slopes of the Park, were lying, half hidden among bracken, huge decaying trunks abounding with Mycetozoa".[20] It may be that there is less dead wood present today; as much as possible should be retained in the future.

The avoidance of further agricultural improvement is also critical to the conservation of the fungi of the Park. Ground compaction, soil disturbance, harrowing and rolling, and the application of fertilisers, lime and herbicides, are all likely to be detrimental.[21] Notwithstanding the good numbers of *Hygrocybe* species, the total number of grassland species recorded to date, about 40, is low compared with what might be expected for old pasture. The range of species may have been reduced by the agricultural improvement of the 1960s and 1970s (see Chapters 6.1 and 6.5).

In conclusion

The record of fungi at Moccas Park so far is interesting and includes some notable species, but considerable scope remains for further productive survey work. If a more comprehensive fungus record is an objective, together with further discoveries of interesting and perhaps uncommon species, the recent trend towards more frequent surveys should be maintained. Regular visits by experienced mycologists at all times of the year are desirable, especially to cover the spring and summer periods.

Notes

1 Blackwell (1998).
2 Anon (1873).
3 Cooke (1880), Cooke (1881).
4 Anon (1902).
5 Wakefield (1927).
6 Smith (1952).
7 British Mycological Society (1996).
8 Purchas & Ley (1889).
9 Author's unpublished data.
10 In September 1999, the BMS database ran to 14,762 species excluding lichens (Paul Kirk pers. comm.).
11 *B. quercinus* is now protected, being listed on Schedule 8 of the Wildlife and Countryside Act 1981. *G. resinaceum* is known from two other Herefordshire parks, Brampton Bryan and Croft Castle, and also from Bodenham Lakes (author's personal records).
12 Ing (1992).
13 Green & Lucas (1992, 1994); they report on field visits in 1992 (15 September and 1 October) and 1994 (10 August).
14 Wakefield (1927).
15 Rald (1985) as reported by Boertmann (1995).
16 Maurice Rotheroe (pers. comm.).
17 Anon (1870) gave the girths of two big birch trees in the Lower Park where none is to be found today. Birch trees were also mentioned by Francis Kilvert in his description of 1876 (Plomer 1940); he is referring to the Upper Park where birch are very rare today.
18 The basic guidelines are given in Alexander, Green & Key (1996).
19 Plomer (1940).
20 Wakefield (1927), Lister (1927).
21 Keizer (1993) reports on the marked effects on fungi of fertiliser applications in forests; Dix & Webster (1995) give examples of changes in the mycoflora following fertilizer treatments and Jansen (1990) points out the particular susceptibility of mycorrhizal fungi. Marren (1998) states that whereas ancient grassland undisturbed by fertiliser or farm machinery may produce 20 or more species of waxcaps *Hygrocybe*, on agriculturally improved pasture there may be just one or two common species or none at all.

References relating to Moccas Park

ANON. 1870. Incidental notes on remarkable trees in Herefordshire. *Transactions of the Woolhope Naturalists' Field Club*, 288-321.

ANON. 1873. The fungus foray and feast of the Woolhope Club, October 1873. *Transactions of the Woolhope Naturalists' Field Club*, 100-117.

ANON. 1902. The Hereford foray, 22-27 September 1902. *Transactions of the British Mycological Society*, 2, 5-12.

BRITISH MYCOLOGICAL SOCIETY. 1996. *Centenary Spring Foray, 1996, species list*. Unpublished.

COOKE, M.C. 1880. The fungus foray. *Transactions of the Woolhope Naturalists' Field Club*, 252-258.

COOKE, M.C. 1881. The fungus foray. *Transactions of the Woolhope Naturalists' Field Club*, 86-89.

GREEN, E.E. & LUCAS, A.J. 1992. *Report and species list*. Unpublished report to English Nature.

GREEN, E.E. & LUCAS, A.J. 1994. *Report and species list*. Unpublished report to English Nature.

LISTER, G. 1927. Mycetozoa gathered during the Hereford foray. *Transactions of the British Mycological Society*, 12, 86-87.

PLOMER, W. 1940. *Kilvert's diary*. Volume three. London: Jonathan Cape.

PURCHAS, W.R. & LEY, A. 1889. *A flora of Herefordshire*. Hereford: Jakeman & Carver.

SMITH, G. 1952. The Hereford foray, 12-19 September 1951. *Transactions of the British Mycological Society*, 35, 168-175.

WAKEFIELD, E.M. 1927. The Hereford foray. *Transactions of the British Mycological Society*, 12, 79-85.

Other references

ALEXANDER, K.N.A., GREEN, E.E. & KEY, R.S. 1996. The management of overmature tree populations for nature conservation - the basic guidelines. *In*: H.J. READ, ed. *Pollard and Veteran Tree Management II*. London: Corporation of London, 122-135.

BLACKWELL, E. 1998. The great fungus meeting at Hereford. *The Journal of the Association of British Fungus Groups*, 2, 16-18.

BOERTMANN, D. 1995. *The genus Hygrocybe (Fungi of northern Europe. Vol. 1)*. Denmark: Svampetryk.

DIX, N. J. & WEBSTER, J. 1995. *Fungal Ecology*. London: Chapman & Hall.

ING, B. 1992. A provisional Red Data List of British Fungi. *The Mycologist*, 6, 124-128.

JANSEN, A.E. 1990. Conservation of fungi in Europe. *The Mycologist*, 4, 83-85.

KEIZER, P.J. 1993. The influence of nature management on the Macromycete flora. *In*: D.N. PEGLER, L. BODDY, B.ING & P.M.KIRK, eds. *Fungi of Europe: investigation, recording and conservation*. Kew: Royal Botanic Gardens, 251-269.

MARREN, P. 1998. Fungal flowers: the waxcaps and their world. *British Wildlife*, 9, 164-172.

RALD, E. 1985. Vokshatte som indikatorarter for mykologisk værdifulde overdrevslokaliteter. *Svampe*, 11, 1-9.

RAYNER, A.D.M. 1993. The fundamental importance of fungi in woodlands. *British Wildlife*, 4, 205-215.

Vascular plants

Dave Simpson,
Peter Thomson,
Stephanie Thomson
and Tom Wall

*.... a route was taken .... to the Deer Park, passing thence round Lawn Pool
(which, owing to the lower average of the rainfall during the last 12 months,
was nearly dry), where* Lysimachia vulgaris *and* Scutellaria galericulata
*were gathered in flower. Botanists will regret to learn that, since the drying
up of this pool, that interesting plant* Utricularia minor, *which we always
took a delight in seeing on its margin, has entirely disappeared.*

Field meeting of the Woolhope Naturalists' Field Club, August 1891.[1]

Ever since those early days, the interest of Moccas Park to botanists has resided principally in the Lawn Pool. Periods of intensive grazing have doubtless reduced the botanical diversity of the grassland of the Lower Park where, in the 1960s and 1970s, the effect was compounded by significant works to improve the agricultural potential. The steep wooded slopes of the Upper Park show clear signs of grazing pressure too: there is no shrub layer or natural regeneration of trees, and the ground flora is less prolific than might be expected. But the Lawn Pool, whilst more island than water, is generally wet enough to reduce grazing pressure and defy any attempt at drainage and improvement and its interest to botanists endures. They will be pleased to learn that notice of the demise of the bladderwort *Utricularia* sp. was premature; its history and specific identity is explored in more detail below.

This chapter begins with an account of the botanical recording and surveys that have been undertaken and then moves on to a discussion of the plant communities of each major habitat type, concluding with notes concerning some of the more interesting species.

Records and surveys

Early published records are limited and fragmentary. The Reverends William Purchas and Augustin Ley in their *Flora of Herefordshire* of 1889 mention Moccas Park as a location for 19 species, most of them recorded by the then owner the Reverend Sir George Cornewall.[2] The report of the Woolhope Club field visit of 1891 cites only the three species named in the quotation above. Two additional species are recorded in 1894 and two more in 1905, and in 1908 Ley makes special mention of the "old marshy pool beds" of Moccas Park as a habitat "in which a vegetation formerly more general [in Herefordshire] lingers", but lists only four of the more interesting wetland plants.[3]

It was not until 1962, when Philip Oswald and Elizabeth Copeland Watts visited the Park on behalf of the Nature Conservancy, making a brief record of plants in the principal habitats, that there was the first attempt at more systematic recording of the vascular plants.[4] Table 4.3.1 provides a summary of this and subsequent surveys. It shows that there has been an increase in activity over the last decade, nevertheless the Park has still not been comprehensively surveyed. Some 259 species have been recorded, but doubtless more remain to be discovered. There is scope too for a study of the cumulative impact of long years of deer grazing and for the development of a better understanding of the origins and history of the plant communities. A full list of the species recorded to date is given in Appendix 4.

Bogbean. *Drawing by Graham Easy.*

Table 4.3.1. Surveys of vascular plants.

Year	Surveyor	Purpose	Number of species recorded in each survey
1962	P. Oswald, E. Copeland Watts[5]	Outline description of habitats; 13 September, 11 October.	100
1976/7	P.T. Harding[6]	Quantitative survey of trees and shrubs; various dates.	30
1982	A. Whitbread[7]	Outline description of habitats; 8 September.	34
1989	S. Thomson, P. Thomson[8]	Listing of plants in part of the Lawn Pool scheduled for dredging; August 1989.	19
1991	C. D. Preston, J. M. Croft[9]	Listing of plants of the Lawn Pool and a 'swampy hollow'; 6 August.	36
1993	N. King, S. Thomson, P. Thomson[10]	Survey of 22 representative plots; four visits, May-September.	147
1998	D. Simpson[11]	Abundance of woodland and grassland plants; 27 March, 15 May.	106
1998	J. Bingham[12]	Outline survey and provisional National Vegetation Classification; 21 August.	157

Plant communities

Deer parks are artificial habitats: long years of deer grazing have modified both the structure of the vegetation and the incidence of palatable species, and further modifications have been brought about through the management of both the trees and the grassland. Moccas Park is no exception, and as a consequence, it is sometimes difficult to relate its plant communities to those described in the National Vegetation Classification (NVC), which aims to describe all British natural and semi-natural plant communities as well as the principal artificial ones.[13] No detailed NVC survey has been carried out, but John Bingham, on the basis of a field visit and the field work reports of Noel King, Stephanie Thomson, Peter Thomson and Dave Simpson, has attempted to assign the main plant communities within the Park to NVC types;[14] the following account draws heavily on his findings.

Common bird's-foot-trefoil

Grassland

Most of the grassland within the Park is 'semi-improved' or 'improved'; it clearly relates to MG6a *Lolium perenne-Cynosurus cristatus* (perennial rye-grass-crested dog's-tail)[15] neutral grassland, and both of the eponymous species are abundant. This is the major permanent pasture type on moist, but freely-draining, agriculturally improved soils in lowland Britain. Typically the incidence of herb species is low and this is the case at Moccas Park. Here the grassland occurs as a mosaic of the typical sub-community and the MG6b *Anthoxanthum odoratum* (sweet vernal grass) sub-community. There are frequent drifts or clumps of bracken *Pteridium aquilinum*, common nettle *Urtica dioica*, creeping thistle *Cirsium arvense* and spear thistle *Cirsium vulgare*. The occasional steep sides of artificial and natural banks in the Lower Park have not been significantly improved and offer an insight into what may once have been more widespread. Here typical species include common dog-violet *Viola riviniana*, common bird's-foot-trefoil *Lotus corniculatus*, field wood-rush *Luzula campestris* and red fescue *Festuca rubra*.[16]

The dense bracken-dominated grassland areas of the Upper Park conform to U20 *Pteridium aquilinum-Galium saxatile* (bracken-heath bedstraw) grassland. There are tiny fragments of the acid grassland community U1d *Festuca ovina-Agrostis capillaris-Rumex acetosella* (sheep's-fescue-common bent-sheep's sorrel), *Anthoxanthum odoratum-Lotus corniculatus* (sweet vernal grass-common bird's-foot-trefoil) sub-community; these fragments are being threatened however by the shade cast by bracken and scrub growing on the deeper adjacent soils. These soils support another acid grassland community U4b *Festuca ovina-Agrostis capillaris-Galium saxatile* (sheep's-fescue-common bent-heath bedstraw), *Holcus lanatus-Trifolium repens* (Yorkshire-fog-white clover) sub-community. Prior to agricultural improvement, this was probably the dominant grassland community on drier ground throughout the Park; at this time species such as tormentil *Potentilla erecta*, lesser trefoil *Trifolium dubium* and mouse-ear-hawkweed *Pilosella officinarum* would have been more widespread.

Guards erected in grassland areas in order to protect newly planted trees from deer and livestock, allow species to prosper which are otherwise suppressed. Colourful examples include cuckooflower *Cardamine pratensis*, primrose *Primula vulgaris* and bluebell *Hyacinthoides non-scripta*. But bluebell may be encountered at many places in the grassland, albeit in a severely checked state.[17] It is, perhaps, a tenacious survivor not just of improvement, but of the woodland from which the Park evolved; it still prospers in the woodland of the Upper Park.

It was reported in 1962 that "a remarkable feature" of the turf of the Lower Park was "the many extremely large and presumably old anthills."[18] Something of the nature of the turf at that time may be seen in a photograph of May 1962 (Figure 4.3.1) taken from behind 'The *Hypebaeus* tree' (see Chapter 3.2) looking across The Lawn towards the Upper Park. The photograph shows what appears to be a very high density of anthills, although none visible in this photograph could be described as "extremely large". Plant species characteristic of these anthills included wild thyme *Thymus polytrichus*, heath speedwell *Veronica officinalis*, heath bedstraw *Galium saxatile* and early hair-grass *Aira praecox*. Within a few years, ploughing had destroyed them; today, with controls on harrowing and rolling negotiated through the Nature Reserve Agreement, they appear to be developing again, but the potential for natural re-colonisation by the characteristic anthill plant species appears to be low.

Another photograph taken in May 1962, from near the south east end of the Lawn Pool looking towards the Upper Park (Figure 4.3.2), shows what appear to be significant quantities of rush *Juncus* spp., and at one time a mosaic of wet grassland and mire may have occurred in parts of the Park. An area west of the Connibury is reported as having been particularly wet and "rushy", with soil "black as sloe";[19] it was drained in the 1960s and 10-12 tons of lime were applied per acre.[20] Today rushes are much less noticeable in the Park, but small pockets of MG10 *Holcus lanatus-Juncus effusus* (soft-rush) rush-pasture occur. This appears to be a secondary community re-invading the wetter parts of the improved grassland.

Figure 4.3.1

The northern part of the Lower Park, May 1962. Looking southwest from behind 'The *Hypebaeus* tree'. Photograph by Peter Skidmore.

Figure 4.3.2

The southern part of the Lower Park, May 1962. Looking south west from near the south east end of the Lawn Pool. Photograph by Peter Skidmore.

A small flushed area adjacent to the perennial stream which runs through the grassland towards the south eastern end of the Park, is one of the more species-rich areas; it has a community conforming to M23 *Juncus effusus/acutiflorus-Galium palustre* (soft/sharp-flowered rush-common marsh-bedstraw) rush-pasture, including common fleabane *Pulicaria dysenterica*, water figwort *Scrophularia auriculata* and marsh pennywort *Hydrocotyle vulgaris*. Other species recorded in flushes and on stream-sides within the Park include lady-fern *Athyrium filix-femina*, opposite-leaved golden-saxifrage *Chrysosplenium oppositifolium*, hemp-agrimony *Eupatorium cannabinum* and glaucous sedge *Carex flacca*.

The principal tree species standing in the grassland of the Lower Park is oak; *Quercus robur* and *Q. petraea* both occur as well as hybrids. Following the demise of elm *Ulmus* spp., the only other native species to occur are field maple *Acer campestre* and ash *Fraxinus excelsior*, and these are heavily outnumbered by beech *Fagus sylvatica*, sweet chestnut *Castanea sativa*, and horse-chestnut *Aesculus hippocastanum*, all of which have been extensively planted. Hawthorn *Crataegus monogyna* was at one time well represented, but many were removed during agricultural improvement. Self-seeded holly *Ilex aquifolium*, ivy *Hedera helix* and elder *Sambucus nigra* all take advantage of the guards erected to protect planted trees from deer and livestock, but are otherwise virtually absent, while spindle *Euonymus europaeus* only occurs just outside the Park pale. Such woody species would presumably have been more widespread but for the long history of intensive grazing. Further details of tree and shrub species, including of recent plantings, can be found in Chapters 3.5 and 6.5.

Woodland

Much of the Upper Park occupies steep north-facing slopes; it is predominantly closed canopy woodland, but there are extensive grassland glades, as described above, woodland edges and also areas with a more open canopy. The dominant tree species is for the most part oak *Quercus* spp. Most have probably been planted, but some may be derived from the original woodland cover, which may also have included yew *Taxus baccata*, wych elm *Ulmus glabra*, large-leaved lime *Tilia platyphyllos*, field maple *Acer campestre* and ash *Fraxinus excelsior*, all of which still occur. Hawthorn *Crataegus monogyna* is the only commonly occurring shrub. Beech *Fagus sylvatica*, sweet chestnut *Castanea sativa* and horse-chestnut *Aesculus hippocastanum*, species which all originate from planting, are frequent. There are also several small plantations of broadleaves and conifers, both in pure and mixed stands. The species and age structure of the trees of the Upper Park are discussed in more detail in Chapter 3.5.

Grazing has eliminated the shrub layer from the woodland and has perhaps favoured the Bluebell dominance of bracken over large areas, because the deer spurn the bracken whilst removing its potential competitors. Bramble *Rubus fruticosus* would be one of these. It is absent throughout areas to which the deer have access, but soon appears in areas from which they are excluded. The woodland falls into the NVC type W10 *Quercus robur-Pteridium aquilinum-Rubus fruticosus* (pedunculate oak-bracken-bramble). It includes extensive areas where bluebell and bracken are dominant, either singly or together, and some of these areas conform more to W25a *Pteridium aquilinum-Rubus fruticosus* (bracken-bramble) under-scrub, *Hyacinthoides non-scripta* (bluebell) sub-community. In some areas bracken dominates without bluebell, suggesting U20 *Pteridium aquilinum-Galium saxatile* (bracken-heath bedstraw), a community derived from grassland rather than woodland, but there are extensive areas where bracken is absent, rare or only occasional.

First impressions suggest that the deer have eaten out the woodland herbs, with the notable exception of bluebell. They may well have checked them, and in some areas reduced their abundance and spread, but a thorough search before bracken emergence, reveals a good range of vernal species, notably wood anemone *Anemone nemorosa*, primrose *Primula vulgaris*, dog's mercury *Mercurialis perennis*, wood-sorrel *Oxalis acetosella*, wood speedwell *Veronica montana*, moschatel *Adoxa moschatellina*, ramsons *Allium ursinum* and wood melick *Melica uniflora*.[21]

Wetland

The Lawn Pool is the only area where there is permanent standing water. The extensive outline of the Pool, shown on maps as encompassing an area of 4.4 ha, belies its true nature. Today there is just a narrow and shallow strip of open water round a substantial island, and even this strip, the product of dredging in the 1980s, dries out except in the wetter summers.

Prior to the dredging, virtually the entire surface had been colonised by swamp, fen and carr. In most years up to and including the 1960s, this vegetation was fired, and this presumably curtailed the spread of shrubs and trees.[22] Then, as today, the entire area was periodically inundated in the winter, but it dried out in summer leaving virtually no open water (see Figures 4.3.3 and 4.3.4). The only consistent exception then, as now, was an area at the south east end of the Pool; even in the remarkably dry summer of 1976 this held a few square yards of water.[23] The quotation which heads this chapter shows however that the drying up of the Pool is not a new phenomenon. There are three smaller pools, referred to hereafter as Bulrush ponds, which become inundated in winter but dry out completely almost every summer.

The vegetation of the Lawn Pool falls into a series of zones which vary in area according to the water level: grassland edge with some bare ground as a result of trampling by livestock, open water (which becomes bare mud in dry years), swamp and woodland. A range of plant communities occurs as a heterogeneous mix, each of them occupying only a small area, which makes NVC determinations difficult. Furthermore, those given below, in common with all those in this chapter, are not based on any detailed survey and must therefore be regarded as only provisional.

The grassland edge conforms to MG13 *Agrostis stolonifera-Alopecurus geniculatus* (creeping bent-marsh foxtail) grassland. Plants in this zone include blinks *Montia fontana* and tufted forget-me-not *Myosotis laxa*. The open water, for which pH values between 6.2 and 7.4 were found in 1998,[24] supports plant communities which have been tentatively ascribed to the A2 *Lemna minor* (common duckweed), A10 *Polygonum amphibium* (= *Persicaria amphibia*) (amphibious bistort) and A16 *Callitriche stagnalis* (common water-starwort) communities. Species other than the eponymous ones include fine-leaved water-dropwort *Oenanthe aquatica* and intermediate water-starwort *Callitriche hamulata*.

Figure 4.3.3

The Lawn Pool, June 1973. Photograph courtesy of the University of Cambridge Committee for Aerial Photography.

Figure 4.3.4

The Lawn Pool, July 1991. This shows the Pool after the dredging of its perimeter and excavation of parts of the west end and centre of the island. Photograph courtesy of the University of Cambridge Committee for Aerial Photography.

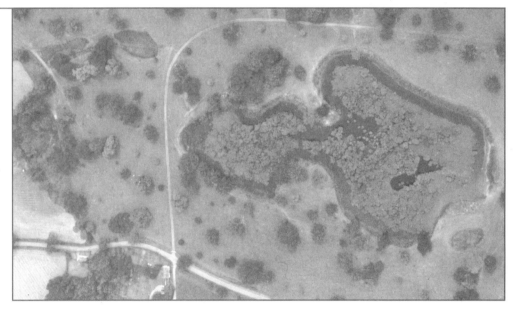

When the Lawn Pool is almost completely dry, the exposed mud supports nodding bur-marigold *Bidens cernua* (known from very few sites in Herefordshire but well represented here), bogbean *Menyanthes trifoliata* (uncommon in the county), celery-leaved buttercup *Ranunculus sceleratus*, water-pepper *Persicaria hydropiper*, marsh pennywort *Hydrocotyle vulgaris* and toad rush *Juncus bufonius*.

Amongst the more obvious plants occurring in the areas of swamp are yellow loosestrife *Lysimachia vulgaris*, water forget-me-not *Myosotis scorpioides*, skullcap *Scutellaria galericulata*, gypsywort *Lycopus europaeus*, marsh speedwell *Veronica scutellata* var. *villosa* and yellow iris *Iris pseudacorus*. Here the plant communities are particularly diverse. S11 *Carex vesicaria* (bladder-sedge) swamp is dominant round most of the Pool (as it is in the pond to the north), but S9 *Carex rostrata* (bottle sedge) swamp, a less rich community, also occurs (as it does in the pond to the south east). There are small areas of S10 *Equisetum fluviatile* (water horsetail) swamp and S8 *Scirpus (= Schoenoplectus) lacustris* ssp. *lacustris* (common club-rush) swamp is present around the edge of deep water in which S12 *Typha latifolia* (bulrush) swamp appears in small patches.

The wooded areas of the island in the Lawn Pool appear to be W5b *Alnus glutinosa-Carex paniculata* (alder-greater tussock-sedge) woodland, *Lysimachia vulgaris* (yellow loosestrife) sub-community. Apart from these species, grey willow *Salix cinerea* ssp. *oleifolia* is common, along with skullcup *Scutellaria galericulata*, soft-rush *Juncus effusus* and yellow iris *Iris pseudacorus,* and, in drier areas, broad buckler-fern *Dryopteris dilatata*, bramble *Rubus fruticosus*, rosebay willowherb *Chamerion angustifolium* and sessile oak *Quercus petraea.*

Noteworthy species, extinctions and survivals

Herefordshire has long been celebrated as one of the very best counties for mistletoe *Viscum album.*[25] Current host species in Moccas Park are field maple *Acer campestre*, hawthorn *Crataegus monogyna*, lime *Tilia* x *vulgaris* and large-leaved lime *Tilia platyphyllos*; there is an old record of ash *Fraxinus excelsior.*[26] The first two are the commonest recorded hosts amongst native species and ash is quite frequently recorded too. Lime is, after cultivated apple *Malus domestica*, the commonest host overall, but large-leaved lime does not appear at all on the well-known published lists of host species.[27]

Moonwort *Botrychium lunaria* and adder's-tongue *Ophioglossum vulgatum* were both recorded in the nineteenth century.[28] The former has not been noted since, but the latter, nowadays a local species in the county, has been observed again over the last few years. Intriguingly, the records often relate to areas which appear to have been agriculturally improved.[29] Intensive grazing by deer may well account for the limited range of other fern species recorded, but this includes lemon-scented fern *Oreopteris limbosperma*, a species of only local occurrence in Herefordshire.[30]

Meadow saffron *Colchicum autumnale* occurs in the grassland of the Upper Park; uncommon nationally, Herefordshire and neighbouring counties form something of a stronghold. The corms were gathered here and elsewhere in Herefordshire during the Second World War for medicinal purposes (see Chapter 2.4), but attempts have been made to eliminate it from pastoral areas of the county because in all its parts it is highly poisonous to livestock.[31] It appears to be avoided by the deer and may flourish in Moccas Park partly because they reduce competition from woody species.

Ivy-leaved bellflower *Wahlenbergia hederacea*, almost certainly now extinct in the county, was recorded in the nineteenth century from "Moccas Park and hill",[32] but possibly only as a result of confusion with a site outside the Park near Depple Wood, where the Reverend Sir George Cornewall showed it to the Woolhope Club in 1891.[33]

Altogether, seven species recorded at the turn of the century have not been identified since (see Appendix 4), but no specific search has been made for them and all could yet be re-discovered. The most significant in the Herefordshire context is small water-pepper *Persicaria minor*, a plant of damp places which is very rare in the county.[34] Seven species recorded in 1962 have not been identified since. These include five grassland species, three of which, including lady's bedstraw *Galium verum* and wild thyme *Thymus polytrichus,* were described as "characteristic" of the anthills which, along with their little sub-community of plants, were lost to agricultural improvement in the 1960s.

Tufted-sedge *Carex elata* (= *stricta*) was placed on record from "old pools in Moccas Park in great abundance" in both 1889 and 1908, but it has not been noted recently and there are very few recent records for Herefordshire.[35] Ley recorded golden dock *Rumex maritimus* and expected it to recur "in favouring seasons",[36] but it is to be found on no other list; it is a plant of seasonally exposed mud and is very rare in the county. Greater tussock-sedge *Carex*

Adder's-tongue

paniculata is uncommon in Herefordshire, but is well established in the Park. The presence of greater spearwort *Ranunculus lingua* was noted by Ley;[37] it survives and, like orange foxtail *Alopecurus aequalis,* first noted by Purchas & Ley and rediscovered in 1998,[38] occurs at few other sites in the county.

However, amongst the wetland species, it is the fortune of the bladderwort *Utricularia* sp., a free floating carnivorous plant which catches tiny invertebrates in its numerous bladder-like traps,[39] which has attracted most comment over the years. There have been successive announcements of the plant's extinction, and three different specific names have been applied to it, despite it seems, only one species having occurred.

Following the first published record of the plant as greater bladderwort *U. vulgaris* in 1889,[40] the Woolhope Club in 1891 recorded its demise under the presumably erroneous guise of lesser bladderwort *U. minor*;[41] its extinction, as *U. vulgaris*, was reported in 1908.[42] A statement of 1951 that "the cleaning out of a pool in Moccas Park has deprived the county of its only recorded station" for *U. vulgaris*,[43] suggests that it had reappeared prior to this event. It was recorded again in 1963 and 1976 as *U. vulgaris*,[44] and has been observed in varying quantities in many subsequent years, always at the south east end of the Lawn Pool. However, in 1998, a wet year, when water was, unusually, sustained round the entire Pool throughout the summer, *Utricularia* sp. was recorded as flowering well around most of the Pool as well as in the pond to its north.[45] In the interim its identity had been reliably determined as bladderwort *U. australis*.[46]

It is to be hoped that this well known plant continues to attract the interest of botanists, and that when visiting the Park they explore and record in other areas too, including the more inaccessible ones. The flora of the Park is not outstanding but there is much of interest in the Lawn Pool and Upper Park, and given a continued moratorium on those agricultural practices which are damaging to the floristic interest, the gradual natural diversification of the grassland flora of the Lower Park should continue.

Notes

1   Anon (1891).
2   Purchas & Ley (1889); in excess of 70 species are referred to as occurring at "Moccas", but only 19 of these are specifically stated as occurring in Moccas Park. No herbaria have been examined for possible Moccas Park specimens.
3   Ley (1894), Anon (1905), Ley (1908).
4   Oswald & Copeland Watts (1962).
5   Oswald & Copeland Watts (1962).
6   Harding (1977).
7   Whitbread (1982).
8   Thomson & Thomson (1989).
9   Preston & Croft (1991).
10 King, Thomson & Thomson (1993).
11 Simpson (1998).
12 Bingham (1998).
13 Rodwell (1991a,b; 1995a,b).
14 King, Thomson & Thomson (1993), Simpson (1998), Bingham (1998).
15 Latin and English names in this chapter follow Stace (1997); where these differ from those used in community names given by Rodwell (1991a,b; 1995a,b), the synonym as used by Stace is given in brackets. A full list of plants recorded in the Park may be found in Appendix 4.
16 Here, as elsewhere where plants are listed, names are given in taxonomic order following Stace (1997), not in order of frequency.
17 A range of factors may check the growth of bluebell. The impact of fallow deer is unknown and the only study we know of relating to the impact of deer on bluebells is that of Cooke (1997), who discusses the impact of grazing by muntjac *Muntiacus reevesi* on bluebells at Monks Wood NNR, where he has also found an effect on primrose (Cooke 1994). Bluebells in the grassland at Moccas Park appear to be checked by grazing, but sheep and cattle graze here as well as fallow deer, and soil conditions and competition from other plant species are doubtless factors too.
18 Oswald & Copeland Watts (1962). The anthills would have been made by the yellow hill ant *Lasius flavus*.
19 Tom Bowen (pers. comm.).
20 John Phipps (pers. comm.).
21 Simpson (1998).

22 Tom Bowen, Sam Davies, Lawrie Whittall and Les Whittal (pers. comms); it was fired once in the 1970s (1976) (Len Slaney, pers. comm.), but has not been since.

23 Len Slaney (pers. comm.).

24 Readings were taken by R. Neville during a survey for the Medicinal Leech Project (see Chapter 5.5).

25 In 1864 Dr Henry Bull published his classic paper 'The mistletoe in Herefordshire' in the *Transactions* of the Woolhope Club (Bull 1864) and the Club has subsequently published many further original observations on the subject. Records of mistletoe on oak *Quercus* spp. have long attracted particular attention, and seven of only eleven authenticated records of mistletoe currently growing on oak in Britain come from Herefordshire (Box, in press). It was a record of mistletoe on oak which drew an anonymous 'Commissioner' of the Woolhope Club to Moccas Park in 1870. He reports that "the discovery of a new Mistletoe-Oak by the Rev. Sir George H. Cornewall, Bart. on the Moccas Estate [but outside the Park], had an irresistible claim on the immediate attention of your Commissioner" (Anon 1870); both the tree and the mistletoe survive today. Having observed this curiosity, the 'Commissioner' (probably Dr Henry Bull) went on to describe and girth some 90 trees in Moccas Park (see Chapters 3.2 - 3.5). There have never been any reports of mistletoe-oaks from within the current boundaries of Moccas Park, but one reported on the west side of Woodbury Hill (Cornewall 1903), may well have stood in Pritchard's Park Wood, which until the eighteenth century fell within the Park boundary (see Chapter 3.1).

26 Anon (1870).

27 It is not listed as a host in the British Isles by Perring (1973) or Briggs (1995, 1999), although neither offers a fully comprehensive listing, nor does it figure in the list of Herefordshire hosts given by Bull (1864). It seems likely however that some recorders fail to distinguish between the two lime species and the hybrid.

28 Purchas & Ley (1889).

29 Observations by Mike Taylor and others (pers. comms).

30 By contrast Brampton Bryan Deer Park in the north of Herefordshire is a very good site for ferns; part of the explanation may lie in deer not having grazed there for many decades.

31 Cooper & Johnson (1984), Mabey (1996).

32 Purchas & Ley (1889); they attribute the record to the Reverend Robert Blight and cast doubt on his description of the location.

33 Anon (1891).

34 Whitehead (1976).

35 Purchas & Ley (1889) and Ley (1908). Whitehead (1976) cites no records, but the Biological Records Centre has three subsequent records for the county.

36 Ley (1908).

37 Ley (1908).

38 Purchas & Ley (1889), Bingham (1998).

39 At any one time up to 1,000 traps will be set on a single plant leading to as many as a quarter of a million captures per plant per year (Friday & Preston 1997).

40 Purchas & Ley (1889).

41 Anon (1891).

42 Ley (1908).

43 Kendrick (1954). It seems that the Moccas Park *Utricularia* has inadvertently been spread to other sites in the county. Following transplantation of other plant species from the Lawn Pool to a pond near Moccas Church (at SO358433) and subsequently onwards to both a garden pond at Bodenham (at SO530513) and one at Little Dewchurch (at SO538327), *Utricularia* has turned up at all three sites (Dr Anthea Brian, pers. comm.).

44 Anon (1963), Whitehead (1976).

45 Bingham (1998).

46 Preston & Croft (1991). *U. vulgaris* and *U. australis* are very closely related and have been confused for years; whilst flowering plants can on close examination be distinguished, vegetative distinctions between the two species are slight and too variable to give an absolutely certain identification. *U. minor* is however a distinct species and this confusion is more surprising (Preston & Croft 1997). Specimens gathered by the Rev. A. Ley on 6 September 1872 and placed in herbaria at the British Museum and Kew have recently been confirmed as *U. australis* (Chris Preston, pers. comm.).

References relating to Moccas Park

ANON. 1870. Incidental notes on remarkable trees in Herefordshire. *Transactions of the Woolhope Naturalists' Field Club*, 288-321.

ANON. 1891. Notes of field meeting, Tuesday, August 25th, 1891. *Transactions of the Woolhope Naturalists' Field Club*, 221-223.

ANON. 1905. Notes additional to the 'Flora of Herefordshire'. *Transactions of the Woolhope Naturalists' Field Club*, 69-152.

ANON. 1963. List of flora found in Moccas Park and district. Manuscript list, English Nature files.

BINGHAM, J. 1998. Moccas Park NNR, National Vegetation Classification report. Report to English Nature.

CORNEWALL, G. 1903. Presidential address. *Transactions of the Woolhope Naturalists' Field Club*, 97-106.

HARDING, P.T. 1977. *Moccas Deer Park, Hereford and Worcester: a report on the history, structure and natural history.* Unpublished report to the Nature Conservancy Council by the Institute of Terrestrial Ecology, Huntingdon.

KENDRICK, F.M. 1954. The botany of Herefordshire. *In*: ANON, ed. *Herefordshire, its natural history, archaeology, and history. Chapters to celebrate the centenary of the Woolhope Naturalists' Field Club.* Hereford: Woolhope Club, 48-59.

KING, N., THOMSON, S.E. & THOMSON, P. 1993. Moccas Park NNR, vegetational recording. Report to English Nature.

LEY, A. 1894. Records of Herefordshire plants additional to those published in the 'Flora of Herefordshire'. Supplement to *Transactions of the Woolhope Naturalists' Field Club*.

LEY, A. 1908. Botany. *Victoria History of the county of Herefordshire*. Vol.1, 39-76. London: Constable.

OSWALD, P. H. & COPELAND WATTS, E. 1962. Report on Moccas Deer Park, Herefordshire. Internal report, Nature Conservancy.

PRESTON, C.D. & CROFT, J.M. 1991. Moccas Park Lake, list of plant species recorded on 6 August 1991. List for Institute of Terrestrial Ecology.

PURCHAS, W.R. & LEY, A. 1889. *A flora of Herefordshire*. Hereford: Jakeman & Carver.

SIMPSON, D. 1998. Notes on the ground flora of Moccas Park, visited 27 March and 15 May 1998. Report to English Nature.

THOMSON, S.E. & THOMSON, P. 1989. Moccas Park lake. Report to Nature Conservancy Council.

WHITBREAD, A. 1982. Moccas Park, Hereford and Worcester; habitat survey. Internal report, Nature Conservancy Council.

WHITEHEAD, L.E. 1976. *Plants of Herefordshire, a handlist*. Hereford: Herefordshire Botanical Society.

Other references

BOX, J.D. In press. Mistletoe *Viscum album* L. (Loranthaceae) on oaks in Britain. *Watsonia*.

BRIGGS, J. 1995. Mistletoe - distribution, ecology and the national survey. *British Wildlife*, 7, 75-82.

BRIGGS, J. 1999. *Kissing goodbye to mistletoe?* London: Plantlife.

BULL, H.G. 1864. The mistletoe in Herefordshire. *Transactions of the Woolhope Naturalists' Field Club*, 59-108.

COOKE, A.S. 1994. Colonisation by muntjac deer *Muntiacus reevesi* and their impact on vegetation. *In*: M.E. MASSEY & R.C. WELCH, eds. *Monks Wood National Nature Reserve. The experience of 40 years 1953-1993*. Peterborough: English Nature, 45-61.

COOKE, A.S. 1997. Effects of grazing by muntjac (*Muntiacus reevesi*) on bluebells (*Hyacinthoides non-scripta*) and a field technique for assessing feeding activity. *Journal of the Zoological Society of London*, 242, 365-369.

COOPER, M.R. & JOHNSON, A.W. 1984. *Poisonous plants in Britain and their effects on animals and man*. London: HMSO.

FRIDAY, L.E. & PRESTON, C.D. 1997. Aquatic plants and communities. *In*: L.E. FRIDAY, ed. *Wicken Fen, the making of a nature reserve*. Colchester: Harley Books, 22-45.

MABEY, R. 1996. *Flora Britannica*. London: Sinclair-Stevenson.

PERRING, F. 1973. Mistletoe. *In*: P.S. GREEN. ed. *Plants: wild and cultivated*. Hampton: Classey, 139-145.

PRESTON, C.D. & CROFT, J.M. 1997. *Aquatic plants in Britain and Ireland*. Colchester: Harley Books.

RODWELL, J.S. 1991a. *British plant communities. Volume 1: woodlands and scrub*. Cambridge: Cambridge University Press.

RODWELL, J.S. 1991b. *British plant communities. Volume 2: mires and heaths*. Cambridge: Cambridge University Press.

RODWELL, J.S. 1995a. *British plant communities. Volume 3: grassland and montane communities*. Cambridge: Cambridge University Press.

RODWELL, J.S. 1995b. *British plant communities. Volume 4: aquatic communities, swamps and tall herb fens*. Cambridge: Cambridge University Press.

STACE, C. 1997. *New flora of the British Isles*. Second edition. Cambridge: Cambridge University Press.

Saproxylic invertebrates

Roger S. Key

and the conservation evaluation of British parklands

.... dying and dead wood provides one of the two or three greatest resources for animal species in a natural forest .... if fallen timber and slightly decayed trees are removed the whole system is impoverished of perhaps more than a fifth of its fauna.

Charles Elton (1966). *The pattern of animal communities.*

Information about saproxylic invertebrates has played an essential role in establishing the importance of some types of British woodlands, in particular wood-pastures, and in defining priorities for the conservation of saproxylic species and their habitats. This chapter explores how this process has developed over a period of more than 20 years and the very important place of Moccas Park and its fauna of saproxylic invertebrates in that process.

Saproxylic invertebrates

Saproxylic species are those that depend on wood, usually but not always dead and decaying wood, for some part of their life-cycle. They include species that feed on wood, decaying or otherwise, those that feed on fungi in or on wood, that predate or parasitise other saproxylic species, and those that depend on other features provided by wood or other saproxylic species, such as the empty burrows of wood-boring insects (Figure 5.1.1).

Many species of saproxylic invertebrates occupy very specific niches, some of which are rare and found only on very ancient trees, for example wood-mould in the heart rot cavities of old oaks. Some saproxylic species also have poor powers of dispersal and colonisation. These factors and the general scarcity of old trees in the present-day landscape of most of Europe, means that many saproxylic species are considered to be among the rarest invertebrates in both Britain and mainland Europe.[1]

Species that exhibit strong fidelity to habitat and limited powers of dispersal, lend themselves to be used as indicators of habitat quality and stability. Many species of saproxylic invertebrates are indicative, in Britain, of long continuity of appropriate ecological conditions associated with ancient trees. Use of such indicator species has enabled important wood-pasture sites to be identified and prioritized for nature conservation, not only for the biotope and its habitats, but also for the species themselves.

It has been estimated that there are more than 1600 species of saproxylic invertebrates in Britain.[2] These species come from many groups, but the majority are beetles (Coleoptera) and flies (Diptera). Knowledge about the occurrence, biology and ecology of such species has been obtained by recording (collecting, observing, breeding and rearing) specimens of both adults and immature stages. Many species have short seasons as adult insects, a few days or a couple of weeks at most, and finding the immature stages of many species often requires small scale disturbance of the dead wood habitat and then rearing larvae or pupae through to the

Some saproxylic insects.
Drawings by Peter Kirby

5
—
1

Figure 5.1.1

Habitats for saproxylic invertebrates. A diagrammatic veteran tree showing some of the important habitats for saproxylic invertebrates. Reproduced by courtesy of the Corporation of London.

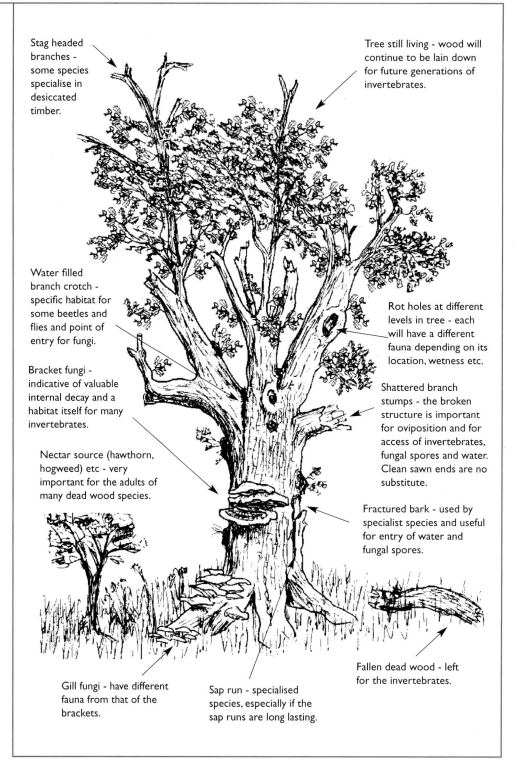

Stag headed branches - some species specialise in desiccated timber.

Tree still living - wood will continue to be lain down for future generations of invertebrates.

Water filled branch crotch - specific habitat for some beetles and flies and point of entry for fungi.

Rot holes at different levels in tree - each will have a different fauna depending on its location, wetness etc.

Bracket fungi - indicative of valuable internal decay and a habitat itself for many invertebrates.

Shattered branch stumps - the broken structure is important for oviposition and for access of invertebrates, fungal spores and water. Clean sawn ends are no substitute.

Nectar source (hawthorn, hogweed) etc - very important for the adults of many dead wood species.

Fractured bark - used by specialist species and useful for entry of water and fungal spores.

Fallen dead wood - left for the invertebrates.

Gill fungi - have different fauna from that of the brackets.

Sap run - specialised species, especially if the sap runs are long lasting.

adult stage.[3] Various trapping techniques have been used to collect adult saproxylic insects, the most effective being various forms of interception trap and emergence traps that retain individuals emerging from specific pieces of timber.[4] However, whether as adults or immature stages, the techniques for finding one species may be inappropriate for many other species.

Because many saproxylic invertebrates are attractive (at least to entomologists), colourful and rare, there is, and always has been, a certain satisfaction in having found such species. Private and museum collections contain many specimens and the British literature is full of records.

Even so, we know little about the detailed ecological requirements of even our commonest saproxylic species and very little indeed of our rarest species.

The activities of a few entomologists, over a period of 150 years, has left a legacy of distributional information and scattered anecdotal descriptions of the habitats of saproxylic species in Britain. When using this information in practical nature conservation we must recognise the limitations of the completeness and relevance of the information. All too often the professional conservation worker has only a list of species for a site, with a few rarities highlighted. This was the case with Moccas Park in the early 1960s. The following sections describe how such lists have been used in establishing nature conservation priorities and actions.

Evaluation of saproxylic species

Indicator species of the mature timber habitat

In 1976, the Nature Conservancy Council (NCC) commissioned the Institute of Terrestrial Ecology to evaluate sites of importance for the conservation of the fauna of what was then referred to as the 'mature timber habitat'. This part-time three-year study concentrated on pasture-woodlands in lowland Britain, which contained what are now referred to as 'veteran trees'. Most of the sites covered by the study were parks, former royal forests and chases and wooded commons. A similar, but longer term programme of site surveys had been in hand for several years to evaluate sites for their epiphyte flora, especially lichens. The individual results of these two studies were described in many, mainly unpublished reports,[5] but the results were also brought together and summarised in a report and a publication by Paul Harding and Francis Rose.[6]

These studies provided a breakthrough in the evaluation of the invertebrate fauna and lichen flora of such sites using simple numerical scoring techniques. In 1974 and 1976, Rose published lists of epiphytic lichens (and bryophytes) that he described as being "faithful to old oak, or mixed deciduous forest in lowland Britain", including preliminary attempts to compare sites based on the presence of these 'indicator' species.[7] After consulting with several nationally recognised experts, Harding compiled lists of species of beetles, flies, spiders, pseudoscorpions and one ant associated with the mature timber habitat.[8] The beetles were graded on a simple three-point scale on the perceived strength of this association, selecting species thought to be indicative of the ecological and historical continuity of their habitat.

Owing to a lack of suitably standardised data on the occurrence of species, the list of beetles as indicators was not used in site-to-site comparisons, but a short study of the literature enabled lists of the 99 most habitat-faithful species of beetles to be compiled for 76 localities.[9] Some years later, with a little more data, 11 sites were compared using a subset of 74 habitat-faithful and nationally threatened species of what were by now known as 'saproxylic' beetles.[10] This was not the first time that a comparison of sites had been attempted using lists of selected species, but it included many more species and more sites.[11]

In the comparison of 11 sites, Moccas Park had the fourth longest list, with only the much larger and better worked localities of Windsor Forest and Great Park, the New Forest and Sherwood Forest achieving higher totals. The fauna of Moccas Park was central to the development of thinking on indicator species. The Park is cited repeatedly in reports and publications as being among the very few sites in Britain where those species with the highest degree of this association with the habitat ("grade 1 species") occur.

The Invertebrate Site Register

In the 1980s, NCC's Invertebrate Site Register (ISR) documented important sites for invertebrates in Britain. In the report for Hereford and Worcester, Moccas Park was described as "A site of national importance - 739 species [of beetle] recorded to date including c. 82 old woodland indicator species, of which 28 are attributable to grade 1 (Harding 1978)".[12] Stuart Ball analyzed the records for Moccas Park in 1989, for the review of the Nature Reserve Agreement then being undertaken by NCC, using the simple Invertebrate Index.[13] Moccas Park scored 4020 for records after 1980, an exceptionally high total. In comparison, Windsor Forest and Great Park, the foremost site for this fauna scored 6530, Sherwood Forest 2110 and Richmond Park 4880. This index scores all species, not just saproxylics, but it is very sensitive to the degree of recording activity and is now seldom used.

Further developments - The Index of Ecological Continuity

Harding's work, ranking beetle species on the strength of their association with saproxylic habitats, led to several similar analyses, including those of hoverflies as indicators of ancient woodlands,[14] and of saproxylic beetles as woodland indicators in the regional context of north/central England.[15]

In 1987, the Royal Entomological Society of London held one of its then rare regional meetings at the University of Leicester on 'Insect indicators of ancient woodland' which was attended by more than 100 people - an unexpectedly large turn-out for such a topic.[16] Keith Alexander of the National Trust proposed an Index of Ecological Continuity (IEC) based on Harding and Rose's list of 196 species,[17] using an approach similar to that developed by Rose for lichen communities in woodland.[18] Alexander ascribed 'points' to the occurrence of particular species at sites employing the grading used by Harding and Rose and based on post-1945 records (later changed to post-1950 for consistency with the ISR).[19]

Ranking of sites

Alexander's methodology was developed further, in 1992, in a paper to a meeting concerning the Conservation of Saproxylic Invertebrates, which was held at Dunham Massey Park, organized by the British Ecological Society.[20] In this paper, a ranked tabulation of key British sites was presented, with Moccas Park now placed third in Britain with an index value of 129. Since then, Alexander has maintained and updated the ranked list and has periodically circulated it to interested parties. Sites scoring 15 or above, of which there are many, are assessed as being of regional importance, those with a value of 25 or above as being of national importance and those with values of 80 or more as being of potential international importance. Using this methodology, some 35 sites are assessed as being of national importance and nine sites as being of international importance.

Moccas Park has remained at third place on this list, the production of which caused some friendly rivalry among beetle recorders and country agency site managers and conservation officers, eager to maintain and promote 'their' site in the rankings. There is competition for third place from Bredon Hill/Elmley Castle Deer Park in neighbouring Worcestershire, a more recently discovered site, where Paul Whitehead has led some intense recording work for several years.[21]

Experimentation with different methods of calculating the IEC, using various arithmetical and geometrical points systems, makes remarkably little difference, if any, to the rankings of the top 15 sites.[22] Moccas Park retains its third place however the scores are calculated, but sites much lower in the ranking vary widely in their position under different scoring systems. With time, it has become clear that the list of species used in the IEC needs revision in the light of recent advances in knowledge of the ecology and ranges of many species.[23]

The Saproxylic Quality Index

In 1997 Adrian Fowles of the Countryside Council for Wales queried the underlying principle behind the IEC as being too dependent on recording effort and overly influenced by the geographical location of a site.[24] These limiting factors had been clearly recognised by Harding in his original 1977 report.

Instead of the IEC, Fowles suggested the development of an index, based on the total number of saproxylic species that have been recorded, rather than just the species of note.[25] This index, the Saproxylic Quality Index (SQI) uses the rarity status of species,[26] rather than the saproxylic groups determined by Harding.[27] SQI goes some way towards taking into account the level of recording undertaken at the site. A minimum of 35 species is needed before the index stabilizes for any site. SQI has the advantage that it can be applied equally to a sample from a site, as well as to a total species list, but equal effort must be made in recording all saproxylic species, not just the rarities.

So far, lists covering all saproxylic species, including all the common ones, are not readily available for all sites, but in refining the index, a wide trawl of cumulative and sample species lists of saproxylic species has been undertaken, from ordinary woodlands as well as parks and wood-pastures throughout Britain. For an accurate assessment, the analyses really need to be performed using data from a defined timespan, rather than a mixture of recent and historical

Table 5.1.1 Saproxylic Quality Index compared with the Index of Ecological Continuity for a selection of parkland sites.

The total numbers of saproxylic species of beetles recorded at each site are given; asterisked sites indicate that comprehensive data have been used from a wide range of sources. At all other sites, the evaluation is based on a single sample survey.

Site	Saproxylic Quality Index	Index of Ecological Continuity	No. saproxylic spp. of beetle
Windsor Forest & Great Park, Berkshire*	847.1	266	365
Richmond Park, Surrey/London*	642.6	140	235
Moccas Park, Herefordshire*	638.4	136	241
Croome Park, Worcestershire	621.5	56	107
Epping Forest, Essex*	598.0	125	256
Ashtead Common, Surrey*	585.6	101	222
Dunham Massey Park, Greater Manchester*	513.8	66	151
Forest of Bere, Hampshire	505.5	46	109
Lullingstone Park, Kent*	486.7	52	105
Staverton Park, Suffolk*	473.6	48	106
Donington Park, Leicestershire*	447.5	43	80
Calke Park, Derbyshire	400.9	47	117
Grimsthorpe Park, Lincolnshire*	387.9	39	99
Powis Castle Park, Powys*	386.5	65	170
Chirk Castle Park, Wrexham*	385.9	67	170
Dinefwr Estate, Carmarthenshire	378.2	58	157
Attingham Park, Shropshire*	363.6	35	88

records. Historically, entomologists have often tended to concentrate on the rarities and may have neglected to record the commoner species, or have not included them when publishing records of species of interest.[28]

Applying this index to the full list of beetles recorded from Moccas Park (see Appendix 5), gives a SQI score of 638.4 using valid records from all dates. Provisional indices have been calculated for almost a hundred additional sites where fairly complete information or comprehensive sample data are available. Some of these have been ranked and are included in Table 5.1.1. More data collation and analysis and, in a few cases, additional surveys may need to be done, before even the most important sites may be compared. For example, appropriate data are not available for the New Forest, the largest wood-pasture site in Britain.

Because of the correction for recording effort, the SQI undoubtedly gives a more realistic comparison between sites than the IEC. Like the IEC, the SQI too has the potential to provide effective threshold values for identifying sites of international and national importance, but it lends itself more easily to meaningful analysis at the regional level. When SQI is fully developed it is hoped that it will give the potential to predict the conservation significance of wood-pastures based on standard methods for rapid surveys, rather than having to undergo the expense and delay inherent in undertaking detailed surveys. It may be some time, however, before sufficient suitable data are available for it to fulfil this potential. The degree of association with continuity of habitat used in the IEC brings added value to its use in analysis of this fauna. Although there are fundamental differences in approach between the methodologies of the two indices, both have particular attractions and an attempt is already being made to bring together the best elements of these two methods of parkland evaluation.

Additional distribution and ecological data for saproxylic species may one day enable us to predict the potential of a site to contain various species and evaluate it against what could reasonably be expected to occur there. Such analyses would have to be based on the known or predicted geographical range of relevant species, the area of a site, and the number and age distribution of the population of trees.

European bio-indicators of site quality

In 1980, the Council of Europe set up a Consultants' Group to identify projects related to invertebrate conservation, which could be incorporated into the Council's future work programme. Several important reports resulted from this initiative; in particular, in 1987, the catalogue of *Invertebrates in need of special protection in Europe*,[29] which drew on earlier and unpublished reports on butterflies, dragonflies and molluscs. This report formed the basis for lists of species to be protected under the Berne Convention and the European Directive on habitats and species.[30] Martin Speight undertook a consultation with entomologists throughout Europe to identify bio-indicators of site quality.[31] A list of species regarded as 'useful in identifying forests of international importance to nature conservation' and a list of European forests 'identified as being of potential international importance by their fauna of saproxylic invertebrates' were prepared. In 1989, the Council of Europe published Speight's report *Saproxylic invertebrates and their conservation*.[32] Speight had used a process, begun in 1982 and similar to that used earlier by Harding and Rose,[33] to compile an inventory of internationally important sites based on a list of saproxylic invertebrates used as bio-indicators of site quality. Moccas Park was one of only five sites included from the United Kingdom and one of the smallest sites identified throughout Europe. Two species recognised in Speight's international criteria are known from Moccas Park, the beetles *Ampedus cardinalis* and *Ischnomera cyanea*. So far, there has been no attempt to develop this methodology further, although the list of bio-indicator species has been revised and the assessment of sites has been extended to cover eastern Europe.[34]

Protection for saproxylic species

Wildlife & Countryside Act

Very few invertebrates are protected by law in Great Britain. The most appropriate legislation for this is Schedule 5 of the 1981 Wildlife & Countryside Act. Listing on Schedule 5 makes the killing or taking of specimens and disturbance of the 'place of shelter' an offence, although *bona fide* researchers can be licensed by English Nature. For a species to be so protected, it or its habitat, must be particularly vulnerable to deliberate human interference, most usually from collecting. Schedule 5 includes only three saproxylic species, *Limoniscus violaceus*, *Lucanus cervus* and *Hypebaeus flavipes*.[35] *Hypebaeus flavipes*, the Moccas beetle, was added to Schedule 5 at the first Quinquennial Review of the Act in 1986.[36] It received full protection in 1987, since when only a few licences have been applied for, to monitor, study or photograph the beetle.

European Directive on habitats and species (1992)

The initial list of invertebrates afforded special protection under the European Directive was derived from the list for the Berne Convention.[37] The Directive did not include any saproxylic species occurring in Britain other than *Limoniscus violaceus* and *Lucanus cervus*. The habitats listed for special protection under the Directive did not include parks and wood-pastures. This is because the selection was based on recognised plant communities and did not consider important structural features of the habitat nor forms of historical management that have created valuable wildlife habitats. Therefore, under the Directive, parkland and wood-pasture did not feature among the habitats that member states are required to conserve as Special Areas of Conservation (SAC). Neither of the listed saproxylic beetles has been recorded at Moccas Park. For these reasons, the Park is not a candidate for SAC status, despite its acknowledged position as a site of international importance using Speight's criteria. Had Moccas Park been a candidate for SAC status it would have attracted considerable attention and probably additional funding for management.

Only a few British sites of importance for saproxylic invertebrates are candidate SACs: the New Forest, Bredon Hill, and Windsor, Sherwood and Epping Forests (see Figure 5.1.2). These are candidates because of the presence of one or both of the above species or because of the presence of other habitat features such as certain types of oak or beech woodland or heathland.

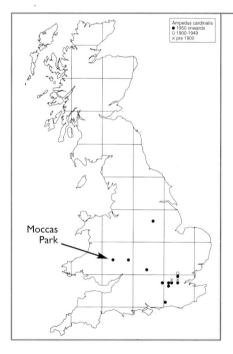

Figure 5.1.2

Distribution of the click beetle *Ampedus cardinalis* in Britain. This beetle is regarded as being a good indicator of important sites for saproxylic invertebrates throughout Europe. It has been recorded at three of the four British sites listed as candidate Special Areas of Conservation for saproxylic species. Reproduced by courtesy of Howard Mendel and the Biological Records Centre, Monks Wood.

5

1

UK Biodiversity Action Plan

The United Kingdom signed the Biodiversity Convention at the Earth Summit at Rio de Janeiro in 1992. Following the publication of *Biodiversity: the UK Action Plan* in 1994, the implementation of this governmental plan has been via the UK Biodiversity Steering Group and several subgroups. The Biodiversity Challenge consortium of voluntary conservation organizations produced two reports to provide a stimulus to the debate in official circles, including lists of species and habitats that were perceived (by the consortium) to be threatened.[38] These lists have formed the basis of official lists of prioritised species published

The UK
Biodiversity
Action Plan
Logo.

by the UK Biodiversity Steering Group.[39] However, the lists were reviewed in 1997 and now include 15 saproxylic species, of which four occur at Moccas Park: *Hypebaeus flavipes*, *Ampedus cardinalis*, *Ampedus rufipennis* and *Gastrallus immarginatus*. A specific conservation action plan has been prepared for the last species and a joint 'priority statement' has been prepared for the other three, in combination with a further seven species that do not occur at Moccas Park.[40] These will be taken forward in conjunction with the Habitat Action Plan for the conservation of parkland and wood-pasture.[41]

Natural Areas - a new approach to nature conservation

English Nature, the statutory conservation agency for England, is currently reviewing the way it evaluates the wildlife resource and determines conservation priorities. English Nature has developed the framework of Natural Areas, areas of coherent biogeographic identity, upon which to target nature conservation effort.[42] Important habitats and species are described in Natural Area profiles and targets set for conservation action, partly based on the Biodiversity

Figure 5.1.3

Moccas Park in relation to English Nature's Natural Areas.
The Park lies within the Black Mountains and Golden Valley Natural Area.

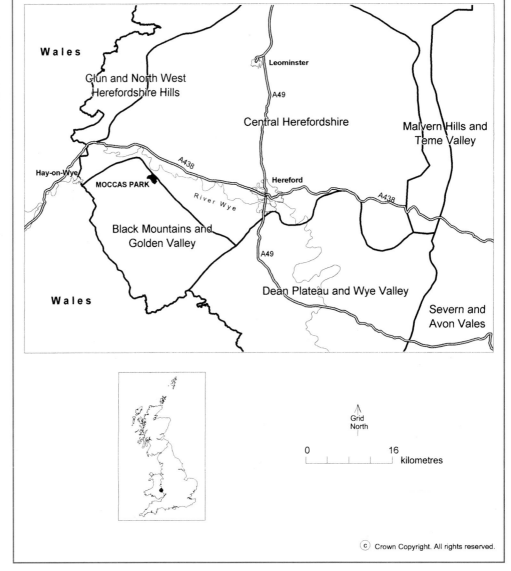

© Crown Copyright. All rights reserved.

Action Plan (above). Moccas Park is included in the Black Mountains and Golden Valley Natural Area, where parklands and saproxylic invertebrates are recognised as key features of nature conservation importance and the Park is cited as the most important site (Figure 5.1.3). Nature conservation targets include identification of the extent and condition of the parkland resource and its fauna. As part of this process, several parkland sites have been, or are currently being notified as Sites of Special Scientific Interest on the basis of their evaluation using the IEC and SQI.

In conclusion

Whatever method of evaluation is used, the saproxylic fauna of Moccas Park makes it one of the three or four most important sites in Britain and one of the few British sites currently recognised to be of international importance for this fauna. The advanced level of knowledge of the fauna of the site has led to its crucial role in the initial development of evaluation methodology. Moccas Park is one of the few sites where the level of information is sufficiently extensive and accessible for more advanced forms of analysis to be tested, analysis which may enable biases induced by varying levels of recording effort to be eliminated. It was, therefore, highly appropriate for Moccas Park to be chosen as the focal point for the 1998 Parklands Symposium.[43] A major theme of the Symposium was the development and integration of evaluation techniques using saproxylic faunas. It is certain that Moccas Park will continue to have a profound influence on the development of such techniques, as it will on other aspects of parkland conservation.

Notes

1   Speight (1989), Good & Speight (1996).
2   Alexander (unpublished).
3   See Hunter (1977), Leseigneur (1972) and Speight (1989) for illustrated examples of the range of niches occupied by saproxylic invertebrates.
4   For examples see Hammond & Harding (1991).
5   Most of the reports are listed in Harding & Rose (1986).
6   Rose & Harding (1978), Harding & Rose (1986).
7   Rose (1974, 1976). Rose (1974) described this epiphyte flora thus "They could therefore be regarded as indicator species in two senses: a. as ecological indicators of the existence of a particular type of forest environment at the present time; b. as historical indicators of lack of environmental change within certain critical limits, over a long period of time." In the same chapter Rose notes that "similar phenomena can be seen among the Coleoptera and Hemiptera in the forest fauna".
8   See Harding (1977). The experts consulted were A.A.Allen, P.J.Chandler, E.A.G.Duffey, F.A.Hunter, C.Johnson, P.E.Jones, P.Skidmore, A.E.Stubbs and R.C.Welch.
9   Harding (1978).
10 Harding & Rose (1986) Appendix 3.
11 Allen (1966) compared the occurrence of 28 species at Windsor Forest with three other sites. Welch & Harding (1974) compared the occurrence of 10 species at Staverton Park with six other sites, including Moccas Park.
12 Steel (1985). Steel's use of the term "old woodland indicator" does not imply a wholly new concept of indicator species; it is one of several examples where Harding's 1977 list was being applied (to some extent incorrectly) by others to a wider range of woodland types, in addition to that which he originally identified and which is now termed 'wood-pasture'.
13 The Invertebrate Index is described by Ball (1986).
14 Stubbs (1982), Whiteley (1987).
15 Garland (1983).
16 For a summary of the meeting see Welch (1988).
17 Harding & Rose (1986).
18 Rose (1976).
19 For a description of the method used see Harding & Alexander (1994).
20 Harding & Alexander (1993).
21 Whitehead (1996).
22 K.N.A.Alexander (unpublished data) and R.S.Key (unpublished data).
23 See also Hammond & Harding (1991).
24 Fowles (1997).
25 Eyre & Rushton (1989) describe the methodolgy for a Species Quality Index using invertebrates. Alexander (unpublished) includes a comprehensive list of British and Irish saproxylic invertebrates, which is available to appropriate specialists.
26 See Hyman & Parsons (1992, 1994).
27 A full description of the Saproxylic Quality Index, together with a list of qualifying species and SQI scores for selected sites are given by Fowles, Alexander & Key (1999).
28 This problem applies even at Moccas Park, see Chapter 5.3.

29 Collins & Wells (1987).
30 The Berne Convention: *Convention on the conservation of European wildlife and natural habitats* (1979). European Community Council (92/43/EEC) *Directive on the conservation of natural and semi-natural habitats of wild fauna and flora*.
31 Dr M.C.D.Speight is an insect ecologist and conservationist with special interests in Diptera and saproxylic faunas in Europe.
32 Speight (1989).
33 Rose & Harding (1978), Harding & Rose (1986).
34 Good & Speight (1996).
35 Only *Hypebaeus flavipes* occurs at Moccas Park, see Chapter 5.2 for more details.
36 *Hypebaeus flavipes* was proposed for addition by the NCC's Chief Scientist's Directorate and West Midlands Region staff. They were concerned about repeated requests from entomologists to collect the species, as well as reports of visits by collectors without permission. They were also mindful that to search for it, other than in early summer, it may be necessary to damage the ancient timber in which it lives.
37 Collins & Wells (1987).
38 Wynne *et al.* (1993, 1995).
39 UK Biodiversity Steering Group (1995), UK Biodiversity Group (1998a).
40 UK Biodiversity Group (1999).
41 UK Biodiversity Group (1998b).
42 English Nature and the Countryside Commission, with help from English Heritage, produced a map of England which depicts the natural and cultural dimensions of the landscape (English Nature/Countryside Commission 1996). This map, and the accompanying descriptions, provide building blocks for landscape and nature conservation in a single, easily understood framework, within which English Nature has defined its Natural Areas.
43 Bullock & Alexander (1998).

References relating to Moccas Park

BULLOCK, D.J. & ALEXANDER, K.N.A. eds. 1998. Parklands - the way forward, 19-21 May 1998, Hereford, Proceedings. *English Nature Research Reports*, No 295.

HARDING, P.T. 1977. *Second report to the Nature Conservancy Council on the fauna of the mature timber habitat.* (CST report No 103). Banbury: Nature Conservancy Council.

HARDING, P.T. 1978. *A bibliography of the occurrence of certain woodland Coleoptera in Britain, with special reference to timber-utilising species associated with old trees in pasture-woodlands.* (CST report No 161). Banbury: Nature Conservancy Council.

HARDING, P.T. & ALEXANDER, K.N.A. 1993. The saproxylic invertebrates of historic parklands: progress and problems. *In*: K.J. KIRBY & C.M. DRAKE, eds. *Dead wood matters: the ecology and conservation of saproxylic invertebrates in Britain.* (English Nature Science No 7.) Peterborough: English Nature, 58-73.

HARDING, P.T. & ALEXANDER, K.N.A. 1994. The use of saproxylic invertebrates in the selection and evaluation of areas of relic forest in pasture-woodlands. *British Journal of Entomology and Natural History*, 7 (Supplement 1), 21-26.

HARDING, P.T. & ROSE, F. 1986. *Pasture-woodlands in lowland Britain. A review of their importance for wildlife conservation.* Huntingdon: Institute of Terrestrial Ecology.

ROSE, F. & HARDING, P.T. 1978. *Pasture-woodlands in lowland Britain and their importance for the conservation of the epiphytes and invertebrates associated with old trees.* (A draft paper produced partly under the NCC/NERC contract HF3/03/118). (CST Report no. 211) Banbury: Nature Conservancy Council.

SPEIGHT, M.C.D. 1989. *Saproxylic invertebrates and their conservation.* Nature and environment series, No 42. Strasbourg: Council of Europe.

STEEL, C. 1985. Review of the sites in England. Provisional Review of Hereford and Worcester. *Invertebrate Site Register Reports*, No 59. London: Nature Conservancy Council.

WELCH, R.C. & HARDING, P.T. 1974. A preliminary list of the fauna of Staverton Park, Suffolk. Part 2, Insecta: Coleoptera. *Suffolk natural history*, 16, 287-304.

Other references

ALEXANDER, K.N.A. (unpublished). *An annotated checklist of the invertebrates of living and decaying timber in Britain and Ireland.*

ALLEN, A.A. 1966. The rarer Sternoxia (Col.) of Windsor Forest. *Entomologist's Record and Journal of Variation*, 78, 14-23.

BALL, S.G. 1986. Terrestrial and freshwater invertebrates with Red Data Book, Notable or habitat indicator status. *Invertebrate Site Register Reports*, 66. Peterborough: Nature Conservancy Council.

COLLINS, N.M. & WELLS, S.M. 1987. *Invertebrates in need of special protection in Europe.* Nature and environment series, No 35. Strasbourg: Council of Europe.

ELTON, C.S. 1966. *The pattern of animal communities.* London: Methuen.

ENGLISH NATURE/COUNTRYSIDE COMMISSION. 1996. *The Character of England, wildlife and natural features.* Peterborough: English Nature/Countryside Commission.

EYRE, M.D. & RUSHTON, S.P. 1989. Quantification of conservation criteria using invertebrates. *Journal of Applied Ecology*, 26, 159-171.

FOWLES, A.P. 1997. The Saproxylic Quality Index: an evaluation of dead wood habitats based on rarity scores, with examples from Wales. *The Coleopterist*, 6, 61-66.

FOWLES, A.P., ALEXANDER, K.N.A. & KEY, R.S. 1999. The Saproxylic Quality Index: evaluating wooded habitats for the conservation of dead-wood Coleoptera. *The Coleopterist*, 8, 121-141.

GARLAND, S.P. 1983. Beetles as primary woodland indicators. *Sorby Record*, 21, 338.

GOOD, J.A. & SPEIGHT, M.C.D. 1996. *Saproxylic invertebrates and their conservation throughout Europe*. Paper T-PVS (96) 31 for the Standing Committee of the Convention on the conservation of European wildlife and natural habitats. Strasbourg: Council of Europe.

HAMMOND, P.M. & HARDING, P.T. 1991. Saproxylic invertebrate assemblages in British woodlands: their conservation significance and evaluation. *In*: H.J. READ, ed. *Pollard and veteran tree management*. London: Corporation of London, 30-37.

HUNTER, F.A. 1977. Ecology of pinewood beetles. *In*: R.G.H. BUNCE & J.N.R. JEFFERS, eds. *Native pinewoods of Scotland*. Cambridge: Institute of Terrestrial Ecology, 42-55.

HYMAN, P.S. & PARSONS, M.S. 1992. A review of the scarce and threatened Coleoptera of Great Britain. Part 1. *UK Nature Conservation*, 3. Peterborough: Joint Nature Conservation Committee.

HYMAN, P.S. & PARSONS, M.S. 1994. A review of the scarce and threatened Coleoptera of Great Britain. Part 2. *UK Nature Conservation*, 12. Peterborough: Joint Nature Conservation Committee.

ROSE, F. 1974. The epiphytes of oak. *In*: M.G. MORRIS & F.H. PERRING, eds. *The British oak, its history and natural history*. Faringdon: Classey.

ROSE, F. 1976. Lichenological indicators of age and environmental continuity in woodlands. *In*: D.H. BROWN, D.L. HAWKSWORTH & R.H. BAILEY, eds. *Lichenology: progress and problems*. London: Academic Press, 279-307.

LESEIGNEUR, L. 1972. Coléoptères Elateridae de la faune de France continental et de Corse. *Bulletin mensuel de la Société linnéenne de Lyon*, 41 (Supplement).

STUBBS, A.E. 1982. Hoverflies as primary woodland indicators with reference to Wharncliffe Wood. *Sorby Record*, 20, 62-67.

UK BIODIVERSITY GROUP 1998a. *Tranche 2 Action Plans - Volume I - vertebrates and vascular plants*. Peterborough: English Nature on behalf of the UK Biodiversity Group.

UK BIODIVERSITY GROUP 1998b. *Tranche 2 Action Plans - Volume II - terrestrial and freshwater habitats*. Peterborough: English Nature on behalf of the UK Biodiversity Group.

UK BIODIVERSITY GROUP 1999. *Tranche 2 Action Plans - Volume III - invertebrates*. Peterborough: English Nature on behalf of the UK Biodiversity Group.

UK BIODIVERSITY STEERING GROUP 1995. *Biodiversity: The UK Steering Group Report*. 2 volumes. London: HMSO.

WELCH, R.C. 1988. Insect indicators of ancient woodland. *Antenna*, 12, 69-71.

WHITEHEAD, P.F. 1996. The notable arboreal Coleoptera of Bredon Hill, Worcestershire, England. *The Coleopterist*, 5, 45-53.

WHITELEY, D. 1987. Hoverflies of the Sheffield area. *Sorby Record, special series*, 6.

WYNNE, G., AVERY, M., CAMPBELL, L., GUBBAY, S., HAWKSWELL, S., JUNIPER, T., KING, M., NEWBERY, P., SMART, J., STEEL, C., STONES, T., STUBBS, A., TAYLOR, J., TYDEMAN, C. & WYNDE, R. 1993. *Biodiversity challenge: an agenda for conservation in the UK*. Sandy: Royal Society for the Protection of Birds.

WYNNE, G., AVERY, M., CAMPBELL, L., GUBBAY, S., HAWKSWELL, S., JUNIPER, T., KING, M., NEWBERY, P., SMART, J., STEEL, C., STONES, T., STUBBS, A., TAYLOR, J., TYDEMAN, C. & WYNDE, R. 1995. *Biodiversity challenge: an agenda for conservation in the UK* (second edition). Sandy: Royal Society for the Protection of Birds.

5/1

Hypebaeus flavipes (F.) (Coleoptera, Melyridae): the so called '*Moccas beetle*'

J. Cooter

Whenever I hear of the capture of rare beetles, I feel like an old war horse at the sound of a trumpet.

Attributed to Charles Darwin (1809-1882).[1]

The early years

Moccas Park was almost certainly first brought to the notice of coleopterists with the finding, by J.R.le B.Tomlin on 26 June 1934, of three female specimens of a beetle new to Britain that were subsequently identified as *Ebaeus abietinus* Abeille.[2] Later, the true identity of the beetle as *Hypebaeus flavipes* (F.) was established from male and female specimens collected in the Park by G.H.Ashe.[3] Because *Hypebaeus flavipes* is typical of the Melyridae, in being markedly sexually dimorphic (Figure 5.2.1), the original misidentification is quite understandable as the characters which distinguish each genus are displayed only by males.

There are few published records of insects from Moccas Park prior to 1934 and G.H.Ashe is generally regarded as being the person to put the Park firmly on the entomological map, though his contemporary, R.W.Lloyd, also did much to establish its reputation.[4] Ashe and Lloyd captured and recorded many rare species during the late 1930s through to the 1950s including, *Aulonothroscus brevicollis*, *Pyrrhidium sanguineum* and *Ernoporicus caucasicus* (see Chapter 5.3). For many years *H. flavipes*, *P. sanguineum* and *E.caucasicus* were known in Britain only from Moccas Park. Now only *H. flavipes* is (at least for the present) known from nowhere else in Britain, the other two Moccas Park specialities having been found at a few additional sites (see Chapter 5.3).

Refinding Hypebaeus flavipes

Many years ago I acquired the set of Fowler's *Coleoptera of the British Islands* that had previously been owned by the late G.H.Ashe.[5] Ashe had had the five volume set interleaved and rebound and over the years added numerous annotations on the

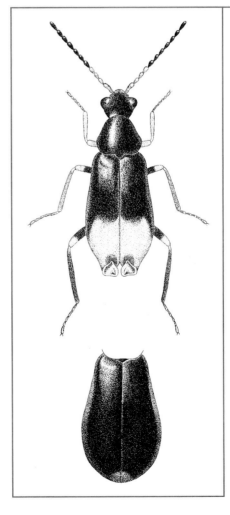

Figure 5.2.1

'**The Moccas beetle**' *Hypebaeus flavipes* (F.). Male (habitus) and female (elytra); same scale. Length = 2·1 mm (elytral apex to anterior margin of head). Original drawing by R.W.J. Read.

5/2

Figure 5.2.2

Sketch (with notes) by G.H.Ashe of the tree in Moccas Park where *Hypebaeus flavipes* was first recorded. Ashe's note reads as follows: "*Hypebaeus flavipes* L. Moccas Park Hereford in numbers. June. Introduced by Tomlin as *Ebaeus abietinus* (Donisthorpe). Blair corrected this 1943 Jan EMM [*Entomologist's monthly Magazine*]. Found by beating old oaks especially those red rotten. Apparently confined to certain trees see map. Especially one with vase shaped trunk. For description see Reitter & fig." [NB Ashe used the word *introduced* to mean that the species had been added to the British list by Tomlin, not an introduction in the sense of the species having been released here from specimens collected somewhere else.]

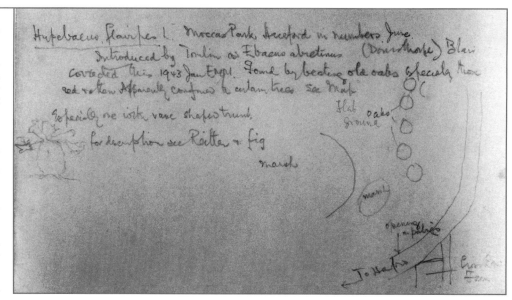

interleaving including, in volume 4 facing page 159, a note about *H. flavipes* with a 'sketch' and location map of the tree under which he swept the beetle (Figure 5.2.2). I made my first visit to Moccas Park in February 1975 and during that summer was easily able to locate 'Ashe's Oak' from the sketch and map and to beat from it specimens of *H. flavipes* on 21 and 26 June and 5 July.[6] Over the years I have found *H. flavipes* on several other ancient oaks in the Park: around the Lawn Pool, on the hillside in the south eastern part and on wind-blown oaks in the northern area. It is generally easy to find from early June to mid-July and sometimes occurs in numbers, a half-dozen specimens on the beating tray at one time not being unusual. Invariably the males appear a week or so before the females, with females surviving for some time after the males have disappeared. In sunny weather, the beetle is very active, an agile runner and readily takes flight. Despite beating the blossoms of hawthorn, field maple and lime regularly over the years, I have never found *H. flavipes* in this way; only by beating the foliage of ancient, usually hollow oaks with 'red-rotten' interiors containing dry, red-coloured dead wood and wood mould or wood dust derived from decayed heartwood. **_Hypebaeus flavipes_ is protected in Britain under the Wildlife and Countryside Act 1981** (see Chapter 5.1).

Hypebaeus flavipes in continental Europe

Hypebaeus flavipes occurs in scattered populations in areas of old woodland in continental Europe, including Scandinavia. Its life-history and ecological requirements are unknown, but it is possible that the larvae are predators on small invertebrates inhabiting burrows in red-rotten oak.

According to Andreas Herrmann, *H. flavipes* is a rare species in Germany and has been found on blossoms or branches of trees standing near large oaks at three sites only in the north east of Niedersachen (north Germany).[7] He once reared four specimens from red-rotten wood mould removed from a hole in a dead standing oak near the village of Grippel, Niedersachen; *Dorcatoma chrysomelina* Sturm and *Pentaphyllus testaceus* (Hellwig) were also present in the mould.

During June 1949, 10 male *H. flavipes* were recorded from a large rotten beech stump riddled with the burrows of sphecid wasps and beetles in the genera *Tomoxia*, *Melasis*, *Sinodendron* and *Ptilinus* at a site near Hornsä, Småland, southern Sweden.[8] Horion states that *H. flavipes* prefers '*Flußauen*' (woodland and trees beside rivers).[9]

Alfons Evers, the acknowledged authority on the Melyridae, finds *H. flavipes* in Germany by beating old hornbeam (*Carpinus betulus*) except in Nikolasee where it occurs on old oak in relict forest.[10] His 29 examples of *H. flavipes*, of which only 10% are males, are from: Saxonia (Leipzig and Dresden); Thueringia (Pössneck and Solkwitz); Hessen (Nassau, Hanan and Schwanheim); Bavaria (Passan); Rhenania (Koblenz); Badenia (Stuhensee (C.Karlsruhe)); Sachsen-Anhalt (Dessan, Harz Mountains (Thale and Ilsenburg)) and Berlin-Brandenburg (Nikolasee).

Notes

1 Crowson (1981).
2 Donisthorpe & Tomlin (1934).
3 Blair & Donisthorpe (1943).
4 See also Chapter 5.4.
5 Fowler (1887-1891).
6 This is the Stag's Horn Oak, now often referred to as 'The *Hypebaeus* tree' (Chapter 3.2).
7 Andreas Herrmann (pers. comm.).
8 Palm (1959).
9 Horion (1953).
10 Alfons Evers (pers. comm.).

References relating to Moccas Park

BLAIR, K.G. & DONISTHORPE, H. St J. 1943. *Hypebaeus flavipes* F. (not *Ebaeus abietinus* Abeille) (Col., Malachiidae) in Britain: a correction. *Entomologist's monthly Magazine,* 79, 16.

DONISTHORPE, H. & TOMLIN, J.R. le B. 1934. *Ebaeus abietinus* Abeille (Malachiidae, Col.) A beetle new to Britain. *Entomologist's monthly Magazine,* 70, 198-199.

Other references

CROWSON, R.A. 1981. *The biology of the Coleoptera.* London: Academic Press.

FOWLER, W.W. 1887-1891. *The Coleoptera of the British Islands.* 5 volumes. London: Reeve.

HORION, A. 1953. *Faunistik der mitteleuropäischen Käfer,* 3, 84-85. Munich: Goeke & Evers.

PALM, T. 1959. Die holz- und rinden-käfer der süd- und mittelschwedischen laufbbäumer. *Opuscula entomologica,* Supplement 16.

5
2

Coleoptera

R. Colin Welch

One thing we know about a divine Creator, supposing one exists, is that he has a particular interest in Coleoptera.

Attributed to Thomas Henry Huxley (1825-1895).[1]

Despite the acknowledged importance of Moccas Park for Coleoptera, it is perhaps surprising that there has never been a comprehensive survey of the beetles of the Park! Present day knowledge of its beetle fauna is based almost entirely on *ad hoc* visits by many specialists over a period of at least 70 years, beginning with George Ashe, Howard Hallett, Robert Lloyd, John Tomlin and, from about 1950, Tony Allen.[2] Since the early 1960s, Moccas Park has been a place of pilgrimage for many British coleopterists, not only because of the rarities for which it is famous, but also because it is rather remote and is not open to public access. However, the relatively small fraternity of British coleopterists is normally generous in sharing information among themselves, and with the conservation agencies, thereby enabling a picture of the beetle fauna to be developed.

Sources of records

More than 60 publications, theses and reports, in nearly as many years, have contained records of Coleoptera from Moccas Park.[3] In addition to these sources, unpublished reports, species lists, letters and other material have been lodged, since 1962, with the Nature Conservancy, Nature Conservancy Council and English Nature.

In 1981, Jonathan Cooter and I drew on these published and unpublished sources in the preparation of an account of the beetle fauna of Moccas Park that also listed 691

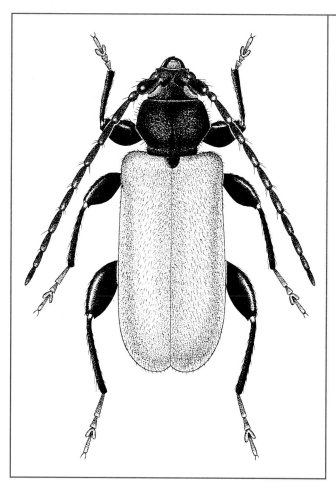

Figure 5.3.1

The longhorn beetle *Pyrrhidium sanguineum.* Length = 9·1 mm (elytral apex to anterior margin of head). Original drawing by R.W.J.Read.

5/3

species known to occur there.[4] To this was added an appendix listing 27 previously unrecorded species, bringing the total to 718 species.[5] The largest source of additional information comes from Cooter's personal records; he has been mainly responsible for increasing the number of Coleoptera known from Moccas Park to over 900 species. A complete catalogue of

unpublished sources has not been prepared, but records from many sources were collated by Stuart Ball in 1989 (see Chapter 5.1).[6] The main unpublished sources used in compiling the 1981 list and the present species list (Appendix 5) are listed at the end of this chapter.

Gaps in knowledge and the need for further work

Most of the coleopterists who have recorded at Moccas Park have concentrated their efforts on the saproxylic species, although a few specialists have examined the aquatic and semi-aquatic fauna of the Lawn Pool and other wet areas in the Park. Few attempts have been made to conduct more general surveys of, for example, tree canopies, pasture grassland, bracken beds or areas of nettles and thistles. As a consequence, there is an apparent absence of several common and widely distributed species which could be expected to occur.

Two major phytophagous families, leaf beetles (Chrysomelidae) and weevils (Curculionidae), appear to be particularly under-represented in the list.[7] Although *Brachypterus glaber*, one of the Nitidulidae associated with nettles, is listed, none of the many species of weevil associated with nettles has been recorded. *Notoxus monoceros* is the only member of the family Anthicidae recorded in the Park, probably because it would seem to be out of place (it occurs mainly at sandy coastal sites), but no species of *Anthicus* has been recorded, probably because it would be considered unremarkable.

Although the list of dung beetles and chafers (Scarabaeidae) is fairly extensive it is interesting to note the presence of *Aphodius porcus*, even if the record dates back to 1929.[8] This species is known to be a 'cuckoo parasite' in burrows of the dor beetle *Geotrupes stercorarius*, but no *Geotrupes* species appear to have been recorded.

Other species typical of open grassland, including several of the larger ground beetles (Carabidae), had not been recorded from the Park until recently, when casual collecting revealed several such species.[9] The canopies of trees have not yet been sampled although techniques such as fogging have been rewarding at other sites.[10] It is probable that a programme of sampling including fogging, pit-fall trapping and intensive sweep-netting of the herbaceous vegetation could add more species to the already impressive list of Coleoptera.

The main objectives of future recording should not be to continue recording the same 'special' species from the same trees, but to complete the picture of the whole beetle fauna throughout the Park and to gain better understanding of the habitat and management requirements of the rare and threatened species. There is also a need for long-term monitoring of the populations of some species, but techniques for this are still in their infancy. For those who are looking for a challenge, there are several 'special' species that have not been seen at Moccas Park for many years, which coleopterists should continue to seek.

The famous three!

The Park is famed for the occurrence of many apparently rare saproxylic species, three of which (*Hypebaeus flavipes*, *Pyrrhidium sanguineum* and *Ernoporicus caucasicus*) have featured prominently in the history of nature conservation at the site (see Chapters 5.1 and 6.1). For comments on Red Data Book (RDB) statuses see below.

❖ ***Hypebaeus flavipes*, Melyridae**
Status: WCA 1981 (schedule 5), RDB 1.
This species is known in Britain only from Moccas Park; see Chapter 5.2.

❖ *Pyrrhidium sanguineum*, Cerambycidae

Status: RDB 2.

The spectacular, carmine-red longhorn beetle, *Pyrrhidium sanguineum* (Figure 5.3.1), was known in Britain from nineteenth century records at widely scattered localities, but all were thought to have been associated with timber introduced from continental Europe.[11] *P.sanguineum* was finally established as a true British species, based on specimens taken by Lloyd at Moccas Park on 12 May 1949, and on several occasions in subsequent years.[12] For more than 20 years this species was found nowhere else in Britain,[13] but it is now known from several woodland and parkland sites in the Welsh border counties (Figure 5.3.2) with post-1980 records from nine 10km grid squares.[14] It is known as a Holocene sub-fossil from Lincolnshire, further confirming that it is native to Britain, but also suggesting that it was formerly more widespread.[15] It appears to breed in freshly broken oak branches and is particularly vulnerable to the removal of newly fallen oak branches from the Park.

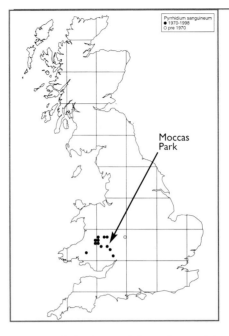

Figure 5.3.2

Distribution of the longhorn beetle *Pyrrhidium sanguineum* in Britain. Reproduced by courtesy of Peter Twinn and the Biological Records Centre, Monks Wood.

❖ *Ernoporicus caucasicus*, Scolytidae[16]

Status: RDB 1.

The third Moccas Park speciality is a small bark beetle, less than 2mm long, associated with small-leaved and hybrid limes (Figure 5.3.3). It was originally thought to be *Ernoporus tiliae*, a species which was known from a few localities in the Midlands. However, in 1969 Allen discovered that specimens, which he had reared from lime twigs collected in Moccas Park during June 1954, were in fact *Ernoporicus caucasicus*, a species new to Britain in modern times.[17] *E.caucasicus* had been recorded previously as Holocene sub-fossil remains in alluvial deposits at Shustoke, Warwickshire, associated with small-leaved and large-leaved lime pollen and fruits, and subsequently at other Holocene sites in similar situations.[18] Other coleopterists subsequently recorded *E.caucasicus* at Moccas Park, but all specimens appear to have been collected from a single, large small-leaved lime growing on the gentle slope just south of the Bodcott (Lawn) Gate. This tree blew down in January 1976 and much of the wood had been removed and burnt by June 1976.[19] In 1980 Cooter collected several specimens of *E.caucasicus* from hybrid limes in the Park,[20] and it has been found subsequently by other coleopterists on hybrid limes, here and at other sites. Recent work by Tony Drane has shown *E.caucasicus* to be widely distributed in the Midlands, occurring in more than twenty 10 km grid squares (Figure 5.3.4); it is probably considerably more common than *E.tiliae*.[21] There are no authenticated records of *E.tiliae* from Moccas Park.

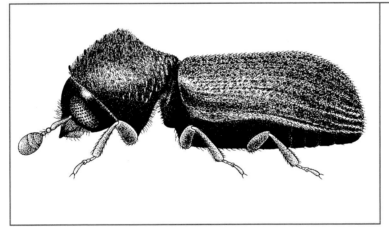

Figure 5.3.3

The lime bark beetle *Ernoporicus caucasicus*. Length = 2 mm (elytral apex to anterior margin of head). Original drawing by R.W.J. Read.

Figure 5.3.4

Distribution of the lime bark beetle _Ernoporicus caucasicus_ in Britain. Reproduced by courtesy of Tony Drane and the Biological Records Centre, Monks Wood.

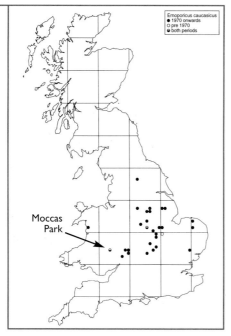

Nationally threatened, rare and uncommon species

This section describes aspects of the occurrence of some of the other more noteworthy species of Coleoptera recorded from the Park. The main method of categorising the national threat status of the British insect fauna is that adopted in 1987 for the Insect Red Data Book, which was updated and expanded for Coleoptera in 1992 and 1994.[22]

The following three species are listed as RDB 1 (Endangered).

❖ **_Anaspis septentrionalis_**, Scraptiidae
Previously known as _Anaspis schilskyana_. John Owen collected one male and one female in the Park in June 1980, and a further pair in June 1981. There are other records, by Cooter, in June and July 1988 and in June in 1990, 1991 and 1993.[23] Unlike other _Anaspis_ species, which occur on hawthorn blossom in May, it occurs on old oak in early June. In Britain, it is known only from Blenheim Park in Oxfordshire, Sherwood Forest in Nottinghamshire, Calke Abbey in Derbyshire and near Aviemore in Scotland.[24]

❖ **_Chrysomela tremula_**, Chrysomelidae
This large leaf beetle is associated with aspen and grey willow. It was recorded by Tomlin from the Park and from at least one other locality within the county.[25] It is now thought to be extinct in Britain, having been seen last in 1957, in Surrey.[26]

❖ **_Malthodes brevicollis_**, Cantharidae
It is believed that the only confirmed occurrence of this small soldier beetle in Britain are from Moccas Park,[27] but a record by Lloyd in 1949 is now thought to be referable to _M.pumilus_, a species which is abundant in the Park. However, Ashe's copy of Fowler's _British Coleoptera_ contains the annotation "vi.1938 in old wood oak + ash".[28] This has a certain authenticity because _M.brevicollis_ is normally found in wood rather than by beating foliage.

Several other saproxylic Coleoptera recorded at Moccas Park are categorised as RDB 2 (Vulnerable).

❖ **_Ampedus cardinalis_**, Elateridae
A red click beetle, which is restricted to a few wood-pasture sites in 11 post-1950 10km grid squares, mainly in the area of Windsor Park and Forest.[29] Its range extends from the New Forest in the south to Sherwood Forest in the north; Moccas Park is the most western locality. It is associated with red-rotten oak. Earlier records from Moccas Park (including that by Hallett under the name of _Elater praeustus_)[30] were confirmed when Peter Hodge recorded it here in May 1980.

❖ **_Ampedus rufipennis_**, Elateridae (Figure 5.3.5)
This red click beetle has a very restricted distribution in Britain. It has been recorded in recent decades only from Moccas Park, Windsor Park and Forest in Berkshire and Bredon Hill in Worcestershire, although Cooter recorded it repeatedly in the 1980s, from a single dead ash tree in a field at Mordiford in Herefordshire.[31] Normally it is associated with rotten wood in beeches.

❖ **_Ischnomera cinerascens_**, Oedemeridae
One female, taken at Moccas Park in May 1965, was not recognised as being this species until 1979 when six specimens were collected at Duncombe Park in Yorkshire and described as new to

Britain.[32]   Later, Howard Mendel confirmed the identity of another specimen, collected by Peter Skidmore in May 1958 at Moccas Park.[33]

❖ *Ischnomera caerulea*, Oedemeridae
This species was recorded by Cooter in May 1988, about 400m north of the Park in the fields between Moccas Court and Park Lodge. Earlier records from the Park may be referable to *I. cyanea*, a more common species.

❖ *Lymexylon navale*, Lymexylonidae
Modern records of this distinctively long, thin beetle were all from the Windsor Forest area and the New Forest until Cooter caught a gravid female at Moccas Park in August 1975. I observed two females ovipositing in freshly sawn oak logs in July 1984 and Andy Godfrey recorded its presence in July 1994.

❖ *Plectophloeus nitidus*, Pselaphidae
This species is known from a few old wood-pastures - Sherwood, Windsor, Blenheim Forests and Moccas Park. It was first found at Moccas by Allen, with *Batrisodes venustus* in May 1950. Cooter took both species together under the thick bark of a huge fallen oak in May 1975.[34] This oak was subsequently damaged by fire and has now been cleared away; *P. nitidus* has not been seen since in the Park.

❖ *Xyletinus longitarsus*, Anobiidae
(Figure 5.3.6) This species was once widely distributed in southern England, but it is now much rarer and was included by Arthur Massee in his 1964 list of rarities from Moccas Park. In recent years, it has been collected from the Park frequently, by Cooter and others, mainly by beating dead oak twigs.[35]

Of the 16 species of Coleoptera recorded from Moccas Park categorised as RDB 3 (Rare), six are closely associated with dead wood in wood-pastures: *Aeletes atomarius* (Histeridae), *Aulonothroscus brevicollis* (Throscidae), *Malthodes crassicornis* (Cantharidae), *Mesosa nebulosa* (Cerambycidae), *Procraerus tibialis* (Elateridae) and *Scraptia testacea* (Scraptiidae). *Nemozoma elongatum* (Trogositidae) is also associated with dead wood, but mainly with elm so that it may be more threatened than its current RDB status implies.

Three species recorded from Moccas Park are categorised as RDB I (Indeterminate), which implies that they merit Red Data Book status but there is not enough information to determine

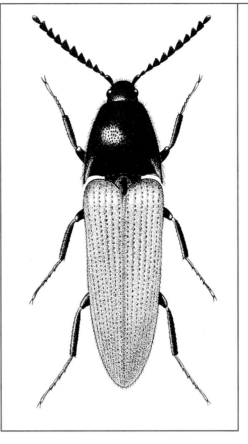

Figure 5.3.5

The click beetle *Ampedus rufipennis*. Length = 11 mm (elytral apex to anterior margin of head). Original drawing by R.W.J. Read.

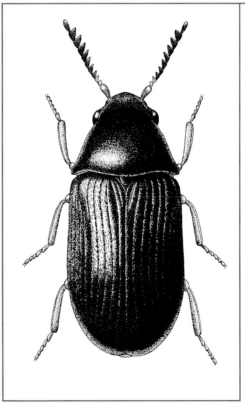

Figure 5.3.6

The beetle *Xyletinus longitarsus*. Length = 6.9 mm (elytral apex to anterior margin of head). Original drawing by R.W.J. Read.

5
3

which category. *Agathidium confusum* (Leiodidae) and *Euplectus nanus* (Pselaphidae) were recorded by Cooter in 1992 and 1994 using flight interception traps.[36] *Philonthus corruscus* (Staphylinidae) was recorded by Tomlin in 1936, but has not been seen since.

A further six species are classed as RDB K (Insufficiently Known), indicating that they may warrant RDB status. Three species are associated with woodlands: *Ptenidium turgidum* (Ptiliidae) occurs within ancient broad-leaved trees, *Hydnobius latifrons* (Leiodidae) probably breeds in subterranean fungi, *Gyrophaena poweri* (Staphylinidae) (see below) and *Mordellistena neuwaldeggiana* (Mordellidae). The last species is often confused with its congeners and its biology is uncertain. The remaining two RDB K species are *Colon dentipes* (Leiodidae) which may have an association with grassland, possibly in wooded areas, and *Schistoglossa viduata* (Staphylinidae) (see below).

Wetland and aquatic species

Most of the species discussed above are associated with trees and woodland. Moccas Park also has an important but less well studied fauna associated with the Lawn Pool and wetland areas nearby. Several species are particularly notable.

❖ **Graphoderus cinereus,** Dytiscidae. Status: RDB 3. The species was known only from the East Anglian fens and East Norfolk, but in 1953 it was found in Woolmer Bog, Hampshire and has since been taken at three localities in Essex, Sussex and Dorset. In March 1966 Robert Angus found it in the marshy part of the Lawn Pool and noted that it was still present in 1973.[37] It was not found by him during his visit in 1990.

❖ **Helophorus nanus** and **Helophorus strigifrons**, Hydrophilidae. Status: both are Scarce. Angus found both species to be numerous in one of the small pools in May 1965 with few in the Lawn Pool. *H.nanus* is a very local species and although *H.strigifrons* is more widely distributed, it is somewhat sporadic in occurrence. Angus reported that both species were in the "ditch-marsh" in April 1990, with a few *H.nanus* in the Lawn Pool.

Four other aquatic RDB 3 species have been recorded from the Lawn Pool, but records of three species (*Bagous collignensis*, *Bagous frit* and *Dryops anglicanus*) require confirmation (see below). The fourth species is *Hydrochus elongatus* (Hydrophilidae), which was recorded by Angus in 1965 and 1973, but not in 1990.

The marshy margins of the Lawn Pool also support several other rare fenland species.

❖ **Schistoglossa viduata**, Staphylinidae. Status: RDB K. Ashe is reported to have taken *S.viduata* "in considerable quantity - by sweeping rushes bordering the lake in Moccas Park".[38] It was also collected by Cooter on two occasions in May 1975. Moccas Park and a West Norfolk fen are believed to be the only sites at which this species has been recorded since 1969.[39]

Other species recorded in this area include the Staphylinidae *Atheta (Dilacra) vilis* and *Stenus formicetorum*. Cooter found the ground beetle *Bembidion quadripustulatum* (Carabidae) to be quite common around the Lawn Pool in 1977. Moccas Park is at the westerly limits of the known distribution of this species in Britain.

Important species not recorded for many years

Several threatened, rare or nationally scarce species, which have appeared on the list of beetles recorded from Moccas Park, have not been recorded in recent decades. Some of these species are now known to have been incorrectly identified, or are too improbable to be accepted (see Corrections section of Appendix 5). Other species have simply not been seen in recent years: some are believed to have declined nationally and may have been lost from the Park, but others may simply have been overlooked. The following species have not been recorded for many years, but, in addition, several species (not listed here) do not appear to have been seen at Moccas Park since the 1970s.

❖ *Abdera flexuosa*, Melandryidae. Recorded in Massee's 1964 list, but not seen since and requires confirmation. It is associated with fungi in dead wood.

❖ *Aderus populneus*, Aderidae. Massee, in his 1964 list, recorded this species and *A.occulatus* 'by beating deciduous trees'. Although the latter occurs widely and is not uncommon in the county, *A.populneus* requires confirmation. Both species are associated with dead wood.

❖ *Anitys rubens*, Anobiidae. Listed by Massee in his 1964 list, but probably based on 1940s records. Cooter reports searching many times in the Park for this characteristic component of the fauna of decaying oaks, but without success.

❖ *Aphodius porcus*, Scarabaeidae. Last recorded 1929. See earlier comments.

❖ *Bagous collignensis* and *Bagous frit* Curculionidae. Massee recorded *B.collignensis* as "subaquatic; banks of lake" in his 1964 list, but there is possible confusion with Tomlin's record of *B.frit* from "Moccas Pool, 26 June 1934, shaken from dead reeds". The identity of any *Bagous* species from the Park requires confirmation.

❖ *Chrysomela tremula*, Chrysomelidae. Last recorded before 1939. See earlier comments.

❖ *Dryops anglicanus*, Dryopidae. Recorded from "Moccas Pool" in June 1939. It has not been found during subsequent visits by appropriate specialists (Angus, Cooter and Garth Foster). According to Cooter, there is some doubt about the reliability of the original identification.

❖ *Gyrophaena poweri*, Staphylinidae. Recorded by Ashe in June 1935. It is associated with fungi in woodland.

❖ *Philonthus corruscus*, Staphylinidae. Recorded by Tomlin in June 1936. The last known British record was from Surrey in 1944. It is associated with decaying straw and carrion.

❖ *Prionus coriarius*, Cerambycidae. Recorded from Moccas Park by Hallett, probably in the 1930s, and also included in Massee's 1964 list. It breeds in the exposed roots and bases of ancient broad-leaved trees, especially oak. The large, cumbersome, adult beetle is crepuscular, but it is easily found where it occurs frequently, such as in West Sussex and Essex. The absence of any recent records from the Park (or from anywhere else in the county) may reflect a national decline in this species.

❖ *Tropideres sepicola*, Anthribidae. Last recorded in 1948. There are few recent British records of this species, which is typical of dead wood in wood-pastures.

The habitat requirements of saproxylic beetles

The range of habitats that is occupied by saproxylic species has been discussed by many other authors.[40] Many factors influence the occurrence of saproxylic Coleoptera, often to varying degrees. These include: tree species, tree age and structure (eg pollard or maiden), tree location (eg exposed or in shade) and the state of decay of wood and species of fungi associated with the decay (Figure 5.3.7). The ways in which these factors interact to determine the availability of any part of a single tree to saproxylic beetles, at any one time, are complex. Also, they are made even more difficult to understand because we have only fragmentary knowledge of the precise requirements of most species in their larval stage (the longest part of the life history of any insect). To add to this complexity, experienced coleopterists, of which many have visited Moccas Park, invariably have their own special techniques for finding species. Few coleopterists will find the same suite of species as their colleagues, even if they collect at the same site on the same day.

Tree species

At Moccas Park most of the rarer saproxylic species have been found breeding in oak or are known to breed in oak. However, *Ernoporicus caucasicus* and *Stenostola dubia* breed only in limes and several other species normally are found breeding in beech, ash or elm. Ancient examples of these other broad-leaved trees, and also both horse and sweet chestnut, all support distinctive suites of saproxylic Coleoptera. The mixture of species of trees in the Park almost certainly influences the species of beetles and the numbers of individuals present. It is worth noting that the stock of trees in the Park has changed over the last 120 years (Chapter 3.4) with probably significant reductions in the numbers of ash and birch, and the loss of all mature elms since the 1960s.

Condition of the tree

Many studies have shown that the state of decay and the associated fungi are just as, if not more, important than the species of tree, in determining whether an individual tree is a suitable breeding site for a given species of beetle. It is important to get the correct perspective on the condition of trees. All species of trees, even closely related species such as native oaks and Turkey oak, grow and decay differently. Conditions suitable for a particular species of beetle may exist for decades or centuries in a native oak, but may last only a few years in a horse chestnut. Rates of decay differ between species due to factors such as the structure and density of the timber, the natural fungal flora of the living tree and the susceptibility of the tree to structural damage.

The habitat requirements of many species of saproxylic insects appear to be so precise that the mere presence of 200 years old oak trees will not ensure their survival. The trees need to contain the right stages of natural decomposition caused by the fungi that occur naturally in the heartwood of all living trees.[41] For example, the larvae of many of the rarer Elateridae breed only in the red-rotten heart wood of ancient decaying oaks. Trees, which have become hollow by the combined actions of fungi and invertebrates, accumulate debris in the hollow which provide a medium for other species of fungi. The fruiting bodies that result from these fungal colonisations attract many species that are specialist feeders on fungi or are predators. Beech and elm often rot in this same manner although beech more characteristically develops rot-holes that support their own unique fauna.

Bark thickness is of prime importance to the numerous sub-cortical species. Oak has a thick insulating bark, which keeps the underlying wood moist for many years. Beech, and to a greater extent lime, has a thin brittle bark which soon splits to allow rapid desiccation of the bark itself and the underlying sap wood and heart wood. A large proportion of those species which complete at least part of their development beneath the bark do so within the first year or two after the death of a branch.

Nectar sources

The adults of many species of saproxylic beetles congregate on open, flat, flower clusters, such as those of hawthorn and elder, and on the flower heads of umbellifers, when they are in full flower. In many cases beetles visit flowers to feed on nectar and pollen and to mate. Some species never feed as adults, but sometimes can be found on such flower heads. Hawthorn, a critically important nectar source in many parks, is now very scarce in the mature state in the Lower Park at Moccas. Many hawthorns were cleared from the Lower Park in the 1960s, during the agricultural improvements. These same changes, mainly to improve the grazing, probably also reduced the numbers of wild flowers in the pasture, although even the Lower Park was heavily over-run with bracken until then. The lack of hawthorn in many parts of the Park also restricts the opportunities for coleopterists to survey and record. Hawthorns in flower are a prime target for coleopterists because of their 'honey-pot' effect on saproxylic species, the emergence of many of which coincides with the flowering of hawthorn and several species of large umbellifers..

Figure 5.3.7

Dead wood habitats.
Drawings by Peter Kirby reproduced by permission of the Joint Nature Conservation Committee.

Dead wood comes in a range of types. Each supports a distinctive invertebrate fauna 1. Sun-baked wood 2. Fungus-infected bark 3. Fine branches and twigs 4. Bracket fungi 5. Birds' nests 6. Stumps 7. Hollow trees 8. Burnt wood 9. Large fallen timber 10. Dead outer branches 11. Rot-holes 12. Standing dead trunks 13. Roots 14. Well-rotted timber 15. Wet fallen wood 16. Red-rotten heartwood

$$\frac{5}{3}$$

Habitats and areas of particular interest

The prime habitats for Coleoptera at Moccas Park are those associated with the large, often ancient, broad-leaved trees. Much of the collecting and recording of beetles has been in the Lower Park, particularly from isolated, ancient, pollard oaks. However, recent work by Cooter, using flight interception traps, suggests that the closed canopy areas in the Upper Park may be just as rewarding for saproxylic and other species. Our perception of the best habitats and areas of particular interest in the Park may be coloured by human factors, such as the accessibility of the old, hollow pollards for collecting and that these trees are on flat ground within easy walking distance of the Park Lodge gate. These factors may be as important in determining our knowledge of the site as are the habitat 'preferences' of the beetles themselves. However, any assessment of Moccas Park and its fauna can be based only on what is known. At the present time we know that the trees of the Lower Park are crucially important for the survival of the saproxylic fauna, but there is growing evidence that the Upper Park is also of importance for many of the same species.

Although the Park is justly famous for the beetles of its ancient, broad-leaved trees, it also contains a selection of exotic conifers. These doubtless support their own specialist fauna although only one species is mentioned in published accounts. In June 1954 Allen found the longhorn beetle *Tetropium gabrieli* "in moderate numbers under the bark of a larch log", and in May 1958 Hunter found pupae "under bark of a dead standing larch".[42] This species has been recorded from several other sites in the region.

The Lawn Pool and associated wetland areas support several uncommon species of aquatic and wetland beetles. The origins of this fauna may lie in the area of ancient wetlands that is believed to have existed along the foot of the Merbach-Woodbury Hill ridge.[43] The periodic fluctuations in water levels and occasional periods of complete drying out of the Lawn Pool do not seem to have had an adverse effect on the known beetle fauna.

The grassland of the Park is grazed by deer, sheep and cattle, and at times the grazing pressure is intense. Much of the grassland was improved for agricultural production in the 1960s and 1970s, with bracken clearance and probably a loss of wild flowers and fungi as the grassland was ploughed, reseeded and fertilized. For these reasons, the grassland is unlikely to support a particularly rich beetle fauna, but, as noted earlier, this fauna does not seem to have been surveyed.

Herbivore dung provides an important food source for a wide range of beetle species, the majority of which are in the families Hydrophilidae, Scarabaeidae and Staphylinidae. Three nationally Scarce species of Scarabaeidae have been recorded from Moccas Park - *Aphodius paykulli*, *A.porcus* and *A.zenkeri*; the last species (Figure 5.3.8) is typically associated with deer dung. Cooter has reported that *A.zenkeri* was particularly common in flight interception traps which he operated during 1992 and 1994 in closed canopy areas of the Upper Park.

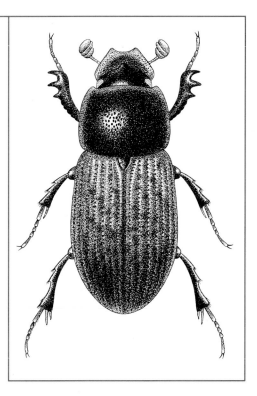

Figure 5.3.8

The dung beetle *Aphodius zenkeri*. Length = 4·6 mm (elytral apex to anterior margin of head). Original drawing by R.W.J. Read.

Moccas Park in national and regional contexts

Although only one species of beetle is now known in Britain only from Moccas Park, the concentration of threatened, rare and nationally scarce species within such a small area continues to make the site nationally and internationally important.[44] The methods of assessing the relative importance of sites for their saproxylic beetles have been described in Chapter 5.1. In the most recent comparative assessment, Moccas Park has been overtaken by Richmond Park in south-west London. However, Richmond Park is nearly seven times larger than Moccas Park and has been the subject of intensive surveys during the last decade.[45]

In the context of the western Midlands of England and eastern Wales, Moccas is distinctly the most important site for its size, but the Bredon Hill/Elmley Park complex in Gloucestershire, which is about twice the size of Moccas Park, is probably a close rival. However, it has not yet been possible to compare Moccas Park with Bredon/Elmley because suitable data are not currently available for the latter site (Chapter 5.1).

Changes in the beetle fauna

Although Moccas Park has been known to coleopterists for the past 60 years, it is only during the last 30 years that visits have become more frequent. Even during this latter period most visitors went there to secure specimens of the 'specialities' of the Park and concentrated their collecting on the ancient oaks and beeches and a few of the lime trees. Published accounts confirm that many of these species have been recorded regularly over the years. It is only in comparatively recent years that new techniques, such as flight interception traps, have been used to advantage with the subsequent addition of many species to the site list.

Some coleopterists have commented that a few species appear to be recorded less frequently, or are found with greater difficulty than formerly, suggesting that the numbers of individuals of a few species may have declined. Given the ageing tree population and the rate at which dead wood has been lost from the Lower Park in the last 35 years, declines in numbers of individuals, of a few species, could be expected. In the absence of any data from monitoring the populations of individual species such suggestions cannot be confirmed.

Past and future site management

Other chapters explore many issues relating to the past and present management of Moccas Park. Some of these issues also have been mentioned in relation to particular species in this chapter. There is the perennial problem, associated with all wood-pasture sites, of how to deal with the diminishing resource of ageing trees and dead wood. The large age gap in the generations of trees in the Park can never be filled, although experiments with the management of individual trees may help to overcome some of the gap. It is probable that, at some time in the future, populations of some species requiring very specialised habitats, found only in the most ancient trees, may become extinct locally. Although much of the surrounding countryside has changed in recent decades, a few of the species that comprise the present day fauna of the Park appear to occur sparsely elsewhere in the region. The future survival of the distinctive beetle fauna of Moccas Park will depend on two main factors:
1) the continuation of management within the Park that is sympathetic to the requirements of the fauna and flora of the site;
2) the management of land surrounding the Park to maintain as many options as possible for mobility of the flora and fauna within this wider landscape.

Notes

1 Crowson (1981).

2 G.H.Ashe (1879-1961), H.M.Hallett (1878-1958), R.W.Lloyd (1868-1958) and J.R.le B.Tomlin (1863-1954) were important British coleopterists of their generation. A.A.Allen (born 1913) has played an important role with respect to Moccas Park (Chapter 6.1). Tomlin compiled the first list of Herefordshire Coleoptera, which was updated by Hallett. Lloyd lived near St Weonards, about 30km south-east of Moccas Park, and was host to many visiting entomologists.

3 For a complete list of publications, theses and reports see the *Bibliography of the Coleoptera of Moccas Park* section of this chapter.

4 J.Cooter has a specialist interest in Coleoptera and is editor of *A coleopterist's handbook*. Having carried out survey work at Moccas Park since 1975, whilst based at Glasgow Museum, he took up the post of Keeper of Natural History at Hereford Museum in January 1979 and has continued to record actively at Moccas Park and its environs.

5 The account of the Coleoptera of Moccas Park and species list were prepared for a meeting of the Historical Ecology Discussion Group (HEDG), held in July 1981, at Hereford. The meeting, *History, land-use and wildlife in south-west Herefordshire*, included a series of discussion papers and a visit to Moccas Park and other sites. In common with most HEDG meetings, no publication resulted from this meeting.

6 Copies of these documents form part of the Invertebrate Site Register archive held at the Biological Records Centre (Centre for Ecology and Hydrology, Monks Wood near Huntingdon).

7 Although some families or groups of beetles have accepted common names (eg ground beetles, ladybirds, water beetles, weevils), many do not and are referred to here only by their scientific name.

8 Tomlin (1950).

9 In July 1993 I collected what I took to be a tawny owl pellet from beneath an oak in the Lower Park. Dissection of its contents revealed the first records for the Park of *Nebria brevicollis* and *Pterostichus melanarius*, two of the commonest British ground beetles, together with *Chlaenius nigricornis*, a Nationally Scarce ground beetle which frequents pond margins and other wetland habitats. During the same visit I also added three species Hydrophilidae and one species Staphylinidae new to the list, which were collected from sheep dung in the Lower Park. During a day's visit on 10 June 1997, Andy Godfrey, when searching for Diptera mainly in wetland habitats, collected 67 species of Coleoptera, 16 of which were first records for the Park.

10 See for example Hammond & Harding (1991).

11 Uhthoff-Kaufmann (1944).

12 Allen & Lloyd (1951).

13 In April 1972 Green (1973) reported obtaining seven specimens at his home in Newport, Monmouthshire, from oak logs originating from a firewood merchant in Hay-on-Wye. This discovery was the impetus for a wider, and more thorough, search for this beetle.

14 Uhthoff-Kaufmann (1995) gives an historical account of *P.sanguineum* reviewing old and recent records. See also Twinn & Harding (1999).

15 Buckland (1981).

16 Tony Drane has recently completed a detailed study of the genus *Ernoporus* in Britain, especially in the East Midlands (Drane 1997). Following recent literature, he suggested that the British perception of the genus *Ernoporus* is incorrect; the species *tiliae* should remain in the genus *Ernoporus*, but both *caucasicus* and *fagi* should be separated into the genus *Ernoporicus* Berger.

17 Allen (1970). He, and subsequent authors, referred to it as *Ernoporus caucasicus*, but see note 16.

18 Kelly & Osborne (1965), Harding (1982).

19 Finally, the butt of this tree was removed by September 1976, but the tree began to regenerate from the stump. Harding (1977) noted that two hybrid limes grew nearby and that there were other lime trees in the Upper Park, which might provide alternative hosts for *E.caucasicus*.

20 Cooter (1981b). Cooter compared his Moccas Park specimens with alleged specimens of *E.tiliae* from Bedford Purlieus in Northamptonshire and Swithland Wood in Leicestershire, collected by Don Tozer, some of which proved to be *E. caucasicus*.

21 Drane's studies have confirmed Cooter's observations that *E.caucasicus* is capable of breeding in both small-leaved and hybrid limes. Drane (1997) noted that *E.caucasicus* breeds frequently in twigs on old maiden or pollarded trees, as well as those on coppiced lime poles, whereas *E.tiliae* is apparently restricted to small-leaved lime, usually coppiced trees. Drane has suggested (pers. comm.) that *E.caucasicus* no longer merits its RDB1 status.

22 See the British Red Data Book for insects (Shirt 1987) and the two volumes of a national review of Coleoptera (Hyman & Parsons 1992,1994). Knowledge of the British fauna increases each year and many species accounts in these volumes are already out of date.

23 Owen (1982), Cooter (1990b & pers. comm.).

24 Levey (1996).

25 Tomlin (1950).

26 Hyman & Parsons (1992).

27 Hyman & Parsons (1992).

28 Cooter (pers. comm.), see also Chapter 5.2.

29 Mendel & Clarke (1996).

30 Hallett (1951).

31 J.Cooter (pers. comm.).

32 Skidmore & Hunter (1981).

33 Mendel (1990).

34 Allen (1951), Cooter (1976).

35 Unpublished lists by A.P.Fowles, R.S.Key and P.F.Whitehead.

36 These records were overlooked by Hyman & Parsons (1994).

37 Angus (1976, 1977).

38 Allen (1963).

39 Hyman & Parsons (1994).

40 See for example Elton (1966), Harding & Rose (1986), Speight (1989).

41 This complex topic is reviewed by Speight (1989).

42 Allen (1955b), Hunter (1959).

43 See Chapters 1.2 and 1.3.

44 See Chapters 5.1 and 5.2.

45 Hammond & Owen (in preparation).

Main unpublished sources of records of Coleoptera from Moccas Park

1962
A.M.Massee: *A list of the rarer and more interesting species of Coleoptera so far known to occur in Moccas Park.* M/S list appended to letter to Dr M.G. Morris dated 30 June 1962.
1964
A.M.Massee: *Some of the more interesting Coleoptera (beetles) and Hemiptera-Heteroptera (plant bugs) recorded at Moccas Deer Park, Moccas, Herefordshire.* M/S list dated 25 November 1964, 8 pages.
1968
F.A.Hunter & P.Skidmore: Letter to J.Thompson (3 October) relating to visit made to Moccas on 28/29 September 1968.
1980
P.J.Hodge: *Coleoptera from Moccas Park 26/26 May 1980.* M/S list in Invertebrate Site Register files, 2 pages.
R.C.Welch: *Coleoptera recorded from Moccas Park, Herefordshire (SO3442) on 26 September 1980.* M/S list, 10 pages.
1981
J.A.Owen: *Moccas Park beetle list.* Computer print-out of list of 26 spp. collected June 1980 with appended M/S list of 16 spp. collected June 1981.
R.C.Welch & J.Cooter: *The Coleoptera of Moccas Park, Herefordshire.* Includes: Appendix 1 - J.Cooter & R.C.Welch: *A list of the Coleoptera known from Moccas Park, Herefordshire*; Appendix 2 - R.C. Welch: *Additions to the list of Coleoptera of Moccas Park* (list of 27 spp. collected by J.A.Owen during 1980 and 1981). Typescript report and species lists prepared for the Historical Ecology Group meeting at Hereford, July 1981, 28 pages.
1984
R.C.Welch: *Moccas Park Coleoptera collected by R.Colin Welch in July 1984.* M/S list of 32 species, 2 pages.
1990
R.B.Angus: Letter to John Bacon (25 April), reporting on a visit to the Park on 4 April 1990. Lists 21 species.
1993
J.A.Owen: *Moccas Park beetle list (Cooter & Welch): revised 28 June 1993.* Computer print-out of 847 spp. 9 pages.
R.C.Welch: *List of Coleoptera recorded by Dr R.Colin Welch during the Forest Entomologists' Group Meeting at Church Stretton, Salop., 5-9 July 1993.* M/S list including 44 species collected at Moccas Park on 7 July 1993. 14 pages + 5 maps.
1994
P.F.Whitehead: *Letter to Andy Godfrey dated 3 September 1994.* Lists 17 species (1 new to the site), 1 page.
1997
R.S.Key: *Beetles at Moccas Park recorded by beating oak on the original* Hypebaeus *tree, and trees in immediate vicinity, on 5 June 1997.* Computer print-out of 16 species, 1 page.
R.C.Welch: *Coleoptera from Moccas Park Herefordshire collected by Dr Andy Godfrey on 10 June 1997.* M/S list of 67 species including 16 additions to the site list, 3 pages.
1998
A.P.Fowles: *Invertebrate records: Moccas Park - A.P.Fowles.* Computer print-out of 18 species of Coleoptera collected in 1990 and 1998, 1 page.

Bibliography of the Coleoptera of Moccas Park

ALLEN, A.A. 1951. *Euplectus nitidus* Fairm. and *Batrisodes venustus* Rchb. (Col., Pselaphidae) in Herefordshire. *Entomologist's monthly Magazine*, 87, 15.

ALLEN, A.A. 1954. *Bolitochara mulsanti* Sharp (Col., Staphylinidae) in Herefordshire and a critical note. *Entomologist's monthly Magazine*, 90, 237.

ALLEN, A.A. 1955a. *Agabus labiatus* Brahm (Col., Dytiscidae) in Herefordshire. *Entomologist's monthly Magazine*, 91, 143.

ALLEN, A.A. 1955b. Coleoptera. Notes on some Longicornia from Herefordshire. *Entomologist's Record and Journal of Variation*, 67, 88-89.

ALLEN, A.A. 1958. *Bibloporus minutus* Raf. (=*höglundi* Palm) (Col., Pselaphidae) in Herefordshire : a definite British record. *Entomologist's monthly Magazine*, 94, 284.

ALLEN, A.A. 1960. *Acrulia inflata* Gyll. (Col., Staphylinidae) in Herefordshire. *Entomologist's monthly Magazine*, 96, 177.

ALLEN, A.A. 1962. George Hamilton Ashe, M.A., B.Sc. - Obituary. *Entomologist's monthly Magazine*, 98, 110.

ALLEN, A.A. 1963. A second Cumberland capture of *Schistoglossa aubei* Bris. (Col., Staphylinidae). *Entomologist's monthly Magazine*, 99, 209.

ALLEN, A.A. 1970. *Ernoporus caucasicus* Lind. and *Leperisinus orni* Fuchs (Col., Scolytidae) in Britain. *Entomologist's monthly Magazine*, 105, 245-9.

ALLEN, A.A. 1971. *Procaerus tibialis* Lac. (Col., Elateridae) in Wilts and Herts. *Entomologist's monthly Magazine*, 107, 12.

ALLEN, A.A. 1974. The British status of *Pyrrhidium sanguineum* L. (Col., Cerambycidae) : a comment. *Entomologist's monthly Magazine*, 109, 98.

ALLEN, A.A. 1975. Two species of *Anaspis* (Col., Mordellidae) new to Britain; with a consideration of the status of *A. hudsoni* Donis., etc. *Entomologist's Record and Journal of Variation*, 87, 269-274.

ALLEN, A.A. 1980. Correction of two further errors concerning *Bolitochara mulsanti* Sharp (Col., Staphylinidae). *Entomologist's monthly Magazine*, 115, 224.

ALLEN, A.A. & LLOYD, R.W. 1951. *Pyrrhidium sanguineum* L. (Col., Cerambycidae) as a British species. *Entomologist's monthly Magazine*, 87, 157-8.

ANGUS, R. 1976. A preliminary note on the British species of *Graphoderus* Sturm, with the additions of *G.bilineatus* Degeer and *G.zonatus* Hoppe to the British List. *The Balfour-Browne Club Newsletter*, 1, 1-3.

ANGUS, R. 1977. Water Beetles at Moccas Park, Herefordshire. *The Balfour-Browne Club Newsletter*, 6, 1-2.

ASHE, G.H. 1942. *Trixagus* (=*Throscus*) *brevicollis* Bonv. (Col., Trixagidae), a species new to Britain. *Entomologist's monthly Magazine*, 78, 287.

ASHE, G.H. 1952. *Atheta* (*Dimetrota*) *sparre-schneideri* Munster (Col., Staphylinidae) in Devon. *Entomologist's monthly Magazine*, 88, 63.

BLAIR, K.G. 1943. *Hypebaeus flavipes* F. (not *Ebaeus abietinus* Abeille) (Col., Malachiidae) in Britain: a correction. *Entomologist's monthly Magazine*, 79, 16.

COOMBS, C.W. & WOODROFFE, G.E. 1955. A revision of the British species of *Cryptophagus* (Herbst) (Coleoptera: Cryptophagidae). *Transactions of the Royal Entomological Society of London*, 106(6), 237-282.

COOTER, J. 1976. A note on some beetles captured at Moccas Park, Herefordshire, during 1975. *Entomologist's Record and Journal of Variation*, 88, 319-320.

COOTER, J. 1978. *Procraerus tibialis* Bois. & Lac., and other beetles in Moccas Park, Herefordshire. *Entomologist's Record and Journal of Variation*, 90, 24.

COOTER, J. 1979a *Bembidion quadripustulatum* Serville (Col., Carabidae) new to Herefordshire. *Entomologist's monthly Magazine*, 113, 234.

COOTER, J. 1979b. *Gnypeta rubrior* Tottenham (Col., Staphylinidae) in Moccas Park, Herefordshire. *Entomologist's monthly Magazine*, 113, 236.

COOTER, J. 1979c. The continued presence of *Pyrrhidium sanguineum* (L.) (Col., Cerambycidae) in Moccas Park, Herefordshire. *Entomologist's monthly Magazine*, 113, 238-239.

COOTER, J. 1979d. A good year for Cerambycidae. *Entomologist's monthly Magazine*, 113, 240.

COOTER, J. 1979e. *Pseudocistela ceramboides* (L.) (Col., Tenebrionidae) in Herefordshire. *Entomologist's monthly Magazine*, 113, 250.

COOTER, J. 1981a A further note on *Pyrrhidium sanguineum* (L.) (Col., Cerambycidae). *Entomologist's monthly Magazine*, 116, 104.

COOTER, J. 1981b. A note on *Ernoporus caucasicus* Lind. (Col., Scolytidae) in Britain. *Entomologist's monthly Magazine*, 116, 112.

COOTER, J. 1982. Yet another note on *Pyrrhidium sanguineum* (L.) (Col., Cerambycidae). *Entomologist's monthly Magazine*, 118, 54.

COOTER, J. 1990a. *Leptusa pulchella* (Mann.)(Col., Staphylinidae) in Herefordshire. *Entomologist's monthly Magazine*, 126, 49

COOTER, J. 1990b. Some beetles from Moccas Park, Herefordshire. *Entomologist's monthly Magazine*, 126, 70.

COOTER, J. 1992. *Xyletinus longitarsus* Jansson (Col., Anobiidae) in Herefordshire. *Entomologist's monthly Magazine*, 128, 183.

COOTER, J. 1994. *Pyrrhidium sanguineum* (L.) (Col., Cerambycidae) on beech. *Entomologist's monthly Magazine*, 130, 194.

DONISTHORPE, H. & TOMLIN, J.R.le B. 1934. *Ebaeus abietinus* Abeille (Malachiidae, Col.), a beetle new to Britain. *Entomologist's monthly Magazine*, 70, 198-199.

DRANE, A.B. 1997. *The taxonomy, status and distribution of* Ernoporus tiliae *(Panzer) and* Ernoporicus caucasicus Lindemann *(Coleoptera, Scolytidae), with particular reference to their occurence in Northamptonshire, Leicestershire and Lincolnshire.* Unpublished thesis for Master of Philosophy, University of Leicester.

GREEN, M.E. 1973. *Pyrrhidium sanguineum* (L.) (Col., Cerambycidae) established as an indigenous species. *Entomologist's monthly Magazine*, 108, 65.

HALLETT, H.M. 1951. The Coleoptera of Herefordshire, First supplement. *Transactions of the Woolhope Naturalists' Field Club*, 279-82.

HARDING, P.T. 1977. *Moccas deer park, Hereford and Worcester: a report on the history, structure and natural history.* Unpublished report to the Nature Conservancy Council by the Institute of Terrestrial Ecology, Huntingdon.

HARDING, P.T. 1978a. *An inventory of areas of conservation value for the invertebrate fauna of the mature timber habitat.* (CST report no. 160). Banbury: Nature Conservancy Council.

HARDING, P.T. 1978b. *A bibliography of the occurrence of certain woodland Coleoptera in Britain, with special reference to timber-utilising species associated with old trees in pasture-woodlands.* (CST report no. 161). Banbury: Nature Conservancy Council.

HORTON, G.A.N. 1980. *Pyrrhidium sanguineum* L. and *Criocephalus rusticus* L. (Col., Cerambycidae) in Monmouthshire. *Entomologist's Record and Journal of Variation*, 92, 52.

HUNTER, F.A. 1959. Collecting longhorn beetles in 1958. *Entomologist's Record and Journal of Variation*, 71, 122-126.

JEANNEL, R. 1954. Un Pselaphide nouveau des Iles Britanniques. *Entomologist's monthly Magazine*, 90, 106-7.

LEVEY, B. 1996. *Anaspis septentrionalis* Champion a senior synonym of *A. schilskyana* Csiki (Scraptiidae). *The Coleopterist*, 5, 58-59.

LLOYD, R.W. 1949. Coleoptera at Moccas Park, Herefordshire. *Entomologist's monthly Magazine*, 85, 22.

LLOYD, R.W. 1950. *Pyrrhidium sanguineum* L. (Col., Cerambycidae), in Herefordshire. *Entomologist's monthly Magazine*, 86, 36.

LLOYD, R.W. 1951. *Plectophloeus nitidus* Fairmaire (Col., Pselaphidae) in Herefordshire. *Entomologist's monthly Magazine*, 87, 62.

MENDEL, H. 1985. *Trixagus brevicollis* (de Bonvouloir) (Col., Throscidae) in Britain. *Entomologist's monthly Magazine*, 121, 95.

MENDEL, H. 1990. The identification of British Ischnomera Stephens (Coleoptera: Oedomeridae). *Entomologist's Gazette*, 41, 209-211.

MORRIS, M.G. 1974. *Pyrrhidium sanguineum* (l.) Col., Cerambycidae) as a breeding species in Britain. *Entomologist's monthly Magazine*, 109, 163.

OWEN, J.A. 1982. *Anaspis schilskyana* Csiki (Col., Scraptiidae) at Moccas Park, Herefordshire. *Entomologist's monthly Magazine*, 118, 68.

PEARCE, E.J. 1954. New aquatic records for Herefordshire. *Entomologist's monthly Magazine*, 90, 247.

PEARCE, E.J. 1954. A second specimen of *Euplectoides pearcei* Jeannel. (Col., Pselaphidae). *Entomologist's monthly Magazine*, 90, 107.

PEARCE, E.J. 1957. Coleoptera : Pselaphidae. *Handbooks for the identification of British insects*, 4(9). London: Royal Entomological Society of London.

SKIDMORE, P. & HUNTER, F.A. 1981. *Ischnomera cinerascens* Pand. (Col., Oedmeridae) new to Britain. *Entomologist's monthly Magazine*, 116, 129-132.

TOMLIN, J.R.le B. 1949. *Herefordshire Coleoptera Part 1*. Hereford: Woolhope Naturalists' Field Club.

TOMLIN, J.R.le B. 1950. *Herefordshire Coleoptera Part 2*. Hereford: Woolhope Naturalists' Field Club.

UHTHOFF-KAUFMANN, R.R. 1944. Is *Pyrrhidium sanguineum* L. (Col., Cerambycidae) a British Insect? *Entomologist's monthly Magazine*, 80, 261-2.

UHTHOFF-KAUFMANN, R.R. 1990. The occurrence of the Callidini Tribe (Col., Cerambycidae) in the British Isles. *Entomologist's Record and Journal of Variation*, 102, 161-166.

UHTHOFF-KAUFMANN, R.R. 1995. A history of *Pyrrhidium sanguineum* (Linnaeus) (Cerambycidae) in Britain. *The Coleopterist*, 4(2): 41-45.

WELCH, R.C. 1981. *Dropephylla grandiloqua* (Luze) (Col., Staphylinidae) at Moccas Park, Herefordshire. *Entomologist's monthly Magazine*, 117, 156.

WELCH, R.C. 1982. *Dropephylla grandiloqua* (Luze) (Col., Staphylinidae) from a second Herefordshire parkland locality. *Entomologist's monthly Magazine*, 118, 166.

WHITEHEAD, P.F. 1990. Notable Coleoptera records - 3. *The Coleopterist*, 5: 54-55.

ZATLOUKAL-WILLIAMS, R.G.Z. 1973. Further records of *Pyrrhidium sanguineum* (L.) (Col., Cerambycidae) in Herefordshire. *Entomologist's monthly Magazine*, 109, 49.

Other references

BUCKLAND, P.C. 1981. Insect remains from beneath the Brigg 'raft'. *In*: S.McGRAIL, ed. *The Brigg 'raft' and her prehistoric environment*. (B.A.R. British Series 89). Oxford: B.A.R., 155-175.

ELTON, C.S. 1966. *The pattern of animal communities*. London: Methuen.

HAMMOND, P.M. & HARDING, P.T. 1991. Saproxylic invertebrate assemblages in British woodlands: their conservation significance and its evaluation. *In*: H.J.READ, ed. *Pollard and veteran tree management*. London: Corporation of London, 30-37.

HAMMOND, P.M. & OWEN, J.A. In preparation. *The beetles of Richmond Park SSSI - a case study*. (English Nature Science series) Peterborough: English Nature.

HARDING, P.T. 1982. A further note on *Ernoporus caucasicus* Lind. (Col., Scolytidae) in Britain. *Entomologist's monthly Magazine*, 118, 166.

HARDING, P.T. & ROSE, F. 1986. *Pasture-woodlands in lowland Britain. A review of their importance for nature conservation*. Huntingdon: Institute of Terrestrial Ecology.

HYMAN, P.S. & PARSONS, M.S. 1992. A review of the scarce and threatened Coleoptera of Great Britain, Part 1. *UK Nature Conservation*, 3. Peterborough: Joint Nature Conservation Committee.

HYMAN, P.S. & PARSONS, M.S. 1994. A review of the scarce and threatened Coleoptera of Great Britain, Part 2. *UK Nature Conservation*, 12. Peterborough: Joint Nature Conservation Committee.

KELLY, M. & OSBORNE, P.J. 1965. Two faunas and floras from the alluvium at Shustoke, Warwickshire. *Proceedings of the Linnean Society of London*, 176, 37-65.

MENDEL, H. & CLARKE, R.E. 1996. *Provisional atlas of the click beetles (Coleoptera: Elateroidea) of Britain and Ireland.* Ipswich: Ipswich Borough Council Museums.

SHIRT, D.B., ed. 1987. *British Red Data Books: 2. Insects.* Peterborough: Nature Conservancy Council.

SPEIGHT, M.C.D. 1989. *Saproxylic invertebrates and their conservation.* Nature and environment series, 42. Strasbourg: Council of Europe.

TWINN, P.F.G. & HARDING, P.T. 1999. *Provisional atlas of the longhorn beetles (Coleoptera, Cerambycidae) of Britain.* Huntingdon: Biological Records Centre.

5
—
3

Diptera

Andy Godfrey

My one desire that day was to get out of the valley and away from the innumerable hordes of flies that infested it.

Robert Gibbings (1942). *Coming down the Wye.*

Sources

The early days

The Diptera (flies) of Moccas Park have not been studied as intensively as the Coleoptera although dipterists seem to have discovered the Park earlier than the coleopterists. Two highly respected dipterists (John Wood and James Collin) collected here on several occasions in the early decades of this century.[1] Wood recorded several uncommon species including *Hercostomus angustifrons* and *Thrypticus nigricauda.*[2] Collin described five species as new to science based on either Wood's specimens, or his own, from the Park: *Hilara griseifrons, Hilara nigrohirta, Anthomyza dissors, Setacera trina* and *Fiebrigella baliola.*[3] Neither Wood's collection, which has been incorporated into the general collection at The Natural History Museum (London), nor Collin's collection and archival material at the Hope Department of Entomology (Oxford) has been examined for records from Moccas Park. A few early records, by Colbran Wainwright,[4] have been traced, but his collection and archives have not been examined. To extract records from such sources is very time consuming and, hitherto, has not been regarded as a priority for work by entomological experts. Thus the early records of Diptera mentioned in this chapter are all of noteworthy species, almost all from published sources.

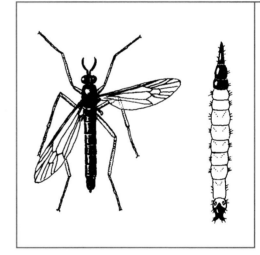

Figure 5.4.1

The snipe fly *Xylophagus ater.* The larvae of this fly prey on other saproxylic insect larvae. Drawing by Peter Kirby reproduced by permission of the Joint Nature Conservation Committee.

5/4

Recent recording

Peter Skidmore has collected in the Park at various times since his first visit in 1959 and his specimens are at Doncaster Museum and Manchester Museum.[5] *Neopachygaster meromelaena* (Stratiomyiidae) is listed from Moccas Park by several people in correspondence during the 1960s and 1970s.[6] Peter Chandler visited and collected at the site in 1972,[7] and a group of dipterists, including Chandler and Alan Stubbs,[8] recorded in the Park in 1977.[9] I have determined material collected by Jonathan Cooter who used an interception trap operated in April to August 1992,[10] and I carried out a survey of the Diptera for English Nature from 30 June to 2 July 1994.[11] More recently, the Park was visited in June 1997 by several dipterists, myself included, during a Dipterists Forum recording week, and members of the Forum visited the Park again in October 1998.

Gaps in knowledge and the need for further work

Our knowledge of the Diptera of Moccas Park is clearly incomplete. The woodland of the Upper Park has yet to be surveyed in detail and may provide favourable conditions for many species given the greater numbers of beeches, more moist conditions in the closed canopy woodland, ground layer and shrub vegetation, and the presence of springs and streams. Within the Lower Park, further recording will certainly reveal more saproxylic species. Probably the most effective ways of locating species would be by using trapping techniques,[12] or by rearing larvae and pupae collected from under bark, in rot holes, at sap runs and in other favoured niches.

Many Diptera families have yet to be studied at Moccas Park. Some, such as sphaerocerids and ephydrids, have been collected but few have been identified. The chironomid fauna of the Lawn Pool has not been examined but would almost certainly reveal interesting species. Even the more popular and accessible groups, such as hoverflies, have not been recorded fully and it would not be difficult to add to the existing list for this particular family.

With the exception of the recent visit in October 1998, almost all the sampling and visits by Dipterists in the 1990s have been between May and early August. Visits in April and September-October would add species that are adult only in spring or autumn, such as many craneflies and fungus gnats.

Nationally threatened, rare and uncommon species

Few species of Diptera with Red Data Book status have been recorded at Moccas Park, but the list is growing.[13] The following species already have Red Data Book status or would probably merit it in any revision of the Red Data list.

❖ *Molophilus lackschewitzianus*, **a cranefly** (Limoniidae)
Status: RDB3.
From interception trap samples taken in 20-24 June 1992 by Jonathan Cooter. A cranefly which is found in woods on clay soils, usually in heavily shaded, deeply cut gullies with streams. The larvae are thought to occur in wet soil. There are only a few, widely scattered records of this species from Wales and England.

❖ *Tasiocera muscula*, **a cranefly** (Limoniidae)
Status: First definite British record of the species.
A minute species swept in 1997 by Ivan Perry beside the woodland stream.[14] Identified by Alan Stubbs.

❖ *Pericoma calcilega*, **an owl-midge** (Psychodidae)
Status: Psychodids have been not given Red Data Book statuses because they are too poorly known. Known from about five localities in Britain.[15]
The species is probably associated with tufa in calcareous streams; I swept it from beside the woodland stream at the south eastern end of the Park in 1994, from around the tufa deposits.

❖ *Colobaea pectoralis*, **a snail-parasite fly** (Sciomyzidae)
Status: RDB2.
Collected by sweeping in small numbers on 10 June 1997 in sedge-dominated damp hollows south east of the Lawn Pool. Pupae of this species have been found in shells of the ramshorn snail *Anisus vortex* beside temporary pools. Most of the recent records have been from the fluctuating 'meres' in Breckland (Norfolk/Suffolk) and from Nottinghamshire, Somerset and Cornwall.

❖ *Heteromeringia nigrimana*, **a clusiid fly** (Clusiidae)
Status: RDB1.
Recorded in 1912. This rare fly is associated with ancient woodlands, with very few known records. Its immature stages are unknown but it probably utilises soft, rotten, dead wood like other clusiids.

❖ *Periscelis winnertzi*, **a periscelid fly** (Periscelidae)

Status: RDB2.

Apparently "not uncommon" in Moccas Park during 1905.[16] Collin recorded it in August 1934 and 1936 (specimens in The Natural History Museum, London). This species is known in Britain only from the New Forest, Wyre Forest and Moccas Park. It is associated with old or damaged broadleaved trees in ancient woodlands and wood-pastures. The biology of the larvae is unknown, but related species develop in sap runs.

❖ *Cordilura aemula*, **a dung-fly** (Scathophagidae)

Status: proposed RDB3.

Taken on two occasions in June 1997 by sweeping beside the Lawn Pool. The life cycle of this species is unknown, but the larvae probably develop in the stems or leaf bases of sedges. Most British records are from fens in East Anglia.

Over 40 species designated as being nationally Scarce have been recorded to date at Moccas Park as indicated in the full species list (Appendix 6).[17] At least 10 of the Scarce species are saproxylics, including the following, which are associated with:[18]

◆ Decaying wood - *Ctenophora pectinicornis*, *Choerades marginatus*;
◆ Sap runs - *Mycetobia pallipes*, *Brachyopa insensilis* and *Aulacigaster leucopeza*;
◆ Rot holes - *Brachypalpus laphriformis*;
◆ Under bark as larvae or pupae - *Neopachygaster meromelaena*, *Megamerina dolium* and possibly *Stegana nigrithorax*.

The early stages of *Fiebrigella baliola* and *F. brevibucca* are virtually unknown but adults have been recorded from old parklands such as Moccas where they tend to occur on or near old trees; a single specimen of *F. brevibucca* has been reared from horse chestnut bark collected in the Park. At least five of the Scarce species are associated with woodland: *Tipula pseudovariipennis*, *Tasiocera robusta*, *Sciophila nonnisilva*, *Platypalpus aurantiacus* and *Pherbellia annulipes*.

A further 11 Scarce species are associated with fens and marshes of which *Speccafrons halophila* appears to be a parasite of spiders in beds of bulrushes, *Eribolus gracilior* is usually swept from marginal vegetation around wetlands, *Chlorops planifrons* is a stem borer of sedges and *Phaonia atriceps* has been reared from pupae found in stems and under sheaths on bulrushes, common reed and sweet-grasses. *Pteromicra glabricula* was taken from tussocks of greater tussock-sedge. Other fenland and marshland species include *Odontomyia tigrina*, *Thrypticus nigricauda*, *Hercostomus nigrilamellatus*, *Platycheirus immarginatus*, *Psacadina verbekei* and *Coniosternum decipiens*. Other habitats with which Scarce species are associated include seepages and flushes (*Molophilus corniger* and both *Oxycera* spp.), grassland (*Chloropus rufinus*), streams (*Dixa maculata*) and peat or bogs (*Hercostomus angustifrons* and possibly *Campsicnemus pumilio*).

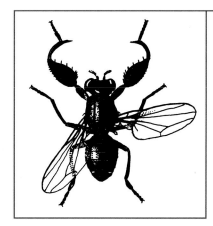

Figure 5.4.2

The shore fly *Ochthera mantis*. This distinctive predatory fly usually occurs beside peaty pools. Drawing by Peter Kirby reproduced by permission of the Joint Nature Conservation Committee.

Moccas Park in national and regional contexts

It has not been possible to compare the Diptera fauna of Moccas Park with that of other ancient parklands because a system for comparison, analogous to that for Coleoptera,[19] has not yet been developed. Long lists of Diptera are available for many wood-pasture sites, and sufficient is known about the habitats of many species of saproxylic Diptera for a Quality Index system to be developed. Detailed Diptera surveys have been, or currently are being, undertaken at several wood-pasture sites that should provide more consistent data for such an assessment system.[20]

Beech is one of the most important species of tree for saproxylic Diptera in Britain (Figure 5.4.3) and they are often the most plentiful trees in many of the classic southern localities for saproxylic Diptera in England such as Windsor Forest and Great Park, the New Forest, Epping Forest and Burnham Beeches. Duncombe Park in North Yorkshire is a more northerly site of importance for saproxylic Diptera; it too has a substantial proportion of mature beech, along with other tree species, with a variety of habitats including woodland with mature trees in which dead wood is allowed to remain and decompose. Similarly, several parks and associated estates in the Midlands support a variety of tree species, including beech, with woodland and scrub and abundant *in situ* dead wood.[21]

In contrast to most of the above sites, Moccas Park is dominated by oaks. It has a much smaller proportion of mature beeches, which are now mainly in the almost closed canopy woodland of the Upper Park. Most of the surviving over-mature beeches are in the Lower Park, in open parkland, but many have been lost during the last 30 years (see Chapter 3.3). There is little shade or shelter around the few surviving beeches in the Lower Park so that any wood that falls from them is exposed, desiccates quickly in direct sunlight and therefore is not available for the many saproxylic Diptera that require moist conditions. These factors may help to explain why Moccas Park appears to have fewer saproxylic Diptera than might be expected.

Habitats and areas of particular interest for Diptera

When compared with beetles (see Chapter 5.3), a much smaller proportion of the more noteworthy flies recorded at Moccas Park are associated with saproxylic habitats. Like many of the saproxylic beetles, saproxylic flies are often difficult to find in any life stage. They often

Figure 5.4.3

Characteristic saproxylic hoverflies. *Criorhina berberina* and *Volucella inflata* on hawthorn blossom in beech parkland. Reproduced by courtesy of Steven J. Falk.

occupy tree cavities, sap runs or decaying limbs and trunks beyond the view or reach of entomologists and possibly have only brief flight periods, usually in May and June. These are the months when collecting from blossom and flower heads, which provide sources of nectar, would be productive for many species of flies and not only for saproxylic species. As has been noted in Chapter 5.3, hawthorn, umbellifers and other typical nectar sources are scare in the Park. Greater use of passive sampling techniques, such as Malaise traps or interception traps, or rearing larvae, could be expected to add several more species of saproxylic Diptera to the current list. Several visits are usually necessary to record saproxylic flies adequately and Moccas Park has been worked much less frequently by dipterists than by coleopterists.

I had problems locating wet tree cavities and active sap runs in June 1994 although dry cavities and red heart rot were frequent. The predominance of oak over beech and the sun-baked nature of much of the dead wood may preclude many saproxylic Diptera, most of which require moist conditions. However, many horse chestnuts had sap runs in 1997 from which the species that are typically associated with this feature were recorded. *Brachypalpoides lentus* was seen basking near a sap run on separate days in June, and *Ctenophora pectinicornis* appeared to have emerged recently from a shattered trunk where a limb had broken off. A small number of saproxylic species, including *Systenus pallipes/pallidus*, *Aulacigaster leucopeza* and *Phaonia cincta*, were reared in 1997 from horse chestnut sap.

Apart from oaks and beech, horse chestnut has proved particularly important for flies associated with sap-runs, including some species more normally associated with elms. One elm speciality, *Odinia meijeri*, was recorded at Moccas Park on several occasions in the 1970s, before all the elms died. Few species have been recorded that are mainly associated with ash. Limes are not particularly noted for their saproxylic Diptera fauna but *Megamerina dolium*, which was swept from the Lawn Pool, has been reared elsewhere from under lime bark.

Many saproxylic Diptera favour shaded conditions in woodland, clearings or woodland edge habitats. Many of the species associated with dead wood actually utilise moss covering the bases of trees or thick coverings of mosses on fallen timber. Other fauna, such as woodlice, millipedes, centipedes and both adult and immature stages of other insects, in damp rotting timber, support parasitic or parasitoid Diptera from several families. Woodlands and woodland edge habitats often provide a variety of sources of nectar and pollen that may attract saproxylic species. Many saproxylic species appear to fly in sheltered conditions, often in dappled shade, along woodland rides and edges. These conditions are not common in the Lower Park, but are present in parts of the Upper Park, which has not been surveyed for Diptera.

The Lawn Pool may prove to be of importance for Diptera. Several uncommon species were recorded in particular from greater tussock-sedge: *Achalcus flavicollis*,[22] *Stilpon graminum* and various chloropids, as well as *Pteromicra glabricula*. Similarly, the low-lying, damp hollows have produced interesting species, most notably the snail-parasite fly *Colobaea pectoralis*.

Several springs and the stream in woodland at the south eastern edge of the Park are also of interest for Diptera. Tufa terraces occur in the stream and the calcareous mud and mosses found here provide suitable conditions for the early stages of *Pericoma calcilega* and two species of *Oxycera*.

Changes in the Diptera fauna at Moccas Park

Although Wood, Collin and Wainwright recorded in the Park in the early decades of this century, there are few documented early records for the Park. The uncommon species recorded by Wood are mainly associated with wetlands. He may have concentrated his efforts on the Lawn Pool (*Thrypticus nigricauda* actually came from here), but none of these species has been re-recorded in recent surveys, possibly due to the low level of recent recording. Conversely, both the *Fiebrigella* species, which were recorded by Collin in 1934, have been re-found and appear to be present in low numbers in the Park.[23]

It is clear that ash was once more plentiful in the Park and elms have been lost due to Dutch elm disease; both losses have probably impoverised the range of habitats available to saproxylic Diptera in the Park.

Site management

Many saproxylic Diptera, for example empids and hoverflies, require flowers because they feed on nectar or pollen. Hawthorn is one of the species most favoured by nectaring insects (beetles as well as flies). Past management of Moccas Park has seen the loss of many hawthorn bushes, which has resulted in a lack of these essential nectar sources for adult flies throughout the Lower Park. This loss will eventually be partially rectified through the inclusion of hawthorn in the planting scheme undertaken since the Park has been a National Nature Reserve.

The water level in the Lawn Pool should be maintained to ensure that the small, but crucial, marginal wetland habitats are not damaged. For example, on my own visits to the Park, water entirely surrounded the island in June 1994, whereas water was present in only the eastern part of the Pool in June 1997. Falls in water levels make it easier for deer and stock to get onto the island, which is the largest area of the Park that is virtually free from grazing. There is also the risk of eutrophication of the water in the Lawn Pool, particularly in dry periods, as wildfowl, deer and stock congregate at the steadily decreasing area of standing water.

Removal of the conifers around the stream with tufa terraces in the south eastern end of the Park and replacing these with native deciduous species would reduce any risk of acidification of the stream which, above the conifers, is biologically of high quality.

Because many of the existing beeches are dying or dead and in advanced states of decomposition, a new generation of beeches has been included in the ongoing planting scheme. However, these recent plantings will not easily bridge the gap to the previous generation of beeches, most of which are probably 200 years old (see Chapter 3.5). Management aimed at maintaining and improving the conservation value of the veteran trees and saproxylic beetles will benefit the Diptera. Of critical importance is the need to retain, preferably *in situ*, as much fallen dead wood as possible.

Notes

1   Dr J.H. Wood (1841-1914) concentrated his entomological pursuits solely within his native Herefordshire and took up Diptera after initially being interested in Microlepidoptera. He was a member of the Woolhope Naturalists' Field Club. His insect collection was originally bequeathed to Hereford Museum, but it was transferred in 1949 to the then British Museum (Natural History) (J. Cooter pers. comm.). J.E. Collin (1876-1968) was probably the leading amateur, British dipterist of his generation. He was the nephew of, assistant to and entomological heir to the great G.H. Verrall (1848-1911).

2   Wood (1913), d'Assis-Fonseca (1976).

3   Pont (1995).

4   C.J. Wainwright (1867-1949) was a leading amateur dipterist who lived for most of his life in Birmingham.

5   For details of P.J. Skidmore see Chapter 6.1.

6   Harding (1977), P.J. Skidmore (pers. comm.).

7   P.J. Chandler has been an active dipterist for more than 30 years and is the national expert on fungus-gnats. He compiled the latest national check list of Diptera (Chandler 1998).

8   A.E. Stubbs has been a driving force in Diptera recording and insect conservation in Britain for more than 30 years; see also Chapter 6.1.

9   Particularly notable records are quoted by Steele (1985).

10 For details of J.Cooter see Chapter 5.3.

11 Godfrey (1994).

12 There are many techniques for passively sampling insects (and other invertebrates) by use of various types of traps. The most favoured types for Diptera are Malaise traps, interception traps and pan traps.

13 For definitions of Red Data Book statuses and nationally Scarce status see Ball (1994). The statuses cited in this Chapter and Appendix 6 are derived from Falk (1991), Falk & Ismay (in preparation) and information made available as part of the Recorder data management system supplied by the Joint Nature Conservation Committee.

14 I.Perry is an experienced amateur dipterist and a member of the Dipterists Forum.

15 Withers (1989 & pers. comm.), Elbourn (1965), Furse *et al.* (1991).

16 Falk & Ismay (in preparation).

17 See note 13 above.

18 The term *saproxylic* is defined in Chapter 5.1.

19 Harding & Alexander (1994), Fowles (1998), see Chapter 5.1.

20 Sites recently surveyed, which may provide comparisons include Bredon Hill/Elmley Castle Deer Park in Worcestershire, Burnham Beeches in Buckinghamshire, Epping Forest in Essex and several Welsh parks.

21 For example, Dunham Massey in Manchester, Clumber in Nottinghamshire, Calke, Chatsworth and Kedleston in Derbyshire and Grimsthorpe in Lincolnshire.

22 *Achalcus flavicollis* has been split recently into several species; it now unclear which species is present at Moccas Park.

23 John Deeming, National Museum of Wales, has confirmed the identifications of the recent *Fiebrigella* records.

References relating to Moccas Park

D'ASSIS-FONSECA, E.C.M. 1976. Dolichopodidae. *Handbooks for the identification of British insects*, 9(5). London: Royal Entomological Society of London.

FALK, S.J. 1991. *A review of the scarce and threatened flies of Great Britain (part 1)*. (Research and Survey in Nature conservation No. 39.) Peterborough: Joint Nature Conservation Committee.

FALK, S.J. & ISMAY, J. (in preparation). *A review of the scarce and threatened flies of Great Britain (part 2)*. Peterborough: Joint Nature Conservation Committee.

GODFREY, A. 1994. *Preliminary survey and appraisal of the Diptera and Heteroptera of Moccas Park National Nature Reserve, Herefordshire.* Unpublished report to English Nature by Ecosurveys Ltd, Spilsby, Lincolnshire.

HARDING, P.T. 1977. *Moccas Deer Park, Hereford and Worcester: a report on the history, structure and natural history.* Unpublished report to the Nature Conservancy Council by the Institute of Terrestrial Ecology, Huntingdon.

HARDING, P.T. & ALEXANDER, K.N.A. 1994. The use of saproxylic invertebrates in the selection and evaluation of areas of relic forest in pasture-woodlands. *British Journal of Entomology and Natural History*, 7 (Supplement 1), 21-26.

PONT, A.C. 1995. *The type-material of the Diptera.* Oxford University Museum Publication No.3. Oxford: Clarendon Press.

STEELE, C. 1985. *Invertebrate Site Register Report No.59 Part 1. Provisional review of Herefordshire and Worcestershire.* Peterborough: Nature Conservancy Council.

WOOD, J.H. 1913. *Thrypticus nigricauda*, a new species, and notes on a few other Dolichopodidae from Herefordshire. *Entomologist's monthly Magazine*, 49, 268-270.

Other references

BALL, S.G. 1994. The Invertebrate Site Register - objectives and achievements. *In*: P.T.HARDING, ed. Invertebrates in the landscape: invertebrate recording in site evaluation and countryside monitoring. *British Journal of Entomology and Natural History*, 7 (Supplement 1), 2-14.

CHANDLER, P.J. ed. 1998. Diptera. *In*: *Checklists of insects in the British Isles* (New Series) Volume 12, Part 1. Royal Entomological Society of London.

ELBOURN, C.A. 1965. The fauna of a calcareous woodland stream in Berkshire. *Entomologist's monthly Magazine*, 101, 25-30.

FOWLES, A.P. 1997. The Saproxylic Quality Index: an evaluation of dead wood habitats based on rarity scores, with examples from Wales. *The Coleopterist*, 6, 61-66.

FURSE, M.T., WINDER, J.M., SYMER, K.L & CLARKE, R.T. 1991. The faunal richness of headwater streams. National Rivers Authority Research and Development Note 221. Marlow: Foundation for Water Research.

GIBBINGS, R. 1942. *Coming down the Wye.* London: Dent.

WITHERS, P. 1989. Moth flies. Diptera: Psychodidae. *Dipterist's digest*, 4, 1-82.

Other invertebrates

Paul T. Harding

.... man is a guest in a world populated mainly by invertebrates ....

Mario Pavan (1986). *A European cultural revolution: The Council of Europe's 'Charter on invertebrates'.*

Sources of records

Most of the intensive survey work on the invertebrates of Moccas Park has been on the beetles (Coleoptera) (Chapter 5.3) and flies (Diptera) (Chapter 5.4). Targeted surveys have been carried out for only two groups, the slugs, snails and pea-mussels (land and freshwater Mollusca) and the spiders (Araneae). Other groups of invertebrates are notably under-recorded, although two species of bird fleas (Siphonaptera) have been the subject of an ecological study in the Park (see Chapter 5.7).[1] Most records of these other groups have been obtained from casual recording or as a by-product of other work. Details of the sources of records are given in Appendix 7.

In 1990, as part of the 10-year Nature Reserve Agreement management review process, Nature Conservancy Council compiled records of the less common species of invertebrates known from the Park. These records are managed as part of the Invertebrate Site Register (ISR) database, which has been updated for some groups up to 1994.[2]

There are possible records of two declining species of butterfly *Boloria selene*, the small pearl-bordered fritillary butterfly (Lepidoptera, Nymphalidae) and *Boloria euphrosyne*, the pearl-bordered fritillary butterfly (Lepidoptera, Nymphalidae), but records of either species at Moccas Park are almost certainly unreliable.[3] Three other uncommon species have been recorded from the Park, for which the records are now considered to be unreliable.[4]

Few of the species, mentioned in this chapter, have English names. In all cases the scientific species name is given first and then an English name, but many of these names refer to a genus or a whole family, not to the individual species.

Gaps in knowledge

The records for groups other than Coleoptera and Diptera do not necessarily reflect the fauna that is probably present. Although the survey of molluscs consisted of only two consecutive days' fieldwork, the overall list of species obtained is representative of this area of Herefordshire. The

Figure 5.5.1

The medicinal leech *Hirudo medicinalis.* This uncommon leech occurs in the Lawn Pool. Photograph by Roger S. Key.

richest habitat within the Park in terms of land snail diversity is the small hillside flush southwest of the Lawn Pool.[5] The surveys of spiders by Mike Taylor have produced an overall list of 116 species and although this list is certainly incomplete, it compares favourably with four other parks where, in some cases, more recording has taken place.[6] But none of the groups listed in Appendix 7 can be considered to have been comprehensively surveyed.

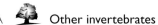

Some potentially important groups of invertebrates have apparently never been recorded in the Park, for example - leaf-hoppers and aphids (Hemiptera: Homoptera), booklice (Psocoptera), lacewings (Neuroptera), mayflies (Ephemeroptera) and springtails (Collembola). Other important groups, such as caddisflies (Trichoptera) and grasshoppers and crickets (Orthoptera) are known from only a few casual records.

Nationally protected, threatened and uncommon species

Of the species recorded in the Park, two have been listed under international conventions/legislation and/or UK legislation and nine others are listed in Red Data Books or National Reviews.[7]

❖ ***Hirudo medicinalis***, the medicinal leech (Annelida, Hirudinea, Hirudinidae) (Figure 5.5.1)
Status: Berne (Appendix III), Habitats Directive (Annex V), WCA 1981 (Schedule 5), UKBAP (Priority species) and RDB3.
H. medicinalis appears to have been reported from the Park by Robert Angus, who found it to be common in the Lawn Pool in 1973.[8] It was not recorded again until a systematic survey was made by Reuben Neville in 1998,[9] when three individual specimens were noted at two sampling points in the Pool. It occurs typically in eutrophic lakes and ponds with dense stands of water plants. Although adult medicinal leeches can feed on the blood of any vertebrates, tadpoles seem to be an important source of food for young specimens.

❖ ***Pisidium pseudosphaerium***, a freshwater pea-mussel (Mollusca, Bivalvia, Sphaeriidae)
Status: UKBAP (Species of conservation concern) and RDB3.
Recorded at Moccas Park at some time in the 1970s by Peter Dance.[10] Its habitat is thought to be transient in character: "clear, clean water in stagnant places choked with aquatic plants, often over a richly organic, even anaerobic, bottom", often occurring with *P. obtusale*.[11] The latter species was found by Ian Killeen during his survey in 1994, but he failed to re-find *P. pseudosphaerium* although the conditions of part of the Lawn Pool apparently remain suitable for it.

Other noteworthy species include the following.
❖ ***Zygiella stroemi***, an orb web spider (Arachnida, Araneae, Araneidae). Status: Scarce.
Recorded by Mike Taylor in 1993. Typically occurs in deep fissures in the bark of trees, particularly oaks.
❖ ***Anthocoris visci***, the mistletoe flower bug (Insecta, Hemiptera, Heteroptera, Cimicidae). Status: Scarce. Recorded by Arthur Massee, some time before 1964. It occurs on mistletoe as a predator of the mistletoe plant-louse *Psylla visci*.
❖ ***Brachythops flavens***, a sawfly (Insecta, Hymenoptera Symphyta, Tenthredinidae). Status: Scarce. Recorded by Andy Godfrey on 10 June 1997. The larvae feed on sedges. This species has a northern and western distribution in Britain.
❖ ***Dolerus megapterus***, a sawfly (Insecta, Hymenoptera Symphyta, Tenthredinidae). Status: Proposed RDB3. The Moccas Park record is attributed to Harold Daltry.[12] The larvae feed on sedges. This species occurs mainly in Scotland, especially on Speyside and Deeside.
❖ ***Crossocerus walkeri***, a solitary wasp (Insecta, Hymenoptera Aculeata, Sphecidae). Status: Scarce. Its nest tunnels are in the dead wood of broadleaved trees and are stocked with small mayflies (Ephemeroptera), usually of the family Baetidae, many of which seem to be associated with rivers or streams with high water quality.
❖ ***Stelis punctulatissima***, a solitary bee (Insecta, Hymenoptera Aculeata, Apidae). Status: Scarce. Recorded by Andy Godfrey in June/July 1994. It is a cleptoparasite of other species of solitary bees; none of the known host species has been recorded from the Park.[13]
❖ ***Synanthedon myopaeformis***, the red-belted clearwing moth (Insecta, Lepidoptera, Sesiidae). Status: Scarce. Recorded by Jonathan Cooter in 1976. Its larvae burrow under

old and cancerous bark of wild and cultivated apple trees (and occasionally other rosaceous fruit and ornamental trees).

❖ **Bryotropha basaltinella,** a micro-moth (Insecta, Lepidoptera, Gelechiidae). Status: Scarce. Recorded by Denzil Ffennell in June 1974, "in outhouse by day", possibly referring to the partly collapsed deer shed in the Park. The larvae are found on moss and the adults are reported as occurring around old thatch.

Characteristic species

Although rare beetles and flies attract most of the entomologists that visit the Park, they, and less specialist visitors, may be aware of a few other invertebrates that could be regarded as being characteristic of Moccas Park at an appropriate time of the year. Here are a few examples.

Figure 5.5.2

The woodland (or ash-grey) slug *Limax cinereoniger.* This nocturnal slug is the largest in Britain. Drawing by Peter Kirby reproduced by permission of the Joint Nature Conservation Committee.

❖ **Limax cinereoniger,** the woodland (or ash-grey) slug (Mollusca, Gastropoda) (Figure 5.5.2). This large, dark grey slug is typical of old woodlands, especially in western Britain.

❖ **Ixodes ricinus,** the sheep tick (Arachnida, Acari, Ixodidae). With large numbers of deer and sheep in the Park for centuries, it is amazing that there seems to have been no record of this common parasite of mammals, until I collected several from my body after surveying trees in August 1997. Perhaps it was just too obvious for anyone to record, but I had never seen it in the Park before 1997.

❖ **Porcellio scaber,** the common rough woodlouse (Crustacea, Isopoda, Oniscidea). This species can be found under almost any piece of bark or log, often in very large numbers. It is one of the most tolerant species of woodlice, occurring in acidic and dry conditions.

❖ **Vespa crabro,** the hornet (Insecta, Hymenoptera Aculeata, Vespidae) (Figure 5.5.3). This giant wasp is common throughout the Park. They nest in hollow trees, sometimes to the annoyance or consternation of visiting coleopterists. They are predatory on other invertebrates.

Figure 5.5.3

The hornet *Vespa crabro.* This impressive insect is common in late summer throughout the Park. Photograph by Roger S. Key.

❖ **Lasius flavus,** the yellow hill ant (Insecta, Hymenoptera Aculeata, Formicidae). Anthills were formerly very plentiful in the Park, but extensive ploughing and re-seeding in the 1960s, and subsequent management of the grassland has reduced the population of yellow hill ants to mainly small, probably short-lived colonies.

❖ **Quercusia quercus,** the purple hairstreak butterfly (Insecta, Lepidoptera, Lycaenidae). This beautiful butterfly is easily missed unless one looks up into the canopy of oak trees, where they feed on honey-dew. They do not fly readily and can most easily be observed in the evening of a warm summer's day. The larvae feed on the buds and young foliage of oaks. Numbers of individuals of this species vary considerably year to year.

❖ **Libellula depressa,** the broad-bodied chaser dragonfly (Insecta, Odonata, Libellulidae). The broad, flattened and pale blue abdomen of a mature male *L.depressa* is easily recognised. Males hold territory aggressively over lengths of the margins of the Lawn Pool, perching on suitably tall and exposed stems or twigs.

The importance of Moccas Deer Park for invertebrates other than Coleoptera and Diptera

Because of the, at best, fragmentary knowledge of most invertebrate groups at Moccas Park, it would be unwise to draw conclusions about the importance of the site for anything other than Coleoptera and Diptera (see Chapters 5.3 and 5.4).

From the other invertebrate groups, *Hirudo medicinalis* and *Pisidium pseudosphaerium* are nationally important, and the former is internationally important. It is perhaps surprising that neither of these species has been the subject of further study at the site, during the time that it has been a National Nature Reserve. On present evidence, the population of *H.medicinalis* in the Lawn Pool may have declined since the 1970s and there is no evidence of *P.pseudosphaerium* being seen for more than 20 years.

Much remains to be discovered at Moccas Park, and although there may not be the noteworthy fauna that distinguishes the beetles at the site, there may yet be some surprises in store for specialists in other groups.

Notes

1   Harper, Marchant & Boddington (1992).

2   Records were compiled by Dr Stuart Ball and incorporated in the *Brief Management Plan* prepared by English Nature (1992). I am grateful to Dr Roger Key for supplying updated listings from the Invertebrate Site Register database at English Nature.

3   *Boloria selene* - Source is the Biological Records Centre database "Moccas Park 1978, recorder not known". This record was mapped in Heath, Pollard & Thomas (1984) despite the obvious uncertainty about who made the record. *Boloria euphrosyne* - Source is a note for the file by John Bacon (NCC Chief Warden, West Midlands) dated 21 February 1991, commenting on the Draft Plan of Management for Moccas Park: "Owner records having probably seen Pearl Bordered Fritillaries in May one year". The present evidence is insufficient to suggest that either species has been recorded with any certainty at Moccas Park in recent times.

4   *Lygus punctatus* (Insecta, Hemiptera, Heteroptera, Miridae) is a nationally scarce species. It was recorded by Massee by sweeping on 9 May 1964 and again in June 1965, and noted by him to be a new record for Herefordshire. The species has been subject to much misidentification (Kirby 1992). As it is known to be associated with Caledonian pine forests in Scotland, mainly on juniper and Scots pine, its occurrence at Moccas Park seems improbable. *Hephanthus nanus* (Insecta, Hemiptera, Homoptera, Cicadellidae), recorded in the Invertebrate Site Register database, is now known to be due to an error in data entry. The record, dated 1965, was listed in Steel (1985). I am grateful to Roger Key of English Nature for resolving my query about this record. *Mompha divisella* (Insects, Lepidoptera, Momphidae) was recorded by Denzil Ffennell in June 1974. Michael Harper considers that *M.divisella* is unlikely to have been recorded as far north as Herefordshire and that the record should be omitted from the present list for Moccas Park, subject to confirmation by examination of Ffennell's collection at the Hope Department in Oxford.

5   Ian Killeen of the Conchological Society surveyed the molluscs in 1994 (Killeen 1994).

6   Mike Taylor of English Nature surveyed the spiders on several occasions in 1993 and 1994. Crocker & Daws (1996) gave the numbers of species of spiders found in three parks in Leicestershire: Bradgate 108, Croxton 34, Donington 63. Harding (1972) listed 73 species from Staverton Park, Suffolk. Duffey (1973) noted that prolonged casual collecting rarely got beyond 200 species at a site, citing as examples Wytham Wood, Oxfordshire (215 species) and Wicken Fen, Cambridgeshire (212 species) compared with the list for Monks Wood, Cambridgeshire (122 species).

7   Included are the following:
Berne Convention on the conservation of European wildlife and natural habitats (1979);
Habitats Directive - The European Community Council Directive (92/43/EEC) on the conservation of natural and semi-natural habitats of wild flora and fauna;
WCA 1981 - Wildlife and Countryside Act 1981;
UKBAP - The UK Biodiversity Action Plan - priority species lists in the Steering Group Report 1995;
RDB - British Red Data Books: 2. Insects (Shirt 1987), British Red Data Books: 3. Invertebrates (Bratton 1991) - which see for the respective Status category definitions (1,2,3,K, etc);
National Reviews - National reviews of the status of several taxonomic groups have been published by NCC/JNCC - see Ball (1994) for a list of reviews and the respective Status category definitions (RDB 1,2,3,K, nationally Scarce, etc).

8   Foster (1977).

9   The survey was undertaken in 11 and 15 June 1998 for the Royal Society for the Protection of Birds, lead partner for the medicinal leech under the UK Biodiversity Action Plan process. The results are from a total of 155 minutes of standard sampling in the Lawn Pool and three nearby pools in the Park. By comparison with results at other sites it is thought likely that numbers at Moccas Park are relatively low. Although the Park is one of 52 sites at which medicinal leech was recorded in 1998, it is notably isolated from all other sites (Ausden & Stork 1999).

10 S.P.Dance is an international expert in Mollusca who worked for some time at the National Museum of Wales. In the 1970s he lived at Clifford and visited Moccas Park on several occasions.

11 Bratton (1991).

12 Benson (1958) lists "Herefordshire: Moccas Park (H.W.Daltry)".

13 Host species are listed in Edwards (1997).

References relating to Moccas Park

AUSDEN, M. & STORK, C. 1999. *Medicinal leech progress report: April 1999.* Unpublished report. Sandy: Royal Society for the Protection of Birds.

BENSON, R.B. 1958. Hymenoptera 2. Symphyta, section (c). *Handbooks for the identification of British insects,* VI, Pt 2(c). London: Royal Entomological Society of London.

FOSTER, G.N. 1977. Editorial note to R.B.ANGUS Water beetles at Moccas Park, Herefordshire. *The Balfour-Browne Club Newsletter,* 6, 1-2.

HARPER, G.H., MARCHANT, A. & BODDINGTON, D.G. 1992. The ecology of the hen flea *Ceratophyllus gallinae* and the moorhen flea *Dasypsyllus gallinulae* in nest boxes. *Journal of animal ecology,* 61, 317-327.

ENGLISH NATURE 1992. *Moccas Park National Nature Reserve, a brief management plan.* Unpublished. Shrewsbury: English Nature West Midlands Team.

KILLEEN, I.J. 1994. *A survey of the land and freshwater Mollusca of Moccas Park NNR, Herefordshire.* Unpublished report to English Nature, Malvern Wells.

STEEL, C. 1985. Review of the sites in England. Provisional review of Hereford and Worcester. *Invertebrate Site Register Reports,* 59. London: Nature Conservancy Council.

Other references

BALL, S.G. 1994. The Invertebrate Site Register - objectives and achievements. *In:* P.T.HARDING, ed. Invertebrates in the landscape: invertebrate recording in site evaluation and countryside monitoring. *British journal of entomology and natural history,* 7 (Supplement 1), 2-14.

BRATTON, J.H. 1991. *British Red Data Books: 3. Invertebrates other than insects.* Peterborough: Joint Nature Conservation Committee.

EDWARDS, R. ed. 1997. *Provisional atlas of the aculeate Hymenoptera of Britain and Ireland. Part 1.* Huntingdon: Biological Records Centre.

HEATH, J., POLLARD, E. & THOMAS, J. 1984. *Atlas of butterflies in Britain and Ireland.* Harmondsworth: Viking.

KIRBY, P. 1992. A review of the scarce and threatened Hemiptera of Great Britain. UK Nature Conservation no. 2. Peterborough: Joint Nature Conservation Committee.

PAVAN, M. 1986. *A European cultural revolution: The Council of Europe's "Charter on invertebrates".* Strasbourg: Council of Europe.

SHIRT, D.B. 1987. *British Red Data Books: 1. Insects.* Peterborough: Nature Conservancy Council.

5/5

Fallow deer: history and management

Tom Wall and
Rory Putman

In The life and letters of the great Earl of Cork *by
Dorothea Townshend,1904, it is recorded that* "Henry Vaughan
of Moccas .... contributed deer for his cousin's park"
at Youghal, co. Cork, about 1617.

Anon (1933). *Transactions of the Woolhope Naturalists' Field Club.*

Fallow deer.
Drawing by Gisèle Wall.

Early references

Fallow deer were introduced, almost certainly by the Normans.[1] They were released into forests and were used over successive centuries to populate the deer parks that proliferated across the British Isles. Richard Boyle, Earl of Cork, stocked his Irish park with deer from various English sources, including some, as we learn above, from Moccas, in about 1617, by courtesy of his cousin Henry Vaughan; this gives us the earliest substantive evidence for the existence of Moccas Deer Park.[2]

Henry Vaughan's widow, Frances, was later to marry a man caught poaching her late husband's remaining deer.[3] This was Edward of the ancient family of Cornewall of Berrington. Doubtless Edward, the poacher, soon turned keeper and safeguarded his herd. His great grand-daughter's husband, Sir George Cornewall, certainly did. Sir George heads a list of gentlemen who placed an advertisement in Pugh's *Hereford Journal* on 9, 16 and 23 January 1772 offering a reward for "intelligence" leading to the prosecution of poachers (Figure 5.6.1). Sir George's concern probably reflected not just the economic value of the deer but also the status and aesthetic value they conferred. This is suggested by the inclusion of deer in two watercolours of Moccas Park by Thomas Hearne, part of a series of nine paintings of the Moccas Estate commissioned from him by Sir George in the 1780s (see Figure 1.1.1).

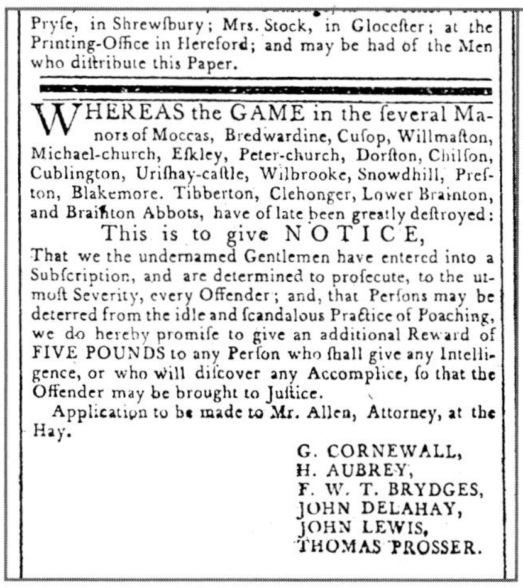

Sir George's Accounts include an entry on February 7 1773 for "thatching the deer house", and the Farm Book for 1786-1799 and Farm Account for 1800-1817 include winter entries in each of the years 1789-1817 for "loads of hay for deer".[4] Cornewall's records also indicate intensive grazing of the Park by livestock. Grazing rights were let and regular payments noted for the pasturing of cattle and horses, and, from the late 1780s, of around 260 sheep for seven months of the year (for further details see Chapter 2.3). Given this level of grazing it is very likely that the deer were in need of winter feed.

Pryfe, in Shrewfbury; Mrs. Stock, in Glocefter; at the Printing-Office in Hereford; and may be had of the Men who diftribute this Paper.

WHEREAS the GAME in the feveral Manors of Moccas, Bredwardine, Cufop, Willmafton, Michael-church, Efkley, Peter-church, Dorfton, Chilfon, Cublington, Urifhay-caftle, Wilbrooke, Snowdhill, Prefton, Blakemore. Tibberton, Clehonger, Lower Brainton, and Braifhton Abbots, have of late been greatly deftroyed:

This is to give NOTICE,

That we the undernamed Gentlemen have entered into a Subfcription, and are determined to profecute, to the utmoft Severity, every Offender; and, that Perfons may be deterred from the idle and fcandalous Practice of Poaching, we do hereby promife to give an additional Reward of FIVE POUNDS to any Perfon who fhall give any Intelligence, or who will difcover any Accomplice, fo that the Offender may be brought to Juftice.

Application to be made to Mr. Allen, Attorney, at the Hay.

G. CORNEWALL,
H. AUBREY,
F. W. T. BRYDGES,
JOHN DELAHAY,
JOHN LEWIS,
THOMAS PROSSER.

Figure 5.6.1

Hereford Journal **advertisement, 1772.** An appeal concerning the prosecution of poachers.

Park pale and park wall

We went through the deer park, among the great ruined weird ghostly oaks.
Coming back we saw some deer that had broken bounds outside the park pales.
Preece said that they kept hounds at Moccas for hunting the stray deer back into the park
and that the deer would be driven in again over the buckleaps.

Francis Kilvert, 17 January 1878.[5]

The keeping of deer necessitates a series of significant commitments; not least is the erection and maintenance of a deer-proof boundary.[6] In the past, this boundary will have been composed entirely of stretches of pale (fence) and of wall. An Ecclesiastical Terrier dated 1677 refers to several areas of land in Moccas parish as being against the pale of Moccas Park.[7] Sir George Cornewall's Account Books of 1777-1785 include a number of entries showing payments for "park wall" and "stone for park wall" (see Chapter 2.3).[8] Presumably these relate to the Deer Park, as may some, at least, of the many references to "paling", and the even more suggestive references to "hauling park pales" and "park paling". Entries in May to August 1786 for "sunk fence" may relate to the stretch of fencing by the roadside near to the Park Lodge where the pale stands in a deep ditch, thereby permitting unobstructed views into and out of the Park. In Sir George's day the Park boundary ran to some 5.2 km in length; today, although the Park has been reduced in size by 41 ha, the boundary is only 200 m shorter.

The park pale was presumably of similar design to that which survives today along 400 m of the roadside boundary near the Park Lodge (Figure 5.6.2). Whitaker refers in 1892 to the pale as being of oak,[9] but sweet chestnut was used for a section replaced recently and 20 years ago a run of 'chestnut paling' (a type of fencing in which thin, close-spaced sweet chestnut pales, of equal length, are wired together and attached to support posts, see Figure 5.6.3) was erected along the roadside between Cross End Farm and Lawn Gate Lodge.

Figure 5.6.2

The park pale, 1974. Photograph by Oliver Rackham.

It would appear that prior to the availability of woven wire fencing, most of the Lower Park was paled and most of the Upper Park was walled. This distribution doubtless reflected convenience. Quarries in the Upper Park would presumably have furnished the stone for the wall, and whilst the pales may have come from the Upper Park too, they were far lighter to transport than the stone would have been.

Today only 500 m of the Park boundary is walled. Long stretches lie derelict and have been replaced by post and wire fences, and some of the stone which made up the wall along the boundary of the area lost to the Park in the 1950s has been carted away for use elsewhere.

Breaches in the boundary are bound to occur from time to time due to branches or trees falling across fences, or a piece of wall collapsing. Until they are found and repaired, these breaches allow deer to leave the Park, but repairs then serve to prevent the return of the escapees. To counter this problem there are today, as in Kilvert's time (and doubtless previously too), what he called "buck leaps" (more commonly referred to as 'deer leaps'). Such leaps exist both in the park pale (Figure 5.6.3) and in the stone wall. The boundary barrier is lower at these points, but low ground on the inside prevents deer from escaping whereas high ground on the outside allows deer to jump back

Figure 5.6.3

Deer leap, 1979. A deer leap on the northern boundary near the Lawn Gate Lodge. Photograph by Paul T. Harding.

into the Park. Today, however, there are no hounds to round up the strays.

Colour, numbers and herd composition

We walked through the Park under the guidance of Mr Bishop, admiring the deer.

Francis Kilvert, 30 August 1872.[10]

What colour were the deer that Kilvert admired? Fallow deer display a great degree of colour variation, including white, 'common-coloured' (chestnut with white spots in summer, but with the coat darkening in winter and the spots becoming indistinct), menil (lighter brown, almost buff, with very bright white spots; in this variation the coat colour remains the same summer and winter) or black. Today, the Moccas Park deer are predominantly what are usually called 'light common', in which the base colour is intermediate between the chestnut of 'true' common and that of menil animals, but with the coats still darkening in winter pelage, when the spots become less distinct (Figure 5.6.4); there is however a small percentage of full menils.[11] Three light bucks were brought from Barrington Park in Oxfordshire in the 1960s in an effort to lighten the colour of the herd and the instruction was given that when culling, lighter coloured animals should be retained.[12] Studies of mating success carried out at other parks, show however, that rigorous selection would probably be necessary in order to influence development of a particular colour variant.[13]

It is difficult to make accurate counts of the herd because of the wariness of the deer, the awkward terrain, the extensive bracken beds and, in parts, the quite dense tree cover. In September 1994 a series of counts suggested a minimum herd size of 260 composed of 80 fawns, 120 yearling and adult does, 36 prickets and 20 bucks older than prickets.[14]

Table 5.6.1 shows a range of estimates of deer numbers recorded over the years. These need however to be treated with some caution. It is not always clear as to which time of year the estimates refer and few of them appear to have been based on any systematic survey.

Fawn to doe ratios in September 1994 suggested that at least 75% of potentially breeding females had successfully reared a fawn to that date, which is well within normal ranges calculated for other park herds. The male herd consisted of 5 or 6 master bucks (breeding animals of about 6 years or older). The ratio of bucks older than yearlings (estimated at around 20) to breeding does (minimum 100-120) indicated a sex-ratio among animals of breeding age of 1:5 or 1:6. In a herd maintained essentially for amenity purposes a higher proportion of mature bucks would be retained, in one managed for venison production, the proportion would be lower, but neither objective dominates at Moccas Park.

Table 5.6.1. Records and references to deer at Moccas Park and their numbers.

Date	Numbers and details	Source
1867	Park named but no details given	Shirley (1867)
1892	180	Whitaker (1892)
1949	50	Whitehead (1950)
1963	"The size of the herd was halved about 18 months ago and is now about 120"	Pritchard & Morris (1963)
1970-77	1970: 150 post cull, condition very poor, felt to be too many in view of livestock numbers. Herd reduced in subsequent years and held at a post cull level of about 100	L. Slaney (gamekeeper) pers. comm.
1974	80; culled every year, with a major cull every four years or so	IRP (1975)
1978	38, spring; significant numbers must have escaped over the previous winter	D. Chandler (gamekeeper) pers. comm.
1986-9	The deer herd was kept to 120 after culling	English Nature (1992)
1988	80-100	Hingston (1988)
1988	120	M.C.M. (1989)
1994	Minimum, post cull, of 180 Minimum summer herd of 260	Putman (1994)
1997/8	Summer herd 315; post cull 220	B. Chester-Master, (manager) and P. Price, (gamekeeper) pers.comm.

Management of the herd

> [Mrs Hicks's] *husband and sons were shooting bucks for venison in the Park.*
> *She said it was the worst park in England for killing bucks, and killed the men as well*
> *as the deer. I saw a herd of bucks near the lodge walking about together*
> *with their sides as tight together as herrings packed in a barrel and their horns*
> *going like a forest. They let me come quite close to them as I had no gun,*
> *though the keepers could not get within a ¼ mile.*

Francis Kilvert, 14 August 1878.[15]

In the absence of culling, the number of animals in an enclosed deer herd would be regulated by food supply; mortality due to starvation would be frequent. Body weights of culled animals provide a good guide to the condition of the herd, the carrying capacity of the Park and the need for supplementary feeding. Series of body weights of yearling males and does recorded between 1979 and 1994 by the former gamekeeper, David Chandler, are shown in summary form in Table 5.6.2.

Table 5.6.2. Weights of Moccas Park deer 1979-1994 (adapted from Putman 1994).

Weights were recorded as larder carcase weights (gralloched carcase,[16] head and feet removed, skin on). Because weights decline somewhat over the winter, weights presented here are standardised as yearling males (prickets): September/October cull only; does: two sets of figures, November/December only and November-February. Note that as not all animals shot were weighed, this table does not indicate the total cull achieved over the period. Data courtesy of D. Chandler.

Yearling males (prickets) : September/October only

Years	1979/80-1983/84	1984/85-1988/89	1989/90-1993/94
Mean weight kg (lbs)	26.5 (58.4)	28.8 (63.3)	28.4 (62.5)
Sample size	80	76	92

Does (includes both mature animals and yearling does): November/December only

Years	1979/80-1983/84	1984/85-1988/89	1989/90-1993/94
Mean weight kg (lbs)	23.3 (51.3)	25.9 (56.9)	24.5 (53.8)
Sample size	42	45	91

Does (includes both mature animals and yearling does): November to February

Years	1979/80-1983/84	1984/85-1988/89	1989/90-1993/94
Mean weight kg (lbs)	23.3 (51.3)	25.0 (55.0)	24.5 (53.8)
Sample size	42	78	111

In fallow deer, yearling males and adult does show the least variance in bodyweight around a calculated population mean and are thus the best indicators of herd condition.[17] The records summarised here do not however distinguish between yearling does and older animals and since weights do not usually stabilise until deer are more than two years old, a mixed age group of this sort will show somewhat higher variance in weight than a sample drawn just from older animals.

The weights show no consistent trend up or down over the 15 year period, despite the fact that the herd is believed to have grown over these years, and they compare well with those from across a range of other parks. Data which were gathered, over a seven-year period, from 7,000 animals across the sex and age range from 25 parks in various parts of England and Wales, indicate that typically, yearling males (September/October only) have a weight of about 25.5 kg (lower than the above means) and does (November to February) 23.4 to 25.2 kg (similar to the above means).[18]

The deer at Moccas Park are not given supplementary feed in all winters as they might be in some other deer parks. The greater abundance of mature mast trees at Moccas Park compared with some other parks may make it less necessary. Certainly, in the prolific, if sporadic, mast years, there can be large quantities of acorns available for the deer as well as good amounts of chestnuts (sweet and horse) and beech mast, all of which they also eat.[19] Studies conducted elsewhere indicate however, that if the average weights of adult does or prickets recorded during the autumn fall below a threshold of 25 kg carcase weight, there is a need for supplementary feeding to get the deer through the winter.[20]

The Park's carrying capacity for deer

*.... [in] the glades of the Park the herds of deer were moving under the brown oaks
and the brilliant green hawthorns ....*

Francis Kilvert, 22 April 1876.[21]

The carrying capacity of a park for deer depends critically on its use by farm livestock. At Moccas, the capacity of the Park to carry significant numbers of farm livestock, in addition to deer, was increased by the ploughing, discing, liming, fertilising and reseeding of the 1960s and 1970s (see Chapter 6.1). Livestock numbers were increased (see Chapter 6.5) and as many as 630 ewes and lambs were grazed in the Park in the late 1980s, as well as 120 deer. Stocking of sheep alongside deer can result in cross-infection of parasites,[22] but this does not seem to have posed a problem at Moccas Park.

Following the improvements to the agricultural potential of the Park, pasture quality was maintained for many years by periodic fertilising, liming, topping, harrowing, rolling and weed control, whilst supplementary feeding of livestock was routine. These measures were progressively phased out however from the late 1980s at the request of Nature Conservancy

Figure 5.6.4

Deer grazing in winter, *circa* **1975.** This view is from just beside the Park Lodge gate looking across to the Lawn Pool. Scraper board engraving by Peter J. Manders.

Council and English Nature and, but for agreed minor exceptions, ceased altogether in 1996. The aim has been to reduce to a minimum artificial inputs to the Park such as fertiliser and concentrated foods. These inputs permit unnaturally high stocking levels with consequent problems of eutrophication leading to damage to lichens (see Chapter 4.1) and of 'poaching' of the ground in winter, thereby encouraging weed infestations. A more natural management regime has meant a reduction in the capacity of the Park to carry livestock, but deer numbers have been allowed to increase.

The 1996/7 level of 300 ewes and their lambs in spring and summer and 100 ewes over the winter, together with a deer herd of 180, rising to 260 after fawning, appeared to be about right. It is believed that in the absence of winter grazing by sheep, an over-winter deer population of up to 370 might be accommodated. Other grazing animals would however be needed in the summer months, because without them, the grasses would quickly mature to flowering spikes and then seed, offering less nutritious forage for the deer.

There is a very marked browse line on all the trees in the Park, and at current grazing levels, and, it would seem, those that have operated for many generations, any chance of establishing new generations of trees or shrubs, whether by planting or natural regeneration, depends entirely on fencing. The incidence of herb species is reduced, palatable adventitious woodland species such as bramble and ivy are virtually eliminated, and unpalatable ones like bracken prosper (see Chapter 4.3). But this is a deer park and it would be perverse to wish for things to be otherwise.

Notes

1   Chapman & Putman (1991).
2   Townshend (1904).
3   Robinson (1869), Reade (1904).
4   Hereford Record Office (HCRO) J56/IV/2, HCRO J56/III/116,117.
5   Plomer (1940). The Preece in question may have been Kilvert's tenant, Thomas Preece of the Rectory Farm, Brobury, or a member of the Preece family who lived at Bredwardine.
6   Other significant commitments are the setting aside of a tract of land on which to keep the deer, the annual cull, and the need, at least in some years, to feed the deer during the winter.
7   Harding (1977).
8   HCRO J56/IV/3.
9   Whitaker (1892).
10 Plomer (1939).
11 Information concerning today's deer herd is drawn largely from a report by Putman (1994) based on observations of the herd in September 1994, discussions with the gamekeeper, David Chandler, and a review of the latter's records. Putman was able to draw on comparative information gathered by his colleagues and himself in detailed studies of herds in 25 parks lying in various parts of England and Wales, including Kentchurch Court, another Herefordshire deer park. Kentchurch, Moccas and Eastnor Parks are now the only active deer parks in the county. There are said to have been 35 parks in Herefordshire in medieval times (Cantor 1983), but some of these may not have been deer parks; there were still 12 deer parks in 1920 (Anon 1974).
12 Len Slaney, pers. comm.
13 Langbein & Thirgood (1989), Langbein (1991). Typically a few males achieve the vast majority of copulations. In one park of some 120 does and 30 mature bucks, only 5 or 6 bucks achieved any matings and the vast majority of does were covered by just three males (Langbein 1991). Thus, for successful colour selection, it would ideally be necessary to make sure that all possible sires were of the chosen colour.
14 Fawn is applied to animals up to one year old, pricket (male) and yearling doe, to animals of between one and two years old.
15 Plomer (1940). Kilvert's account indicates that Mr Hicks was a gamekeeper; he probably lived at Park Lodge.
16 Gralloched means eviscerated.
17 Putman & Langbein (1992).
18 From data cited in Putman (1994).
19 In one study population, oaks in a good year bore an average of 50,000 acorns with some yielding as many as 90,000 (Jones 1959). There are some 1,000 mature oak trees growing in Moccas Park but many will not be very productive. Assuming an average yield of 20,000 acorns, and working on the basis of 220-250 acorns per kilo for pedunculate oak (Forestart, pers. comm.) this would indicate that a crop of some 85 metric tonnes of acorns might be forthcoming in a good acorn year. This is only a speculative figure and the crop will of course be shared amongst a very wide range of animals, including sheep, but it is indicative of the potentially high input of feed at a time when deer need to build up their body weights for the winter.
20 Putman & Langbein (1992).
21 Plomer (1940).
22 See for example Hawkins (1988) and Putman & Langbein (1992).

References relating to Moccas Park

ANON. 1933. Notes of field meeting to Monnington and Moccas. *Transactions of the Woolhope Naturalists' Field Club*, xi-xviii.

ANON. 1974. Notes of field meeting to Moccas and Eastnor Parks. *Transactions of the Woolhope Naturalists' Field Club*, 144.

ENGLISH NATURE. 1992. *Moccas Park National Nature Reserve: Brief Management Plan.* West Midlands Team, Shrewsbury, unpublished.

HARDING, P.T. 1977. *Moccas Deer Park, Hereford and Worcester: a report on the history, structure and natural history.* Unpublished report to the Nature Conservancy Council by the Institute of Terrestrial Ecology, Huntingdon.

HINGSTON, F. ed. 1988. *Deer parks and deer of Great Britain.* Buckingham: Sporting & Leisure Press.

I.R.P. 1975. Hereford Branch, Moccas Estate. *Quarterly Journal of Forestry*, 69, 113-115.

M.C.M. 1989. Three Counties Division, Moccas Park. *Quarterly Journal of Forestry*, 83, 135- 137.

PLOMER, W. 1939, 1940. *Kilvert's diary.* Volumes two and three. London: Jonathan Cape.

PRITCHARD, T.O. & MORRIS, M.G. 1963. Annex to unpublished paper to the Nature Conservancy's Committee for England. E/M/63/94.

PUTMAN, R.J. 1994. *Survey and description of the deer herd at Moccas Park NNR.* Unpublished report to English Nature.

READE, C. 1904. *Memorials of old Herefordshire.* London: Bemrose and Sons.

ROBINSON, C.J. 1869. *A history of the castles of Herefordshire and their lords.* London: Longman.

SHIRLEY, E.P. 1867. *Some account of English deer parks.* London: John Murray.

TOWNSHEND, D. 1904. *The life and letters of the great Earl of Cork.* London: Duckworth.

WHITAKER, J. 1892. *A descriptive list of the deer-parks and paddocks of England.* London: Ballantyne, Hanson and Co.

WHITEHEAD, G.K. 1950. *Deer and their management in the deer parks of Great Britain and Ireland.* London: Country Life.

Other references

CANTOR, L. 1983. *The medieval parks of England, a gazetteer.* Loughborough: Loughborough University.

CHAPMAN, N.G. & PUTMAN, R.J. 1991. Fallow deer. *In*: G.B.CORBET & S.HARRIS. *The Handbook of British Mammals.* Oxford: Blackwell, 508-518.

HAWKINS, D. 1988. The parasitic interrelationships of deer and sheep on the Knebworth Park Estate, near Stevenage. *Deer*, 7, 296-300.

JONES, E.W. 1959. Biological flora of the British Isles. *Quercus. Journal of Ecology*, 47, 169-222.

LANGBEIN, J. 1991. *Effects of density and age on body condition, reproductive performance, behaviour and survival of fallow deer.* PhD thesis, University of Southampton.

LANGBEIN, J. & THIRGOOD, S.J. 1989. Variation in mating systems of fallow deer in relation to ecology. *Ethology*, 83, 195-214.

PUTMAN, R.J. & LANGBEIN, J. 1992. Effects of stocking density, feeding and herd management on mortality of park deer. *In*: R. BROWN, ed. *Biology of deer.* New York: Springer-Verlag, 180-188.

Birds

David Boddington
and Alan Marchant

In June 1873, I noticed a pair of these birds [pied flycatchers]
*at the eastern end of Moccas pool. From their anxiety
they had probably a nest of young ones in the immediate vicinity.*

Rev. Clement Ley quoted by H G Bull (1888) in
Notes on the Birds of Herefordshire. Contributed by members of the Woolhope Club.

P arks such as Moccas, with their abundance of old trees, provide many sites for hole nesting birds such as pied flycatcher, and, in turn, opportunities for studies of their breeding biology. It is ironic that at Moccas Park these opportunities have been realised entirely through the use of nest boxes.

The Nest Box Scheme of what was then the Herefordshire and Radnorshire Nature Trust was launched at Moccas Park and elsewhere in 1963. The scheme aimed to encourage all small hole-nesting species but there was the particular hope that it would assist the eastward expansion of the Welsh and west Herefordshire population of pied flycatchers. The successful achievement of this objective was highlighted in *The Atlas of Breeding Birds in Britain and Ireland*[1] and it is highly appropriate that the pied flycatcher should be the emblem of the Herefordshire Nature Trust.

At Moccas Park, as elsewhere, the pied flycatcher has been the principal beneficiary of the scheme. The story of the pied flycatcher at Moccas Park is outlined below; this is followed by a note of the results of some detailed research into the ecology of the fleas that are parasitic on birds using nest boxes, and a summary of observations on some of the other bird species which use 'tit boxes' (boxes for the larger hole nesting species have not been erected and information on these species is scant). Notes on other species recorded over the years are included, and the section concludes with a discussion of future survey and monitoring work, and of management to conserve and enhance the ornithological interest of the Park.

Pied flycatcher

Pied flycatchers at Moccas Park

In his *Birds of Herefordshire* Bull refers to the pied flycatcher as "a rare visitant to this county",[2] and Ley's observation, as quoted above, would appear to be the first recorded evidence of 'probable breeding' in Herefordshire; confirmation did not come until 1889.[3] At this period, the pied flycatcher was abundant as a breeding species only in north Wales and northwest England.[4]

The tree in which pied flycatchers are understood to have first bred in the Park survived, latterly as a decaying hulk, until about 1990.[5] But, by then, the species was very well established. In 1940 the Hon. Guy Charteris had found a "colony" nesting in natural tree holes in the Park,[6] and when, in 1963, 12 boxes were erected in the Park, one was occupied by pied flycatchers. Sixty boxes were in place by 1967 and pied flycatchers used 15 of them.[7]

Pied flycatchers take readily to nest boxes, which are actually preferred to natural cavities, making it possible to attract almost the whole breeding population within an area into boxes.[8] This situation applies at Moccas Park, where nowadays use of natural tree holes by pied flycatchers is rare. Males are on occasion polygamous, so the number of occupied nest boxes indicates the number of breeding females in the population.

Moccas Park was, from the start, among the eight Nest Box Scheme sites in Herefordshire where systematic recording of breeding species was carried out, and this continues today, along with ringing, notably of pied flycatchers. The number of nest boxes in the Park occupied by pied flycatchers has ranged from 6-28 over the years 1965-1999 with an average of 14.4 (Appendix 9). This is out of a total of some 60 available boxes (range, over the years, 38 to 70). Nest box availability is not apparently a constraint on the numbers of pairs that breed, as total occupancy by all species is usually less than 50%.

All nestling pied flycatchers, and as many adults as possible, are ringed. Recaptures of Herefordshire pied flycatchers ringed as adults, including birds from Moccas Park, has shown the greater site fidelity of males: 96% of 58 males were re-caught at the original ringing location, as against 73% of 170 females. Of 323 nestlings ringed in Herefordshire, including Moccas Park, over the years 1980-1986 and subsequently recaptured, 39% were caught again at their natal site; there was no difference in site fidelity between males and females. Over the years there have been many recaptures of birds ringed at Moccas Park at nesting sites in Monmouthshire, Powys, Gloucestershire and Shropshire. Recoveries have also been reported from Spain, Algeria and Morocco; these are presumably of birds on passage, because the wintering area is in West Africa south of the Sahara.[9]

Bird nest boxes, their occupants and their fleas

Species other than pied flycatcher recorded breeding in nest boxes at Moccas Park are, in descending order of frequency, blue tit, great tit, marsh tit, coal tit, redstart and nuthatch; occupancy rates for the years 1965-1998 are shown in Appendix 9. Data were gathered from the boxes over the years 1974-83 in order to establish breeding timetables for a number of species as shown in Figure 5.7.1. These timetables illustrate the later breeding season of the migrant species, pied flycatcher and redstart, showing why in areas where nest holes are limited the migrants can lose out to the earlier breeding resident species.

Figure 5.7.1

Breeding timetables of birds occupying nest boxes, 1974-1983. Adapted from Harper, Marchant & Boddington (1992) and reproduced by permission of the editor of the *Journal of Animal Ecology*.

Only nests from which at least one young successfully flew are included. N = average start date of nest building; FE = average date of laying first egg; LE = average date of laying last egg; F = average date when young left the nest. Only one estimate of date F is available for coal tit.

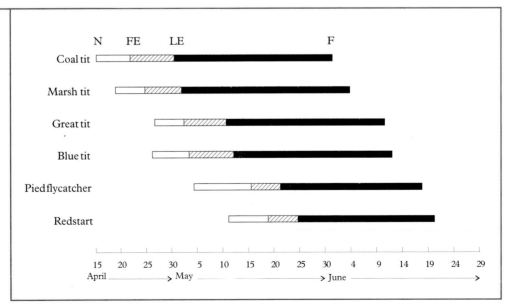

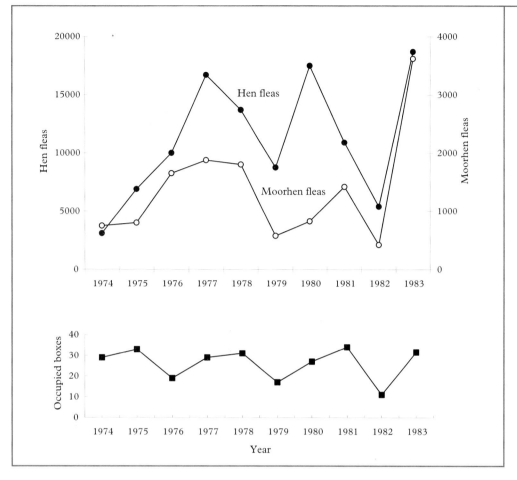

Figure 5.7.2

**The numbers of hen
and moorhen fleas
and of occupied nest
boxes, 1974-1983.**
Adapted from Harper,
Marchant & Boddington
(1992) and reproduced
by permission of the
editor of the *Journal of
Animal Ecology*.

The timetables were established as part of a study, carried out principally at Moccas Park, into the ecology of the fleas that are parasitic on birds using nest boxes.[10] This study investigated the populations and dispersal of the hen flea *Ceratophyllus gallinae* and the moorhen flea *Dasypsyllus gallinulae*. Estimates of the populations of both species in the nest boxes at Moccas Park were related to environmental data, in particular the breeding timetables of the host birds.

Figure 5.7.2 shows the numbers of each of the two main species of flea found in the nests of the seven bird species using nest boxes at Moccas Park. Five other species of flea were found in a few of the nests, all but one of them were fleas of small mammals; their presence may be explained by the use of nest boxes by wood mice *Apodemus sylvaticus* after the departure of the birds.[11]

The study found that the hen flea was hosted and dispersed primarily by blue tits and the numbers found in the nests of pied flycatchers depended on blue tit numbers. The moorhen flea was more abundant in marsh tit, coal tit and redstart nests than in pied flycatcher and other tit nests. The factors controlling the numbers of moorhen fleas remain obscure but it was demonstrated that the population size of the hen flea is dependent on the length of time the nest is maintained above air temperature.

Other bird species

The systematic monitoring of the nest boxes over the last 34 years has given opportunities for casual observations of other species but no time for more systematic survey. The annotated systematic list in Appendix 8 is the product of these casual observations combined both with those of other birdwatchers and with records from published and manuscript sources. The following account mentions some of the more typical and the more interesting species occurring in the principal habitats.

The Lower Park

Raven

Most bird observations come from the Lower Park. This occupies about half of the total area; it is parkland dotted with open-grown trees, most of them mature oaks, growing over close-cropped grass with no undergrowth other than patches of nettles, thistles and bracken. This and the other habitats of the Park are described in more detail in Chapters 1.2. and 4.3.

The avifauna of the Lower Park includes, in particular, a range of hole and cavity nesting species. Apart from the 'tit box' species already mentioned, jackdaw, starling, great spotted woodpecker, little owl and spotted flycatcher are probably the commonest. But the attention of visitors may first be drawn by the Park's ravens squabbling noisily with the resident buzzards. The ravens nest in most years near the top of the tallest tree in the Park, a Wellingtonia. It has been suggested that a raven nest at Moccas in 1926 (presumably in the Park) may well have been the first in Herefordshire since the extinction of ravens in the county in about 1880.[12]

The Upper Park

Much of the Upper Park is closed canopy woodland but the area is interspersed with occasional very large glades. There is virtually no understorey and the field layer is dominated by bracken; oak is the dominant tree species. Adjacent areas of coniferous woodland account for occasional visits by crossbills.

Most of the breeding species of the Lower Park are also found in the Upper Park, together with chiffchaff, willow and wood warblers and the occasional tree pipit. It is only in the few small areas from which deer are excluded that the cover is dense enough to attract blackcap and garden warbler. Elsewhere, blackbird and song thrush respond on occasion to the lack of an understorey by nesting low down amongst what little cover is available; indeed a song thrush nest was once found on the ground amongst bracken.

Great spotted woodpecker

The Upper and Lower Parks and the Lawn Pool are all used for game shooting. The principal quarry species are pheasant and mallard. Pheasants have been released in the Park annually since the mid 1970s,[13] and there are currently two pheasant release pens in the Upper Park. Mallard are regularly encouraged to the Lawn Pool by artificial feeding and birds were released there in 1984 and 1997.[14] Carrion crows and jackdaws nesting in the Park are controlled by the sporting tenant in the interests of game and agriculture.

The Lawn Pool

Little grebe

The Lawn Pool lies in the Lower Park, it extends to 4.4 ha but includes significant areas of fen and carr and relatively little open water. The Pool has dried up almost entirely in dry summers over the last century or more, but the occurrence appears to be more frequent nowadays, limiting the Pool's value to wetland species. Nevertheless, moorhen, coot, mallard and Canada goose nest every year and in some years little grebe, tufted duck and mute swan do so too; grey heron, teal and black-headed gull have bred in the past. Goosanders have started appearing in recent years; they wander, particularly in the spring, from the nearby River Wye (which, at one point, meanders to within 500 m of the Pool), as may occasional migrant visitors such as green sandpiper. The numbers of mallard build up in autumn and winter as do those of teal, and up to 100 of the latter have been recorded. Of the common wetland passerines only reed buntings breed nowadays; reed and sedge warbler have bred in the past but probably were never numerous. In some years Canada geese are shot under licence during the closed season and recoveries include birds ringed as adults at Llangorse Lake, Powys (2), Ellesmere, Shropshire and Scar House Reservoir in North Yorkshire.[15]

The future: survey, monitoring and management

Long standing biological studies such as that of the Moccas Park nest boxes are rare, and this fact alone provides a reason for continuing with it. The study gives opportunities for the long term monitoring of changes in the abundance, breeding performance and breeding seasons of a range of hole nesting species, most notably pied flycatcher. Additionally, the recapture rate for ringed pied flycatchers is high compared with that for many other species, thereby providing a relatively good return of information on the ringing effort expended.[16] This range of factors makes the nest box study well worth keeping up.

Parks such as Moccas are often regarded as being rich in certain specialist hole nesting bird species, but there appears to be little definite information about the diversity and density of breeding birds to be found in such wood-pastures, particularly those made up of the low density of trees to be found in the Lower Park at Moccas. In the only known study, at Windsor Forest and Great Park, it was found that open parkland, with widely spaced ancient trees in grassland, supported extremely low numbers of species and individuals, of which the commonest breeders were stock doves and jackdaws, there being very few small birds.[17] A survey of the Lower Park at Moccas would probably also reveal relatively low numbers of individuals when compared with woodland, but a larger range of species. It would be worthwhile to test this surmise through field survey, building on the data gathered through the nest box scheme and relating bird diversity and density to tree density and ground cover.

Maintenance of the considerable ornithological interest of Moccas Park depends on maintenance of its habitats. Apart from the obvious requirement of seeking to ensure the survival and eventual replacement of the ancient trees, the diversification of the underlying sward (in terms both of species and structure), the development of ant colonies and the retention of dead fallen timber, should all be encouraged. Such policies will all help enhance the invertebrate populations on which the birds depend.

The Lawn Pool is an important element of the ornithological interest of the Park and if it is indeed drying up, this will lead to the decline and indeed loss of several wetland species. The efforts already in hand to maintain areas of open water should be beneficial. Sustaining open water through periods of dry weather is less straight forward but the removal of the excess cover of trees and scrubs would help reduce transpirational losses.

Moccas Park has for more than a century been regarded as one of the most interesting bird sites in Herefordshire. It is to be hoped that further study and appropriate management will confirm, maintain and indeed enhance that interest.

Notes

1 Sharrock (1976).
2 Bull (1888).
3 Anon (1890).
4 Holloway (1996).
5 The tree was shown to David Boddington in the 1960s by Dr Charles Walker, then the leading authority on the birds of Herefordshire, who reported that in one year it had housed nests of blue tit, pied flycatcher, redstart and great spotted woodpecker.
6 Walker & Smith (1975).
7 The full records for the years 1963 and 1964 have unfortunately been destroyed.

8 Boddington & Marchant (1983), Lundberg & Alatalo (1993).

9 Cramp & Perrins (1993).

10 Harper, Marchant & Boddington (1992).

11 The other species of fleas were *Ctenophthalmus nobilis*, *Megabothris turbidus*, *Rhadinopsylla pentacantha*, *Orchopeas howardi* and *Ceratophyllus garei*.

12 See Ammonds (1982), however Walker & Smith (1975) state that a pair of ravens had nested "close to Hereford" since 1924.

13 Len Slaney, former gamekeeper *per* Tom Wall (pers. comm.).

14 Tom Wall (pers. comm.).

15 Tom Wall (pers. comm.).

16 Of 939 nestlings ringed over the years 1968 to 1985, 39 (4.2%) were subsequently re-trapped at Moccas Park or reported from elsewhere. Of 94 adults caught and ringed over the years 1968 to 1982, 37 (39.4%) were re-trapped at Moccas Park or reported from elsewhere.

17 Counts were made by Ted Green; they are reported in Fuller (1995). Other studies have concentrated on wood-pastures with a considerably higher density of trees. For example a study of wood-pasture in the New Forest by Smith, Burges & Parks (1992), used areas having a mean of 92.3 trees per hectare. If forestry plantations are excluded, as well as trees and shrubs planted since the 1960s, the counts of trees made by Harding (1977) give densities of only 15 trees per hectare in the Upper Park at Moccas, and 10 trees per hectare in the Lower Park.

References relating to Moccas Park

AMMONDS, T.R. 1982. Experience of the raven in north Herefordshire. *Herefordshire Ornithological Club Report*, 1982, 70-72.

BODDINGTON, D.G. & MARCHANT, A. 1983. Some notes on the birds of Moccas Park, Herefordshire. *Herefordshire Ornithological Club Report*, 1983, 115-116.

BULL, H.G. 1888. *Notes on the Birds of Herefordshire. Contributed by members of the Woolhope Club*. Hereford: Jakeman & Carver.

HARDING, P.T. 1977. *Moccas Deer Park, Hereford and Worcester: a report on the history, structure and natural history*. Unpublished report to the Nature Conservancy Council by the Institute of Terrestrial Ecology, Huntingdon.

HARPER, G.H., MARCHANT, A. & BODDINGTON, D.G. 1992. The ecology of the hen flea *Ceratophyllus gallinae* and the moorhen flea *Dasypsyllus gallinulae* in nest boxes. *Journal of Animal Ecology*, 61, 317-327.

WALKER, C.W. & SMITH, A.J. 1975. *Herefordshire Birds*. Hereford: Woolhope Naturalists' Field Club.

Other references

ANON, 1890. The collection of eggs of British birds belonging to Dr. Robert Williams, of the Croase House, Kingsland. *Transactions of the Woolhope Naturalists' Field Club*, 49.

CRAMP, S. & PERRINS, C.M. eds. 1993. *The Birds of the Western Palearctic*. Vol. VII. Oxford: Oxford University Press.

FULLER, R.J. 1995. *Bird life of woodland and forest*. Cambridge: Cambridge University Press.

HOLLOWAY, S. 1996. *The Historical Atlas of Breeding Birds in Britain and Ireland: 1875-1900*. London: T. & A.D. Poyser.

LUNDBERG, A. & ALATALO, R. V. 1992. *The Pied Flycatcher*. London: T. & A.D. Poyser.

SHARROCK, J.T.R 1976. *The Atlas of Breeding Birds in Britain and Ireland*. Tring: British Trust for Ornithology.

SMITH, K.W., BURGES, D.J. & PARKS, R.A. 1992. Breeding bird communities of broadleaved plantation and ancient pasture woodlands in the New Forest. *Bird Study*, 39, 132-141.

Other vertebrates

Tom Wall

Those grey old men of Moccas .... with such tales to tell, as when they whisper
them to each other in the midsummer nights, make .... the long ears of the hares
and rabbits stand on end.

From the diary of the Reverend Francis Kilvert, 22 April 1876.[1]

Kilvert could well have seen brown hare and rabbit in Moccas Park, but this is poetical whimsy not zoological observation. It is however an indication of how little attention has been paid to the 'other vertebrates' of the Park - fish, amphibians, reptiles and mammals - that to this day Kilvert's list is the longest to find its way into print! This chapter reviews what little fragmentary knowledge there is, and mentions all species that have been recorded.[2] It is based on the observations of a number of individuals, most notably those who have worked as the Moccas Estate's gamekeeper over the years, and on occasional observations of my own over the period 1991-98.

Fish, reptiles and amphibians

There are no records of fish. They doubtless occur, but recolonisation following the virtual drying up of the Lawn Pool, something that has been noted on occasion since at least 1891 (Chapter 4.3), may take time. Common toad, common frog and smooth newt are all seen from time to time.[3] Common frog tadpoles have been found in several places, including the Lawn Pool, where common toad and smooth newt also breed. Slow-worm and grass snake are encountered only occasionally.

Figure 5.8.1

Polecat. Drawing by Guy Troughton, reproduced by courtesy of The Vincent Wildlife Trust.

Mammals

A single record of muntjac dates from 1984,[4] but it is only over the last few years that deer stalkers have started to see them at all frequently in surrounding woods.[5] The herd of fallow deer is discussed in Chapter 5.6, and the impact it has on the vegetation of the Park in Chapter 4.3. The only commonly encountered mammal species, apart from the fallow deer, are grey squirrel and rabbit. In common with the deer, both are introduced species, and like the deer they have a considerable impact on the vegetation of the Park. Grey squirrels colonised Herefordshire from the south east, reaching Bredwardine (and hence presumably Moccas Park) by 1938.[6] They have long been very common in the Park, despite attempts at control by shooting and the use of warfarin baits, and as many as 300 have been shot in one year.[7] They can significantly damage saplings of beech, willow spp. and oak sometimes too.

The red squirrel will certainly have occurred in the Park, although there is no record of it. Red squirrels are said to have reached a population peak in Herefordshire at the beginning of the twentieth century but to have declined subsequently.[8] They were still being seen in various parts of Herefordshire in the early 1950s, including in the parish of Moccas in 1950,[9] but they died out soon thereafter.[10]

The significant horseshoe-shaped mound in the east of the Park is known locally as the 'Connibury'. It is tempting to speculate both on a derivation from 'coney' (rabbit) and 'bury' (burrow), and on the possibility of the breeding of rabbits in the Park for food in the distant past. However, the mound appears natural and is far bigger than the artificial 'pillow-mounds' which are found in some other Parks and are believed to have functioned as artificial rabbit-warrens.[11] Rabbits were certainly extremely common in the Park prior to the arrival of myxomatosis in 1954.[12] Today they are quite common again, especially in the Lower Park, where, despite sporadic control, many burrows may be found amongst tree roots. Badger tunnels may sometimes be found in similar situations but active setts are more in evidence in the Upper Park. Moles are most evident in the Lower Park, but they have not been common over recent years, nor have hedgehogs.[13] Hares are seen only very occasionally, and then usually in the Upper Park.

Polecats (Figure 5.8.1) were all but eliminated from the English Midlands by about 1900 but they hung on in Wales and western Herefordshire. They started to re-colonise the rest of the county following the relaxation of gamekeeping during and following the First World War, and there was a build up of records in Herefordshire from 1919 onwards.[14] The earliest documented record from Moccas Park is not until 1960, but they were doubtless present prior to this and gamekeepers and others have reported them on occasion since.[15] Otters may have bred in the Park in the 1950s;[16] mink did in the 1980s but they are infrequently encountered nowadays.[17] Gamekeepers report the frequent shooting or trapping of fox, stoat and weasel.

The only survey of small mammals (shrews, voles, mice, rats and dormice) so far undertaken was for common dormouse, in 1991. Not surprisingly, in view of the lack of cover and paucity of species such as bramble, honeysuckle and hazel with which dormice are associated, none was found.[18] Wood mice have been found using bird nest boxes,[19] and several other small mammal species will be present, but the lack of ground cover, in both grassland and woodland, due to grazing by deer and livestock, will depress population levels.[20] This is likely to have a 'knock-on' effect on the populations of predators of small mammals, notably fox, badger, owls and kestrel.[21]

All the bat species occurring in Britain feed on insects associated with trees, whilst trees, particularly old ones rich in cracks, holes and cavities, also provide breeding, roosting and hibernating sites for several bat species.[22] Moccas Park offers therefore some promising bat habitat, particularly as it includes the water, fen and carr of the Lawn Pool which provide good hunting opportunities too. But there are as yet very few specific records of bats for the Park. A barbastelle was seen in 1961,[23] (it is a rare species, and there is only one other Herefordshire record).[24] The next bat record was not until August 1998 when work with bat detectors revealed the presence of both the 45 kilohertz and the 55 kilohertz phonotypes of pipistrelle bat,[25] but observations of what were believed to be whiskered bats were not confirmed.[26] Future bat survey work clearly deserves a high priority.

Notes

1 Plomer (1940).
2 The following is a list of all the species of mammals recorded from the Park; nomenclature follows Corbet & Harris (1991):
Badger *Meles meles*
Barbastelle *Barbastella barbastellus*
Brown hare *Lepus europaeus*
Fallow deer *Dama dama*
Fox *Vulpes vulpes*
Grey squirrel *Sciurus carolinensis*
Hedgehog *Erinaceus europaeus*
Mink *Mustela vison*
Mole *Talpa europaea*
Muntjac *Muntiacus reevesi*
Otter *Lutra lutra*
Pipistrelle bat *Pipistrellus pipistrellus*
Polecat *Mustela putorius*
Rabbit *Oryctolagus cuniculus*
Red squirrel *Sciurus vulgaris*
Stoat *Mustela erminea*
Weasel *Mustela nivalis*
Wood mouse *Apodemus sylvaticus*
Other species mentioned in the text are whiskered bat *Myotis mystacinus* (not confirmed) and common dormouse *Muscardinus avellanarius* (not found).
3 The following is a list of all the species of amphibians and reptiles recorded from the Park; nomenclature follows Frazer (1983):
Common frog *Rana temporaria*
Common toad *Bufo bufo*
Grass snake *Natrix natrix*
Slow-worm *Anguis fragilis*
Smooth newt *Triturus vulgaris*
4   R. C. Welch via the Biological Records Centre.
5 David Chandler (pers. comm.).
6 Mellor (1954).
7 Len Slaney, former gamekeeper (pers. comm.); in the year when 300 grey squirrels were shot (1972 or 1973), Richard Chester-Master was offering a bounty of "three bob a tail" on behalf of the Moccas Estate.
8 Mellor (1954).
9 Mellor (1954).
10 Shorten (1954), Arnold (1993).
11 Blenheim Park provides a number of examples (Bond 1997).
12 Les Whittal and Tom Bowen, local residents, remember when there were "millions" of rabbits in the Park (pers. comm.).
13 Len Slaney recalls that hedgehogs were common in the 1970s (pers. comm.), but Phil Price, the current gamekeeper, does not see them often (pers. comm.).
14 Johnny Birks (pers. comm.), Mellor (1954).
15 K. C. Walton, C. W. Walker and J. D. S. Birks via the Biological Records Centre; Len Slaney and David Chandler (pers. comm.), both worked as gamekeepers in and around the Park.
16 Tom Bowen (pers. comm.) recalls that on at least one occasion he saw a family party of otters crossing the road in the direction of the River Wye.
17 David Chandler (pers. comm.) recalls catching a family party of mink, probably in the 1980s, as they emerged from a culvert leading from the Park. The current status of mink is as reported by Phil Price (pers. comm.).
18 Paige Mitchell (pers. comm.).
19 Harper, Marchant & Boddington (1992).
20 Reeve & Jones (1996) found that grassland habitats in Richmond Park supported only low populations of small mammals; they attributed this in part to inadequate cover as a consequence of grazing by deer and rabbits. Putman (1994) reported that in the New Forest five species of small mammal were present except where grazing was heavy, here only wood mice maintained their density, all other species were rare or absent.
21 Putman (1994).
22 Holmes (1996).
23 Peter Skidmore (pers. comm.); it was found under the loose bark of a beech tree, probably in May.
24 The only other Herefordshire record of barbastelle known to the Bat Conservation Trust is from Abbey Dore in 1990 (pers. comm.).
25 The two phonotypes are widely recognised and data on echolocation, DNA and other differences have been used to prepare a case for them to be named as two different species; this case will be considered by the International Commission on Zoological Nomenclature (Bat Conservation Trust pers. comm.).
26 Andrew McLeish (pers. comm.) on behalf of the Shropshire Bat Group.

References relating to Moccas Park

HARPER, G.H., MARCHANT, A. & BODDINGTON, D.G. 1992. The ecology of the hen flea *Ceratophyllus gallinae* and the moorhen flea *Dasypsyllus gallinulae* in nest boxes. *Journal of Animal Ecology*, 61, 317-327.

PLOMER, W. 1940. *Kilvert's diary*. Volume 3. London: Jonathan Cape.

Other references

ARNOLD, H.R. 1993. *Atlas of mammals in Britain*. (Institute of Terrestrial Ecology research publication no. 6). London: HMSO.

BOND, J. 1997. Woodstock Park in the sixteenth and seventeenth centuries. *In*: J. BOND & K. TILLER, eds. *Blenheim: landscape for a palace*. Stroud: Sutton, second edition, 55-66.

CORBET, G.B. & HARRIS, S. 1991. *The handbook of British mammals*. Third edition. Oxford: Blackwell.

FRAZER, D. 1983. *Reptiles and amphibians in Britain*. London: Collins.

HOLMES, M. 1996. Ancient trees - their importance to bats. *In*: H.J. READ, ed. *Pollard and veteran tree management II*. London: Corporation of London, 19-20.

MELLOR, J.E.M. 1954. The mammals of Herefordshire. *In*: ANON, ed. *Herefordshire, its natural history, archaeology and history*. Chapters to celebrate the centenary of the Woolhope Naturalists' Field Club. Hereford: Woolhope Club, 94-106.

PUTMAN, R.J. 1994. Effects of grazing and browsing by mammals on woodlands. *British Wildlife*, 5, 205-213.

REEVE, N.J. & JONES, K.E. 1996. A trapping survey of small mammals in Richmond Park, Surrey and some implications for future conservation management. *The London Naturalist*, 75, 81-90.

SHORTEN, M. 1954. *Squirrels*. London: Collins.

Establishing the nature conservation status

Paul T. Harding

Moccas Park is a must and should be scheduled as a Nature Reserve forthwith ....

Arthur Massee, August 1962, in a letter to Michael Morris.[1]

Introduction

Although Moccas Park had been famous, over several generations, for its distinctive landscape and large trees (see Chapter 3.2 and inside front cover), awareness of the wider importance of the Park for wildlife has emerged gradually. This awareness began in the 19th century with fungi (Chapter 4.2) and vascular plants (Chapter 4.3) and expanded to include other taxa, especially beetles (Chapters 5.1, 5.2 and 5.3), mainly from the 1930s onwards.

The importance of Moccas Park was not recognised until comparatively late in the tortuous process of choosing representative examples of Britain's wildlife habitats. It was not included in the list of "areas worthy of protection" compiled by The Honourable Nathaniel Rothschild in 1915.[2] Nor was it identified in the list of proposed nature reserves drawn up under the auspices of the Nature Reserves Investigation Committee (NRIC) during the 1939-45 War, or by the official Wild Life Conservation Special (the Huxley) Committee of 1947.[3] Even if it had been considered, the importance of parkland as a distinctive biotope was not properly recognised until the late 1960s.[4]

The story of how Moccas Park came to be acknowledged for its importance for wildlife, leading to its National Nature Reserve status, gives an insight into the workings of nature conservation in the 1960s and 1970s. It also highlights the role of a few individuals characterised by their commitment and perseverance.

1962 to 1964

Three deaths in the family

Moccas Park, as part of the Cornewall estate, was managed in a manner that was generally benign for wildlife throughout the 56 years that Sir Geoffrey and Sir William Cornewall were responsible for the estate.[5] Sir Geoffrey died in January 1951 and his younger brother and heir, Sir William, died in May 1962. Only eight months later, in January 1963, their cousin and Sir William's heir, Lt. Colonel William Chester-Master also died. The death of three owners within 12 years, left the new heir to the Moccas estate, Richard Chester-Master, with many new responsibilities and very considerable death duty commitments.[6]

The Chester-Master family arms.

Entomologists take the lead

The death of Sir William in 1962 prompted some leading British field entomologists to alert the Nature Conservancy (NC) to the importance of Moccas Park and to their concern about its future. The news of Sir William's death was first communicated to the nature conservation community by Peter Skidmore, in a letter to Christopher Cadbury dated 21 May 1962, in the context of involving the "Hereford Naturalists' Trust" in safeguarding Moccas Park.[7] In early June 1962, Skidmore's close friend, Eric Hunter, wrote to Tom Pritchard stressing the importance of the site.[8] Pritchard immediately sought the involvement of Michael Morris who wrote to Tony Allen on 26 July 1962 seeking his advice because Allen had visited the site several times (most recently in 1954).[9] Allen's four page reply (30 July 1962) summarised as much as was known about the entomology of the site, including a list of "Rare and more interesting species of Coleoptera", with three species (*Pyrrhidium sanguineum*, *Hypebaeus flavipes* and *Ernoporicus* (formerly *Ernoporus*) *caucasicus*) then known nowhere else in Britain.

Figure 6.1.1

Arthur Massee
Photograph courtesy of The *Entomologist's Monthly Magazine*.

Arthur Massee (Figure 6.1.1) wrote to Morris, on 1 August 1962 stating that "Moccas Park is a must and should be scheduled as a 'Nature Reserve' forthwith....For the area to be scheduled as a SSSI [Site of Special Scientific Interest] means literally little or nothing".[10] Morris, replying to Elizabeth Copeland Watts at the NC's Shrewsbury office on 9 August 1962, mentioned the letters from Allen and Massee, quoting Allen that Moccas Park holds an "almost unique concentration of rare species in a quite small space".[11]

Hunter had suggested that Moccas Park might be "a remnant of original oak forest". Morris followed up this suggestion with Archie Archibald.[12] In his response to Morris, Archibald commented that, although he had not visited the site, "it seems to me highly improbable...that it is 'a piece of original oak forest' or anything of the sort". This exchange illustrates two aspects of much of the thinking at that time - the under-estimation both of the degree to which the supposed "oak forest" was as much a product of cultural as of natural processes, and of the importance of parkland for nature conservation.

Involvement of the Herefordshire and Radnorshire Nature Trust[13]

Discussion about the future of Moccas Park was closely linked with the development of this new Trust. The Trust was mentioned first in Skidmore's original letter to Cadbury. Dr Charles Walker, Chairman of the Trust, was actively involved with discussions and meetings about the Park and, in 1963, a proposal was made that the Trust might acquire part of the Park, if it was offered by the Estate Duty Office. In principle, the Trust felt that it might be able to maintain 40-80 ha in the Park but following discussions and a site visit, it was decided that the Park was too important to be split up. As it was, the Trust gained access to the Park and other areas to install and monitor nest boxes (Chapter 5.7), but failed to secure any form of simple nature reserve agreement, despite further negotiations with the Estate in 1970.

Rumours of threats from forestry

Several entomologists expressed concern that the Park might fall into the hands of the Forestry Commission or a commercial forestry company. In a letter written in mid January 1963, Walker informed Pritchard that Lt. Colonel William Chester-Master had "died suddenly last Saturday". In the same letter, Walker noted that "Clore has bought up a lot of property in the neighbourhood, including adjacent woods - I don't know whether he will be wanting Moccas or not!".[14]

Nature Conservancy Committee for England in action

Copeland Watts, Walker and Philip Oswald visited Moccas Park on 13 September 1962, and Morris and Copeland Watts visited on 11 October 1962.[15] Reports on these visits, and information gleaned mainly by Morris from entomologists and published sources, were used to prepare a paper for the NC's Committee for England meeting on 29 January 1963. By this time, it was known that Lt. Colonel Chester-Master had died and that death duty liability on his estate was likely to be considerable.

The friendship between Massee and Morris was critical to getting Moccas Park brought onto the Agenda for the meeting on 29 January. Massee was a member of the Committee, and Morris was able to provide him with advice on probable delays and lack of interest at high levels in the administration of the Conservancy. The entomological *maquis* became active and at least a dozen letters were sent to the Director-General (DG) of NC by entomologists (including Allen, Freddy Buck, Colin Johnson, Eric Philp and Ken Side).[16] Pritchard was also promoting the cause of Moccas from the perspective of the NC's Midlands Region, which at that time had only four National Nature Reserves (NNR).

Massee's comment on the meeting on 29 January demonstrates the opposition he believed he faced from the NC's senior officers. "When I entered the Meeting Room Worthington, Frazer and the D-G looked daggers drawn at me - so after my three years [on the Committee] I shall be turfed out".[17] Or perhaps this comment was coloured by Massee's puckish sense of humour.

In the event, due largely to the excellent paper prepared by Morris and Pritchard, the letters and Massee's characteristically forceful advocacy at the meeting, the Committee agreed that Moccas Park should be notified as a SSSI. It also recommended "(i) that an approach be made to the Estate Duty Office for the area to be accepted in lieu of Death Duty and (ii) that subject to (i) above, the Hereford County Naturalists' Trust be requested to assume responsibility for its future management", subject to the agreement "of the Executors of the

Estate to offer the park in this way". At this stage, the area under consideration was only 40-80 ha, although Morris and Pritchard, in March 1963, both stressed the importance of safeguarding the whole site.

SSSI and PNNR

Moccas Park was notified as a SSSI in September 1963. At its meeting on 3 October 1963, the NC's Committee for England again considered Moccas Park and agreed that it "was of National Nature Reserve status and should be preserved as a whole" and that it should "be adopted as a Proposed National Nature Reserve" (PNNR). Nicholson sent a letter to this effect to the owner on 15 January 1964. Pritchard reported to the Entomological Liaison Committee on 12 November 1963 that he was "in close touch with the agents, but that the creation of a NNR was a question of priorities; there was no immediate danger to the site".[18] Massee reported to the Entomological Liaison Committee on 3 March 1964 that "The owner was not at present prepared to part with the land or to enter into a Nature Reserve Agreement, but he agreed to keep the area in its present state".

Changes in management

News of proposals by the Estate to carry out "reclamation" of the Park had broken on 15 January 1964 (the same day as the DG's letter to Richard Chester-Master regarding PNNR status) causing a flurry of activity at the highest levels in the NC. Jamie Johnstone was authorised by the DG to give the case top priority.[19] Following telephone conversations with the agent for the Estate (John Phipps) on 22 January and the tenant (Michael Minoprio) on 23 January, Pritchard noted that they were seeking early discussions about financial arrangements. Site meetings were held at Moccas on 27 January and 24 February 1964. Pritchard and Johnstone represented the NC, and Chester-Master and Phipps represented the Estate.

At the first meeting the NC put several specific proposals to Chester-Master, but he made it clear that he did not wish to sell, or to commit himself to a lease or a Nature Reserve Agreement (NRA). It was a cordial meeting at which it was agreed that Massee (and Minoprio) should attend a second meeting to discuss the scientific implications of the reclamation proposals. In his record of this second meeting, Johnstone noted that the Estate expressed its intentions:

❖ "to recapture some of the conditions in the park that he [R.C.-M.] thought existed 80 to 100 years ago";
❖ "to see part of the sward improved in some parts with ant hills levelled";
❖ "no wish to destroy the scientific interest or to get rid of the herd of deer";
❖ "to graze cattle and sheep and agreed not to plough or use toxic chemicals on the land".

Massee promoted the idea of a phased programme of tree planting, including oaks from seed from the park, and some limes. In a follow-up letter to Phipps, Johnstone stressed the agreement that trees in the park would remain, fallen timber would not be removed and would be kept close to the trees from which it fell, herbage under the trees would be left undisturbed and toxic chemicals would not be used. In his reply, Phipps stated that timber would continue to be felled, as in the past, but excluding the very old trees.[20]

During the summer of 1964 an outline application was submitted to the County Council, on behalf of the Estate, for a single house in the Park, between Cross End Farm and the Lawn Pool. The NC concluded that there were no major scientific grounds for objection to the application, but fortunately the house was never built.

The Estate made rapid progress with "reclamation" of the Park. Writing to Pritchard on 11 November 1964, Minoprio stated that "The first 85 acres [34.4 ha] of this has been accomplished and we are deciding now what the next move is". His plan was to plough and re-seed bracken infested land in "two relatively flat areas, one of about 20 acres directly above the park pool and another of, in all about 30 acres, on the east side of the park". In his reply, after consulting Massee, Pritchard noted these plans without objection.[21] If all this work was completed, about 45% of Park was reclaimed; in effect almost all of the open canopy area. About 0.05 ha were lost from the Park when the western gateway (Lawn Gate) was closed and fenced to allow vehicular access to Lawn Gate Lodge from the public road. Renamed, Lawn Gate Cottage, the building and land were sold by the Estate in the late 1970s.

1965 to 1976

Lichens - a new importance

Up to the late 1960s the main nature conservation features of Moccas Park were the rare insects, especially beetles, and the old trees. Francis Rose and Brian Coppins, both leading lichenologists, visited the site in April 1968 and surveyed the lower part of the Park. In his report on the visit, Rose stressed the importance of the Park for its lichen flora, based on knowledge at that time (Chapter 4.1). Also, taking into account its entomological importance, he commented that the Park "should certainly be regarded as a site whose conservation is *vital*. It comes in the 'living museum-piece' category and is quite irreplaceable".

Nature Conservation Review (NCR)

In the late 1960s, the NC embarked on a major review of nature conservation priorities in Britain, including extensive surveys of flora and fauna.[22] Moccas Park was listed as a Grade 1 site in the NCR and was therefore regarded as being a prime candidate for NNR status.

The schedule of SSSIs in Herefordshire was reviewed in October 1969 and completely revised in 1975, but neither exercise brought about a change in the conservation status of Moccas Park.

Continued involvement by the Nature Conservancy (Council)

During the remainder of the 1960s, the NC had little contact with either the Estate or with the entomologists, who continued to visit the Park. Following a routine visit in 1971 in his role as the local NC officer, Chris Fuller reported to John Thompson his concern about the paucity of fallen timber and the planting of exotic trees in the Park.[23] Fuller and Thompson met Chester-Master in December 1971 to discuss, *inter alia*, tree planting and the retention of fallen and dead wood. Following this meeting Thompson obtained agreement from the NC Headquarters to begin negotiation of a SSSI Management Agreement, under Section 15 of the Countryside Act 1968. Thompson invited George Peterken to advise on tree planting requirements in such an agreement. Peterken and Paul Harding visited the Park in August 1972, followed by a meeting with Phipps and Fuller.[24]

Peterken's report formed the basis for proposals put to the Estate by Thompson in February 1973. In addition to tree planting and the retention of dead wood, Peterken proposed the planting of hawthorns (as nectar sources for insects), protection of some areas from spring grazing (to allow herbs to flower) and the creation of some hanging dead branches in oaks (to provide oviposition sites for the beetle *Pyrrhidium sanguineum*). These proposals met with little favour with the Estate at the time, and they were reluctant to enter into any formal agreement with the NC. This reluctance on the part of the Estate continued for several more years, despite the gentle persistence of Mervyn Evans working with Thompson and, from 1976, Noel King.[25] A meeting on 22 October 1974 resulted in the Estate offering to include small-leaved limes *Tilia cordata* in future plantings and to some branches being sawn-through as proposed, but neither was carried out. King and Harding visited the Park in September 1976 and recorded the recently planted trees.

1977 to 1981

Progress to a Nature Reserve Agreement

Evidence for the unique importance of pasture-woodlands, including parks, was beginning to emerge from the work of several research scientists particularly concerned with woodland conservation.[26] This evidence was improved by surveys commissioned by the NC and its successor, the Nature Conservancy Council (NCC).[27] As part of this work, Harding, working under contract to the NCC, undertook a study of the history, structure and natural history of Moccas Park which was summarised as part of a larger report on the contract.[28]

The Institute of Terrestrial Ecology's report on the Moccas Park study was revised sightly at the request of the NCC West Midlands Region.[29] This revised report was used in a move to open up closer communication between the NCC and Richard Chester-Master and members of the Baunton Trust, with a view to establishing a National Nature Reserve by means of a Nature Reserve Agreement (NRA).[30] On 11 July 1977, King and Harding met Richard Chester-Master and his family at their home near Cirencester. In his notes on the meeting, King records that Chester-Master "said that although he [R.C.-M.] had been reluctant to proceed with any formal agreement with the NCC over the site, he was now prepared to do so". Harding subsequently made proposals for restocking the park with up to 1000 trees, spread over the entire area. The co-operation between the NCC and the Estate was developed further at a meeting of representatives of both, on site, on 29 September 1977 when Chester-Master agreed to consider the terms of a draft NRA. On 20 October 1977 King had a meeting with Harding, Alan Stubbs and Jonathan Cooter to establish the scientific requirements of the proposed NRA.[31]

Progress towards finalising the NRA was slow and painstaking, with considerable re-drafting over several months, but the Agreement was finally signed on 11 May 1979.[32] The formal Declaration of the NNR was not made until 24 March 1981. Nearly 17 years after Skidmore, Hunter, Massee and Allen had advocated that it should become a 'Nature Reserve', Moccas Park became Britain's (and probably the world's) first parkland National Nature Reserve.

Notes

1 By permission of Dr M.G.Morris.
2 Rothschild & Marren (1997).
3 Sheail & Adams (1980).
4 The treatment of Staverton Park, Suffolk, illustrates the point. Although Staverton was included in both the Rothschild and NRIC lists, the distinguished botanist and ecologist, Sir Edward Salisbury, visited this site and his recommendation was accepted that Staverton should be removed from the Huxley Committee list on the grounds that the trees were the remnants of an old plantation, rather than an ancient woodland (Sheail 1976).
5 In 1914, just before Sir Geoffrey inherited, the Cornewall estate was estimated to be about 4050 ha in extent.
6 By 1963, the estate had been reduced to just over 1215 ha.
7 Dr P. Skidmore is a highly experienced entomologist and an international authority on Diptera. He retired recently from the position of Curator of Natural History at Doncaster Museum. C.J.Cadbury CBE (1908-1995) was President of the Society for the Promotion of Nature Reserves and its successor the Royal Society for Nature Conservation, from 1962 to 1988.
8 F.A. (Eric) Hunter has a special interest in saproxylic Coleoptera. He retired recently from a varied and successful career with the Ministry of Agriculture, Fisheries and Food. Dr T.O.Pritchard was the NC Regional Officer for the Midlands during the 1960s and went on to hold senior posts with the NC/NCC in Wales and with the Countryside Council for Wales.

9   Dr M.G.Morris was the Entomologist with the NC's newly formed Conservation Research Section, at Monks Wood near Huntingdon. He went on to become Head of Furzebrook Research Station with the Institute of Terrestrial Ecology. A.A.Allen has occupied a unique role in British entomology for nearly six decades, especially as a leading authority on the occurrence and ecology of Coleoptera. His output of papers and short informative notes, based on unrivalled experience in the field and in taxonomy, is legendary.

10 Dr A.M.Massee (1899-1967), usually referred to as Dr Massee or simply A.M.M., was a leading horticultural entomologist and an enthusiastic and skilled collector of British insects, especially Heteroptera and Coleoptera. He played an active role in nature conservation, nationally and also locally in south east England, especially in Kent. Dr M.G.Morris had recently completed his PhD at East Malling Research Station, supervised by Massee, and had established a close friendship with his mentor. Morris and Massee visited several sites (including Moccas Park) to put the entomological interest of the sites on record, based on Massee's personal experience and his legacy of knowledge from contacts with entomologists of earlier generations.

11 E.Copeland Watts was Assistant Regional Officer to Dr Pritchard in the early 1960s.

12 J.F.Archibald was a member of the NC's Woodland Research Section at Monks Wood from 1960 to 1962 and went on to work in the NC's South West England Region.

13 Founded in 1963, but split into the two individual county trusts in 1986 and renamed as the Herefordshire Nature Trust and the Radnorshire Wildlife Trust.

14 The industrialist Sir Charles Clore had bought the nearby Guy's Estate in 1959. John Phipps (who subsequently became the agent for the Moccas Estate) has commented that there was "no question of him [Clore] ever purchasing the Park, nor of it being bought by the Forestry Commission", so these concerns would seem to have been groundless.

15 P.H.Oswald was the NC's Warden at Rostherne Mere NNR in Cheshire.

16 The term *maquis* is used advisedly; the entomologists concerned, whether correctly or not, perceived that they formed a resistance movement in opposing bureaucracy and prejudice which tended to overlook the importance of invertebrates in establishing priorities in nature conservation. Initially, Moccas Park was doubly blighted, being a park (regarded as an artificial habitat) of interest mainly for invertebrates! The Director General of the NC at this time was the redoubtable E.M.(Max) Nicholson, CB CVO.

17 Dr E.Barton Worthington, a leading freshwater ecologist of his generation, was Deputy Director-General (Scientific) of the NC. Dr J.F.D.Frazer was Conservation Officer, England of the NC.

18 The Entomological Liaison Committee was a short lived group of a few leading field entomologists, and entomologists on the NC's own staff, that provided for liaison on insect conservation and gave advice to the NC, especially the Committee for England.

19 J.V. Johnstone was Senior Land Agent at the NC.

20 In the positions taken at this early stage by the Estate and the NC it is possible to detect two different, equally ill-defined, and in both cases probably illusory, 'visions' of the Park. That of the Estate was for a productive, green, healthy and tidy Park and that of the NC was based on an interpretation of the Park, as described by Francis Kilvert, full of old trees and dead wood.

21 The decision by the NC to accept all the proposals for ploughing and reseeding of parts of the Park seems to have overlooked any botanical or entomological interest of the areas of rough grassland that were to be treated. Massee's advice was sought, but his concern was always about the trees and dead wood, and apparently not with other habitats at the site.

22 Ratcliffe (1977).

23 C.Fuller was the Assistant Regional Officer in the Midland Region of the NC from 1967 to 1976 and is now an Area Officer with the Countryside Council for Wales. J.A.Thompson was Regional Officer for the Midlands (later West Midlands) Region of the NC/NCC from 1966 to 1990.

24 Dr G.F.Peterken OBE was a member of the Woodland Management Section at Monks Wood until 1974 when he transferred to NCC as the woodland specialist in the Chief Scientist Team. P.T.Harding was assistant to Peterken in the Woodland Management Section at Monks Wood from 1971 to 1974.

25 D.M.Evans was the NCC's Regional Land Agent from 1974 to 1997. N.E.King was Assistant Regional Officer for Herefordshire and Worcestershire with the NCC from 1976 to 1985 and Senior Officer for Gloucestershire, Herefordshire and Worcestershire from 1985 to 1991.

26 See Peterken (1969), Rackham (1974, 1976), Rose (1974), Stubbs (1972), Welch & Harding (1974).

27 See Rose & Harding (1978), Harding & Rose (1986).

28 In 1974 Harding joined the staff of the newly formed Institute of Terrestrial Ecology, still based at Monks Wood. He worked in the Sub-division of Invertebrate Ecology, headed by Morris. The full report was Harding (1977a).

29 Harding (1977b).

30 The Baunton Trust was set up in the 1950s by Lt. Colonel Chester-Master. Half the Moccas Estate (including the Park) was added to the Trust in 1967; the rest of the Estate was added in 1992. Richard Chester-Master was a beneficiary of the Trust.

31 A.E.Stubbs was Senior Entomologist in the NCC's Chief Scientist Team. He is a specialist in Diptera with a particular interest in saproxylic fauna. For information on J.Cooter see Chapters 5.2 and 5.3.

32 The Nature Reserve Agreement was for 21 years from 29 September 1978.

References relating to Moccas Park

HARDING, P.T. 1977a. Appendix 2 - Moccas Deer Park, Hereford and Worcester. *In*: HARDING, P.T. 1977. *Second report to the Nature Conservancy Council on the fauna of the mature timber habitat* (CST Report No. 103). Banbury: Nature Conservancy Council.

HARDING, P.T. 1977b. *Moccas Deer Park, Hereford and Worcester: a report on the history, structure and natural history*. Unpublished report to the Nature Conservancy Council by the Institute of Terrestrial Ecology, Huntingdon.

RATCLIFFE, D.A. ed. 1977. *A nature conservation review*. Cambridge: Cambridge University Press.

6

1

Other references

HARDING, P.T. & ROSE, F. 1986. *Pasture-woodlands in lowland Britain.* Huntingdon: Institute of Terrestrial Ecology.

PETERKEN, G.F. 1969. Development of vegetation in Staverton Park, Suffolk. *Field Studies*, 3, 1-39.

RACKHAM, O. 1974. The oak tree in historic times. *In*: M.G. MORRIS & F.H. PERRING. eds. *The British oak.* Faringdon: Classey, 62-79.

RACKHAM, O. 1976. *Trees and woodland in the British landscape.* London: Dent.

ROSE, F. 1974. The epiphytes of oak. *In*: M.G. MORRIS & F.H. PERRING. eds. *The British oak.* Faringdon: Classey, 250-273.

ROSE, F. & HARDING, P.T. 1978. *Pasture-woodlands in lowland Britain and their importance for the conservation of the epiphytes and invertebrates associated with old trees.* (CST Report No. 211). Banbury: Nature Conservancy Council.

ROTHSCHILD, M. & MARREN, P. 1997. *Rothschild's reserves: time and fragile nature.* Rehovet, Israel: Balaban Publishers & Colchester: Harley Books.

SHEAIL, J. 1976. *Nature in trust.* Glasgow & London: Blackie.

SHEAIL, J. & ADAMS, W.M. eds. 1980. Worthy of preservation: a gazetteer of sites of high biological or geological value, identified since 1912. *University College London, Discussion papers in conservation*, 28.

STUBBS, A.E. 1972. Wildlife conservation and dead wood. *Journal of the Devon Trust for Nature Conservation*, supplement, 1-18.

WELCH, R.C. & HARDING, P.T. 1974. A preliminary list of the fauna of Staverton Park, Suffolk. Part 2, Insecta: Coleoptera. *Suffolk natural history*, 16, 287-304.

6
1

$$\frac{6}{1}$$

Priorities of the Estate

Francis Chester-Master

Landscape parks [of the eighteenth century] *in England are usually studied as 'works of art'*.... [but] *the members of the aristocracy and gentry who lived in and paid for these landscapes had more complex interests and needs .... they were creating landscapes with a wide range of functions .... parks were homes, farms and forestry enterprises as well as being pictures.*

Tom Williamson (1993). The landscape park: economics, art and ideology.

Today, as in the eighteenth century, Moccas Park has a wide range of functions. The functions during both periods have been similar, leading to parallels between the management of the Park by Sir George Cornewall, owner between 1771 and 1819 (see Chapter 2.3), and by the Trustees of the Baunton Trust (a trust for the benefit of the Chester-Master family, cousins to the Cornewalls), owners since 1967. These parallels include agricultural improvement, deer management, securing the Park boundary, works to the Lawn Pool, felling, planting, surveys, plans, and the celebration of the Park through art.[1] The need to view Moccas Park in the context of the wider Moccas Estate is also common to both periods.[2] The agricultural and forestry contexts of the day are of course critical too, and national policies on agriculture and forestry, as well as those in respect of heritage, and not least, nature conservation, are all influential in setting priorities.

Moccas Park within the context of the Moccas Estate

The Moccas Estate (hereafter referred to as 'the Estate') comprises 789 hectares of farm and woodland on the southern banks of the River Wye around the villages of Moccas and Bredwardine. Moccas Court lies at the eastern end of the Estate, and along with the nearby village of Moccas, forms its core.

Moccas Court (Figure 6.2.1) was built for Sir George Cornewall in 1775-84; initial drawings were provided by Robert Adam, but the final design was by Anthony Keck.[3] In 1778 'Capability' Brown provided a plan for an extensive area of parkland running from Moccas Court to Moccas Park; the plan formed the basis for Sir George Cornewall's remodelling of this part of the Estate (see Chapter 2.3). The Court is sited so as to take advantage, in particular, of the views of the River Wye to the north and west, and of the parkland to the south and the south west, where Moccas Park itself rises sharply to form the horizon. The Park's dominance as a landscape feature and its linkage to the Court through the area of designed parkland (Figure 6.2.2) underlines its value to the Estate as an amenity of great scenic and historic importance.

Figure 6.2.1

Moccas Court. Viewed from the south with the River Wye just beyond the house, 1999. Photograph by Derek Foxton.

6/2

Figure 6.2.2

Moccas Park and Moccas Court, a view looking north east from the top of the Park. The white cottage to the right of the tree trunk is the Park Lodge. In front of the Lodge lies the road from Moccas to Bredwardine which bisects the photograph and marks the north eastern boundary of Moccas Park. Beyond the road a run of parkland leads up to Moccas Court which is visible to the left of the tree trunk near the top of the photograph; it is approximately 2.5 km distant from the photographer. Moccas Church is visible directly above the Lodge. Within Moccas Park itself, and to the left of the tree trunk, part of the Lawn Pool is visible and beyond it an area of flood water. Photograph by Peter Wakely, May 1994.

The ownership and management of the sporting rights on the Estate (including the Park) rests outside the Trust, with members of the family. The Estate shoot is run through a syndicate. The syndicate members pay a contribution to the running costs and employ a gamekeeper who lives at the Park Lodge. Roughly a quarter of the pheasant shooting on the Estate takes place in the Park and a similar proportion of the less frequent duck shooting. The shoot manager and the keeper are responsible for the management of the Park's herd of fallow deer (see Chapter 5.6). The Trust retains responsibility for the deer fencing and wall around the Park boundary.

All the farmland on the Estate is let, including the 257 ha 'Home Farm', the tenant of which is a member of the family. The Home Farm encompasses Moccas Park (139 ha, of which 68 ha is grazing) and 113 ha of arable land; the balance of the farm is woodland.

The Baunton Trust employs two part-time foresters to manage the 45 ha of woodland on the Estate. Management grant is paid by the Forestry Commission, through its Woodland Grant Scheme, on four small forestry plantations in the Upper Park (total area 5.1 ha). Several areas of natural regeneration are also supported by this scheme.

It is impossible however to convey the importance of Moccas Park to the Moccas Estate. Its contribution is not just practical, it adds significantly to the amenity, scenic and historic value of the Estate.

Management objectives

The Baunton Trust, the 'Home Farm' and the shoot are separate legal and financial entities. These entities have diverse objectives in relation to the Park, but in practice there is generally consensus on all the major management and conservation issues. This consensus is facilitated by overlapping interests. For example, any potential conflict between the grazing requirements of livestock and deer, is reconciled through the responsibility for both lying with the same family member.

The objectives of the various interests in relation to the Park are as follows.

Baunton Trust

❖ To ensure that the capital value of the Estate is maintained, and where possible enhanced, for the benefit of the current and future generations.

❖ To generate a commercial agricultural income from the Park through letting it to the Home Farm.

❖ To manage the Park, its landscape, individual parkland trees and woodland with the aim firstly of maintaining and enhancing its amenity, landscape, and conservation value to the Estate, and secondly of generating income to reinvest in such management.

❖ To continue to recognise and respect the Park's national importance for the conservation of both nature and the historic heritage.

'The Home Farm'

❖ Bearing in mind the rental paid for the Park to the Baunton Trust, to make profitable use of its grazing potential by managing and encouraging a productive sward in line with normal best practice for grassland management.

The Shoot

❖ To take advantage of the sporting potential that the Park offers for high quality pheasant and duck shooting.

❖ To manage the deer as a wild herd aiming to:
- promote quality (notably bodyweights) through selective culling
- ensure a stable and sustainable herd size through selective culling
- restrict the entry of other deer through continued maintenance of the boundary fence
- recycle income from venison sales so as to offset the costs of employing a keeper for the shoot
- avoid artificial feeding in order to safeguard the wild nature of the herd.

Summary

In summary, it is the intention of all the interests on the Estate to ensure that the Park is managed now, and in the future, as a place where the veteran trees are protected and their successors are encouraged within the landscape of a well grazed deer park. This needs to be done in a way that sensibly balances modern nature conservation practices with the intentions of those who moulded the Park in the late eighteenth century, whilst continuing to recognise the importance of amenity, agricultural, sporting and commercial considerations.

Since 1977 the Estate has believed that the best way of realising its objectives is through a Nature Reserve Agreement with the statutory nature conservation authority (formerly Nature Conservancy Council, now English Nature). The first Agreement was entered into in 1979 (see Chapter 6.1). The delicate balancing of the Estate's objectives with those of English Nature through the Nature Reserve Agreement is discussed in Chapter 6.4.

Notes

1 Over and above his agricultural and forestry activities in Moccas Park, Sir George Cornewall commissioned plans and surveys from John Lambe Davis and 'Capability' Brown, both of which involved the Park (see Chapter 2.3), and two watercolours from Thomas Hearne, the leading topographical artist of the day, including one of the Moccas Oak (Morris 1989) (Figure 1.1.1). Modern equivalents relating to the Park (albeit facilitated rather than commissioned by the Baunton Trust), include the plans and surveys of Harding (1977) and Phibbs (1993a, b), the paintings of Diane Barker and the photography of Jeremy Moore (Moore 1990).

2 Chapter 2.3 also mentions the context of Sir George Cornewall's trading and colonial interests.

3 Thompson (1976).

References relating to Moccas Park

HARDING, P.T. 1977. *Moccas Deer Park, Hereford and Worcester: a report on the history, structure and natural history.* Unpublished report to the Nature Conservancy Council by the Institute of Terrestrial Ecology, Huntingdon.

MOORE, J. 1990. *After the wildwood; an exploration of people and trees.* Exhibition brochure. Wrexham: Wrexham Library Arts Centre.

MORRIS, D. 1989. *Thomas Hearne and his landscape.* London: Reaktion Books.

PHIBBS, J.L. 1993a. *Moccas Court, Herefordshire: notes on the landscaping of the deer park.* Report by Debois Landscape Survey Group for English Nature.

PHIBBS, J.L. 1993b. *Moccas Court, Herefordshire: notes on the landscaping of the deer park above the bracken line.* Report by Debois Landscape Survey Group for English Nature.

Other references

THOMPSON, N. 1976. Moccas Court, Herefordshire - I. *Country Life*, 160, 1474-1477.

WILLIAMSON, T. 1993. The landscape park: economics, art and ideology. *Journal of Garden History*, 13, 49-55.

Integrating the conservation of the natural and historic heritage

John Thompson
and Tom Wall

The English landscape, and therefore its habitats and wildlife, is a largely human artefact. From the macro level of the existence and distribution of moorland and heath, to the detailed level of protected natural or historic sites offering protective refuges for the other interests, there is clearly a symbiotic relationship.

Graham Fairclough of English Heritage (1995).
From: *The sum of all its parts: an overview of the politics of integrated management in England.*

ENGLISH HERITAGE

ENGLISH NATURE

P revious chapters have made clear the major importance of Moccas Park both as a wildlife site and as an historic park incorporating elements of landscape design. This dual importance is not, however, unusual. Twenty seven of the 56 English lowland wood-pastures listed by Paul Harding and Francis Rose as being of importance for wildlife conservation,[1] are also included on English Heritage's *Register of Parks and Gardens of Special Historic Interest in England*. Not surprisingly, the reverse applies too: parks of outstanding landscape or historic importance are frequently also of great value for their natural features. This dual importance means that 84 sites, including Moccas Park, are not only on English Heritage's *Register* but have also been notified, at least in part, by English Nature as Sites of Special Scientific Interest.[2]

This combination of natural and historic interest may arise in several ways. A landscape park may, by chance or intent, encompass valuable pre-existing 'natural' features, such as old trees, long established grasslands, wetlands and rocks.[3] The designer may prescribe new plantings, or create new features, which develop special nature conservation value over time, such as trees or shrubs offering particular habitat niches for insects or birds, artificial lakes important for birds or dragonflies, and garden buildings providing roosting sites for bats.[4] The nature conservation interest may also arise through the passage of time,[5] for example the development of dead wood and tree-cavities of value to insects, bats and birds.

Francis Kilvert's description of Moccas Park in 1876 illustrates three cases in point: his "grey old men" will have been pre-existing 'natural' features, the "brilliant green hawthorns" may have formed part of the landscape design, while the "fallow wood" was "the gathering ruin and decay probably of centuries";[6] all contribute to the outstanding nature conservation importance of the Park.

An integrated approach to the management of the natural and historic heritage of parks and other sites has developed only quite recently;[7] it is a process in which Moccas Park has played a part. In 1992 English Nature and English Heritage signed *A Statement of Intent for the Conservation of the Natural and Archaeological Environment*, which established procedures to ensure that the respective interests of the two organisations are taken into account in the management of land including Sites of Special Scientific Interest and registered historic parks.

This chapter discusses the priorities for the conservation of the natural and historic heritage at Moccas Park and the development of an integrated approach to their conservation.

Priorities for the conservation of the natural heritage

Moccas Park's primary importance for nature conservation is as a habitat for a range of insects, in particular beetles, which depend for most of their life cycles on decaying wood. It was concern for the conservation of this insect habitat which led in 1963 to the notification of the Park as a Site of Special Scientific Interest (see Chapter 6.1).

Survey work in 1968 suggested that Moccas Park might be of national importance for epiphytic lichens.[8] Subsequent survey and re-evaluation showed that the lichen flora was in fact of no more than regional importance, and revealed that it was suffering from pollution derived both from the intensification of pasture management that had occurred in the Park and atmospheric sources, as is explained in more detail in Chapter 4.1. This has meant that low intensity grassland management has assumed an important place on the nature conservation agenda. Wetland management has too, with the growing recognition of the importance of the Lawn Pool as a wildlife habitat, especially for plants and invertebrates (see, in particular, Chapters 4.3, 5.3 and 5.5).

The priorities of tree, dead wood, grassland and wetland conservation frame the principal management prescriptions in the National Nature Reserve Management Plan;[9] they are as follows:

Tree and dead wood management
* Maintain the existing trees, whether standing or fallen, and all stages of decaying wood.
* Establish a new generation of pollards, and seek to prematurely age selected maiden trees.
* Perpetuate the habitat by planting trees grown from Moccas Park seed, including hawthorn as a nectar source for invertebrates, and other species for their lichen potential (notably smooth-barked tree species, and walnut as an elm substitute).

Grassland management
* Maintain appropriate grazing levels, cease fertiliser and lime applications and ensure that any necessary weed control is very carefully targeted.

Wetland management
* Retain fen and swamp communities by control of tree and shrub cover.
* Retain areas of open water.

Priorities for the conservation of the historic heritage

Official recognition of the historic importance of Moccas Park did not come until 1986, when a large part of the Moccas Estate, including all of Moccas Park, was included as a Grade II* site on English Heritage's *Register of Parks and Gardens of Special Historic Interest in England*; the site boundary, as revised in 1999, is shown in Figure 6.3.1. This grading denotes that the site is "of great historic interest".[10]

English Heritage refers to the site as 'Moccas Court', the name of the country house built between 1775 and 1784 by Sir George and Lady Catherine Cornewall, owners of the Moccas Estate. But the Park is an integral part of the registered landscape, it has major intrinsic importance and is also a key element of the ensemble that makes up the great historic interest of Moccas. Key elements of this ensemble are illustrated in James Wathen's 'View of Moccas' of 1788 (Figure 6.3.2)[11] which shows Brobury Scar, the River Wye, the recently completed Moccas Court, Moccas Church and the pale and trees of the Park.

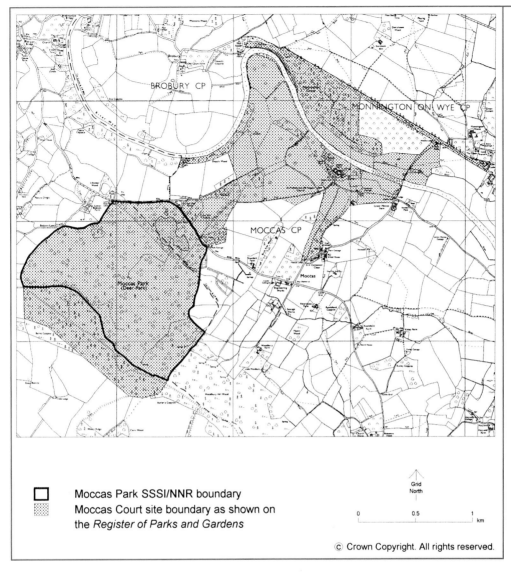

© Crown Copyright. All rights reserved.

Figure 6.3.1

The boundaries of the Moccas Park Site of Special Scientific Interest and of the Moccas Court site on the *Register of Parks and Gardens of Special Historic Interest in England.*

Moccas Park SSSI/NNR boundary
Moccas Court site boundary as shown on the *Register of Parks and Gardens*

Grid North

0   0.5   1 km

The entry in the *Register*, which was revised in 1999, includes a description of the history and features of Moccas Park. It does not give prescriptions for site management, but conservation is, of course, implicit in the registration. Elements of interest which are specifically mentioned are the 'Capability' Brown plan, the veteran trees (including pollards), the Park's picturesque character, the Lawn Pool, the park pale, the park wall, areas of ridge and furrow, the limekiln and quarries.

From the point of view of landscape design, the particular importance of Moccas Park has been highlighted in Chapter 3.1. Much of this importance lies in the range of landscape styles that are detectable. Sir George Cornewall was owner throughout the period 1771-1819, which encompassed much of the heyday of English landscape design. During this period he was exposed to the direct influence of the leading practitioners and theoreticians of the period: 'Capability' Brown, Humphry Repton, Richard Payne Knight and Uvedale Price, and in his management of the Park he responded, in part it seems, to them all.

Integrated management

Because of its direct involvement in the management of Moccas Park, the responsibility for integrating the conservation of the natural and historic heritage has lain with English Nature and its predecessor bodies, rather than with English Heritage. However, for such integration

Figure 6.3.2

View of Moccas in Herefordshire the seat of Sir George Cornewall Bart taken from Brobury Scar 1788, by James Wathen. The pale of Moccas Park lies to the right of Moccas Court. Photograph by Kenneth J. Hoverd.

to take place, there is the need not just for willingness, which would not have been lacking, but also for information, which has not necessarily been available, and for liaison.

Nature Conservancy Council staff had, since the 1970s, been aware of 'Capability' Brown's *Plan for the intended alterations at Moccas Court*, and knew that it extended into the Park, including the area known as The Lawn.[12] However, no guidance was available as to the nature and extent of landscape planting here or elsewhere in the Park.

In 1989, John Phibbs, an historic landscape consultant, visited Moccas Park. He subsequently wrote to John Thompson, then Regional Officer of the Nature Conservancy Council, alerting him to the presence of the Park on English Heritage's *Register*.[13] He expressed his concern that Nature Conservancy Council and the Moccas Estate were not paying due attention to historic landscape considerations when selecting locations for new tree planting. As a result, certain spaces and views within the Park, which he believed had been intentionally left unplanted in the past, were now being planted up and lost. Stimulated by Phibbs's letter, new management prescriptions requiring both an investigation of the evidence for elements of landscape design in the distribution of trees in the Park, and a review of nature conservation management in the light of this investigation, were included in the first formal Management Plan for the National Nature Reserve.[14]

Furthermore, in 1992, the Moccas Estate and English Nature hosted a workshop entitled 'Nature Conservation and Historic Parks'; it was organised by the Garden History Society and was held at the Court and Park. The workshop, which included English Heritage representation, sought to develop understanding between those seeking to conserve wildlife sites and designed landscapes. Situations in which differences of view had previously arisen were explored and a series of recommendations and points of view emerged.[15] Those with particular relevance to Moccas Park were as follows:

❖ New planting: nature conservation management needs to take account of the design of historic landscapes rather than simply putting in trees wherever there is a space.
❖ The practice of leaving dead wood on standing trees and fallen wood lying on the ground is not opposed by historic landscape conservationists.

❖ Intensive grassland management is not a requirement of historic landscape conservation and should be avoided.

❖ The retention of shrubs such as hawthorn to provide nectar sources is usually compatible with historic landscape conservation.

❖ The reintroduction of pollarding ought to be checked against historic precedent so as to avoid the risk of compromising the historic landscape interest.

Later in 1992, English Nature commissioned investigations of the historic landscape of Moccas Park, possibly the first such investigations to be instigated by the statutory nature conservation agency. The reports that followed,[16] developed and interpreted information first gathered by Paul Harding in 1976/77.[17] They highlighted the particular patterns in the cover, species distribution, age and management of trees within the Park and attributed them to design periods; additionally, field archaeology, drives, view points and views were mapped. Recommendations were made as to future planting and pollarding, and existing planting locations judged to be incompatible with the historic pattern of planting were pinpointed. As a result, English Nature decided to move 55 trees to new locations, because whilst from the point of view of nature conservation it is vital to establish a new generation of trees, their precise locations are not usually of great significance.

A further recommendation was to reduce tree and scrub cover on the island in the Lawn Pool so as to restore views across and through the Park. This is seen as compatible with nature conservation requirements, and some work has been undertaken, but it has been limited by the desire of the Estate's shoot to retain cover in the perceived interest of duck shooting.

English Nature has striven to integrate the conservation of the natural and historic heritage in its work at Moccas Park. It has perhaps been slow however to involve English Heritage more directly, notably in carrying out surveys and giving advice, and is likely to look for more such input in the future.

Conclusion

Richard Mabey has observed that Francis Kilvert's description of Moccas Park is "a forceful demonstration that the features responsible for [its] ecological importance and aesthetic appeal are not so far removed from each other".[18] Part of this aesthetic appeal comes from Moccas Park being a designed landscape of historic importance, and the overlap between this historic heritage and the natural heritage of the Park is such that the conservation of both can be readily integrated. Indeed, this book is itself a significant testimony to the integrated approach that is now being followed.

6 / 3

Notes

1   Harding & Rose (1986).
2   Eighty-four sites represents approximately 7% of the 1,282 sites on the *Register* in October 1999 (English Heritage, unpublished listings).
3   The ancient trees of Windsor Great Park are a good example of a pre-existing natural feature.
4   Just two examples are the nationally important dragonfly assemblage at Eridge Park Sussex, which is also of outstanding interest for its lichens (English Nature, Site of Special Scientific Interest citation, 1986, unpublished), and the large bat roost in a garden building at Osborne House, Isle of Wight. A rather different example is the botanical interest of 'The Salisburys', lawns at Chatsworth, Derbyshire, laid by 'Capability' Brown in the 1760s (Gilbert & Hopkins 1983). At Moccas Park a rare beetle *Ernoporicus caucasicus* occurs in the twigs of hybrid lime trees planted probably in the early eighteenth century (see Chapters 5.3 and 3.5) and tree creepers roost in cavities they have excavated in the bark of Wellingtonias planted probably in about 1860 (see Chapter 3.5).
5   Dunham Massey Park is a case in point.
6   Plomer (1940).
7   See, for example, Thompson (1992), Gay (1995), Berry & Brown (1995) and Thomas & Wells (1999).
8   An epiphyte is a plant growing on another plant without being parasitic on it, for example lichens and mosses which grow on trees.

9   English Nature (1992), English Nature (1999).
10 Grading relates to the national context. The sequence of grades, the percentage in each grade and their relative level of importance are as follows: Grade I (10%) "of exceptional historic interest"; Grade II★ (28%) "of great historic interest"; Grade II (62%) "of special historic interest" (English Heritage (1993) and Harriet Jordan (pers. comm.)).
11 Whitehead & Shoesmith (1994).
12 This was made clear in Harding (1977).
13 It is a measure of the inadequate liaison of the time, that the presence of Moccas Park on the *Register* was not general knowledge within Nature Conservancy Council, and did not inform thinking concerning site management. Knowledge of the SSSI status of *Register* sites is understood to have been equally limited in English Heritage.
14 English Nature (1992).
15 Garden History Society (1992).
16 Phibbs (1993a, 1993b).
17 Harding (1977).
18 Mabey (1980).

References concerning Moccas Park

ENGLISH NATURE. 1992. *Moccas Park National Nature Reserve Brief Management Plan.* Unpublished.

ENGLISH NATURE. 1999. *Moccas Park National Nature Reserve Brief Management Plan; first revision.* Unpublished.

HARDING, P.T. 1977. *Moccas Deer Park, Hereford and Worcester: a report on the history, structure and natural history.* Unpublished report to the Nature Conservancy Council by the Institute of Terrestrial Ecology, Huntingdon.

MABEY, R. 1980. *The common ground. A place for nature in Britain's future.* London: Hutchinson.

PHIBBS, J.L. 1993a. *Moccas Court, Herefordshire: notes on the landscaping of the deer park.* Report by Debois Landscape Survey Group for English Nature.

PHIBBS, J.L. 1993b. *Moccas Court, Herefordshire: notes on the landscaping of the deer park above the bracken line.* Report by Debois Landscape Survey Group for English Nature.

PLOMER, W. 1940. *Kilvert's diary.* Volume 3. London: Jonathan Cape.

WHITEHEAD, D. & SHOESMITH, R. 1994. *James Wathen's Herefordshire, 1770-1820. A collection of his sketches and paintings.* Almeley: Logaston Press.

Other references

BERRY, A.Q. & BROWN, I.W., eds. 1995. *Managing ancient monuments: an integrated approach.* Mold: Clwyd County Council.

ENGLISH HERITAGE. 1993. Criteria for the assessment of sites for the Register of Parks and Gardens. Information sheet, November 1993.

FAIRCLOUGH, G. 1995. The sum of all its parts: an overview of the politics of integrated management in England. In: A.Q. BERRY & I.W. BROWN, eds. *Managing ancient monuments: an integrated approach.* Mold: Clwyd County Council, 17-28.

GARDEN HISTORY SOCIETY. 1992. *Nature conservation and historic parks.* Suggestions following on from a Workshop held at Moccas Court. Unpublished note.

GAY, H. 1995. Integrated conservation of natural and historical aspects of the countryside. *Journal of Architectural Conservation*, 3, 70-89.

GILBERT, O.L. & HOPKINS, D.H. 1983. The ancient lawns at Chatsworth. *The Garden*, 108, 471-474.

HARDING, P.T. & ROSE, F. 1986. *Pasture-woodlands in lowland Britain. A review of their importance for wildlife conservation.* Huntingdon: Institute of Terrestrial Ecology.

THOMAS, R.C. & WELLS, D. 1999. Nature conservation and historic properties: an integrated approach. In: J. GRENVILLE, ed. *Managing the historic rural landscape.* London: Routledge, 149-162.

THOMPSON, J.A. 1992. *Nature and landscape: harmony or acrimony?* English Heritage Internal Report. Unpublished. Subsequently a summary of this report was published in *English Heritage Conservation Bulletin*, October 1992, 16-17.

Estate management and conservation: striking a balance

Francis Chester-Master
and Tom Wall

.... part of the skill of medieval deer farmers lay in their ability to integrate deer farming into a wider context. They had the power to privilege the deer, and often did so, but in practice a sort of balance was struck between often conflicting interests.

Jean Birrell (1992). Deer and deer farming in medieval England.

Chapters 6.2 and 6.3 outlined the estate management and nature conservation priorities at Moccas Park; this chapter examines how, where these priorities differ, they are reconciled through the Nature Reserve Agreement under which the Park is managed; it also considers the conservation of the historic heritage. The objectives of parkland management may have evolved over the centuries, but as is indicated in the epigraph, the existence of diverse interests is not new, nor is the necessity to strike a balance between them.

The Chester-Master family arms.

This chapter covers the period up to the end of September 1999 when the current Nature Reserve Agreement expired. A new Agreement is under negotiation; it has not been concluded however at the time of writing, and the comments and judgements made in this chapter relate only to previous negotiations and Agreements.

ENGLISH NATURE

Throughout this chapter, 'the Moccas Estate', or simply 'the Estate', is used as a shorthand term embracing three entities whose interests are seen as essentially the same: the Baunton Trust (owners of the Park), the 'Home Farm' (tenant) and the shoot (which uses the Park along with the rest of the Moccas Estate). The term 'the Council' is used to embrace both the Nature Conservancy Council and its successor, English Nature (formally the Nature Conservancy Council for England).

6/4

The main priorities of the Moccas Estate and of the Council

Table 6.4.1 provides a simplified résumé of the main priorities of the Moccas Estate and of the Council in respect of Moccas Park. These priorities are expressed as a series of counterpoised objectives and an assessment is made of the degree to which they converge. The areas of divergence have been reconciled through the Nature Reserve Agreement and its Management Policy.

Table 6.4.1. The main priorities of the Moccas Estate and of the Council in respect of Moccas Park and an assessment of the degree to which these priorities converge.

| Issue | Priorities of | | Convergence/ Divergence of priorities |
	Moccas Estate	The Council	
Estate management and nature conservation			
Stewardship	Maintain and ideally enhance the resource and its capital value	Practise sustainable nature conservation management	Convergence with some differences of emphasis
Financial considerations	Safeguard income	Ensure value for money on any payments made	Convergence through negotiation
Parkland management (Lower Park)	Cherish and perpetuate the Park, its old trees, amenity, landscape and wildlife	Conserve the old trees, flora and fauna, including by the 'premature ageing' of some trees by pollarding	Convergence
	Limit the quantity and spread of fallen timber in the grassland	Maintain all dead, standing and fallen timber	Divergence
	Plant a new generation of timber trees, especially oak, beech and sweet chestnut	Plant new trees, including hawthorn, appropriate to the conservation interest	Convergence with some differences of emphasis
Forestry (Upper Park)	Carry out silvicultural management, notably in the plantations, and maintain the sporting potential	Maintain all dead and fallen timber; perpetuate deciduous tree cover; remove conifers	Differences of emphasis and timing rather than any real divergence
Grassland management and grazing	Manage so as to achieve productive pasture	Encourage 'extensive' management and grazing with low inputs and outputs	Divergence
Lawn Pool	Retain a reasonable amount of cover for duck shooting	Remove substantial areas of tree and shrub cover	Differences of emphasis
	Retain open water	Retain open water	Convergence
Sporting	Realise the duck and pheasant shooting potential	Avoid intensification	Any divergence of interests is not fundamental
Deer	Manage as a healthy wild herd within a secure boundary	Encourage continued management of a healthy wild herd	Convergence
Scientific research and survey	Welcome research and survey which extends knowledge of the Park	Encourage research and survey, particularly where it guides conservation management	Convergence
Access	Welcome access by interested and responsible visitors	Explore opportunities for enhanced public appreciation of the Park	Convergence
The historic heritage			
Designed landscape	Take due account of landscape considerations	Respect the historic pattern of tree planting, species and management	Convergence
Historic features	Conserve, in so far as finances permit, the existing lengths of park pale and park wall	Encourage the conservation of the existing lengths of park pale and park wall	Convergence
	Retain ridge and furrow, quarries, limekiln	Encourage the retention of ridge and furrow, quarries, limekiln	Convergence

Issues on which priorities differ

The management of fallen dead wood in the Lower Park

Dead wood, both standing and fallen, is of vital importance in the life cycles of a range of organisms, notably invertebrate species, for which the Park has particular importance (see Chapter 5.1). Other elements of the parkland habitat are vital to these species too, notably flowers as food sources for the adults of insects whose larvae develop in dead wood. It is however the management of the fallen dead wood element of the habitat that has engendered most discussion between the parties.

The original Nature Reserve Agreement established a series of principles which sought to meet the Council's requirements, whilst limiting and localising the visual impact of fallen dead wood and recognising potential financial loss. These principles were developed over the years into a series of guidelines which are listed in Chapter 6.5.

The Estate has always recognised the crucial importance to the nature conservation interest of dead wood. It does however believe that the conservation value of the dead wood resource needs to be balanced with landscape, amenity and farming considerations. In the past allowing all dead wood to lie where it fell reduced grazing areas, and nettles proliferated around the fallen timber. In addition, the Estate believes that fallen trees have had an adverse impact on the appearance of the parkland, particularly around the Lawn Pool. From an estate management perspective, the requirement that all timber larger than brushwood and twigs (interpreted as being all timber in excess of six inches (15cm) in diameter) should be offered to the Council at its market value, has put an unnecessary administrative and financial burden on both parties.

In the light of these views, the Estate has proposed a new approach in respect of the Lower Park, designed to satisfy the main priorities of both parties. This would involve the Estate when it requires fallen timber for firewood or planking, removing half, while leaving the balance for nature conservation purposes. The balance would include the decayed and fractured timber, which is of particular nature conservation value. The advantages of this approach would be a reduction in administration for both parties and the absence of any financial outlay for the Council; its practical implementation is currently under discussion.

Grassland management and grazing

The Estate wishes to maximise the grazing potential and also sees amenity value in a well tended sward with few thistles and nettles and little in the way of bracken. The Council however has become increasingly concerned over the years by the numbers of livestock grazing the Park, and the management (harrowing, rolling, topping and herbicide use) and nutrient inputs (lime, fertilisers and supplementary feeding) required to sustain them. It has sought to move towards a more 'extensive' system with minimal or no inputs and reduced stocking levels. It sees this as preferable from a number of points of view, including the conservation of lichens and fungi (see Chapters 4.1 and 4.2) and the enhancement of the structure and floristic interest of the grassland (see Chapter 4.3). The Nature Reserve Agreement of 1979 was varied in 1992 in order to meet these concerns and further changes were introduced in 1996 (see Chapter 6.5).

The farm tenant pays a commercial rent to the Baunton Trust. This is set at a level which reflects the agricultural potential of the Park when managed as an improved grassland sward. The various changes to the Agreement have reduced the profitability of the grazing and as a result the Agreement allows for the tenant to receive an annual compensation payment.

Capital value

The Baunton Trust has a responsibility to see that the capital value of the Park is maintained. The Trustees' concern is that a less intensively managed sward, with increased quantities of dead wood, could lead to a reduction in capital value. In contrast, it is the Council's hope that, in the medium to long term, management to safeguard the natural and historic importance of the site (including perhaps the marketing of organically reared livestock and deer) might prove to be as reliable a way of maintaining both capital value and income as a more intensive farming enterprise.

Sporting interests

At one time no pheasants were released in the Park. This has changed over the years, as is explained in Chapter 6.5, but currently the management of the Park's sporting interest is low key. Intensification of the sporting interest would be a matter of concern to the Council. For example, mallard were released and artificially fed on the Lawn Pool in 1984 and 1997. The Council was concerned as to the impact on aquatic life of such disturbance and the nutrient enrichment that might have resulted.

Additionally, the shoot sees the clearance of significant areas of scrub growth on the island in the Pool as being counter to its interests because of the resultant reduction in cover. The nature conservation interest however would be best served by maintaining a larger area of open habitat. It has also been suggested that the landscape interest would benefit from such clearance as it would restore views within the Park.[1]

Whereas issues such as these are the subject of ongoing consultations, it should be recognised that parks can be subjected to recreational uses such as golf courses and motocross events which are far less compatible with their conservation than unintensive management in the sporting interest.

The Nature Reserve Agreement

Table 6.4.1 is the sort of analysis which will have influenced the negotiation of the original Nature Reserve Agreement. The Agreement is the legal instrument through which shared priorities are developed into management projects and guidelines; these are laid out in a Management Policy annexed to the Agreement. The Baunton Trust, its farm tenant (who manages the shoot) and the Council are signatories to this Agreement.

Contexts change over the years, knowledge develops, priorities evolve and the economic and farming climate fluctuates. In order to take account of this, the original Agreement of 1978 has been varied and replaced; the dates and durations of the various agreements are shown in Table 6.4.2.

Table 6.4.2. Nature Reserve Agreements between the Moccas Estate and the Council.

Form of agreement	Start date (date of signature)	End/ Expiry date
Nature Reserve Agreement	29 September 1978 (11 May 1979)	Due to run to 29 September 1999 (21 years), this Agreement was overtaken by the new Agreement of 1996
Variation to the original Agreement	30 September 1991 (16 September 1992)	As above
New Nature Reserve Agreement	29 September 1996 (14 July 1997)	29 September 1999

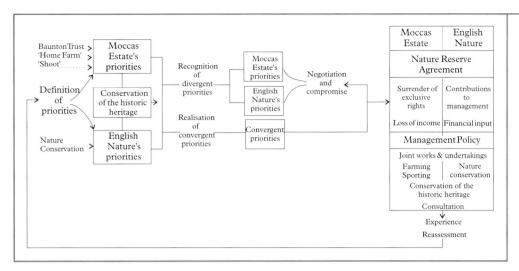

Figure 6.4.1

The processes involved in arriving at the Nature Reserve Agreement and its Management Policy.

Reaching an Agreement

Figure 6.4.1 seeks to illustrate the process of enquiry and negotiation which has led to the conclusion of Nature Reserve Agreements for Moccas Park National Nature Reserve. The process has generated agreement on many shared priorities. The resolution of the differences that remain has required compromise on both sides.

The Agreement for Moccas Park specifies a range of positive management works, such as tree planting, to which the Council makes contributions of money and/or labour. It also details compensatory payments. The level of payments and contributions that have been agreed reflects the degree to which the Estate is suffering loss of income.

The Agreement dates from a period when compensatory payments calculated on the basis of 'loss of profits foregone' were the norm. Nowadays the Council makes payments for positive nature conservation management. Securing the desired grassland management through appropriate grazing by a managed deer herd and by livestock would be an example of this. The new Agreement currently under discussion aims to accommodate this change in a manner satisfactory to both parties.

Both parties have always shared a concern for the conservation of the historic heritage. A lack of information as to the Park's history and the rôle of design in its present make-up has been a limitation which has only recently begun to be remedied (see Chapter 3.1). English Nature's responsibility to take account of the historic heritage in its management of National Nature Reserves was formalised in 1992 through a statement of intent drawn up with English Heritage (see Chapter 6.3).

Concluding remarks

The Nature Reserve Agreement grew out of the decision taken by the late Mr Richard Chester-Master to enter into a partnership with the Council to assist in the conservation of Moccas Park. This led to its designation as the first parkland National Nature Reserve. The Agreement sought to strike a balance between estate management and nature conservation. It was based on shared priorities, and where there were differences of emphasis, compromise met the needs of both parties. Consultation is ongoing and forms a fund of understanding and experience which feeds back into the periodic reassessment of priorities. With the expiry of the current Agreement in September 1999, a reassessment of priorities is in hand at the time of writing. We are confident that each side's priorities can continue to be met in the future.

Notes

1   Phibbs (1993).

Reference relating to Moccas Park

PHIBBS, J.L. 1993. *Moccas Court, Herefordshire: notes on the landscaping of the deer park.* Report by Debois Landscape Survey Group to English Nature.

Other reference

BIRRELL, J. 1992. Deer and deer farming in medieval England. *Agricultural History Review*, 40.2, 112-126.

6
4

Management in practice

John Bacon and
Tom Wall

.... from the twenty ninth day of September one thousand nine hundred and seventy eight the land shall be managed as a nature reserve in such manner and upon such terms as hereinafter provided .... the general estate management and the farming of the land shall be carried out by the Owners and the Tenant in accordance with the Agreed Management Policy.

Extract from the first Nature Reserve Agreement between the Owners, the Tenant and Nature Conservancy Council.

Nature reserves may be thought of, and indeed defined, as areas of land set aside exclusively for nature. However, since its inception in 1978, Moccas Park National Nature Reserve has been managed simultaneously as a nature reserve, as part of a farm, as part of a shoot and as part of a forestry enterprise. It has been managed with an eye to amenity and landscape too. It is of course a deer park and there has therefore been the ongoing need to manage the deer herd as well. This chapter describes management as practised in these various spheres between the Septembers of 1978 and 1999 by the Nature Conservancy Council and English Nature (referred to collectively hereafter as 'the

Council') and the various interests on the Moccas Estate;[1] activities prior to 1978 are also outlined where this helps to put subsequent work into context.[2]

Figure 6.5.1

Tree planting.
Sam Davies (left) and Brian Davies (right, no relation) tree planting in the Lower Park, March 1979. Photograph by Eric Pithers.

Recognition of the range of overlapping, and sometimes conflicting, activities and objectives that have been pursued over the years, is crucial to an understanding of how Moccas Park has functioned as a National Nature Reserve. All these activities have been carried out within the context of the original Nature Reserve Agreement of 1978, the Variation of 1991 to that Agreement, and the new Agreement of 1996. In the Variation and the new Agreement the balance has moved increasingly towards nature conservation and away from commercial use of the Park as a grazing unit, and the Council has made a significant financial commitment in order to bring about this change. From 29 September 1999 a new Nature Reserve Agreement is due to come into force; its terms have not been finalised at the time of writing but are likely to differ in some respects from those described below.

Among the many things learned at this, the first parkland National Nature Reserve, have been strategies for balancing the needs of nature conservation management with those of the other activities which are part and parcel of an English deer park. Indeed, one of the rôles of Moccas Park National Nature Reserve, as referred to at the start of this book, has been that of an open-air workshop and classroom in nature conservation management, and one of the purposes of this chapter is to highlight and pass on the experience that has been gained in the open-air of Moccas Park since 1978.

Staffing

The Council and all members of its staff .... [are granted] .... free right of access
.... for the purposes of carrying out the Council's functions ....[3]

It is sometimes assumed that all nature reserves are under the constant daily care of a resident nature reserve warden, but in general this is only true of the biggest or busiest reserves. Moccas Park has never had a nature reserve warden as such, and the visits of the Council's staff, from bases never less than 50 km away, have sometimes had to be at monthly or even longer intervals due to their many other responsibilities; it has meant also that most of the practical nature reserve management work has been carried out by contractors rather than the Council's own staff.[4] The 'at arm's length' nature of the Council's involvement and management has meant that it has not been as comprehensive or as well documented as would have been desirable.

In respect of the Estate, there has been the much more constant oversight of a locally based agent, as well as a gamekeeper living at the Park Lodge, and local farm and estate staff. The Estate is owned by the Baunton Trust (a trust for the benefit of the Chester-Master family); for much of the period no member of the Chester-Master family has had a main residence at Moccas, but the family has maintained a close and regular interest and involvement.[5]

Tree planting

Council will undertake the planting and establishment of 100 trees
in each of the first ten years of the agreed term.

In 1968 the Estate, under new ownership, had started to meet the pressing need for new trees to be planted in the Park, where there had been virtually no planting for nearly 150 years. Approximately half of the 74 individual trees then planted, all of them in or immediately adjacent to the Lower Park, were oak, sweet chestnut or beech; but, following perhaps the spirit of the time, the balance included 18 specimen conifers and a range of exotic broadleaves. Perceptions of what it is appropriate to plant in parks such as Moccas have

Figure 6.5.2

A recently planted tree. A young oak planted near 'The *Hypebaeus* tree', probably the oldest tree in the Park (see Chapter 3.2). Photograph by Peter Wakely, May 1994.

changed since then, and the accent today is very much on respecting the historically established mix of tree species; indeed four cypresses planted in 1968 were felled in 1997.[6]

Following on from the start made by the Moccas Estate in 1968, the original Nature Reserve Agreement prescribed the planting of 1,000 individual trees which were to be "well distributed throughout the land" but sited "with a view to minimising interference with agricultural operations". Given that there were only about 1,700 trees in the Park at that time,[7] this was an ambitious level of planting. It was a response to the urgent need for a significant injection of young trees to renew an aging stock.

The planting plan in the Nature Reserve Agreement was based on the advice of Paul Harding who had recently completed a survey of the trees of the entire Park.[8] Seven hundred and twenty of the 1,000 trees were to be oak, 170 beech, 20 ash, 20 field maple and 20 small-leaved lime, with the species of an additional 50 trees being determined by the owners at a later date. The species composition respected the existing dominance of oak, and the strong representation of beech; choice of the minority species reflected the incidence of other native species in the Park.

There was also the need to perpetuate the habitat of the beetle *Ernoporicus caucasicus* which at that time was known in Britain only at Moccas Park, and on only one tree, a small-leaved lime. This was the only small-leaved lime out of 13 limes in the Park, and it had blown down in January 1976![9]   Hawthorn is another particularly significant species for nature conservation (as explained below); the owners did not want hawthorn to be included in the planting plan, but 60 have been planted through informal agreement.

The planting programme outlined in the Nature Reserve Agreement was initiated by the Council in March 1979 (Figures 6.5.1 and 6.5.2) and in excess of 1,000 trees have now been planted. The planting rhythm has been scaled down gradually in the 1990s, and since the 1995/96 season has been reduced to an annual figure of just ten trees per year. Details of what has been planted to date are given below. There is also an ongoing cycle of maintenance involving weed control, repairs to the guards which protect each tree against deer and livestock, occasional pruning, and replacement of failures.

Approaches to parkland planting have become increasingly sophisticated over the years since the Agreement of 1978 was drawn up. The planting at Moccas Park has proceeded without a detailed "Master Plan" such as that now in place for Blenheim Park, Oxfordshire, with its careful weighting of "natural regeneration", "continuous replacement" and "sequential replanting" as ways of achieving a balanced tree structure.[10] Nor has there been the quest for background silvicultural information on "survivorship curves", "death rates" and "recruitment rates" that is informing work at Duncombe Park National Nature Reserve, North Yorkshire.[11] In the case of Moccas Park, a simple approach, applied with flexibility, has generally proved very adequate, and has seen the establishment of a major cohort of new trees. This is the foundation on which future manipulation of the balance of species and age structure, through additional recruitment, pollarding, or, if need be, premature fellings, can be based. But, if the generation gap that was evident in the 1960s is not to recur, it is vital that planting should either be ongoing, albeit at a low level, or that substantial new cohorts are established at intervals not exceeding 50 years.

Planting in the Lower Park

Up to the end of 1999, 695 trees had been planted in the Lower Park; this compares with a pre- existing tree stock of 598 trees. The species composition of the plantings is shown in Figure 6.5.3; this can be compared with Figure 3.5.1, which shows the species composition of the pre-existing tree stock. All the oak, and most of the other trees, have been propagated from seed gathered in the Park.[12]

The dominance of oak has been perpetuated in the new plantings,[13] but there has been an attempt to bolster the representation of both hawthorn and field maple. Hawthorns were frequent in the Lower Park prior to the agricultural improvement that took place in the 1960s/70s, reaching, it is said, densities of up to one every 40 yards.[14] Hawthorn blossom is an important source of nectar for some beetle species and other invertebrates,[15] while the bark of field maple is suitable for a number of epiphytes.[16] The proportion of ash has been kept high too, reflecting its former importance in the Park.[17] It is probable that there were

Figure 6.5.3

The numbers and species of trees planted in the Lower Park, 1968-1999. All but 74 of these trees were planted by the Council.

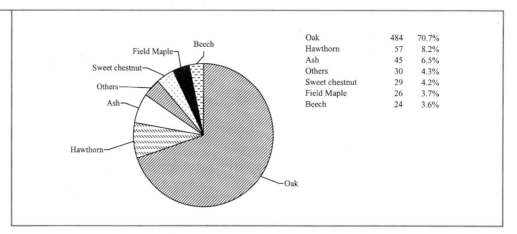

Oak	484	70.7%
Hawthorn	57	8.2%
Ash	45	6.5%
Others	30	4.3%
Sweet chestnut	29	4.2%
Field Maple	26	3.7%
Beech	24	3.6%

few elms in the Park even before the advent of Dutch elm disease in the 1970s (see Chapter 3.4). Elm has importance for lichens and invertebrates but because of the disease it was excluded from the planting proposals.

The proportion of beech in new plantings is lower than was envisaged in the Nature Reserve Agreement and it lags behind that of the established tree population, as does the proportion of sweet chestnut, while no horse chestnuts have been planted as yet. There are good nature conservation and landscape reasons for maintaining the representations of all three species,[18] and this is something to which attention should turn in future. The few limes planted to date appear to be hybrids,[19] and the lack of small-leaved lime ought to be made good, even though *E. caucasicus* has now been found on hybrid lime at Moccas Park as well as on limes at more than 20 sites elsewhere in the country (see Chapter 5.3).

Planting in the Upper Park

Between 1978 and 1999, 349 individual trees were planted by the Council throughout the Upper Park, either in gaps in the canopy or in glades; this compares with a pre-existing tree stock of approximately 1,025 trees. All the oaks and most of the other trees had been propagated from seed gathered in the Park. The species composition of these plantings is shown in Figure 6.5.4; this can be compared with Figure 3.5.3, which shows the numbers of trees prior to these plantings. Additionally, since 1966, 14 small plantations of trees have been established by the Estate and the Council; they are discussed in the forestry section below.

Comments made in relation to the planting in the Lower Park are again applicable. If the species composition prior to planting is to be perpetuated, good numbers of beech, sweet chestnut and horse chestnut need to be planted in future. There is also a place for small numbers of large-leaved lime and yew, both of which are present here but not in the Lower Park.

Figure 6.5.4

The numbers and species of trees planted in the Upper Park, 1979-1999. The trees shown in this chart were all planted by the Council. Additional plantings made by the Estate and the Council within deer exclosures are excluded.

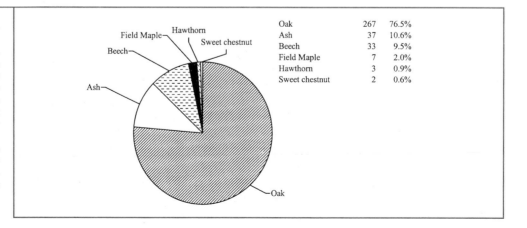

Oak	267	76.5%
Ash	37	10.6%
Beech	33	9.5%
Field Maple	7	2.0%
Hawthorn	3	0.9%
Sweet chestnut	2	0.6%

Tree management

Tree numbering

Council may introduce a numbering system for standing trees ....

The mapping and numbering of the trees enables them to be readily identified for the purposes of recording and management. In the case of newly planted trees, numbers can be attached to the tree guards. Various techniques have been tried for numbering the long-established trees. For many years 2.5 cm diameter aluminium alloy discs were used. The numbered discs were secured using aluminium alloy nails and were placed in holes cut through the bark of a root buttress in order to expose the sap wood in which the nails could be anchored. Regular maintenance was necessary however, because the bark soon grew back over the holes.[20] In 1998 a new method was adopted using 4 cm by 2.5 cm individually numbered galvanised metal timber labels. These are attached above the reach of deer and livestock, using one 8 cm long aluminium alloy nail driven only 2 cm into the tree.[21] The label hangs free so that it is pushed out along the nail by the expanding trunk of the tree. The only drawback noted to date, albeit an important one, is that at least when new, the labels can appear intrusive.

Tree pollarding

.... the parties will meet .... to discuss management details and any variations ....
which might be necessary or desirable.

Ancient pollard oaks such as 'The *Hypebaeus* Tree' (Chapters 3.2 and 5.2) have a multitude of habitat niches and a longevity not equalled by maiden trees.[22] It is unlikely, however, that any tree in the Park has been pollarded or re-pollarded within the last century, indeed it is a practice that has largely died out throughout the British Isles. The possibility of future pollarding or re-pollarding was not mentioned in the Nature Reserve Agreement (such issues were not to the fore at that time), but, from an early date, the Council's staff proposed the creation of new pollards as a desirable variation to be discussed with the Owners.

It was not, however, until the winter of 1990/91 that agreement was reached for the first three of, to date, just 16 oak and one beech of 10-30 years of age, to be pollarded. The majority have done well, but after producing good early growth, six of the first oaks to be pollarded died, as did the beech; all the oak suffered infestations of mildew.[23] Subsequent pollarding has proceeded more cautiously, with some established branches being left rather than all being removed at once, and this appears to be a more successful method. In the absence of either written record or oral tradition, pollarding is proceeding by just such a process of trial and error, with experience at Moccas Park and elsewhere being shared amongst a growing band of practitioners.[24]

There is, however, a huge age gap between these newly pollarded trees and the few ancient pollards to be found in the Park today, and very few of the trees in intermediate generations are pollards. With this in mind, since 1992 eight oaks estimated to be between 150 and 200 years old have been 'topped' in an attempt to

Figure 6.5.5

A 'giraffe pollard'. An oak tree in the Lower Park, number 149, after 'topping'. Photograph by Peter Wakely, May 1994.

6
—
5

initiate the development of surrogates for more long-established pollards (Figure 6.5.5). Trees of this age in the Park appear to have developed in close-grown stands, and thus have relatively clean stems without low forks or vigorous low side-branches which would offer good 'pollarding' points. It has therefore been necessary to make them into 'giraffe pollards' by truncating them at an average height of some 7 metres, as against a traditional pollarding height of 2 to 3 metres. Truncation has in all cases been just above side-branches and all the trees have produced vigorous new shoots at or near this point. It is hoped that these trees will not only continue to produce vigorous growth but also that pollarding will induce premature decay, giving opportunities for colonisation by fungi and invertebrates.[25]

The safeguard of ancient and over-mature trees

The conditions which have led to the retention of the high scientific interest
of the parkland will be continued ....

Important though it is to pursue these strategies for accelerating the development of niches suitable, in particular, for saproxylic invertebrates, the safeguard of the existing ancient and over-mature trees is the first priority. The oldest oak pollards tend to have small and relatively well balanced crowns; current thinking is that they should not be re-pollarded because to do so might be a risky strategy with no certain dividends. Since 1992 single mature oak and alder pollards have however been re-pollarded, and eight

Figure 6.5.6

Tree surgery. Work in progress to safeguard tree number 276 against windblow, Lower Park, February 1993. Photograph by Tom Wall.

amongst the older oak trees that appeared most vulnerable to windblow, as well as single beech, ash and walnut, have been selectively lopped so as to enhance their stability (Figure 6.5.6).

Dead wood

In view of their importance to nature conservation, dead trees
and fallen timber .... shall be treated as follows ....

The retention or removal of dead trees and fallen timber is the issue which over the years has generated most debate between the Council and the Estate (Figure 6.5.7). Amenity, proliferation of weeds,[26] loss of firewood, waste of timber value and loss of grazing, have all been matters of concern to the Estate; the vital importance of decaying wood to the principal interest of the Reserve has been the major concern of the Council. Practice has varied over the years, but the letter and spirit of the original Nature Reserve Agreement have guided both parties in developing the following arrangements, which may well however change under the terms of the new Agreement:

❖ In the Upper Park all fallen wood is left *in situ*.
❖ In the Lower Park twigs and branches less than six inches in diameter may be removed by the Owners; an exception is made however in the case of lime, because the beetle *Ernoporicus caucasicus* breeds in lime twigs.

❖ If fallen timber is felt by the Estate to be obtrusive or causing inconvenience, it may, by agreement, be moved to less sensitive locations. When this occurs, timber is to be left in as long lengths as possible and out of direct sunlight (this helps prevent rapid desiccation and consequent loss of value to invertebrates).

Figure 6.5.7

Dead wood. One of the veteran oaks collapsed onto grassland in the Lower Park, September 1989. Photograph by Paul T. Harding.

❖ Where tree surgery is undertaken, all wood, of whatever size, which is free of decay, is removed from the Park but all other wood is left on site.

❖ Invertebrates may lay eggs in recently fallen and severed branches and trunks during Spring, Summer and Autumn; if this occurs, subsequent removal of this timber would lead to a loss to the Park of part at least of the next generation of these organisms. In order to attempt to pre-empt this, if wood is to be removed during these seasons it must be taken away as soon as is possible after it falls, and removal of timber that falls during the Winter must be done before the middle of April.

❖ Compensation may be paid for loss of timber value or grazing.

As explained in Chapter 3.5, current volumes of fallen dead wood in the Lower Park appear low by comparison with woodland sites, and dead standing trees also are scarce.

Grazing

Grazing of the land by sheep and cattle will continue.

Records of livestock numbers are somewhat fragmentary, but those available, together with numbers of deer, are shown in Table 6.5.1.[27] The record is taken back to 1964 in order to provide an historical context.

Figure 6.5.8

Grazing. Sheep in the Lower Park, May 1994. Photograph by Peter Wakely.

The record shows that cattle grazing has declined over the years and that sheep grazing has increased (Figure 6.5.8). It had been hoped that through the provisions of the revised Nature Reserve Agreement of 1991 there would be a return to a more diverse grazing regime, with cattle reintroduced to replace some of the sheep. But the young livestock then available proved too excitable, inexperienced and difficult to control in such an extensive grazing unit, which encompasses some dangerously steep terrain and the highly poisonous meadow saffron and yew. Cattle grazing was not persevered with at that time, but a suckler herd grazed the Park in late summer in 1998 and 1999, helping to achieve the desired balance and intensity of grazing.

The Variation of 1991 to the original Agreement was the product of complex negotiations through which the Estate agreed to accept compensation for a significant reduction in livestock numbers. This went with undertakings to cease lime and fertiliser applications and significantly curtail supplementary feeding. These aspects are discussed further below.

The new Agreement of 1996 included for the first time a provision that "no stock treated with avermectins should be allowed to graze the land", or, if they had been so treated, that they should be kept off the land "until the avermectin residues are no longer present in the dung".[28] Avermectins are a group of chemicals several of which are used as veterinary medicines to control parasites in livestock. Residues of these medicines are excreted and may poison invertebrates, including flies and beetles, that colonise dung. In addition to the direct effects on invertebrates, concern has been expressed as to the indirect effects on predatory species, such as bats, through a reduction in food supply, and to the effects on aquatic invertebrates when livestock defecate in pools and water courses.[29] Whilst no study has yet been undertaken to quantify the impact of avermectins on wildlife, a precautionary approach is appropriate at an important wildlife site such as Moccas Park.

Table 6.5.1. Grazing levels 1964-1999.

Period	Deer	Sheep	Cattle	Ponies
1964-79	100-120	Regularly: 200-300 ewes Peak: 400-500 ewes	Regularly: 30-50 Peak: 90-100	All year: 5-10.
1980-85	120	Gradual build up	Numbers reduced	?
1986-90	120	Mid April to May/June: 630 ewes and their lambs June to mid February: gradual reduction leaving 300 ewes over-wintering	September - December: 20	?
1991-97	180	April-September: 300 ewes and their lambs October-March: 100 ewes	1992 and 1993, April-September: maximum 50; none thereafter	0
1998-99	180	All year: 100 ewes, with lambs at foot in Spring and Summer	July-September: 50, with calves at foot	0

Grassland management

Fertilisation by lime and slag would be continued .... controlled spraying may be undertaken by the Owners in consultation with the Council .... areas of the upper portions of the land might be ploughed and re-seeded.

During the period 1964-1972 the Lower Park was ploughed in parts and disced in others, hawthorn bushes were grubbed out, some areas were drained, extensive areas of anthills were levelled, slag and lime was applied and the grassland (most of which had previously been covered in dense, tall bracken) was re-seeded so that grazing could be intensified.[30] A further area, sometimes referred to as the 'Secret Meadow', which lies in the western part of the Upper Park above Bodcott Plantation, and extends to some 2 ha, was worked in much the same way in 1979/80.

Following these agricultural improvements, pasture quality was maintained by the periodic spreading of slag, and by fertilising, liming, topping, harrowing and rolling, while supplementary feeding of livestock was routine. It is now believed that these agricultural activities have had an adverse affect on the nature conservation interest of the Park, and in particular on its lichen flora, as described in Chapter 4.1. Accordingly, from the late 1980s, these activities were progressively phased out by negotiation of compensatory arrangements in the Management Agreement, and, but for agreed minor exceptions, they ceased altogether in 1996. The aim has been to reduce to a minimum the external nutrient inputs to the Park, such as fertilisers and concentrated foods for livestock and deer, and to return to a more 'natural' regime of low inputs and low outputs which will have been the norm in deer parks in the past. A more 'natural' management regime has meant a reduction in both the quantity and quality of forage; livestock numbers have been reduced accordingly, whilst deer numbers have been allowed to increase (see Chapter 5.6).

Thistles and nettles

The spread of creeping thistle, spear thistle and nettle may have been encouraged by the intensification of grassland management and 'poaching' of the ground due to high stocking levels. The control of these species is felt by the Estate to be essential from an agricultural and an amenity point of view. There is little or no nature conservation case *per se* for their control, indeed thistles and nettles are important to many invertebrates, but the Council has cooperated, and generally led, on control. This is for two reasons: firstly so as to guard against the proliferation of nettles and thistles becoming an issue which might hinder cooperation on more significant matters, and secondly so as to be satisfied that control is carried out with the interests of other species to the fore.

For some years the Lower Park was topped once or twice (exceptionally three times) each summer, in the hope that this would help in weed control as well as keep the Park looking 'tidy'. Topping was supported by the Council, as it was felt to be preferable to the former practice of spraying using a boom-sprayer mounted on a tractor, an activity which

Figure 6.5.9

Weed-wiper trials.
Mervyn Owen, English Nature Estate Worker, trialling a prototype of the 'Allman Eco-Wipe' in the Lower Park, using a mix of dye and water, June 1992. Photograph by Tom Overbury (Royal Agricultural College).

was likely to be damaging to plants other than the weed species. The frequency and timing of topping is critical if it is to be effective, and it is possible that the topping of the Park may actually have strengthened rather than weakened the hold of creeping thistle, by stimulating the formation of new shoots and reducing competition from grasses.[31] At best it proved ineffective as a control measure, and in 1987 the Council and the Agricultural Development and Advisory Service carried out trials at Moccas Park to test the effectiveness of a weed-wiper mounted on a tractor as a way of controlling thistles. A weed-wiper is designed to apply herbicide to the target species only, and should thus prove less damaging to the environment than the spraying of herbicide which is inevitably less discriminate. These trials identified design limitations in the weed-wipers then available, particularly when they were used on undulating ground, and in 1992 and 1993 the Park was used as a trial site by English Nature and the Royal Agricultural College for prototypes of a new, ground-hugging, weed-wiper (Figure 6.5.9),[32] which was subsequently marketed as the 'Allman Eco-Wipe'. The effectiveness of weed-wipers for thistle control at Moccas Park using clopyralid (in a formulation marketed as 'Dow Shield') has generally been high (Figure 6.5.10).

Figure 6.5.10

Thistle control.
An area lying between the Lawn Pool and the road, photographed in June 1993, before the application of herbicide to the stand of thistles using a prototype of the 'Allman Eco-wipe', and in summer 1996, after wiping in 1993, 1994 and 1995. Photographs by Tom Wall.

Nettles tend to be more clumped in their distribution than are thistles, and they often occur under trees where tractor access is difficult. In this case spot-spraying by the Council of triclopyr (principally in a formulation marketed as 'Broadshot') using knapsack sprayers, has proved the most practical method and it has proved effective, particularly in controlling the large and frequent clumps which proliferated in the western half of the Lower Park.[33]

Bracken

When thistles were topped during the summer months, bracken was cut too and this doubtless helped to check any potential spread of bracken in the grassland of the Lower Park. Since topping has ceased, bracken has become more obvious to the eye and possibly more widespread too. Again, this is not really a nature conservation issue, indeed bracken, provided it is not dominant, adds structural diversity to the sward, thereby encouraging a range of invertebrate and vertebrate species. From an agricultural standpoint however, it is viewed with very considerable concern, particularly as memories of the 'reclamation' of the grassland of the Park from a sea of bracken are still fresh.[34]

6 / 5

Accordingly, over the years 1996-98, the Council agreed to, and carried out, the spot-spraying of bracken using asulam (in a formulation marketed as 'Asulox'), concentrating on the 'Secret Meadow' and the upper reaches of the Lower Park. Such spot-spraying localises the application of a herbicide to which a number of other species are susceptible,

Figure 6.5.11

Bracken rolling. Brian Otterburn adjusting his 'Parkland Bracken Breaker' so as to run it off-set under low tree branches, the Lower Park, 6 June 1997. The towing balls permit the towing of additional units, whether off-set, or in-line through gateways. This model was developed in association with English Nature, the Royal Agricultural College, the Veteran Trees Initiative and the Ancient Tree Forum. Photograph by John Bacon.

notably all other fern species including adder's-tongue, an uncommon fern which has been noticed in the grassland over recent years (see Chapter 4.3).[35] The alternative techniques of bracken pulling and bruising were both demonstrated at a Veteran Trees Initiative demonstration day organised by English Nature at Moccas Park in 1997 (Figure 6.5.11) and a bracken roller was used in the Park in 1999;[36] these non-herbicide control methods offer options for the future, including for the control of thistles and common nettle.[37]

Intensity of management

In addition to the direct and indirect effects that agricultural intensification may have had on the lichens, there also have been potential or actual effects on other key elements of the nature conservation interest. Ploughing, re-seeding, fertilising and herbicide applications will have reduced the incidence of herb species in the grassland. This may in turn

Figure 6.5.12

Harrows in the Lower Park, 1991. Photograph by Tom Wall.

have had some effect on the value of the grassland to adult saproxylic invertebrates through the removal of potential pollen and nectar sources. Harrowing (Figure 6.5.12) and rolling will have prevented the formation of anthills.[38] Ploughing may have destroyed uncommon species of fungi which are now found only in the small areas of old grassland that persist on banks and dips inaccessible to the plough.[39] But, most critically, agricultural intensification may well have had a detrimental effect on the trees themselves, by damaging root systems and fungal mycorrhiza,[40] but also through drainage, fertilizer and herbicide applications and soil compaction.[41]

The low-key management of the agriculturally improved pasture within the Park, and the conservation of the remaining areas of unimproved pasture, are therefore regarded by the Council as important to the retention and enhancement of the value of the Park for its grassland flora, fungi, lichens and invertebrates and to the well-being of the trees themselves. But the impact that this has on the agricultural interests of the Estate has to be carefully weighed and considered.

Forestry

> .... the Owners [covenant] to carry out forestry .... operations ....
> in such manner as may .... be agreed with the Council ....

Between 1966 and 1982 the Estate, in the interests of forestry and game management, established four small plantations with a total area of 5.1 ha on the lower slopes of the Upper Park, within which a range of predominantly coniferous species, was established. The biggest of these was the Woodbury Plantation (3.2 ha) lying on the eastern boundary of the Park. Additionally, in the early 1980s the Council established 10 small deer exclosures with a total area of 0.6 ha, again on the lower slopes of the Upper Park, within which oak and beech were planted.

The Estate's predominantly coniferous plantations were never welcomed by the Council, who felt that they were not in tune with the character of the Park, either in terms of their species or their configurations. The straight western edge of the Woodbury Plantation was 'scalloped' in 1998, which helped to reveal some of the fine parkland trees round which the conifers had been planted, and one of the other plantations is due for clear-felling in the near future. Within the remaining plantations selective fellings will, in the medium to long term, favour any broadleaved trees that are present.

The Upper Park is included as one of the woodland compartments on the Moccas Estate falling within a Woodland Grant Scheme which was approved by the Forestry Commission in 1992 and reviewed in 1998. Whilst the Scheme applies to the whole of the Upper Park, only the small predominantly coniferous plantations referred to above are specifically identified for management, together with areas set aside for natural regeneration. In 1994, in a joint venture between the Estate, the Council and the Commission, an open area of approximately 1 ha lying near the old limekiln in the south eastern part of the Park was cleared of bracken (by cutting and herbicide application) and fenced against deer, livestock, hares and rabbits, to allow the natural regeneration of trees and shrubs. A further similar area, approximately 1.7 ha in size, is currently being established near the Bodcott Plantation at the western end of the Upper Park. These are not however new endeavours, a plot for natural regeneration was established by the Estate in 1978, but it yielded only a few sweet chestnut trees.[42]

In 1978, six oaks were felled by the Estate at the top of the Park and at least 59 more were taken from the west side of the Upper Park in 1987. One dead and one moribund oak were felled near the Bodcott Plantation in 1998.

Wetland works

> .... the Owners or the Council might consider ....
> the carrying out of dredging works to Lawn Pool ....

Older residents remember that up to the 1960s the "segs" (sedges) and "bulrushes" growing over much of the Lawn Pool were fired, possibly every year, which scorched and checked the "black sallies" (willows) and kept the Pool open; the judgment at that time was that this would help to encourage more duck.[43] It may be that as a consequence of the cessation of this management, much of the island in the centre of the Pool started to get overgrown with willows and alders. To allow the island to become a solid mass of willow and alder would significantly reduce its biological diversity; furthermore, views across the Pool are now regarded as an important element of the landscape design and these are obstructed by tree and scrub growth.[44]

A significant number of alders were removed or coppiced by the Council in the centre of the island in 1989, as described below, but nowadays the shoot wishes to see good cover retained round the fringes of the island. Accordingly, further tree and shrub clearance work, which the Council commenced in 1995, has so far been confined to the felling of willows in

Figure 6.5.13

Dredging of the perimeter of the Lawn Pool, October 1983. Noel King (Nature Conservancy Council's Assistant Regional Officer) on the right, and the drag-line operator (name not known), standing on the north side of the Pool. Photograph by Eric Pithers.

the centre of the west end of the island and, at the east end, pushing back the alders and willows that were encroaching from the island into its surrounding 'moat'; further work may be undertaken in future. Stumps were treated with herbicide to prevent regrowth, but this was not always successful.[45]

Various excavations have aimed to extend the area of open water which, by 1973, was minimal; these excavations have generally been seen as in the interests of both shooting and nature conservation. An aerial photograph taken in 1973 which is reproduced as Figure 4.3.3 shows the Pool before these excavations were undertaken; one taken in 1991, reproduced as Figure 4.3.4, shows the Pool after most of the excavations had been completed. The various excavations are listed below; unless otherwise stated they were carried out by the Estate:[46]

- the mid 1970s, four or five small craters were made in the western end of the island using explosives.
- In the early 1980s, a narrow channel was cut into the island at its north end using a 'transport box' on the back of a tractor.
- In 1983, almost the entire perimeter of the Pool was excavated using a dragline (Figure 6.5.13), effectively creating a 'moat' around a central island (the only part left untouched was at the extreme east end); the spoil was spread adjacent to the Pool.
- In 1989, working from the promontory on its south side, the Council created an area of open water approximately 35 m in diameter in the centre of the island; it was dug to a clay bottom which was reached at a depth of about 1.8 m; at the same time some alders were pulled out and others were coppiced; the spoil was subsequently taken away.
- In 1990, the Council made a substantial excavation near the centre of the island in the western lobe of the Pool; it was approximately 60 m long, averaged 12 m in width and extended to a depth of about 1 m; the spoil was subsequently taken away.
- In 1992, the Council used an excavator to scoop out a small area at the extreme east end of the Pool; the spoil was taken away.

Walls and fences

.... repair and maintenance of boundary fences ....

The present boundary of Moccas Park is some 5 km in length. Presumably at one time the entire boundary was either paled or walled. Today only 400 m is made up of traditional park paling and just 500 m of stone wall (see respectively Figure 5.6.2 and Figure 4.1.2. Otherwise, 500 m is modern 'chestnut paling',[47] and the remaining 3,600 m is post and wire fence. Repair and replacement costs are a heavy burden, particularly in respect of the traditional paling and walling, but these lengths have particular historic value and they are also of interest as lichen habitats (Chapter 4.1). New park paling costs £39 per m to supply and erect (for a life span of perhaps 30 years), walling comes at a similar cost, but for labour only (life span of 40 years), modern 'chestnut paling' approximately £8 per m to supply and erect (life span of 30 years) and post and wire fencing £6 per m (life span of 20 years). The Estate meets the cost of repair and replacement of the boundary (pale, wall and fences) assisted by an annual contribution from the Council.

In 1976, a fence was erected across the Park running in a south westerly direction from near Cross End Farm right to the boundary fence at the top of the Park. It was a stock fence, enabling the Park to be divided roughly in two for grazing purposes; it did not stop deer movements, but on occasions deer accidentally got caught up in it. It was a visual intrusion, interrupting views through the Park. By 1995 it had outlived its useful life, and all but the short stretch between the road and the Lawn Pool was removed by the Council; the stretch left standing still proves to be of use when livestock are being gathered.

Deer management

> .... deer control .... will continue

Deer management is the *sine qua non* of a deer park. At Moccas Park it is the responsibility of those who manage the Estate's shoot; stalking is not let on a commercial basis. The Council has no direct involvement in the management of the deer, but it is keenly interested in this aspect of Moccas Park, has commissioned a report and recommendations on the management of the deer herd,[48] and contributes to the cost of the cull. Deer management is discussed in more detail in Chapter 5.6.

Shooting

> *Shooting for duck and pheasant will continue ....*

Until the 1970s, the sporting interest of the Moccas Estate lay principally in the salmon fishing on the River Wye, and the shooting of duck and wild pheasant. The release of small numbers of pheasants (800-1,000 in all) began in the 1970s, but it was not until about 1976 that any were released in the Park.[49] For some years now, there have been two release pens in the Upper Park, and approximately one quarter of the pheasant shooting on the Estate takes place in the Park.[50] Pheasants are fed in the Upper Park prior to and during the shooting season, and rides are cut in the bracken so as to aid access for the beaters and to provide flushing points. The track bulldozed through the Upper Park by the Estate in 1980 is also important in providing access for the shoot.[51]

The Park is also important with respect to duck shooting. The Lawn Pool is not the only duck haunt on the Estate but it is one of the most important, and although generally no more than 50 duck are shot each year, it provides perhaps one quarter of the duck shooting on the Estate as a whole. Ducks are encouraged in by feeding, and in 1984 and 1997 mallard were released on the Pool. Such releases are unwelcome to the Council who fear that they may have a detrimental impact on the ecology of the Pool, and the Estate has agreed not to release birds in future.

Pest control

Limited control of pest species may need to be undertaken ....

The Estate's gamekeeper controls some recognised pest species in the interests of game preservation, farming and forestry. The most frequently targeted species are grey squirrel and rabbit, but corvids, especially jackdaw and carrion crow, are controlled too, as are fox, mole and mustelids. Whilst this control is not regarded as damaging to the nature conservation interest, it is not generally seen as being beneficial, with the exception of the control of grey squirrels which can cause severe damage, notably to sapling beech and oak trees in the Upper Park. Here, despite efforts to control them, squirrels compromise the successful establishment of a new generation of trees. Squirrel control is by shooting and the use of warfarin baits in hoppers of recognised design. In some recent years small numbers of Canada geese have been shot under licence during the closed season. This is to prevent them nesting on the Lawn Pool, where they are thought to be liable to disturb other waterfowl, foul adjacent pasture, and, when water levels are low, compromise water quality.

Access and scientific survey and research

Notwithstanding .... the Owners [and] the Tenant .... all other persons shall only be permitted to enter upon the land with the previous consent of the Council.

It has always been the policy of both the owners and the Council that those with a *bona fide* interest should be allowed to visit the Park. Indeed, from the start, special provision was made for access by members of what was then the Herefordshire and Radnorshire Nature Trust as well as for the residents of the parish of Moccas. For reasons of safety, pheasant shooting, deer culling, and preventing undue disturbance to the deer and water birds, open access to the Park is not appropriate, but in recent years there has been an increase in the number of guided walks arranged for natural history societies and similar groups and for the wider public too.

Figure 6.5.14

Lichen monitoring. Ray Woods examining a lichen recording quadrat in the Lower Park, February 1992 (see Chapter 4.1). To his left is John Henry Looney and to his right, Tim Harvey. Photograph by Tom Wall.

Council has always been keen to encourage scientific survey and research and this has been supported by the owners. Indeed, but for the many permits issued over the years, this book would have been a great deal less comprehensive.

Amenity and landscape design

The main use of the land being grazing by livestock will be continued with sporting and amenity continued in conjunction with the agricultural and nature conservation interests.

Amenity - the quality of being pleasant or agreeable - lies in the eye of the beholder, and this fact has led to some lively debates between the parties to the Nature Reserve Agreement. The

Figure 6.5.15

A view in the Lower
Park, *circa* 1990.
Photograph by Jeremy
Moore.

Estate has tended towards a perception of amenity which includes a certain amount of tidiness and smoothness of texture; the Council has favoured nature conservation policies which result in irregularity and roughness. The treatment of fallen dead wood exemplifies the two approaches: on the one hand 'cut up and stack, or, better still, remove'; on the other 'leave as fallen'. Goodwill on both sides has usually led to a workable compromise.

Whilst the Nature Reserve Agreement mentions 'amenity', it does not consider issues of landscape design. John Phibbs, a landscape consultant, who first visited Moccas Park in 1989, advised the Council that in his opinion there were distinct design elements within the Park and that the choice of location for some of the recent tree planting did not take adequate account of landscape considerations. He gives his reading of the landscape of Moccas Park in Chapter 3.1.

If one looks at Moccas Park with the notion of design in mind, patterns soon become evident. They can be seen, for example, in the distribution of the trees as a whole (scattered or grouped in different areas), of the ancient trees (often on or near banks) and of particular species (notably horse chestnut). And there are open spaces (small and large), planted knolls and open vales, and views both within and out of the Park. Given that the Park owes much to design as well as to nature, conservationists can feel confident about planting non-native species such as horse and sweet chestnut which are clearly such an important element of the present-day make-up of the Park as well as having nature conservation value in their own right.

The open spaces are one of the most important elements in the 'design' and in general these had not been planted, partly at least because of the requirement in the Nature Reserve Agreement that plantings should be sited "with a view to minimising interference with agricultural operations". Elsewhere, the relocation within the Lower Park in 1993/94 of 55 trees (out of a total of in excess of 600 trees planted there to that date), met the principal reservations that had been raised on landscape grounds. Since then, locations for new plantings have followed the suggestions given by John Phibbs in reports commissioned by the Council.[52]

In conclusion

The parties agree to consult with each other on such occasions as circumstances may require in order to promote to the utmost extent the fulfilment of this policy.

As has been indicated from time to time in the preceding account, the parties have needed to consult with each other on many occasions! The Estate and the Council have approached the conservation of the Park from different angles and with different perceptions and in consequence have often pulled in different directions. But good things have been achieved, a lot has been learned by both parties, and there is now a deeper understanding of each other's point of view. It is to be hoped both that this understanding can be welded into a clear view of the practical management that is necessary in order to conserve Moccas Park into the future, and that the lessons learned here at the first parkland National Nature Reserve will continue to be applied at parkland and veteran tree sites elsewhere in the country.

Notes

1   Nature Conservancy Council was signatory to the first Nature Reserve Agreement (1978), its successor, English Nature (Nature Conservancy Council for England) to its subsequent variation (1991) and the new Agreement of 1996. The term 'the Estate' is used in this chapter to embrace the owners of the Park (the Baunton Trust), the agricultural tenant of 'the Home Farm', whose holding includes the Park, and the Estate's shoot.

2   As detailed in Chapter 6.1, the first recommendations on management for nature conservation were made by the Nature Conservancy in the 1960s. Formal proposals were put forward in 1973 and expanded in Harding (1977a,b). They formed the basis for the nature conservation management undertaken through the Nature Reserve Agreement.

3   This, and all the succeeding quotations, are taken from the Nature Reserve Agreement of 1978 and its Management Plan.

4   From 1978 onwards, the members of the staff of the Council who have had the greatest involvement have been Mervyn Evans (Land Agent), Noel King (Assistant Regional Officer), Eric Pithers and John Bacon (successive Chief Wardens whose duties included management of the Reserve), Tom Wall (Site Manager), Mike Taylor (Assistant Site Manager) and Helen Stace (Conservation Officer). Sam Davies of Woodbury, Moccas, a local contractor, has planted virtually all the trees in the Park over the last 20 years, as well as doing a range of other works. Tree surgery has been carried out by Mark Parsons of Rhosgoch.

5   From 1978 onwards the principal representatives of the Estate have been the late Richard Chester-Master and latterly his sons Francis and Ben; John Phipps, who was agent for many years; the gamekeepers who have undertaken the crucial work of deer management (David Chandler, for most of the period, and latterly Phil Price); Nigel Bridges, farm manager, and Tom and Bill Bowen, farm staff; and Elwyn Jones, woodman.

6   A European larch and a Chinese thuja were felled at the same time.

7   Harding (1977a).

8   Harding (1977a).

9   Harding (1977a). Since 1976 the small-leaved lime has re-sprouted from the surviving root system.

10 Cobham & Hutton (1997).

11 Clayden (1996).

12 Seed collection commenced in November 1976. Whilst, following the advice of Paul Harding (1977b), acorns have been sought from the best specimens of ancient and over-mature trees, poor seed years and the depredations notably of deer, livestock and pheasants have led to acorns being harvested from other trees too.

13 The oaks have been propagated from Moccas Park acorns and therefore, following the evidence of Percy (1986), are more likely to be pedunculate or hybrids than sessile oak. Percy identified 56% of 231 of the established oak trees in the Lower Park as pedunculate and only 9% as sessile, the balance being hybrids. For many years seed of oak and other species was propagated by the Forestry Commission's nursery at Alice Holt.

14 Tom Bowen, former farm manager (pers. comm.); John Phipps, former agent, recalls a rather lower frequency (pers. comm.).

15 Speight (1989) has observed that flowers are probably as critical to the survival of some saproxylic invertebrates (those dependent on wood and associated habitats; for a full definition see Chapter 5.1) as are the appropriate larval habitats, notably in the rotting timber. This is because flowers provide the pollen and nectar on which the adults depend for food. Hawthorn is regarded as the most important early summer nectar source and many species of insects, including saproxylic species, appear to have life cycles adapted so that the peak of adult emergence coincides with the peak of hawthorn blossom (Kirby 1992).

16 Harding & Rose (1986).

17 Anon (1870).

18 Beech is second only to oak in its nature conservation importance as a parkland tree, and the losses of mature beech from the Park over the last two decades have been greater than those of any other species (Harding 1990). Beech mast is a valuable food source for deer and many other species. The mast of both sweet and horse chestnut is also eaten by the deer, and the flowers and sap runs of horse chestnut are important for a number of insects. All three species are also of considerable significance to the landscape of the Park (see Chapter 3.1).

19 Wall (1996); the two limes planted by the Estate are a red-twigged lime and an American lime (from information in English Nature files).

20 It was also found that discs were damaged, possibly by birds or grey squirrels (Fretwell & Green 1996) or, particularly on sweet chestnut, became corroded.

21 The method is as described by Fretwell & Green (1996).

22 Rackham (1991).

23 This experience is not unique, see White (1996), Coleman (1996).

24 See for example Mitchell (1989), Read (1991), Wall (in Read 1996) and Read (in press).

25 Pollarding is one of the techniques for the "induction of premature senility in trees" advocated by Speight (1989) with a view to developing habitat for saproxylic invertebrates.

26 Nettles and thistles tend to proliferate round dead wood. This appears to be a consequence of enhanced nutrient inputs and ground disturbance brought about by the process of decay and the tendency of livestock to congregate at these points. The dead wood then impedes access, thus hampering weed control.

27 The figures for livestock are taken from the National Nature Reserve Management Plan (English Nature 1992), discussions with local people and personal observations. The figures for deer are taken from Chapter 5.6; they are the herd size after the annual cull.

28 The period over which avermectins persist in livestock varies greatly according to the method of treatment, but it can be as long as 6 months (Cooke 1997).

29 Cooke (1997).

30 English Nature (1992); the account given there is based on discussions with Tom Bowen who was farm manager at that time.

31 Bacon (1994).

32 Bacon (1994).

33 Experience at Moccas Park has demonstrated the risk of vapour drift if triclopyr is used in warm weather, and this has led to the promulgation of advice as to application in relation to air temperature (Cooke 1995). In situations where sensitive and important vegetation occurs nearby, temperatures above 15°C should be avoided, and triclopyr should certainly not be used if the air temperature is higher than 20°C, or is likely to exceed 20°C on the day of application. In warm springs it can sometimes be difficult to find days suitable for the application of triclopyr.

34 Up until the 1950s 'fern' was harvested in the Park as a crop, see Chapter 2.4.

35 Apart from ferns and dock species, a range of other plants show susceptibility to Asulox (Brown & Robinson 1997).

36 The machines demonstrated were a prototype of the Alvan Blanch 'Eco-puller' (developed through collaboration with English Nature and the Royal Agricultural College) and the 'Parkland' version of the 'Otterburn Bracken Breaker' (developed through collaboration with English Nature, the Royal Agricultural College, The Ancient Tree Forum and the Veteran Trees Initiative) (Bacon 1994, 1995, 1997, 1998a).

37 See Bacon & Coleshaw (1999).

38 The ground level inside the longer-standing guards round planted trees is sometimes more than 30 cm higher than that outside, apparently as a result of the activity of yellow hill ants which find sanctuary here (Helen Stace pers. comm.).

39 Ted Green (pers. comm.); see Chapter 4.2.

40 Mycorrhizal fungi associated with the roots of some plants are thought to enhance greatly the uptake, by the roots, of mineral nutrients and water, and to afford some protection against pathogenic root-infecting fungi (Rayner 1993).

41 Alexander & Green (1993), Alexander (1995), White (1998).

42 John Phipps (pers. comm.).

43 Tom Bowen, Sam Davies and Les Whittal (pers.comms).

44 Phibbs (1993a).

45 The Husqvarna 'root cutting chainsaw' developed through collaboration with English Nature and the Royal Agricultural College may in future provide a useful non-herbicide alternative (Bacon 1998b).

46 The approximate locations are shown in Strutt (1997).

47 The chestnut-paling is composed of vertical pales 1.8 m tall, approximately 4 cm wide, held together by three horizontal line wires; the pales are set 7-10 cm apart.

48 Putman (1994).

49 Len Slaney (pers. comm.).

50 Ben Chester-Master (pers. comm.).

51 Unfortunately the cutting of this new track now makes it more difficult to discern the historical pattern of paths and drives within the Upper Park.

52 Phibbs (1993a,b).

References relating to Moccas Park

ANON. 1870. Incidental notes on remarkable trees in Herefordshire. *Transactions of the Woolhope Naturalists' Field Club*, 288-321.

ENGLISH NATURE. 1992. *Moccas Park National Nature Reserve: Brief Management Plan.* West Midlands Team, Shrewsbury, unpublished.

HARDING, P.T. 1977a. *Moccas deer park, Hereford and Worcester: a report on the history, structure and natural history.* Unpublished report to the Nature Conservancy by the Institute of Terrestrial Ecology, Huntingdon.

HARDING, P.T. 1977b. *Moccas deer park. Proposed tree planting.* Unpublished proposals to the Nature Conservancy by the Institute of Terrestrial Ecology, Huntingdon.

HARDING, P.T. 1990. *Damage to ecologically important trees in selected pasture-woodlands resulting from winter storms and summer drought in 1990.* Huntingdon: Institute of Terrestrial Ecology, unpublished.

PERCY, H. 1986. *Moccas Park National Nature Reserve - tree inventory.* Unpublished report to Nature Conservancy Council.

PHIBBS, J. L. 1993a. *Moccas Court, Herefordshire: notes on the landscaping of the deer park.* Unpublished report to English Nature.

PHIBBS, J. L. 1993b. *Moccas Court, Herefordshire: notes on the landscaping of the deer park above the bracken line.* Unpublished report to English Nature.

PUTMAN, R.J. 1994. *Survey and description of the deer herd at Moccas Park NNR.* Unpublished report to English Nature.

STRUTT, J.A. 1997. *Ice melt channels, dead ice hollows and/or a landscaped pool? A stratigraphic investigation of the depth and nature of deposits to determine the shape and origin of the aquatic basin of the Lawn Pool, Moccas Park National Nature Reserve.* Lancaster University, BSc dissertation.

WALL, T. 1996. Strategies for nature conservation in parklands: some examples from Moccas Park National Nature Reserve. *In:* H. READ, ed. *Pollard and veteran tree management II.* London: Corporation of London, 42-49.

Other references

ALEXANDER, K.N.A. 1995. Historic parks and pasture-woodlands: the National Trust resource and its conservation. *In:* D.J. BULLOCK & H.J. HARVEY, eds. The National Trust and nature conservation: 100 years on. *Biological Journal of the Linnean Society,* 56 (suppl.), 155-175.

ALEXANDER, K.N.A. & GREEN, E. E. 1993. Deadwood - eyesore or ecosystem. *Enact* 1 (1), 11-14.

BACON, J.C. 1994. A prickly problem. *Enact* 2 (1), 12-15.

BACON, J.C. 1995. Removing the prickles. *Enact* 3 (2), 10-11.

BACON, J.C. 1997. Bracken breaking - a bruising battle. *Enact* 5 (3), 19-22.

BACON, J.C. 1998a. Pulling tall weeds. *Enact* 6 (2), 7-9.

BACON, J.C. 1998b. Modernising the mattock. *Enact* 6 (4), 15-18.

BACON, J.C. & COLESHAW, T. 1999. *Practical Solutions: equipment, techniques and ideas for wildlife management.* Peterborough: English Nature.

BROWN, R. & ROBINSON, R. 1997. *Bracken management handbook.* Ongar: Rhône-Poulenc Agriculture.

CLAYDEN, D. 1996. Data collection and analysis of veteran tree populations: a plea for co-ordination - with an example from Duncombe Park NNR/SSSI, North Yorkshire. *In:* H. READ, ed. *Pollard and veteran tree management II.* London: Corporation of London, 55-64.

COBHAM, R. & HUTTON, P. 1997. Blenheim: present management and future restoration. *In:* J. BOND & K. TILLER, eds. *Blenheim: Landscape for a Palace.* Stroud: Sutton, 133-150.

COLEMAN, N. 1996. Maiden pollarding at Thorndon Country Park. *In:* H. READ, ed. *Pollard and veteran tree management II.* London: Corporation of London, 89-90.

COOKE, A. 1995. Avoiding vapour drift damage from triclopyr formulations. *Pollution News,* 11, 4-5.

COOKE, A. 1997. *Avermectin use in livestock.* Farming and Wildlife Advisory Group leaflet.

FRETWELL, K. & GREEN, E.E. 1996. Methods for tagging trees. *In:* H. READ, ed. *Pollard and veteran tree management II.* London: Corporation of London, 138-139.

HARDING, P.T. & ROSE, F. 1986. *Pasture-woodlands in lowland Britain. A review of their importance for wildlife conservation.* Huntingdon: Institute of Terrestrial Ecology.

KIRBY, P. 1992. *Habitat management for invertebrates: a practical handbook.* Sandy: RSPB.

MITCHELL, P.L. 1989. Repollarding large neglectied pollards: a review of current practice and results. *Arboricultural Journal,* 13, 125-142.

RACKHAM, O. 1991. Introduction to pollards. *In:* H. READ, ed. *Pollard and Veteran Tree Management.* London: Corporation of London, 6-10.

RAYNER, A.D.M. 1993. The fundamental importance of fungi in woodlands. *British Wildlife,* 4, 205-215.

READ, H. ed. 1991. *Pollard and veteran tree management.* London: Corporation of London.

READ, H. ed. 1996. *Pollard and veteran tree management II.* London: Corporation of London.

READ, H. In press. *Veteran trees: a guide to good management.* Peterborough: English Nature.

SPEIGHT, M.C.D. 1989. *Saproxylic invertebrates and their conservation.* Nature and Environment Series, 42. Strasbourg: Council of Europe.

WHITE, J. 1996. Progress with re-pollarding old oaks and new work on ash. *In:* H. READ, ed. *Pollard and veteran tree management II.* London: Corporation of London, 75-76.

WHITE, J. 1998. Site and tree management. *In:* D.J. BULLOCK & K.N.A. ALEXANDER, eds. *Parklands - the way forward.* English Nature Research Report number 295. Peterborough: English Nature.

A vision for the future

Tom Wall,
Paul T. Harding
and Helen Stace

The objectives and targets cover habitat conservation, restoration and expansion. Key components include the need, by 2002 to initiate the expansion of 500 ha of wood-pasture or parkland, in appropriate areas, to help reverse fragmentation ....

UK Biodiversity Group (1998). *Lowland wood-pasture and parkland. A Habitat Action Plan.*

A vision, but first a retrospective: two hundred years ago Herefordshire was a hotbed of parkland thinking, planting and making. Up and down the county, landowners, theoreticians, designers and practitioners were at work, creating new parks or adapting those dating from earlier centuries. Humphry Repton, building on the early lead of 'Capability' Brown, was advising at Moccas, Garnons, Stoke Edith, Sufton Court, Belmont, The Weir and Hampton Court.[1] Nurserymen such as Edwin Wheeler, John Davenport and James Cranstone were laying out and planting grounds at The Mynde and Allensmore Court.[2] Richard Payne Knight and Uvedale Price, arbiters of national educated taste in such matters, were designing, theorising and evangelising on their estates at Downton and Foxley. And, at Moccas, there was a synthesis. As we have learned (see Chapter 2.3) Brown had advised here, as did Repton; the landowner, Sir George Cornewall, used and adapted their advice, aided and influenced by Webster, his gardener and forester. Uvedale Price, who lived just 8 km away advised too, as did Richard Payne Knight, a friend and regular visitor, born and brought up 10 km away at Wormsley Grange.

The UK Biodiversity Action Plan logo.

Two hundred years on, Herefordshire is again at the forefront of parkland thinking and action and Moccas Park is again in the thick of things. This, the first parkland National Nature Reserve, has been the site for parkland workshops and demonstrations; the Park, as part of Herefordshire's Georgian parkland legacy, was an important component of *The Picturesque Landscape* exhibition, sponsored by English Nature, which opened in Hereford in 1994;[3] and in 1998, Moccas Park and Hereford were the venues for the national Parklands Symposium.[4]

We look to a future in which Moccas Park continues to be at the forefront, the exemplar of integrated action to conserve the natural and historic interest of the UK's parklands.

Habitat Action Plans

The national context for the future is *Lowland Wood-pasture and Parkland: A Habitat Action Plan,*[5] which forms part of the *UK Biodiversity Action Plan.* The *Habitat Action Plan* calls for the conservation of the current extent of lowland wood-pasture and parkland, of which there are some 10-20,000 ha. It advocates the initiation, by 2002, of a programme to expand by 500 ha the area of wood-pasture or parkland, and calls for a programme to restore 2,500 ha of derelict wood-pasture and parkland to favourable ecological condition by 2010. Linked to

7

it are *Action Plan* proposals for the conservation of a group of rare beetle species that depend on dead wood.[6] The county context is the *Herefordshire Habitat Action Plan for Wood-pasture and Parkland* that is currently being worked up by the Herefordshire Biodiversity Forum; it will set targets for the county.

The opportunity exists to make Moccas Park the standard bearer for both the national and county action plans. Conservation, restoration and expansion are the watchwords. Our vision is one in which they are realised to the full at and around Moccas Park, first of all through initiatives within the *Biodiversity Action Plan* timescales, and subsequently through the continuity of management over succeeding centuries, which is essential to the conservation of parklands.

Conservation

It is to be hoped that the conservation of Moccas Park itself will be assured and enhanced through the new Nature Reserve Agreement that currently is under negotiation. Survey is needed to increase our knowledge of certain important groups as the basis for their conservation, notably fungi, Diptera, aculeate Hymenoptera, Heteroptera, Lepidoptera, spiders and bats. Research is required too, in order to refine nature conservation management. Key topics include the nectar and pollen requirements of the rarer invertebrates; the habitat requirements of the developmental stages of these invertebrates; and the impact of locally and externally derived pollution on lichens and fungi. Dialogue is essential so as to ensure that the conservation of the natural and historic interest go forward together.

The importance for conservation of other parkland at Moccas and in the two local Natural Areas (the Black Mountains and Golden Valley and the Central Herefordshire Natural Areas, see Chapter 5.1) needs to be assessed. This will be the basis for reviewing the number and extent of parkland Sites of Special Scientific Interest and for planning conservation initiatives. Such planning and subsequent action at Moccas Park, and elsewhere, will be entirely dependent on the prior establishment of active partnerships between landowners, voluntary bodies, local authorities and statutory agencies.

Restoration

Over recent decades, areas of former parkland at Moccas and in surrounding areas have been converted to arable farmland and commercial forestry plantations, but some veteran trees persist, and there are many more in surrounding areas. Several old orchards survive locally too. This is a related form of wood-pasture with high nature conservation interest and historic and landscape importance; it has particular resonance in this county of cider, perry and mistletoe, and neatly complements the parkland interest of the area. This combination of former parkland, veteran trees and old orchards provides the framework for a substantial restoration initiative.

Expansion

What better place than Moccas to initiate the expansion of the parkland resource? (Figure 7.1.1). The existing parkland has been secured over recent decades, now opportunities to create new parkland on surrounding land need to be explored. For example, Brown's Plan of 1778 might be revisited, and the broad parkland link he proposed between Moccas Court and Moccas Park revived. Opportunities to the west and the east could be investigated too, or to the south where, up until the eighteenth century, parkland ran over the ridge and down into the Golden Valley (see Chapter 3.1). Given such expansion, the reservoir of species surviving at Moccas Park would have the opportunity to spread through newly created parkland areas and, providing links are established, colonise other Wye Valley parklands.

Figure 7.1.1

Aerial view looking northeast across Moccas Park to Moccas Court and beyond, June 1973. The Park lies in the foreground; the Court stands left of centre towards the top of the photograph and beyond it Monnington and the woods of Garnons and Foxley. Part of Brobury Scar is visible to the left of Moccas Court as is a loop of the River Wye. Photograph courtesy of the University of Cambridge Committee for Aerial Photography.

Into the future

Moccas Park is an emblematic site, an apt standard bearer for initiatives to conserve the natural and historic interest of parkland and wood-pasture in and beyond the twenty first century. Those named in the first paragraph of this chapter, who, two hundred years ago, conserved existing parklands in Herefordshire and designed and planted new ones, showed a boldness, creativity and vision of which we are the beneficiaries. Let us draw inspiration from their example, build on the work done since 1978, when Moccas Park became a National Nature Reserve, and use the Biodiversity Action Plan as the platform for initiatives that will, in their turn, bear fruit over future centuries.

This chapter is not the place to formulate precise plans, these are for local discussion and decision, but we hold to a vision of Moccas Park secured for the future, expanded and, ideally, linked to other parklands in the area. The vision is of a parkland, wood-pasture and orchard network spreading from the Golden Valley into Central Herefordshire, building on historical precedent and the strong parkland, veteran tree, orchard and native woodland resource of the area.[7] Sites like Moccas Park, where topography has aided survival, would be the starting points, some sites formerly of high natural and historic interest could be restored, others created *de novo*. Orchards, woodlands and hedgerow trees would form vital links in the network; farming and forestry would of course continue as the major land uses, but the overall objectives would be to expand the parkland resource, re-create links and reverse fragmentation.

Whilst the *Habitat Action Plan* provides the rationale and context for our vision, what of the necessary funding? Consideration is currently being given to securing alternative funding options for parkland initiatives in pursuit of Biodiversity Action Plan targets.[8] For Moccas

Park to be in the vanguard of such funding would honour those who secured its place as the first parkland National Nature Reserve and those, and there are many of them, who have contributed to the researching, writing and production of this book.

If our vision were realised, it would be a worthy memorial to those who have shaped, managed and maintained Moccas Park over the centuries. A memorial both to the many anonymous individuals who have planted and pollarded, fenced and walled, cut and culled, observed and recorded, created and conserved, and to those who have figured by name in the story that has been told in these pages, including St Dyfrig, de Fresne, Vaughan, Cornewall, Brown, Webster, Kilvert, Massee and Chester-Master.

Notes

1   Daniels (1999).
2   Whitehead (1994).
3   Daniels & Watkins (1994).
4   Bullock & Alexander (1998).
5   UK Biodiversity Group (1998).
6   In particular *Saproxylic beetles; Grouped Species Statement,* in UK Biodiversity Group (1999).
7   Notable parkland sites in the area include Garnons, Foxley, Whitfield and Kentchurch, respectively 5, 8, 12 and 18 km from Moccas Park. The holly orchards of the Olchon Valley, part of the Black Mountains, lie 12 km to the south west.
8   Notes of the Lowland wood-pasture and Parkland Advisory Group meeting, 18 June 1999; unpublished.

References

BULLOCK, D.J. & ALEXANDER, K. eds. 1998. Parklands - the way forward, 19-21 May 1998, Hereford, Proceedings. *English Nature Research Reports*, No 295.

DANIELS, S. 1999. *Humphry Repton. Landscape gardening and the geography of Georgian England.* New Haven & London: Yale University Press.

DANIELS S. & WATKINS, C. eds. 1994. *The picturesque landscape: visions of Georgian Herefordshire.* Nottingham: University of Nottingham.

UK BIODIVERSITY GROUP. 1998. *Tranche 2 Action Plans. Vol II Terrestrial and freshwater habitats. Lowland wood-pasture and parkland. A Habitat Action Plan.* Peterborough: English Nature.

UK BIODIVERSITY GROUP. 1999. *Tranche 2 Action Plans. Vol VI Terrestrial and freshwater species and habitats. Saproxylic beetles; Grouped Species Statement.* Peterborough: English Nature.

WHITEHEAD, D. 1994. Sense with sensibility: landscaping in Georgian Herefordshire. *In:* S. DANIELS & C. WATKINS, eds. *The picturesque landscape: visions of Georgian Herefordshire.* Nottingham: University of Nottingham, 16-33.

Acknowledgements

Paul T. Harding and
Tom Wall

With a little help from my friends.

Song title. Lennon - McCartney (1967).

In this book we bring together the work of 22 authors (see pages 269-272). We, as editors, are most grateful to them for their willingness to share their knowledge and understanding of the Park, to write and revise their contributions and then to wait, with remarkable patience, for rather too long for their work to appear in print. We are very grateful to the illustrators (see pages 273-275) whose work forms an essential part of the book. We should also like to thank many of the authors and illustrators for their help in other ways.

Several of the authors kindly read and commented on chapters other than their own, and others have helped in this way too. Our thanks go to Henry Arnold, John Bingham, Johnny Birks, Ben Chester-Master, David Evans, Mervyn Evans, Chris Fuller, Ted Green, Phil Grice, Elizabeth Haworth, Colin Hindmarch, Sue Holland, Richard Jefferson, Harriet Jordan, Noel King, Keith Kirby, James Marsden, Tony Mitchell-Jones, Michael Morris, John Phipps, Eric Pithers, John Port, Chris Preston, Francis Rose, Maurice Rotheroe, Ron Shoesmith, John Sheail, Paul Stamper, Rachel Thomas, Les Waters and Rob Williams.

We owe thanks to the following colleagues and others for their help in a variety of ways:
Coral Walton (Coral Design Management) for her imaginative work on the design and layout of the entire book;
Jeanette Hall (English Nature) for the major task of sourcing and negotiating permission for use of the illustrations, as well as assistance in other ways;
Gisèle Wall for assistance in the field, data handling and analysis, and the preparation of charts and diagrams;
Amanda Giles, Rachel Thomas and Les Waters (English Nature) for their support and encouragement through the Veteran Trees Initiative;
Helen Stace (English Nature) for her patience and assistance;
Derek Foxton, Ken Hoverd, Éilis Kirby and John Read who all provided original illustrative material especially for this book;
Sue Ellis, John Lincoln, Stuart Burgess and Alex Geairns (English Nature) who, successively, oversaw the design and production over a protracted period;
Michael Harper and Mike Taylor for contributing their records for the lists of moths and spiders respectively;
English Nature's Geographic Information Unit and Julie Gaunt (Centre for Ecology and Hydrology) for preparing some of the maps, and Henry Arnold (Centre for Ecology and Hydrology) for preparing the species distribution maps;
Alison Ely, Marjorie King and Jayne Power for help with some of the typing;
and finally to John Thompson (formerly of English Nature) for encouraging us in our initial ideas for the book.

We, the other authors and the illustrators are also grateful to the following individuals for their help in many different ways:
D.M.Ackland, Keith Alexander, A.A.Allen, Robert Angus, Michael Archer, Malcolm Ausden, Stuart Ball, Tom Bowen, John Box, Anthea Brian, Nick Campbell, David Chandler, Peter

8
—
1

Chandler, R.Cooke, Johnny Coppin, Sam Davies, Peter Dance, Tony Drane, Timothy Duke, Adrian Fowles, Hazel Fryer, Rob Fuller, Oliver Gilbert, Bill Harriman, David Hatfield, Mark Hill, Peter Hodge, Liz Howe, Mike Howe, Sue Hubbard, Eric Hunter, Philip Jones, Ian Killeen, Paul Kirk, Gerald Legg, Andrew McLeish, David Lockwood, Paige Mitchell, Reuben Neville, John Owen, D.M.Parker, Ivan Perry, George Peterken, Sophie Piebenga, Donald Pigott, Phil Price, W.R.Pye, W.J.L.Roberts, Ivor Saunders, Mark Shaw, Jonathan Sleath, Len and Shirley Slaney, D. and V.Soper, Alan Stubbs, Jim Tonkin, John White, Paul Whitehead, Lawrie Whittall, Les Whittal and Alex Williams.

An important part of the information contained in this book was gathered over the last 130 years or more by members of the Woolhope Naturalists' Field Club and published in the Club's *Transactions*. Without this sustained endeavour, our text would have been less complete and the illustrations sparse. We are very grateful to the Club for permission to use both information and illustrations from the *Transactions* in this publication.

We and the other authors have had assistance from the following organisations:
ADAS Agromet Unit, Bat Conservation Trust, British Ecological Society, English Heritage, English Nature's Library and Typing Services, Forestart, Hereford City Library, Hereford Record Office, Institute of Freshwater Ecology, Institute of Terrestrial Ecology, Joint Nature Conservation Committee, Leverhulme Trust, Ministry of Defence, Royal Society for the Protection of Birds, University of Cambridge.

This book would not have been published without the support of English Nature, in particular through the Veteran Trees Initiative, and additional funding provided by the Centre for Ecology and Hydrology and two anonymous donors. Further financial support for the publication came from Herefordshire Council.

We are very grateful to Philippa Harding, Gisèle Wall and our respective families for putting up with our particular obsession with Moccas Park for many years.

Finally, thanks are due to the Chester-Master family and the Baunton Trust for welcoming the prolonged interest in the minutiae of their Park. Their willingness and that of their forebears, over many decades, to permit ready access to the Park by naturalists and others, has enabled the gathering of much of the information contained in this book. Long may it continue.

8
—
1

List of authors

... those that find places valuable and interesting .... gain great pleasure from interpreting them to others.

Graham Barrow (1993). Environmental interpretation and conservation in Britain. *In*: F.B.Goldsmith and A.Warren, eds. *Conservation in progress*. London: Wiley.

JOHN BACON, BA, is Senior Land Management Officer in English Nature's Lowlands Team, finding practical solutions to difficult conservation land management problems. Following time on the family farm, he has worked since 1968 in nature conservation in locations from Kent to the Isle of Rum. From 1985 to 1993 he was Chief Warden in Nature Conservancy Council's West Midlands Region, and over much of this time he had direct responsibility for Moccas Park NNR. Whilst involved in all habitats he is especially interested in grazing, including for the conservation of butterflies and other invertebrates, on which subjects he has published widely.
English Nature, Northminster House, Peterborough, PE1 1UA.

TED BLACKWELL, I Eng, FI Plant E, is a retired engineering manager. A member, since 1965, of the British Mycological Society, he has in retirement devoted his energies to mycology, surveying sites in Herefordshire and surrounding counties. Currently chairman of the Herefordshire Fungus Study Group, he has a particular interest in the computerisation of Herefordshire fungus records. He is joint author of *Checklist of Shropshire Fungi* (1997) and an occasional contributor of papers to the British Mycological Society's *KEYS* publications and the Society's Newsletter.
7 Ashley Walk, Orleton, Ludlow, Shropshire, SY8 4HD.

DAVID BODDINGTON, MB, ChB, MSc, has recently completed fifty years of bird ringing, mostly in Herefordshire, where he worked as a rural General Medical Practitioner. He was an Army Medical Officer and Nature Conservancy Warden on St Kilda in 1958-9. Since 1969, he has supervised the nest box studies at Moccas Park. On retirement he took a postgraduate degree in ecology. He is a member of the Woolhope Club and a past Chairman of the Herefordshire Nature Trust.
The Down House, Bromyard, Herefordshire, HR7 4QH.

FRANCIS CHESTER-MASTER, BSc, ARICS, FAAV, has known Moccas Park all his life and for the last three years has lived in Moccas Parish. Following a spell in publishing he trained as a Chartered Surveyor and worked for eight years for Strutt & Parker, but he now runs his own land management company in Builth Wells. He has managed the Moccas Estate on behalf of the Baunton Trust since 1992. He is Vice Chairman of the local branch of the Royal Institute of Chartered Surveyors and is a committee member of the Herefordshire branch of the Countryside Landowners' Association, Wye Salmon Fisheries Owners' Association and the Wye Preservation Trust.
Chester-Master Limited, Dolgarreg, North Road, Builth Wells, Powys, LD2 3DD.

JON COOTER, BSc, FRES, AMA, is Senior Collections Officer for Herefordshire Heritage Services. He edited (and wrote much of) the *Coleopterist's Handbook* (1993), is a recognised authority on the family *Leiodidae* and has published many papers on beetle taxonomy. His first visit to Moccas Park was in 1975, and since then he has been a frequent visitor, latterly becoming a Voluntary Warden. Through survey and publication he has done more than anyone to confirm the particular importance of the Park for beetles. Further afield, recent highlights of his thirty years of experience in entomology have included visits to China and Kazakhstan, sponsored by the Royal Society, and curatorial work at Geneva Natural History Museum.
Hereford Museum, Broad Street, Hereford, HR4 9AU.

8

2

STEPHEN DANIELS, MA, MSc, PhD, is Professor of Cultural Geography at the University of Nottingham. He is the author of *Humphry Repton: landscape gardening and the geography of Georgian England* (1999), *Fields of vision: landscape imagery and national identity in England and the United States* (1993) and a number of other works on the history and theory of landscape and geography. He was editor (with Charles Watkins) of *The Picturesque Landscape: visions of Georgian Herefordshire* (1994) to which both David Whitehead and Tom Wall contributed.
School of Geography, The University, Nottingham, NG7 2RD.

LISA DUMAYNE-PEATY, BA, PhD, is a Lecturer in Geography at the University of Birmingham, with a decade of research experience in environmental change, palaeoecology and palynology. She has a particular interest in environmental archaeology and her publications include several concerning the human impact on the environment during the Romano-British period. Much of her research has been in northern England, so, geographically speaking, the work she has supervised at Moccas Park since 1996 has been a new departure.
School of Geography and Environmental Sciences, University of Birmingham, Edgbaston, Birmingham, B15 2TT

ANDY GODFREY, BSc, MSc, FRES, was formerly employed in the natural history departments of several museums and as an entomologist with the Nature Conservancy Council. Since 1991, he has worked in ecological consultancies, specialising in invertebrate surveys. He worked for Ecosurveys Ltd when they were commissioned by English Nature in 1994 to carry out an entomological survey of Moccas Park. He has a particular interest in Diptera and has published lists for a wide range of sites across the country.
90 Bence Lane, Darton, Barnsley, South Yorkshire, S75 5DA.

PAUL HARDING, MIBiol, has worked in nature conservation and ecological research almost continuously since 1962. Since 1982, he has been Head of the Biological Records Centre, working mainly with volunteer specialists throughout the Britain and Ireland. During the late 1970s he carried out surveys and assessments of important parks in Britain and has produced many reports and publications including, with Francis Rose, *Pasture-woodlands in lowland Britain* (1986). He has maintained a particular interest in Moccas Park, and in the Marches generally, since first visiting the Park in 1972. In 1977 he prepared the first comprehensive report on the importance of the Park for nature conservation.
Centre for Ecology and Hydrology, Monks Wood, Abbots Ripton, Huntingdon, PE17 2LS.

ROGER KEY, BSc, PhD, FRES, was at one time the Radnor Development Officer for the Herefordshire and Radnorshire Nature Trust; more recently he was Head of Terrestrial Invertebrate Zoology with the Nature Conservancy Council and he is now Senior Invertebrate Ecologist in English Nature's Lowlands Team. Amongst his many publications are several concerning invertebrates in dead wood and ancient tree ecology, and he helped to set up English Nature's Veteran Trees Initiative. He is a frequent broadcaster and widely published photographer. His occasional visits to Moccas Park started in 1981.
English Nature, Northminster House, Peterborough, PE1 1UA.

ALAN MARCHANT was born in Herefordshire. He trained and still works as an Architectural Draughtsman. Ornithology is a hobby that he has followed for many years. His activities have included the editorship, for ten years, of the Herefordshire Ornithological Club Annual Report, census work throughout the County, bird ringing, and, since 1972, the weekly recording of the nest boxes at Moccas Park.
79 Nicholson Court, Hereford, HR4 9TD.

JOHN PHIBBS, BA, MSc, has been involved in the management of historic parks and gardens for some 20 years. He has a particular interest in the relationship between the post-medieval countryside and the English landscape movement and has lectured and published on both 'Capability' Brown and Humphry Repton. A committee member of the Garden History Society,

8
—
2

he is principal of the Debois Landscape Survey Group. He first visited Moccas Park in 1989 since when English Nature has commissioned from him two studies of the landscaping of the Park.
Macaroni Downs Farm, Eastleach, Cirencester, Gloucestershire, GL7 3PU.

RORY PUTMAN, BA, DPhil, was for 20 years head of the University of Southampton's Deer Management Research Group, before deciding in 1994 to move back to Scotland to live. He now works from home as an independent ecological and deer management consultant, while also holding a Research Chair in Environmental Biology at the Manchester Metropolitan University. In 1994 he was commissioned by English Nature to look at the deer herd at Moccas Park and make recommendations for its future management.
Ach Na Criche, Drimnin, Morvern, Argyll, PA34 5XZ.

SUSANNE SEYMOUR, BA, PhD, is a Lecturer in Geography at the University of Nottingham. She has published a range of works on the interpretation of estate landscapes in the eighteenth century and is currently researching issues of empire and gender. With her colleagues, Stephen Daniels and Charles Watkins, she has researched not only the Moccas and Grenada Estates of Sir George Cornewall but also the estate of his near neighbour, Uvedale Price, at Foxley. This work has been funded by the Leverhulme Trust.
School of Geography, The University, Nottingham, NG7 2RD.

DAVE SIMPSON has worked in practical nature conservation for more than 20 years, including as an ecological and botanical surveyor and consultant. He has assisted with tree surveys at Moccas Park, carried out surveys of the ground flora and habitats, especially in the Upper Park, and compiled an annotated bibliography of the Park. He has lived in the Marches since 1980 and is currently growing and distributing organically grown vegetables, whilst continuing to explore the area.
Flat 3, Broadward Hall, Clungunford, Craven Arms, Shropshire, SY7 0QA.

HELEN STACE, BA, MA, is English Nature's Conservation Officer for Herefordshire. She started work for the Nature Conservancy Council in 1981 in south east Scotland. From 1987 she was Conservation Officer for South Humberside before moving to Herefordshire in 1994. Currently she looks after Eastnor Park and Brampton Bryan Park Sites of Special Scientific Interest, and in 1998 she took over the management of Moccas Park NNR. She has a keen interest in veteran trees and invertebrates.
English Nature, Bronsil House, Eastnor, nr Ledbury, Herefordshire, HR8 1EP.

JOHN THOMPSON, BSc, worked at East Malling Research Station before joining the Nature Conservancy as a Warden Naturalist in East Anglia. He became Regional Officer in the Midlands Region in 1966, when his long involvement with Moccas Park began. As Nature Conservation Adviser to English Heritage from 1990 to 1993, he developed links between those involved in landscape and nature conservation and liaised over joint interests in historic parks such as Moccas. He works in 'retirement' as an ecological consultant and enjoys being an 'amateur' naturalist.
Shotton Cottage, Godings Lane, Harmer Hill, Shrewsbury, Shropshire SY4 3HB.

PETER THOMSON, BSc, is a retired lecturer in Geography. He has a particular interest in geology and provided geological information for this publication. His marriage to **STEPHANIE**, who is recorder for Herefordshire for the Botanical Society of the British Isles, confirmed his interest in plants. Peter and Stephanie have visited Moccas Park occasionally since the early 1960s recording both flowering plants and fungi. In 1993, they carried out a survey of the vascular plants in the Park, together with Noel King, formerly the Nature Conservancy Council's Conservation Officer for Herefordshire. Peter has been a member of the Woolhope Club since the 1960s. Stephanie and Peter, with members of the Herefordshire Botanical Society, are currently working on an Atlas of the Herefordshire Flora.
Hall Pool, Marden, Hereford, HR1 3EN.

TOM WALL, BA, has worked in nature reserve management since 1974, initially with the Wildfowl Trust and subsequently with the Nature Conservancy Council and English Nature. He currently manages National Nature Reserves in Shropshire and Herefordshire, including, from 1991 to 1998, Moccas Park. Work at Downton Gorge NNR, Herefordshire, a 'Picturesque' landscape garden, has led to several papers. He has been heavily involved too at Brampton Bryan Park SSSI, also in Herefordshire. He is a member of the Woolhope Club.
English Nature, Holly Mead, 18 Kempton, Lydbury North, Shropshire, SY7 0JG.

CHARLES WATKINS, BSc, PhD, FLS, is Reader in Rural Geography at the University of Nottingham. Amongst the books which he has written or edited are *Woodland management and conservation* (1990), *Ecological effects of afforestation: studies in the history and ecology of afforestation in Western Europe* (1993), *Rights of way: policy, culture and management* (1996) and *European woods and forests, studies in cultural history* (1998). He was editor (with Stephen Daniels) of *The Picturesque Landscape: visions of Georgian Herefordshire* (1994). His family home is in Herefordshire and he is a member of the Woolhope Club.
School of Geography, The University, Nottingham, NG7 2RD.

COLIN WELCH, PhD, BSc, DIC, ARCS, FRES, joined the Nature Conservancy at Monks Wood in 1965, as Woodlands Entomologist, staying on as an employee of the Institute of Terrestrial Ecology until his retirement in 1995. Over the years, he has surveyed the Coleoptera of woodlands the length and breadth of the country. This work continues in retirement but now he has more time to pursue his personal interest in rove beetles. He first visited Moccas Park in 1980 and on this and subsequent visits has added many species to the beetle list.
The Mathom House, Hemington, nr Oundle, Peterborough, PE8 5QJ.

DAVID WHITEHEAD, MA, FSA, has, since 1970, lived and taught in Herefordshire, latterly specialising in its architectural and landscape history. He has written extensively on West Midland country estates especially those involving Humphry Repton and John Nash. He is Chairman of the Picturesque Society, Editor of the Herefordshire and Worcester Gardens Trust Newsletter and a Past President of the Woolhope Club. Recently he carried out a review for English Heritage of the parks and gardens of Herefordshire. He first visited Moccas Park more than 20 years ago.
60 Hafod Road, Hereford, HR1 1SQ.

RAY WOODS, BSc, is Area Officer, East Wales, for the Countryside Council for Wales. He has worked in wildlife conservation for over 25 years and he lectures and broadcasts on countryside subjects. Author of the *Flora of Radnorshire* (1993), he is currently working on a Lichen Flora of Brecknock. He is a past President of the British Lichen Society and, with Alan Orange, has published a *Catalogue and Conservation Evaluation of Welsh Lichens* (1999). He first visited Moccas Park some 20 years ago and on occasional visits since then has advised and assisted in lichen survey work.
Countryside Council for Wales, Eden House, Ithon Road, Llandrindod Wells, LD1 6AS.

List of illustrators

When we came down into the Park again .... there was a looking over and comparing of sketches and Mrs Crichton by general request sat down on the bank to make a sketch of the scene ....

From the Diary of Reverend Francis Kilvert, Friday 30 August 1872.

Some chapter authors have also contributed photographs; their names appear in the previous list. Unattributed drawings are taken from English Nature's collection, on all of which it holds the copyright.

HEATHER ANGEL has been a leading international natural history photographer for some 30 years; her work has been published very extensively, including in numerous books of her own.

DIANE BARKER was born in Worcestershire; she is a professional artist and photographer whose work includes many watercolours of trees at Moccas Park.

LANCELOT 'CAPABILITY' BROWN (1716-1783), fashioned some of England's most celebrated landscapes and may be regarded as its greatest landscape designer; his 'natural' parklands rank as major works of European art.

HENRY GRAVES BULL (1818-1885) was a physician, stalwart of the Woolhope Club, mycologist, botanist, ornithologist (*Birds of Herefordshire* 1888), pomologist (*Herefordshire Pomona* 1877-85) and tree enthusiast.

NATHANIEL DANCE (1736-1811) was a portrait painter and foundation member of the Royal Academy; one of his best known portraits is of Captain Cook. Son of George Dance senior, architect of the Mansion House.

JOHN LAMBE DAVIS was an eighteenth century surveyor.

GRAHAM EASY is an ornithologist and botanist whose line drawings have appeared in *Nature in Cambridgeshire* for many years; he illustrated *Aquatic plants in Britain and Ireland* (C.D. Preston & J.M. Croft 1997).

STEVE FALK is a professional ecologist and also a freelance illustrator specialising in detailed paintings of insects for identification guides.

DEREK FOXTON is a retired dentist. A life-long photographer, he is author and illustrator of five books on Hereford, where he lives.

ROBERT GIBBINGS (1889-1958) was a wood-engraver, sculptor, teacher, author (including *Coming down the Wye* 1942) and publisher.

THOMAS HEARNE (1744-1817) was one of the most admired and influential topographical artists of his day, his watercolours of landscapes, townscapes and ruins, include many of Herefordshire.

KEN HOVERD undertakes specialist rectified survey and architectural photography. He took all the photographs for *James Wathen's Herefordshire 1770-1820* (D. Whitehead & R. Shoesmith 1994).

ÉILIS KIRBY is a graduate in Fine Art who has also worked in nature conservation, surveying dormice in Herefordshire and trees at Moccas Park.

PETER KIRBY is a freelance ecologist specialising in invertebrate conservation. His publications include *Habitat Management for Invertebrates: a practical handbook* (1992) which he both wrote and illustrated.

FRANK E. LANCASTER is a building surveyor who has profited from retirement near Llandrindod Wells to pursue his particular interests in fungi and photography.

SIR THOMAS LAWRENCE (1769-1830) was the leading portrait painter of his day; the last great portrait painter in the eighteenth century tradition he was devoted to the memory and example of Reynolds (q.v.).

G.R. LEWIS (1782-1871) was a portrait painter who also published illustrations of Kilpeck and Shobdon Churches and *British Forest Trees*.

PETER MANDERS lives in Hereford and has been a professional artist for 50 years specialising in pen and ink drawings of the county, and caricatures, notably of jazz musicians.

JEREMY MOORE is a professional photographer who specialises in Welsh landscapes but took photographs of Moccas Park when preparing his exhibition *After the Wildwood* (1990).

TOM OVERBURY is a lecturer at the Royal Agricultural College; he has worked with English Nature on developing machinery for nature conservation management, notably a weed-wiper, a weed puller and a bracken roller.

HEATHER PERCY surveyed trees in Moccas Park for the Nature Conservancy Council in 1985/86; in addition to mapping and measuring, she made sketches of 82 trees.

ERIC PITHERS was Chief Warden for Nature Conservancy Council's West Midlands Region from 1975 to 1985. From 1978 he had responsibility for Moccas Park NNR, initiating the tree planting programme in that year

BENJAMIN T. POUNCY (died 1799), was an English engraver whose early work was generally of antiquarian subjects but he subsequently devoted himself to landscapes.

WALTER PRITCHARD (1867-1947) was a master tailor and cutter. His multitude of interests ranged from photography to ballooning. A keen member of the Woolhope Club, he was a great friend of Alfred Watkins (q.v.).

OLIVER RACKHAM is a Fellow of Corpus Christi College, Cambridge; his books include *The History of the Countryside* (1986) and *The Last Forest: the story of Hatfield Forest* (1989).

JOHN READ has had a life-long interest in beetles; his meticulous eye for detail is evident in his distinctive 'habitus' portraits which are much in demand for specialist books and journals.

SIR JOSHUA REYNOLDS (1723-1792) was the leading portrait painter of his day; first President of the Royal Academy his is arguably the most important figure in the history of British painting.

GEORGE ROMNEY (1734-1802) was a portrait painter, notably of women and children; he is best known for his many studies of Lady Hamilton.

TREVOR ROWLEY is a landscape historian and a director at the University of Oxford; his many publications include *The making of English Landscapes: Hereford* (1976) and *Landscape of the Welsh Marches* (1986).

SAMUEL SHELLEY (*circa* 1750-1808) was a miniature painter, book illustrator and founder member of the Water-colour Society.

PETER SKIDMORE is an international authority on Diptera; he retired recently from the position of Curator of Natural History at Doncaster Museum. The first of his occasional visits to Moccas Park was in 1958.

WORTHINGTON G. SMITH (1835-1917) was a book and periodical illustrator (notably of fungi), author and mycologist; he regularly attended Woolhope Club fungus forays of which he drew humorous cartoons.

JAMES SOWERBY (1757-1822) illustrated many and diverse books on natural history of which the most famous is *English Botany* (1790-1814; text by J.E. Smith, 36 vols, 2500 plates).

J.G. STRUTT (1790-1864) was an English landscape painter and etcher. His volumes of etched plates include *Sylva Britannica* (1825) and *Deliciæ Sylvarum* (1828).

GUY TROUGHTON is a biology graduate and professional wildlife illustrator.

PETER WAKELY was Photographer for the Nature Conservancy and its successors, 1957-97; his work figures widely in English Nature publications, notably *England's National Nature Reserves* (Marren 1994) and *English Nature Magazine*.

JAMES WATHEN (1751-1828), Herefordian, merchant glover and primitive artist, published many drawings of houses and townscapes; they are now of considerable historical interest (see also Ken Hoverd).

ALFRED WATKINS (1855-1935) was a miller, brewer, bee-keeper, archaeologist, photographer, inventor, originator of the ley line theory (*The Old Straight Track* 1925) and leader of public opinion in his home town of Hereford.

8

3

A check list of the lichens

Compiled by
Ray Woods

APPENDIX **1**

Nomenclature

Sequence and nomenclature follow O.W.PURVIS, B.J.COPPINS, P.W.JAMES. 1993. Checklist of lichens of Great Britain and Ireland. *Bulletin of the British Lichen Society*, 72 (Supplement) 1-75.

Sources

GOSLING, M.M. 1994. *A survey of lichens on rocks, fences and trees at Moccas Park NNR.* Report to English Nature.
GOSLING, M.M. 1996. *Moccas Park NNR lichen survey.* Report to English Nature.
GOSLING, M.M.& SANDELL, K.A. 1993. *Lichen survey and monitoring, Moccas Park NNR Herefordshire.* Report to English Nature.
HARVEY,T. & LOONEY, J.H.H. 1992. *Lichen monitoring, Moccas Park NNR, Herefordshire.* Report to English Nature by Ecosurveys Ltd.
ROSE, F. 1986. Manuscript list of lichen species recorded in 1968, 1981 and 1986. In English Nature files.
ROSE, F. & COPPINS, B.J. 1968. Manuscript list of lichen species. In English Nature files.
SANDELL, K.A. & GOSLING, M.M. 1988. *Moccas Park NNR Lichen Survey.* Report to Nature Conservancy Council.

Habitats

Lichens found on trees and dead wood: all records are of species recorded since 1968. Species marked '+' have not been seen since 1982. Species marked 'R' are used by Francis Rose to calculate his 'Revised index of ecological continuity' (ROSE, F. 1976. Lichenological indicators of age and environmental continuity in woodlands. *In*: D.H.BROWN, D.L.HAWKSWORTH & R.H.BAILEY, eds. *Lichenology: progress and problems.* London: Academic Press, 279-307).

Lichens found on the park pale, park wall and rock outcrops: all records are from Gosling (1994).

SPECIES	HABITATS				
	Trees and dead wood		Park pale	Park wall	Rock outcrops
Acarospora fuscata				✓	
Acrocordia gemmata	✓	+			
Anisomeridium biforme	✓	+			
A. nyssaegenum	✓				
Arthonia arthonioides				✓	
A. impolita	✓				
A. punctiformis	✓	+			
A. radiata	✓				
A. spadicea	✓				
A. vinosa	✓	R			
Arthopyrenia punctiformis	✓	+			
Bacidia bagliettoana				✓	
B. incompta	✓				
B. phacodes	✓				
B. rubella	✓				
B. sabuletorum				✓	✓
B. vezdae	✓				
Baeomyces rufus					✓
Buellia griseovirens	✓				
B. punctata	✓		✓		
Calicium glaucellum	✓	+			
C. salicinum	✓				
C. viride	✓				
Caloplaca citrina	✓			✓	✓

SPECIES

HABITATS

	Trees and dead wood	Park pale	Park wall	Rock outcrops
Caloplaca crenularia			✓	
C. flavescens			✓	
C. flavovirescens			✓	
C. holocarpa			✓	
C. isidiigera			✓	
C. lucifuga	✓			
Candelaria concolor	✓			
Candelariella reflexa	✓	✓		
C. vitellina	✓	✓	✓	
C. xanthostigma	✓			
Catillaria atropurpurea	✓	R		
Cetraria chlorophylla	✓			
Chaenotheca brunneola	✓			
C. chrysocephala	✓			
C. ferruginea	✓			
C. trichialis	✓			
Chrysothrix candelaris	✓			
Cladonia chlorophaea			✓	✓
C. coniocraea	✓			
C.digitata	✓			
C. fimbriata	✓		✓	✓
C. furcata	✓	+		
C. macilenta	✓			✓
C. polydactyla	✓	+		
C. pyxidata	✓	+	✓	
C. squamosa var. subsquamosa	✓	+		
Clauzadea monticola				✓
Cliostomum griffithii	✓			
Collema crispum			✓	
Cyphelium inquinans	✓			
Cystocoleus ebeneus				✓
Dimerella pineti	✓			
Diploicia canescens	✓		✓	
Diploschistes scruposus			✓	
Diplotomma alboatrum	✓	+		
Dirina massiliensis f. sorediata			✓	
Enterographa crassa	✓	R		
E. hutchinsiae				✓
Evernia prunastri	✓	✓		
Foraminella ambigua		✓		
Fuscidea lightfootii	✓	+		
Graphis elegans	✓	+		
G. scripta	✓			
Gyalecta flotowii	✓	+		
G. ulmi				✓
Gyalideopsis anastomosans	✓			
Hypocenomyce scalaris	✓	✓		
Hypogymnia physodes	✓	✓		
H. tubulosa	✓	✓		
Imshaugia aleurites	✓	✓		
Lecanactis abietina	✓			✓
L. premnea	✓	R		
L. subabietina	✓	+		
Lecania cyrtella	✓			
L. erysibe			✓	
Lecanora albescens			✓	
L. campestris			✓	
L. chlarotera	✓	✓		
L. conferta			✓	
L. confusa	✓	+		
L. conizaeoides	✓	✓		
L. dispersa	✓		✓	

SPECIES   HABITATS

SPECIES	Trees and dead wood	Park pale	Park wall	Rock outcrops
Lecanora expallens	✓	✓		
L. orosthea			✓	
L. pulicaris	✓			
L. saligna	✓			
L. soralifera			✓	
L. sublivescens	✓			
L. sulphurea			✓	
L. symmicta		✓		
L. varia	✓			
Lecidella elaeochroma	✓			
L. scabra	✓		✓	
L. stigmatea			✓	
Lepraria incana agg.	✓		✓	✓
Lepraria spp.	✓			
Leproloma membranaceum				✓
L. vouauxii			✓	
Leproloma spp.				✓
Micarea bauschiana				✓
M. denigrata	✓			
M. lignaria		✓		
Mycoblastus sterilis	✓	✓		
Normandina pulchella	✓			
Ochrolechia androgyna	✓			
O. parella	✓		✓	✓
O. subviridis	✓	✓		
O. turneri	✓	✓		
Opegrapha atra	✓			
O. gyrocarpa			✓	
O. niveoatra	✓			
O. rufescens	✓	+		
O. sorediifera	✓			
O. varia	✓			
O. vermicellifera	✓			
O. vulgata	✓			
Opegrapha spp.			✓	
Parmelia caperata	✓		✓	✓
P. elegantula	✓			
P. exasperata	✓	+		
P. glabratula	✓			
P. glabratula ssp glabratula		✓		
P. pastillifera	✓	+		
P. perlata	✓			
P. revoluta	✓			
P. saxatilis	✓		✓	
P. subaurifera	✓			
P. subrudecta	✓		✓	
P. sulcata	✓		✓	
Parmeliopsis ambigua	✓			
Peltigera horizontalis	✓	+R		✓
P. lactucifolia	✓		✓	✓
P. membranacea	✓	+	✓	✓
P. praetextata				✓
P. rufescens				on lime kiln
Pertusaria albescens	✓			
P. albescens var. corallina	✓		✓	
P. amara	✓			
P. coccodes	✓			
P. corallina			✓	
P. flavida	✓			
P. hemisphaerica	✓			
P. hymenea	✓			
P. leioplaca	✓			

SPECIES

HABITATS

Species	Trees and dead wood		Park pale	Park wall	Rock outcrops
Pertusaria multipuncta	✓	+			
P. pertusa	✓			✓	
P. pseudocorallina				✓	
Phaeophyscia orbicularis	✓				
Phlyctis argena	✓				
Physcia adscendens	✓		✓	✓	
P. tenella	✓			✓	
P. tribacia	✓				
Physciopsis adglutinata	✓				
Physconia distorta	✓				
P. enteroxantha	✓				
P. grisea	✓				
P. perisidiosa	✓		✓		
Placynthiella icmalea	✓		✓		
Platismatia glauca	✓				
Polysporina simplex				✓	
Porina aenea	✓				
P. leptalea	✓	R			
Porpidia cinereoatra				✓	
P. crustulata				✓	✓
P. macrocarpa					✓
P. tuberculosa				✓	✓
Protoblastenia rupestris					✓
Pseudevernia furfuracea	✓				
Psilolechia lucida				✓	✓
Pyrenula chlorospila	✓	R			
Pyrrhospora quernea	✓				
Ramalina farinacea	✓				
R. fastigiata	✓	+			
R. fraxinea	✓				
Rhizocarpon obscuratum				✓	
Rinodina exigua	✓				
R. gennarii				✓	
R. roboris	✓				
Schismatomma decolorans	✓				
Scoliciosporum chlorococcum	✓	+			
S. umbrinum				✓	
Sphinctrina turbinata	✓				
Tephromela atra				✓	
Thelopsis rubella	✓	+R			
Trapelia placodioides				✓	
Trapeliopsis flexuosa	✓		✓		
T. granulosa	✓				
T. pseudogranulosa	✓				
Usnea ceratina	✓	+			
U. subfloridana	✓		✓		
Verrucaria muralis				✓	✓
V. nigrescens				✓	
Xanthoria candelaris	✓		✓		
X. parietina	✓			✓	
X. polycarpa	✓		✓		

A check list of the mosses and liverworts

Compiled by
Ray Woods

APPENDIX 2

Taxonomy follows M.O.HILL, C.D.PRESTON & A.J.E. SMITH. 1991, 1992, 1994. *Atlas of the bryophytes of Britain and Ireland.* Three volumes. Colchester: Harley Brooks.

Sources

PORT, P.J. & PORT, C. 1978. *Bryophyte Survey of Moccas Deer Park Herefordshire.* Report to Nature Conservancy Council.
ROSE, F. 1986. Manuscript list of lichen species recorded in 1968 and 1986. In English Nature files.
SLEATH, J. D. 1998. Manuscript list of bryophyte species. In English Nature files.
WOODS, R. Various dates. Casual records.

Mosses

POLYTRICHACEAE
Polytrichum longisetum
P. formosum
P. juniperinum
Atrichum undulatum

DITRICHACEAE
Pleuridium acuminatum

DICRANACEAE
Ceratodon purpureus
Dichodontium pellucidum
Dicranella heteromalla
Dicranoweisia cirrata
Dicranum bonjeanii
D. scoparium
D. majus
Campylopus paradoxus
C. introflexus
Fissidentaceaea
Fissidens viridulus
F. bryoides
F. taxifolius
F. cristatus

ENCALYPTACEAE
Encalypta vulgaris

POTTIACEAE
Tortula intermedia
T. laevipila
T. muralis
Barbula cylindrica
B. sinuosa
B. recurvirostra
Schistidium apocarpum

GRIMMIACEAE
Grimmia pulvinata
Racomitrium aciculare
R. affine

FUNARIACEAE
Funaria hygrometrica
Physcomitrium pyriforme

BRYACEAE
Orthodontium lineare
Pohlia carnea
Bryum pallens
B. capillare
B. bicolor
B. rubens

MNIACEAE
Mnium hornum
M. stellare
Rhizomnium punctatum
Plagiomnium affine
P. undulatum
P. rostratum

AULACOMNIACEAE
Aulacomnium androgynum

ORTHOTRICHACEAE
Zygodon viridissimus var. viridissimus
Z. viridissimus var. stirtonii
Z. baumgartneri
Orthotrichum lyellii
O. affine
O. stramineum
O. diaphanum
Ulota crispa

LEUCODONTACEAE
Pterogonium gracile

NECKERACEAE
Neckera crispa
N. complanata
Homalia trichomanoides

THAMNIACEAE
Thamnobryum alopecurum

THUIDIACEAE

Heterocladium heteropterum

Anomodon viticulosus

Thuidium tamariscinum

AMBLYSTEGIACEAE

Cratoneuron filicinum

Amblystegium serpens

A. tenax

A. riparium

Drepanocladus aduncus

Calliergon giganteum

C. cuspidatum

BRACHYTHECIACEAE

Isothecium myurum

I. myosuroides

Homalothecium sericeum

Brachythecium rutabulum

B. rivulare

B. velutinum

B. populeum

Pseudoscleropodium purum

Cirriphyllum piliferum

C. crassinervum

Rhynchostegium riparioides

R. murale

R. confertum

Eurhynchium striatum

E. praelongum

E. swartzii

E. speciosum

PLAGIOTHECIACEAE

Plagiothecium succulentum

P. nemorale

Isopterygium elegans

HYPNACEAE

Hypnum cupressiforme

H. cupressiforme var. resupinatum

H. andoi

H. jutlandicum

Ctenidium molluscum

Rhytidiadelphus triquetrus

R. squarrosus

R. loreus

Pleurozium schreberi

Hylocomium splendens

Liverworts

PSEUDOLEPICOLEACEAE

Blepharostoma trichophyllum

CALYPOGEIACEAE

Calypogeia fissa

C. arguta

CEPHALOZIACEAE

Cephalozia bicuspidata

JUNGERMANNIACEAE

Jungermannia atrovirens

J. pumila

J. gracillima

Nardia scalaris

SCAPANIACEAE

Scapania scandica

S. nemorea

GEOCALYCACEAE

Lophocolea bidentata

L. heterophylla

Chiloscyphus polyanthos

C. polyanthos var. polyanthus

PLAGIOCHILACEAE

Plagiochila porelloides

P. asplenioides

PTILIDIACEAE

Ptilidium ciliare

PORELLACEAE

Porella arboris-vitae

P. platyphylla

FRULLANIACEAE

Frullania tamarisci

F. dilatata

LEJEUNEACEAE

Lejeunea cavifolia

L. ulicina

PELLIACEAE

Pellia epiphylla

P. endiviifolia

METZGERIACEAE

Metzgeria furcata

LUNULARIACEAE

Lunularia cruciata

CONOCEPHALACEAE

Conocephalum conicum

RICCIACEAE

Riccia huebeneriana

R. fluitans

A check list of the fungi

Compiled by
Edward Blackwell

APPENDIX 3

Sources and references

WNFC	24.10.1873	Woolhope Naturalists' Field Club Foray (Anon 1873).
WNFC	08.10.1880	Woolhope Naturalists' Field Club Foray (Cooke 1880).
WNFC	02.10.1881	Woolhope Naturalists' Field Club Foray (Cooke 1881).
FoH	pre 1889	*A Flora of Herefordshire* (no dates given) (Purchas & Ley 1889).
VHCH	pre 1908	Victoria History of the County of Hereford (no dates given) (Page 1908)
BMS	30.09.1926	British Mycological Society, Hereford Foray (Wakefield 1927, Lister 1927).
BMS	15.09.1951	British Mycological Society, Hereford Foray (Smith 1952).
FF	17.10.1959	Fred Fincher, Herefordshire Botanical Society (Oswald & Copeland Watts 1962).
JTP	1963	Record by J. T. Palmer (specimen in Kew Herbarium).
GNG	31.05.1964	Dr G. N. Greenhalgh, The University, Liverpool (manuscript list).
FF	11.09.1971	Fred Fincher, Herefordshire Botanical Society (manuscript list).
NM	13.10.1979	N. Mansbridge, Eaton Bishop Women's Institute (manuscript list).
SET	02.10.1980	S. E. Thomson, Herefordshire Botanical Society (manuscript list).
G+L	15.09.1992	E. E. Green and A. J. Lucas (Green & Lucas 1992).
G+L	01.10.1992	E. E. Green and A. J. Lucas (Green & Lucas 1992).
EB+	05.05.1994	E. Blackwell, F. E. Lancaster and S. E. Thomson (manuscript list).
G+L	10.08.1994	E. E. Green and A. J. Lucas (Green & Lucas 1994).
EB+	06.10.1994	E. Blackwell, F. E. Lancaster and R. J. Mantle (manuscript list).
BMS	05.04 1996	British Mycological Society, Centenary Spring Foray (BMS 1996).

ANON. 1873. The fungus foray and feast of the Woolhope Club, October 1873. *Transactions of the Woolhope Naturalists' Field Club*, 100-117.

ANON. 1902. The Hereford foray, 22-27 September 1902. *Transactions of the British Mycological Society*, 2, 5-12.

BRITISH MYCOLOGICAL SOCIETY. 1996. Centenary Spring Foray, 1996, species list.

COOKE, M.C. 1880. The fungus foray. *Transactions of the Woolhope Naturalists' Field Club*, 252-258.

COOKE, M.C. 1881. The fungus foray. *Transactions of the Woolhope Naturalists' Field Club*, 86-89.

GREEN, E.E. & LUCAS, A.J. 1992. Report and species list. Unpublished report to English Nature.

GREEN, E.E. & LUCAS, A.J. 1994. Report and species list. Unpublished report to English Nature.

LISTER, G. 1927. Mycetozoa gathered during the Hereford foray. *Transactions of the British Mycological Society*, 86-87.

OSWALD, P.H. & COPELAND WATTS, E. 1962. Report on Moccas Deer Park, Herefordshire. Internal report, Nature Conservancy.

PAGE, W. 1908. Victoria History of the County of Hereford. London: Constable.

PURCHAS, W.R. & LEY, A. 1889. *A flora of Herefordshire*. Hereford: Jakeman & Carver.

SMITH, G. 1952. The Hereford foray, 12-19 September 1951. *Transactions of the British Mycological Society*, 35, 168-175.

WAKEFIELD, E.M. 1927. The Hereford foray. *Transactions of the British Mycological Society*, 12, 79-85.

Taxonomic and nomenclatural references

There is neither a comprehensive nor a currently accepted published checklist of British fungi. To span the range of taxonomic groups it is necessary to refer to a number of authoritative works. Names of fungi in the various taxonomic groups (as far as can be determined from the record) generally follow those used in the principal works listed below. Author citations have been omitted from the list, being absent in any case from much of the recorded data. Where the current species name differs from that under which the species was first recorded, the latter is given in brackets.

Agaricales

The majority of Agaric records are of species in the sense of the *New Checklist of Agarics and Boleti* (Dennis, Orton & Hora 1960). However, Agaric and Bolete taxonomic arrangement and synonymy have undergone considerable revision since then, and in those instances where its nomenclature has been superseded (or new species or combinations introduced) reference has been made to the other works listed below.

DENNIS, R.W.G., ORTON, P.D. & HORA F.B. 1960. New Checklist of Agarics and Boleti. *Transactions of the British Mycological Society.* 43 (Supplement).

HENDERSON, D.M., ORTON, P.D. & WATLING, R. 1969. *British Fungus Flora. Agarics and Boleti: Introduction.* Edinburgh: Royal Botanic Garden.

> WATLING, R. 1970. *Part 1 Boletaceae, Gomphidiaceae, Paxillaceae.*
>
> ORTON, P.D. & WATLING, R. 1979. *Part 2 Coprinaceae.*
>
> WATLING, R. 1982. *Part 3 Bolbitiaceae.*
>
> ORTON, P.D. 1986. *Part 4 Pluteaceae.*
>
> WATLING, R. & GREGORY, N. M. 1987. *Part 5 Strophariaceae and Coprinaceae.*
>
> WATLING, R. & GREGORY, N. M. 1990. *Part 6 Crepidotaceae, Pleurotaceae and other pleurotoid agarics.* (Includes gilled Aphyllophorales).
>
> WATLING, R., GREGORY, N.M. & ORTON, P.D. 1993. *Part 7 Cortinariaceae.*

MOSER, M. 1983. *Keys to Agarics and Boleti (Polyporales, Boletales, Agaricales, Russulales.* (Translated by S. Plant from *Die Röhrlinge und Blätterpliz*). London: Roger Phillips. (For Agaricales only).

RAYNER, R.W. 1985. *Keys to the British Species of Russula.* London: British Mycological Society.

Non-gilled Aphyllophorales, Auriculariales, Cantharellales, Dacrymycetales, Exobasidiales, Tremellales, and Gasteromycetes (Lycoperdales, Nidulariales, Phallales, Sclerodermatales)

ELLIS, M.B. & ELLIS, J.P. 1990. *Fungi Without Gills.* London: Chapman & Hall.

Ascomycota

CANNON, P.F., HAWKSWORTH, D.L. & SHERWOOD-PIKE, M.A. 1985. *The British Ascomycotina, an annotated checklist.* Slough: Commonwealth Agricultural Bureaux.

Rusts

WILSON, M. & HENDERSON, D.M. 1996. *British Rust Fungi.* Cambridge: Cambridge University Press.

Smuts

MORDUE, J. E. M. & AINSWORTH, C.G. 1984. *Ustilaginales of the British Isles.* Mycological Paper 154. Slough: Commonwealth Agricultural Bureaux.

Peronosporaceae

FRANCIS, S.M. & WATERHOUSE, G.M. 1988. List of *Peronosporaceae* reported from the British Isles. *Transactions of the British Mycological Society,* 91, 1-62.

Myxomycota

ING, B. 1999. *The Myxomycetes of Britain and Ireland - an identification handbook.* Slough: Richmond Publishing.

Mitosporic fungi

Generally:

ELLIS, M.B. & ELLIS, J.P. 1997. *Microfungi on Land Plants.* Slough: Richmond Publishing.

ELLIS, M.B. & ELLIS, J.P. 1998. *Microfungi on Miscellaneous Substances.* Slough: Richmond Publishing.

Additionally, where not covered by the above:

GROVE, W.B. 1935, 1937. *British Stem and Leaf Fungi.* Vol.1, Vol.2. Cambridge: Cambridge University Press.

MOORE, W.C. 1959. *British Parasitic Fungi.* Cambridge: Cambridge University Press.

Species name	Last recorded	Source

Basidiomycota

AGARICALES

Species name	Last recorded	Source
Agaricus arvensis	1992	G+L
Agaricus augustus	1992	G+L
Agaricus bisporus	1992	G+L
Agaricus campestris	1994	G+L
Agaricus comtulus	1959	FF
Agaricus haemorrhoidarius	1992	G+L
Agaricus macrosporus	1992	G+L
Agaricus placomyces	1994	G+L
Agaricus semotus	1994	G+L
Agaricus silvicola	1992	G+L
Agaricus xanthodermus	1992	G+L
Agrocybe erebia (Pholiota erebia)	1926	BMS
Agrocybe semiorbicularis	1994	G+L
Amanita aspera	1992	G+L
Amanita citrina	1992	G+L
Amanita excelsa	1994	EB+
Amanita fulva (Amanitopsis fulva)	1951	BMS
Amanita pantherina	1971	FF
Amanita phalloides	1926	BMS
Amanita rubescens	1992	G+L
Amanita vaginata	1994	G+L
Armillaria bulbosa	1994	G+L
Armillaria mellea s.l.	1994	EB+
Arrhenia acerosa	1994	G+L
Bolbitius aleuriatus (Pleurotus aleuriatus)	1951	BMS
Bolbitius reticulatus (Pluteolus aleuriatus)	1951	BMS
Bolbitius vitellinus	1992	G+L
Calocybe carnea (Tricholoma carneum)	1951	BMS
Calocybe constricta (Lepiota constricta)	1926	BMS
Calyptella capula	1994	G+L
Chaetocalathus craterellus (Pleurotellus patelloides)	1951	BMS
Chromocyphella muscicola (Cyphella galeata Fr.)	1873	WNFC
Clitocybe cerussata	1992	G+L
Clitocybe clavipes	1994	G+L
Clitocybe dealbata	1926	BMS
Clitocybe ditopa	pre 1908	VHCH
Clitocybe flaccida	1992	G+
Clitocybe fragrans	1994	G+L
Clitocybe gibba (Clitocybe infundibuliformis)	1992	G+L
Clitocybe hydrogramma (Omphalia hydrogramma)	1951	BMS
Clitocybe incilis	1926	BMS
Clitocybe nebularis	1992	G+L
Clitocybe phyllophila	1992	G+L
Clitocybe rivulosa	1951	BMS
Clitocybe vibecina	1992	G+L
Clitopilus cretatus	1951	BMS
Clitopilus prunulus	1992	G+L
Collybia acervata	1980	SET
Collybia butyracea	1994	EB+
Collybia cirrhata	1994	G+L
Collybia dryophila	1994	EB+
Collybia fusipes	1992	G+L
Collybia kuehneriana (Collybia erythropus)	1992	G+L
Collybia peronata	1994	EB+
Conocybe arrhenii (Pholiota togularis)	1951	BMS
Conocybe lactea	1994	G+L
Conocybe tenera	1994	EB+
Conocybe togularis s.l. (Pholiota togularis)	1951	BMS
Coprinus atramentarius	1994	EB+
Coprinus comatus	1994	EB+
Coprinus disseminatus	1979	NM

Species name	Last recorded	Source
Coprinus domesticus	1994	G+L
Coprinus freisii	1951	BMS
Coprinus lagopus	1994	EB+
Coprinus micaceus	1992	G+L
Coprinus niveus	1951	BMS
Coprinus picaceus	1951	BMS
Coprinus plicatilis	1994	EB+
Cortinarius anomalus	1979	NM
Cortinarius cinnamomeus	1994	G+L
Cortinarius elatior	1951	BMS
Cortinarius glandicolor	1951	BMS
Cortinarius hinnuleus	1994	G+L
Cortinarius psammocephalus	1951	BMS
Cortinarius torvus	1971	FF
Crepidotus applanatus	1994	EB+
Crepidotus mollis	1951	BMS
Crepidotus variabilis	1951	BMS
Cystoderma amianthinum (Lepiota amianthina)	1951	BMS
Dermoloma atrocinereum (Tricholoma atrocinereum)	1951	BMS
Dermoloma cuneifolium (Dermoloma cuneiforme (sic))	1994	G+L
Entoloma aprile	1992	G+L
Entoloma chalybaeum v. lazulinum (Leptonia lazulina)	1994	G+L
Entoloma eulividum (Entoloma lividum)	1951	BMS
Entoloma euchroum (Leptonia euchroa)	1951	BMS
Entoloma hirtipes	1996	BMS
Entoloma incana	pre 1908	VHCH
Entoloma jubatum	1926	BMS
Entoloma neglectum (Eccilia cancrina)	1951	BMS
Entoloma nidorosum	1994	G+L
Entoloma pascuum (Nolanea pascua)	1926	BMS
Entoloma papillatum	1926	BMS
Entoloma porphyrophaeum	1951	BMS
Entoloma sericeum	1994	EB+
Entoloma sinuatum (Entoloma lividum)	1951	BMS
Flammulina velutipes	1992	G+L
Galerina hypnorum (Galera hypnorum)	1951	BMS
Galerina unicolor (Pholiota marginata)	1926	BMS
Gymnopilus junonius	1994	EB+
Gymnopilus penetrans	1994	G+L
Hebeloma crustuliniforme	1992	G+L
Hebeloma longicaudum	1980	SET
Hebeloma mesophaeum	1994	EB+
Hebeloma radicosum	1994	G+L
Hemimycena cucullata (Mycena gypsea sensu Kuhner)	1951	BMS
Hygrocybe calyptraeformis (Hygrophorus calyptraeformis)	1971	FF
Hygrocybe chlorophana	1994	EB+
Hygrocybe clivalis (Hygrophorus clivalis Fr.)	1926	BMS
Hygrocybe coccinea	1994	EB+
Hygrocybe colemanniana	1992	G+L
Hygrocybe conica	1994	EB+
Hygrocybe fornicata (Hygrophorus fornicata)	1873	WNFC
Hygrocybe intermedia (Hygrophorus intermedius)	1951	BMS
Hygrocybe konradii (Hygrophorus obrusseus)	1951	BMS
Hygrocybe laeta	1992	G+L
Hygrocybe lepidopus (Hygrophorus lepidopus Rea)	1926	BMS
Hygrocybe nigrescens	1994	G+L
Hygrocybe nitrata (Hygrophorus nitratus)	1951	BMS
Hygrocybe nivea (Hygrophorus niveus)	1926	BMS
Hygrocybe obrussea (Hygrophorus obrusseus)	1951	BMS
Hygrocybe persistens v. langei (Hygrocybe langei)	1992	G+L
Hygrocybe pratensis v. pratensis (Hygrocybe pratensis)	1992	G+L
Hygrocybe psittacina	1992	G+L
Hygrocybe psittacina v. perplexa (Hygrophorus sciophanus)	1951	BMS
Hygrocybe punicea (Hygrophorus puniceus)	1926	BMS
Hygrocybe reai (Hygrophorus reai)	1926	BMS

Species name	Last recorded	Source
Hygrocybe russocoriacea (Hygrophorus russocoriaceus)	1873	WNFC
Hygrocybe sciophana (Hygrophorus sciophanus)	1951	BMS
Hygrocybe turunda (Hygrophorus turundus)	1926	BMS
Hygrocybe unguinosa	1992	G+L
Hygrocybe virginea v. virginea (Hygrocybe nivea)	1992	G+L
Hygrocybe vitellina	1992	G+L
Hygrophorus eburneus v. eburneus (Hygrocybe eburneus (sic))	1992	G+L
Hypholoma ericaeum (Psilocybe ericaea)	1926	BMS
Hypholoma fasciculare	1994	EB+
Hypholoma sublateritium	1994	EB+
Hypholoma udum	1996	BMS
Hypsizygus tessulatus (Pleurotus tessulatus)	pre 1908	VHCH
Inocybe asterospora (Astrosporina asterospora)	1951	BMS
Inocybe cincinnata	1926	BMS
Inocybe cookei	1951	BMS
Inocybe corydalina	1971	FF
Inocybe deglubens	1951	BMS
Inocybe fastigiata	1980	SET
Inocybe geophylla	1994	EB+
Inocybe geophylla v. lilacina	1994	EB+
Inocybe microspora	1994	EB+
Inocybe obscura	1951	BMS
Inocybe phaeocomis (Inocybe cincinnata)	1926	BMS
Inocybe phaeocomis v. major (Inocybe obscura)	1951	BMS
Inocybe pyriodora	1951	BMS
Inocybe rimosa	1926	BMS
Inocybe sp. (identity uncertain) (Inocybe scabella)	1951	BMS
Kuehneromyces mutabilis (Galerina mutabilis)	1994	G+L
Laccaria amethystea	1994	EB+
Laccaria bicolor	1992	G+L
Laccaria laccata	1994	EB+
Laccaria tortilis	1992	G+L
Lacrymaria lacrymabunda (Lacrymaria velutina)	1994	G+L
Lacrymaria pyrotricha (Hypholoma pyrotrichum)	1926	BMS
Lepiota aspera (Lepiota friesii)	1992	G+L
Lepiota cristata	1994	G+L
Lepista nuda	1994	EB+
Leucoagaricus leucothites (Lepiota leucothites)	1979	NM
Lyophyllum decastes (Lyophyllum aggregatum)	1980	SET
Macrolepiota konradii	1992	G+L
Macrolepiota mastoidea	1994	EB+
Macrolepiota procera	1992	G+L
Macrolepiota rhacodes	1994	EB+
Macrolepiota rhacodes v. hortensis	1992	G+L
Marasmiellus ramealis (Marasmius ramealis)	1959	FF
Marasmius chordalis	1994	G+L
Marasmius oreades	1992	G+L
Marasmius rotula	1994	G+L
Marasmius undatus	1951	BMS
Melanoleuca humilis (Tricholoma humile)	pre 1908	VHCH
Melanophyllum echinatum	1994	G+L
Melanotus horizontalis	1994	G+L
Mycena acicula	1951	BMS
Mycena adonis	1951	BMS
Mycena aetites	1994	EB+
Mycena bulbosa	1951	BMS
Mycena epipterygia	1951	BMS
Mycena filopes	1959	FF
Mycena flavoalba	1926	BMS
Mycena galericulata	1994	EB+
Mycena galopus	1951	BMS
Mycena haematopus	1994	EB+
Mycena inclinata	1994	EB+
Mycena leptocephala	1994	G+L
Mycena metata	1926	BMS

APPENDIX 3

Species name	Last recorded	Source
Mycena olivaceomarginata (Mycena avenacea (sensu Kuhner?))	1951	BMS
Mycena pelianthina	1951	BMS
Mycena polygramma	1992	G+L
Mycena pura	1994	G+L
Mycena sanguinolenta	1994	G+L
Mycena speirea	1951	BMS
Mycena vitilis	1959	FF
Nolanea pascua (nom. conf.) (Nolanea papillata)	1926	BMS
Omphalina rustica	1926	BMS
Oudemansiella longipes (Collybia longipes)	1951	BMS
Oudemansiella mucida	1994	EB+
Oudemansiella radicata	1992	G+L
Panaeolina foenisecii (Panaeolus foenisecii)	1994	G+L
Panaeolus campanulatus	1992	G+L
Panaeolus fimicola	1994	EB+
Panaeolus rickenii	1994	EB+
Panaeolus semiovatus (Annelaria seperata)	1926	BMS
Panellus stipticus (Panus stipticus)	1951	BMS
Phaeomarasmius erinaceus (Naucoria erinacea)	1951	BMS
Pholiota curvipes	1994	G+L
Pholiota gummosa	1992	G+L
Pholiota highlandensis	1994	G+L
Pholiota squarrosa	1926	BMS
Pholiota tuberculosa	1992	G+L
Pluteus cervinus	1994	EB+
Pluteus cinereofuscus	1951	BMS
Pluteus luteovirens	1994	G+L
Pluteus nanus	1951	BMS
Pluteus phlebophorus	1951	BMS
Pluteus romellii (Pluteus nanus v. lutescens)	1926	BMS
Pluteus salicinus	1994	G+L
Pluteus umbrosus	1951	BMS
Psathyrella atomata	1951	BMS
Psathyrella candolleana	1994	EB+
Psathyrella caudata	1959	FF
Psathyrella gracilis	1979	NM
Psathyrella piluliformis	1994	EB+
Psathyrella sp.? (name unknown) (Psathyrella campestris)	1992	G+L
Psathyrella spadiceo-grisea	1994	EB+
Psilocybe semilanceata	1994	EB+
Resupinatus applicatus (Pleurotus applicatus)	1926	BMS
Resupinatus trichotis	1996	BMS
Rhodotus palmatus (Agaricus (Pleurotus) subpalmatus)	1873	WNFC
Rickenella fibula	1994	EB+
Rickenella setipes (Omphalia fibula v.. swartzii)	1951	BMS
Simocybe centunculus (Ramicola centunculus)	1994	G+L
Stropharia aeruginosa	1980	SET
Stropharia coronilla?	1964	GNG
Stropharia semiglobata	1994	EB+
Tephrocybe rancida (Collybia rancida)	1951	BMS
Tricholoma albobrunneum	1994	EB+
Tricholoma argyraceum	1926	BMS
Tricholoma lascivum	1994	EB+
Tricholoma saponaceum	1992	G+L
Tricholoma sejunctum	1992	G+L
Tubaria furfuracea	1994	G+L
Volvariella bombycina (Volvaria bombycina)	1951	BMS

APHYLLOPHORALES

Species name	Last recorded	Source
Abortiporus biennis (Heteroporous biennis)	1994	G+L
Athelia teutoburgensis (Corticium flavescens)	1926	BMS
Bjerkandera adusta	1996	BMS
Buglossoporus pulvinus	1994	G+L
Bulbillomyces farinosus	1994	G+L

Species name	Last recorded	Source
Ceriporiopsis aneirina (Sporotrichum geochroum)	pre 1889	FoH
Chondrostereum purpureum	1996	BMS
Clavaria rosella	pre 1889	FoH
Clavaria tenuipes	1926	BMS
Clavaria vermicularis	1951	BMS
Clavaria zollingeri (Clavulinopsis zollingeri)	1992	G+L
Clavulina amethystina	1926	BMS
Clavulina cinerea (Clavaria cinerea)	1926	BMS
Clavulina cristata	1994	EB+
Clavulina rugosa (Clavaria rugosa)	1926	BMS
Clavulina rugosa v. macrospora? (Clavaria gigaspora)	1926	BMS
Clavulinopsis corniculata	1992	G+L
Clavulinopsis fusiformis	1994	EB+
Clavulinopsis helvola	1992	G+L
Clavulinopsis luteoalba (Clavaria luteoalba)	1926	BMS
Clavulinopsis subtilis	1992	G+L
Clavulinopsis umbrinella (Clavaria umbrina)	1873	WNFC
Coniophora puteana	1994	G+L
Coriolus hirsutus (Polystictus hirsutus)	1926	BMS
Coriolus versicolor	1994	EB+
Craterellus cornucopioides	1951	BMS
Daedaleopsis confragosa	1996	BMS
Datronia mollis	1996	BMS
Fistulina hepatica	1994	EB+
Ganoderma adspersum	1996	BMS
Ganoderma applanatum s.l. (Ganoderma applanatum)	1992	G+L
Ganoderma lucidum (Polyporus lucidus)	1873	WNFC
Ganoderma resinaceum	1994	G+L
Grifola frondosa	1994	EB+
Hapalopilus nidulans	1994	G+L
Hymenochaete rubiginosa	1996	BMS
Hyphodontia alutaria	1996	BMS
Hyphodontia aspera (Grandina granulosa)	1880	WNFC
Hyphodontia pruni	1996	BMS
Inonotus dryadeus	1996	BMS
Inonotus hispidus	1992	G+L
Inonotus radiatus	1994	EB+
Laetiporus sulphureus	1996	BMS
Lentinellus cochleatus (Lentinus cochleatus)	1926	BMS
Leptoporus mollis (Trametes mollis)	1880	WNFC
Meripilus giganteus	1994	EB+
Merulius tremellosus	1994	G+L
Mycoacia uda	1994	G+L
Peniophora cinerea	1926	BMS
Peniophora quercina	1996	BMS
Perenniporia fraxinea (Fomes fraxineus)	1951	BMS
Phaeocyphellopsis ochraceus (Solenia ochracea Pers.)	pre 1908	VHCH
Phanerochaete filamentosa	1994	G+L
Phanerochaete velutina	1996	BMS
Phellinus ferreus	1996	BMS
Phellinus ferruginosus (Polyporus ferruginosus)	1926	BMS
Phlebia livida	1996	BMS
Phlebia ochraceofulva	1926	BMS
Phlebia radiata	1994	G+L
Physisporinus sanguinolentus	1994	G+L
Piptoporus betulinus (Polyporus betulinus)	1926	BMS
Pleurotus ostreatus	1994	G+L
Pleurotellus chioneus (Pleurotus chioneus)	1951	BMS
Podoscypha multizonata (Thelephora multizonata)	1873	WNFC
Polyporus squamosus	1994	EB+
Polyporus varius	1979	NM
Postia balsamea (Polyporus amorphus)	1926	BMS
Postia fragilis (Polyporus fragilis)	1880	WNFC
Postia stiptica (Polyporus stipticus)	1926	BMS
Pseudotrametes gibbosa (Trametes gibbosa)	1964	GNG

APPENDIX 3

Species name	Last recorded	Source
Pulchericium caeruleum	1994	G+L
Ramariopsis crocea? (Clavaria curta Fr.)	pre 1908	VHCH
Ramariopsis kunzei (Clavaria kunzei)	1926	BMS
Rigidoporus ulmarius (Polyporus ulmarius)	1926	BMS
Schizopora paradoxa	1996	BMS
Serpula himantioides	1996	BMS
Sistotrema brinkmannii	1996	BMS
Skeletocutis amorpha (Polyporus amorphus)	1926	BMS
Stereum gausapatum	1996	BMS
Stereum hirsutum	1996	BMS
Stereum rameale	1994	G+L
Stereum rugosum	1996	BMS
Thelephora terrestris	1992	G+L
Tomentella bryophila (Hypochnus ferrugineus)	1926	BMS
Tomentella hoehnelii	1926	BMS
Trametes ochracea	1996	BMS
Trechispora cohaerens (Corticium confine)	1926	BMS
Trechispora farinacea	1996	BMS
Trechispora hymenocystis (Poria hymenocystis)	1926	BMS
Trechispora mollusca (Poria hymenocystis)	1926	BMS
Vuilleminia comedens	1996	BMS

AURICULARIALES

Auricularia auricula-judae	1996	BMS
Auricularia mesenterica	1994	G+L

BOLETALES

Boletus aereus	1992	G+L
Boletus albidus	1992	G+L
Boletus badius	1994	G+L
Boletus chrysenteron	1994	EB+
Boletus edulis	1980	SET
Boletus erythropus	1994	G+L
Boletus impolitus	1951	BMS
Boletus lanatus	1992	G+L
Boletus piperatus	1979	NM
Boletus porosporus	1992	G+L
Boletus pruinatus	1992	G+L
Boletus pulverulentus	1992	G+L
Boletus reticulatus	1926	BMS
Boletus subtomentosus	1994	G+L
Boletus versicolor	1994	G+L
Gyroporus castaneus	1994	G+L
Hygrophoropsis aurantiaca	1992	G+L
Leccinum versipelle (Boletus verispellis)	1951	BMS
Paxillus involutus	1992	G+L
Phylloporus rhodoxanthus	1994	G+L
Strobilomyces floccopus (Strobilomyces strobilaceus)	1971	FF
Suillus grevillei	1994	EB+
Tylopilus felleus	1971	FF

CANTHARELLALES

Cantharellus cibarius	1994	EB+
Cantharellus cinereus (Craterellus cinereus)	1971	FF

DACRYMYCETALES

Calocera cornea	1992	G+L
Calocera viscosa	1992	G+L
Dacrymyces concavus	1996	BMS
Dacrymyces stillatus	1994	G+L

Species name	Last recorded	Source
HYMENOGASTRALES		
Hymenogaster tener	1963	JTP
LYCOPERDALES		
Bovista nigrescens	1996	BMS
Bovista plumbea	1996	BMS
Calvatia excipuliformis	1992	G+L
Calvatia gigantea	1992	G+L
Calvatia utriformis	1992	G+L
Lycoperdon atropurpureum	1951	BMS
Lycoperdon lividum (Lycoperdon spadiceum)	1994	G+L
Lycoperdon molle	1951	BMS
Lycoperdon perlatum	1994	EB+
Lycoperdon pyriforme	1996	BMS
Vascellum pratense (Lycoperdon depressum)	1951	BMS
NIDULARIALES		
Crucibulum laeve (Crucibulum vulgare)	1959	FF
PHALLALES		
Mutinus caninus	1971	FF
Phallus impudicus	1992	G+L
RUSSULALES		
Lactarius blennius	1994	EB+
Lactarius camphoratus	1951	BMS
Lactarius chrysorrheus	1992	G+L
Lactarius cimicarius	1992	G+L
Lactarius hepaticus	1994	G+L
Lactarius pallidus	1951	BMS
Lactarius piperatus	1992	G+L
Lactarius pterosporus	1994	EB+
Lactarius pyrogalus	1926	BMS
Lactarius quietus	1992	G+L
Lactarius subdulcis	1994	EB+
Lactarius subumbonatus (Lactarius serifluus)	1951	BMS
Lactarius tabidus	1980	SET
Lactarius vellereus	1992	G+L
Russula amoena (Russulla punctata Gill.)	1926	BMS
Russula atropurpurea	1992	G+L
Russula brunneoviolacea	1992	G+L
Russula cyanoxantha	1994	EB+
Russula emeticella (Russula fragilis)	1926	BMS
Russula farinipes	1951	BMS
Russula foetens	1994	EB+
Russula fragilis	1926	BMS
Russula laurocerasi	1994	G+L
Russula lepida	1992	G+L
Russula lutea	1994	G+L
Russula mairei	1992	G+L
Russula nigricans	1992	G+L
Russula ochroleuca	1992	G+L
Russula pectinata	1980	SET
Russula pseudointegra	1992	G+L
Russula puellaris	1994	G+L
Russula sanguinea (Russula rosacea)	1926	BMS
Russula solaris	1951	BMS
Russula sororia	1992	G+L
Russula vesca	1994	EB+
Russula virescens	1926	BMS
Russula xerampelina	1992	G+L

Species name	Last recorded	Source
SCLERODERMATALES		
Scleroderma citrinum (Scleroderma aurantium)	1926	BMS
Scleroderma verrucosum	1994	EB+
Sphaerobolus stellatus	1951	BMS
TREMELLALES		
Exidia glandulosa	1994	EB+
Exidia truncata	1994	EB+
Sebacina incrustans	1926	BMS
Tremella mesenterica	1994	EB+
TULASNELLALES		
Oliveonia fibrillosa	1996	BMS
UREDINALES		
Phragmidium fragariae (Phragmidium fragariastri)	1951	BMS
Phragmidium mucronatum (Phragmidium disciflorum)	1951	BMS
Phragmidium potentillae (Frommea obtusa)	1951	BMS
Puccinia buxi	1951	BMS
Puccinia calcitrapae (Puccinia cirsii)	1951	BMS
Puccinia caricina	1996	BMS
Puccinia chaerophylli	1951	BMS
Puccinia chrysosplenii	1951	BMS
Puccinia circaeae	1951	BMS
Puccinia glechomatis	1926	BMS
Puccinia graminis	1996	BMS
Puccinia hieracii v. hieracii (Puccinia taraxaci)	1951	BMS
Puccinia major	1951	BMS
Puccinia malvacearum	1951	BMS
Puccinia primulae	1951	BMS
Puccinia punctata	1951	BMS
Puccinia punctiformis (Puccinia suaveolens)	1951	BMS
Puccinia veronicae	1951	BMS
Pucciniastrum vaccinii	1889	FoH
Puccinia violae	1951	BMS
Pucciniastrum circaeae	1951	BMS
Uromyces dactylidis	1951	BMS
Uromyces nerviphilus (Uromyces flectens)	1951	BMS
Uromyces rumicis	1951	BMS
USTILAGINALES		
Doassansiopsis hydrophila (Doassansia martianoffiana)	1951	BMS
Sphacelotheca hydropiperis	1951	BMS

Ascomycota

Species name	Last recorded	Source
CLAVICIPITALES		
Claviceps nigricans	1880	WNFC
Claviceps purpurea	1994	G+L
Cordyceps militaris	1951	BMS
Epichloe typhina	1951	BMS
Hypomyces aurantius	1926	BMS
Hypomyces rosellus (Penicillium hypomycelis)	pre 1889	FoH
DIAPORTHALES		
Diaporthe leiphaemia	1996	BMS
Hypospilina pustulata	1996	BMS

APPENDIX 3

Species name	Last recorded	Source
DIATRYPALES		
Diatrype disciformis	1994	G+L
Diatrype stigma	1994	G+L
Diatrypella quercina	1996	BMS
Eutypa acharii	1964	GNG
Eutypa scabrosa	1994	EB+
DOTHIDEALES		
Acanthophiobolus helicosporus (Ophiosphaeria gracilis)	1951	BMS
Berlesiella nigerrima	1964	GNG
Hysterium angustatum	1996	BMS
Leptosphaeria acuta	1996	BMS
Leptosphaeria doliolum	1951	BMS
Leptospora rubella	1996	BMS
Lophiostoma vagabundum	1996	BMS
Mycosphaerella punctiformis	1996	BMS
Paraphaeosphaeria michotii	1996	BMS
Pleospora scirpicola	1996	BMS
Rhopographus filicinus	1996	BMS
Splanchnonema ampullaceum (Massariella curreyi)	1964	GNG
Venturia rumicis	1996	BMS
ERYSIPHALES		
Microsphaera alphitoides	1994	EB+
HELOTIALES		
Arachnoscypha aranea (Arachnopeziza aranea)	1951	BMS
Ascocoryne sarcoides	1994	G+L
Bisporella citrina (Calycella claroflava)	1926	BMS
Bisporella sulfurina	1951	BMS
Bulgaria inquinans	1994	EB+
Calloria neglecta	1996	BMS
Catinella olivacea	1926	BMS
Dasyscyphus apalus	1996	BMS
Dasyscyphus bicolor	1996	BMS
Dasyscyphus caeruleoalbus	1951	BMS
Dasyscyphus controversus	1951	BMS
Dasyscyphus fugiens	1996	BMS
Dasyscyphus niveus	1996	BMS
Dasyscyphus virgineus	1996	BMS
Geoglossum cookeianum	1992	G+L
Haglundia perelegans	1951	BMS
Hyaloscypha daedaleae	1996	BMS
Hyaloscypha hyalina	1951	BMS
Hymenoscyphus fructigenus	1996	BMS
Lachnellula willkommii (Trichoscypha willkommii)	1951	BMS
Microglossum olivaceum (Mitrula olivacea Sacc.)	pre 1908	VHCH
Microglossum viride	1926	BMS
Micropodia pteridina	1996	BMS
Mollisia caricina	1951	BMS
Mollisia cinerea	1996	BMS
Mollisia ligni	1996	BMS
Myriosclerotinia curreyana	1996	BMS
Niptera pulla	1951	BMS
Orbilia xanthostigma	1926	BMS
Poculum petiolorum (Cyathicula petiolorum)	pre 1908	VHCH
Psilachnum asemum (Dasyscyphus helotioides)	1951	BMS
Rutstroemia echinophila (Phialea echinophila)	1951	BMS
Trichoglossum hirsutum	1992	G+L
Unguicularia costata	1996	BMS

APPENDIX 3

Species name	Last recorded	Source
HYPOCREALES		
(Nectria aurea - not recognised, current name not traced)	1880	WNFC
Hypocrea rufa	1994	G+L
Nectria cinnabarina	1996	BMS
Nectria episphaeria	1996	BMS
Nectria peziza	1994	G+L
Nectriopsis aureonitens (Hypomyces aureonitens Tul.)	pre 1908	VHCH
PEZIZALES		
Aleuria aurantia	1959	FF
Ascobolus furfuraceus (Ascobolus stercorarius)	1951	BMS
Helvella crispa	1992	G+L
Helvella lacunosa	1994	EB+
Humaria hemisphaerica (Lachnea hemisphaerica)	1951	BMS
Peziza badia	1992	G+L
Peziza micropus	1994	EB+
Peziza proteana v. sparassoides (Gyromitra phillipsii)	1951	BMS
Sarcoscypha coccinea s.l. (Sarcoscypha coccinea)	1926	BMS
Scutellinia scutellata (Cilaria scutellata)	1926	BMS
POLYSTIGMATALES		
Phomatospora therophila	1951	BMS
Phyllachora junci	1994	G+L
RHYTISMATALES		
Ascodichaena rugosa (Dichaena quercina)	1926	BMS
Colpoma quercinum	1996	BMS
Hypohelion scirpinum (Leptothyrium scirpinum)	1951	BMS
SORDARIALES		
Acanthonitschkea tristis (Calyculosphaeria tristis)	1964	GNG
Bertia moriformis	1996	BMS
Lasiosphaeria ovina (Leptospora ovina)	1926	BMS
Lasiosphaeria spermoides (Leptospora spermoides)	1926	BMS
SPHAERIALES		
Anthostomella punctulata	1951	BMS
Ceriophora palustris (Didymosphaeria palustris)	1951	BMS
Chaetosphaerella phaeostroma	1996	BMS
Chaetosphaeria myriocarpa	1964	GNG
Daldinia concentrica	1996	BMS
Hyponectria buxi	1951	BMS
Hypoxylon chestersii	1996	BMS
Hypoxylon confluens	1996	BMS
Hypoxylon fragiforme	1994	EB+
Hypoxylon howeianum	1994	G+L
Hypoxylon multiforme (Xylaria multiforme (sic))	1994	G+L
Hypoxylon nummularium	1994	EB+
Hypoxylon rubiginosum	1964	GNG
Hypoxylon serpens	1964	GNG
Niesslia exosporioides	1951	BMS
Lopadostoma turgidum (Diatrype turgida)	pre 1889	FoH
Phomatospora therophila	1951	BMS
Rosellinia aquila	1994	EB+
Ustulina deusta	1992	G+L
Xylaria carpophila	1996	BMS
Xylaria filiformis	1994	G+L
Xylaria hypoxylon	1994	EB+

Species name	Last recorded	Source

Mastigomygotina

PERONOSPORALES

Species name	Last recorded	Source
Albugo candida (Cystopus candida)	1951	BMS
Paraperonospora leptosperma (Peronospora leptosperma)	1951	BMS
Peronospora affinis	1951	BMS
Peronospora aparines	1951	BMS
Peronospora farinosa	1951	BMS
Peronospora grisea	1951	BMS
Peronospora parasitica	1951	BMS
Phytophthora syringae	1951	BMS
Pseudoperonospora humuli	1951	BMS
Pseudoperonospora urticae	1951	BMS

Myxomycota

ACRASIALES

Pocheina rosea	1996	BMS

CERATIOMYXALES

Ceratiomyxa fruticulosa	1926	BMS

LICEALES

Cribraria argillacea	1926	BMS
Cribraria aurantiaca	1994	EB+
Cribraria cancellata (Dictydium cancellatum)	1951	BMS
Cribraria cancellata v. fusca (Dictydium cancellatum v. fuscum)	1926	BMS
Cribraria vulgaris	1926	BMS
Enteridium lycoperdon	1994	EB+
Licea minima	1996	BMS
Licea parasitica	1996	BMS
Lycogala conicum	1951	BMS
Tubifera ferruginosa	1994	EB+

PHYSARALES

Badhamia utricularis	1996	BMS
Diderma effusum	1996	BMS
Didymium difforme	1926	BMS
Didymium nigripes	1951	BMS
Didymium squamulosum	1996	BMS
Fuligo septica	1951	BMS
Fuligo candida	1926	BMS
Mucilago crustacea (Mucilago spongiosa)	1951	BMS
Phyrarum leucophaeum	pre 1889	FoH
Physarum nutans	1951	BMS
Physarum robustum	1996	BMS
Physarum viride	1951	BMS

STEMONITALES

Collaria elegans (Comatricha elegans)	1926	BMS
Comatricha laxa	1926	BMS
Comatricha nigra	1996	BMS
Enerthenema papillatum	1996	BMS
Paradiacheopsis fimbriata	1996	BMS
Paradiacheopsis solitaria	1996	BMS
Stemonitis fusca	1994	EB+
Stemonitopsis typhina (Comatricha typhoides)	1926	BMS
Symphytocarpus amaurochaetoides (Stemonitis fusca v.. confluens)	1926	BMS

APPENDIX 3

Species name	Last recorded	Source
TRICHIALES		
Arcyria affinis (Arcyria incarnata v. fulgens List.)	1926	BMS
Arcyria cinerea	1996	BMS
Arcyria denudata	1996	BMS
Arcyria incarnata	1951	BMS
Arcyria obvelata (Arcyria nutans)	1951	BMS
Arcyria pomiformis	1951	BMS
Metatrichia floriformis	1996	BMS
Metatrichia vesparium (Hemitrichia vesparium)	1926	BMS
Perichaena depressa	1996	BMS
Trichia affinis	1996	BMS
Trichia botrytis	1996	BMS
Trichia botrytis v. cerifera	1996	BMS
Trichia contorta v. contorta	1996	BMS
Trichia decipiens	1996	BMS
Trichia persimilis	1926	BMS
Trichia scabra	1996	BMS
Trichia varia	1996	BMS
MITOSPORIC FUNGI		
(Monilia aurea - not recognised, current name not traced)	1926	BMS
(Rhinotrichum thwaitesii - not recognised, current name not traced)	1926	BMS
Alysidium conidial state (dubium?)	1996	BMS
Bispora antennata (Bispora moniliodes Cda.)	pre 1908	VHCH
Botrytis argillacea	1964	GNG
Brachysporium bloxami	1996	BMS
Diplodia taxi (Phoma taxa)	pre 1889	FoH
Eleutheromyces subulatus	pre 1889	FoH
Epicoccum purpurascens (Epicoccum nigrum)	1951	BMS
Lemmoniera aquatica	1951	BMS
Leptostroma donacinum	1996	BMS
Leptostroma juncacearum	1996	BMS
Leptothyrium scirpinum	1951	BMS
Libertella faginea	1926	BMS
Menispora ciliata	1964	GNG
Neottiospora caricina	1951	BMS
Periconia atra	1951	BMS
Periconia cookei	1996	BMS
Periconia minutissima	1996	BMS
Ramularia calcea	1926	BMS
Ramularia rubella	1996	BMS
Sepedonium chrysospermum	1994	EB+
Tetracladium marchalianum	1951	BMS
Tetraploa aristata	1996	BMS
Torula herbarum	1951	BMS
Tricladium angulatum	1951	BMS
Trichothecium roseum	pre 1889	FoH
Tubercularia vulgaris	1994	EB+

The following pleomorphic species were recorded as anamorphs and appear in the above list under the anamorph name, which corresponds with the teleomorph name as follows:

ANAMORPH	TELEOMORPH
Alysidium conidial state (dubium?)	Botryobasidium aureum
Leptothyrium scirpinum	Hypoderma scirpinum
Libertella faginea	Quaternaria quaternata
Sepedonium chrysospermum	Apiocrea chrysospermum
Tetraploa arista	Massarina tetraploa
Tubercularia vulgaris	Nectria cinnabarina

A check list of the vascular plants

Compiled by
Dave Simpson,
Peter Thomson,
Stephanie Thomson
and Tom Wall

Sources of records

1889-1908

PURCHAS, W.R. & LEY, A. 1889. *A flora of Herefordshire.* Hereford: Jakeman & Carver.

ANON. 1891. Notes of field meeting, Tuesday, August 25th, 1891. *Transactions of the Woolhope Naturalists' Field Club.*

LEY, A. 1894. Records of Herefordshire plants additional to those published in the 'Flora of Herefordshire'. Supplement to the *Transactions of the Woolhope Naturalists' Field Club.*

ANON. 1905. Notes additional to the 'Flora of Herefordshire'. *Transactions of the Woolhope Naturalists' Field Club,* 69-152.

LEY, A. 1908. Botany. *Victoria history of the county of Herefordshire.* Vol. 1, 39-76. London: Constable.

1962

OSWALD, P.H. & COPELAND WATTS, E. 1962. Report on Moccas Deer Park, Herefordshire. Internal report, Nature Conservancy.

1976-1999

HARDING, P.T. 1977. Moccas Deer Park, Hereford and Worcester: a report on the history, structure and natural history. Unpublished report to the Nature Conservancy Council by the Institute of Terrestrial Ecology, Huntingdon.

WHITBREAD, A. 1982. Moccas Park, Hereford and Worcester; habitat survey. Internal report, Nature Conservancy Council.

THOMSON, S.E. & THOMSON, P. 1989. Moccas Park lake. Report to Nature Conservancy Council.

WALL, T. 1991-1999. Occasional casual records from field notebooks.

PRESTON, C.D. & CROFT, J.M. 1991. Moccas Park lake, list of plant species recorded on 6 August 1991. List for Institute of Terrestrial Ecology.

WHITE, J. 1992. Identifications of some of the exotic tree species from leaf samples. Notes on English Nature files.

KING, N., THOMSON, S.E. & THOMSON, P. 1993. Moccas Park NNR, vegetational recording. Report to English Nature.

SIMPSON, D. 1998. Notes on the ground flora of Moccas Park, visited 27 March and 15 May 1998. Report to English Nature.

BINGHAM, J. 1998. Moccas Park NNR, National Vegetation Classification report following visit on 21 August 1998. Report to English Nature.

Nomenclature

Sequence and nomenclature follow C. STACE. 1997. *New flora of the British Isles.* Second edition. Cambridge: Cambridge University Press.

Frequency

Frequency ratings relate only to the present time; they are not based on detailed survey and are given as an indication only. They are as follows: D = Dominant; A = Abundant; F = Frequent; O = Occasional; R = Rare. These ratings relate to the habitat in which the species is found and not to the Park as a whole. Where two or more frequency ratings are given, they relate respectively to the habitats in which the species occurs as listed in the 'Habitat' column. Where a rating is prefaced by L (= locally) this indicates a local frequency within the habitat in question. Several exotic tree species occur as one or two specimens only.

Habitat

G = grassland (predominantly the Lower Park; records include tree species growing in the parkland); W = woodland (the Upper Park); P = the Lawn Pool (including the fen and carr at its centre) and ponds as described in Chapter 4.3; F = flushes. Where a species has not been recorded in the current period, an entry has been made in the habitat column only if the habitat in which the species occurred was stated in the original record.

Family and species names

Family and species names		Periods			Habitat	Present frequency
		1889 to 1908	1962	1976 to 1999		
EQUISETACEAE	**Horsetail family**					
Equisetum fluviatile	Water horsetail		✓	✓	P	O
E. arvense	Field horsetail			✓	F	O
OPHIOGLOSSACEAE	**Adder's-tongue family**					
Ophioglossum vulgatum	Adder's-tongue	✓		✓	G	R
Botrychium lunaria	Moonwort	✓			G	
POLYPODIACEAE	**Polypody family**					
Polypodium interjectum	Intermediate polypody		✓	✓	W	R
DENNSTAEDTIACEAE	**Bracken family**					
Pteridium aquilinum	Bracken		✓	✓	G W	F(LD) F(LD)
THELYPTERIDACEAE	**Marsh fern family**					
Oreopteris limbosperma	Lemon-scented fern			✓	W	R
ASPLENIACEAE	**Spleenwort family**					
Asplenium trichomanes	Maidenhair spleenwort		✓	✓	W	R
WOODSIACEAE	**Lady-fern family**					
Athyrium filix-femina	Lady-fern			✓	W	R
DRYOPTERIDACEAE	**Buckler-fern family**					
Dryopteris filix-mas	Male-fern		✓	✓	W P	R O
D. dilatata	Broad buckler-fern			✓	W	R
PINACEAE	**Pine family**					
Abies grandis	Giant fir			✓	W	R
Pseudotsuga menziesii	Douglas fir			✓	W	O
Picea sp.	Spruce sp.			✓	W	O
Larix decidua	European larch			✓	G W	R R
L. x marschlinsii	Hybrid larch			✓	W	O
Cedrus deodara	Deodar			✓	G	R
Pinus sylvestris	Scots pine			✓	G W	R O
TAXODIACEAE	**Redwood family**					
Sequoia sempervirens	Coastal redwood			✓	G W	R O
Taxodium distichum	Swamp cypress			✓	G	R
Sequoiadendron giganteum	Wellingtonia		✓	✓	G	R
CUPRESSACEAE	**Juniper family**					
Chamaecyparis lawsoniana	Lawson's cypress			✓	G	R
Thuja plicata	Western red cedar			✓	W	O
TAXACEAE	**Yew family**					
Taxus baccata	Yew			✓	W	R
RANUNCULACEAE	**Buttercup family**					
Anemone nemorosa	Wood anemone			✓	W	R(LA)
Ranunculus acris	Meadow buttercup			✓	G	O
R. repens	Creeping buttercup		✓	✓	G	F
R. sceleratus	Celery-leaved buttercup		✓	✓	P	R
R. lingua	Greater spearwort	✓	✓	✓	P	O
R. flammula	Lesser spearwort		✓	✓	P	O
R. ficaria	Lesser celandine			✓	G W	F O(LF)
R. peltatus	Pond water-crowfoot			✓	P	O
Aquilegia vulgaris	Columbine	✓				
PLATANACEAE	**Plane family**					
Platanus x hispanica	London plane			✓	G	R
ULMACEAE	**Elm family**					
Ulmus glabra	Wych elm			✓	W	R
URTICACEAE	**Nettle family**					
Urtica dioica	Common nettle		✓	✓	G W	F O(LF)
JUGLANDACEAE	**Walnut family**					
Juglans regia	Walnut			✓	G	R

Family and species names		Periods			Habitat	Present frequency
		1889 to 1908	1962	1976 to 1999		
FAGACEAE	**Beech family**					
Fagus sylvatica	Beech		✓	✓	G W	F F(LD)
Castanea sativa	Sweet chestnut		✓	✓	G W	F F
Quercus cerris	Turkey oak			✓	G	R
Q. ilex	Evergreen oak			✓	G	R
Q. petraea	Sessile oak			✓	W P	A O
Q. petraea x Q. robur				✓	G W	F F
Q. robur	Pedunculate oak		✓	✓	W P	A(LD) A
Q. rubra	Red oak			✓	G	R
BETULACEAE	**Birch family**					
Betula pendula	Silver birch		✓	✓	W	R
Alnus glutinosa	Alder		✓	✓	W P	R F(LD)
Carpinus betulus	Hornbeam			✓	G	R
Corylus avellana	Hazel			✓	W	R
CHENOPODIACEAE	**Goosefoot family**					
Chenopodium urbicum	Upright goosefoot	✓				
PORTULACACEAE	**Blinks family**					
Montia fontana	Blinks			✓	P	O
CARYOPHYLLACEAE	**Pink family**					
Moehringia trinervia	Three-nerved sandwort			✓	W	R
Stellaria media	Common chickweed			✓	G W	O O
S. holostea	Greater stitchwort			✓	G W	R R
S. graminea	Lesser stitchwort		✓	✓	G	R
S. uliginosa	Bog stitchwort		✓	✓	F	O
Cerastium fontanum	Common mouse-ear			✓	G	O
Sagina procumbens	Procumbent pearlwort			✓	P	O
Silene dioica	Red campion			✓	W	R
POLYGONACEAE	**Knotweed family**					
Persicaria amphibia	Amphibious bistort		✓	✓	P	F
P. lapathifolia	Pale persicaria			✓	P	O
P. hydropiper	Water-pepper		✓	✓	P	F
P. minor	Small water-pepper	✓			P	
Polygonum arenastrum	Equal-leaved knotgrass			✓	G	O
Rumex acetosella	Sheep's sorrel			✓	G	R
R. acetosa	Common sorrel			✓	G	O
R. crispus	Curled dock			✓	G	R
R. conglomeratus	Clustered dock		✓	✓	P	O
R. sanguineus	Wood dock			✓	P F	O O
R. maritimus	Golden dock	✓			P	
CLUSIACEAE	**St John's-wort**					
Hypericum tetrapterum	Square-stalked St John's-wort		✓		W	
H. humifusum	Trailing St John's-wort		✓	✓	G	R
TILIACEAE	**Lime family**					
Tilia platyphyllos	Large-leaved lime			✓	W	R
T. platyphyllos 'rubra'				✓	G	R
T. x vulgaris	Lime			✓	G W	R R
T. cordata	Small-leaved lime			✓	W	R
T. americana	American lime			✓	G	R
VIOLACEAE	**Violet family**					
Viola riviniana	Common dog-violet		✓	✓	G W	O O
V. reichenbachiana	Early dog-violet			✓	W	R
SALICACEAE	**Willow family**					
Salix cinerea ssp. oleifolia	Grey willow			✓	W P	O F
BRASSICACEAE	**Cabbage family**					
Cardamine pratensis	Cuckooflower		✓	✓	G P	O O
C. flexuosa	Wavy bitter-cress		✓	✓	W F	O(LF) O
Coronopus didymus	Lesser swine-cress			✓	P	O
PRIMULACEAE	**Primrose family**					
Primula vulgaris	Primrose		✓	✓	G W	O O
Lysimachia nemorum	Yellow pimpernel			✓	G	O
L. nummularia	Creeping-Jenny			✓	G	R
L. vulgaris	Yellow loosestrife	✓	✓	✓	P	F

APPENDIX 4

Family and species names		Periods			Habitat	Present frequency
		1889 to 1908	1962	1976 to 1999		
GROSSULARIACEAE	**Gooseberry family**					
Ribes nigrum	Black currant			✓	W	R
SAXIFRAGACEAE	**Saxifrage family**					
Chrysosplenium oppositifolium	Opposite-leaved golden-saxifrage		✓	✓	W F	O(LF) O
ROSACEAE	**Rose family**					
Rubus fruticosus agg.	Bramble			✓	W P	R O
Potentilla anserina	Silverweed			✓	G P	R F
P. erecta	Tormentil		✓	✓	G	R
P. anglica	Trailing tormentil		✓		G	
P. reptans	Creeping cinquefoil			✓	G P	O O
P. sterilis	Barren strawberry		✓	✓	G W	R R
Geum urbanum	Wood avens			✓	W	R
Agrimonia procera	Fragrant agrimony	✓				
Aphanes arvensis	Parsley-piert			✓	G	R
Rosa arvensis	Field-rose			✓	G	R
Prunus lusitanica	Portugal laurel			✓	G	R
Malus sylvestris	Crab apple			✓	G W	R R
Sorbus aucuparia	Rowan			✓	W	R
Crataegus monogyna	Hawthorn		✓	✓	G W	F F
FABACEAE	**Pea family**					
Lotus corniculatus	Common bird's-foot-trefoil		✓	✓	G	O
L. pedunculatus	Greater bird's-foot-trefoil			✓	P	R
Vicia sativa	Common vetch			✓	G	R
Lathyrus pratensis	Meadow vetchling			✓	F	R
Medicago lupulina	Black medick			✓	G	R
Trifolium repens	White clover	✓	✓	✓	G	A
T. dubium	Lesser trefoil		✓	✓	G	A
T. pratense	Red clover			✓	G	R
HALORAGACEAE	**Water-milfoil family**					
Myriophyllum spicatum	Spiked water-milfoil	✓			P	
M. alterniflorum	Alternate water-milfoil	✓			P	
LYTHRACEAE	**Purple-loosestrife family**					
Lythrum salicaria	Purple-loosestrife		✓	✓	P	F
L. portula	Water-purslane		✓	✓	P	O
ONAGRACEAE	**Willowherd family**					
Epilobium hirsutum	Great willowherb			✓	P	F
E. obscurum	Short-fruited willowherb			✓	P	O
E. brunnescens	New Zealand willowherb			✓	F	R
Chamerion angustifolium	Rosebay willowherb			✓	G P	R O
Circaea lutetiana	Enchanter's-nightshade		✓	✓	W	O
VISCACEAE	**Mistletoe family**					
Viscum album	Mistletoe		✓	✓	G W	R R
AQUIFOLIACEAE	**Holly family**					
Ilex aquifolium	Holly			✓	G W	R R
EUPHORBIACEAE	**Spurge family**					
Mercurialis perennis	Dog's mercury		✓	✓	W	O(LA)
POLYGALACEAE	**Milkwort family**					
Polygala vulgaris	Common milkwort			✓	G	R
HIPPOCASTANACEAE	**Horse-chestnut family**					
Aesculus hippocastanum	Horse-chestnut		✓	✓	G W	F O(LD)
ACERACEAE	**Maple family**					
Acer platanoides	Norway maple			✓	G W	R R
A. campestre	Field maple		✓	✓	G W	O R
A. pseudoplatanus	Sycamore			✓	W	R
SIMAROUBACEAE	**Tree-of-heaven family**					
Ailanthus altissima	Tree-of-heaven			✓	G	R
OXALIDACEAE	**Wood-sorrel family**					
Oxalis acetosella	Wood-sorrel		✓	✓	G W	O O(LA)
GERANIACEAE	**Crane's-bill family**					
Geranium robertianum	Herb-Robert		✓	✓	W	O

APPENDIX 4

Family and species names		Periods			Habitat	Present frequency
		1889 to 1908	1962	1976 to 1999		
BALSAMINACEAE	**Balsam family**					
Impatiens glandulifera	Indian balsam			✓	F	R
ARALIACEAE	**Ivy family**					
Hedera helix	Ivy			✓	W	R
APIACEAE	**Carrot family**					
Hydrocotyle vulgaris	Marsh pennywort	✓	✓	✓	P F	O(LF) F
Conopodium majus	Pignut			✓	G W	R R
Oenanthe fistulosa	Tubular water-dropwort	✓		✓	P	R
O. aquatica	Fine-leaved water-dropwort		✓	✓	P	O
Apium nodiflorum	Fool's-water-cress			✓	F	O
Angelica sylvestris	Wild angelica			✓	P F	O O
Heracleum sphondylium	Hogweed	✓		✓	G	R
APOCYNACEAE	**Periwinkle family**					
Vinca major	Greater periwinkle			✓	G	R
SOLANACEAE	**Nightshade family**					
Solanum dulcamara	Bittersweet			✓	P	O
MENYANTHACEAE	**Bogbean family**					
Menyanthes trifoliata	Bogbean			✓	P	O
BORAGINACEAE	**Borage family**					
Myosotis scorpioides	Water forget-me-not			✓	P	F
M. laxa ssp. caespitosa	Tufted forget-me-not		✓	✓	P	O
M. arvensis	Field forget-me-not			✓	G	R
LAMIACEAE	**Deadnettle family**					
Stachys sylvatica	Hedge woundwort			✓	W	R
Scutellaria galericulata	Skullcap	✓	✓	✓	P F	O O
Teucrium scorodonia	Wood sage			✓	W	R
Glechoma hederacea	Ground-ivy		✓	✓	W	O
Prunella vulgaris	Selfheal		✓	✓	G	O
Thymus polytrichus	Wild thyme		✓		G	
Lycopus europaeus	Gypsywort		✓	✓	P	F
Mentha arvensis	Corn mint		✓	✓	P	F
M. aquatica	Water mint			✓	P F	F F
CALLITRICHACEAE	**Water-starwort family**					
Callitriche stagnalis	Common water-starwort			✓	P	F
C. hamulata	Intermediate water-starwort			✓	P	F
PLANTAGINACEAE	**Plantain family**					
Plantago major	Greater plantain		✓	✓	G	O
P. lanceolata	Ribwort plantain		✓	✓	G	F
OLEACEAE	**Ash family**					
Fraxinus excelsior	Ash		✓	✓	G W	O O
SCROPHULARIACEAE	**Figwort family**					
Scrophularia nodosa	Common figwort			✓	W F	R R
S. auriculata	Water figwort			✓	P	O
Digitalis purpurea	Foxglove		✓	✓	W	O(LF)
Veronica serpyllifolia	Thyme-leaved speedwell		✓	✓	G	O
V. officinalis	Heath speedwell		✓	✓	G	R
V. chamaedrys	Germander speedwell		✓	✓	G W	O O
V. montana	Wood speedwell		✓	✓	W	O
V. scutellata var. villosa	Marsh speedwell			✓	P	R
V. filiformis	Slender speedwell			✓	W F	R R
LENTIBULARIACEAE	**Bladderwort family**					
Utricularia australis	Bladderwort	✓		✓	P	F
CAMPANULACEAE	**Bellflower family**					
Campanula rotundifolia	Harebell		✓	✓	G	R
RUBIACEAE	**Bedstraw family**					
Galium palustre	Common marsh-bedstraw		✓	✓	P F	R R
G. verum	Lady's bedstraw		✓		G	
G. mollugo	Hedge bedstraw			✓	G	R
G. saxatile	Heath bedstraw		✓	✓	G	R
G. aparine	Cleavers			✓	G P	R R

APPENDIX 4

Family and species names		Periods			Habitat	Present frequency
		1889 to 1908	1962	1976 to 1999		
CAPRIFOLIACEAE	**Honeysuckle family**					
Sambucus nigra	Elder			✓	G W	R R
Lonicera periclymenum	Honeysuckle			✓	W	R
ADOXACEAE	**Moschatel family**					
Adoxa moschatellina	Moschatel			✓	W	R(LA)
VALERIANACEAE	**Valerian family**					
Valeriana dioica	Marsh valerian			✓	F	O
DIPSACACEAE	**Teasel family**					
Succisa pratensis	Devil's-bit scabious		✓		G	
ASTERACEAE	**Daisy family**					
Cirsium vulgare	Spear thistle		✓	✓	G	F(LA)
C. palustre	Marsh thistle		✓	✓	G F	F O
C. arvense	Creeping thistle		✓	✓	G	A(LD)
Centaurea nigra	Common knapweed			✓	G	R
Hypochaeris radicata	Cat's-ear			✓	G	R
Leontodon autumnalis	Autumn hawkbit		✓	✓	G	O
L. saxatilis	Lesser hawkbit		✓	✓	G	R (LF)
Taraxacum agg.	Dandelion			✓	G	R
Crepis capillaris	Smooth hawk's-beard			✓	G	R
Pilosella officinarum	Mouse-ear-hawkweed		✓	✓	G	R
Gnaphalium uliginosum	Marsh cudweed		✓	✓	P	O
Inula helenium	Elecampane	✓				
Pulicaria dysenterica	Common fleabane			✓	F	R
Bellis perennis	Daisy			✓	G	O
Achillea millefolium	Yarrow		✓	✓	G	O
Bidens cernua	Nodding bur-marigold	✓		✓	P	O(LD)
Senecio jacobaea	Common ragwort			✓	W	R
Eupatorium cannabinum	Hemp-agrimony			✓	P	R
ALISMATACEAE	**Water-plantain family**					
Alisma plantago-aquatica	Water-plantain		✓	✓	P	O
POTAMOGETONACEAE	**Pondweed family**					
Potamogeton natans	Broad-leaved pondweed			✓	P	O
P. polygonifolius	Bog pondweed	✓	✓		P	
ARACEAE	**Lords-and ladies family**					
Arum maculatum	Lords-and-ladies			✓	G W	O O
LEMNACEAE	**Duckweed family**					
Lemna minor	Common duckweed		✓	✓	P	F
L. minuta	Least duckweed			✓	P	O
JUNCACEAE	**Rush family**					
Juncus bufonius	Toad rush		✓	✓	P	O
J. articulatus	Jointed rush			✓	P F	O O
J. acutiflorus	Sharp-flowered rush			✓	P F	R F
J. inflexus	Hard rush		✓	✓	P	O
J. effusus	Soft-rush		✓	✓	G W P	O O(LF) O
J. conglomeratus	Compact rush		✓	✓	G P	O O
Luzula campestris	Field wood-rush		✓	✓	G	O(LF)
CYPERACEAE	**Sedge family**					
Eleocharis palustris	Common spike-rush			✓	P	O
Schoenoplectus lacustris	Common club-rush	✓	✓	✓	P	O(LF)
Carex paniculata	Greater tussock-sedge			✓	P	O(LF)
C. divulsa ssp. divulsa	Grey sedge			✓	G	R
C. remota	Remote sedge			✓	F	R
C. ovalis	Oval sedge		✓	✓	G	O
C. echinata	Star sedge			✓	F	O
C. hirta	Hairy sedge			✓	G	F
C. acutiformis	Lesser pond-sedge			✓	P	R
C. rostrata	Bottle sedge			✓	P	F
C. vesicaria	Bladder-sedge	✓	✓	✓	P	A
C. strigosa	Thin-spiked wood-sedge	✓				
C. flacca	Glaucous sedge			✓	F	F
C. viridula ssp. oedocarpa	Yellow-sedge			✓	F	O
C. elata	Tufted-sedge	✓			P	

Family and species names		1889 to 1908	Periods 1962	1976 to 1999	Habitat	Present frequency
POACEAE	**Grass family**					
Festuca rubra	Red fescue			✓	G	F
F. ovina	Sheep's-fescue		✓	✓	G	R
Lolium perenne	Perennial rye-grass			✓	G	D
Vulpia bromoides	Squirreltail fescue			✓	G	R
Cynosurus cristatus	Crested dog's-tail		✓	✓	G	A
Poa annua	Annual meadow-grass		✓	✓	G	O
P. trivialis	Rough meadow-grass			✓	G	A
Dactylis glomerata	Cock's-foot			✓	G	O
Glyceria fluitans	Floating sweet-grass		✓	✓	P	O
Melica uniflora	Wood melick			✓	W F	R R
Arrhenatherum elatius	False oat-grass			✓	G	O
Deschampsia cespitosa	Tufted hair-grass		✓	✓	W	O(LF)
Holcus lanatus	Yorkshire-fog			✓	G W	O O(LA)
H. mollis	Creeping soft-grass			✓	W	O
Aira caryophyllea	Silver hair-grass			✓	G	R
A. praecox	Early hair-grass		✓		G	
Anthoxanthum odoratum	Sweet vernal-grass		✓	✓	G	A
Phalaris arundinacea	Reed canary-grass		✓	✓	P	F
Agrostis capillaris	Common bent		✓	✓	G	D
A. gigantea	Black bent			✓	P	R
A. stolonifera	Creeping bent			✓	P	O
Alopecurus geniculatus	Marsh foxtail			✓	P	O
A. aequalis	Orange foxtail	✓		✓	P	R
Phleum pratense	Timothy			✓	G	O
Brachypodium sylvaticum	False brome		✓	✓	W	O(LF)
SPARGANIACEAE	**Bur-reed family**					
Sparganium erectum	Branched bur-reed		✓	✓	P	O
S. erectum ssp. neglectum		✓			P	
TYPHACEAE	**Bulrush family**					
Typha latifolia	Bulrush		✓	✓	P	O
LILIACEAE	**Lily family**					
Colchicum autumnale	Meadow saffron			✓	W	O(LF)
Hyacinthoides non-scripta	Bluebell			✓	G W	O F(LD)
Allium ursinum	Ramsons			✓	W	R(LA)
IRIDACEAE	**Iris family**					
Iris pseudacorus	Yellow iris			✓	P	O
DIOSCOREACEAE	**Black bryony family**					
Tamus communis	Black bryony			✓	W	R
ORCHIDACEAE	**Orchid family**					
Dactylorhiza fuchsii	Common spotted-orchid			✓	G	R

APPENDIX 4

A check list of the Coleoptera

Compiled by
R. Colin Welch
and J. Cooter

Sources and verification of records

The following list has been compiled from all known published records, plus those contained in various manuscript and typescript lists held by English Nature (formerly the Nature Conservancy Council). In addition, several coleopterists have made their own personal records available to us and without their assistance the following check list would have been much less complete.

Most modern records have been verified, confirmed by our own collecting or are judged by us to be accurate. One of us (J.C.) has been visiting Moccas Park regularly since 1975; during this time particular efforts have been made to confirm the presence of many of the rarer and unusual species recorded by the early coleoperists and for which no museum specimen has, to date, been located. Eight species have been omitted from the main check list for the reasons described in the Addendum. A further eight species preceded by **??** in the list are regarded as doubtful records in need of confirmation. Four more species are preceded by **?** indicating that this taxon has been split into two or more separate species as the result of recent taxonomic studies.[1]

Systematics and nomenclature

The naming of insects, conjoined with the ticklish question of priorities of names, seems to be the passion of many entomologists as surely as it is the bête noire *of many more.*

E. F. Linssen (1959). *Beetles of the British Isles.*

The sequence of families and genera, and the general nomenclature adopted in the following list, is based on the most recent comprehensive British check list prepared by R.D. Pope in 1977.[2] This national check list is now considerably out of date. In the absence of a comprehensive revision of the national check list, several published taxonomic and nomenclatural revisions have been incorporated here, together with some of the specific changes that are already in use by British coleopterists. Many of these changes have been brought forward in past issues of the Royal Entomological Society's journal *Antenna*, or published in short notes and papers in specialist journals. Other important revisions have been included in publications on particular genera and families.[3]

Threatened, scarce and indicator species

The first column to the right of the species list gives the latest Red Data Book (RDB 1 to 3, RDB K) and Nationally Notable categories as defined and listed in reviews of the status of British Coleoptera.[4] Since the publication of these reviews, the Nationally Notable status used by Hyman and Parsons is now referred to as Nationally Scarce, but their original statuses are used here. Nationally Notable was divided in Category A (Na) and Category B (Nb) based on the number of 10 km squares or biological vice-counties from which the species had been recorded.[5]

The second column to the right of the species list indicates the saproxylic species that are regarded as being especially characteristic of ancient woodlands with continuity of saproxylic habitat and in particular of ancient wood-pastures.[6] The term 'Ancient Woodland Indicators' (AWI) has been applied to these species by some authors (see Chapter 5.1); the three categories (1 to 3) are indicative of the 'faithfulness' of the species to this biotope, 1 being the most 'faithful'.

APPENDIX 5

Status

CARABIDAE
Cychrus caraboides rostratus (L.)
Carabus nemoralis Müller
C. problematicus gallicus Gehin
C. violaceus L.
Leistus rufomarginatus (Duftschmidt)
Nebria brevicollis (F.)
Notiophilus biguttatus (F.)
N. rufipes Curtis
Elaphrus cupreus Duftschmidt
E. riparius (L.)
Loricera pilicornis (F.)
Dyschirius globosus (Herbst)
Clivina fossor (L.)
Patrobus atrorufus (Ström)
Trechus quadristriatus (Schrank)
? Asaphidion flavipes sensu auct.
Bembidion articulatum (Panzer)
B. assimile Gyllenhal
B. bruxellense Wesmael
B. clarki Dawson   Nb
B. dentellum (Thunberg)
B. doris (Panzer)
B. guttula (F.)
B. harpaloides Serville
B. lampros (Herbst)
B. lunulatum (Fourcroy)
B. mannerheimi Sahlberg
B. properans Stephens
B. quadrimaculatum (L.)
B. quadripustulatum Serville   Nb
Pterostichus cupreus (L.)
P. diligens (Sturm)
P. gracilis (Dejean)   Nb
P. madidus (F.)
P. melanarius (Illiger)
P. niger (Schaller)
? P. nigrita (Paykull)
P. strenuus (Panzer)
P. vernalis (Panzer)
P. versicolor (Sturm)
Abax parallelepipedus (Piller & Mitterpacher)
Calathus piceus (Marsham)
Synuchus nivalis (Panzer)
Agonum assimile (Paykull)
A. dorsale (Pontoppidan)
A. fuliginosum (Panzer)
A. gracile Sturm
A. marginatum (L.)
A. muelleri (Herbst)
A. obscurum (Herbst)
A. piceum (L.)
A. thoreyi Dejean
A. viduum (Panzer)
Amara plebeja (Gyllenhal)
Harpalus rufipes (Degeer)
Bradycellus collaris (Paykull)
B. harpalinus (Serville)
Stenolophus mixtus (Herbst)
Acupalpus consputus (Duftschmidt)   Nb
A. dubius Schilsky
Chlaenius nigricornis (F.)   Nb
Demetrias atricapillus (L.)
Dromius agilis (F.)

Status

Dromius angustus Brullé
D. meridionalis Dejean
D. quadrimaculatus (L.)
D. quadrinotatus (Zenker in Panzer)

HALIPLIDAE
Haliplus lineolatus Mannerheim
H. ruficollis (Degeer)
H. wehnckei Gerhardt

NOTERIDAE
Noterus clavicornis (Degeer)

DYTISCIDAE
Laccophilus minutus (L.)
Hyphydrus ovatus (L.)
Hygrotus decoratus (Gyllenhal)   Nb
H. inaequalis (F.)
Coelambus impressopunctatus (Schaller)
Hydroporus angustatus Sturm
H. erythrocephalus (L.)
H. nigrita (F.)
H. palustris (L.)
H. planus (F.)
H. pubescens (Gyllenhal)
Suphrodytes dorsalis (F.)
Graptodytes granularis (L.)   Nb
Porhydrus lineatus (F.)
Copelatus haemorrhoidalis (F.)
Agabus biguttatus (Olivier)
A. bipustulatus (L.)
A. guttatus (Paykull)
A. labiatus (Brahm)
A. melanocornis Zimmerman
A. nebulosus (Forster)
A. sturmii (Gyllenhal)
A. unguicularis Thomson   Nb
Ilybius quadriguttatus (Lacordaire & Boisduval)
Rhantus exsoletus (Forst.)
Colymbetes fuscus (L.)
Graphoderus cinereus (L.)   RDB 3
Dytiscus semisulcatus Müller
D. marginalis L.

GYRINIDAE
Gyrinus natator (L.)
G. substriatus Stephens
Orectochilus villosus (Müller)

HYDROPHILIDAE
Georissus crenulatus (Rossi)   Na
Hydrochus elongatus (Schaller)   RDB 3
Helophorus aequalis Thomson
H. aquaticus (L.)
H. arvernicus Mulsant   Nb
H. brevipalpis Bedel
H. flavipes (F.)
H. grandis Illiger
H. minutus F.
H. nanus Sturm   Nb
H. obscurus Mulsant
H. strigifrons Thomson   Nb
Coelostoma orbiculare (F.)
? Sphaeridium bipustulatum F.

5 APPENDIX

	Status	
Cercyon analis (Paykull)		
C. atomarius (F.)		
C. convexiusculus Stephens		
C. haemorrhoidalis (F.)		
C. melanocephalus (L.)		
C. pygmaeus (Illiger)		
C. quisquillius (L.)		
C. unipunctatus (L.)		
Megasternum obscurum (Marsham)		
Hydrobius fuscipes (L.)		
Anacaena bipustulata (Marsham)	Nb	
A. globulus (Paykull)		
A. limbata (F.)		
A. lutescens (Stephens)		
Laccobius biguttatus Gerhardt		
Helochares lividus (Forster)	Nb	
H. obscurus (Müller)	Nb	
Enochrus affinis (Thunberg)	Nb	
E. bicolor (F.)	Nb	
E. coarctatus (Gredler)		
E. fuscipennis (Thompson)		
E. ochropterus (Marsham)	Nb	
E. testaceus (F.)		
Cymbiodyta marginella (F.)		
Chaetarthria seminulum (Herbst)	Nb	

HISTERIDAE

	Status	
Plegaderus dissectus Erichson	Nb	AWI 3
Abraeus globosus (Hoffmann)		
Aeletes atomarius (Aubé)	RDB 3	AWI 1
Gnathoncus buyssoni Auzat	Na	
Dendrophilus punctatus (Herbst)		
Carcinops pumilio (Erichson)		
Paromalus flavicornis (Herbst)		
Onthophilus striatus (F.)		

HYDRAENIDAE

Ochthebius minimus (F.)	
Hydraena riparia Kugelann	
Limnebius truncatellus (Thunberg)	

PTILIIDAE

	Status	
Nossidium pilosellum (Marsham)	N	
Ptenidium gressneri Erichson	N	AWI 2
P. intermedium Wankowicz		
P. laevigatum Erichson		
P. nitidum (Heer)		
P. turgidum Thomson	RDB K	AWI 2
Ptiliolum fuscum (Erichson)		
Ptinella aptera (Guérin-Méneville)		
P. cavelli (Broun)		
P. errabunda Johnson		
Pteryx suturalis (Heer)		
Nephanes titan (Newman)		
Acrotrichis fascicularis (Herbst)		
A. insularis (Mäklin)		
A. intermedia (Gillmeister)		
A. rossketheni Sundt		
A. rugulosa Rosskothen		

LEIODIDAE

	Status
Hydnobius latifrons (Curtis)	RDB K
Leiodes ferruginea (F.)	

	Status	
Leiodes litura Stephens		
L. oblonga (Erichson)	N	
L. calcarata (Erichson)		
L. strigipenne Daffner		
Liocyrtusa vittata (Curtis)		
Colenis immunda (Sturm)		
Anisotoma humeralis (F.)		
A. orbicularis (Herbst)		
Agathidium atrum (Paykull)		
A. confusum Brisout	RDB 1	
A. nigrinum Sturm		
A. nigripenne (F.)		
A. rotundatum Gyllenhal		
A. seminulum (L.)		
A. varians Beck		
Ptomophagus subvillosus (Goeze)		
Nargus velox (Spence)		
Choleva angustata (F.)		
Sciodrepoides fumata (Spence)		
S. watsoni (Spence)		
Catops coracinus Kellner		
C. fuliginosus Erichson		
C. kirbii (Spence)		
C. nigrita Erichson		
C. tristis (Panzer)		
Colon brunneum (Latreille)		
C. dentipes (Sahlberg)	RDB K	
C. serripes (Sahlberg)		

SILPHIDAE

Nicrophorus vespilloides Herbst	
Necrodes litoralis (L.)	
Thanatophilus rugosus (L.)	
Oiceptoma thoracicum (L.)	
Silpha atrata L.	

SCYDMAENIDAE

	Status	
Neuraphes angulatus (Müller & Kunze)		
N. plicicollis Reitter	N	
Stenichnus bicolor (Denny)		AWI 3

SCAPHIDIIDAE

Scaphidium quadrimaculatum (Olivier)	
Scaphisoma agaricinum (L.)	
S. boleti (Panzer)	

STAPHYLINIDAE

	Status
Micropeplus fulvus Erichson	
M. staphylinoides (Marsham)	
Metopsia retusa (Stephens)	
Megarthrus depressus (Paykull)	
Proteinus atomarius Erichson	
P. brachypterus (F.)	
P. ovalis Stephens	
Olophrum piceum (Gyllenhal)	
Phyllodrepoidea crenata (Gravenhorst)	N
Lesteva heeri Fauvel	
L. longoelytra (Goeze)	
Eusphalerum luteum (Marsham)	
E. minutum (F.)	
E. primulae (Stephens)	
E. torquatum (Marsham)	
Acrulia inflata (Gyllenhal)	
Phyllodrepa floralis (Paykull)	

APPENDIX 5

	Status			Status	
Dropephylla deville (Bernhauer)			Philonthus cruentus (Gmelin in L.)		
D. gracilicornis (Fairmaire & Laboulbène)	N		P. decoratus (Gravenhorst)		
D. ioptera (Stephens)			P. ebeninus (Gravenhorst)	N	
D. vilis (Erichson)			P. fimetarius (Gravenhorst)		
Hapalaraea pygmaea (Paykull)			P. laminatus (Creutzer)		
Omalium excavatum Stephens			P. politus (L.)		
O. italicum Bernhauer			P. quisquiliarus (Gyllenhal)		
O. oxycanthae Gravenhorst			P. rectangulus Sharp		
O. rugatum Mulsant & Rey	N		P. sordidus (Gravenhorst)		
Phloeonomus punctipennis Thomson			P. splendens (F.)		
Phloeostiba plana (Paykull)			P. succicola Thomson		
Xylodromus concinnus (Marsham)			P. tenuicornis Mulsant & Rey		
Philorinum sordidum (Stephens)			P. umbratilis (Gravenhorst)		
Siagonum quadricorne Kirby			P. varians (Paykull)		
Coprophilus striatulus (F.)			P. varius (Gyllenhal)		
Syntomium aeneum (Müller)			P. ventralis (Gravenhorst)		
Carpelimus bilineatus Stephens			Gabrius pennatus Sharp		
C. elongatulus (Erichson)			G. splendidulus (Gravenhorst)		
C. rivularis (Motschulsky)			Staphylinus olens (Müller)		
Platystethus arenarius (Fourcroy)			Creophilus maxillosus (L.)		
P. cornutus (Gravenhorst)			Quedius cruentus (Olivier) var virens Rottenburg		
P. nitens (Sahlberg)			Q. fumatus (Stephens)		
Anotylus inustus (Gravenhorst)			Q. longicornis Kraatz	Nb	
A. rugosus (F.)			Q. maurus (Sahlberg)		AWI 3
A. sculpturatus (Gravenhorst)			Q. mesomelinus (Marsham)		
A. tetracarinatus (Block)			Q. scitus (Gravenhorst)	Nb	AWI 3
Oxtelus laqueatus (Marsham)			Q. ventralis (Aragona)	Nb	AWI 3
Stenus biguttatus (L.)			Q. xanthopus Erichson	Nb	AWI 3
S. boops Ljungh			Trichophya pilicornis (Gyllenhal)	Nb	
S. cicindeloides (Schaller)			Habrocerus capillaricornis (Gravenhorst)		
S. clavicornis (Scopoli)			Mycetoporus lepidus (Gravenhorst)		
S. comma Le Conte			M. longulus (Mannerheim)		
S. formicetorum Mannerheim			M. rufescens (Stephens)		
S. fulvicornis Stephens			M. splendidulus (Gravenhorst)		
S. impressus Germar			Lordithon exoletus (Erichson)		
S. juno (Paykull)			L. lunulatus (L.)		
S. latifrons Erichson			L. thoracicus (F.)		
S. pallitarsis Stephens			L. trinotatus (Er.)		
S. picipes Stephens			Sepedophilus bipunctatus (Gravenhorst)	Nb	
S. pubescens Stephens			S. littoreus (L.)		
S. solutus Erichson			S. lusitanicus Hammond		
S. subaeneus Erichson			S. marshami (Stephens)		
S. tarsalis Ljungh			S. nigripennis (Stephens)		
Euaesthetus ruficapillus Boisduval & Lacordaire			Tachyporus atriceps Stephens		
Paederus fuscipes Curtis		?	T. chrysomelinus (L.)		
P. littoralis Gravenhorst			T. dispar (Paykull)		
P. riparius (L.)			T. hypnorum (F.)		
Lathrobium brunnipes (F.)			T. nitidulus (F.)		
L. elongatum (L.)			T. obtusus (L.)		
L. quadratum (Paykull)			T. pallidus Sharp		
L. ripicola Czwalina	N		T. transversalis Gravenhorst		
L. terminatum Gravenhorst			Tachinus humeralis Gravenhorst		
Sunius propinquus (Brisout)			T. marginellus (F.)		
Rugilis erichsoni (Fauvel)			T. rufipennis Gyllenhal	RDB 3	
R. orbiculatus (Paykull)			T. signatus Gravenhorst		
Othius angustus Stephens			T. subterraneus (L.)		
O. punctulatus (Goeze)			Deinopsis erosa (Stephens)		
Atrecus affinis (Paykull)			Cypha hanseni Palm		
Gyrohypnus atratus (Heer)			C. longicornis (Paykull)		
G. fracticornis (Müller)			Oligota apicata Erichson	N	
Xantholinus linearis (Olivier)			O. picipes (Stephens)		
Erichsonius cinerascens (Gravenhorst)			O. pusillima (Gravenhorst)		
Philonthus albipes (Gravenhorst)			Myllaena dubia (Gravenhorst)		
P. corruscus (Gravenhorst)	RDB 1		M. gracilis (Matthews)		

	Status		Status	
Myllaena minuta (Gravenhorst)		Atheta (Datomicra) celata (Erichson)		
Hygronoma dimidiata (Gravenhorst)		A. (Datomicra) dadopora Thomson		
Gyrophaena affinis Mannerheim		A. (Datomicra) nigra (Kraatz)		
G. angustata (Stephens)	N	A. (Datomicra) sordidula (Erichson)		
G. fasciata (Marsham)		A. (s.str.) brunneipennis (Thomson)		
G. gentilis Erichson		A. (s.str.) castanoptera (Mannerheim)		
G. joyi Wendeler	N	A. (s.str.) gramminicola (Gravenhorst)		
G. latissima (Stephens)		A. (s.str.) hypnorum (Kiesenwetter)		
G. minima Erichson		A. (s.str.) incognita (Sharp)		
G. nana (Paykull)		A. (s.str.) pertyi (Heer)		
G. poweri Crotch	RDB K	A. (s.str.) triangulum (Kraatz)		
G. strictula Erichson		A. (s.str.) xanthopus (Thomson)		
Placusa depressa Mäklin	N	A. (Lohse Gp I) britanniae Bernhauer & Scheerpeltz		
P. pumilio (Gravenhorst)		A. (Lohse Gp I) crassicornis (F.)		
P. tachyporoides (Waltl)	N	A. (Lohse Gp I) coriaris (Kraatz)		
Anomognathus cuspidatus (Erichson)		A. (Lohse Gp I) crassicornis (F.)		
Leptusa fumida Kraatz		A. (Lohse (Gp I) fungicola (Thomson)		
L. pulchella (Mannerheim)		A. (Lohse Gp I) intermedia (Thomson)		
L. ruficollis (Erichson)		A. (Lohse Gp I) laticollis (Stephens)		
Bolitochara bella Mäklin		A. (Lohse Gp I) oblita (Erichson)		
B. lucida (Gravenhorst)		A. (Lohse Gp I) ravilla (Erichson)		
B. mulsanti Sharp	N	A. (Lohse Gp I) repanda (Mulsant & Rey)		
B. obliqua Erichson		A. (Dimetrota) atramentaria (Gyllenhal)		
Autalia impressa (Olivier)		A. (Dimetrota) cinnamoptera (Thomson)		
A. rivularis (Gravenhorst)		A. (Dimetrota) laevana (Mulsant & Rey)		
Tachyusa atra (Gravenhorst)		A. (Dimetrota) marcida (Erichson)		
T. coarctata Erichson		A. (Dimetrota) nigripes (Thomson)		
Gnypeta carbonaria (Mannerheim)		A. (Chaetida) longicornis (Gravenhorst)		
G. rubrior Tottenham		Thamiaraea hospita (Märkel)	N	
Schistoglossa gemina (Erichson)	N	Drusila canaliculata (F.)		
S. viduata (Erichson)	RDB K	Phloeopora teres (Gravenhorst)		
Aloconota (s.str.) gregaria (Erichson)		P. testacea (Mannerheim)		
Amischa analis (Gravenhorst)		Ilyobates nigricollis (Paykull)		
A. bifoveolatus (Mannerheim)		Chiloporata longitarsis (Erichson)		
A. decipiens (Sharp)		Ocyusa maura (Erichson)		
Dochmonota clancula (Erichson)	N	Mniusa incrassata (Mulsant & Rey)		
Geostiba circellaris (Gravenhorst)		Oxypoda alternans (Gravenhorst)		
Plataraea brunnea (F.)		O. amoena Fairmaire & Laboulbène	N	
Atheta (Philhygra) britteni Joy		O. annularis Mannerheim		
A. (Philhygra) elongatula (Gravenhorst)		O. elongatula Aubé		
A. (Philhygra) hygrobia (Thomson)	N	O. lentula (Erichson)		
A. (Philhygra) obtusangula Joy		O. lividipennis Mannerheim		
A. (Philhygra) palustris (Kiesenwetter)		O. procerula Mannerheim		
A. (Dilacra) vilis (Erichson)		O. umbrata (Gyllenhal)		
A. (Enalodroma) hepatica (Erichson)		Dexiogyia corticina (Erichson)	N	
A. (Bessobia) fungivora (Thomson)		Haploglossa pulla (Gyllenhal)		
A. (Bessobia) occulata (Erichson)		Tinotus morion (Gravenhorst)		
A. (Lohse Gp III & IV) euryptera (Stephens)		Aleochara (Coprochara) bipustulata (L.)		
A. (Lohse Gp III & IV) liturata (Stephens)		A. (s.str.) curtula (Goeze)		
A. (Anopleta) corvina (Thomson)		A. (Baryodma) intricata Mannerheim		
A. (Microdota) amicula (Stephens)		A. (Xenochara) funebris Wollaston		
A. (Microdota) boreella Brundin		A. (Xenochara) lanuginosa (Gravenhorst)		
A. (Microdota) indubia (Sharp)		A. (Xenochara) sparsa (Heer)		
A. (Microdota) liliputana (Brisout)	Nb	A. (Xenochara) tristis Gravenhorst		
A. (Lohse Gp II) cadaverina (Brisout)				
A. (Lohse Gp II) gagatina (Baudi)		**PSELAPHIDAE**		
A. (Lohse Gp II) pallidicornis (Thomson)		Bibloporus bicolor (Denny)		
A. (Mocyta) amplicollis (Mulsant & Rey)		B. minutus Raffray	Nb	AWI 2
A. (Mocyta) clientula (Erichson)		Bibloplectus ambiguus (Reichenbach)		
A. (Mocyta) fungi (Gravenhorst)		B. spinosus Raffray	N	
A. (Acrotona) aterrima (Gravenhorst)		Euplectus fauveli Guillebeau	N	
A. (Acrotona) muscorum (Brisout)		E. infirmus Raffray		
A. (Acrotona) parvula (Mannerheim)		E. karsteni (Reichenbach)		
A. (Datomicra) canescens (Sharp)		E. nanus (Reichenbach)	RDB I	AWI I

APPENDIX 5

Status

Euplectus piceus Motschulsky

Plectophloeus nitidus (Fairmaire)	RDB 2	AWI 1
Batrisodes venustus (Reichenbach)	Na	AWI 2

Bryaxis curtisi (Leach)

Tychus niger (Paykull)

Rybaxis laminata (Motschulsky)

R. longicornis (Leach)

Brachygluta haematica (Reichenbach)

LUCANIDAE

Dorcus parallelipipedus (L.)

Sinodendron cylindricum (L.)	AWI 3

TROGIDAE

Trox scaber (L.)

SCARABAEIDAE

Colobopterus fossor (L.)

C. haemorrhoidalis (L.)

Aphodius ater (Degeer)

A. borealis (Gyllenhal)

A. contaminatus (Herbst)

A. depressus (Kugelann)

A. equestris (Panzer)

A. fimetarius (L.)

A. foetans (F.)

A. ictericus (Laicharting)

A. luridus (F.)

A. obliteratus (Panzer)

A. paykulli Bedel	Nb
A. porcus (F.)	Nb

A. prodromus (Brahm)

A. pusillus (Herbst)

A. rufipes (L.)

A. sphacelatus (Panzer)

A. zenkeri Germar	Nb

Onthophagus coenobita (Herbst)

O. similis (Scriba)

Serica brunnea (L.)

Melolontha melolontha (L.)

CLAMBIDAE

Clambus punctulus (Beck)

C. gibbula (Leconte)

SCIRTIDAE

Elodes marginata (F.)

E. minuta (L.)

Microcara testacea (L.)

Cyphon coarctatus Paykull

C. hilaris Nyholm

C. ochraceus Stephens

C. padi (L.)

C. palustris Thomson

C. pubescens (F.)	Nb

Scirtes hemisphaericus (L.)

BYRRHIDAE

Byrrhus pilula (L.)

HETEROCERIDAE

Heterocerus fenestratus (Thunberg)

H. marginatus (F.)

Status

DRYOPIDAE

?? Dryops anglicanus Edwards	RDB 3
D. auriculatus (Fourcroy)	Nb
D. striatellus (Fairmaire & Brisout)	RDB 3

BUPRESTIDAE

Agrilus angustulus (Illiger)	Nb
A. laticornis (Illiger)	Nb

ELATERIDAE

Ampedus balteatus (L.)

A. cardinalis (Schiödte)	RDB 2	AWI 1
A. quercicola (du Buysson)	Nb	AWI 1
A. rufipennis (Stephens)	RDB 2	AWI 1
Procraerus tibialis (Boisduval & Lacordaire)	RDB 3	AWI 1
Oedostethus quadripustulatus (F.)	Na	

Melanotus villosus (Fourcroy)

Stenagostus rhombeus (Olivier)		AWI 3

Athous bicolor (Goeze)

A. haemorrhoidalis (F.)

A. vittatus (F.)

Hemicrepidius hirtus (Herbst)

Ctenicera cuprea (F.)

Calambus bipustulatus (L.)	Nb	AWI 3

Prosternon tessellatum (L.)

Agriotes acuminatus (Stephens)

A. obscurus (L.)

A. pallidus (Illiger)

A. sordidus (Illiger)	RDB 3

A. sputator (L.)

Dalopius marginatus (L.)

Adrastus pallens (F.)

Denticollis linearis (L.)

THROSCIDAE

Aulonothroscus brevicollis (de Bonvouloir)	RDB 3	AWI 1

Trixagus carinifrons (de Bonvouloir)

T. dermestoides (L.)

T. elateroides sensu auctt. Brit.	RDB 3

EUCNEMIDAE

Melasis buprestoides (Paykull)	Nb	AWI 3

CANTHARIDAE

Podabrus alpinus (Paykull)

Cantharis cryptica Ashe

C. decipiens Baudi

C. lateralis L.

C. nigricans (Müller)

C. pallida Goeze

C. pellucida F.

C. rustica Fallén

C. thoracica (Olivier)

Rhagonycha fulva (Scopoli)

R. lignosa (Müller)

R. testacea (L.)

Malthinus flaveolus (Herbst)

M. frontalis (Marsham)	Nb

M. seriepunctatus Kiesenwetter

?? Malthodes brevicollis (Paykull)	RDB 1	AWI 1
M. crassicornis (Mäklin)	RDB 3	AWI 2
M. guttifer Kiesenwetter	Nb	

M. marginatus (Latreille)

5 APPENDIX

	Status	
Malthodes maurus (Laporte de Castelnau)	Nb	
M. pumilus (Brébisson)		
LYCIDAE		
Platycis minuta (F.)	Nb	AWI 3
DERMESTIDAE		
Dermestes murinus L.		
Attagenus pellio (L.)		
Megatoma undata (L.)	Nb	
Ctesias serra (F.)	Nb	AWI 3
Anthrenus fuscus Olivier		
ANOBIIDAE		
Ptinomorphus imperialis (L.)	Nb	
Grynobius planus (F.)		
Dryophilus pusillus (Gyllenhal)		
Ochina ptinoides (Marsham)		
Xestobium rufovillosum (Degeer)		AWI 3
Hemicoelus fulvicornis (Sturm)		
Anobium punctatum (Degeer)		
Habrobregmus denticollis (Creutzer in Panzer.)	Nb	
Ptilinus pectinicornis (L.)		
Xyletinus longitarsus Jansson	RDB 2	AWI 3
Dorcatoma chrysomelina Sturm		AWI 2
D. dresdensis Herbst	Na	AWI 2
D. flavicornis (F.)	Nb	AWI 3
D. serra Panzer	Na	AWI 2
Anitys rubens (Hoffmann)	Nb	AWI 1
PTINIDAE		
Ptinus fur (L.)		
P. subpilosus Sturm	Nb	AWI 2
LYCTIDAE		
Lyctus linearis (Goeze)	Nb	
PHLOIOPHILIDAE		
Phloiophilus edwardsi (Stephens)	Nb	AWI 3
TROGOSITIDAE		
Nemozoma elongatum (L.)	RDB 3	
CLERIDAE		
Tillus elongatus (L.)	Nb	AWI 3
Opilo mollis (L.)	Nb	AWI 3
Necrobia violacea (L.)		
MELYRIDAE		
Dasytes aeratus Stephens		
Hypebaeus flavipes (F.)	RDB 1	AWI 1
Malachius bipustulatus (L.)		
M. viridis (F.)		
Anthocomus fasciatus (L.)		
LYMEXYLIDAE		
Lymexylon navale (L.)	RDB 2	AWI 1
KATERETIDAE		
Kateretes rufilabris (Latreille)		
NITIDULIDAE		
Brachypterus glaber (Stephens)		
Carpophilus mutilatus Erichson		
C. sexpustulatus (Fb.)		AWI 3

	Status	
Meligethes aeneus (F.)		
M. atratus (Olivier)		
Epuraea aestiva (L.)		
E. deleta Sturm		
E. florea Erichson		
E. guttata (Olivier)	Nb	
E. melanocephala (Marsham)		
E. melina Erichson		
E. unicolor (Olivier)		
Nitidula bipunctata (L.)		
Omosita colon (L.)		
O. depressa (L.)		
O. discoidea (F.)		
Soronia grisea (L.)		
Pocadius ferrugineus (F.)		
Cryptarcha strigata (F.)	Nb	
C. undata (Olivier)	Nb	
Glischrochilus quadripunctatus (L.)		
RHIZOPHAGIDAE		
Rhizophagus bipustulatus (F.)		
R. dispar (Paykull)		
R. nitidulus (F.)		AWI 3
R. perforatus Erichson		
SPHINDIDAE		
Sphindus dubius (Gyllenhal)	Nb	
Aspidophorus orbiculatus (Gyllenhal)		
CUCUJIDAE		
Pediacus dermestoides (F.)		AWI 3
Cryptolestes ferrineus (Stephens)		
Notolaemus unifasciatus (Latreille)	Na	AWI 2
SILVANIDAE		
Silvanus unidentatus (Olivier)		AWI 3
Psammoecus bipunctatus (F.)		
CRYPTOPHAGIDAE		
Telmatophilus caricic (Olivier)		
T. typhae (Fallén)		
Paramecosoma melanocephalum (Herbst)		
Henoticus serratus (Gyllenhal)		
Cryptophagus acuminatus Coombs & Woodroffe		
C. dentatus (Herbst)		
C. labilis Erichson	N	
C. pubescens Sturm		
C. ruficornis Stephens	N	
C. scanicus (L.)		
Antherophagus nigricornis (F.)		
Caenoscelis subdeplanata Brisout		
Atomaria (Anchicera) atra (Herbst)		
A. (Anchicera) atricapilla Stephens	N	
A. (Anchicera) fuscata (Schoenherr)		
A. (A.) lewisi Reitter		
A. (Anchicera) mesomela (Herbst)		
A. (Anchicera) pusilla (Paykull)		
A. (Anchicera) rubella Kraatz		
A. (Anchicera) testacea Stephens		
A. (s.str.) fimetarii (F.)		
A. (s.str.) linearis Stephens		
A. (s.str.) nigrirostris Mannerheim		
A. (s.str.) pulchra (Paykull)		

APPENDIX 5

Status

BIPHYLIDAE

Biphyllus lunatus (F.)		AWI 3

EROTYLIDAE

Triplax aenea (Schaller)		AWI 3
T. russica (L.)		AWI 3
Dacne bipustulata (Thunberg)		
D. rufifrons (F.)		

PHALACRIDAE

Phalacrus caricis Srurm		
P. substriatus (Gyllenhal)		
Olibrus aeneus (F.)		
Stilbus testaceus (Panzer)		

CERYLONIDAE

Cerylon ferrugineum Stephens		
C. histeroides (F.)		

CORYLOPHIDAE

Orthoperus mundus Matthews		

COCCINELIDAE

Coccidula rufa (Herbst)		
Stethorus punctillum Weise		
Scymnus (Pullus) auritus Thunberg		
S. (Pullus) haemorrhoidalis Herbst		
Anisosticta novemdecipunctata (L.)		
Adalia bipunctata (L.)		
A. decempunctata (L.)		
Coccinella septempunctata L.		
C. unidecimpunctata L.		
Calvia (Propylea) quatuordecimpunctata (L.)		
Calvia (s.str.) quattuordecimguttata (L.)		
Halyzia sedecimguttata (L.)		

ENDOMYCHIDAE

Endomychus coccineus (L.)		

LATHRIDIIDAE

Stephostethus lardarius (Degeer)		
Aridius bifasciatus (Reitter)		
A. nodifer (Westwood)		
Lathridius consimilis Mannerheim	N	AWI 1
L. minutus (L.)		
Enicmus histrio Joy & Tomlin		
E. testaceus (Stephens)		
E. transversus (Olivier)		
Adistemia watsoni (Wollaston)		
Corticaria alleni Johnson	N	AWI 1
C. elongata (Gyllenhal)		
Corticarina fuscula (Gyllenhal)		
C. similata (Gyllenhal)		
Cortinicara gibbosa (Herbst)		

CISIDAE

Octotemnus glabriculus (Gyllenhal)		
Sulcacis affinis (Gyllenhal)		
Cis (Orthocis) festivus (Panzer)	Nb	
C. (Orthocis) pygmaeus (Marsham)		
C. (s.str.) bidentatus (Olivier)		
C. (s.str.) bilamellatus Wood		
C. (s.str.) boleti (Scopoli)		
C. (s.str.) fagi (Waltl)		

Cis (s.str.) hispidus (Paykull)		
C. (s.str.) nitidus (F.)		
Ennearthron cornutum (Gyllenhal)		

Status

MYCETOPHAGIDAE

Pseudotriphyllus suturalis (F.)		AWI 3
Triphyllus bicolor (F.)		AWI 3
Litargus connexus (Fourcroy)		
Mycetophagus atomarius (F.)		AWI 3
M. mulitpunctatus (F.)		
M. piceus (F.)	Nb	AWI 3
M. populi (F.)	Na	
M. quadriguttatus Müller	Na	
M. quadripustulatus (L.)		
Typhaea stercorea (L.)		

COLYDIIDAE

Bitoma crenata (F.)		AWI 3

TENEBRIONIDAE

Eledona agaricola (Herbst)	Nb	AWI 3
Corticeus bicolor (Olivier)		
Cylindronotus laevioctostriatus (Goeze)		
Lagria hirta (L.)		
Prionychus ater (F.)	Nb	AWI 3
Pseudocistela ceramboides (L.)	Nb	AWI 2
Isomira murina (L.)		

TETRATOMIDAE

Tetratoma fungorum F.		AWI 3

SALPINGIDAE

Lissodema quadripustulatum (Marsham)	Nb	
Vincenzellus ruficollis (Panzer)		
Rhinosimus planirostris (F.)		
R. ruficollis (L.)		

PYROCHROIDAE

Pyrochroa coccinea (L.)	Nb	AWI 3
P. serraticornis (Scopoli)		

MELANDRYIDAE

	Orchesia micans (Panzer)	Nb	
	O. undulata Kraatz		AWI 3
	Abdera biflexuosa (Curtis)	Nb	AWI 3
??	A. flexuosa (Paykull)	Nb	
	A. quadrifasciata (Curtis)	Na	AWI 1
	Phloiotrya vaudoueri Mulsant	Nb	AWI 2
	Melandrya caraboides (L.)	Nb	AWI 3
	Conopalpus testaceus (Olivier)	Nb	AWI 3

SCRAPTIIDAE

Scraptia testacea Allen	RDB 3	AWI 1
Anaspis costae Emery		
A. frontalis (L.)		
A. garneysi Fowler		
A. humeralis (F.)		
A. lurida Stephens		
A. maculata Fourcroy		
A. pulicaria Costa		
A. regimbarti Schilsky		
A. septentrionalis Champion	RDB 1	AWI 1
A. thoracica (L.)		

5 · APPENDIX

MORDELLIDAE	Status	
Mordellistena abdominalis (F.)		
M. neuwaldeggiana (Panzer)	RDB K	

OEDEMERIDAE		
? Ischnomera caerulea (L.)	RDB 2	AWI 3
I. cinerascens Pandelle	RDB 2	AWI 1
I. cyanea (F.)	Nb	
I. sanguinicollis (F.)	Nb	AWI 1
Oedemera lurida (Marsham)		

ANTHICIDAE		
Notoxus monoceros (L.)		

ADERIDAE		
Aderus oculatus (Paykull)	Nb	AWI 3
?? A. populneus (Creutzer in Panzer)	Nb	

CERAMBYCIDAE		
Prionus coriarius (L.)	Na	AWI 3
Tetropium gabrieli Weise		
Rhagium bifasciatum (F.)		
R. mordax (Degeer)		
Stenocorus meridianus (L.)		
Grammoptera ruficornis (F.)		
Alosterna tabacicolor (Degeer)		
Judolia cerambyciformis (Schrank)		
Leptura maculata Poda		
L. melanura L.		
Molorchus minor (L.)		
M. umbellatarum (von Schreber)	Na	
Pyrrhidium sanguineum (L.)	RDB 2	AWI 1
Phymatodes alni (L.)	Nb	
P. testaceus (L.)		AWI 3
Clytus arietis (L.)		
Anaglyptus mysticus (L.)		
Mesosa nebulosa (F.)	RDB 3	AWI 2
Pogonocherus hispidulus (Piller & Mitterpacher)		
Leiopus nebulosus (L.)		
Stenostola dubia (Laicharting)	Nb	
Tetrops praeusta (L.)		

BRUCHIDAE		
Bruchus atomarius (L.)	Nb	
Bruchidius ater (Marsham)		

CHRYSOMELIDAE		
Donacia simplex F.		
D. vulgaris Zschach		
Plateumaris discolor (Panzer)		
P. sericea (L.)		
Orsodacne cerasi (L.)		
O. lineola (Panzer)	Nb	
Lema cyanella (L.)		
Oulema lichenis Voet		
O. melanopa (L.)		
Cryptocephalus pusillus F.		
Chrysolina polita (L.)		
Gastrophysa polygoni (L.)		
Phaedon armoraciae (L.)		
Prasocuris junci (Brahm)		
P. phellandrii (L.)		
?? Chrysomela tremula F.	RDB 1	
Phyllodecta laticollis Suffrian		

	Status	
Galerucella calmariensis (L.)		
G. lineola (F.)		
G. nymphaeae (L.)		
G. sagittariae (Gyllenhal)		
G. tenella (L.)		
Lochmaea crataegi (Forster)		
Phyllobrotica quadrimaculata (L.)		
Phyllotreta aenea Allard		
P. atra (F.)		
P. exclamationalis (Thunberg)		
P. tetrasigma (Comolli)		
P. undulata Kutschera		
Aphthona nonstriata (Goeze)		
Longitarsus luridus (Scopoli)		
L. lycopi (Foudras)	Nb	
Altica ericeti (Allard)		
A. lythri Aubé		
Crepidodera ferruginea (Scopoli)		
Chalcoides aurata (Marsham)		
C. aurea (Fourcroy)		
Epitrix pubescens (Koch)		
Chaetocnema hortensis (Fourcroy)		
Sphaeroderma rubidum (Graëlls)		
Cassida flaveola Thunberg		

ANTHRIBIDAE		
Tropideres sepicola (F.)	RDB 2	AWI 1
Brachytarsus fasciatus (Forster)	Na	

ATTELABIDAE		
Rhynchites aequatus (L.)		

APIONIDAE		
Omphalapion hookeri (Kirby)		
Acanaphodus (s.str.) onopordi (Kirby)		
Ceratapion gibbirostre (Gyllenhal)		
Protapion fulvipes (Geoffroy)		
Perapion (s.str.) violaceum (Kirby)		
Apion frumentarium (L.)		
Ischnopterapion (Chlorapion) virens (Herbst)		
Oxystoma subulatum (Kirby)		
Eutrichapion (s.str.) ervi (Kirby)		

CURCULIONIDAE		
Otiorhynchus desertus Rosenhauer	Nb	
Phyllobius argentatus (L.)		
P. calcaratus (F.)		
P. maculicornis Germar		
P. pyri (L.)		
Polydrusus cervinus (L.)		
P. mollis (Ström)	Nb	
P. pterygomalis Boheman		
P. undatus (F.)		
Barypithes araneiformis (Schrank)		
B. pellucidus (Boheman)		
Strophosoma melanogrammus (Forster)		
Sitona lepidus Gyllenhal		
S. lineatus (L.)		
S. suturalis Stephens		
Hypera plantaginis (Degeer)		
Cionus alauda (Herbst)		
C. hortanulus (Fourcroy)		
C. nigritarsis Reitter		
Magdalis cerasi (L.)	Nb	

APPENDIX 5

	Status			Status	
Magdalis ruficornis (L.)			Gymnetron villosulum Gyllenhal		
Tanysphyrus lemnae (Paykull)			Rhynchaenus avellanae (Donovan)		
Rhyncolus lignarius (Marsham)			R. fagi (L.)		
R. truncorum (Germar)			R. pilosus (F.)		
Trachodes hispidus (L.)	Nb		R. quercus (L.)		
?? Bagous collignensis (Herbst)	RDB 3		R. rusci (Herbst)		
?? B. frit (Herbst)	RDB 3				
Notaris acridulus (L.)			**SCOLYTIDAE**		
N. bimaculatus (F.)	Nb		Scolytus intricatus (Ratzeburg)		
Thryogenes festucae (Herbst)			S. multistriatus (Marsham)		
T. nereis (Paykull)			S. scolytus (F.)		
Ceutorhynchus cochleariae (Gyllenhal)			Hylesinus crenatus (F.)		
C. erysimi (F.)			Kissophagus hederae (Schmitt)	Nb	
C. floralis (Paykull)			Dryocoetinus villosus (F.)		
Sirocalodes depressicollis (Gyllenhal)			Xyloterus domesticus (L.)		AWI 3
Nedyus quadrimaculatus (L.)			X. signatus (F.)	Nb	AWI 3
Anthonomus (s.str.) pedicularis (L.)			Ernoporicus caucasicus (Lindemann)	RDB 1	AWI 1
Curculio glandium Marsham			E. fagi (F.)	Na	AWI 3
C. nucum L.			Xyleborus saxeseni (Ratzeburg)		AWI 3
C. pyrrhoceras Marsham					
C. venosus (Gravenhorst)			**PLATYPODIDAE**		
Mecinus pyraster (Herbst)			Platypus cylindrus (F.)	Nb	AWI 3

Addendum to Appendix 5

Corrections to the list of Coleoptera recorded from Moccas Park

Compiled by R.Colin Welch and J.Cooter

With increasing knowledge of the biology and taxomomy of British Coleoptera, and as a result of intensive surveys of Moccas Park in recent decades, several early records appear to be erroneous or very doubtful. The following species, which were included in earlier lists, have been omitted from the above check list. For the references cited in the notes on the following species, see the *Bibliography of the Coleoptera of Moccas Park* in Chapter 5.3.

Helophorus laticollis Thompson (Hydrophilidae)
Listed by Massee but shown by Angus to be *H. strigifrons* Thompson.[7]

Zorochros minimus (Boisduval & Lacordaire) (Elateridae)
Tomlin recorded this species as 'common at Moccas June to September',[8] but this probably refers to the River Wye at Moccas and not a record from within the Park.

Atomaria (s.str.) *badia* Erichson (Cryptophagidae)
Recorded by Massee as *A. sahlbergi* Sjöberg, collected by 'sweeping grass'.[9] This species is restricted to Caledonian pine forests of the Scottish Highlands.[10]

Vellius dilatatus (L.) (Staphylinidae)
Recorded by Massee, although it was not included in his earlier (1962) list of 'rarer and more interesting species'.[11] J.C. has failed to find it, during extensive surveys, either in the Park or anywhere else in the county. This species inhabits the nests of hornets, *Vespa crabro* L. and, although large and distinctive, the adult beetle is very seldom encountered. Although hornets are still common, nesting in the hollow oaks in the Park, the presence of *Vellius dilatatus* must remain in doubt until confirmed by a recent specimen. Its current distribution is centred on the New Forest, Hampshire.

Scymnus (Pullus) nigrinus Kugelann (Coccinellidae)
Listed by Massee 'on oak'.[12] This record probably refers to *S.(Pullus) auritus* Thunberg, which occurs on oaks, while *S. (P.) nigrinus* is associated with pines. The published distribution map for this species shows no records for south central Wales, West Midlands or south western England.[13]

Abdera triguttata (Gyll.) (Melandryidae)
This species is regarded by Hyman and Parsons as primarily restricted to Scotland; the early Moccas Park record by Massee 'in fungi' has not been included here and awaits confirmation.[14]

Scraptia fuscula Müll. (Scraptiidae)
Any records for this species probably refer to *S. testacea* Allen because the former species is thought to be restricted to the Windsor Forest area.

Anoplodera scutellata F. (Cerambycidae)
Recorded by Massee as *Leptura scutellata* 'in decaying deciduous trees'.[15] Neither Allen nor Hunter referred to this species in their accounts of this family occurring at Moccas Park,[16] and it has not been reported there since. Moccas Park appears to be outside its present known distribution in Britain and therefore the record requires confirmation.[17]

Notes

1   Booth (1988), Luff (1990), Speight, *et al* (1986), Van Berge Henegonwen (1989).
2   Kloet & Hincks (1977).
3   Cooter (1996), Johnson (1993), Mendel & Clarke (1996), Morris (1991, 1993), Twinn & Harding (1999).
4   Hyman & Parsons (1992, 1994).
5   Ball (1994).
6   Harding & Rose (1986).
7   Massee (1964), Angus (1977).
8   Tomlin (1950).
9   Massee (1964).
10 Johnson (1993).
11 Massee (1964).
12 Massee (1964).
13 Pope (1973).
14 Massee (1964), Hyman & Parsons (1992).
15 Massee (1964).
16 Allen (1955), Hunter (1959).
17 Twinn & Harding (1999).

References

ALLEN, A.A. 1955. Coleoptera. Notes on some Longicornia from Herefordshire. *Entomologist's Record and Journal of Variation*, 67, 88-89.

ANGUS, R. 1977. Water Beetles at Moccas Park, Herefordshire. *The Balfour-Browne Club Newsletter*, 6, 1-2.

BALL, S.G. 1994. The Invertebrate Site Register - objectives and achievements. *In*: P.T.HARDING, ed. Invertebrates in the landscape: invertebrate recording in site evaluation and countryside monitoring. *British journal of entomology and natural history*, 7 (Supplement 1), 2-14.

BOOTH, R.E. 1988. The identity of *Tachyporus chrysomelinus* (Linnaeus) and the separation of *T. dispar* (Paykull) (Coleoptera; Staphylinidae. *Entomologist*, 107, 127-133.

COOTER, J. 1996. Annotated keys to the British Leiodinae (Col., Leiodidae). *Entomologist's monthly Magazine*, 132, 205-272.

HARDING, P.T. & ROSE, F. 1986. *Pasture-woodlands in lowland Britain. A review of their importance for nature conservation.* Huntingdon: Institute of Terrestrial Ecology.

HUNTER, F.A. 1959. Collecting longhorn beetles in 1958. *Entomologist's Record and Journal of Variation*, 71, 122-126.

HYMAN, P.S. & PARSONS, M.S. 1992. A review of the scarce and threatened Coleoptera of Great Britain, Part 1. *UK Nature Conservation*, 3. Peterborough: Joint Nature Conservation Committee.

HYMAN, P.S. & PARSONS, M.S. 1994. A review of the scarce and threatened Coleoptera of Great Britain, Part 2. *UK Nature Conservation*, 12. Peterborough: Joint Nature Conservation Committee.

JOHNSON, C. 1993. *Provisional atlas of the Cryptophagidae - Atomariinae (Coleoptera) of Britain and Ireland.* Huntingdon: Biological Records Centre.

KLOET, G.S. & HINCKS, W.D. 1977. A check list of British Insects, Second Edition, Coleoptera and Strepsiptera, revised by R.D.Pope. *Handbooks for the Identification of British Insects*, 11 (3), London: Royal Entomological Society.

LINSSEN, E.F. 1959. *Beetles of the British Isles* (First series). London: Warne.

LUFF, M.L. 1990. *Pterostichus rhaeticus* Heer (Col., Carabidae), a British species previously confused with *P. nigrita* (Paykull). *Entomologist's monthly Magazine*, 126, 245-249.

MASSEE, A.M. 1964. *Some of the more interesting Coleoptera (beetles) and Hemiptera-Heteroptera (plant bugs) recorded at Moccas Deer Park, Moccas, Herefordshire.* Unpublished list dated 25 November 1964, 8 pages, in English Nature files.

APPENDIX 5

MENDEL, H. & CLARKE, R.E. 1996. *Provisional atlas of the click beetles (Coleoptera: Elateroidea) of Britain and Ireland.* Ipswich: Ipswich Borough Council Museums.

MORRIS, M.G. 1991. A taxonomic check list of the British Ceutorhynchinae, with notes, particularly on host plant relationships (Coleoptera: Curculionidae). *Entomologist's Gazette*, 42, 255-265.

MORRIS, M.G. 1993. "British Orthocerous Weevils": Corrections and new information (Coleoptera, Curculionoidea). *Entomologist's monthly Magazine*, 129, 23-29.

POPE, R.D. 1973. The species of *Scymnus (s.str)*, *Scymnus (Pullus)* and *Nephus* (Col., Coccinellidae) occurring in the British Isles. *Entomologist's monthly Magazine*, 109, 3-39.

SPEIGHT, M.C.D., MARTINEZ, M. & LUFF, M.L. 1986. The *Asaphidion* (Col.: Carabidae) species occurring in Great Britain and Ireland. *Proceedings and Transactions of the British Entomological and Natural History Society*, 19, 17-21.

TOMLIN, J.R.le B. 1950. *Herefordshire Coleoptera Part 2.* Hereford: Woolhope Naturalists' Field Club.

TWINN, P.F.G. & HARDING, P.T. 1999. *Provisional atlas of the longhorn beetles (Coleoptera, Cerambycidae) of Britain.* Huntingdon: Biological Records Centre.

VAN BERGE HENEGONWEN, A. 1989. *Sphaeridium marginatum* reinstated as a species distinct from *S.bipustulatum* (Coleoptera: Hydrophilidae). *Entomologische berichten*, 49, 168-170.

APPENDIX 5

A check list of the Diptera

Compiled by
Andy Godfrey

In the following check list the nomenclature follows Chandler (1998). A key to the numbered sources of records is given at the end of the check list.

	Year	Source	Status
TRICHOCERIDAE			
Trichocera regelationis	1992	11	
TIPULIDAE			
Ctenophora pectinicornis	1997	12	
Nephrotoma quadrifaria	1994	10	
Nephrotoma guestfalica	1994	10	
Tipula couckei	1994	10	
Tipula fascipennis	1994	10	
Tipula flavolineata	1992	11	
Tipula fulvipennis	1992	11	
Tipula irrorata	1994	10	
Tipula meigeni	1992	11	
Tipula pruinosa	1994	10	
Tipula pseudovariipennis	1992	11	
Tipula scripta	1992	11	
Tipula solstitialis	1994	10	
Tipula unca	1994	10	
LIMONIIDAE			
Limonia nubeculosa	1992, 1994	10,11	
Limonia phragmitidis	1994, 1997	10,13	
Neolimonia dumetorum	1994	10	
Dicranomyia mitis	1992	11	
Dicranomyia modesta	1994, 1997	10,13	
Helius flavus	1994	10	
Paradelphomyia senilis	1994	10	
Epiphragma ocellare	1992, 1994	10,11	
Austrolimnophila ochracea	1992	11	
Pseudolimnophila sepium	1994	10	
Phylidorea fulvonervosa	1994	10	
Symplecta hybrida	1994	10	
Erioptera divisa	1994	10	
Erioptera lutea	1994	10	
Erioptera nielseni	1994	10	
Ilisia maculata	1994	10	
Ilisia occoecata	1994	10	
Ormosia hederae	1992	11	
Ormosia nodulosa	1992	11	
Molophilus appendiculatus	1994	10	
Molophilus cinereifrons	1994	10	
Molophilus corniger	1994	10	Scarce
Molophilus lackschewitzianus	1992	11	RDB3
Molophilus obscurus	1994	10	
Tasiocera muscula	1997	19	First positive British record
Tasiocera robusta	1994	10	Scarce
PEDIICIDAE			
Pedicia rivosa	1997	13	
Tricyphona immaculata	1992	11	
PSYCHODIDAE			
Pericoma calcilega	1994	10	Few British records

	Year	Source	Status
PTYCHOPTERIDAE			
Ptychoptera albimana	1994	10	
Ptychoptera contaminata	1992	11	
Ptychoptera lacustris	1992	11	
DIXIDAE			
Dixa maculata	1992	11	Scarce
Dixa nubilipennis	1992	11	
Dixella aestivalis	1994	10	
THAUMALEIDAE			
Thaumalea testacea	1997	13	
ANISOPODIDAE			
Sylvicola cinctus	1992	11	
Sylvicola punctatus	1992, 1997	11,13	
MYCETOBIIDAE			
Mycetobia pallipes	1994, 1997	10,13	Scarce
BIBIONIDAE			
Bibio johannis	1992	11	
Bibio marci	1992	11	
Bibio nigriventris	1976	20	
Bibio pomonae	1992	11	
Bibio venosus	1992	11	
Dilophus febrilis	1992	11	
BOLITOPHILIDAE			
Bolitophila cinerea	1994	14	
Bolitophila hybrida	1994	14	
Bolitophila saundersii	1994	14	
DIADOCIDIIDAE			
Diadocidia ferruginosa	1992	22	
DITOMYIIDAE			
Symmerus annulatus	1992	22	
KEROPLATIDAE			
Macrocera angulata	1992, 1994	14,22	
Macrocera centralis	1961	3	
Macrocera faciata	1972, 1994	14,23	
Macrocera stigma	1961, 1972	3,23	
Macrocera vittata	1992	22	
Macrorrhyncha flava	1992	22	
Platyura marginata	1992	22	
Orfelia fasciata	1992	22	
Orfelia nemoralis	1992	22	
Orfelia nigricornis	1992	22	
Orfelia unicolor	1992	22	
Pyratula zonata	1992	22	

APPENDIX 6

	Year	Source	Status
MYCETOPHILIDAE			
Mycomya cinerascens	1992	22	
Mycomya circumdata	1992	22	
Mycomya marginata	1992, 1994	14,22	
Mycomya prominens	1992	22	
Mycomya sigma	1992	22	
Mycomya trilineata	1994	14	
Mycomya wankowiczii	1992	22	
Mycomya winnertzi	1992, 1994	14,22	
Leptomorphus walkeri	1992	22	
Syntemna hungarica	1992	22	
Phthinia mira	1992	22	
Sciophila nonnisilva	1992	22	Scarce
Acnemia nitidicollis	1992	22	
Monoclona rufilatera	1992	22	
Coelosia flava	1994	14	
Apolephthisa subincana	1992	22	
Boletina basalis	1992	22	
Boletina dubia	1992	22	
Boletina gripha	1992	22	
Boletina plana	1972, 1992	22,23	
Boletina sciarina	1992	22	
Boletina trivittata	1992	22	
Saigusaia flaviventris	1992	22	
Synapha fasciata	1992	22	
Synapha vitripennis	1972, 1992	3,22,23	
Leia crucigera	1972	23	
Tetragoneura sylvatica	1992	22	
Docosia fuscipes	1992	22	Scarce
Docosia gilvipes	1992	22	
Docosia sciarina	1992	22	
Anatella ciliata	1992	22	
Anatella longisetosa	1992	22	
Anatella simpatica	1992	22	
Anatella setigera	1992	22	
Tarnania nemoralis	1992	22	
Synplasta excogitata	1992	22	
Allodiopsis rustica	1994	14	
Exechia bicincta	1934	24	
Exechia dorsalis	1992	22	
Exechia fusca	1992	22	
Exechiopsis leptura	1992	22	
Exechiopsis membranacea	1992	22	Scarce
Exechiopsis subulata	1992	22	
Pseudexechia trisignata	1992	22	
Allodia lugens	1992	22	
Allodia ornaticollis	1992	22	
Allodia pyxidiiformis	1992	22	
Allodia grata	1992	22	
Stigmatomeria crassicorne	1992	22	
Brevicornu griseicolle	1977, 1992	3,22	
Brevicornu sericoma	1992, 1994	14,22	
Cordyla crassicornis	1977, 1992	3,22	
Cordyla fissa	1992	22	
Cordyla fusca	1994	14	
Cordyla murina	1992	22	
Trichonta atricauda	1992, 1994	14,22	
Trichonta foeda	1992	22	
Trichonta melanura	1992	22	
Trichonta submaculata	1992	22	
Trichonta terminalis	1992	22	
Trichonta xenosa	1994	14	

	Year	Source	Status
Phronia basalis	1992	22	
Phronia biarcuata	1992, 1994	14,22	
Phronia braueri	1992	22	
Phronia cineraescens	1977, 1994	3,14,22	
Phronia conformis	1992, 1994	14,22	
Phronia coritanica	1992	22	
Phronia disgrega	1992	22	
Phronia forcipata	1992, 1994	14,22	
Phronia nigricornis	1992, 1994	14,22	
Phronia notata	1992	22	
Phronia siebeckii	1994	14	
Phronia strenua	1992	22	
Phronia tenuis	1992	22	
Dynatosoma fuscicorne	1972, 1992	22,23	
Dynatosoma reciprocum	1992	22	
Mycetophila abiecta	1992	22	
Mycetophila adumbrata	1992	22	
Mycetophila alea	1994	14	
Mycetophila britannica	1992	22	
Mycetophila curviseta	1992, 1994	14,22	
Mycetophila edwardsi	1992, 1994	14,22	
Mycetophila formosa	1994	14	
Mycetophila fungorum	1992	22	
Mycetophila hetschkoi	1994	14	
Mycetophila lunata	1994	14	
Mycetophila marginata	1992	22	
Mycetophila ocellus	1992	22	
Mycetophila ornata	1992	22	
Mycetophila perpallida	1992	22	
Mycetophila pictula	1992	22	
Mycetophila pumila	1992	22	
Mycetophila rudis	1994	14	
Mycetophila spectabilis	1992	22	
Mycetophila trinotata	1992	22	
Mycetophila unipunctata	1992	22	
Mycetophila vittipes	1992	22	
Zygomyia humeralis	1992	22	
Zygomyia pictipennis	1992	22	
Zygomyia pseudohumeralis	1992	22	
Zygomyia valeriae	1992	22	
Zygomyia valida	1992	22	
Zygomyia vara	1992	22	
Sceptonia costata	1992	22	Scarce
Sceptonia membranacea	1992	22	
Sceptonia nigra	1992	22	
Platurocypta punctum	1992	22	
Platurocypta testata	1992, 1994	14,22	
SCATOPSIDAE			
Colobostema nigripenne	1994	10	
Cookella albitarsis	1994	10	
Scatopse notata	1992	11	
Thripomorpha paludicola	1994	10	
Anapausis soluta	1992	11	
STRATIOMYIDAE			
Beris chalybata	1992, 1997	11,13	
Beris fuscipes	1994	10	
Beris vallata	1976, 1994	10,20	
Chorisops tibialis	1994	10	
Nemotelus nigrinus	1994	10	
Oxycera pardalina	1994	10	Scarce

APPENDIX 6

	Year	Source	Status
Oxycera pygmaea	1994	10	Scarce
Pachygaster atra	1994	10	
Neopachygaster meromelaena	1960s, 1976	3,7	Scarce
Chloromyia formosa	1976, 1994	10,20	
Microchrysa flavicornis	1994	10	
Sargus iridatus	1976, 1994	10,20	
Odontomyia tigrina	1994, 1997	10,13	Scarce

XYLOPHAGIDAE

	Year	Source	Status
Xylophagus ater	1992	11	

RHAGIONIDAE

	Year	Source	Status
Chrysopilus asiliformis	1976, 1994	10,20	
Chrysopilus cristatus	1976, 1994	10,11,20	
Ptiolina nigra	1992	11	Scarce
Rhagio lineola	1992	11	
Rhagio scolopaceus	1976, 1997	11,13,20	
Rhagio tringarius	1976, 1994	10,20	

TABANIDAE

	Year	Source	Status
Chrysops caecutians	1976, 1994	10,20	
Haematopota pluvialis	1976, 1997	10,13,20	
Hybomitra bimaculata	1997	18	
Hybomitra distinguenda	1992	11	
Tabanus autumnalis	1994, 1997	10,18	
Tabanus bromius	1992, 1994	10,11	

ASILIDAE

	Year	Source	Status
Machimus atricapillus	1976, 1992	11,20	
Choreades marginatus	1960s	3	Scarce
Leptogaster cylindrica	1976, 1997	10,13,20	
Dioctria linearis	1976, 1997	18,20	

HYBOTIDAE

	Year	Source	Status
Drapetis ephippiata	1994, 1997	10,13	
Drapetis parilis	1992	11	
Drapetis simulans	1992	11	
Crossopalpus humilis	1992	11	
Crossopalpus minimus	1992	11	
Crossopalpus nigritellus	1992	11	
Stilpon graminum	1997	13	
Tachypeza nubila	1992	11	
Tachydromia aemula	1992	11	
Tachydromia umbrarum	1994	10	
Platypalpus agilis	1992, 1997	11,13	
Platypalpus aurantiacus	1992	11	Scarce
Platypalpus calceatus	1994	10	
Platypalpus candicans	1994, 1997	10,13	
Platypalpus ciliaris	1992, 1997	11,18	
Platypalpus longiseta	1992, 1997	10,11,13	
Platypalpus minutus s.s.	1994	10	
Platypalpus nigritarsis	1992	11	
Platypalpus notatus	1992	11	
Platypalpus pallidicornis	1997	13	
Platypalpus parvicauda	1997	18	
Platypalpus pallidiventris	1992, 1994	10,11	
Platypalpus pectoralis	1992, 1994	10,11	
Platypalpus verralli	1992	11	

HYBOTIDAE

	Year	Source	Status
Hybos femoratus	1994, 1997	10,13	
Hybos culiciformis	1992	11	
Bicellaria intermedia	1992	11	

	Year	Source	Status
Bicellaria pilosa	1992	11	
Ocydromia glabricula	1994, 1997	10,13	
Leptopeza flavipes	1997	18	
Trichina clavipes	1994	10	
Oedalea flavipes	1997	18	
Oedalea holmgreni	1992, 1997	10,11,13,18	
Oedalea stigmatella	1992, 1997	11,13	
Euthyneura myrtilli	1992, 1994	10,11	

MICROPHORIDAE

	Year	Source	Status
Microphor anomalus	1994	10	
Microphor crassipes	1997	13	
Microphor holosericeus	1992, 1997	11,13	

EMPIDIDAE

	Year	Source	Status
Gloma fuscipennis	1992, 1994	10,11	
Rhamphomyia anomalipennis	1992	11	
Rhamphomyia crassirostris	1992	11	
Rhamphomyia flava	1992, 1997	11,18	
Rhamphomyia longipes	1997	13	
Rhamphomyia micropyga	1992	11	Scarce
Rhamphomyia tarsata	1994	10	
Empis aestiva	1992, 1994	10,11	
Empis albinervis	1992, 1997	10,11,18	
Empis chioptera	1992	11	
Empis grisea	1992	11	
Empis livida	1994	10	
Empis nuntia	1992	11	
Empis scutellata	1997	18	
Empis tessellata	1992	11	
Hilara anglodanica	1997	13,18	
Hilara cornicula	1997	18	
Hilara fuscipes	1994, 1997	10,18	
Hilara galactoptera	1997	13	
Hilara griseifrons	1913, 1994	2,10,18	
Hilara litorea	1992	11	
Hilara lurida	1994	10	
Hilara monedula	1997	13	
Hilara nigrohirta	1913	2	
Hilara obscura	1994	10	
Hilara thoracica	1994	10	
Heleodromia immaculata	1992	11	
Phyllodromia melanocephala	1994	10	
Dolichocephala irrorata	1992	11	

DOLICHOPODIDAE

	Year	Source	Status
Sciapus platypterus	1992, 1994	10,11	
Dolichopus brevipennis	1994	10	
Dolichopus latielimbatus	1994	10	
Dolichopus nubilus	1994	10	
Dolichopus picipes	1992	11	
Dolichopus pennatus	1997	18	
Dolichopus plumipes	1994, 1997	10,13	
Dolichopus popularis	1992, 1994	10,11	
Dolichopus trivialis	1994, 1997	10,18	
Dolichopus ungulatus	1992, 1997	10,11,13,18	
Hercostomus angustifrons	1910, 1991	1, 25	Scarce
Hercostomus assimilis	1997	13	
Hercostomus cupreus	1992	11	
Hercostomus metallicus	1994	10	
Hercostomus nanus	1997	18	
Hercostomus nigrilamellatus	1997	18	Scarce
Hercostomus silvestris	1997	18	

APPENDIX **6**

	Year	Source	Status
Sybistroma crinipes	1997	13,18	
Sybistroma obscurellus	1992	11	
Poecilobothrus nobilitatus	1994	10	
Medetera abstrusa	1992	11	
Medetera flavipes	1994	10	
Medetera impigra	1992	11	
Medetera muralis	1992	11	
Medetera truncorum	1994	10	
Thrypticus laetus	1913	1	
Thrypticus nigricauda	1912	1	Scarce
Rhaphium appendiculatum	1992, 1997	10,11,13,18	
Rhaphium commune	1997	13	
Rhaphium crassipes	1997	18	
Rhaphium elegantulum	pre-1913	1	
Rhaphium micans	Date not given	5	Scarce
Syntormon bicolorellum	1994	10	
Systenus pallidus	1997	14	
Systenus pallipes/pallidus (female)	1994	10	
Achalcus cinereus	1997	13	
Achalcus flavicollis gp.	1997	13	
Neurigona pallida	1997	18	
Chrysotus cilipes	1994	10	
Chrysotus gramineus	1992, 1994	10,11	
Chrysotus laesus	1994	10	
Argyra diaphana	1992, 1997	11,18	
Argyra leucocephala	1992, 1994	10,11	
Argyra perplexa	1994	10	
Campsicnemus curvipes	1992, 1994	10,11	
Campsicnemus loripes	1992	11	
Campsicnemus pumilio	Date not given	5	Scarce
Campsicnemus scambus	1994	10	
Sympycnus desoutteri	1994, 1997	10,13,18	
Anepsiomyia flaviventris	1997	13	
Micromorphus albipes	1994, 1997	10,13	
Chrysotimus molliculus	1994	10	

LONCHOPTERIDAE

	Year	Source	Status
Lonchoptera bifurcata	1994	10	
Lonchoptera lutea	1992, 1994	10,11	
Lonchoptera tristis	1992, 1994	10,11	

OPETIIDAE

	Year	Source	Status
Opetia nigra	1997	13	

PLATYPEZIDAE

	Year	Source	Status
Agathomyia viduella	1994	10	

PIPUNCULIDAE

	Year	Source	Status
Verrallia aucta	1994	10	
Dorylomorpha anderssoni	1997	13,18	Proposed Scarce
Eudorylas fuscipes	1997	18	

SYRPHIDAE

	Year	Source	Status
Syrphus ribesii	1976	20	
Eupeodes corollae	1994	10	
Dasysyrphus albostriatus	1977	4	
Parasyrphus annulatus	1977	4	
Melanostoma mellinum	1992	11	
Melanostoma scalare	1992, 1997	11,13	
Platycheirus albimanus	1976, 1992	11,20	
Platycheirus granditarsa	1994	10	
Platycheirus immarginatus	1976	20	Scarce

	Year	Source	Status
Platycheirus rosarum	1994	10	
Pipiza noctiluca	1977	4	
Lejogaster metallina	1976, 1994	10,20	
Melanogaster hirtella	1994	10	
Brachyopa insensilis	1994	10	Scarce
Sphegina clunipes	1997	13	
Neoascia tenur	1994, 1997	10,13	
Volucella pellucens	1994	10	
Xylota segnis	1992, 1994	10,11	
Xylota sylvarum	1992	11	
Brachypalpoides lentus	1997	12,13,18	
Chalcosyrphus nemorum	1976	20	
Brachypalpus laphriformis	1977, 1997	4,13	Scarce
Syritta pipiens	1994	10	
Criorhina berberina	1992	11	
Criorhina floccosa	1977, 1992	4,11	
Anasimia contracta	1994	10	
Anasimia lineata	1994	10	
Helophilus hybridus	1992, 1994	10,11	
Helophilus pendulus	1992, 1994	10,11	
Parhelophilus versicolor	1994	10	
Eristalis arbustorum	1994	10	
Eristalinus sepulchralis	1994	10	
Myathropa florea	1976, 1992	11,20	

CONOPIDAE

	Year	Source	Status
Conops strigatus	1913	6	Scarce

TEPHRITIDAE

	Year	Source	Status
Terellia ruficauda	1994	10	
Terellia serratulae	1997	13	
Urophora stylata	1994	10	
Tephritis formosa	1994	10	

ULIDIIDAE

	Year	Source	Status
Seioptera vibrans	1994, 1997	10,18	
Herina frondescentiae	1994	10	

MICROPEZIDAE

	Year	Source	Status
Neria cibaria	1992, 1997	10,11,18	
Neria commutata	1992, 1997	11,13	
Cnodacophora sellata	1994	10	

MEGAMERINIDAE

	Year	Source	Status
Megamerina dolium	1994	10	Scarce

PSILIDAE

	Year	Source	Status
Chamaepsila rosae	1992	11	
Chamaepsila rosae/nigricornis (f)	1997	13	
Loxocera aristata	1994	10	
Chyliza leptogaster	1997	18	

DRYOMYZIDAE

	Year	Source	Status
Neuroctena anilis	1992, 1997	10,11,13	
Dryomyza decrepita	1994	10	

LAUXANIIDAE

	Year	Source	Status
Minettia inusta	1992	11	
Minettia longipennis	1997	18	
Sapromyza sexpunctata	1994	10	
Peplomyza litura	1994	10	
Lyciella pallidiventris	1994, 1997	10,18	
Lyciella platycephala	1992, 1997	11,13	

	Year	Source	Status
Lyciella rorida	1997	18	
Lyciella stylata	1992	13	
Tricholauxania praeusta	1994, 1997	10,13	
HELEOMYZIDAE			
Suillia atricornis	1992	11	
Suillia flavifrons	1994	10	
Suillia humilis	1997	18	
Suillia variegata	1992, 1994	10,11	
Heteromyza oculata	1997	18	
Tephrochlamys rufiventris	1992	11	
Eccoptomera microps	1994	10	
Eccoptomera obscura	1992	11	
Morpholeria ruficornis	1992	13	
Scoliocentra villosa	1994	10	
Scoliocentra dupliciseta	1992	11	
Heleomyza serrata	1992	11	
Trixoscelis frontalis	1994	10	
CHYROMYIDAE			
Chyromya flava	1992	11	
SEPSIDAE			
Themira germanica	Date not given	8	Scarce
Themira superba	1994	10	Scarce
Sepsis cynipsea	1992	11	
Sepsis fulgens	1992, 1994	10,11	
Sepsis orthocnemis	1994, 1997	10,13	
Sepsis punctum	1994	10	
Sepsis violacea	1992	11	
SCIOMYZIDAE			
Colobaea pectoralis	1997	13	RDB2
Pherbellia annulipes	1997	13,18	Scarce
Pherbellia dubia	1994	10	
Pteromicra glabricula	1997	13	Scarce
Tetanura pallidiventris	1997	18	
Elgiva cucularia	1994	10	
Hydromya dorsalis	1992, 1994	10,11	
Limnia paludicola	1994	10	
Pherbina coryleti	1994	10	
Psacadina verbekei	1997	13	
Renocera pallida	1997	13,18	
Sepedon sphegea	1994, 1997	10,13	
Sepedon spinipes	1997	13	
Tetanocera elata	1994, 1997	10,13	
Tetanocera ferruginea	1997	18	
Tetanocera hyalipennis	1994	10	
SPHAEROCERIDAE			
Lotophila atra	1994	10	
PALLOPTERIDAE			
Palloptera quinquemaculata	1997	13	
Palloptera umbellatarum	1994	10	
LONCHAEIDAE			
Lonchaea scutellaris	1994	10	
PIOPHILIDAE			
Prochyliza nigrimana	1997	18	
Allopiophila luteata	1992	11	
Parapiophila vulgaris	1992	11	

	Year	Source	Status
OPOMYZIDAE			
Geomyza tripunctata	1992, 1994	10,11	
Opomyza florum	1994	10	
Opomyza germinationis	1976, 1997	10,11,13,20	
CLUSIIDAE			
Clusia flava	1992	11	
Clusiodes albimanus	1992	11	
Heteromeringia nigrimana	1912	16	RDB1
CARNIIDAE			
Meonura triangularis	1992	11	Scarce
Meonura vagans	1992	11	
ACARTOPHTHALMIDAE			
Acartophthalmus nigrinus	1992	11	
PERISCELIDAE			
Periscelis winnertzi	1905, 1936	16	RDB2
AULACIGASTRIDAE			
Aulacigaster leucopeza	1994, 1997	12,13,15	Scarce
ANTHOMYZIDAE			
Anthomyza dissors	1934	2	
Anthomyza gracilis	1994	10	
Anthomyza neglecta	1997	13	
Paranthomyza nitida	1994	10	
Anagnota bicolor	1997	13	Scarce
ASTEIDAE			
Leiomyza scatophagina	1997	13	
CAMILLIDAE			
Camilla flavicauda	1994	10	
Camilla glabra	1994, 1997	10,13	
EPHYDRIDAE			
Notiphila caudata	1994	10	
Hydrellia griseola	1997	13	
Hydrellia maura	1992, 1997	10,11,13	
Philygria maculipennis	1992	11	
Axysta cesta	1994	10	
Ochthera mantis	1994	10	
Setacera trina	1911	2	
Limnellia quadrata	1992, 1994	10,11	
Scatella silacea	1997	13	
DIASTATIDAE			
Diastata fuscula	1992, 1997	11,13	
DROSOPHILIDAE			
Stegana nigrithorax	1992	11	Scarce
Leucophenga maculata	1994, 1997	10,12,13	
Scaptomyza graminum	1992	11	
Scaptomyza pallida	1992, 1994	10,11	
Drosophila andalusiaca	1994	10	
Drosophila fenestrarum	1992	11	
Drosophila funebris	1994	10	
Drosophila phalerata	1992	11	
Drosophila picta	1992	13	
Drosophila subobscura	1992	11	

	Year	Source	Status
AGROMYZIDAE			
Cerodontha capitata	1994	10	
Cerodontha denticornis	1994, 1997	10,13	
CHLOROPIDAE			
Calamoncosis glyceriae	1997	13	
Fiebrigella baliola	1934, 1997	2,10,11,15,17	Scarce
Fiebrigella brevibucca	1934, 1994	10,17	Scarce
Oscinisoma cognatum	1997	13	
Oscinisoma germanicum	1911	21	
Speccafrons halophila	1997	13	Scarce
Tricimba cincta	1992, 1997	11,13	
Dicraeus vagans	1994	10	
Eribolus gracilior	1997	13	Scarce
Eribolus nana	1934	21	
Oscinella frit	1992, 1997	10,11,13	
Oscinella hortensis	1994	10	
Oscinella nitidissima	1994	10	
Rhopalopterum fasciola	1997	13	
Elachiptera cornuta	1992, 1997	10,11,13	
Elachiptera diastema	1997	13	
Elachiptera tuberculifera	1992	11	
Meromyza triangulina	1994	10	
Meromyza zachvatkini	1994	10	
Pseudopachychaeta heleocharis/			
approximatonervis (male)	1997	13	Scarce
Diplotoxa messoria	1997	13	
Cetema elongatum	1994	10	
Cetema elongatum/simile (female)	1997	13	
Chlorops limbatus	1992, 1997	10,11,13	
Chlorops planifrons	1997	13	Scarce
Chlorops hypostigma	1992, 1994	10,11	
Chlorops pumilionis	1994	10	
Chlorops rufinus	1934	21	Scarce
Thaumatomyia glabra	1977, 1997	13,21	
Thaumatomyia notata	1992, 1997	11,13	
TACHINIDAE			
Dexiosoma caninum	1992	11	
Macquartia praefica	1994	10	
Oswaldia muscaria	1992	11	
Zaira cinerea	1997	13	
Ocytata pallipes	1992	11	
RHINOPHORIDAE			
Tricogena rubricosa	1997	13	
SARCOPHAGIDAE			
Oebalia cylindrica	1994	10	
Oebalia minuta	1997	13	
Sarcophaga carnaria	1992	11	
Sarcophaga incisilobata	1994	10	
Sarcophaga subvicina	1992, 1997	10,11,18	
Sarcophaga variegata	1992, 1994	10,11	
CALLIPHORIDAE			
Calliphora vicina	1992, 1994	10,11	
Calliphora vomitoria	1992, 1994	10,11	
Pollenia amentaria	1997	13	
Pollenia angustigena	1992	11	
Pollenia pediculata	1994	10	
Pollenia rudis	1992	11	
Pollenia viatica	1992	11	

	Year	Source	Status
SCATHOPHAGIDAE			
Cordilura aemula	1997	13,18	Proposed RDB2
Cordilura ciliata	1997	13,18	
Cordilura pudica	1997	13	
Cleigastra apicalis	1997	13,18	
Megaphthalma pallida	1992	11	
Spaziphora hydromyzina	1992	11	
Coniosternum decipiens	1992	11	Scarce
Scathophaga furcata	1992	11	
Scathophaga inquinata	1992, 1994	10,11	
Scathophaga lutaria	1994	10	
Scathophaga stercoraria	1992, 1994	10,11	
Scathophaga taeniopa	1992	11	
ANTHOMYIIDAE			
Chirosia grossicauda	1992, 1997	11,18	
Lasiomma seminitidum	1994, 1997	10,13,18	
Lasiomma strigilatum	1997	9	
Zaphne ambigua	1997	13,18	
Anthomyia liturata	1997	9	
Anthomyia procellaris	1997	9	
Eustalomyia festiva	1994	10	
Delia florilega	1994, 1997	9,10	
Delia platura	1997	9	
Hylemya nigrimana	1992	11	
Hylemya vagans	1997	9	
Hylemya variata	1994, 1997	9,10,13	
Hylemyza partita	1997	9,18	
Pegoplata aestiva	1992, 1997	9,10,11	
Pegoplata infirma	1992, 1997	9,11	
Emmesomyia socia	1992	11	
Adia cinerella	1997	9	
Mycophaga testacea	1997	18	
FANNIIDAE			
Fannia armata	1992, 1997	11,11	
Fannia lepida	1992	11	
Fannia parva	1992, 1997	11,13	
Fannia monilis	1997	13	
Fannia pauli	1997	13	
Fannia polychaeta	1992	11	
Fannia postica	1997	13	
Fannia serena	1994	10	
Fannia sociella	1992-1994	10,11	
MUSCIDAE			
Polietes lardarius	1997	13	
Eudasyphora cyanella	1992	11	
Neomyia cornicina	1994	10	
Musca autumnalis	1997	13	
Azelia cilipes	1992	11	
Azelia nebulosa	1994, 1997	10,13	
Potamia littoralis	1992	11	
Thricops semicinereus	1992	11	
Hydrotaea dentipes	1992	11	
Hydrotaea irritans	1992	11	
Muscina prolapsa	1962	3	
Phaonia atriceps	1994	10	Scarce
Phaonia cincta	1997	15	
Phaonia errans	1992	11	
Phaonia pallida	1992, 1997	11,13	
Phaonia palpata	1992, 1994	10,11	
Phaonia rufiventris	1992	11	

APPENDIX 6

	Year	Source	Status
Phaonia subventa	1992	11,15	
Phaonia valida	1992	11	
Helina depuncta	1992, 1997	11,13	
Helina evecta	1992	11	
Helina impuncta	1992, 1994	10,11	
Helina pertusa	1992	11	
Helina pubiseta	1992	11	
Mydaea ancilla	1992	11	
Lispe tentaculata	1994	10	
Lispocephala erythrocera	1997	13	
Schoenomyza litorella	1994	10	
Coenosia albicornis	1992	11	
Coenosia mollicula	1992	11	
Coenosia tigrina	1992, 1997	10,11,13	

Key to the numbered sources of records

1   Quoted in Wood (1913).
2   Species described as new to science by James Collin from Moccas Park (Pont 1995).
3   Skidmore (1985) and pers. comm.
4   Collected and determined by A.E. Stubbs (listed in Invertebrate Site Register).
5   Listed for Moccas Pool in d'Assis-Fonseca (1976) [J.H. Wood record?].
6   Collected by C.J. Wainwright and listed in Smith (1959).
7   Collected by J. Cooter (listed in Harding 1977 and Invertebrate Site Register).
8   Listed in Pont (1979) [J.H. Wood record?].
9   Recorded 8 June 1997. D.M. Ackland.
10   Survey 30 June 1994 - 2 July 1994, collected and determined by A. Godfrey. Godfrey (1994).
11   Collected J. Cooter using interception trap April-August 1992 and determined by A. Godfrey.
12   Collected 6 June 1997. Collected and determined by A. Godfrey.
13   Collected 10 June 1997. Collected and determined by A. Godfrey.
14   Collected A. Godfrey 30 June 1994 - 2 July 1994, determined by P.J. Chandler.
15   Collected 6 June 1997 and subsequently reared. Determined by A. Godfrey.
16   1934 and 1936 specimens in the general collection, Natural History Museum, London. 1905 and 1934 records listed in Falk & Ismay (in preparation).
17   Record in Collin (1946).
18   Collected 8 June 1997 and determined by I. Perry.
19   Collected 8 June 1997 and determined by A.E. Stubbs.
20   Collected 26-30 June 1976 and identified by J. Cooter. Determinations checked by A. Brindle.
21   Specimens in Oxford University Museum pers. comm. D.M. Ackland.
22   Collected J. Cooter using interception trap April-August 1992 and determined by P.J. Chandler.
23   Collected and determined by P.J. Chandler.
24   Collected James Collin (Chandler pers.comm.).
25   Collected and determined by P. Hodge, 26 June 1991.

References

D'ASSIS-FONSECA, E.C.M. 1976. Dolichopodidae. *Handbooks for the identification of British insects*, 9(5). London: Royal Entomological Society of London.

CHANDLER, P.J. ed. 1998. Diptera. *In: Checklists of insects in the British Isles* (New Series) Volume 12, Part 1. Royal Entomological Society of London.

COLLIN, J.E. 1946. The British Genera and Species of Oscinellinae (Diptera, Chloropidae). *Transactions of the Royal Entomological Society of London*, 97 (5), 117-8

FALK, S.J. & ISMAY, J. (in preparation). *A review of the scarce and threatened flies of Great Britain (part 2).* Peterborough: Joint Nature Conservation Committee.

GODFREY, A. 1994. *Preliminary survey and appraisal of the Diptera and Heteroptera of Moccas Park National Nature Reserve, Herefordshire.* Unpublished report to English Nature by Ecosurveys Ltd, Spilsby, Lincolnshire .

HARDING, P.T. 1977. *Moccas deer park, Hereford and Worcester: a report on the history, structure and natural history.* Unpublished report to the Nature Conservancy Council by the Institute of Terrestrial Ecology, Huntingdon.

PONT, A.C. 1979. Sepsidae, Diptera, Cyclorrhapha, Acalypterata. *Handbooks for the identification of British insects*, 10(5c). London: Royal Entomological Society of London.

APPENDIX 6

PONT, A.C. 1995. *The type-material of the Diptera.* Oxford University Museum Publication No.3. Oxford: Clarendon Press.

SKIDMORE, P. 1985. *The Biology of the Muscidae of the World.* Leiden: Junk.

SMITH, K.G.V. 1959. The Distribution and Habitats of the British Conopidae (Diptera). *Transactions of the Society for British Entomology,* 13 (7), 113-136.

WOOD, J.H. 1913. *Thrypticus nigricauda,* a new species, and notes on a few other Dolichopodidae from Herefordshire. *Entomologist's monthly Magazine,* 49, 268-270.

APPENDIX
6

A check list of the invertebrates
other than Coleoptera and Diptera

Compiled by
Paul T. Harding

In the following check list the endnote for each taxonomic group includes the source of the nomenclature used and brief details of the sources of records.

Status

Status

MOLLUSCA

Gastropoda (slugs & snails)[1]
ELLOBIIDAE
Carychium minimum
LIMNAEIDAE
Lymnaea truncatula
L. palustris
L. peregra
PLANORBIDAE
Planorbis planorbis
Bathyomphalus contortus
Gyraulus albus
Armiger crista
Hippeutis complanatus
SUCCINEIDAE
Succinea putris
COCHLICOPIDAE
Azeca goodalli
Cochlicopa lubrica
VERTIGINIDAE
Columella aspera
VALLONIIDAE
Acanthinula aculeata
ENDODONTIDAE
Punctum pygmaeum
Discus rotundatus
ARIONIDAE
Arion ater (rufus)
A. subfuscus
A. silvaticus
A. distinctus
A. intermedius
VITRINIDAE
Vitrina pellucida
ZONITIDAE
Vitrea contracta
Nesovitrea hammonis
Aegopinella pura
A. nitidula
Oxychilus cellarius
O. alliarius
Zonitoides nitidus
LIMACIDAE
Limax maximus
L. cinereoniger
L. marginatus
Deroceras laeve
D. reticulatum
EUCONULIDAE
Euconulus fulvus
CLAUSILIIDAE
Clausilia bidentata

HELICILDAE
Trichia hispida
Cepaea nemoralis

Bivalvia (mussels & pea-mussels)[2]
SPHAERIIDAE
Sphaerium lacustre
Pisidium obtusale
P. pseudosphaerium   BAP, RDB3

ANNELIDA

Polychaeta: Hirudinea (leeches)[3]
HIRUDINIDAE
Haemopis sanguisuga
Hirudo medicinalis (medicinal leech)   Berne, WCA, BAP, RDB3

ARTHROPODS OTHER THAN INSECTS

Arachnida: Acari - Metastigmata (ticks)[4]
IXODIDAE
Ixodes ricinus (sheep tick)

Arachnida: Araneae (spiders)[5]
AMAUROBIIDAE
Amaurobius fenestralis
A. similis
DICTYNIDAE
Dictyna arundinacea
Lathys humilis
DYSDERIDAE
Harpactea hombergi
SEGESTRIIDAE
Segestria senoculata
CLUBIONIDAE
Clubiona brevipes
C. compta
C. pallidula
C. stagnatilis
C. terrestris
ZORIDAE
Zora spinimana
ANYPHAENIDAE
Anyphaena accentuata
EUSPARASSIDAE
Micrommata virescens
THOMISIDAE
Diaea dorsata
Xysticus audax
X. cristatus
Philodromus aureolus

APPENDIX 7

Status

Status

Philodromus cespitum
P. dispar
P. praedatus
LYCOSIDAE
Pardosa amentata
P. lugubris
P. nigriceps
P. proxima
P. pullata
Trochosa ruricola
Pirata hygrophilus
P. latitans
P. piraticus
P. piscatorius
PISAURIDAE
Pisaura mirabilis
AGELENIDAE
Textrix denticulata
Tegenaria duellica
Coelotes atropos
MIMETIDAE
Ero furcata
THERIDIIDAE
Steatoda bipunctata
Anelosimus vittatus
Theridion bimaculatum
T. impressum
T. mystaceum
T. pallens
T. sisyphium
T. tinctum
T. varians
Enoplognatha ovata
Pholcomma gibbum
TETRAGNATHIDAE
Tetragnatha extensa
T. montana
Pachygnatha degeeri
Meta mengei
M. merianae
M. segmentata
ARANEIDAE
Gibbaranea gibbosa
Araneus diadematus
A. quadratus
A. sturmi
A. triguttatus
Larinioides cornutus
Nuctenea umbratica
Agalenatea redii
Araniella cucurbitina
A. opistographa
Zygiella atrica
Z. stroemi   Scarce
Z. x-notata
Cyclosa conica
LINYPHIIDAE
Walkenaeria acuminata
W. antica
Dicymbium nigrum
D. tibiale
Gnathonarium dentatum
Gongylidium rufipes
Dismodicus bifrons

Hypomma cornutum
Gonatium rubens
Maso sundevalli
Peponocranium ludicrum
Oedothorax fuscus
O. gibbosus
O. retusus
Monocephalus fuscipes
Gongylidiellum vivum
Micrargus subaequalis
Erigonella hiemalis
Savignya frontata
Diplocephalus cristatus
D. picinus
Milleriana inerrans
Erigone atra
E. dentipalpis
Porrhomma microphthalmum
P. pygmaeum
Meioneta rurestris
Centromerita concinna
Saaristoa abnormis
Bathyphantes gracilis
B. nigrinus
Diplostyla concolor
Drapetisca socialis
Labulla thoracica
Lepthyphantes alacris
L. cristatus
L. flavipes
L. mengei
L. minutus
L. pallidus
L. tenebricola
L. tenuis
L. zimmermanni
Linyphia hortensis
L. triangularis
Neriene clathrata
N. montana
N. peltata
Microlinyphia pusilla

Arachnida: Opiliones (harvest-spiders)[6]
PHALANGIIDAE
Rilaena triangularis

Arachnida: Pseudoscorpiones (pseudoscorpions)[7]
CHERNETIDAE
Lamprochernes nodosus
Chernes cimicoides

Crustacea: Isopoda, Oniscidea (woodlice)[8]
ONISCIDAE
Oniscus asellus
PHILOSCIIDAE
Philoscia muscorum
PORCELLIONIDAE
Porcellio scaber

Diplopoda (millipedes)[9]
JULIDA, BLANIULIDAE
Proteroiulus fuscus

Status

INSECTS

Hemiptera: Homoptera (leaf hoppers)[10]
CICADELLIDAE
Typhlocyba rosae
PSYLLIDAE
Psylla visci

Hemiptera: Heteroptera (true bugs)[11]
ARADIDAE
Aradus depressus
ANEURIDAE
Aneurus avenius
RHOPALIDAE
Myrmus mirmiformis
LYGAEIDAE
Heterogaster urticae
Scolopostethus thomsoni
TINGIDAE
Tingis cardui
NABIDAE
Nabis rugosus
CIMICIDAE
Temnostethus gracilis
T. pusillus
Anthocoris confusus
A. nemoralis
A. nemorum
A. visci   Scarce
Orius majusculus
O. niger
MIRIDAE
Deraeocoris lutescens
Lopus decolor
Amblytylus nasutus
Harpocera thoracica
Phylus coryli (=pallipes)
P. melanocephalus
Psallus assimilis
P. confusus (=diminutus)
P. perrisi
P. mollis (=masseei)
P. salicis
P. varians
P. wagneri
Plagiognathus arbustorum
P. chrysanthemi
Cyllecoris histrionicus
Dryophilocoris flavoquadrimaculatum
Heterotoma merioptera
Orthotyllus prasinus
O. tenellus
O. marginalis
Pithanus maerkeli
Lygus punctatus   Scarce
Liocoris tripustulatus
Orthops cervinus
O. viscicola
Lygocoris contaminatus
L. pabulinus
L. spinolai
Mirus striatus
Calocoris norvegicus
C. quadrimaculatus

Status

Stenotus binotatus
Phytocoris reuteri
Stenodema calcaratun
S. laevigatum
Trigonotylus ruficornis
Leptopterna dolobrata
SALDIDAE
Saldula saltatoria
GERRIDAE
Gerris thoracicus
NAUCORIDAE
Ilyocoris cimicoides
PLEIDAE
Plea minutissima (=leachei)
CORIXIDAE
Hesperocorixa moesta

Hymenoptera: Symphyta (sawflies)[12]
TENTHREDINIDAE
Strongylogaster lineata
Brachythops flavens   Scarce
Selandria serva
Dolerus aericeps
D. cothurnatus
D. megapterus   Proposed RDB3
D. niger
Athalia circularis
A. glabricollis
A. lugens
Rhogogaster chlorosoma
Tenthredo scrophulariae
Pachyprotasis rapae
Nematus myosotidis

Hymenoptera: Parasitica (parasitic 'wasps')[13]
ICHNEUMONIDAE
Iscnoceros rusticus
Xorides praecatorius
Trychosis legator
Itamoplex (=Cryptus) titubator
Ophion ventricosus
Coelichneumon comitator
BRACONIDAE
Spathius exarator
Hypodoryctes (=Wachsmannia) spathiiformis

Hymenoptera: Aculeata (ants, bees and wasps)[14]
DRYINIDAE
Aphelops melaleucus
Anteon infectum
A. scapulare
CHRYSIDIDAE
Chrysis angustula
C. cyanea
C. ignita
TIPHIIDAE
Tiphia minuta
FORMICIDAE
Myrmica rubra
Lasius flavus (yellow hill ant)
POMPILIDAE
Dipogon nitidus
D. subintermedius

APPENDIX 7

Status

VESPIDAE

Vespa crabro L. (hornet)

SPHECIDAE

Trypoxylon clavicerum

Crossocerus annulipes

C. cetratus

C. dimidiatus

C. elongatulus

C. podagricus

C. quadrimaculatus

C. walkeri   Scarce

Ectemnius cavifrons

E. cephalotes

Rhopalum coarctatum

Psen dahlbomi

Passaloecus corniger

COLLETIDAE

Hylaeus cummunis

ANDRENIDAE

Andrena bucecephala

A. haemorrhoa

HALICTIDAE

Lasiglossum albipes

L. calceatum

L. fulvicorne

L. lativentris

L. morio

MEGACHILIDAE

Stelis punctulatissima   Scarce

Chelostoma campanularum

Osmia rufa

Megachile versicolor

ANTHOPHORIDAE

Nomada flava

N. panzeri

APIDAE

Bombus pascuorum

Lepidoptera: Rhopalocera (butterflies) [15]

HESPERIDAE

Thymelicus sylvestris (small skipper)

Ochlodes venata (large skipper)

PIERIDAE

Pieris brassicae (large white)

P. rapae (small white)

P. napi (green-veined white)

Anthocaris cardamines (orange tip)

LYCAENIDAE

Quercusia quercus (purple hairstreak)

Lycaena phlaeas (small copper)

Polyommatus icarus (common blue)

NYMPHALIDAE

Vanessa atalanta (red admiral)

Cynthia cardui (painted lady)

Aglais urticae (small tortoishell)

Inachis io (the peacock))

Parage aegeria (speckled wood)

Lasiommata megera (the wall)

Pyronia tithonus (the gatekeeper

Maniola jurtina (meadow brown)

Aphantopus hyperantus (the ringlet)

Status

Lepidoptera (moths) [16]

HEPIALIDAE

Hepialus humuli (ghost moth)

H. lupulinus (common swift)

NEPTICULIDAE

Ectoedemia albifasciella

Stigmella oxycanthella

INCURVARIIDAE

Adela reaumurella

PSYCHIDAE

Narycia monilifera

Luffia ferchaultella

TINEIDAE

Nemapogon cloacella (cork moth)

N. variatella

Triaxomera parasitella

Tineola bisselliella (common clothes moth)

Niditinea fuscella (brown-dotted clothes moth)

LYONETIIDAE

Lyonetia clerkella (apple leaf miner)

GRACILLARIIDAE

Caloptilia robustella

Phyllonorycter harrisella

P. quercifoliella

P. salicicolella

P. maestingella

SESIIDAE

Synanthedon myopaeformis (red-belted clearwing)   Scarce

CHOREUTIDAE

Anthophila fabriciana

YPONOMEUTIDAE

Argyresthia laevigatella

A. glaucinella

Ypsolopha alpella

Y. sylvella

Y. parenthesella

Y. ustella

COLEOPHORIDAE

Coleophora laricella (larch case-bearer)

C. caespititiella

ELACHISTIDAE

Elachista canapennella

E. rufocinerea

Cosmiotes freyerella

OECOPHORIDAE

Telechrysis tripuncta

Alabonia geoffrella

Carcina quercana

Diurnea phryganella

Depressaria daucella

D. ultimella

Agonopterix heracliana

GELECHIIDAE

Bryotropha basaltinella   Scarce

B. terrella

COSMOPTERIGIDAE

Dystebenna stephensi

TORTRICIDAE

Agapeta hamana

Pandemis cerasana (barred fruit-tree tortrix)

P. heparana (dark fruit-tree tortrix)

Status

Archips podana (large fruit-tree tortrix)
A. xylosteana (variegated golden tortrix)
Clepsis spectrana (cyclamen tortrix)
C. consimilana
Ptycholoma lecheana
Ditula angustiorana (red-barred tortrix)
Aleimma loeflingiana
Tortrix viridana (green oak tortrix)
Acleris ferrugana
A. literana
Olethreutes lacunana
Bactra furfurana
Eudemis profundana
Epinotia cruciana (willow tortrix)
Zeiraphera isertana
Gypsonoma dealbana
Epiblema cirsiana
Pammene splendidulana
P. argyrana
P. populana
PYRALIDAE
Chrysoteuchia culmella
Crambus perlella
Agriphila straminella
A. tristella
A. inquinatella
Scoparia ambigualis
Dipleurina lacustrata
Eudonia mercurella
Elophila nymphaeata (brown china-mark)
Evergestis pallidata
Pleuroptya ruralis (mother of pearl)
Achroia grisella (lesser wax moth)
Aphomia sociella (bee moth)
THYATIRIDAE
Thyatira batis (peach blossom)
GEOMETRIDAE
Alsophila aescularia (March moth)
Cyclophora punctaria (maiden's blush)
Idaea aversata (riband wave)
Xanthorhoe designata (flame carpet)
X. spadicearia (red twin-spot carpet)
X. montanata (silver-ground carpet)
X. fluctuata (garden carpet)
Scotopteryx luridata (July belle)
Epirrhoe alternata (common carpet)
Eulithis populata (northern spinach)
Colostygia pectinataria (green carpet)
Epirrita dilutata (November moth)
Perizoma alchemillata (small rivulet)
Eupithecia pulchellata (foxglove pug)
E. exiguata (marbled pug)
E. vulgata (common pug)
E. subfuscata (grey pug)
E. lariciata (larch pug)
Plagodis dolabraria (scorched wing)
Opisthograptis luteolata (brimstone moth)

Status

Ennomos quercinaria (August thorn)
E. erosaria (September thorn)
Selenia dentaria (early thorn)
Apocheima pilosaria (pale brindled beauty)
Biston strataria (oak beauty)
B. betularia (peppered moth)
Agriopis aurantiaria (scarce umber)
Erannis defoliaria (mottled umber)
Peribatodes rhomboidaria (willow beauty)
Alcis repandata (mottled beauty)
Ectropis bistortata (the engrailed)
Cabera pusaria (common white wave)
C. exanthemata (common wave)
Campaea margaritata (light emerald)
SPHINGDAE
Smerinthus ocellata (eyed hawk-moth)
Laothoe populi (poplar hawk-moth)
LYMANTRIIDAE
Orgyia antiqua (the vapourer)
Calliteara pudibunda (pale tussock)
Euproctis similis (yellow-tail)
Lymantria monacha (black arches)
ARCTIIDAE
Thumatha senex (round-winged muslin)
Eilema griseola (dingy footman)
Artcia caja (garden tiger)
Spilosoma lubricipeda (white ermine)
S. lutea (buff ermine)
Tyria jacobaeae (the cinnabar)
NOCTUIDAE
Agrotis exclamationis (heart and dart)
Axylia putris (the flame)
Ochropleura plecta (flame-shoulder)
Noctua pronuba (large yellow underwing)
N. comes (lesser yellow underwing)
Diarsia mendica (ingrailed clay)
D. rubi (small square-spot)
Xestia triangulum (double square-spot)
Anaplectoides prasina (green arches)
Lacanobia thalassina (pale-shouldered brocade)
Orthosia cruda (small quaker)
O. populeti (lead-coloured drab)
Mythimna straminea (southern wainscot)
M. comma (shoulder-striped wainscot)
Dryobotodes eremita (brindled green)
Amphipyra berbera (Svensson's copper underwing)
A. tragopoginis (mouse moth)
Rusina ferruginea (brown rustic)
Euplexia lucipara (small angle shades)
Cosmia trapezina (the dun-bar)
Apamea monoglypha (dark arches)
A. crenata (clouded-bordered brindle)
Oligia strigilis (marbled minor)
Mesapamea secalis (common rustic)
Celaena haworthii (Haworth's minor)
Autographa pulchrina (beautiful golden Y)

Status

Status

Odonata (damselflies and dragonflies)[17]
CALOPTERYGIDAE
Calopteryx splendens (banded demoiselle)
LESTIDAE
Lestes sponsa (emerald damselfly)
COENAGRIONIDAE
Pyrrhosoma nymphula (large red damselfly
Coenagrion puella (azure damselfly)
Enallagma cyathigerum (common blue damselfly)
Ischnura elegans (blue-tailed damselfly)
AESHNIDAE
Aeshna mixta (migrant hawker)
GOMPHIDAE
Gomphus vulgatissimus (club-tailed dragonfly)
LIBELLULIDAE
Libellula depressa (broad-bodied chaser)
Sympetrum striolatum (common darter)
S. sanguineum (ruddy darter)

Orthoptera (grasshoppers & crickets)[18]
TETTIGONIIDAE
Meconema thalassinum (oak bush-cricket)
Pholidoptera griseoaptera (dark bush-cricket)
TETRIGIDAE
Tetrix subulata (slender ground-hopper)

ACRIDIDAE
Chorthippus brunneus (field grasshopper)
C. parallelus (meadow grasshopper)

Siphonaptera (fleas)[19]
HYSTRICHOPSYLLIDAE
Ctenophthalmus nobilis
Rhadinopsylla pentacantha
CERATOPSYLLIDAE
Orchopeas howardi
Dasyphyllus gallinulae
Megabothris turbidus
Ceratophyllus garei
C. gallinae

Trichoptera (caddisflies)[20]
LIMNEPHILIDAE
Grammotaulius nigropunctatus
Limnephilus auricula
L. vittatus
BERAEIDAE
Beraea pullata

Notes

1 Gastropoda - Nomenclature: Kerney (1999). Source of records: Killeen (1994).
2 Bivalvia - Nomenclature: Kerney (1999). Source of records: Killeen (1994); *P.pseudosphaerium*, listed in ISR database citing Foster (1983), but recorded by S.P.Dance in 1973 (letter to P.T.Harding dated 15 November 1976).
3 Hirudinea - Nomenclature: Elliott & Tullett (1982). Sources of records: ISR database 1973 citing G.N.Foster (see Foster 1977), see also Chapter 5.5.
4 Metastigmata - Nomenclature: Martyn (1988), Source of record: recorded in August 1997 by P.T.Harding.
5 Araneae - Nomenclature: Roberts (1985, 1987). [The nomenclature of British spiders is undergoing further revision and Roberts' check list is no longer considered to be wholly valid. However, it was the check list used by the recorders (below) when submitting their records. The systematics used by Roberts is followed to generic level, but within genera species are listed here in alphabetical order. Eds]. Sources of records: collected and identified by M.Taylor (November 1993, May and September 1994); collected by J.Cooter (June 1992, June/July 1995, June 1998) and identified by S.A.Williams.
6 Opiliones - Nomenclature: Hillyard & Sankey (1989). Sources of records: recorded in August 1977 by P.Skidmore; collected by J.Cooter (June 1992) and identified by S.A.Williams.
7 Pseudoscorpiones - Nomenclature: Legg & Jones (1988). Sources of records: ISR database (unknown dates or before 1970); collected by J.Cooter in May 1977 and identified by P.E.Jones.
8 Oniscidea - Nomenclature: Oliver & Meechan (1993). Source of records: recorded on various dates by P.T.Harding.
9 Diplopoda - Nomenclature: Blower (1985). Source of record: recorded in October 1977 by P.T.Harding.
10 Homoptera - Nomenclature: Kloet & Hincks (1964). Source of records: list prepared in 1964 by A.M.Massee.
11 Heteroptera - Nomenclature: Kloet & Hincks (1964). Sources of records: lists and notes by A.M.Massee (August 1963, June 1965); recorded by J.Cooter in 1994; Godfrey (1994).
12 Symphyta - Nomenclature: Kloet & Hincks (1978). Sources of records: recorded by J.Cooter in 1976 and 1978, by A.Godfrey in June 1997 and by D.M.Ackland in June 1997; H.W.Daltry in Benson (1958).
13 Parasitica - Nomenclature: Kloet & Hincks (1978). Sources of records: collected by J.Cooter and A.Godfrey in the 1990s and identfied by M.R.Shaw.
14 Aculeata - Nomenclature: Kloet & Hincks (1978) with some revisions (*fide* M.E.Archer). Sources of records: recorded by J.Cooter in the 1970s and 1980s; collected by A.Godfrey in 1994 and identified by M.E.Archer; recorded by E.A.. and M.A.Howe in June 1997.
15 Butterflies - Nomenclature: Emmet & Heath (1989). Sources of records: casual records from 1970s onwards mainly by J.Cooter, A.P.Fowles, P.T.Harding, P.J.Hodge, D.M.Parker, D.and V.Soper and T.Wall; see also Chapter 5.5.
16 Lepidoptera (moths) – Nomenclature: Emmet (1991). Sources of records: mainly by M.W.Harper (July 1974 and various dates from 1979 to 1997), others by D.W.H.Ffennell (June 1974) and casual records by J.Cooter, A.P.Fowles and M.A.and E.A.Howe.
17 Odonata - Nomenclature: Merritt, Moore & Eversham (1996). Sources of records: casual records mainly from the 1990s by A.Godfrey, N.J.Osley, D.M.Parker, P.Skidmore, D.and V.Soper, T.Wall; also Garner (1993).
18 Orthoptera - Nomenclature: Marshall & Haes (1988). Sources of records: casual records in 1977 from ISR archive and database; casual records in the 1990s by A.P.Fowles, A.Godfrey and P.T.Harding.
19 Siphonaptera - Nomenclature: Kloet & Hincks (1976). All records are from 1974-83 (Harper, Marchant & Boddington 1992).
20 Trichoptera - Nomenclature: Barnard (1985). Sources of records: J.Cooter in Miles (1984); recorded by A.Godfrey in 1997.

APPENDIX 7

References relating to Moccas Park

BENSON, R.B. 1958. *Hymenoptera 2. Symphyta, section (c).* (Handbooks for the identification of British insects, Vol VI, Pt 2(c)). London: Royal Entomological Society of London.

FOSTER, A. 1983. *A national review of non-marine molluscs. Invertebrate Site Register report No. 14.* London: Nature Conservancy Council.

FOSTER, G.N. 1977. Editorial note to R.B. ANGUS Water beetles at Moccas Park, Herefordshire. *The Balfour-Browne Club Newsletter*, 6, 1-2.

GARNER, P.G. 1993. Herefordshire Odonata. *The Flycatcher*, 59, 17-25.

GODFREY, A. 1994. *Preliminary survey and appraisal of the Diptera and Heteroptera of Moccas Park National Nature Reserve, Herefordshire.* Unpublished report to English Nature by Ecosurveys Ltd, Spilsby, Lincolnshire.

HARPER, G.H., MARCHANT, A. & BODDINGTON, D.G. 1992. The ecology of the hen flea *Ceratophyllus gallinae* and the moorhen flea *Dasypsyllus gallinulae* in nest boxes. *Journal of animal ecology*, 61, 317-327.

KILLEEN, I.J. 1994. *A survey of the land and freshwater Mollusca of Moccas Park NNR, Herefordshire.* Unpublished report to English Nature, Malvern Wells.

MILES, B.E. 1984. Some Herefordshire Trichoptera (Caddis-flies). *Transactions of the Woolhope Naturalists' Field Club*, 44. 301-309.

Other references

BARNARD, P.C. 1985. An annotated check-list of the Trichoptera of Britain and Ireland. *Entomologist's Gazette*, 36, 31-45.

BLOWER, J.G. 1985. *Millipedes.* Synopses of the British fauna (New series) No.35. London: E.J. Brill/W. Backhuys.

ELLIOTT, J.M. & TULLETT, P.A. 1982. *Provisional atlas of the freshwater leeches of the British Isles.* FBA Occasional Publication No.14. Ambleside: Freshwater Biological Association.

EMMET, A.M. 1991. Life history and habits of the British Lepidoptera. In: EMMET, A.M. & HEATH, J. eds. *The moths and butterflies of Great Britain and Ireland, 7, Part 2, Lasiocampidae - Thyatiridae.* Colchester: Harley Books.

EMMET, A.M. & HEATH, J. 1989. *The moths and butterflies of Great Britain and Ireland, 7, Part 1, Hesperiidae-Nymphalidae, The butterflies.* Colchester: Harley Books.

HILLYARD, P.D. & SANKEY, J.H.P. 1989. *Harvestmen.* Synopses of the British fauna (New series) No.4 (2nd edition). Leiden: E.J. Brill.

KERNEY, M.P. 1999. *Atlas of the non-marine molluscs of Britain and Ireland.* Colchester: Harley Books.

KLOET, G.S. & HINCKS, W.D. 1964. *A checklist of Britsh insects (2nd edition, revised). Part 1: Small orders and Hemiptera.* (Handbooks for the identification of British insects, Vol XI, Part 1). London: Royal Entomological Society of London.

KLOET, G.S. & HINCKS, W.D. 1976. *A checklist of Britsh insects (2nd edition, completely revised). Part 5: Diptera and Siphonaptera.* (Handbooks for the identification of British insects, Vol XI, Part 5). London: Royal Entomological Society of London.

KLOET, G.S. & HINCKS, W.D. 1978. *A checklist of Britsh insects (2nd edition, completely revised). Part 4: Hymenoptera.* (Handbooks for the identification of British insects, Vol XI, Part 4). London: Royal Entomological Society of London.

LEGG, G. & JONES, R.E. 1988. *Pseudoscorpions.* Synopses of the British fauna, (New series), No.40. Leiden: E.J. Brill.

MARSHALL, J.A. & HAES, E.C.M. 1988. *Grasshoppers and allied insects of Great Britain and Ireland.* Colchester: Harley Books.

MARTYN, K.P. 1988. *Provisional atlas of the ticks (Ixodoidea) of the British Isles.* Huntingdon: Biological Records Centre.

MERRITT, R., MOORE, N.W. & EVERSHAM, B.C. 1996. *Atlas of the dragonflies of Britain and Ireland.* London: HMSO.

OLIVER, P.G. & MEECHAN, C.J. 1993. *Woodlice.* Synopses of the British fauna (New series) No.49. Shrewsbury: Field Studies Council.

ROBERTS, M.J. 1985. *The spiders of Great Britain and Ireland, 1, Atypidae-Theridiosomatidae.* Colchester: Harley Books.

ROBERTS, M.J. 1987. *The spiders of Great Britain and Ireland, 2, Linyphiidae.* Colchester: Harley Books.

APPENDIX 7

A check list of the birds

Compiled by
David Boddington,
Alan Marchant
and Tom Wall

Nomenclature

Sequence and Latin names follow the *Checklist of Birds of Britain and Ireland*, British Ornithologists' Union, 6th edition, 1992. For some species the *Checklist* advocates new English names but it also lists those in current usage. This species list uses the latter.

Sources

BULL, H.G. 1888. *Notes on the Birds of Herefordshire. Contributed by members of the Woolhope Club.* Hereford: Jakeman & Carver.

HARDING, P.T. 1977. *Moccas Deer Park, Hereford and Worcester: a report on the history, structure and natural history.* Unpublished report to the Nature Conservancy Council by the Institute of Terrestrial Ecology, Huntingdon. Includes a bird list compiled by J.L. Fox.

HEREFORDSHIRE ORNITHOLOGICAL CLUB (1951-1997). *Annual bird reports.*

OSWALD, P. & COPELAND WATTS, E. 1962. Report on Moccas Deer Park, Herefordshire. Internal report, Nature Conservancy. Includes a bird list compiled by C.W. Walker.

TRANSACTIONS (1886-1950). *Transactions of the Woolhope Naturalists' Field Club.*

WALKER, C.W. 1963. List of birds seen in Moccas Deer Park in 1963. Report to Nature Conservancy.

WALKER, C.W. & SMITH, A.J. 1975. *Herefordshire Birds.* Hereford: Woolhope Naturalists' Field Club.

Personal records of David Boddington and Alan Marchant (1967-1998) and Tom Wall (1991-1998).

It is often difficult to know for certain whether records published as "at Moccas" refer to the Park itself. Some such records have been eliminated, but others have been included on the basis of circumstantial evidence that they do indeed relate to the Park.

HOC = Annual report of the Herefordshire Ornithological Club.

1. Breeding Species

BREEDING STATUS

Current:	There was evidence of breeding in the years 1994-1998 as well as previously.
Former:	There was no evidence of breeding in the years 1994-1998, but there was previously.

BREEDING PAIRS

Less than five:	It is thought that the breeding population is/was less than 5 pairs in number; the actual number is given, where known.
Five or more:	It is thought that the breeding population is/was 5 or more pairs in number.

		Breeding status		Breeding pairs		Notes
		Current breeder	Former breeder	Less than five	Five or more	
Little Grebe	*Tachybaptus ruficollis*	✓		1		Probably bred in some years in the 1960s-80s; breeding confirmed in 1993 and 1995
Heron	*Ardea cinerea*		✓	1		Bred 1985 and 1986
Mute Swan	*Cygnus olor*	✓		1		Bred 1991, 1993, 1995, 1996, cygnets were seen in the first three years but they may not have fledged
Canada Goose	*Branta canadensis*	✓		✓		Regular
Teal	*Anas crecca*		✓	✓		1-3 pairs bred in the 1960s but there has been no confirmed record since then
Mallard	*A. platyrhynchos*	✓			✓	Regular
Tufted Duck	*Aythya fuligula*	✓		✓		Irregular, two broods in 1993
Sparrowhawk	*Accipiter nisus*	✓		✓		Regular

APPENDIX 8

		Breeding status		Breeding pairs		Notes
		Current breeder	Former breeder	Less than five	Five or more	
Buzzard	Buteo buteo	✓		✓		Regular
Kestrel	Falco tinnunculus	✓		✓		Regular
Hobby	F. subbuteo		✓	1		Irregular
Red-legged Partridge	Alectoris rufa		✓	✓		Irregular
Grey Partridge	Perdix perdix		✓	✓		Irregular
Pheasant	Phasianus colchicus	✓			✓	Regular
Moorhen	Gallinula chloropus	✓			✓	Regular
Coot	Fulica atra	✓			✓	Regular
Woodcock	Scolopax rusticola		✓	✓		Breeding never confirmed and no breeding season records since the 1980s, but it is probably overlooked
Black-headed Gull	Larus ridibundus		✓		✓	50 pairs were thought to have nested in 1969 (HOC) but there are no earlier or later records
Stock Dove	Columba oenas	✓			✓	Regular
Woodpigeon	C. palumbus	✓			✓	Regular
Turtle Dove	Streptopelia turtur		✓	✓		"'At least one pair in 1963" (Walker 1963)
Cuckoo	Cuculus canorus	✓		✓		Regular
Barn Owl	Tyto alba		✓	1		Carrying food to nest hole, 1963 (HOC)
Little Owl	Athene noctua	✓		✓		Regular
Tawny Owl	Strix aluco	✓		✓		Regular
Green Woodpecker	Picus viridis	✓		✓		Regular
Great Spotted Woodpecker	Dendrocopos major	✓		✓		Regular
Lesser Spotted Woodpecker	D. minor	✓		✓		Regular
Woodlark	Lullula arborea		✓	✓		Extinct; all records are of birds "at Moccas" in the 1960s (HOC) they may refer to the area of former parkland now coniferised which lies to the south of the present Park boundary
Tree Pipit	Anthus trivialis	✓		✓		Regular
Wren	Troglodytes troglodytes	✓			✓	Regular
Dunnock	Prunella modularis	✓		✓		Regular
Robin	Erithacus rubecula	✓			✓	Regular
Redstart	Phoenicurus phoenicurus	✓			✓	Regular
Blackbird	Turdus merula	✓			✓	Regular
Song Thrush	T. philomelos	✓			✓	Regular
Mistle Thrush	T. viscivorus	✓		✓		Regular
Sedge Warbler	Acrocephalus schoenobaenus		✓	✓		Extinct; up to 3 pairs bred in the 1960s and '70s but none since (HOC)
Reed Warbler	A. scirpaceus		✓	✓		Extinct; 1 pair bred in 1975, but none has since (HOC)
Whitethroat	Sylvia communis			✓		Irregular
Garden Warbler	S. borin	✓			✓	Regular
Blackcap	S. atricapilla	✓			✓	Regular
Wood Warbler	Phylloscopus sibilatrix	✓			✓	Regular
Chiffchaff	P. collybita	✓			✓	Regular
Willow Warbler	P. trochilus	✓			✓	Regular
Goldcrest	Regulus regulus	✓		✓		Regular
Spotted Flycatcher	Muscicapa striata	✓			✓	Regular
Pied Flycatcher	Ficedula hypoleuca	✓			✓	Regular
Long-tailed tit	Aegithalos caudatus	✓		✓		Irregular
Marsh Tit	Parus palustris	✓		✓		Regular
Coal Tit	P. ater	✓			✓	Regular
Blue Tit	P. caeruleus	✓			✓	Regular
Great Tit	P. major	✓			✓	Regular
Nuthatch	Sitta europaea	✓			✓	Regular
Treecreeper	Certhia familiaris	✓			✓	Regular
Jay	Garrulus glandarius	✓		✓		Regular
Magpie	Pica pica	✓		✓		Regular
Jackdaw	Corvus monedula	✓			✓	Regular
Carrion Crow	C. corone	✓			✓	Regular
Raven	C. corax	✓		1		Regular
Starling	Sturnus vulgaris	✓			✓	Regular
Tree Sparrow	Passer montanus	✓		✓		Irregular
Chaffinch	Fringilla coelebs	✓			✓	Regular
Greenfinch	Carduelis chloris	✓		✓		Irregular
Bullfinch	Pyrrhula pyrrhula	✓		✓		Irregular
Reed Bunting	Emberiza schoeniclus	✓		✓		Regular

2. Non-breeding species

FREQUENCY

Frequent: Seen on a daily basis at the appropriate season.
Regular: Seen often at the appropriate season, but not on a daily basis.
Irregular: Five or more records over the last 30 years, but sightings remain unpredictable and infrequent.
Exceptional: Less than five records over the last 30 years.

		Frequent	Regular	Irregular	Exceptional	Notes
Bittern	Botaurus stellaris				✓	One, several times, Jan. 1998 (B. Chester-Master, P. Price)
Pink-footed Goose	Anser brachyrhynchus				✓	One with Canada Geese, 1977 and 1978 (HOC)
Snow Goose	A. caerulescens				✓	One with Canada Geese, 1986 (HOC)
Mandarin Duck	Aix galericulata				✓	Three recent records on the occasion of duck shoots
Goosander	Mergus merganser			✓		1-4 birds since 1995
Goshawk	Accipiter gentilis		✓			A recent arrival with records increasing
Osprey	Pandion haliaetus				✓	One in 1964
Peregrine	Falco peregrinus			✓		A recent increase in records
Water Rail	Rallus aquaticus				✓	Doubtless overlooked
Lapwing	Vanellus vanellus			✓		
Snipe	Gallinago gallinago		✓			
Curlew	Numenius arquata			✓		
Redshank	Tringa totanus			✓		
Greenshank	T. nebularia			✓		
Green Sandpiper	T. ochropus			✓		
Common Gull	Larus canus			✓		
Lesser Black-backed Gull	L. fuscus			✓		
Collared Dove	Streptopelia decaocto		✓			
Swift	Apus apus	✓				
Skylark	Alauda arvensis			✓		
Sand Martin	Riparia riparia		✓			
Swallow	Hirundo rustica	✓				
House Martin	Delichon urbica	✓				
Meadow Pipit	Anthus pratensis			✓		
Pied Wagtail	Motacilla alba yarrellii		✓			
Wheatear	Oenanthe oenanthe				✓	One record, 1 May 1976 (HOC)
Fieldfare	Turdus pilaris	✓				
Redwing	T. iliacus	✓				
Grasshopper Warbler	Locustella naevia				✓	One record, 1965 (HOC)
Lesser Whitethroat	Sylvia curruca			✓		
Willow Tit	Parus montanus			✓		
Rook	Corvus frugilegus		✓			
House Sparrow	Passer domesticus		✓			
Brambling	Fringilla montifringilla			✓		
Goldfinch	Carduelis carduelis			✓		
Siskin	C. spinus			✓		
Redpoll	C. flammea			✓		
Crossbill	Loxia curvirostra			✓		
Hawfinch	Coccothraustes coccothraustes				✓	
Yellowhammer	Emberiza citrinella				✓	

APPENDIX 8

Bird nest box occupation
by pied flycatchers and other bird species 1965-1999

Compiled by
David Boddington

Sources

All figures for 1965 and 1966 are taken from an anonymous list in English Nature files. David Boddington and Alan Marchant supplied the figures for numbers of boxes and numbers of pied flycatchers for the years 1967-1999 and for all other species from 1972 to 1999. Figures for species other than pied flycatcher for the years 1967 to 1971 are taken from the anonymous list. The boxes were not monitored in 1995.

Year	No. of boxes	Pied fly.	Total of species other than pied fly.	Species other than pied flycatcher						Grand total
				Blue tit	Great tit	Marsh tit	Coal tit	Redstart	Nuthatch	
1965	38	6	9	2	4	0	0	3	0	15
1966	60	12	23	7	9	1	0	6	0	35
1967	60	15	10	6	2	0	0	2	0	25
1968	58	14	10	0	4	0	2	4	0	24
1969	57	11	9	3	6	0	0	0	0	20
1970	57	11	11	3	5	0	0	3	0	22
1971	57	13	9	2	3	1	1	2	0	22
1972	57	13	14	7	4	2	0	1	0	27
1973	57	8	9	5	1	3	0	0	0	17
1974	59	12	18	13	3	2	0	0	0	30
1975	65	13	22	14	8	0	0	0	0	35
1976	68	8	11	6	2	2	1	0	0	19
1977	70	11	19	11	7	1	0	0	0	30
1978	70	12	19	7	10	1	0	0	1	31
1979	70	8	9	7	1	0	0	1	0	17
1980	70	14	13	7	5	0	0	1	0	27
1981	70	16	18	11	5	0	1	1	0	34
1982	70	9	2	2	0	0	0	0	0	11
1983	70	14	17	5	9	0	1	2	0	31
1984	70	14	14	7	7	0	0	0	0	28
1985	70	20	13	7	5	0	0	1	0	33
1986	70	14	7	2	5	0	0	0	0	21
1987	70	16	13	10	3	0	0	0	0	29
1988	70	24	18	14	3	0	0	1	0	42
1989	65	28	3	2	1	0	0	0	0	31
1990	65	22	10	8	1	0	0	1	0	32
1991	67	20	5	4	1	0	0	0	0	25
1992	65	13	11	6	5	0	0	0	0	24
1993	65	12	7	3	3	0	0	1	0	19
1994	65	17	4	4	0	0	0	0	0	21
1996	65	16	7	5	0	0	1	1	0	23
1997	61	15	7	5	2	0	0	0	0	22
1998	68	18	10	7	3	0	0	0	0	28
1999	69	21	9	6	2	0	0	1	0	30

APPENDIX 9

Transcript of Sir George Cornewall's Account Book
July 20 to December 31 1785

Transcribed by Tom Wall

		£	s	d
1785	Extras - B^t on	**507**	**19**	**9½**
July 20:	Davies [?]Colleb	2	8	6
	D° [Erasures] [?]Lee	5	12	3½
	D° Masters	3	13	6
	D° Harrison	1	15	
	D° fishing tackle	1	2	6
	D° dif things	8	2	11½
28:	[?]Aird - Men at sundries	1	1	
	D° Bevan, on acc^t park wall	10	10	
	D° Expence [?]to [?]Hereford	0	1	
	D° Men mowing weeds	0	11	
	D° Williams	0	19	6
	D° [?]Letter [?]woman	0	4	6
30:	D° in full for park wall to			
	Enclosures (46.15.0 p^d before)	5	17	4
	[Erasures]			
	D° - 262 perch ditch cleaning	3	9	10
Augst 1:	Mrs Elliot [?]Inst to [?]Candlemas	5		
	Evans, wheat & bread to Poor	3	12	
7:	Maddox	2	7	8
	[?]Aird - Men at sundries	0	11	
	D° - Williams	1	2	6
	D° - Mowing weeds - turnpikes	0	3	6
19:	D° - Men at sundries	0	12	
	D° - Bevan 13 perch park wall	11	14	
	D° - hauling 6 [?]day : lime for d°	0	14	
	D° - moving stones for d°	0	9	
	D° - Williams	1	4	7
16:	Bells at Hereford	2	2	
	Races	24		
2[?]5:	[?]Aird - Men at sundries	1	4	
	D° Watkins - Smith	3	2	1½
	D° [?]Bethell in Monnington Wood	0	11	
	D° Williams	0	12	
	D° Bevan - 9 perch park wall	[?]8	2	
		620	12	1

		£	s	d
27:	Subscription to Wye Navigation	5	5	
	[?]Aird - Men at sundries	0	16	[?]1
	D° - turnpikes [?]d°	0	14	3
	D° - Williams	0	14	3
Sept 3 :	D° - Men at sundries	0	10	2
	D° - Penny - care of plantations	0	10	6
	D° - Bevan 12 perch park wall	10	16	
6:	Harry	0	14	7
	[?] Mr [?]Thallowes - Baronetage Cert.	12	4	10
	Davies	1	9	1
10:	[?]Aird - Men at sundries	0	11	6
	D° Powel	1	1[?]8	11
	D° Williams	1	1	
	D° stamps, paper & pens	1	1	4
14:	Rooms etc at Weymouth	3	3	
	Bells at [?]Ross	1	1	
17:	[?]Aird - Bevan 12 perch park wall	10	16	
23:	Master of Ceremonies ball Weymouth	2	2	
24:	[?]Aird - Men at sundries	0	[?]8	
	D° cleaning hedges	0	8	[?]6
Oct [?]1 :	D° Men at sundries	0	12	
	D° Bevan 11 perch park wall	9	18	
	D° carrying lime to d°.	0	9	4
	D° jams to gate of d°.	0	2	6
	D° Williams - 3 weeks bills	2	8	
	D° mowing before house	0	10	6
11:	Hounds at Weymouth	2	2	
13:	Lodging at d°	28	7	
	D°. for stable man	1	5	
	[?]Aird - mowing etc before house	0	18	
	D°. Williams	0	9	6
	D°. Stocking trees	0	3	
	D°. cleaning of [?]Mearfield ditch	1	4	
		735	**1**	**10**

		£	s	d
	B⁺ on	735	I	10
Oct 15:	[?]Aird - Men mowing by house	0	9	2
	D° d° at sundries	0	5	
	D° Bevan 11 perch park wall	9	18	
	D° Williams - day bills	I	2	
	D° Women stonepicking	0	6	
22:	D° d° - d° -	0	4	
	D° Men at sundries	0	14	2
	D° Williams	I	4	5
29:	D° Men at sundries	I	5	2
	D° Bevan 10 perch park wall	9		
	D° [?]4.8 lime for d°	I	I	
	D° carriage of d°	0	11	I
	D° Williams putting up Pound	I	10	
	D° Team expence to Hereford fair	0	6	6
	D° women stonepicking	0	4	
Nov	Infirmary - 2 years	21		
	Charity school	5	5	
	George at Diddlebury	4	4	
21:	[?]Aird - Men at sundries	0	10	
	D° Bevan 9 perch park wall	8	2	
	D° Williams	0	18	
	D° Cox - stocking trees	0	6	
19:	D° Men at sundries	I	2	11
	D° women stonepicking	0	6	
	D° Cox	0	3	6
	D° Williams	0	12	
26:	D° d°	0	6	
	D° men at sundries	0	12	
	D° d° [?]thatching paddock shed	0	10	6
	D° [?]d° Preece mowing the lawn	0	10	6
	D° Cox, filling saw pits	0	3	
Dec 3:	D° d° d°	0	3	
	D° Men at sundries	0	10	
	D° d° stocking hedge	0	15	5
		809	I	8

APPENDIX 10

		£	s	d
Dec 3:	[?]Aird - Bevan 5 perch park wall	4	10	
	D° - laying [?]clenny plantation hedge	0	12	3
10:	D° Men at sundries [?]& hedge stocking	1	8	
	D° Bevan, raising stone, park wall	6	6	
	D° - Williams	1	2	6
	D° d° - pales Ch field & garden	2	19	6
12:	Mrs Mr Berkelay - given	10		
16:	[?]Aird - Men at sundries	0	8	4
	D° [?]padlocks & turnpikes	0	7	5
	D° Williams	1	7	9
22:	D° Men at sundries	0	9	2
	[?]Welson raising [?]200 tiles	2	10	
	[?]Coxe	0	3	7
31:	D° Men at Ice house etc	2	4	2
	D° Bevan on acc[t] park wall	2	2	
	D° Williams	1	16	0
	D° Hedge towards Byford	0	11	3
		847	**19**	**7**
	The above includes for park wall	174	14	6½
	Mr Romney portraits	81	18	0
	[?]Downman d°	10	10	0
	Green on acc[t] [?]organ	52	10	0
	Hauling timber park pales	9	9	4
		329	**1**	**10½**

Notes

The meaning of the superscript 'd' (30 July) and superscript 'st' (August 1) are unclear.

[]	Square brackets indicate insertions made by the transcriber.
[?]	Indicates that the word that follows is particularly difficult to read and may not have been transcribed correctly.
[Erasures]	Indicates an entry that has been crossed out.
D° and d°	= ditto.
B[t]	= brought, as in "brought on" ie brought forward from a previous page.
dif[f]	= different.
acc[t]	= account.

The figure columns show pounds (£), shillings (s) and pence (d).

Index

Page numbers in italics indicate an illustration or map.

References in brackets associated with individuals indicate that, at the time(s) referred to in the text, they were:
1   an employee of one or more of the following - English Nature (EN), Institute of Terrestrial Ecology (ITE) Institute of Freshwater Ecology (IFE), Nature Conservancy (NC), Nature Conservancy Council (NCC) and / or
2   concerned with Moccas Park or the Moccas Estate in the primary capacity of an artist, botanist, entomologist, etc.

All species recorded at Moccas Park are included in the appropriate check list (see Appendices), but only the species mentioned in the text of Sections 1 to 7, that are particularly noteworthy, have been indexed.